Lecture Notes in Artificial Intelligence   2850

Edited by J. G. Carbonell and J. Siekmann

Subseries of Lecture Notes in Computer Science

T0226298

Springer
Berlin
Heidelberg
New York
Hong Kong
London
Milan
Paris
Tokyo

Moshe Y. Vardi   Andrei Voronkov (Eds.)

Logic for Programming, Artificial Intelligence, and Reasoning

10th International Conference, LPAR 2003
Almaty, Kazakhstan, September 22-26, 2003
Proceedings

 Springer

Series Editors

Jaime G. Carbonell, Carnegie Mellon University, Pittsburgh, PA, USA
Jörg Siekmann, University of Saarland, Saarbrücken, Germany

Volume Editors

Moshe Y. Vardi
Rice University
Department of Computer Science
6100 S. Main Street, Houston, TX 77005-1892, USA
E-mail: vardi@cs.rice.edu

Andrei Voronkov
University of Manchester
Department of Computer Science
Kilburn Building, Oxford Road, Manchester M13 9PL, UK
E-mail: voronkov@cs.man.ac.uk

Cataloging-in-Publication Data applied for

A catalog record for this book is available from the Library of Congress
Bibliographic information published by Die Deutsche Bibliothek
Die Deutsche Bibliothek lists this publication in the Deutsche Nationalbibliografie;
detailed bibliographic data is available in the Internet at <http://dnb.ddb.de>.

CR Subject Classification (1998): I.2.3, I.2, F.4.1, F.3, D.2.4, D.1.6

ISSN 0302-9743
ISBN 3-540-20101-7 Springer-Verlag Berlin Heidelberg New York

Springer-Verlag Berlin Heidelberg New York
a member of BertelsmannSpringer Science+Business Media GmbH
http://www.springer.de

© Springer-Verlag Berlin Heidelberg 2003
Printed in Germany

Typesetting: Camera-ready by author, data conversion by Steingräber Satztechnik GmbH
Printed on acid-free paper   SPIN 10960424   06/3142   5 4 3 2 1 0

Preface

This volume contains the papers presented at the Tenth International Conference on Logic for Programming, Artificial Intelligence, and Reasoning (LPAR 2003), held on September 22–26, 2003, in Almaty, Kazakhstan, together with the Fourth International Workshop on Implementation of Logics.

There were 65 submissions, of which 8 belonged to the special submission category of experimental papers, intended to describe implementations or comparisons of systems, or experiments with systems. Each submission was reviewed by at least three program committee members and an electronic program committee meeting was held via the Internet. We are very grateful to the 32 program committee members for their efforts and for the quality of their reviews and discussions. Finally, the committee decided to accept 27 papers. The program also included five invited talks, by Franz Baader, Serikzhan Badaev, Dexter Kozen, Sergei Goncharov, and Thomas Wilke.

Apart from the program committee, we would also like to thank the other people who have made LPAR 2003 possible: the external reviewers and the local organizers Serikzhan Badaev and Anna Romina.

The Internet-based submission software and the program-committee discussion software were provided by the second co-chair.

July 2003

Moshe Y. Vardi
Andrei Voronkov

Conference Organization

Program Chairs

Moshe Y. Vardi (Rice University, USA)
Andrei Voronkov (University of Manchester, UK)

Program Committee

Matthias Baaz (Technische Universität Wien)
Maurice Bruynooghe (Katholieke Universiteit Leuven)
Patrick Cousot (ENS Paris)
Evgeny Dantsin (Roosevelt University)
Volker Diekert (Universität Stuttgart)
Thomas Eiter (Technische Universität Wien)
Amy Felty (University of Ottawa)
Enrico Franconi (Free University of Bozen-Bolzano)
Harald Ganzinger (Max-Planck-Institut, Saarbrücken)
Philippa Gardner (Imperial College)
Erich Grädel (RWTH Aachen)
Sergio Greco (Università della Calabria)
Jan Friso Groote (Eindhoven University of Technology)
Miki Hermann (Ecole Polytechnique)
Neil D. Jones (University of Copenhagen)
Bakhadyr Khoussainov (University of Auckland)
Claude Kirchner (LORIA)
Teodor Knapik (Université de la Réunion)
Orna Kupferman (Hebrew University)
Daniel Leivant (Indiana University-Bloomington)
Christopher Lynch (Clarkson University)
Maarten Marx (Universiteit van Amsterdam)
William McCune (Argonne National Laboratory)
Ron van der Meyden (University of New South Wales)
Dale Miller (INRIA)
Michel Parigot (University of Paris 7)
Teodor C. Przymusinski (University of California at Riverside)
Ulrike Sattler (Technische Universität Dresden)
Jörg Siekmann (DFKI, Saarbrücken)
Jean-Marc Talbot (Université des Sciences et Techniques de Lille)
Toby Walsh (University College Cork)
Frank Wolter (University of Liverpool)

Local Organization

Serikzhan Badaev
Anna Romina

External Reviewers

Amal Ahmed
Alessandro Artale
Raffaella Bernardi
Achim Blumensath
Witold Charatonik
Eric Deplagne
Clare Dixon
Alfredo Fernandez-Valmayor
Christophe Fouquere
Hui Gao
Rob Goldblatt
Bruno Guillaume
Furio Honsell
Marcin Jurdzinski
Konstantin Korovin
Francisco J. Lopez-Fraguas
A.R.D. Mathias
Mohammad Reza Mousavi
Hans de Nivelle
Bert Van Nuffelen
David Pearce
Germán Puebla
Sethu Ramesh
Jussi Rintanen
Jaime Sanchez
Stefan Schwoon
Viorica Sofronie-Stokkermans
Sergio Tessaris
Hans Tompits
Olga Tveretina
Jacqueline Vauzeilles
Sofie Verbaeten
Shuly Wintner
Jeffrey Zucker

Ofer Arieli
Chita Baral
Dietmar Berwanger
Cristiano Calcagno
Andrea Corradini
Joelle Despeyroux
Uwe Egly
Olivier Fissore
Filippo Furfaro
David Gilis
Gianluigi Greco
Ian Hodkinson
Marieke Huisman
Yevgeny Kazakov
Martin Leucker
Ian Mackie
Arjan J. Mooij
Joachim Niehren
Damian Niwinski
Luigi Palopoli
Nikolay Pelov
David Pym
Christophe Ringeissen
Sasha Rubin
David Schmidt
Alexander Serebrenik
Eugenia Ternovska
Sophie Tison
John Tucker
Wim Vanhoof
Joost Vennekens
Uwe Waldmann
Stefan Woltran
Mark van der Zwaag

Conferences Preceding LPAR 2003

RCLP'90, Irkutsk, Soviet Union
RCLP'91, Leningrad, Soviet Union, aboard the ship "Michail Lomonosov"
LPAR'92, St. Petersburg, Russia, aboard the ship "Michail Lomonosov"
LPAR'93, St. Petersburg, Russia
LPAR'94, Kiev, Ukraine, aboard the ship "Marshal Koshevoi"
LPAR'99, Tbilisi, Republic of Georgia
LPAR 2000, Reunion Island, France
LPAR 2001, Havana, Cuba
LPAR 2002, Tbilisi, Republic of Georgia

Table of Contents

From Tableaux to Automata for Description Logics 1
   F. Baader, J. Hladik, C. Lutz, F. Wolter

Disproving False Conjectures 33
   S. Autexier, C. Schürmann

A Formal Proof of Dickson's Lemma in ACL2 49
   F.J. Martín–Mateos, J.A. Alonso, M.J. Hidalgo, J.L. Ruiz–Reina

Imperative Object-Based Calculi in Co-inductive Type Theories 59
   A. Ciaffaglione, L. Liquori, M. Miculan

Congruence Closure with Integer Offsets 78
   R. Nieuwenhuis, A. Oliveras

A Machine-Verified Code Generator 91
   C. Walther, S. Schweitzer

A Translation Characterizing the Constructive Content
of Classical Theories.. 107
   M. Baaz, C.G. Fermüller

Extensions of Non-standard Inferences to Description Logics
with Transitive Roles 122
   S. Brandt, A.-Y. Turhan, R. Küsters

Extended Canonicity of Certain Topological Properties of Set Spaces 137
   B. Heinemann

Algebraic and Model Theoretic Techniques for Fusion Decidability
in Modal Logics 152
   S. Ghilardi, L. Santocanale

Improving Dependency Pairs 167
   J. Giesl, R. Thiemann, P. Schneider-Kamp, S. Falke

On Closure under Complementation of Equational Tree Automata
for Theories Extending AC 183
   K.N. Verma

Completeness of *E*-Unification with Eager Variable Elimination.......... 198
   B. Morawska

Computable Numberings 213
    S. Badaev

Handling Equality in Monodic Temporal Resolution 214
    B. Konev, A. Degtyarev, M. Fisher

Once upon a Time in the West – Determinacy, Definability, and Complexity
of Path Games 229
    D. Berwanger, E. Grädel, S. Kreutzer

Ordered Diagnosis 244
    D. Van Nieuwenborgh, D. Vermeir

Computing Preferred Answer Sets in Answer Set Programming 259
    T. Wakaki, K. Inoue, C. Sakama, K. Nitta

A Syntax-Based Approach to Reasoning about Actions and Events 274
    Q. Bao Vo, A. Nayak, N. Foo

Minimizing Automata on Infinite Words 289
    T. Wilke

Gandy's Theorem for Abstract Structures without the Equality Test 290
    M. Korovina

Efficient SAT Engines for Concise Logics:
Accelerating Proof Search for Zero-One Linear Constraint Systems 302
    M. Fränzle, C. Herde

NP-Completeness Results for Deductive Problems on Stratified Terms 317
    T. Boy de la Tour, M. Echenim

Is Cantor's Theorem Automatic? 332
    D. Kuske

Automatic Structures of Bounded Degree 346
    M. Lohrey

An Optimal Automata Approach to LTL Model Checking
of Probabilistic Systems 361
    J.-M. Couvreur, N. Saheb, G. Sutre

A Logical Study on Qualitative Default Reasoning with Probabilities 376
    C. Beierle, G. Kern-Isberner

On Structuring Proof Search for First Order Linear Logic 389
    P. Bruscoli, A. Guglielmi

Strict Geometry of Interaction Graph Models 407
    F. Honsell, M. Lenisa, R. Redamalla

Connection-Based Proof Construction in Non-commutative Logic 422
    D. Galmiche, J.-M. Notin

Author Index.. 437

From Tableaux to Automata
for Description Logics[*]

Franz Baader[1], Jan Hladik[1], Carsten Lutz[1], and Frank Wolter[2]

[1] Theoretical Computer Science, TU Dresden,
D-01062 Dresden, Germany,
{baader,hladik,lutz}@tcs.inf.tu-dresden.de
[2] Department of Computer Science, University of Liverpool,
Liverpool L69 7ZF, U.K.,
frank@csc.liv.ac.uk

Abstract. This paper investigates the relationship between automata-
and tableau-based inference procedures for Description Logics. To be
more precise, we develop an abstract notion of what a tableau-based algorithm is, and then show, on this abstract level, how tableau-based algorithms can be converted into automata-based algorithms. In particular,
this allows us to characterize a large class of tableau-based algorithms
that imply an ExpTime upper-bound for reasoning in the description
logics for which such an algorithm exists.

1 Introduction

Description logics (DLs) [1] are a family of knowledge representation languages
which can be used to represent the terminological knowledge of an application
domain in a structured and formally well-understood way. The name *description
logics* is motivated by the fact that, on the one hand, the important notions of
the domain are described by *concept descriptions*, i.e., expressions that are built
from atomic concepts (unary predicates) and atomic roles (binary predicates)
using the concept and role constructors provided by the particular DL. On the
other hand, DLs differ from their predecessors, such as semantic networks and
frames [21, 25], in that they are equipped with a formal, *logic*-based semantics,
which can, e.g., be given by a translation into first-order predicate logic.

Knowledge representation systems based on description logics (DL systems)
[22, 30] provide their users with various inference capabilities (like subsumption
and instance checking) that allow them to deduce implicit knowledge from the
explicitly represented knowledge. In order to ensure a reasonable and predictable
behavior of a DL system, these inference problems should at least be decidable,
and preferably of low complexity. Consequently, the expressive power of the DL
in question must be restricted in an appropriate way. If the imposed restrictions
are too severe, however, then the important notions of the application domain

---

[*] Partially supported by the EU Network of Excellence CoLogNET and the German
Research Foundation (DFG).

M.Y. Vardi and A. Voronkov (Eds.): LPAR 2003, LNAI 2850, pp. 1–32, 2003.
© Springer-Verlag Berlin Heidelberg 2003

can no longer be expressed. Investigating this trade-off between the expressivity of DLs and the complexity of their inference problems has been one of the most important issues in DL research (see [9] for an overview of complexity results).

The focus of this research has, however, changed in the last 15 years. In the beginning of the 1990ies, DL researchers investigated the border between tractable and intractable DLs [11, 12], and systems that employed so-called structural subsumption algorithms, which first normalize the concept descriptions, and then recursively compare the syntactic structure of the normalized descriptions, were still prevalent [19, 20, 23, 24]. It quickly turned out, however, that structural subsumption algorithms can handle only very inexpressive languages, and that one cannot expect a DL of reasonable expressive power to have tractable inference problems. For expressive DLs, tableau-based inference procedures turned out to be quite useful. After the first such tableau-based subsumption algorithm was developed by Schmidt-Schauß and Smolka [27] for the DL $\mathcal{ALC}$, this approach was extended to various other DLs and also to other inference problems such as the instance problem (see [4] for an overview).

Most of these early tableau-based algorithms for DLs were of optimal worst-case complexity: they treated DLs with a PSPACE-complete subsumption problem, and the algorithms needed only polynomial space. Thus, by designing a tableau-based algorithm for such a DL one could solve two problems simultaneously: prove an optimal complexity upper-bound, and describe an algorithm that is easy to implement and optimize [2], thus yielding a practical reasoning system for this DL. [15] and RACER [13] are based on very expressive DLs (like $\mathcal{SHIQ}$ [18]), which have an ExpTime-complete subsumption problem. high worst-case complexity of the underlying logics, the systems FaCT and RACER behave quite well in realistic applications. This is mainly due to the fact that their implementors have developed a great variety of sophisticated optimization techniques for tableau-based algorithms (see [16] for an overview of these techniques). Tableau-based algorithms are, however, notoriously bad at proving ExpTime upper-bounds.[1] In many cases, ExpTime upper-bounds are easily established using automata-based approaches (see, e.g., Section 5.3 in [7]). However, to the best of our knowledge, there exist no practical DL reasoners based on automata techniques. two different algorithms for every ExpTime-complete DL, an automata-based one for establishing the exact worst-case complexity, and a tableau-based one for the implementation.

This paper investigates the (rather close) relationship between automata- and tableau-based algorithms. To be more precise, we develop an abstract notion of what a tableau-based algorithm is, and then show, on this abstract level, how tableau-based algorithms can be converted into automata-based algorithms. In particular, this allows us to characterize a large class of tableau-based algorithms that imply an ExpTime upper-bound for reasoning in the DLs for which such an algorithm exists. We consider this to be a very useful result since, in many cases, it eliminates the need for developing two algorithms for the same DL: one

---

[1] treats the case of $\mathcal{ALC}$ with general concept inclusions (GCIs), and even in this simple case the algorithm is very complicated.

can now design a tableau-based algorithm, use our general result to obtain an ExpTime upper-bound, and then base a practical implementation on the very same algorithm. We illustrate the usefulness of our framework by reproving the known ExpTime upper-bounds for the description logic $\mathcal{ALC}$ with general concept inclusions [26], and for the extension $\mathcal{ALCQI}$ of $\mathcal{ALC}$ by qualified number restrictions and inverse roles [8].

In the next section, we introduce the abstract notion of a tableau system. In order to motivate and illustrate the technical definitions, we first consider the example of a tableau-based algorithm for $\mathcal{ALC}$ with general concept inclusions. In Section 3, we define additional restrictions on tableau systems that ensure an exponential upper-bound on reasoning. This upper-bound is shown via a translation of tableau systems into looping tree automata. In Section 4, we show how tableau systems can directly be used to obtain a tableau-based decision procedure, which can be the basis for an optimized implementation. The main problem to be solved there is to ensure termination of the tableau-based algorithm. In Section 5, we apply the abstract framework to a more complex DL: we design a tableau system for the DL $\mathcal{ALCQI}$, thus giving an alternative proof of the known ExpTime upper-bound for reasoning in this DL. Finally, in Section 6, we discuss possible variants and extensions of the abstract framework.

2 Formalizing Tableau Algorithms

In this section, we develop an abstract formalization of tableau algorithms. To this end, we first discuss the standard tableau-based algorithm for the basic description logic $\mathcal{ALC}$, and then use this concrete example as a guide when devising the abstract framework.

2.1 A Tableau Algorithm for $\mathcal{ALC}$

We start with introducing the syntax and semantics of $\mathcal{ALC}$:

Definition 1 ($\mathcal{ALC}$ Syntax). *Let* N_C *and* N_R *be pairwise disjoint and countably infinite sets of* concept names *and* role names. *The set of* $\mathcal{ALC}$*-concepts* $CON_{\mathcal{ALC}}$ *is the smallest set such that*

- *every concept name is an* $\mathcal{ALC}$*-concept, and*
- *if* C *and* D *are* $\mathcal{ALC}$*-concepts and* r *is a role name, then the following expressions are also* $\mathcal{ALC}$*-concepts:* $\neg C$, $C \sqcap D$, $C \sqcup D$, $\exists r.C$, $\forall r.C$.

A general concept inclusion (GCI) *is an expression* $C \sqsubseteq D$, *where both* C *and* D *are* $\mathcal{ALC}$*-concepts. A finite set of GCIs is called* $\mathcal{ALC}$*-TBox. We use* $TBOX_{\mathcal{ALC}}$ *to denote the set of all* $\mathcal{ALC}$*-TBoxes.*

As usual, we will use $\top$ as abbreviation for an arbitrary propositional tautology, $\bot$ for $\neg\top$, and $C \to D$ for $\neg C \sqcup D$.

Note that there exist several different TBox formalisms that vary considerably w.r.t. expressive power (see [3]). The kind of TBoxes adopted here are among the most general ones available. They are supported by modern DL reasoners such as FaCT and RACER.

Like all DLs, $\mathcal{ALC}$ is equipped with a Tarski-style set-theoretic semantics.

Definition 2 ($\mathcal{ALC}$ Semantics). *An interpretation $\mathcal{I}$ is a pair $(\Delta^{\mathcal{I}}, \cdot^{\mathcal{I}})$, where $\Delta^{\mathcal{I}}$ is a non-empty set, called the* domain, *and $\cdot^{\mathcal{I}}$ is the* interpretation function. *The interpretation function maps each concept name A to a subset $A^{\mathcal{I}}$ of $\Delta^{\mathcal{I}}$ and each role name r to a subset $r^{\mathcal{I}}$ of $\Delta^{\mathcal{I}} \times \Delta^{\mathcal{I}}$. It is extended to arbitrary $\mathcal{ALC}$-concepts as follows:*

$$(\neg C)^{\mathcal{I}} := \Delta^{\mathcal{I}} \setminus C^{\mathcal{I}}$$
$$(C \sqcap D)^{\mathcal{I}} := C^{\mathcal{I}} \cap D^{\mathcal{I}}$$
$$(C \sqcup D)^{\mathcal{I}} := C^{\mathcal{I}} \cup D^{\mathcal{I}}$$
$$(\exists r.C)^{\mathcal{I}} := \{d \in \Delta^{\mathcal{I}} \mid \text{There is } e \in \Delta^{\mathcal{I}} \text{ with } (d,e) \in r^{\mathcal{I}} \text{ and } e \in C^{\mathcal{I}}\}$$
$$(\forall r.C)^{\mathcal{I}} := \{d \in \Delta^{\mathcal{I}} \mid \text{For all } e \in \Delta^{\mathcal{I}}, \text{ if } (d,e) \in r^{\mathcal{I}}, \text{ then } e \in C^{\mathcal{I}}\}$$

The interpretation $\mathcal{I}$ is a model *of the $\mathcal{ALC}$-concept C iff $C^{\mathcal{I}} \neq \emptyset$, and it is a model of the TBox $\mathcal{T}$ iff $C^{\mathcal{I}} \subseteq D^{\mathcal{I}}$ holds for all $C \sqsubseteq D \in \mathcal{T}$.*

The main inference problems related to a TBox are satisfiability and subsumption of concepts.

Definition 3 ($\mathcal{ALC}$ Inference Problems). *The $\mathcal{ALC}$-concept C is* satisfiable *w.r.t. the TBox $\mathcal{T}$ iff C and $\mathcal{T}$ have a common model, and C is* subsumed by *the $\mathcal{ALC}$-concept D w.r.t. the TBox $\mathcal{T}$ (written $C \sqsubseteq_{\mathcal{T}} D$) iff $C^{\mathcal{I}} \subseteq D^{\mathcal{I}}$ holds for all models $\mathcal{I}$ of $\mathcal{T}$.*

Since $C \sqsubseteq_{\mathcal{T}} D$ iff $C \sqcap \neg D$ is unsatisfiable w.r.t. $\mathcal{T}$, it is sufficient to design a satisfiability algorithm. We now discuss the standard tableau-based satisfiability algorithm for $\mathcal{ALC}$. This algorithm has first been described in [27]; more modern accounts can, e.g., be found in [4]. It can rightfully be viewed as the ancestor from which all state-of-the-art tableau-based algorithms for description logics are descended. Such algorithms are nowadays the standard approach for reasoning in DLs, and they underlie modern and efficient reasoning systems such as FaCT and RACER, which are based on DLs that are much more expressive than $\mathcal{ALC}$.

Tableau algorithms are characterized by an underlying data structure, a set of completion rules, and a number of so-called clash-triggers. To decide the satisfiability of an input concept C w.r.t. an input TBox $\mathcal{T}$, the algorithm starts with an initial instance of the data structure constructed from C and $\mathcal{T}$, and repeatedly applies completion rules to it. This rule application can be viewed as an attempt to construct a model for the input, or as making implicit knowledge explicit. Rule application continues until either one of the clash-triggers applies, which means that the attempt to construct a model has failed, or all implicit knowledge has been made explicit without encountering a clash-trigger. In the latter case, the algorithm has succeeded to construct (a representation of) a model. To be more precise, the tableau algorithms considered in this paper may be non-deterministic, i.e., there may exist completion rules that yield more

R⊓	if $C_1 \sqcap C_2 \in \mathcal{N}(a)$ and $\{C_1, C_2\} \not\subseteq \mathcal{N}(a)$ then $\mathcal{N}(a) := \mathcal{N}(a) \cup \{C_1, C_2\}$
R⊔	if $C_1 \sqcup C_2 \in \mathcal{N}(a)$ and $\{C_1, C_2\} \cap \mathcal{N}(a) = \emptyset$ then $\mathcal{N}(a) := \mathcal{N}(a) \cup \{C\}$ for some $C \in \{C_1, C_2\}$
R∃	if $\exists r.C \in \mathcal{N}(a)$ and there is no r-successor b of a with $C \in \mathcal{N}(b)$, then generate a new successor b of a, and set $\mathcal{E}(a, b) := r$ and $\mathcal{N}(b) := \{C\}$
R∀	if $\forall r.C \in \mathcal{N}(a)$ and b is an r-successor of a with $C \notin \mathcal{N}(b)$ then set $\mathcal{N}(b) := \mathcal{N}(b) \cup \{C\}$
R$\mathcal{T}$	if $C \sqsubseteq D \in \mathcal{T}$ and $\mathsf{nnf}(C \to D) \notin \mathcal{N}(a)$ then set $\mathcal{N}(a) := \mathcal{N}(a) \cup \{\mathsf{nnf}(C \to D)\}$

Fig. 1. Completion rules for $\mathcal{ALC}$.

than one possible outcome. In this case, the algorithm returns "satisfiable" iff there exists at least *one* way to apply the non-deterministic rules such that a model of the input is obtained. Note that only the choice of the outcome of non-deterministic rules is true "don't know" non-determinism (and thus requires backtracking), whereas the order of rule applications is basically "don't care" non-determinism.

Before we can define the data structure underlying the $\mathcal{ALC}$ tableau algorithm, so-called completion trees, we must introduce some notation. Given an $\mathcal{ALC}$-concept C, its *negation normal form* is an equivalent[2] concept such that negation occurs only in front of concept names. Such a concept can easily be computed by pushing negation as far as possible into concepts, using de Morgan's rules and the usual duality rules for quantifiers. We will denote the negation normal form of C by $\mathsf{nnf}(C)$. If C is an $\mathcal{ALC}$-concept and $\mathcal{T}$ an $\mathcal{ALC}$-TBox, then we use $\mathsf{sub}(C, \mathcal{T})$ to denote the set of all subconcepts of the concepts in the set

$$\{\mathsf{nnf}(C)\} \cup \bigcup_{D \sqsubseteq E \in \mathcal{T}} \{\mathsf{nnf}(D \to E)\}.$$

Definition 4 (Completion Trees). *Let C be an $\mathcal{ALC}$-concept and $\mathcal{T}$ an $\mathcal{ALC}$-TBox. A completion tree[3] for C and $\mathcal{T}$ is a labeled tree[3] $T = (V, E, \mathcal{N}, \mathcal{E})$ of finite out-degree such that (V, E) is a tree, each node $a \in V$ is labeled with a subset $\mathcal{N}(a)$ of $\mathsf{sub}(C, \mathcal{T})$ and each edge $(a, b) \in E$ is labeled with a role name $\mathcal{E}(a, b)$ occurring in C or $\mathcal{T}$.*

The completion rules are given in Figure 1, where R⊔ is the only non-deterministic rule. To decide satisfiability of a concept C w.r.t. a TBox $\mathcal{T}$, the

---

[2] Two concepts are equivalent iff they subsume each other w.r.t. the empty TBox.

[3] Here and in the following, a tree is an acyclic directed graph (V, E) with a unique root where every node other than the root is reachable from the root and has exactly one predecessor. The edge relation E is a sub*set* of $V \times V$, and thus the successors of a given node are not ordered.

$\mathcal{ALC}$ tableau algorithm starts with the initial completion tree

$$T_{C,\mathcal{T}} := (\{x\}, \emptyset, \{x \mapsto \{\mathsf{nnf}(C)\}\}, \emptyset)$$

and repeatedly applies completion rules. Rule application stops in one of the following two cases:

1. the obtained completion tree $T = (V, E, \mathcal{N}, \mathcal{E})$ *contains a clash*, i.e. there is a node $a \in V$ and a concept name A such that $\{A, \neg A\} \subseteq \mathcal{N}(a)$;
2. T is *saturated*, i.e. no more completion rule is applicable to T.

If we consider only empty TBoxes (and thus drop the R$\mathcal{T}$ rule), then the described algorithm terminates for any input and any sequence of rule applications. Things are not so simple if we admit non-empty TBoxes: because of the R$\mathcal{T}$ rule, the algorithm need not terminate, both on satisfiable and on unsatisfiable inputs. For example, rule application to the concept $\top$ and the TBox $\{\top \sqsubseteq \exists R.\top\}$ continues indefinitely. However, the algorithm then computes an infinite "increasing" sequence of completion trees: in each step, the tree and its node labels may only grow but never shrink. In case of non-termination, there thus exists a unique completion tree computed by this run of the algorithm "in the limit". Thus, both terminating and non-terminating runs of the algorithm "compute" a unique completion tree. This (possibly infinite) completion tree is called *saturated* iff no more completion rule is applicable to it.

The tableau algorithm for $\mathcal{ALC}$ is sound and complete in the following sense:

- *Soundness.* If the algorithm computes a saturated and clash-free completion tree for the input $C, \mathcal{T}$, then C is satisfiable w.r.t. $\mathcal{T}$.
- *Completeness.* If the input $C, \mathcal{T}$ is satisfiable, then there is a run of the algorithm that computes a saturated and clash-free completion tree for this input.

Given these notions of soundness and completeness, it should be clear that we want our algorithm to compute saturated completion trees. Obviously, any terminating run of the algorithm yields a saturated completion tree. For this reason, the order of rule applications is in this case "don't care" non-deterministic. For a non-terminating run, this is only true if we require completion rules to be applied in a *fair*[4] manner. Ensuring fairness is a simple task: we can, e.g., always apply completion rules to those nodes in the tree that are as close to the root as possible. This yields a fair strategy since the out-degree of completion trees constructed for an input $C, \mathcal{T}$ is bounded by the cardinality of the set $\mathsf{sub}(C, \mathcal{T})$.

Although the procedure as described until now does not necessarily terminate and thus is no decision procedure for satisfiability, quite surprisingly we will see that it already provides us with enough information to deduce an Exp-Time upper-bound for $\mathcal{ALC}$-concept satisfiability (and thus, in particular, with a decidability result). This will be shown by a translation into a tree automaton,

---

[4] Intuitively, fairness means that rules are applied such that every applicable rule will eventually be applied unless it is made inapplicable by the application of other rules.

which basically accepts saturated and clash-free completion trees for the input. We view this as a rather convenient feature of our framework: to obtain an Exp-Time decision procedure, it is sufficient to design a sound and complete tableau algorithm and not even bother to prove termination, a usually hard task (see Section 3 for details). Moreover, we will show in Section 4 that a given non-terminating sound and complete tableau procedure can always be turned into a terminating sound and complete procedure. This yields a tableau-based *decision* procedure, which is, however, not necessarily of ExpTime complexity.

2.2   The General Framework

We now develop a general notion of tableau algorithms. It is in the nature of this endeavor that our formalism will be a rather abstract one. We start with defining the core notion: tableau systems. Intuitively, the purpose of a tableau system is to capture all the details of a tableau algorithm such as the one for $\mathcal{ALC}$ discussed in the previous section. The set $\mathfrak{I}$ of inputs used in the following definition can be thought of as consisting of all possible pairs $(C, \mathcal{T})$ of concepts C and TBoxes $\mathcal{T}$ of the DL under consideration.

Definition 5 (Tableau System). *Let $\mathfrak{I}$ be a set of* inputs. *A* tableau system *for $\mathfrak{I}$ is a tuple*

$$S = (\mathsf{NLE}, \mathsf{EL}, \cdot^S, \mathcal{R}, \mathcal{C}),$$

where NLE *and* EL *are sets of* node label elements *and* edge labels, *respectively, and $\cdot^S$ is a function mapping each input $\Gamma \in \mathfrak{I}$ to a tuple*

$$\Gamma^S = (\mathsf{nle}, \mathsf{el}, \mathsf{ini})$$

such that

- nle $\subseteq$ NLE *and* el $\subseteq$ EL *are finite;*
- ini *is a subset of $\wp(\mathsf{nle})$, where $\wp(\cdot)$ denotes powerset.*

The definitions of $\mathcal{R}$ and $\mathcal{C}$ depend on the notion of an S-pattern, which is a finite labeled tree

$$(V, E, n, \ell),$$

of depth at most one with $n : V \to \wp(\mathsf{NLE})$ and $\ell : E \to \mathsf{EL}$ node and edge labeling functions.

- $\mathcal{R}$, *the collection of* completion rules, *is is a function mapping each S-pattern to a finite set of non-empty finite sets of S-patterns;*
- $\mathcal{C}$, *the collection of* clash-triggers, *is a set of S-patterns.*

To illustrate tableau systems, we now define a tableau system $S_{\mathcal{ALC}}$ that describes the $\mathcal{ALC}$ tableau algorithm discussed in the previous section. Intuitively, NLE is the set of elements that may appear in node labels of completion trees, *independently* of the input. In the case of $\mathcal{ALC}$, NLE is thus simply $\mathrm{CON}_{\mathcal{ALC}}$.

Similarly, EL is the set of edge labels, also independently of the input. In the case of $\mathcal{ALC}$, EL is thus the set of role names N_R.

The function $\cdot^S$ describes the impact of the input on the form of the constructed completion trees. More precisely, nle fixes the node label elements that may be used in a completion tree for a particular input, and el fixes the edge labels. Finally, ini describes the possible initial node labels of the root of the completion tree. Note that the initial root label is not necessarily unique, but rather there can be many choices—a possible source of (don't know) non-determinism that does not show up in the $\mathcal{ALC}$ algorithm.

To illustrate the function $\cdot^S$, let us define it for the tableau system $S_{\mathcal{ALC}}$. For simplicity, we write $\mathsf{nle}_{S_{\mathcal{ALC}}}(C,\mathcal{T})$ to refer to the first element of the tuple $(C,\mathcal{T})^{S_{\mathcal{ALC}}}$, $\mathsf{el}_{S_{\mathcal{ALC}}}(C,\mathcal{T})$ to refer to the second element of the tuple $(C,\mathcal{T})^{S_{\mathcal{ALC}}}$, and so forth. For each input $C, \mathcal{T} \in \mathsf{CON}_{\mathcal{ALC}} \times \mathsf{TBOX}_{\mathcal{ALC}}$, we have

$$\mathsf{nle}_{S_{\mathcal{ALC}}}(C,\mathcal{T}) = \mathsf{sub}(C,\mathcal{T});$$
$$\mathsf{el}_{S_{\mathcal{ALC}}}(C,\mathcal{T}) = \{r \in N_R \mid r \text{ appears in } C \text{ or } \mathcal{T}\};$$
$$\mathsf{ini}_{S_{\mathcal{ALC}}}(C,\mathcal{T}) = \{\{\mathsf{nnf}(C)\}\}.$$

It remains to formalize the completion rules and clash-triggers. First observe that, in the $\mathcal{ALC}$ tableau, every clash-trigger, every rule premise, and every rule consequence concerns only a single node either alone or together with its successors in the completion tree. This observation motivates our definition of patterns, which formalize clash-triggers as well as pre- and post-conditions of completion rules. The collection of completion rules $\mathcal{R}$ maps patterns to finite sets of finite sets of patterns. Intuitively, if P is a pattern and $\{P_1, \ldots, P_k\} \in \mathcal{R}(P)$, then this means that a rule of the collection can be applied to completion trees matching the pattern P, non-deterministically replacing the "area" matching P with an "area" matching one of the patterns $P_1, \ldots, P_k$ (we will give a formal definition of this later on). If $\{P_1, \ldots, P_k\} \in \mathcal{R}(P)$, then we will usually write

$$P \rightarrow_{\mathcal{R}} \{P_1, \ldots, P_k\}$$

to indicate the rule induced by this element of $\mathcal{R}(P)$. Similar to the application of such a rule, a completion tree contains a clash if this completion tree matches a pattern in $\mathcal{C}$.

To illustrate this, let us again consider the case of $\mathcal{ALC}$. For $\mathcal{ALC}$, the set of clash-triggers $\mathcal{C}$ consists of all patterns whose root label contains both A and $\neg A$ for some concept name A. Thus, a completion tree contains a clash if one of its nodes labels contains A and $\neg A$ for some concept name A.

With one exception, the collection of completion rules is defined by a straightforward translation of the rules in Figure 1. For each pattern $P = (V, E, n, \ell)$ with root v_0, $\mathcal{R}(P)$ is the smallest set of finite sets of patterns such that the following holds:

R⊓   if the root label $n(v_0)$ contains the concept $C \sqcap D$ and $\{C, D\} \not\subseteq n(v_0)$, then $\mathcal{R}(P)$ contains the singleton set $\{(V, E, n', \ell)\}$, where $n'(v) = n(v)$ for all $v \in V \setminus \{v_0\}$ and $n'(v_0) = n(v_0) \cup \{C, D\}$;

RⵙⴴⵙⴴR⊔ if the root label $n(v_0)$ contains the concept $C \sqcup D$ and $\{C, D\} \cap n(v_0) = \emptyset$, then $\mathcal{R}(P)$ contains the set $\{(V, E, n', \ell), (V, E, n'', \ell)\}$, where $n'(v) = n''(v) = n(v)$ for all $v \in V \setminus \{v_0\}$ and $n'(v_0) = n(v_0) \cup \{C\}$ and $n''(v_0) = n(v_0) \cup \{D\}$;

R∃ if the root label $n(v_0)$ contains the concept $\exists r.C$, $u_1, \ldots, u_m$ are all the sons of v_0 with $\ell(v_0, u_i) = r$, and $C \notin n(u_i)$ for all $i, 1 \le i \le m$, then $\mathcal{R}(P)$ contains the set $\{P_0, P_1, \ldots, P_m\}$, where
- $P_0 = (V_0, E_0, n_0, \ell_0)$, where u_0 is a node not contained in V, $V_0 = V \cup \{u_0\}$, $E' = E \cup \{(v_0, u_0)\}$, $n_0 = n \cup \{u_0 \mapsto \{C\}\}$, $\ell' = \ell \cup \{(v_0, u_0) \mapsto r\}$,
- for $i = 1, \ldots, m$, $P_i = (V, E, n_i, \ell)$, where $n_i(v) = n(v)$ for all $v \in V \setminus \{u_i\}$ and $n_i(u_i) = n(u_i) \cup \{C\}$;

R∀ if $n(v_0)$ contains the concept $\forall r.C$, $\ell(r, v_1) = r$ for some $v_1 \in V$, and $C \notin n(v_1)$, then $\mathcal{R}(P)$ contains $\{(V, E, n', \ell)\}$, where $n'(v) = n(v)$ for all $v \in V \setminus \{v_1\}$ and $n'(v_1) = n(v_1) \cup \{C\}$;

R𝒯 if $C \sqsubseteq D \in \mathcal{T}$ and $\mathsf{nnf}(C \to D) \notin n(v_0)$, then $\mathcal{R}(P)$ contains the set $\{(V, E, n', \ell)\}$, where $n'(v) = n(v)$ for all $v \in V \setminus \{v_0\}$ and $n'(v_0) = n(v_0) \cup \{\mathsf{nnf}(C \to D)\}$.

The exception is the treatment of existential restrictions. The rule in Figure 1 is deterministic: it always generates a *new* r-successor of the given node. In contrast, the rule handling existential restrictions introduced above (don't know) non-deterministically chooses between generating a new successor or re-using one of the old ones. Basically, this is the price we have to pay for having a very general framework. The reason why one can always create a new individual when treating existential restrictions in $\mathcal{ALC}$ is that $\mathcal{ALC}$ is invariant under bisimulation [5], and thus one can duplicate successors in models without changing validity. We could have tailored our framework such that the deterministic rule for $\mathcal{ALC}$ can be used, but then we basically would have restricted its applicability to DLs invariant under bisimulation (see Section 6 for a more detailed discussion of this issue).

Let us now continue with the general definitions. Tableau systems are a rather general notion. In fact, as described until now they are too general to be useful for our purposes. For example, tableau algorithms described by such tableau systems need not be monotonic: completion rules could repeatedly (even indefinitely) add and remove the same piece of information. To prevent such pathologic behavior, we now formulate a number of conditions that "well-behaved" tableau systems are supposed to satisfy. For the following definitions, fix a set of inputs $\mathfrak{I}$ and a tableau system $S = (\mathsf{NLE}, \mathsf{EL}, \cdot^S, \mathcal{R}, \mathcal{C})$ for $\mathfrak{I}$. Before we can define admissibility of tableau systems, we must introduce an "inclusion relation" between patterns.

Definition 6. Let $P = (V, E, n, \ell)$ and $P' = (V', E', n', \ell')$ be S-patterns. We write $P \precsim P'$ iff the following conditions are satisfied: there is an injection $\pi : V \to V'$ that maps the root of P to the root of P' and satisfies the following conditions:
- for all $x \in V$, we have $n(x) \subseteq n'(\pi(x))$;

- for all $x, y \in V$, if $(x, y) \in E$, then $(\pi(x), \pi(y)) \in E'$ and
  $\ell(x, y) = \ell'(\pi(x), \pi(y))$;

If π is the identity on V, then we write $P \preceq P'$ (and $P \prec P'$ if, additionally, $P \neq P'$). If π is a bijection and $n(x) = n'(\pi(x))$ for all $x \in V$, then we write $P \sim P'$. To make the injection (bijection) π explicit, we sometimes write $P \precsim_\pi P'$ ($P \sim_\pi P'$).

Let $\Gamma \in \mathfrak{J}$ be an input. We say that P is a *pattern for* Γ iff the labels of all nodes in P are subsets of $\mathsf{nle}_S(\Gamma)$ and the labels of all edges in P belong to $\mathsf{el}_S(\Gamma)$. The pattern P is *saturated* iff $\mathcal{R}(P) = \emptyset$.

Definition 7 (Admissible). *The tableau system S is called* admissible *iff it satisfies, for all S-patterns $P = (V, E, n, \ell)$ and $P' = (V', E', n', \ell')$, the following conditions:*

1. *If $P \rightarrow_\mathcal{R} \{P_1, \ldots, P_k\}$, then $P \prec P_i$ for all $i, 1 \leq i \leq k$.*
2. *If $P \rightarrow_\mathcal{R} \{P_1, \ldots, P_k\}$, P' is saturated, and $P \precsim P'$, then there exists an $i, 1 \leq i \leq k$, such that $P_i \precsim P'$.*
3. *For all inputs $\Gamma \in \mathfrak{J}$, if P is a pattern for Γ and $P \rightarrow_\mathcal{R} \{P_1, \ldots, P_k\}$, then the patterns P_i are patterns for Γ.*
4. *If $P \in \mathcal{C}$ and $P \precsim P'$, then $P' \in \mathcal{C}$.*

It is in order to discuss the intuition underlying the above conditions. Condition 1 basically says that rule application always adds nodes or elements of node labels. Condition 2 can be understood as follows. Assume that a (non-deterministic) rule is applicable to P and that P' is a "superpattern" of P that is saturated (i.e., all applicable rules have already been applied). Then the non-deterministic rule can be applied in such a way that the obtained new pattern is still a subpattern of P'. Intuitively, this condition can be used to reach P' from P by repeated rule application. Condition 3 says that, by applying completion rules for some input Γ, we stay within the limits given by the values of the $\cdot^S$ function. Condition 4 states that applicability of clash-triggers is monotonic, i.e., if a pattern triggers a clash, all its "superpatterns" also trigger a clash.

It is easy to see that these conditions are satisfied by the tableau system $S_{\mathcal{ALC}}$ for $\mathcal{ALC}$. For Condition 1, this is obvious since the rules only add nodes or elements of node labels, but never remove them. Condition 3 holds since rules only add subconcepts of existing concepts to the node label. Condition 4 is also clear: if the label of the root of P contains A and $\neg A$, then the label of the root of every superpattern also contains A and $\neg A$.

The most interesting condition is Condition 2. We illustrate it by considering the treatment of disjunction and of existential restrictions in $S_{\mathcal{ALC}}$. First, assume that $P \rightarrow_\mathcal{R} \{P_1, P_2\}$ where the root label of P contains $C \sqcup D$ and the root labels of P_1 and P_2 are obtained from the root label of P by respectively adding C and D. If $P \precsim P'$, then the root label of P' also contains $C \sqcup D$. If, in addition, P' is saturated, then its root label already contains C or D. In the first case, $P' \precsim P_1$ and in the second $P' \precsim P_2$.

Second, consider the rules handling existential restrictions. Thus, let $P \precsim P'$, and assume that the root label of P contains the existential restriction $\exists r.C$ and that the root of P has m r-successors $u_1, \ldots, u_m$. Then the existential restriction $\exists r.C$ induces the rule $P \to_\mathcal{R} \{P_0, \ldots, P_m\}$ where the patterns $P_0, \ldots, P_m$ are as defined above. If, in addition, P' is saturated, then its root has an r-successor whose label contains C. If this is a "new" r-successor (i.e., one not in the range of the injection π that ensures $P \precsim P'$), then $P_0 \precsim P'$.[5] Otherwise, there is an r-successor u_i of the root of P such that the label of $\pi(u_i)$ in P' contains C. In this case, $P_i \precsim P'$.

We now introduce S-trees, the abstract counterpart of completion trees, and define what it means for a pattern to match into an S-tree.

Definition 8 (S-Tree, Matching). *An S-tree is a labeled tree $T = (V, E, n, \ell)$ with finite out-degree, a countable set of nodes V, and the node and edge labeling functions $n : V \to \wp(\mathsf{NLE})$ and $\ell : E \to \mathsf{EL}$.*

Any node $x \in V$ defines a pattern T, x, the neighborhood of x in T, as follows: $T, x := (V', E', n', \ell')$ where

- *$V' = \{x\} \cup \{y \in V \mid (x, y) \in E\}$;*
- *E', n', ℓ' are the restrictions of E, n, ℓ to V';*

If $P = (V', E', n', \ell')$ is an arbitrary S-pattern and $x \in V$, then we say that P matches x in T iff $P \sim T, x$ (see Definition 6).

For the tableau system for $\mathcal{ALC}$ introduced above, $S_{\mathcal{ALC}}$-trees are exactly the completion trees defined in Section 2.

We are now ready to describe rule application on an abstract level. Intuitively, the rule $P \to_\mathcal{R} \{P_1, \ldots, P_k\}$ can be applied to the node x in the tree T if $P \sim T, x$, and its application yields the new tree T', which is obtained from T by adding new successor nodes of x and/or extending the node labels, as indicated by some P_i. This intuition is formalized in the following definition.

Definition 9 (Rule Application). *Let S be an admissible tableau system, $T = (V, E, n, \ell)$ be an S-tree, and $P \to_\mathcal{R} \{P_1, \ldots, P_k\}$ be a rule of S. The S-tree $T' = (V', E', n', \ell')$ is obtained from T by application of this rule to a node $x \in V$ iff the following holds:*

1. *$V \subseteq V'$;*
2. *$E' = E \cup \{(x, y) \mid y \in V' \setminus V\}$;*
3. *ℓ' extends ℓ, i.e., $\ell(y, z) = \ell'(y, z)$ for all $(y, z) \in E$;*
4. *$P \sim_\pi T, x$ for some bijection π;*
5. *$P_i \sim_{\pi'} T', x$ for some $i, 1 \le i \le k$ and bijection π' extending π;[6]*
6. *for all $y \in V$ with $y \notin \mathsf{ran}(\pi)$, we have $n(y) = n'(y)$.*

---

[5] This shows that we cannot replace $\precsim$ by $\preceq$ in the statement of Condition 2. In fact, we cannot be sure that the new successor introduced in P_0 has the same name as the new successor in P'.

[6] Note that Condition 1 in the definition of admissibility implies that P_i differs from P in that the root may have additional successors, and that the node labels may be larger. Thus, π' differs from π in that the additional successors of the root are mapped to the elements of $V' \setminus V$.

Thus, rule application may add some new successors of x, may extend the labels of the existing successors of x and of x itself, and otherwise leaves the edge relation and the node and edge labels unchanged. For a fixed rule $P \to_{\mathcal{R}} \{P_1, \ldots, P_k\}$, a fixed choice of P_i, and a fixed node x in T, the results of the rule application is unique up to the names of the new nodes in $V' \setminus V$. It is easy to check that, in the case of $S_{\mathcal{ALC}}$, rule application as defined above captures precisely the intuitive understanding of rule application employed in Section 2.

To finish our abstract definition of tableau algorithms, we need some way to describe the set of S-trees that can be obtained by starting with an initial S-tree for an input Γ, and then repeatedly applying completion rules. This leads to the notion of S-trees for Γ.

Definition 10 (S-Tree for Γ). *Let S be an admissible tableau system, and let Γ be an input for S. The set of S-trees for Γ is the smallest set of S-trees such that*

1. *All initial S-trees for Γ belong to this set, where an initial S-tree for Γ is of the form*
$$(\{v_0\}, \emptyset, \{v_0 \mapsto \Lambda\}, \emptyset)$$
where v_0 is a node and $\Lambda \in \mathsf{ini}_S(\Gamma)$.
2. *If T is an S-tree for Γ and T' can be obtained from T by the application of a completion rule, then T' is an S-tree for Γ.*
3. *If $T_0, T_1, \ldots$ is an infinite sequence of S-trees for Γ with $T_i = (V_i, E_i, n_i, \ell_i)$ such that*
   (a) *T_0 is an initial S-tree for Γ and*
   (b) *for all $i \geq 0$, T_{i+1} can be obtained from T_i by the application of a completion rule,*
   then the tree $T^\omega = (V, E, n, \ell)$ is also an S-tree for Γ, where
   - *$V = \bigcup_{i \geq 0} V_i$,*
   - *$E = \bigcup_{i \geq 0} E_i$,*
   - *$n = \bigcup_{i \geq 0} n_i$, and*
   - *$\ell = \bigcup_{i \geq 0} \ell_i$.*

Rule application may terminate after finitely many steps or continue forever. The last case of Definition 10 deals with such infinite sequences of rule applications. The S-tree T^ω can be viewed as the limit of the sequence of S-trees $T_0, T_1, \ldots$ This limit exists since admissibility of S implies that rule application is monotonic, i.e., it extends S-trees by new nodes or by additional elements in node labels, but it never removes nodes or elements of node labels.

Let us now define when an S-tree is saturated and clash-free.

Definition 11 (Saturated, Clash-Free). *Let S be an admissible tableau system. We say that the S-tree $T = (V, E, n, \ell)$ is*

- *saturated if, for every node x in T and every pattern P, $P \sim T, x$ implies $\mathcal{R}(P) = \emptyset$;*
- *clash-free if, for every node x in T and every $P \in \mathcal{C}$, we have $P \not\sim T, x$.*

Saturatedness says that no completion rule is applicable to the S-tree, and an S-tree is clash-free if no clash-trigger can be applied to any of its nodes.

Finally, we define soundness and completeness of tableau systems w.r.t. a certain property of its set of inputs. If the inputs are pairs consisting of a concept and a TBox, the property is usually satisfiability of the concept w.r.t. the TBox.

Definition 12 (Sound, Complete). *Let $\mathcal{P} \subseteq \mathfrak{I}$ be a property. The tableau system S is called*
- *sound for $\mathcal{P}$ iff, for any $\Gamma \in \mathfrak{I}$, the existence of a saturated and clash-free S-tree for Γ implies that $\Gamma \in \mathcal{P}$;*
- *complete for $\mathcal{P}$ iff, for any $\Gamma \in \mathcal{P}$, there exists a saturated and clash-free S-tree for Γ.*

It should be noted that the algorithmic treatment of tableau systems requires a stronger notion of completeness: an additional condition is needed to ensure that the out-degree of S-trees is appropriately bounded (see Definition 13 and Definition 20 below).

Taking into account the known soundness and completeness results for the $\mathcal{ALC}$ tableau algorithm described in Figure 1, it is straightforward to check that the tableau system $S_{\mathcal{ALC}}$ is sound and complete w.r.t. satisfiability of concepts w.r.t. TBoxes. Note, in particular, that saturated S-trees for an input Γ are precisely those S-trees for Γ that can be obtained by exhaustive or infinite and *fair* rule application.

3   ExpTime Automata-Based Decision Procedures from Tableau Systems

In this section, we define the class of "ExpTime-admissible" tableau systems. If such a tableau system is sound and complete for a property $\mathcal{P}$, then it gives rise to an ExpTime algorithm for deciding $\mathcal{P}$.[7] In the case where $\mathcal{P}$ is satisfiability of description logic concepts w.r.t. a (general) TBox, this means that the mere existence of an ExpTime-admissible tableau system for the DL implies an Exp-Time upper-bound for concept satisfiability w.r.t. (general) TBoxes in this DL. The ExpTime upper-bound is shown via a translation of the inputs of the Exp-Time-admissible tableau system into certain automata working on *infinite* trees. For this reason, ExpTime-admissible tableau systems need *not* deal with the issue of termination. Indeed, non-terminating tableau algorithms such as the one for $\mathcal{ALC}$ with general TBoxes introduced in Section 2.1 may yield ExpTime-admissible tableau systems.

Throughout this section, we consider a fixed set of inputs $\mathfrak{I}$ and a fixed tableau system $S = (\mathsf{NL}, \mathsf{EL}, \cdot^S, \mathcal{R}, \mathcal{C})$ for $\mathfrak{I}$, which is sound and complete w.r.t. some property $\mathcal{P}$.[7] As usual, the exponential upper-bound of deciding $\mathcal{P}$ is assumed to be in the "size" of the input $\Gamma \in \mathfrak{I}$. Thus, we assume that the set

---

[7] More precisely, we must demand a slightly stronger version of completeness, as introduced in Definition 13 below.

of inputs is equipped with a size function, which assigns to an input $\Gamma \in \mathfrak{I}$ a natural number, its size $|\Gamma|$.

3.1   Basic Notions

Recall that a tableau system S is sound and complete for a property $\mathcal{P}$ if, for any input Γ, we have $\Gamma \in \mathcal{P}$ iff there exists a (potentially infinite) saturated and clash-free S-tree for Γ. The fundamental idea for obtaining an ExpTime upper-bound for deciding $\mathcal{P}$ is to use automata on infinite trees to check for the existence of a clash-free and saturated S-tree for a given input Γ. More precisely, each input Γ is converted into a tree automaton $\mathcal{A}_\Gamma$ such that there exists a clash-free and saturated S-tree for Γ iff $\mathcal{A}_\Gamma$ accepts a non-empty language. Since tree automata work on trees of some fixed out-degree, this approach only works if the (size of the) input determines such a fixed out-degree for the S-trees to be considered. This motivates the following definition.

Definition 13 (p-Complete). *Let p be a polynomial. The tableau system S is called p-complete for $\mathcal{P}$ iff, for any $\Gamma \in \mathcal{P}$, there exists a saturated and clash-free S-tree for Γ with out-degree bounded by $p(|\Gamma|)$.*

Throughout this section, we assume that there exists a polynomial p such that the fixed tableau system S is p-complete w.r.t. the property $\mathcal{P}$ under consideration.

The tableau system $S_{\mathcal{ALC}}$ defined in Section 2 is easily proved to be i-complete, with i being the identity function on the natural numbers: using the formulation of the rules, it is easily proved that the out-degree of every $S_{\mathcal{ALC}}$-tree for the input $(C, \mathcal{T})$ is bounded by the number of concepts of the form $\exists r.D$ in $\mathsf{sub}(C, \mathcal{T})$ and thus also by

$$|(C, \mathcal{T})| := |C| + \sum_{C_1 \sqsubseteq C_2 \in \mathcal{T}} (|\mathsf{nnf}(C_1 \rightarrow C_2)|),$$

where $|E|$ denotes the length of the concept E.

It should be noted that most standard description logic tableau algorithms also exploit p-completeness of the underlying logic: although this is not made explicit in the formulation of the algorithm itself, it is usually one of the central arguments in termination proofs. The intuition that p-completeness is *not* an artefact of using an automata-based approach is reinforced by the fact that a similar strengthening of completeness is needed in Section 4, where we construct tableau-based decision procedures from tableau systems.

To ensure that the automaton $\mathcal{A}_\Gamma$ can be computed and tested for emptiness in exponential time, we require the function $\cdot^S$ of the tableau system S and the rules of S to exhibit an "acceptable" computational behavior. This is captured by the following definition. In this definition, we assume that all patterns are appropriately encoded in some finite alphabet, and thus can be the input for a decision procedure. The *size of a pattern* P is the sum of the sizes of its node and edge labels, where the size of a node label is the sum of the sizes of its node label elements.

Definition 14 (ExpTime-Admissible). *The tableau system S is called Exp-Time-admissible iff the following conditions are satisfied:*

1. *S is admissible (see Definition 7);*
2. *$\text{ini}_S(\Gamma)$ and $\text{el}_S(\Gamma)$ can be computed in time exponential in $|\Gamma|$, and the size of each edge label in $\text{el}_S(\Gamma)$ is polynomial in $|\Gamma|$;*
3. *the cardinality of $\text{nle}_S(\Gamma)$ and the size of each node label element in $\text{nle}_S(\Gamma)$ is polynomial in $|\Gamma|$, and $\text{nle}_S(\Gamma)$ can be computed in time exponential in $|\Gamma|$;*
4. *for each pattern P it can be checked in time exponential in the size of P whether, for all patterns P', $P' \sim P$ implies $\mathcal{R}(P') = \emptyset$;*
5. *for each pattern P it can be checked in time exponential in the size of P whether there is a clash-trigger $P' \in \mathcal{C}$ such that $P' \sim P$.*

Note that Point 2 of ExpTime-admissibility implies that, for each $\Gamma \in \mathfrak{I}$, the cardinality of the sets $\text{ini}_S(\Gamma)$ and $\text{el}_S(\Gamma)$ are at most exponential in $|\Gamma|$. The cardinality of the set of node label elements $\text{nle}_S(\Gamma)$ is explicitly required (in Point 3) to be polynomial. For the actual set of node labels (which are sets of node label elements), this yields an exponential upper-bound on its cardinality, but the size of each node label is polynomial in $|\Gamma|$. Since p-completeness implies that we consider only S-trees T of out-degree bounded by $p(|\Gamma|)$, and since the sizes of edge and node labels are polynomial in $|\Gamma|$, the size of each neighborhood T, x is polynomial in $|\Gamma|$. Thus, the fourth point ensures that the saturatedness condition can be checked in time exponential in $|\Gamma|$ for a given neighborhood T, x of T. The fifth point yields the same for clash-freeness.

Most standard description logic tableau algorithms for ExpTime-complete DLs trivially satisfy the conditions of ExpTime-admissibility. For example, it is easy to show that the tableau system $S_{\mathcal{ALC}}$ defined in Section 2 is ExpTime-admissible. We have already shown admissibility of $S_{\mathcal{ALC}}$, and Point 2 and 3 are immediate consequences of the definitions of $\text{ini}_{S_{\mathcal{ALC}}}$, $\text{nle}_{S_{\mathcal{ALC}}}$, and $\text{el}_{S_{\mathcal{ALC}}}$. To see that Points 4 and 5 are satisfied as well, first note that the definition of the rules and clash-triggers in $S_{\mathcal{ALC}}$ is invariant under isomorphism of patterns. For this reason, the decision problem in Point 4 reduces to checking whether a given pattern P is saturated (see the definition of this notion below Definition 6), and the decision problem in Point 5 reduces to checking whether a given pattern is a clash-trigger. As an example, we consider the rule handling existential restrictions. Let $P = (V, E, n, \ell)$ be a pattern with root v_0, and assume that $\exists r.C \in n(v_0)$. This existential restriction contributes a set of patterns to $\mathcal{R}(P)$ iff $C \notin n(u)$ for all r-successors u of v_0. Obviously, this can be checked in time polynomial in the size of the pattern.

The remainder of the present section is concerned with converting tableau systems into automata-based decision procedures, as outlined above. The major challenge is to bring together the different philosophies underlying tableau algorithms and automata-based approaches for deciding concept satisfiability: tableau algorithm actively try to *construct* a model for the input by applying rules, as reflected in the Definitions 9 and 10, whereas automata are based on the concept of "acceptance" of a tree, i.e., they verifying whether a *given* tree actually describes a model. Of course, the emptiness test for the automaton then again checks whether such a tree exists. Due to these different perspectives, it is not straightforward to construct automata that directly check for the existence of S-trees for an input Γ. To overcome this problem, we first introduce the (less constructive) notion of S-trees *compatible with Γ*, and investigate the relationship of this notion to S-trees *for Γ*, as introduced in Definition 10.

Definition 15 (S-Tree Compatible with Γ). *Let Γ be an input and $T = (V, E, n, \ell)$ an S-tree with root v_0. Then T is compatible with Γ iff it satisfies the following conditions:*

1. *$n(x) \subseteq \wp(\mathsf{nle}_S(\Gamma))$ for each $x \in V$;*
2. *$\ell(x, y) \in \mathsf{el}_S(\Gamma)$ for each $(x, y) \in E$;*
3. *there exists $\Lambda \in \mathsf{ini}_S(\Gamma)$ such that $\Lambda \subseteq n(v_0)$;*
4. *the out-degree of T is bounded by $p(|\Gamma|)$.*

Below, we will show that, given an ExpTime-admissible tableau system S that is sound and p-complete for some property $\mathcal{P}$ and an input Γ for S, we can construct a looping tree automaton of size exponential in the size of Γ that accepts exactly the saturated and clash-free S-trees compatible with Γ. Since the emptiness problem for looping tree automata can be decided in time polynomial (actually, linear) in the size of the automaton, this shows that the existence of saturated and clash-free S-trees compatible with Γ can be decided in exponential time. Since S is sound and p-complete for $\mathcal{P}$, we have $\Gamma \in \mathcal{P}$ iff there is a saturated and clash-free S-tree for Γ. Thus, we must investigate the connection between S-trees for Γ and S-trees compatible with Γ. This is done in the next lemma.

In the proof of the lemma, we need sub-tree relations between S-trees in analogy to the inclusion relations "$\precsim$" and "$\preceq$" between patterns introduced in Definition 6. These relations are defined on trees exactly as for patterns, and we also use the same relation symbols for them.

Lemma 1. *There exists a clash-free and saturated S-tree that is compatible with Γ iff there exists a clash-free and saturated S-tree for Γ.*

Proof. The "if" direction is straightforward: let $T = (V, E, n, \ell)$ be a clash-free and saturated S-tree for Γ. Since S is sound and p-complete for $\mathcal{P}$, we can w.l.o.g. assume that the out-degree of T is bounded by $p(|\Gamma|)$. It is not hard to show that T is compatible with Γ, i.e. satisfies Conditions 1 to 4 of Definition 15:

- Each initial S-tree satisfies Conditions 1 and 2 of compatibility, and Condition 3 of admissibility ensures that rule application adds only node label elements from $\mathsf{nle}_S(\Gamma)$ and edge labels from $\mathsf{el}_S(\Gamma)$.
- Each initial S-tree satisfies Condition 3 of compatibility, and rule application cannot delete elements from node labels.
- Since we assume the out-degree of T to be bounded by $p(|\Gamma|)$, Condition 4 of compatibility is also satisfied.

Now for the "only if" direction. Let $T = (V, E, n, \ell)$ be a clash-free and saturated S-tree with root v_0 that is compatible with Γ. To construct a clash-free and saturated S-tree for Γ, we first construct a (possibly infinite) sequence

$$T_1 \preceq T_2 \preceq T_3 \preceq \cdots$$

of S-trees for Γ such that $T_i \precsim_{\pi_i} T$ for all $i \geq 1$. The construction will be such that the injections π_i that yield $T_i \precsim T$ also build an increasing chain, i.e., π_{i+1} extends π_i for all $i \geq 1$. In the construction, we use a countably infinite set V' from which the nodes of the trees T_i are taken. We fix an arbitrary enumeration $x_0, x_1, \ldots$ of V', and write $x < y$ if $x \in V'$ occurs before $y \in V'$ in this enumeration. We then proceed as follows:

- Since T is compatible with Γ, there exists $\Lambda \in \mathsf{ini}_S(\Gamma)$ such that $\Lambda \subseteq n(v_0)$. Define T_1 to be the initial S-tree $(\{x_0\}, \emptyset, \{x_0 \mapsto \Lambda\}, \emptyset)$. Obviously, $T_1 \precsim_{\pi_1} T$ for $\pi_1 := \{x_0 \mapsto v_0\}$.
- Now, assume that $T_i \precsim_{\pi_i} T$ is already constructed. If T_i is saturated, then T_i is the last tree in the sequence. Otherwise, choose the least node x in T_i (w.r.t. the fixed ordering $<$ on V') such that $P \sim T_i, x$ for some pattern P that is not saturated, i.e. there exists a rule $P \to_{\mathcal{R}} \{P_1, \ldots, P_k\}$. Since $T_i \precsim_{\pi_i} T$, we have $P \precsim T, \pi_i(x)$. Since T is saturated, the pattern $T, \pi_i(x)$ is saturated. By Condition 2 of admissibility, we have $P_j \precsim T, \pi_i(x)$ for some j with $1 \leq j \leq k$. We apply the rule $P \to_{\mathcal{R}} \{P_1, \ldots, P_k\}$ to x in T_i such that $P_j \sim T_{i+1}, x$. If T_{i+1} contains new nodes, then they are taken from V'. Admissibility yields $T_i \preceq T_{i+1}$ and the fact that $P_j \precsim T, \pi_i(x)$ implies that we can define an injection π_{i+1} such that $T_{i+1} \precsim_{\pi_{i+1}} T$.

In the definition of the clash-free and saturated S-tree T^* for Γ, we distinguish two cases:

1. if the constructed sequence is finite and T_n is the last tree in the sequence, then set $T^* := T_n$;
2. otherwise, let T^* be the S-tree T^ω obtained from the sequence $T_1, T_2, \ldots$ as in Case 3 of Definition 10.

In both cases, T^* is obviously an S-tree for Γ by definition. In addition, we have $T^* \precsim_\pi T$ where π is the injection obtained as the union of the injections π_i for $i \geq 1$.

It remains to be shown that T^* is clash-free and saturated. We concentrate on the second case, where $T^* = T^\omega$, since the first case is similar, but simpler. Clash-freeness is an easy consequence of $T^* \precsim T$. In fact, by Condition 4 of admissibility, clash-freeness of T implies that $T^* \precsim T$ is also clash-free.

To show saturatedness of T^*, we must look at T^* and its relationship to the trees T_i in more detail. Since $T_i \preceq T^* \precsim T$ and the out-degree of T is bounded by $p(|\Gamma|)$, the out-degrees of the trees T_i and T^* are also bounded by $p(|\Gamma|)$. For a given node x of T^*, we consider its neighborhood T^*, x. Since the rules of S only add nodes or elements of node labels (see Condition 1 in the definition of admissibility), and since the out-degree of x is bounded by $p(|\Gamma|)$ and the set

$\mathsf{nle}_S(\Gamma)$ is finite, there is an i such that x is a node of T_i and "the neighborhood of x does not change after step i," i.e., $T_i, x = T_{i+1}, x = \ldots = T^*, x$.

Now assume that T^* is not saturated, i.e., there exists a node x in T^* to which a rule applies, i.e., $P \sim T^*, x$ for some pattern P with $\mathcal{R}(P) \neq \emptyset$. Let i be such that $T_i, x = T_{i+1}, x = \ldots = T^*, x$. Thus, for $j \geq i$, a rule applies to the node x in T_i. In the construction of the sequence $T_1, T_2, T_3, \ldots$, we apply a rule only to the least node to which a rule is applicable. Consequently, from the ith step on, we only apply rules to nodes $y \leq x$. Since there are only finitely many such nodes (see the definition of the order $<$ above), there is one node $y \leq x$ to which rules are applied infinitely often. However, each rule application strictly increases the number of successors of y, or the label of y or of one of its successors. This contradicts the fact that the out-degree of y in the trees T_i is bounded by $p(|\Gamma|)$ and all node labels are subsets of the finite set $\mathsf{nle}_S(\Gamma)$. ☐

3.2 Accepting Compatible S-Trees Using Looping Automata

Recall that we assume our tableau system S to be sound and p-complete w.r.t. a property $\mathcal{P}$. By Lemma 1, to check whether an input has property $\mathcal{P}$, it thus suffices to verify the existence of a saturated and clash-free S-tree that is compatible with Γ. In this section, we show how this can be done using an automata-based approach.

As usual, the automata work on k-ary infinite trees (for some fixed natural number k) whose nodes are labeled by elements of a finite label set and whose edges are ordered, i.e., we can talk about the i-th son of a node. To be more precise, let M be a set and $k \geq 1$. A k-ary M-tree is a mapping $T : \{1, \ldots, k\}^* \to M$ that labels each node $\alpha \in \{1, \ldots, k\}^*$ with $T(\alpha) \in M$. Intuitively, the node αi is the i-th child of α. We use ϵ to denote the empty word, corresponding to the root of the tree.

Definition 16 (Looping Tree Automata). *A looping tree automaton $\mathcal{A} = (Q, M, I, \Delta)$ working on k-ary M-trees consists of a finite set Q of states, a finite alphabet M, a set $I \subseteq Q$ of initial states, and a transition relation $\Delta \subseteq Q \times M \times Q^k$.*

A run of $\mathcal{A}$ on an M-tree T is a mapping $R : \{1, \ldots, k\}^* \to Q$ such that $R(\epsilon) \in I$ and

$$(R(\alpha), T(\alpha), R(\alpha 1), \ldots, R(\alpha k)) \in \Delta$$

for each $\alpha \in \{1, \ldots, k\}^*$. The language of k-ary M-trees accepted by $\mathcal{A}$ is

$$L(\mathcal{A}) := \{T \mid \text{there is a run of } \mathcal{A} \text{ on the } k\text{-ary } M\text{-tree } T\}.$$

Note that, in contrast to the S-trees considered above, the trees defined here are infinite trees of a *fixed* arity k, where edges are not labeled, but ordered. It is, however, not hard to convert S-trees compatible with a given input into k-ary M-trees for appropriate k and M. This is achieved by (i) "padding" with additional dummy nodes, and (ii) representing edge labels via node labels.

Definition 17 (Padding). *Let $\Gamma \in \mathfrak{I}$ be an input and $T = (V, E, n, \ell)$ an S-tree with root $v_0 \in V$ that is compatible with Γ. For each $x \in V$, we use $d(x)$ to denote the out-degree of x in T. We assume that the successors of each node $x \in V$ are linearly ordered and that, for each node $x \in V \setminus \{v_0\}$, $s(x) = i$ iff x is the i-th successor of its predecessor. We inductively define a function m from $\{1, \ldots, p(|\Gamma|)\}^*$ to $V \cup \{\sharp\}$ (where $\sharp \notin V$) as follows:*

- *$m(\epsilon) = v_0$;*
- *if $m(\alpha) = x$, $(x, y) \in E$, and $s(y) = i$, then $m(\alpha i) = y$;*
- *if $m(\alpha) = x$ and $d(x) < i$, then $m(\alpha i) = \sharp$;*
- *if $m(\alpha) = \sharp$, then $m(\alpha i) = \sharp$ for all $i \in \{1, \ldots, p(|\Gamma|)\}$.*

Let $\mathsf{tl}_S(\Gamma)$ denote the set $(\wp(\mathsf{nle}_S(\Gamma)) \times \mathsf{el}_S(\Gamma)) \cup \{(\sharp, \sharp)\}$. The padding P_T of T is the $p(|\Gamma|)$-ary $\mathsf{tl}_S(\Gamma)$-tree defined by setting

1. *$P_T(\epsilon) = (n(v_0), e_0)$ where e_0 is an arbitrary (but fixed) element of $\mathsf{el}_S(\Gamma)$;*
2. *$P_T(\alpha) = (n(x), \Theta)$ if $\alpha \neq \epsilon$, $m(\alpha) = x \neq \sharp$, and $\ell(y, x) = \Theta$ where y is the (unique) predecessor of x in T;*
3. *$P_T(\alpha) = (\sharp, \sharp)$ if $m(\alpha) = \sharp$.*

We now define, for each input $\Gamma \in \mathfrak{I}$, a looping automaton $\mathcal{A}_\Gamma$ that accepts a non-empty language iff there exists a saturated and clash-free S-tree that is compatible with Γ.

Definition 18 (Automaton for Input Γ). *Let $\Gamma \in \mathfrak{I}$ be an input and $h = p(|\Gamma|)$. The automaton $\mathcal{A}_\Gamma$ is defined as follows:*

- *$Q := M := \mathsf{tl}_S(\Gamma)$;*
- *$I := \{(\Psi, e_0) \mid \Lambda \subseteq \Psi \text{ for some } \Lambda \in \mathsf{ini}_S(\Gamma)\}$;*
- *$((\Lambda_0, \Theta_0), (\Lambda, \Theta), (\Lambda_1, \Theta_1), \ldots, (\Lambda_h, \Theta_h)) \in \Delta$ iff the following two conditions are satisfied:*
  1. *$(\Lambda_0, \Theta_0) = (\Lambda, \Theta)$;*
  2. *either $\Lambda_0 = \Lambda_1 = \cdots = \Lambda_h = \sharp$,*
     or there is a $0 \leq k \leq h$ such that $\Lambda_0, \ldots, \Lambda_k$ differ from $\sharp$, $\Lambda_{k+1} = \cdots = \Lambda_h = \sharp$, and the pattern $P^* = (V^*, E^*, n^*, \ell^*)$ defined as
     - *$V^* := \{i \mid 0 \leq i \leq k\}$,*
     - *$E^* := \{(0, i) \mid i \in V^* \setminus \{0\}\}$,*
     - *$n^* = \{i \mapsto \Lambda_i \mid i \in V^*\}$, and*
     - *$\ell^* := \{(0, i) \mapsto \Theta_i \mid i \in V^* \setminus \{0\}\}$*
     satisfies the following conditions:
     (a) for each pattern P with $P \sim P^*$, P is saturated (i.e. $\mathcal{R}(P) = \emptyset$);
     (b) for each pattern $P \in \mathcal{C}$, we have $P \not\sim P^*$.

The following lemma shows that the automaton $\mathcal{A}_\Gamma$ accepts exactly the paddings of saturated and clash-free S-trees compatible with Γ. Consequently, it accepts a non-empty set of trees iff there exists a saturated and clash-free S-tree compatible with Γ.

Lemma 2. *Let $\Gamma \in \mathfrak{I}$ be an input. Then*

$$L(\mathcal{A}_\Gamma) = \{P_T \mid T \text{ is a saturated and clash-free } S\text{-tree compatible with } \Gamma\}.$$

Proof. First, assume that T is a saturated and clash-free S-tree compatible with Γ. We claim that P_T itself is a run of $\mathcal{A}_\Gamma$ on P_T. In fact, $P_T(\epsilon) \in I$ is an immediate consequence of the definition of padding and Condition 3 in the definition of S-trees compatible with Γ. Now, consider some node α of P_T. The first condition in the definition of Δ is satisfied since we have P_T as run on itself. Thus, consider the second condition. If $P_T(\alpha) = (\sharp, \sharp)$, then the definition of padding implies that all the successor nodes of α also have label $(\sharp, \sharp)$, and thus the second condition in the definition of Δ is satisfied. Otherwise, it is easy to see that the pattern P^* defined in the second condition in the definition of Δ is also a pattern in T. Since T is saturated and clash-free, P^* thus satisfies (a) and (b) in the second condition in the definition of Δ. This completes the proof that P_T is a run of $\mathcal{A}_\Gamma$ on P_T, and thus shows that $P_T \in L(\mathcal{A}_\Gamma)$.

Second, assume that $\widehat{T}$ is a tree accepted by $\mathcal{A}_\Gamma$. Because of the first condition in the definition of Δ, $\widehat{T}$ itself is a run of $\mathcal{A}_\Gamma$ on $\widehat{T}$. The definitions of Q, I, and Δ imply that there is an S-tree T compatible with Γ such that $P_T = \widehat{T}$. This tree can be obtained from $\widehat{T}$ by removing all the padding. It remains to be shown that T is saturated and clash-free. Thus, consider a node x of T, and let α be the corresponding node in $P_T = \widehat{T}$. Since x is a node in T, the node α has a label different from $(\sharp, \sharp)$. Let us now consider the transition from α to its successor nodes. It is easy to see that the pattern P^* defined in the second condition in the definition of the transition relation coincides with T, x. Thus (a) and (b) in this condition imply that no rule and no clash-trigger is applicable to x.   □

We are now ready to prove the main result of this section: the ExpTime upper-bound induced by ExpTime-admissible tableau systems.

Theorem 1. *Let $\mathfrak{I}$ be a set of inputs, $\mathcal{P} \subseteq \mathfrak{I}$ a property, and p a polynomial. If there exists an ExpTime-admissible tableau system S for $\mathfrak{I}$ that is sound and p-complete for $\mathcal{P}$, then $\mathcal{P}$ is decidable in ExpTime.*

Proof. Let $\Gamma \in \mathfrak{I}$ be an input. To decide whether $\Gamma \in \mathcal{P}$, we construct the automaton $\mathcal{A}_\Gamma$ and then check whether it accepts a non-empty language. By Lemmas 1 and 2, this algorithm is correct. Thus, it remains to be shown that it can be executed in exponential time. To see that the automaton $\mathcal{A}_\Gamma$ can be constructed in time exponential in $|\Gamma|$, note that, by Conditions 2 and 3 of ExpTime-admissibility, we can compute $\wp(\mathsf{nle}_S(\Gamma))$ and $\mathsf{el}_S(\Gamma)$ in time exponential in $|\Gamma|$, and thus the same holds for $\mathsf{tl}_S(\Gamma) = Q = M$, and I. The transition relation Δ can be computed in exponential time due to the Conditions 4 and 5 of ExpTime-admissibility and the fact that p is a polynomial. Since the automaton can be computed in exponential time, its size is at most exponential in $|\Gamma|$. Thus, it remains to note that the emptiness test for looping tree automata can be realized in polynomial time [29].   □

Since we have shown that the tableau system $S_{\mathcal{ALC}}$ is ExpTime-admissible as well as sound and p-complete (for some polynomial p) for satisfiability of $\mathcal{ALC}$-concepts w.r.t. (general) TBoxes, we can immediately put Theorem 1 to work:

Corollary 1. *$\mathcal{ALC}$-concept satisfiability w.r.t. TBoxes is in ExpTime.*

4 Tableau-Based Decision Procedures from Tableau Systems

The tableau systems described in Section 2.2 cannot immediately be used as tableau-based decision procedures since rule application need not terminate. The purpose of this section is to show that, under certain natural conditions, the addition of a straightforward cycle detection mechanism turns them into (terminating) decision procedures. The resulting procedures are structurally similar to standard tableau-based algorithms for description logics, such as the ones underlying systems like FaCT and RACER. In contrast to the ExpTime algorithm constructed in the previous section, the procedures obtained here are usually not worst-case optimal—a price we have to pay for more easily implementable and optimizable decision procedures.

Fix a set of inputs $\mathfrak{I}$ and a tableau system $S = (\mathsf{NLE}, \mathsf{EL}, \cdot^S, \mathcal{R}, \mathcal{C})$ for $\mathfrak{I}$. As in the previous section, we require that S has a number of computational properties. Since we do not consider complexity issues in this section, it is sufficient for our purposes to impose effectiveness (and not efficiency) constraints. We start with modifying Definition 14:

Definition 19 (Recursive Tableau System). *S is called* recursive *iff the following conditions are satisfied:*

1. *S is admissible (see Definition 7);*
2. *$\mathsf{ini}_S(\Gamma)$ can be computed effectively;*
3. *for each pattern P it can be checked effectively whether, for all patterns P', $P' \sim P$ implies $\mathcal{R}(P') = \emptyset$; if this is not the case, then we can effectively determine a rule*

$$P' \to_{\mathcal{R}} \{P_1, \ldots, P_k\}$$

   and a bijection π such that $P' \sim_\pi P$.
4. *for each pattern P it can be checked effectively whether there is a clash-trigger $P' \in \mathcal{C}$ such that $P' \sim P$.*

The main difference between this definition and Definition 14 is Condition 3, which now requires that, besides checking the applicability of rules, we can effectively apply at least one rule whenever some rule is applicable at all. Another difference is that we do not actually need to compute the sets $\mathsf{el}_S(\Gamma)$ and $\mathsf{nle}_S(\Gamma)$ in order to apply rules.

Analogously to the case of ExpTime-admissibility, it can be verified that the tableau system $S_{\mathcal{ALC}}$ is recursive. In particular, for the second part of Condition 3 we can again use the fact that the rules of $S_{\mathcal{ALC}}$ are invariant under isomorphism

---

Preconditions: Let $\mathfrak{I}$ be a set of inputs, $\mathcal{P} \subseteq \mathfrak{I}$ a property, f a recursive function, and S a recursive tableau system for $\mathfrak{I}$ that is sound and f-complete for $\mathcal{P}$.

Algorithm: Return true on input $\Gamma \in \mathfrak{I}$ if the procedure tableau(T) defined below returns true for at least one initial S-tree T for Γ. Otherwise return false.

procedure tableau(T)

If $P \sim T, x$ for some $P \in C$ and node x in T or the out-degree of T exceeds $f(|\Gamma|)$,
  then return false.

If no rule is applicable to a non-blocked node x in T,
  then return true.

Take a a non-blocked node x in T and a rule $P \to_{\mathcal{R}} \{P_1, \ldots, P_k\}$ with $P \sim T, x$.

Let T_i be the result of applying the above rule such that $P_i \sim T_i, x$, for $1 \le i \le k$.

If at least one of tableau(T_1), tableau(T_2), . . . , tableau(T_k) returns true,
  then return true.

Return false.

Fig. 2. Decision procedure for $\mathcal{P}$.

of patterns: this means that it suffices to compute, for a given non-saturated pattern P, a set of patterns $\{P_1, \ldots, P_k\}$ such that $P \to_{\mathcal{R}} \{P_1, \ldots, P_k\}$. It is easy to see that this can be effectively done for the rules of $S_{\mathcal{ALC}}$.

We now define a more relaxed variant of Definition 13.

Definition 20 (f-Complete). *Let $f : \mathbb{N} \to \mathbb{N}$ be a recursive function. The tableau system S is called f-complete for $\mathcal{P}$ iff, for any $\Gamma \in \mathcal{P}$, there exists a saturated and clash-free S-tree for Γ with out-degree bounded by $f(|\Gamma|)$.*

Since we have already shown that $S_{\mathcal{ALC}}$ is p-complete for some polynomial p, $S_{\mathcal{ALC}}$ is clearly f-complete for the (computable) function f induced by the polynomial p.

In order to implement a cycle detection mechanism, we introduce the notion of blocking: given an S-tree $T = (V, E, n, \ell)$, we denote by E^* the transitive and reflexive closure of E and say that $x \in V$ is *blocked* iff there exist distinct $u, v \in V$ such that uE^*x, vE^*x, and $n(u) = n(v)$. Note that this corresponds to the well-known "equality-blocking" technique that is used in various DL tableau algorithms [4, 17].

The tableau-based decision procedure for $\mathcal{P}$ induced by the tableau system S is described in Figure 2. Note that the selection of rules and nodes in the "else" part of the procedure tableau is "don't care" non-deterministic: for the soundness and completeness of the algorithm, it does not matter which rule we apply when to which node.

Let us verify that the individual steps performed by the algorithm in Figure 2 are actually effective:

– the initial trees for an input Γ can be computed effectively, since $\text{ini}_S(\Gamma)$ can be computed effectively by Condition 2 of Definition 19;

- the condition in the first "if" statement can be checked effectively by Condition 4 of Definition 19 and since f is a recursive function;
- the applicability of rules can be checked by the first part of Condition 3 of Definition 19;
- finally, that we can effectively take a rule and apply it to a node x follows from the second part of Condition 3 of Definition 19.

We now turn to termination, soundness, and completeness of the algorithm.

Lemma 3 (Termination). *Suppose the preconditions of Figure 2 are satisfied. Then the algorithm of Figure 2 terminates for any input $\Gamma \in \mathfrak{I}$.*

Proof. Let $\Gamma \in \mathfrak{I}$. The number of initial trees for Γ is finite and can be computed effectively. Hence, it is sufficient to show that the procedure tableau terminates on any initial tree for Γ. For each step in which the procedure does not immediately return true or false, a node is added to the tree or $n(x)$ properly increases for some node x (due to Condition 1 of admissibility). Hence, since $n(x) \subseteq \wp(\mathsf{nle}_S(\Gamma))$ for any node x and any tree constructed during a run of tableau, it is sufficient to show that both the out-degree and the depth of the trees constructed is bounded. But the out-degree of the trees is bounded by $f(|\Gamma|)$ (more precisely, as soon as one rule application yields a tree with out-degree larger than $f(|\Gamma|)$, the algorithm returns false in the next step) and the length of E-paths does not exceed $2^{|\mathsf{nle}_S(\Gamma)|}$ since rules are not applied to blocked nodes. $\square$

Lemma 4 (Soundness). *Suppose the preconditions of Figure 2 are satisfied. If the algorithm of Figure 2 returns true on input Γ, then $\Gamma \in \mathcal{P}$.*

Proof. Suppose the algorithm returns true on input Γ. Then the algorithm terminates with a clash-free S-tree $T = (V, E, n, \ell)$ whose out-degree does not exceed $f(|\Gamma|)$ and such that no rule is applicable to a non-blocked node in T. As S is sound for $\mathcal{P}$, it is sufficient to show that there exists a saturated and clash-free S-tree for Γ. To this end we construct a clash-free and saturated S-tree

$$T' = (V', E', n', \ell')$$

which is compatible with Γ (from which, by Lemma 1, we obtain a clash-free and saturated S-tree for Γ). Say that a node $x \in V$ is *directly blocked* if it is blocked but its predecessor is not blocked. If y is the (uniquely determined) node $y \neq x$ with yE^*x and $n(x) = n(y)$, then y is said to *block* x.

Now, V' consists of all non-empty sequences $\langle v_0, x_1, \ldots, x_n \rangle$, where v_0 is the root of V, the $x_1, \ldots, x_n \in V$ are directly blocked or not blocked, and $(x_i, x_{i+1}) \in E$ if x_i is not blocked or x_i is blocked by some $y \in V$ such that $(y, x_{i+1}) \in E$. Define E' by setting, for $\boldsymbol{x} = \langle v_0, x_1, \ldots, x_n \rangle \in V'$ and $\boldsymbol{y} \in V'$, $(\boldsymbol{x}, \boldsymbol{y}) \in E'$ iff there exists x_{n+1} such that $\boldsymbol{y} = \langle v_0, x_1, \ldots, x_n, x_{n+1} \rangle$. Define n' by setting $n'(\langle v_0, x_1, \ldots, x_n \rangle) = n(x_n)$. Finally, define ℓ' by

- $\ell'(\langle v_0, x_1, \ldots, x_n \rangle, \langle v_0, x_1, \ldots, x_n, x_{n+1} \rangle) = \ell(x_n, x_{n+1})$ if x_n is not blocked;
- $\ell'(\langle v_0, x_1, \ldots, x_n \rangle, \langle v_0, x_1, \ldots, x_n, x_{n+1} \rangle) = \ell(y, x_{n+1})$ if x_n is blocked and y blocks x_n.

We show that T' is a clash-free and saturated S-tree which is compatible with Γ. Compatibility is readily checked using the definition of T'. Since T is clash-free and no rule is applicable to a non-blocked node of T, we can prove clash-freeness and saturatedness of T' by showing that any S-pattern P that matches T', x for some node x in T' also matches a T, x for some non-blocked node x in T. Thus, assume that $P \sim_\tau T', \langle v_0, x_1, \ldots, x_n \rangle$, for some bijection τ. If x_n is not blocked, then $P \sim_{\tau'} T, x_n$, where τ' is obtained from τ by composing τ with the mapping that assigns x_n to $\langle v_0, x_1, \ldots, x_n \rangle$ and x_{n+1} to each successor $\langle v_0, x_1, \ldots, x_n, x_{n+1} \rangle$ of $\langle v_0, x_1, \ldots, x_n \rangle$. Similarly, if x_n is blocked by y, then $P \sim_{\tau'} T, y$, where τ' is obtained from τ by composing τ with the mapping that assigns y to $\langle v_0, x_1, \ldots, x_n \rangle$ and x_{n+1} to each successor $\langle v_0, x_1, \ldots, x_n, x_{n+1} \rangle$ of $\langle v_0, x_1, \ldots, x_n \rangle$. □

Lemma 5 (Completeness). *Suppose the preconditions of Figure 2 are satisfied. If $\Gamma \in \mathcal{P}$, then the algorithm of Figure 2 returns* true *on input Γ.*

Proof. Suppose $\Gamma \in \mathcal{P}$. Since S is f-complete for $\mathcal{P}$, there exists a clash-free and saturated S-tree $T = (V, E, n, \ell)$ for Γ whose out-degree does not exceed $f(|\Gamma|)$. We use T to "guide" the algorithm to an S-tree of out-degree at most $f(|\Gamma|)$ in which no clash-trigger applies and no rule is applicable to a non-blocked node. This will be done in a way such that all constructed S-trees T' satisfy $T' \precsim T$.

For the start, we need to choose an appropriate initial S-tree T_1. Let v_0 be the root of T. Since S-trees for Γ are also compatible with Γ, the definition of compatibility implies that there exists $\Lambda \in \mathsf{ini}_S(\Gamma)$ such that $\Lambda \subseteq n(v_0)$. Define T_1 to be the initial S-tree $(\{v_0\}, \emptyset, \{v_0 \mapsto \Lambda\}, \emptyset)$. Clearly, $T_1 \precsim T$. We start the procedure tableau with the tree T_1.

Now suppose that tableau is called with some S-tree T' such that $T' \precsim T$. If no rule is applicable to a non-blocked node in T', we are done: since $T' \precsim T$ and T is clash-free and of out-degree at most $f(|\Gamma|)$, the same holds for T'. Now suppose that a rule is applicable to a non-blocked node in T'. Assume that the tableau procedure has chosen the rule $P \to_\mathcal{R} \{P_1, \ldots, P_k\}$ with $P \sim T', x$. Since $T' \precsim_\tau T$ for some τ, we have $P \precsim T, \tau(x)$. Since T is saturated, $T, \tau(x)$ is saturated. By Condition 2 of admissibility, we have $P_j \precsim T, \tau(x)$ for some $j, 1 \leq j \leq k$. So we "guide" the tableau procedure to continue exploring the S-tree T'_j obtained from T' by applying the rule $P \to_\mathcal{R} \{P_1, \ldots, P_k\}$ such that $P_j \sim T'_j, x$. Now, $P_j \precsim T, \tau(x)$ implies $T'_j \precsim T$.

Since the tableau procedure terminates on any input, the "guidance" process will also terminate and thus succeeds in finding an S-tree of out-degree at most $f(|\Gamma|)$ in which no clash-trigger applies and no rule is applicable to a non-blocked node. Hence, tableau(T_1) returns true. □

The three lemmas just proved imply that we have succeeded in converting the tableau system S into a decision procedure for $\mathcal{P}$.

Theorem 2. *Suppose the preconditions of Figure 2 are satisfied. Then the algorithm of Figure 2 effectively decides $\mathcal{P}$.*

5   A Tableau System for $\mathcal{ALCQI}$

As an example for a more expressive DL that can be treated within our framework, we consider the DL $\mathcal{ALCQI}$, which extends $\mathcal{ALC}$ with qualified number restrictions and inverse roles. Qualified number restrictions $((\geqslant m\,r.C)$ and $(\leqslant m\,r.C))$ can be used to state constraints on the number of r-successors belonging to a given concept C, and the inverse roles allow us to use both a role r and its inverse r^- when building a complex concept.

Definition 21 ($\mathcal{ALCQI}$ Syntax and Semantics). *Let $\mathsf{N_C}$ and $\mathsf{N_R}$ be pairwise disjoint and countably infinite sets of concept and role names. The set of $\mathcal{ALCQI}$-roles is defined as $\mathsf{ROL}_{\mathcal{ALCQI}} := \mathsf{N_R} \cup \{r^- \mid r \in \mathsf{N_R}\}$.*
The set of $\mathcal{ALCQI}$-concepts $\mathsf{CON}_{\mathcal{ALCQI}}$ is the smallest set such that

- *every concept name is a concept, and*
- *if C and D are $\mathcal{ALCQI}$-concepts and $r \in \mathsf{ROL}_{\mathcal{ALCQI}}$ is a role, then $\neg C, C \sqcap D, C \sqcup D, (\leqslant m\,r.C)$ and $(\geqslant m\,r.C)$ are also $\mathcal{ALCQI}$-concepts.*

TBoxes are defined as in the case of $\mathcal{ALC}$, i.e., they are finite sets of GCIs $C \sqsubseteq D$ where $C, D \in \mathsf{CON}_{\mathcal{ALCQI}}$.
The semantics of $\mathcal{ALCQI}$ is defined as for $\mathcal{ALC}$, where the additional constructors are interpreted as follows:

$$(r^-)^{\mathcal{I}} := \{(y, x) \mid (x, y) \in r^{\mathcal{I}}\},$$
$$(\leqslant m\,r.C)^{\mathcal{I}} := \{d \in \Delta^{\mathcal{I}} \mid \#\{y \mid (d, y) \in r^{\mathcal{I}} \land y \in C^{\mathcal{I}}\} \le m\},$$
$$(\geqslant m\,r.C)^{\mathcal{I}} := \{d \in \Delta^{\mathcal{I}} \mid \#\{y \mid (d, y) \in r^{\mathcal{I}} \land y \in C^{\mathcal{I}}\} \ge m\},$$

where $\#S$ denotes the cardinality of the set S.

Although the constructors $\exists r.C$ and $\forall r.C$ are not explicitly present in $\mathcal{ALCQI}$, they can be simulated by $(\geqslant 1\,r.C)$ and $(\leqslant 0\,r.\neg C)$, respectively. Thus, $\mathcal{ALCQI}$ really extends $\mathcal{ALC}$.

The definition of negation normal form (and thus of the function nnf) can easily be extended to $\mathcal{ALCQI}$ (see, e.g., [14]), and the same is true for the function sub. In addition, we define the *closure* of the $\mathcal{ALCQI}$ concept C and the TBox $\mathcal{T}$ as

$$\mathsf{cl}(C, \mathcal{T}) := sub(C, \mathcal{T}) \cup \{\mathsf{nnf}(\neg D) \mid D \in sub(C, \mathcal{T})\}.$$

In order to simplify the treatment of inverse roles, we denote *the inverse* of the $\mathcal{ALCQI}$-role r by $\bar{r}$, i.e., $\bar{r} = r^-$ if r is a role name, and $\bar{r} = s$ if $r = s^-$ for a role name s.

Completion trees for $\mathcal{ALCQI}$ look like completion trees for $\mathcal{ALC}$, with the only difference that edges may also be labeled with inverse roles. In fact, to handle a number restriction of the form $(\geqslant 1\,r^-.C)$ (which corresponds to the existential restriction $\exists r^-.C$) in the label of the node v, the tableau algorithm may introduce an r^--successor of v.

The fact that edges can also be labeled by inverse roles complicates the treatment of number restrictions by tableau rules. For a given node, we need to count the number of other nodes it is related to via the role r. Without inverse roles, this is quite easy: we just take the direct successors reached by an edge labeled with r. With inverse roles, we must also count the direct predecessor if the corresponding edge is labeled with $\bar{r}$. However, our framework only allows for patterns of depth one, and thus the rules cannot simultaneously look at a node together with its direct predecessor *and* its direct successors. To overcome this problem, we introduce new concept names $M_{r,C}$ for every pair r, C appearing in a number restriction $(\geqslant m\, r.C)$ or $(\leqslant m\, r.C)$. The intuitive meaning of these "marker concepts" is the following: if the label of node v contains $M_{r,C}$, then the edge leading to v from its direct predecessor u is labeled with $\bar{r}$ and the label of u contains C. Since the root node of the tree does not have a predecessor, these concepts are not allowed to appear in the root node. We will ensure this by enforcing that the root label contains $\neg M_{r,C}$. Given a concept C and a TBox $\mathcal{T}$, the set of necessary marker concepts is

$$\mathsf{M}_{\mathsf{C},\mathcal{T}} := \{M_{r,C}, \neg M_{r,C} \mid \{(\geqslant m\, r.C), (\leqslant m\, r.C)\} \cap \mathsf{cl}(C,\mathcal{T}) \neq \emptyset \text{ for some } m\}.$$

Definition 22 ($S_{\mathcal{ALCQI}}$). *The tableau system $S_{\mathcal{ALCQI}}$ is defined as follows:* $\mathsf{NLE} := \mathsf{CON}_{\mathcal{ALCQI}}$ *is the set of all $\mathcal{ALCQI}$-concepts,* $\mathsf{EL} := \mathsf{ROL}_{\mathcal{ALCQI}}$ *is the set of all $\mathcal{ALCQI}$-roles, and the function $\cdot^{S_{\mathcal{ALCQI}}}$ assigns to any input pair $(C,\mathcal{T})$ the following tuple $(\mathsf{nle}_{S_{\mathcal{ALCQI}}}, \mathsf{el}_{S_{\mathcal{ALCQI}}}, \mathsf{ini}_{S_{\mathcal{ALCQI}}})$:*

$$\mathsf{nle}_{S_{\mathcal{ALCQI}}}(C,\mathcal{T}) := \mathsf{cl}(C,\mathcal{T}) \cup \mathsf{M}_{\mathsf{C},\mathcal{T}},$$
$$\mathsf{el}_{S_{\mathcal{ALCQI}}}(C,\mathcal{T}) := \{r, r^- \mid r \in \mathsf{N_R} \text{ occurs in } C \text{ or } \mathcal{T}\},$$
$$\mathsf{ini}_{S_{\mathcal{ALCQI}}}(C,\mathcal{T}) := \{\{\mathsf{nnf}(C)\} \cup \{\neg M_{r,C} \mid \neg M_{r,C} \in \mathsf{M}_{\mathsf{C},\mathcal{T}}\}\}.$$

The rules and clash-triggers of $S_{\mathcal{ALCQI}}$ are introduced in the next two definitions.

In order to define the rules and clash-triggers, we need to count the r-neighbors of a given node v in an $S_{\mathcal{ALCQI}}$-tree, i.e., the nodes that are either r-successors of v or the (unique) predecessor of v in case v is an $\bar{r}$-successor of this predecessor. The problem is that we must do this in a pattern, where the predecessor is not explicitly present. Instead, we use the presence of the marker concepts $M_{r,D}$ in the label of v.[8] Let P be a pattern with root v_0. We say that v_0 *has k r-neighbors containing D* iff

- either $M_{r,D}$ is not in the label of v_0 and v_0 has exactly k r-successors whose labels contain D;
- or $M_{r,D}$ is in the label of v_0 and v_0 has exactly $k - 1$ r-successors whose labels contain D.

---

[8] The rules and clash-triggers are defined such that the presence of the marker concept $M_{r,D}$ in the label of a node v in a saturated and clash-free $S_{\mathcal{ALCQI}}$-tree implies that v is an $\bar{r}$-successor of its father w and that the label of w contains D.

In addition to the rules handling conjunctions, disjunctions, and the TBox axioms, $S_{\mathcal{ALCQI}}$ has three rules[9] that treat number restrictions. Before introducing them formally, we give brief intuitive explanations of these rules:

R⩾ To satisfy an at-least restriction ($\geqslant m\,r.C$), the rule creates the necessary neighbors one-by-one. In a single step, it adds $M_{r,C}$ to the label of the root of the pattern, or it adds C to the label of an existing r-successor of the root, or it creates a new r-successor of the root with label $\{C\}$.

RC If the root label of the pattern contains the at-most restriction ($\leqslant m\,r.C$), then this so-called *choose-rule* adds either the concept C or the concept $\mathsf{nnf}(\neg C)$ to the label of all r-successors of the root. In addition, this rule also takes the (not explicitly present) predecessor node into account by "guessing" whether the given node is an $\bar{r}$-successor of its predecessor and whether the label of this predecessor contains C. This is done by adding either $M_{r,C}$ or $\neg M_{r,C}$ to the label of the root.

R↑ This rule propagates the information contained in the marker concepts to the predecessor node, i.e., if the label of an $\bar{r}$-successor of the root contains $M_{r,C}$, then we add C to the label of the root; if the label of an $\bar{r}$-successor of the root contains $\neg M_{r,C}$, then we add $\neg C$ to the label of the root.

Definition 23 (The Rules of $S_{\mathcal{ALCQI}}$). *Let $P = (V, E, n, \ell)$ be a pattern with root v_0. Then $\mathcal{R}(P)$ is the smallest set of finite sets of patterns that contains all the sets of patterns required by the R⊓, R⊔, and R$\mathcal{T}$ rules, and in addition the following sets:*

R⩾₁ *if the root label $n(v_0)$ contains the concept ($\geqslant m\,r.C$) as well as the concept $M_{r,C}$, and there are less than $m - 1$ nodes v for which $\ell(v_0, v) = r$ and $C \in n(v)$, then $\mathcal{R}(P)$ contains the set $\{P_0, P_1, \ldots, P_t\}$, where $\{u_1, \ldots, u_t\}$ consists of all sons of v_0 with $\ell(v_0, u_i) = r$ and $C \notin n(u_i)$ and*
   1. *$P_0 = (V_0, E_0, n_0, \ell_0)$, where $u_0 \notin V$, $V_0 = V \cup \{u_0\}$, $E_0 = E \cup \{(v_0, u_0)\}$, $n_0 = n \cup \{u_0 \mapsto \{C\}\}$, and $\ell_0 = \ell \cup \{(v_0, u_0) \mapsto r\}$,*
   2. *for $1 \leq i \leq t$, $P_i = (V, E, n_i, \ell)$, where $n_i(v) = n(v)$ for all $v \in V \setminus \{u_i\}$ and $n'_i(u_i) = n_i(u_i) \cup \{C\}$;*

R⩾₂ *if the root label $n(v_0)$ contains the concept ($\geqslant m\,r.C$), but not the concept $M_{r,C}$, and if there are less than m nodes v for which $\ell(v_0, v) = r$ and $C \in n(v)$, then $\mathcal{R}(P)$ contains the set $\{P_{-1}, P_0, P_1, \ldots, P_t\}$, where t and $P_0, \ldots, P_t$ are defined as in the R⩾₁-rule, and*
   3. *$P_{-1} = (V, E, n_{-1}, \ell)$, where $n_{-1}(v) = n(v)$ for all $v \in V \setminus \{v_0\}$ and $n_{-1}(v_0) = n(v_0) \cup \{M_{r,C}\}$;*

RC₁ *if the root label $n(v_0)$ contains the concept ($\leqslant m\,r.C$) and $\ell(v_0, v_1) = r$ for some $v_1 \in V$ with $n(v_1) \cap \{C, \mathsf{nnf}(\neg C)\} = \emptyset$, then $\mathcal{R}(P)$ contains the set $\{(V, E, n', \ell), (V, E, n'', \ell)\}$, where $n'(v_1) = n(v_1) \cup \{C\}$, $n''(v_1) = n(v_1) \cup \{\mathsf{nnf}(\neg C)\}$, and $n'(v) = n''(v) = n(v)$ for all $v \in V \setminus \{v_1\}$;*

---

[9] For better readability, each rule will be split into two sub-rules.

RC$_2$ *if the root label $n(v_0)$ contains the concept $(\leqslant m\,r.C)$, but neither $M_{r,C}$ nor $\neg M_{r,C}$, then $\mathcal{R}(P)$ contains the set $\{(V, E, n', \ell), (V, E, n'', \ell)\}$, where $n'(v_0) = n(v_0) \cup \{M_{r,C}\}$, $n''(v_0) = n(v_0) \cup \{\neg M_{r,C}\}$ and $n'(v) = n''(v) = n(v)$ for all $v \in V \setminus \{v_0\}$;*

R↑$_1$ *if there is a son v_1 of the root v_0 with $M_{r,C} \in n(v_1)$ and $\ell(v_0, v_1) = \overline{r}$, but $C \notin n(v_0)$, then $\mathcal{R}(P)$ contains the singleton set $\{P'\}$, where $P' = (V, E, n', \ell)$ and $n'(v) = n(v)$ for all $v \in V \setminus \{v_0\}$ and $n'(v_0) = n(v_0) \cup \{C\}$;*

R↑$_2$ *if there is a son v_1 of the root v_0 with $\neg M_{r,C} \in n(v_1)$ and $\ell(v_0, v_1) = \overline{r}$, but $\mathsf{nnf}(\neg C) \notin n(v_0)$, then $\mathcal{R}(P)$ contains the singleton set $\{P'\}$, where $P' = (V, E, n', \ell)$ and $n'(v) = n(v)$ for all $v \in V \setminus \{v_0\}$ and $n'(v_0) = n(v_0) \cup \{\mathsf{nnf}(\neg C)\}$.*

In $S_{\mathcal{ALCQI}}$, we also need two additional clash-triggers. First, we have a clash whenever the label of the node v contains a marker concept that is in conflict with the actual label of the edge connecting the predecessor of v with v. Second, we need a clash-trigger that detects that an at-most restriction is violated.

Definition 24. *The set of clash-triggers $\mathcal{C}$ contains all the clash triggers of $S_{\mathcal{ALC}}$, and additionally*

- *all patterns (V, E, n, ℓ) such that there exists an edge $(v, w) \in E$, roles r, s, and a concept C with $\ell(v, w) = r$, $M_{s,C} \in n(w)$, and $r \neq \overline{s}$;*
- *all patterns (V, E, n, ℓ) with root v_0 such that $(\leqslant m\,r.C) \in n(v_0)$ and v_0 has more than m r-neighbors containing C.*

Admissibility, ExpTime-admissibility, and recursive admissibility of $S_{\mathcal{ALCQI}}$ can be shown as for $S_{\mathcal{ALC}}$. The proof of soundness and completeness is similar to known soundness and completeness proofs for tableau algorithms for DLs containing qualified number restrictions and inverse roles (see, e.g., [18]). In order to have p-completeness for an appropriate polynomial p, we must assume that numbers in number restrictions are given in unary coding, i.e., the number m really contributes with m to the size of the input. As an immediate consequence of Theorem 1, we obtain the following upper-bound for the satisfiability problem in $\mathcal{ALCQI}$.

Corollary 2. $\mathcal{ALCQI}$-*concept satisfiability w.r.t. TBoxes is in ExpTime.*

6   Variants and Extensions

When defining the abstract notion of a tableau system, we had several degrees of freedom. The decisions we made were motivated by our desire to stay as close as possible to the "usual" tableau-based algorithms for DLs while at the same time obtaining a notion that is as general as possible. While writing the paper, we have noticed that several decisions could have been made differently. In the following, we mention three alternative decisions, one leading to a restricted variant and two leading to extensions of the framework. Embedding the two extensions into our framework is the subject of future work.

6.1   Changing the Definition of Subpatterns

Recall that our treatment of existential restrictions in the tableau system $S_{\mathcal{ALC}}$ differs from the usual treatment in tableau-based algorithms for $\mathcal{ALC}$ in that it leads to a non-deterministic rule, which chooses between generating a new r-successor or re-using an old one. In contrast, the usual rules treating existential restrictions always generate a new successor.

Why could we not employ the usual rule for handling existential restrictions? The reason is that then the tableau system would not be admissible. In fact, the proof that Condition 2 of Definition 7 is satisfied for $S_{\mathcal{ALC}}$ (given below Definition 7) strongly depends on the fact that r-successors can be re-used. To be more precise, assume that P is a pattern whose root label consists of $\exists r.A$ for a concept name A, and whose root has exactly one successor u_1, which is an r-successor with an empty label. Let P' be the pattern that is obtained from P by adding A to the label of u_1. Obviously, $P \precsim P'$ and P' is saturated. However, if we consider the pattern P_1 that is obtained from P by adding a new r-successor with label $\{A\}$, then $P_1 \not\precsim P'$. Thus, the deterministic rule $P \to_{\mathcal{R}} \{P_1\}$ does not satisfy Condition 2 of Definition 7.

Could we change the framework such that the usual deterministic rule for handling existential restrictions becomes admissible? One way to achieve this would be to change the definition of the subpattern relation $\precsim$ (see Definition 6) by removing the requirement that π be injective. In fact, with this new definition, we would have $P_1 \precsim P'$ in the example above. By consistently replacing the old version of $\precsim$ with this new version, we would obtain a framework where all the results of Sections 3 and 4 still hold, and where the usual deterministic rule for handling existential restrictions in $\mathcal{ALC}$ is admissible.

Why did we not use this modified framework? Intuitively, if we use a non-injective mapping π in the definition of $\precsim$, then the actual number of r-successors of a given node is irrelevant as long as we have one successor of each "type." Thus, a clash-trigger that fires if a certain number of successors is exceeded (like the one used in Section 5) does not make sense. In fact, with the modified definition of $\precsim$, a pattern $P \in \mathcal{C}$ having at least m successors of the root node could be a subpattern of a pattern T, x where x has only one successor. Thus, the modified framework could not treat a DL like $\mathcal{ALCQI}$, where the number of successors (and not just their type) counts. For DLs like $\mathcal{ALC}$, where the number of successors of a given type is irrelevant,[10] the modified framework could be used, and would probably lead to simpler rules. However, we think that number restrictions are important enough in DLs to justify the use of a framework that can handle them, even if this leads to a somewhat more complex treatment of other constructors.

---

[10] This follows from the bisimulation invariance of $\mathcal{ALC}$, which is an immediate consequence of bisimulation invariance of its syntactic variant, multi-modal K_m [5].

6.2   Using Larger Patterns

In our current framework, patterns (the clash-triggers and left-hand sides of rules) are trees of depth at most one, i.e., we consider one node and its direct successors when defining rules and clash-triggers. In some cases, it would be more convenient to have larger patterns available. A case in point are DLs with inverse roles (like $\mathcal{ALCQI}$), where it would be more convenient to have not only the direct successors of a node available, but also its direct predecessor. In our definition of the tableau system for $\mathcal{ALCQI}$, we had to employ special markers to memorize whether the predecessor belongs to a certain concept. Though this works, it is not very natural, and it leads to rather complicated rules. Thus, a natural extension motivated by $\mathcal{ALCQI}$ and similar DLs is to consider patterns consisting of a node together with its direct predecessor and its direct successors. This would yield a new framework that is close to two-way automata [28].

Why have we not made this extension? Including the predecessor of a node in the definition of patterns is an extension that appears to be tailored to the treatment of DLs with inverse roles. Thus, it has the flavor of an ad-hoc extension, with the clear danger that adding another constructor may motivate yet another extension of the framework.

Is there a more general extension? Instead of restricting patterns to being certain trees of depth 2, a more general extension would be to use as patterns trees of some fixed depth k or patterns whose depth is bounded by some function of the input size. We conjecture that it is possible to extend our framework in this direction while retaining the results shown in this paper. In contrast to the extension of patterns by predecessor nodes, this appears to require some more work, though.

6.3   Allowing for Global Information

In the present framework, rules are local in that they consider only one node and its direct successors. The extension mentioned in the previous subsection extends the scope of rules but leaves it still local (bounded by the depth of patterns). In some cases, it would be convenient to be able to access global information that can influence the behavior of rules and can also be changed by rules.

Is such global information useful? A typical example where it would be convenient to allow for global information are DLs with so-called nominals, i.e., concept names that must be interpreted as singletons, and thus stand for a single element of the interpretation domain. Assume that N is such a nominal. If N occurs in the label of two different nodes of a completion tree, then this means that these nodes represent the same individual in the corresponding model, and thus the whole label sets of these nodes must coincide in a saturated and clash-free completion tree. Thus, rules and clash-triggers that are designed to realizing this are concerned with information about nodes that may be quite far apart from each other in the tree. One way of ensuring this could be to have, in addition to the completion tree with its local node labels, a global book-keeping component that contains information about the labels of all nominals. A rule that encounters the nominal N in the label of node v may then use the information in the book-keeping component for nominal N to extend the label of v, but it may also extend the book-keeping component based on what is found in the label of v. Thus, through this book-keeping component, information can be passed between nodes that are far apart from each other in the tree.

Is this extension too general? We believe that this extension is harmless as long as the number of possible "states" of the book-keeping component is appropriately bounded by the size of the input. Of course, this depends on the exact definition of the book-keeping component and its interaction with rules and clash-triggers. The integration of such a book-keeping component into our framework and the proof that the results shown in the present paper still hold in this extended framework is a subject of future research.

References

1. F. Baader, D. Calvanese, D. McGuinness, D. Nardi, and P. F. Patel-Schneider, editors. *The Description Logic Handbook: Theory, Implementation, and Applications.* Cambridge University Press, 2003.
2. F. Baader, E. Franconi, B. Hollunder, B. Nebel, and H.-J. Profitlich. An empirical analysis of optimization techniques for terminological representation systems or: Making KRIS get a move on. *Applied Artificial Intelligence. Special Issue on Knowledge Base Management,* 4:109–132, 1994.
3. F. Baader and W. Nutt. Basic description logics. In *[1]*, pages 43–95. 2003.
4. F. Baader and U. Sattler. An overview of tableau algorithms for description logics. *Studia Logica,* 69:5–40, 2001.
5. P. Blackburn, M. de Rijke, and Y. Venema. *Modal Logic,* volume 53 of *Cambridge Tracts in Theoretical Computer Science.* Cambridge University Press, 2001.
6. R. J. Brachman and H. J. Levesque, editors. *Readings in Knowledge Representation.* Morgan Kaufmann, Los Altos, 1985.
7. D. Calvanese and G. DeGiacomo. Expressive description logics. In *[1]*, pages 178–218. 2003.
8. G. De Giacomo and M. Lenzerini. TBox and ABox reasoning in expressive description logics. In L. C. Aiello, J. Doyle, and S. C. Shapiro, editors, *Proc. of the 5th Int. Conf. on the Principles of Knowledge Representation and Reasoning (KR'96),* pages 316–327. Morgan Kaufmann, Los Altos, 1996.
9. F. Donini. Complexity of reasoning. In *[1]*, pages 96–136. 2003.
10. F. Donini and F. Massacci. EXPTIME tableaux for $\mathcal{ALC}$. *Acta Informatica,* 124(1):87–138, 2000.
11. F. M. Donini, M. Lenzerini, D. Nardi, and W. Nutt. The complexity of concept languages. In J. Allen, R. Fikes, and E. Sandewall, editors, *Proc. of the 2nd Int. Conf. on the Principles of Knowledge Representation and Reasoning (KR'91),* pages 151–162. Morgan Kaufmann, Los Altos, 1991.
12. F. M. Donini, M. Lenzerini, D. Nardi, and W. Nutt. Tractable concept languages. In *Proc. of the 12th Int. Joint Conf. on Artificial Intelligence (IJCAI'91),* pages 458–463, Sydney (Australia), 1991.
13. V. Haarslev and R. Möller. RACER system description. In *Proc. of the Int. Joint Conf. on Automated Reasoning (IJCAR 2001),* 2001.

14. B. Hollunder and F. Baader. Qualifying number restrictions in concept languages. In *Proc. of the 2nd Int. Conf. on the Principles of Knowledge Representation and Reasoning (KR'91)*, pages 335–346, 1991.

15. I. Horrocks. Using an expressive description logic: FaCT or fiction? In *Proc. of the 6th Int. Conf. on Principles of Knowledge Representation and Reasoning (KR'98)*, pages 636–647, 1998.

16. I. Horrocks. Implementation and optimization techniques. In *[1]*, pages 306–346. 2003.

17. I. Horrocks and U. Sattler. A description logic with transitive and inverse roles and role hierarchies. *J. of Logic and Computation*, 9(3):385–410, 1999.

18. I. Horrocks, U. Sattler, and S. Tobies. Practical reasoning for very expressive description logics. *J. of the Interest Group in Pure and Applied Logic*, 8(3):239–264, 2000.

19. R. MacGregor. The evolving technology of classification-based knowledge representation systems. In J. F. Sowa, editor, *Principles of Semantic Networks*, pages 385–400. Morgan Kaufmann, Los Altos, 1991.

20. E. Mays, R. Dionne, and R. Weida. K-REP system overview. *SIGART Bull.*, 2(3), 1991.

21. M. Minsky. A framework for representing knowledge. In J. Haugeland, editor, *Mind Design*. The MIT Press, 1981. A longer version appeared in *The Psychology of Computer Vision* (1975). Republished in [6].

22. R. Möller and V. Haarslev. Description logic systems. In *[1]*, pages 282–305. 2003.

23. P. F. Patel-Schneider, D. L. McGuiness, R. J. Brachman, L. Alperin Resnick, and A. Borgida. The CLASSIC knowledge representation system: Guiding principles and implementation rational. *SIGART Bull.*, 2(3):108–113, 1991.

24. C. Peltason. The BACK system — an overview. *SIGART Bull.*, 2(3):114–119, 1991.

25. M. R. Quillian. Word concepts: A theory and simulation of some basic capabilities. *Behavioral Science*, 12:410–430, 1967. Republished in [6].

26. K. Schild. A correspondence theory for terminological logics: Preliminary report. In *Proc. of the 12th Int. Joint Conf. on Artificial Intelligence (IJCAI'91)*, pages 466–471, 1991.

27. M. Schmidt-Schauß and G. Smolka. Attributive concept descriptions with complements. *Artificial Intelligence*, 48(1):1–26, 1991.

28. M. Y. Vardi. Reasoning about the past with two-way automata. In *Proc. of the 25th Int. Coll. on Automata, Languages and Programming (ICALP'98)*, volume 1443 of *Lecture Notes in Computer Science*, pages 628–641. Springer-Verlag, 1998.

29. M. Y. Vardi and P. Wolper. Automata-theoretic techniques for modal logics of programs. *J. of Computer and System Sciences*, 32:183–221, 1986. A preliminary version appeared in *Proc. of the 16th ACM SIGACT Symp. on Theory of Computing (STOC'84)*.

30. W. A. Woods and J. G. Schmolze. The KL-ONE family. In F. W. Lehmann, editor, *Semantic Networks in Artificial Intelligence*, pages 133–178. Pergamon Press, 1992. Published as a special issue of *Computers & Mathematics with Applications*, Volume 23, Number 2–9.

Disproving False Conjectures

Serge Autexier[1,2,*] and Carsten Schürmann[3,**]

[1] FR 6.2 Informatik, Saarland University
[2] German Research Center for Artificial Intelligence (DFKI), Saarbrücken, Germany,
autexier@dfki.de
[3] Yale University, New Haven, USA,
carsten@cs.yale.edu

Abstract. For automatic theorem provers it is as important to disprove false conjectures as it is to prove true ones, especially if it is not known ahead of time if a formula is derivable inside a particular inference system. Situations of this kind occur frequently in inductive theorem proving systems where failure is a common mode of operation. This paper describes an abstraction mechanism for first-order logic over an arbitrary but fixed term algebra to second-order monadic logic with 0 successor functions. The decidability of second-order monadic logic together with our notion of abstraction yields an elegant criterion that characterizes a subclass of unprovable conjectures.

1 Introduction

The research on automated theorem proving is inspired by Leibniz' dream to develop a "lingua characteristica" together with a "calculus ratiocinator" in order to mechanize logical reasoning. He advocated using the purely rational and incorruptible mechanized reasoners in order to decide whether a given logical consequence holds or not. While this vision has spurred a lot of research devoted to proving *true* conjectures, disproving *false* conjectures that occur frequently in proof assistants, inductive theorem provers, and logical programming systems has attracted far less interest.

In fact, in most theorem proving systems, the default mode of operation is failure: conjectures are often entered in the hope that they are correct, the proof by cases is typically triggered by failure to prove a given subgoal, and even in logic programming, backtracking is always preceded by failure to construct a proof of a subgoal be it in Horn logic or hereditary Harrop logic [9].

In practice, the development of conjectures is an evolutionary process and typically a true conjecture is the result of a sequence of false conjectures and their disproofs. Thus, research on automatic disproving of false conjectures is equally important as automatic proving of true conjectures. Automatic disproving is of

* This work was supported by the German Academic Exchange Service DAAD & the Deutsche Forschungsgemeinschaft (DFG) under grant Hu-737/1-2.

** This work was supported in part by the National Science Foundation NSF under grants CCR-0133502 and INT-9909952.

M.Y. Vardi and A. Voronkov (Eds.): LPAR 2003, LNAI 2850, pp. 33–48, 2003.
© Springer-Verlag Berlin Heidelberg 2003

increasing relevance in the context of formal software development [2, 3], where early detection of flaws in programs reduces the overall development cost.

The key idea underlying our technique presented in this paper consists of the definition of a representational abstraction function of first-order logic formulas into a decidable fragment of second-order logic, namely second-order monadic logic without successor functions, S0S [10]. The abstraction function is effectively polynomial-time computable, preserves the structural form of the original formula, and most importantly preserves non-provability. Second-order monadic logic is decidable, and therefore disproving a conjecture in S0S implies contrapositively that the original conjecture could not have been provable either. The decision procedure of S0S is PSPACE-complete [14], but will always report true or false. Only if no proof in S0S exists, we can be sure that the conjecture is indeed false. If a proof exists, in terms of provability, nothing can be learned from it. However, the proof may contain vital information that can assist the theorem prover to try to prove the conjecture, a question which we will consider in future work.

In preliminary studies [11], we have developed a similar criterion for the first-order meta-logic $\mathcal{M}_{\omega}^{+}$ for the logical framework LF [6], although without negation, disjunction, or implication. Besides truth and falsehood we did not consider any other logical constants or predicates. The abstraction mechanism presented in this paper, on the other hand, scales to first-order logic with equational theories (e.g. Peano Arithmetic) and is based on Leibniz equality which is prevalent in many higher-order theorem proving systems [1, 13].

The paper is organized as follows: In Sec. 2 we define syntax and sequent calculi of first-order and second-order monadic logics. The abstraction of first-order logic formulas to second-order logic formulas and the relevant meta theory is presented in Sec. 3. Some of the proofs in that section are omitted because of space restrictions and can be found in [4]. In Sec. 4 we extend our techniques to first-order logic with equality and show in Sec. 5 that the class of disprovable formulas includes formulas with infinite counter-models. In Sec. 6 we present details about the implementation of the technique before concluding and assessing results in Sec. 7.

2   First-Order Logic and Second-Order Monadic Logic

We recapitulate the definitions of first-order and second-order monadic logic with 0 successors (S0S) as well as the decidability result of second-order modal logic [10] that is relevant for the technique presented in this paper.

2.1   First-Order Logic

Definition 1 (First-Order Logic Formulas). *Let $\mathcal{T}(\mathcal{C}, \mathcal{V})$ be a term algebra freely generated from a set of constant symbols $\mathcal{C}$ and a list of pairwise different variable symbols $\mathcal{V}$. Let $\mathcal{P}$ be a set of predicates. Then first-order logic formulas are defined by*

Terms: $VC(x) := [x]$ $VC(c) = [c]$ $VC(f(t_1, \ldots, t_n)) := \bigoplus_{i=1}^{n} VC(t_i)$
Formulas: $VC(P(t_1, \ldots, t_n)) := \bigoplus_{i=1}^{n} VC(t_i)$ $VC(\top) = VC(\bot) := []$
$VC(F_1 \supset F_2) = VC(F_1 \wedge F_2) := VC(F_1) \oplus VC(F_2)$
$VC(\neg F) := VC(F)$ $VC(\forall x. F) = VC(\exists x. F) := VC(F) \setminus \{x\}$

Fig. 1. List of constants and free variables in formulas and terms, where $[x]$ denotes the singleton list with the variable x, $[c]$ the singleton list with the constant c, $\oplus$ denotes the concatenation of lists, and $L \setminus \{x\}$ denotes the list obtained from L by removing any occurrence of the variable x.

$$\textit{First-order Logic Formulas: } F ::= P(t_1 \ldots t_n) \mid \top \mid \bot \mid F_1 \supset F_2 \mid F_1 \wedge F_2 \mid \neg F$$
$$\mid \forall x. F \mid \exists x. F$$

where $t_1, \ldots, t_n \in \mathcal{T}(\mathcal{C}, \mathcal{V})$ and $P \in \mathcal{P}$. In first-order logic, we write x, y, z for variables. For formulas F and terms t we write $VC(F)$ and $VC(t)$ to refer to the list[1] of free variables and constants in F and t (cf. Fig. 1).

Substitutions are capture avoiding and play an important role in this paper, especially in the proof of the soundness Theorem 2. We do not distinguish between substitutions for first-order or second-order monadic logic.

Definition 2 (Substitutions). *A substitution σ is a syntactically defined object $\sigma ::= \cdot \mid \sigma, t/x$. As usual, we write $\sigma(x)$ to apply σ to the variable x and the domain of a substitution is the set of variables for which $\sigma(x)$ is defined. The domain of a substitution is always finite.*

Definition 3 (First-Order Substitution Application). *We denote by $[\sigma]t$ and $[\sigma]F$ the standard application of σ to first-order terms and formulas.*

A sequent calculus for classical first-order logic is given in Fig. 2. All rules are standard. The subscript $_1$ in the rule names identifies the quantifier rules as first-order. The superscript ^{a} indicates that a is fresh in $\Gamma \implies \forall x. F$ for $\forall_1 I^a$ and in $\Gamma \implies H$ for $\exists_1 E^a$. First-order logic provides a foundation of several theorem proving systems, Spass, INKA, and others, and we illustrate its use with our running example about binary trees.

Example 1 (Binary Trees). In first-order logic, properties of trees and paths can be expressed as formulas ranging over terms generated by a term algebra that consists of two constant symbols here (for the empty path) and leaf (for leaves in a tree), two unary function symbols left and right (for paths denoting respectively left and right subtrees), and one binary function symbol node (for non-leaf nodes of trees). We use the validtree and validpath as unary predicates that describe the well-formedness of trees and paths, respectively, mirror and reflect as binary predicates, where $\text{mirror}(t, t')$ stands for t' is a tree that is derived from t by subtreewise exchanging left and right subtrees, and $\text{reflect}(p, p')$ for p' is a path

---

[1] We define $VC(t)$ as a list of variables and constants as the order of the symbols simplifies the proofs. However, the reader may think of $VC(t)$ as a set.

$$\overline{\Gamma, F \Longrightarrow \Delta, F} \ \text{ax} \qquad \overline{\Gamma \Longrightarrow \Delta, \top} \ \top\text{R} \qquad \overline{\Gamma, \bot \Longrightarrow \Delta} \ \bot\text{L}$$

$$\frac{\Gamma \Longrightarrow \Delta}{\Gamma, F \Longrightarrow \Delta} \ \text{weak L} \qquad \frac{\Gamma \Longrightarrow \Delta}{\Gamma \Longrightarrow F, \Delta} \ \text{weak R}$$

$$\frac{\Gamma \Longrightarrow \Delta, F \quad \Gamma \Longrightarrow \Delta, G}{\Gamma \Longrightarrow \Delta, F \wedge G} \ \wedge\text{R} \qquad \frac{\Gamma, F, G, \Longrightarrow \Delta}{\Gamma, F \wedge G \Longrightarrow \Delta} \ \wedge\text{L}$$

$$\frac{\Gamma \Longrightarrow \Delta, F, G}{\Gamma \Longrightarrow \Delta, F \vee G} \ \vee\text{R} \qquad \frac{\Gamma, F \Longrightarrow \Delta \quad \Gamma, G \Longrightarrow \Delta}{\Gamma, F \vee G \Longrightarrow \Delta} \ \vee\text{L}$$

$$\frac{\Gamma, F \Longrightarrow \Delta, G}{\Gamma \Longrightarrow \Delta, F \supset G} \ \supset\text{R} \qquad \frac{\Gamma, \Longrightarrow \Delta, F \quad \Gamma, G \Longrightarrow \Delta}{\Gamma, F \supset G \Longrightarrow \Delta} \ \supset\text{L}$$

$$\frac{\Gamma, F \Longrightarrow \Delta}{\Gamma \Longrightarrow \Delta, \neg F} \ \neg\text{R} \qquad \frac{\Gamma \Longrightarrow \Delta, F}{\Gamma, \neg F \Longrightarrow \Delta} \ \neg\text{L}$$

$$\frac{\Gamma \Longrightarrow \Delta, [a/x]F}{\Gamma \Longrightarrow \Delta, \forall x. F} \ \forall_1 \text{R}^a \qquad \frac{\Gamma, \forall x. F, [t/x]F \Longrightarrow \Delta}{\Gamma, \forall x. F \Longrightarrow \Delta} \ \forall_1 \text{L}$$

$$\frac{\Gamma \Longrightarrow \Delta, \exists x. F, [t/x]F}{\Gamma \Longrightarrow \Delta, \exists x. F} \ \exists_1 \text{R} \qquad \frac{\Gamma, [a/x]F \Longrightarrow \Delta}{\Gamma, \exists x. F \Longrightarrow \Delta} \ \exists_1 \text{L}^a$$

$$\frac{\Gamma, F \Longrightarrow \Delta \quad \Gamma \Longrightarrow F, \Delta}{\Gamma \Longrightarrow \Delta} \ \text{Cut}(F)$$

Fig. 2. Sequent Calculus for Classical First-Order Logic.

that is derived from p by exchanging constant left by right and vice versa. A set of axioms that relate terms is given in Fig. 3.

A property about binary trees that one may be interested in is to show that mirrored subtrees are preserved under reflecting paths which can be formally expressed as

$$\forall t. \forall s. \forall p. (\text{validtree}(t) \wedge \text{validtree}(s) \wedge \text{validpath}(p) \wedge \text{subtree}(t, p, s))$$
$$\supset \exists t'. \exists s'. \exists p'. (\text{validtree}(t') \wedge \text{validtree}(s') \wedge \text{validpath}(p') \wedge \text{subtree}(t', p', s')$$
$$\wedge \text{mirror}(t, t') \wedge \text{reflect}(p, p') \wedge \text{mirror}(s, s'))$$

Without induction principles, this theorem is not provable in first-order logic. □

2.2 Second-Order Monadic Logic without Successor Functions

Second-order monadic logic without successor functions (S0S) restricts atomic formulas to the form $P(x)$ or $X(x)$ where $x \in \mathcal{V} \cup \mathcal{C}$ is either a variable or a constant, P is a unary predicate, and X is a unary variable that ranges over unary predicates.

Definition 4 (Second-Order Logic Formulas S0S). *Let $\mathcal{T}(\mathcal{C}, \mathcal{V})$ be a term algebra with constants and variables only, and $\mathcal{P}$ be defined as above in Definition 1 and $\mathcal{W}$ a list of pairwise distinct second-order variable names. Second-order monadic logic formulas are defined by*

---

validtree(leaf)

$\forall t_1. \forall t_2.$ validtree$(t_1) \wedge$ validtree$(t_2) \supset$ validtree$(\text{node}(t_1, t_2))$

validpath(here)

$\forall p.$ validpath$(p) \supset$ validpath$(\text{left}(p))$

$\forall p.$ validpath$(p) \supset$ validpath$(\text{right}(p))$

mirror(leaf, leaf)

$\forall t_1. \forall t_1'. \forall t_2. \forall t_2'.$ mirror$(t_1, t_1') \wedge$ mirror$(t_2, t_2') \supset$ mirror$(\text{node}(t_1, t_2), \text{node}(t_2', t_1'))$

reflect(here, here)

$\forall p. \forall p'.$ reflect$(p, p') \supset$ reflect$(\text{left}(p), \text{right}(p'))$

$\forall p. \forall p'.$ reflect$(p, p') \supset$ reflect$(\text{right}(p), \text{left}(p'))$

$\forall t.$ subtree(t, here, t)

$\forall t_1. \forall t_2. \forall p. \forall t'.$ subtree$(t_1, p, t') \supset$ subtree$(\text{node}(t_1, t_2), \text{left}(p), t')$

$\forall t_1. \forall t_2. \forall p. \forall t'.$ subtree$(t_2, p, t') \supset$ subtree$(\text{node}(t_1, t_2), \text{right}(p), t')$

Fig. 3. Sample set of axioms defining properties of trees.

$$\frac{\Gamma \Longrightarrow [p/X]A, \Delta}{\Gamma \Longrightarrow \forall X.\, A, \Delta} \; \forall \mathsf{R}^p \qquad \frac{\Gamma, \forall X.\, A, [P/X]A \Longrightarrow \Delta}{\Gamma, \forall X.\, A \Longrightarrow \Delta} \; \forall \mathsf{L}$$

$$\frac{\Gamma \Longrightarrow [P/X]A, \exists X.\, A, \Delta}{\Gamma \Longrightarrow \exists X.\, A, \Delta} \; \exists \mathsf{R} \qquad \frac{\Gamma, [p/x]A \Longrightarrow \Delta}{\Gamma, \exists x.\, A \Longrightarrow \Delta} \; \exists \mathsf{L}^p$$

Fig. 4. Additional Rules for second-order logic.

SOS formulas: $G ::= P(x) \mid P(c) \mid X(x) \mid X(c) \mid \top \mid \bot \mid G_1 \supset G_2 \mid G_1 \wedge G_2$
$\mid \neg G \mid \forall x.\, G \mid \exists x.\, G \mid \forall X.\, G \mid \exists X.\, G$

where $x \in \mathcal{V}$, $c \in \mathcal{C}$, $X \in \mathcal{W}$ and $P \in \mathcal{P}$. In second-order monadic logic, we write x, y, z for variables, and X, Y, Z for variables that range over predicates.

The sequent calculus for classical SOS is obtained by adding four left and right rules for the second-order quantifiers to the respective first-order natural deduction calculi as depicted in Fig. 4 where P is any predicate from $\mathcal{P}$ and p is new with respect to the sequent. Since we consider second-order monadic logic without successors, $t \in \mathcal{V} \cup \mathcal{C}$ in rules $\exists_1\mathsf{I}$ and $\forall_1\mathsf{E}$, respectively. For the purpose of our paper the main result about second-order monadic logic is that it is decidable, which has been proved by Rabin [10].

Theorem 1 (Rabin, 1969). *Second-order monadic logic with k successor functions is decidable.* □

3   Abstraction

It is well-known that brute force search for proofs of conjectures may easily exhaust system resources regarding space and time. If a conjecture is true, the traversal of the search space in one way or another is necessary to find the derivation that is known to exist. Often, however, interim conjectures are not necessarily known to be derivable. These situations arise frequently in systems where induction principles are not axiomatized but encoded via special elimination rules. In many inductive theorem provers, therefore, failure to find a derivation in the non-inductive fragment indicates that subsequent case analyses are necessary and failure is therefore the predominant way of operation.

Of course, before a theorem prover can meaningfully fail, it must have visited every node in the search space that is potentially infinite. Alternatively, following the algorithm outlined in this paper, it is often possible to disprove formally a conjecture. Our proposed technique relies on an abstraction into second-order monadic logic without successor functions that is known to be decidable. If the abstracted formula is false, by the soundness of abstraction (Theorem 2), the original formula is false as well. Therefore, following the proposed classifications of abstractions by Giunchiglia and Walsh [5][2], our notion of abstraction satisfies the properties of a TI abstraction with a consistent abstract space. For the domain of first-order logic, first-order monadic logic would suffice as abstract space, but equality (see Sec. 4) requires the use of second-order monadic logic.

The abstraction can be intuitively explained as follows. A derivation $\cdot \implies P(t_1, \ldots, t_n)$ must contain information about the individual t_i's in one form or another. Without axiomatizing this relation, we instead propose to approximate it, and we rewrite $P(t_1, \ldots, t_n)$ to a conjunction of unary atomic formulas $P(x)$ and $P(c)$ for any variable x and any constant c that occurs in the terms. The abstraction preserves the structure of a formula, and is defined as follows.

Definition 5 (Abstraction).

$$\alpha(\top) := \top \tag{1}$$
$$\alpha(\bot) := \bot \tag{2}$$
$$\alpha(F_1 \vee F_2) := \alpha(F_1) \vee \alpha(F_2) \tag{3}$$
$$\alpha(F_1 \wedge F_2) := \alpha(F_1) \wedge \alpha(F_2) \tag{4}$$

$$\alpha(F_1 \supset F_2) := \alpha(F_1) \supset \alpha(F_2) \tag{5}$$
$$\alpha(\neg F) := \neg(\alpha(F)) \tag{6}$$
$$\alpha(\forall x. F) := \forall x. \alpha(F) \tag{7}$$
$$\alpha(\exists x. F) := \exists x. \alpha(F) \tag{8}$$

$$\alpha(P(t_1, \ldots, t_n)) := \bigwedge_{x \in VC(P(t_1, \ldots, t_n))} P(x) \tag{9}$$

The cases (1)–(8) are straightforward, which leaves (9) to be explained. In (9) $\bigwedge_{x \in VC(P(t_1, \ldots, t_n))} P(x)$ is the conjunction of formulas defined by

$$\bigwedge_{x \in []} P(x) := \top, \quad \bigwedge_{x \in [x']} P(x) := P(x'), \quad \text{and} \quad \bigwedge_{x \in [x'] \oplus L} P(x) := P(x') \wedge \left(\bigwedge_{x \in L} P(x) \right)$$

Example 2. We illustrate the technique by abstracting the axioms depicted in Fig. 3. The result is shown in Fig. 5.

---

[2] This paper also provides an overview of different abstraction mechanisms.

validtree(leaf)

$\forall t_1. \forall t_2.$ validtree$(t_1) \wedge$ validtree(t_2)validtree$(t_1) \wedge$ validtree(t_2)

validpath(here)

$\forall p.$ validpath$(p) \supset$ validpath(p)

$\forall p.$ validpath$(p) \supset$ validpath(p)

mirror(leaf) $\wedge$ mirror(leaf)

$\forall t_1. \forall t_1'. \forall t_2. \forall t_2'.$ mirror$(t_1) \wedge$ mirror$(t_1') \wedge$ mirror$(t_2) \wedge$ mirror(t_2')

$\supset$ mirror$(t_1) \wedge$ mirror$(t_2) \wedge$ mirror$(t_2') \wedge$ mirror(t_1')

reflect(here) $\wedge$ reflect(here)

$\forall p. \forall p'.$ reflect$(p) \wedge$ reflect$(p') \supset$ reflect$(p) \wedge$ reflect(p')

$\forall p. \forall p'.$ reflect$(p) \wedge$ reflect$(p') \supset$ reflect$(p) \wedge$ reflect(p')

$\forall t.$ subtree$(t) \wedge$ subtree(here) $\wedge$ subtree(t)

$\forall t_1. \forall t_2. \forall p. \forall t'.$ subtree$(t_1) \wedge$ subtree$(p) \wedge$ subtree$(t') \supset$

subtree$(t_1) \wedge$ subtree$(t_2) \wedge$ subtree$(p) \wedge$ subtree(t')

$\forall t_1. \forall t_2. \forall p. \forall t'.$ subtree$(t_2) \wedge$ subtree$(p) \wedge$ subtree$(t') \supset$

subtree$(t_1) \wedge$ subtree$(t_2) \wedge$ subtree$(p) \wedge$ subtree(t')

Fig. 5. Abstractions of the sample set of axioms.

The following lemma ensures that the abstraction of any first-order logic formula is always a second-order monadic formula with respect to S0S.

Lemma 1. *For any first-order logic formula F, $\alpha(F)$ is a second-order monadic formula without successor functions, and it holds $VC(F) = VC(\alpha(F))$.*

We now address the question of how substitutions and abstraction interact. Following Definition 2 the standard definition of substitutions may contain non-monadic terms, which complicates the interaction with abstraction. Consider the following example. Let $P(f(x,y))$ be a predicate and $\sigma = g(u,v)/x$ a substitution. Applying σ naively to the result of abstraction $P(x) \wedge P(y)$ would yield $P(g(u,v)) \wedge P(y)$, which is not an S0S formula and differs from

$$\alpha([\sigma](P(f(x,y)))) = \alpha(P(f(g(u,v),y))) = P(u) \wedge P(v) \wedge P(y).$$

Thus, substitution application of σ to t differs from the standard form of application, since it is required to flatten the structure of atomic formulas, as well. It is defined over the structure of t and σ, simultaneously.

Definition 6 (Flattening Substitution Application). *We denote by $[\![\sigma]\!](t)$ and $[\![\sigma]\!](F)$ the application of the homomorphic extension of σ to second-order terms and formulas defined by:*

$$[\![\sigma]\!](P(x)) := \bigwedge_{y \in VC(\sigma(x))} P(y) \tag{10}$$

$$\llbracket \sigma \rrbracket(\neg F) := \neg(\llbracket \sigma \rrbracket(F)) \tag{11}$$

$$for \circ \in \{\wedge, \vee, \supset\} \quad \llbracket \sigma \rrbracket(F_1 \circ F_2) := \llbracket \sigma \rrbracket(F_1) \circ \llbracket \sigma \rrbracket(F_2) \tag{12}$$

$$for\ Q \in \{\forall, \exists\} \quad \llbracket \sigma \rrbracket(Qx.\,F) := Qx.\,\llbracket \sigma, x/x \rrbracket(F) \tag{13}$$

where $(\sigma, x/x)$ denotes the substitution that maps x to x and otherwise is identical to σ.

Substitutivity in first-order logic and S0S commute with abstraction, which is the crucial property used at several occasions in the proof of the soundness Theorem 2.

Lemma 2. *Let F be a first-order logic formula and σ a first-order substitution. Then it holds:*

$$\alpha(\llbracket \sigma \rrbracket F) = \llbracket \sigma \rrbracket(\alpha(F))$$

Unfortunately, the proof theory of second-order monadic logic is not defined in terms of flattening substitution application, but rather in terms of the standard form of application, as used in the quantifier rules in Fig. 2. However, there is a direct relationship between flattening substitution application and renaming substitutions ρ

$$\rho ::= \cdot \mid \rho, y/x \mid \rho, c/x.$$

A renaming ρ can only substitute variables or constants for variables because no successor functions are available.

This relationship is captured by extending the notion of abstraction α that currently maps only atomic formulas into conjunctions of monadic S0S predicates, to map substitutions σ into renaming substitutions ρ. Intuitively, $\alpha(\sigma)$ computes the witness substitution for the S0S quantifier rules.

$$\begin{aligned} \alpha(\cdot) \quad &= \cdot \\ \alpha(\sigma, t/x) &= \alpha(\sigma), y/x \quad \text{for some } y \in VC(\sigma(x)) \end{aligned}$$

If σ maps x to t, the corresponding ρ maps x to some variable or constant that occurs in t. Substitution abstraction is hence a necessary step to embed substitutions that arise in first-order logic derivations in S0S, but is it the right choice? Does it preserve the derivability of abstracted sequents?

The answer to this question is contingent on a suitable choice of abstraction to first-order logic derivations that we describe inductively. Abstracting a derivation tree proceeds by replacing each formula in the tree by its abstraction. Axioms $\Gamma, P(t_1, \ldots, t_n) \vdash P(t_1, \ldots, t_n), \Delta$, for example, are mapped into $\alpha(\Gamma), \alpha(P(t_1, \ldots, t_n)) \vdash \alpha(P(t_1, \ldots, t_n)), \alpha(\Delta)$. It remains to show that the abstracted derivation is really an S0S derivation which we do in two steps.

First, we show that the choice of renaming substitution is well chosen and compatible with the previous notion of flattening substitution application (see Definition 6). In the interest of brevity, we write $\llbracket \Gamma \rrbracket$ for a context that consists of $\llbracket \sigma_1 \rrbracket F_1 \ldots \llbracket \sigma_n \rrbracket F_n$, and $[\Gamma]$ for a context of the form $[\alpha(\sigma_1)]F_1 \ldots [\alpha(\sigma_n)]F_n$. Second, we prove soundness of our abstraction.

Lemma 3 (Compatibility). *If $[\![\Gamma]\!] \Longrightarrow [\![\Delta]\!]$ is the result of abstracting a derivation then $[\Gamma] \Longrightarrow [\Delta]$.*

Proof. By induction on the derivation of $\Gamma \Longrightarrow \Delta$. The proof is quite straightforward. We only show three representative cases.

Case: $\dfrac{}{[\![\Gamma]\!], [\![\sigma]\!]P \Longrightarrow [\![\sigma]\!]P, [\![\Delta]\!]}$ ax

Similarly, we obtain $[\Gamma], [\sigma]P \Longrightarrow [\sigma]P, [\Delta]$ by the ax rule.

Case: $\dfrac{[\![\Gamma]\!], \forall x.\, [\![\sigma, x/x]\!]F, [t/x][\![\sigma, x/x]\!]F \Longrightarrow [\![\Delta]\!]}{[\![\Gamma]\!], \forall x.\, [\![\sigma, x/x]\!]F \Longrightarrow [\![\Delta]\!]}$ $\forall$L .

Since we are considering substitutions in SOS, the term t must always be a variable or a constant. By renaming we obtain that $[t/x][\![\sigma, x/x]\!]F = [\![\sigma, t/x]\!]F$, on which we can apply the induction hypothesis.

$$[\Gamma], \forall x.\, [\sigma, x/x]F, [\sigma, t/x]F \Longrightarrow [\Delta]$$

We can always rewrite the formula $[\sigma, t/x]F$ as $[t/x][\sigma, x/x]F$ by factoring out the renaming substitution and a renewed application of $\forall$L yields the desired

$$[\Gamma], \forall x.\, [\sigma, x/x]F \Longrightarrow [\Delta]$$

Case: $\dfrac{[\![\Gamma]\!] \Longrightarrow [a/x][\![\sigma, x/x]\!]F[\![\Delta]\!]}{[\![\Gamma]\!] \Longrightarrow, \forall x.\, [\![\sigma, x/x]\!]F[\![\Delta]\!]}$ $\forall$R^a .

As above, by renaming we obtain that $[a/x][\![\sigma, x/x]\!]F = [\![\sigma, a/x]\!]F$, on which we can apply the induction hypothesis.

$$[\Gamma] \Longrightarrow [\sigma, a/x]F, [\Delta]$$

We can always rewrite the term $[\sigma, a/x]F$ as $[a/x][\sigma, x/x]F$ by factoring out the renaming substitution. After discharging the parameter a, a renewed application of $\forall$L^a yields the desired

$$[\Gamma] \Longrightarrow \forall x.\, [\sigma, x/x]F, [\Delta]$$ $\square$

The translation into monadic second-order logic reduces an intrinsically undecidable problem to a decidable one and allows us to conclude from the disproof of an abstracted conjecture that the original conjecture could not have been true. The following theorem establishes that relationship with the benefit that it defines implicitly a procedure to disprove false conjectures: Using the abstraction, convert a conjecture from first-order logic into second-order monadic logic, and then run an implementation of a decision procedure for SOS. This insight can be seen as the central contribution of this work.

Theorem 2 (Soundness). *The abstraction α of derivations in first-order logic into derivations of first-order monadic logic without successor functions preserves the non-provability of formulas: If $\Gamma \Longrightarrow \Delta$ then $\alpha(\Gamma) \Longrightarrow \alpha(\Delta)$.*

Proof. By induction on the derivation of $\Gamma \Longrightarrow \Delta$. We only show the two challenging cases for the universal quantifier. All others are analogous.

Case:
$$\frac{\Gamma \Longrightarrow \Delta, \forall x.\, F, [a/x]F}{\Gamma \Longrightarrow \Delta, \forall x.\, F} \ \forall\mathsf{I}^a :$$

$$
\begin{array}{ll}
\alpha(\Gamma) \Longrightarrow \alpha(\Delta, \forall x.\, F, [a/x]F) & \text{by induction hypothesis} \\
\alpha(\Gamma) \Longrightarrow \alpha(\Delta, \forall x.\, F), [\![a/x]\!]\alpha(F) & \text{by Lemma 2} \\
\alpha(\Gamma) \Longrightarrow \alpha(\Delta, \forall x.\, F), [a/x]\alpha(F) & \text{by Lemma 3} \\
\alpha(\Gamma) \Longrightarrow \alpha(\Delta, \forall x.\, F) & \text{by } \forall\mathsf{R}
\end{array}
$$

Case:
$$\frac{\Gamma, \forall x.\, F, [t/x]F \Longrightarrow \Delta}{\Gamma, \forall x.\, F \Longrightarrow \Delta} \ \forall\mathsf{E} :$$

$$
\begin{array}{ll}
\alpha(\Gamma, \forall x.\, F, [t/x]F) \Longrightarrow \alpha(\Delta) & \text{by induction hypothesis} \\
\alpha(\Gamma, \forall x.\, F), [\![t/x]\!]\alpha(F) \Longrightarrow \alpha(\Delta) & \text{by Lemma 2} \\
\alpha(\Gamma, \forall x.\, F), [\alpha(t/x)]\alpha(F) \Longrightarrow \alpha(\Delta) & \text{by Lemma 3} \\
\alpha(\Gamma, \forall x.\, F) \Longrightarrow \alpha(\Delta) & \text{by } \forall\mathsf{L}
\end{array}
$$

$\square$

Example 3 (Mirrored Subtrees). Let F_0 be the conjunction of all axioms from Fig. 3 and $\alpha(F_0)$ the conjunction of all axioms from Fig. 5. Recall the problem from Example 1 of proving that a reflected path p in a mirrored tree t' leads to the same subtree as mirroring the subtree s that is found at p in the original tree t.

$$
\begin{aligned}
F_0 \supset \forall t.\, \forall s.\, \forall p.\, &(\mathsf{validtree}(t) \wedge \mathsf{validtree}(s) \wedge \mathsf{validpath}(p) \wedge \mathsf{subtree}(t, p, s)) \\
&\supset \exists t'.\, \exists s'.\, \exists p'.\, (\mathsf{validtree}(t') \wedge \mathsf{validtree}(s') \wedge \mathsf{validpath}(p') \wedge \mathsf{subtree}(t', p', s') \\
&\wedge \mathsf{mirror}(t, t') \wedge \mathsf{reflect}(p, p') \wedge \mathsf{mirror}(s, s'))
\end{aligned}
$$

In second-order monadic logic without successors the abstracted version of this formula is not provable either.

$$
\begin{aligned}
F_0 \supset \forall t.\, \forall s.\, \forall p.\, &(\mathsf{validtree}(t) \wedge \mathsf{validtree}(s) \wedge \mathsf{validpath}(p) \\
&\wedge \mathsf{subtree}(t) \wedge \mathsf{subtree}(p) \wedge \mathsf{subtree}(s)) \\
&\supset \exists t'.\, \exists s'.\, \exists p'.\, (\mathsf{validtree}(t') \wedge \mathsf{validtree}(s') \wedge \mathsf{validpath}(p') \\
&\wedge \mathsf{subtree}(t') \wedge \mathsf{subtree}(p') \wedge \mathsf{subtree}(s') \\
&\wedge \mathsf{mirror}(t) \wedge \mathsf{mirror}(t') \wedge \mathsf{reflect}(p) \wedge \mathsf{reflect}(p') \wedge \mathsf{mirror}(s) \wedge \mathsf{mirror}(s'))
\end{aligned}
$$

Consequently, there is no need to invoke a first-order theorem prover, because by Theorem 2 it is determined to fail. On the other hand with induction, analyzing cases over p yields three conjectures whose abstractions are all provable in SOS assuming a few necessary but simple lemmas about binary trees and their abstractions, which we omit from this presentation. $\square$

The abstraction has many applications. For example, by trial and error it can be helpful to determine which axioms are indispensable for proof search. We also suspect that the proof derivations of the abstracted formula contains much information that is useful to guide a theorem prover during the proof search process.

4   Treating Primitive Equality

The decision procedure defined in the previous sections is restricted to first-order logic without primitive equality. Thus, equality is treated like any other binary predicate and an equation $s = t$ is abstracted to the monadic formula $(\bigwedge_{x \in VC(s=t)} = (x))$.

In order to support primitive equality in an adequate way we extend the abstraction function to primitive equality and abstract equations to

$$\alpha(s = t) := \forall X. \left(\bigwedge_{x \in VC(s)} X(x) \right) \supset \left(\bigwedge_{x \in VC(t)} X(x) \right)$$
$$\wedge \forall X. \left(\bigwedge_{x \in VC(t)} X(x) \right) \supset \left(\bigwedge_{x \in VC(s)} X(x) \right)$$

Differently to the first-order case without equality, second-order quantifiers are necessary to range over predicates, such as subtree, mirror, or reflect.

Remark 1. This mapping is inspired by the Leibniz' definition of equality in higher-order logic, which is $s =_{Leibniz} t := \forall P. P(s) \supset P(t)$ with the only difference that besides the covariant it also involves the contravariant direction of implication. Without $\forall X. \left(\bigwedge_{x \in VC(t)} X(x) \right) \supset \left(\bigwedge_{x \in VC(s)} X(x) \right)$, for example, primitive equality would not be adequately captured in SOS. In higher-order logic P may be instantiated with any predicate $p_{\iota \to o}$ as well as with $\lambda x. \neg p(x)$, while in SOS the latter is not possible. However, the latter is necessary in order to obtain for each p not only $p(s) \supset p(t)$, but also the converse $p(t) \supset p(s)$, as used in the base case of Lemma 4.

It can be easily seen that the abstraction of a first-order equation is a second-order monadic formula due to the quantifier over X.

In the presence of primitive equality, we add the following rules to complete the sequent calculus for first-order logic with primitive equality. For those rules we denote by $C_{|u \leftarrow v}$ the replacement of exactly one occurrence of u with v in C.

$$\frac{}{\Gamma \Longrightarrow t = t, \Delta} \text{ refl} \qquad \frac{\Gamma, s = t \Longrightarrow F_{|t \leftarrow s}, \Delta}{\Gamma, s = t \Longrightarrow F, \Delta} \text{ Sub}_l^r \qquad \frac{\Gamma, s = t \Longrightarrow F_{|s \leftarrow t}, \Delta}{\Gamma, s = t \Longrightarrow F, \Delta} \text{ Sub}_r^r$$

$$\frac{\Gamma, F_{|t \leftarrow s}, s = t \Longrightarrow \Delta}{\Gamma, F, s = t \Longrightarrow \Delta} \text{ Sub}_l^l \qquad \frac{\Gamma, F_{|s \leftarrow t}, s = t \Longrightarrow \Delta}{\Gamma, F, s = t \Longrightarrow \Delta} \text{ Sub}_r^l$$

where for Sub-rules none of the variables in s and t are bound in F.

Lemma 4. *Any SOS sequent of the form* $\Gamma, \alpha(s = t), \alpha(F_{|s \leftarrow t}) \Longrightarrow \alpha(F), \Delta$ *or* $\Gamma, \alpha(s = t), \alpha(F) \Longrightarrow \alpha(F_{|s \leftarrow t}), \Delta$ *is provable.*

Proof. The proof is by induction over the structure of F.

Base Case: $F = P(t_1, \ldots, t_n)$: In that case it holds

$$\alpha(F_{|s \leftarrow t}) = \alpha(P(t_1, \ldots, t_n)_{|s \leftarrow t}) = \bigwedge_{x \in VC(P(t_1, \ldots, t_n)_{|s \leftarrow t})} P(x)$$

and $\alpha(F) = \alpha(P(t_1, \ldots, t_n)) = \bigwedge_{x \in VC(P(t_1, \ldots, t_n))} P(x)$. Note that by definition of VC there exist lists L, L' such that $VC(P(t_1, \ldots, t_n)_{|s \leftarrow t}) = L \oplus VC(t) \oplus L'$ and $VC(P(t_1, \ldots, t_n)) = L \oplus VC(s) \oplus L'$. Furthermore,

$$\alpha(s = t) = \forall X. \left(\bigwedge_{x \in VC(t)} X(x) \right) \supset \left(\bigwedge_{x \in VC(s)} X(x) \right)$$
$$\wedge \forall X. \left(\bigwedge_{x \in VC(s)} X(x) \right) \supset \left(\bigwedge_{x \in VC(t)} X(x) \right)$$

By instantiating the first X with P and the observation that $VC(s)$ is a sublist of $VC(P(t_1, \ldots, t_n))$ and $VC(t)$ is a sublist of $VC(P(t_1, \ldots, t_n)_{|s \leftarrow t})$, it is trivial to see that there is a proof for

$$\Gamma, \forall X. \left(\bigwedge_{x \in VC(t)} X(x) \right) \supset \left(\bigwedge_{x \in VC(s)} X(x) \right)$$
$$\wedge \forall X. \left(\bigwedge_{x \in VC(s)} X(x) \right) \supset \left(\bigwedge_{x \in VC(t)} X(x) \right), \bigwedge_{x \in VC(P(t_1, \ldots, t_n)_{|s \leftarrow t})} P(x)$$
$$\Longrightarrow \bigwedge_{x \in VC(P(t_1, \ldots, t_n))} P(x), \Delta$$

The case for $\Gamma, \alpha(s = t), \alpha(F) \Longrightarrow \alpha(F_{|s \leftarrow t}), \Delta$ is analogous, except that we must instantiate the second X. This is were the adequacy of the abstraction of an equation to both $\forall X. \left(\bigwedge_{x \in VC(s)} X(x) \right) \supset \left(\bigwedge_{x \in VC(t)} X(x) \right)$ and $\forall X. \left(\bigwedge_{x \in VC(t)} X(x) \right) \supset \left(\bigwedge_{x \in VC(s)} X(x) \right)$ is formally visible.

Induction Step: We proceed by case analysis over the structure of F:

1. $F = \neg F'$: It is obvious to see that $\alpha(\neg(F')_{|s \leftarrow t}) = \neg(\alpha(F'_{|s \leftarrow t}))$. Then

$$\cfrac{\cfrac{\Gamma', \alpha(s = t), \alpha(F') \Longrightarrow \alpha(F'_{|s \leftarrow t}), \Delta \quad \text{I.H.}}{\Gamma', \neg(\alpha(F'_{|s \leftarrow t})), \alpha(s = t), \alpha(F') \Longrightarrow \Delta} \; \neg \text{L}}{\Gamma', \neg(\alpha(F'_{|s \leftarrow t})), \alpha(s = t) \Longrightarrow \neg\alpha(F'), \Delta} \; \neg \text{R}$$

2. $F = F_1 \wedge F_2$: Without loss of generality we assume that s occurs in F_1. Again, it is obvious to see that $\alpha((F_1 \wedge F_2)_{|s \leftarrow t}) = \alpha(F_1|_{s \leftarrow t}) \wedge \alpha(F_2)$. Then we have to prove $\Gamma', \alpha(F_1|_{s \leftarrow t}) \wedge \alpha(F_2), \alpha(s = t) \Longrightarrow \alpha(F_1) \wedge \alpha(F_2), \Delta$.

$$\cfrac{\cfrac{\cfrac{\Gamma', \alpha(F_1|_{s \leftarrow t}), \alpha(s = t) \Longrightarrow \alpha(F_1), \Delta \quad \text{I. H.}}{\Gamma', \alpha(F_1|_{s \leftarrow t}), \alpha(F_2), \alpha(s = t) \Longrightarrow \alpha(F_1), \Delta} \; \text{weak L}}{\Gamma', \alpha(F_1|_{s \leftarrow t}) \wedge \alpha(F_2), \alpha(s = t) \Longrightarrow \alpha(F_1), \Delta} \; \wedge \text{L} \quad \cfrac{\quad}{\Gamma', \alpha(F_1|_{s \leftarrow t}), \alpha(F_2), \alpha(s = t) \Longrightarrow \alpha(F_2), \Delta} \; \text{ax}}{\Gamma', \alpha(F_1|_{s \leftarrow t}) \wedge \alpha(F_2), \alpha(s = t) \Longrightarrow \alpha(F_1) \wedge \alpha(F_2), \Delta} \; \wedge \text{R}$$

3. $F = \forall x. F'$: Again, it trivially holds that $\alpha((\forall x. F')_{|s \leftarrow t}) = \forall x. \alpha(F'_{|s \leftarrow t})$. Note that x does neither occur in s nor in t. Then we have to prove $\Gamma', \forall x. \alpha(F'_{|s \leftarrow t}), \alpha(s = t) \Longrightarrow \forall x. \alpha(F'), \Delta$:

$$\dfrac{\dfrac{\dfrac{\dfrac{\dfrac{\Gamma', \alpha([a/x]F'_{|s\leftarrow t}), \alpha(s=t) \Longrightarrow \alpha([a/x]F'), \Delta}{\Gamma', [a/x]\alpha(F'_{|s\leftarrow t}), \alpha(s=t) \Longrightarrow [a/x]\alpha(F'), \Delta} \; \text{Lemma } 2 \times 2}{\Gamma', [\alpha(a)/x]\alpha(F'_{|s\leftarrow t}), \alpha(s=t) \Longrightarrow [\alpha(a)/x]\alpha(F'), \Delta} \; \text{Lemma } 3 \times 2}{\Gamma', \forall x.\,\alpha(F'_{|s\leftarrow t}), [\alpha(a)/x]\alpha(F'_{|s\leftarrow t})\alpha(s=t) \Longrightarrow [\alpha(a)/x]\alpha(F'), \Delta} \; \text{weak L}}{\Gamma', \forall x.\,\alpha(F'_{|s\leftarrow t}), \alpha(s=t) \Longrightarrow [\alpha(a)/x]\alpha(F'), \Delta} \; \forall\text{L}}{\Gamma', \forall x.\,\alpha(F'_{|s\leftarrow t}), \alpha(s=t) \Longrightarrow \forall x.\,\alpha(F'), \Delta} \; \forall\text{R} \qquad \text{I.H.}$$

4. The remaining cases are analogous.   □

The soundness theorem with respect to first-order logic with primitive equality is then

Theorem 3. *The abstraction α of first-order logic formulas with primitive equality to second-order monadic logic formulas preserves the non-provability.*

Example 4. Let F_0, and $\alpha(F_0)$ as in Example 3. A formula in first-order logic that concludes that any subtree in a tree t at path p is unique is

$$F_0 \supset \forall p.\, \forall p'.\, \forall t.\, \forall s.\, \forall s'.\, \mathsf{subtree}(t, p, s) \wedge \mathsf{subtree}(t, p', s') \supset s = s'.$$

Its abstraction expands the equality predicate as described above.

$$F_0 \supset \forall p.\, \forall p'.\, \forall t.\, \forall s.\, \forall s'.\, \mathsf{subtree}(t) \wedge \mathsf{subtree}(p) \wedge \mathsf{subtree}(s)$$
$$\wedge \mathsf{subtree}(t) \wedge \mathsf{subtree}(p') \wedge \mathsf{subtree}(s')$$
$$\supset (\forall X.\, X(s) \supset X(s')) \wedge (\forall X.\, X(s') \supset X(s)).$$

The resulting formula is not provable in SOS and can therefore not be proved in first-order logic with primitive equality by Theorem 3. On the other hand with induction, if one would consider cases over p, abstraction yields three cases, each of which is provable in SOS.   □

5 About the Subclass of Unprovable Formulas

The question now arises which class of false conjectures can be tackled by the presented technique. Although we have no formal characterization for that class of formulas, we know that it includes first-order logic formulas that have only infinite counter-models. To see this consider the non-valid first-order logic formula in Fig. 6 and assume $\mathcal{I}$ is a counter-model that falsifies that formula. Then $\mathcal{I}(\varphi) = \bot$ entails that (1) $\mathcal{I}$ validates the left-hand side of the implication and (2) falsifies $\exists x.\, \neg P(x)$. From (1) it follows that the interpretations of P, $>$, and $=$ must be infinite. A possible infinite interpretation for P is $\lambda x.\top$. The abstraction $\alpha(\varphi)$ is also invalid with respect to SOS, also by interpreting P as $\lambda x.\top$. Thus, with our technique we can disprove first-order logic formulas that have no finite counter-models.

FOL formula: $\varphi := (\exists x.\, P(x) \wedge \forall x.\, \exists y.\, P(x) \supset (y > x \wedge P(y)) \wedge$
$\forall x, y, z.\, (x > y \wedge y > z) \supset x > z \wedge \forall x.\, x \neq x) \supset \exists x.\, \neg P(x)$

SOS formula: $\alpha(\varphi) := (\exists x.\, P(x) \wedge \forall x.\, \exists y.\, P(x) \supset (> (y) \wedge > (x) \wedge P(y)) \wedge$
$\forall x, y, z.\, (> (x) \wedge > (y) \wedge > (z)) \supset> (x) \wedge > (z) \wedge$
$\forall x.\, \neg(\forall X.\, X(x) \supset X(x) \wedge \forall X.\, X(x) \supset X(x))) \supset \exists x.\, \neg P(x)$

Fig. 6. Disproven first-order logic formula with infinite counter-model.

6   Implementation

The procedure for disproving false conjectures has been implemented in the MAYA system [3]. MAYA is an in-the-large verification tool for structured specifications. It is based on the notion of development graphs and incorporates an efficient management of change to preserve and adjust proof information when changing the specification. Each node of the development graph corresponds to an axiomatically defined theory and the procedure presented in this paper can be used to disprove false conjectures with respect to some theory. The implementation abstracts the first-order logic subset Φ of the axioms defining a theory to second-order monadic logic. To disprove a false conjecture ψ, the validity of the SOS formula $\alpha(\Phi \supset \psi)$ is checked.

In order to decide the validity of an SOS formula, rather than implementing our own SOS decision procedure, we have linked MAYA with the MONA system [8]. Although MONA implements only a decision procedure for *weak* second-order monadic logic, it is still useful since it is conservative over *full* second-order monadic logic without successor functions. Counter-models found in MONA are also counter-models in the more general setting. To our knowledge there is no available implementation of a full SOS decision procedure.

7   Conclusion

We have outlined a technique to disprove false conjectures in first-order logic with and without equality over a given and fixed term algebra. The central idea is that of abstraction. Formulas are transformed into second-order monadic logic without successor functions, which is known to be decidable. We have shown that the abstraction is sound, which means it preserves provability. Thus the absence of a proof in second-order monadic logic entails that the initial conjecture is unprovable, as well.

As related work we consider the tableau method [12] as well as combinations of model generation with automated theorem provers, such as the SCOTT system [7]. The tableau method not only detects unsatisfiability of the negated conjecture but also generates models for it. This is similar to the use of model generating systems during refutation proofs, as done in the SCOTT system. Thus, certain classes of false conjectures can be detected by generating counter-models. However, the relationship between these classes and the class characterized by the procedure presented in this paper is unclear yet and is left for future work.

Further future work is planned in different directions: First, we plan to investigate how to obtain from a counter-example for a non-valid SOS formula a counter-example for the original first-order logic formula, which would be highly beneficial especially in MAYA's application context which is formal software development. Also we assume it to be helpful to develop a characterization for the subclass of unprovable first-order logic formulas. Secondly, we plan to experiment with abstractions that preserve more of the term structures when mapping first-order logic formulas to second-order monadic logic formulas. Thereby we would leave the SOS fragment and employ larger fragments of second-order monadic logic, e.g. SkS. Preserving the structure should result in an increased efficiency for equational first-order logic theories. A third line of research will consist of using second-order logic proofs as proof plans to guide the actual proof search for the initial first-order logic formulas.

References

1. P. B. Andrews, M. Bishop, and C. E. Brown. System Description: TPS: A Theorem Proving System for Type Theory. In *Proceedings of CADE-17*, pages 164–169.

2. S. Autexier, D. Hutter, B. Langenstein, H. Mantel, G. Rock, A. Schairer, W. Stephan, R. Vogt, and A. Wolpers. Vse: Formal methods meet industrial needs. *International Journal on Software Tools for Technology Transfer, Special issue on Mechanized Theorem Proving for Technology, Springer*, September 1998.

3. S. Autexier, D. Hutter, T. Mossakowski, and A. Schairer. The development graph manager MAYA. In H. Kirchner and C. Ringeissen, editors, *Proceedings 9th Int. Conference on Algebraic Methodology And Software Technology (AMAST'02)*, 2002.

4. S. Autexier and C. Schürmann. Disproving False Conjectures. SEKI Technical Report SR-2003-06, CS Dep., Saarland University, Saarbrücken, Germany, 2003.

5. F. Giunchiglia and T. Walsh. A theory of abstraction. *Artificial Intelligence*, 57(2-3):323–389, 1992.

6. R. Harper, F. Honsell, and G. Plotkin. A framework for defining logics. *Journal of the Association for Computing Machinery*, 40(1):143–184, January 1993.

7. K. Hodgson and J. Slaney. Development of a semantically guided theorem prover. In R. Goré, A. Leitsch, and T. Nipkow, editors, *Automated Reasoning*, LNAI 2083, pages 443–447. Springer, June 2001.

8. N. Klarlund. Mona & fido: The logic-automaton connection in practice. In *Computer Science Logic, CSL '97*, LNCS 1414, 1998.

9. G. Nadathur and D. Miller. An overview of λProlog. In K. A. Bowen and R. A. Kowalski, editors, *Fifth International Logic Programming Conference*, pages 810–827, Seattle, Washington, August 1988. MIT Press.

10. M. O. Rabin. Decidability of second-order theories and automata on infinite trees. *Transactions of the American Mathematical Society*, 141:1–35, 1969.

11. C. Schürmann and S. Autexier. Towards proof planning for $\mathcal{M}_\omega^+$. *Electronic Notes in Theoretical Computer Science*, 70(2), 2002.

12. R. Smullyan. *First-Order Logic*. Springer, 1968.

13. J. Siekmann *et.al.* Proof development with ΩMEGA. In A. Voronkov, editor, *Proceedings of CADE-19*, LNAI 2392, pages 144–149. Springer, 2002.

14. M. Y. Vardi. The complexity of relational query languages (extended abstract). In *Proceedings of the 14th Annual ACM Symposium on Theory of Computing*, pages 137–146, 1982.

A Formal Proof of Dickson's Lemma in ACL2[*]

F.J. Martín–Mateos, J.A. Alonso, M.J. Hidalgo, and J.L. Ruiz–Reina

Computational Logic Group, Dept. of Computer Science and Artificial Intelligence,
University of Seville, E.T.S.I. Informática,
Avda. Reina Mercedes, s/n. 41012 Sevilla, Spain,
http://www.cs.us.es/{~fmartin,~jalonso,~mjoseh,~jruiz}

Abstract. Dickson's Lemma is the main result needed to prove the termination of Buchberger's algorithm for computing Gröbner basis of polynomial ideals. In this case study, we present a formal proof of Dickson's Lemma using the ACL2 system. Due to the limited expressiveness of the ACL2 logic, the classical non-constructive proof of this result cannot be done in ACL2. Instead, we formalize a proof where the termination argument is justified by the multiset extension of a well-founded relation.

1 Introduction

Dickson's Lemma is the main result needed to prove the termination of Buchberger's algorithm [2] for computing Gröbner basis of polynomial ideals. Thus, a formal proof of this result is needed by any formal termination proof of this algorithm. In particular, if we use the ACL2 system [7] to define and verify Buchberger's algorithm, a formal proof of Dickson's Lemma is essential, in order to reason about it in ACL2. This is our motivation for doing the formal proof of Dickson's Lemma. Since ACL2 consists of a programming language (an extension of an applicative subset of Common Lisp), a logic describing the programming language and a theorem prover supporting deduction in the logic, a formally verified Buchberger's algorithm in ACL2 would allow an environment in which proving and computing would be intermixed.

The ACL2 logic is a subset of first-order logic, without quantifiers and with a principle of proof by induction. Due to this limited expressiveness, it is not possible to reproduce the classical non-constructive proof of Dickson's Lemma as it is usually presented in the literature. The proof we present here is constructive and it is mainly based on a multiset extension of a well-founded relation. In the mechanization of this proof, we use a tool for defining multiset well-founded relations in ACL2 in an automated way, a tool that we used previously in other formalizations [13] and that can now be reused.

Dickson's Lemma is usually stated as follows:

Theorem 1 (Dickson's Lemma). *Let $n \in \mathbb{N}$ and $\{m_k : k \in \mathbb{N}\}$ be an infinite sequence of monomials in the variables $\{X_1, \ldots, X_n\}$. Then, there exist indices $i < j$ such that m_i divides m_j.*

---

[*] This work has been supported by project TIC2000-1368-C03-02 (Ministry of Science and Technology, Spain) and FEDER funds.

M.Y. Vardi and A. Voronkov (Eds.): LPAR 2003, LNAI 2850, pp. 49–58, 2003.

Given a fixed set of variables $V = \{X_1, \ldots, X_n\}$, we can naturally identify the set of n-variate monomials (with variables in V) with the set $\mathbb{N}^n$ of n-tuples of natural numbers: a monomial $X_1^{e_1} X_2^{e_2} \ldots X_n^{e_n}$ can be seen as the n-tuple $\langle e_1, \ldots, e_n \rangle$. The divisibility relation between monomials is then identified with the relation $\leq^n$ on $\mathbb{N}^n$, defined as $\langle k_1, \ldots, k_n \rangle \leq^n \langle l_1, \ldots, l_n \rangle$ if and only if $k_i \leq l_i$ for all $1 \leq i \leq n$. In the sequel, we will identify tuples and monomials in this sense. Thus, Dickson's Lemma can be reformulated stating that for every infinite sequence $\{f_k : k \in \mathbb{N}\}$ of n-tuples of natural numbers there exist indices $i < j$ such that $f_i \leq^n f_j$.

As we said above, the classical proof of Dickson's Lemma is non-constructive (see [1], for example), and thus it is not suitable for being formalized in the ACL2 logic. The proof we describe in the following is based on the same ideas as some constructive proofs already present in the literature [10, 14], and it essentially shows a well-founded measure that can be associated to the initial segments of the sequence of tuples and that decreases whenever a tuple in the sequence is not divided by any of the previous tuples.

2   Formalizing the Proof in ACL2

The ACL2 logic is a quantifier-free, first-order logic with equality, describing an applicative subset of Common Lisp. The syntax of terms is that of Common Lisp and the logic includes axioms for propositional logic and for a number of Lisp functions and data types. Rules of inference of the logic include those for propositional calculus, equality and instantiation. One important rule of inference is the *principle of induction*, that permits proofs by well-founded induction on the ordinal ε_0. The theory has a constructive definition of the ordinals up to ε_0, in terms of lists and natural numbers, given by the predicate e0-ordinalp and the order e0-ord-<. Although this is the only built-in well-founded relation, the user may define new well-founded relations from that, by previously providing an order-preserving ordinal function.

By the *principle of definition*, new function definitions are admitted as axioms only if there exists a measure in which the arguments of each recursive call decrease with respect to a well-founded relation; in this way, it is ensured that no inconsistencies are introduced by new definitions. Usually, the system can prove automatically this property using a predefined ordinal measure on Lisp objects and the relation e0-ord-<. Nevertheless, if the termination proof is not trivial, the user has to explicitly provide a measure on the arguments and a well-founded relation ensuring termination.

The ACL2 theorem prover mechanizes the logic, being particularly well suited for obtaining automated proofs based on simplification and induction. For a detailed description of ACL2, we refer the reader to the ACL2 book [6].

For the sake of readability, the ACL2 expressions in this paper are presented using a notation closer to the usual mathematical notation than its original Common Lisp syntax. Some of the functions are also used in infix notation. The complete proof can be found in http://www.cs.us.es/~fmartin/acl2/dickson/.

2.1 Formulation of Dickson's Lemma

To formalize Dickson's Lemma in the ACL2 logic, we consider a constant N (that is, a 0-ary function) representing the number of variables, and a unary function f, representing the infinite sequence of monomials given as N-tuples of natural numbers. These functions are abstractly defined by means of the encapsulate mechanism, which allows the user to introduce new function symbols by axioms constraining them to have certain properties. To ensure consistency, local witness functions having the same properties have to be exhibited. Inside an encapsulate construct, the properties stated need to be proved for the local witnesses, and outside, they work as assumed axioms. In this case, the assumed properties about N and f are the following[1]:

ASSUMPTION: N-is-natural->-0
$$N \in \mathbb{N} \wedge 0 < N$$

ASSUMPTION: f-sequence-of-N-tuples
$$i \in \mathbb{N} \rightarrow [\text{len}(f(i)) = N \wedge \text{natural-listp}(f(i))]$$

where natural-listp checks if its argument is a list of natural numbers (we use lists of length n to represent n-tuples).

Here, the encapsulate mechanism behaves like an universal quantifier over the functions abstractly defined with it. So, any theorem proved about these functions is true for any functions with the same properties as the ones assumed in the encapsulate construct, by means of functional instantiation (see [6] for details). This is the case for the ACL2 formalization of Dickson's Lemma: as the infinite sequence of monomials is abstractly defined via encapsulate, the proved properties about it are valid for any infinite sequence of monomials.

Let us now define the functions needed to state Dickson's Lemma. First, the function tuple-<= implements the divisibility relation (that is, the relation $\leq^n$):

DEFINITION:
$$T_1 \text{ tuple-<= } T_2 \Leftrightarrow$$
   if $\text{endp}(T_1)$ **then** $\text{endp}(T_2)$
   elseif $\text{endp}(T_2)$ **then** $\text{endp}(T_1)$
   elseif $\text{car}(T_1) \in \mathbb{N} \wedge \text{car}(T_2) \in \mathbb{N}$
         then $\text{car}(T_1) \leq \text{car}(T_2) \wedge \text{cdr}(T_1) \text{ tuple-<= } \text{cdr}(T_2)$
   else nil

The following function get-tuple-<=-f has two arguments, a natural number j and a N-tuple T, and it returns the largest index i such that $i < j$ and $f(i)$ tuple-<= T whenever such index exists (nil otherwise):

DEFINITION:
   get-tuple-<=-f$(j,T) =$
      if $j \in \mathbb{N}$ **then if** $j = 0$ **then nil**
                        elseif $f(j-1)$ tuple-<= T **then** $j-1$
                        else get-tuple-<=-f$(j-1,T)$
      else nil

---

[1] The local witnesses are irrelevant to our description of the proof.

Finally, the following function `dickson-indices` receives as input an index k and uses `get-tuple-<=-f` to recursively search a pair of indices $i < j$ such that $j \geq k$ and `f`(i) `tuple-<=` `f`(j):

DEFINITION:
    `dickson-indices`$(k) =$
        if $k \in \mathbb{N}$ then let i be `get-tuple-<=-f`$(k,$`f`$(k))$
                        in if $i \neq$ nil then $\langle i, k \rangle$
                            else `dickson-indices`$(k + 1)$
        else nil

Let us assume for the moment that we have proved that the function `dickson-indices` terminates and that this definition has been admitted by the system. Then the following property is easily proved as direct consequence of the definitions of the functions involved:

THEOREM: `dickson-lemma`
    $[k \in \mathbb{N} \wedge$ `dickson-indices`$(k) = \langle i, j \rangle] \rightarrow [i < j \wedge$ `f`(i) `tuple-<=` `f`$(j)]$

This theorem ensures that for any infinite sequence of monomials $\{f_k : k \in \mathbb{N}\}$, there exists $i < j$ such that f_i divides f_j (and the function `dickson-indices` explicitly provides these values). Thus, it is a formal statement of Dickson's Lemma in ACL2.

The hard part is the termination proof of the function `dickson-indices`. For that purpose, we have to explicitly provide to the system a measure on the input argument and prove that the measure decreases with respect to a given well-founded relation in every recursive call. We present the details in the next subsections.

2.2   A Well-Founded Measure

Before giving a formal definition of the termination measure, we give some intuition by means of an example. Let $\{f_k : k \in \mathbb{N}\}$ be an infinite sequence of pairs of natural numbers. Let us assume that $f_0 = \langle 3, 2 \rangle$, $f_1 = \langle 1, 5 \rangle$ and $f_2 = \langle 2, 1 \rangle$. In figure 1, we sequentially represent (by the shaded regions) the set of tuples that are divisible by some element of the sequence.

Thus, in each step, the non-shaded region represents the set of tuples that can be the next in the sequence without being divisible by the previous tuples. The main idea is that for every tuple of the sequence that is not divisible by any of the previous tuples, this "free space" decreases with respect to a well-founded relation.

Let us precise this intuitive idea. We can have a compact representation of the non-shaded regions by means of *patterns*. A **pattern** is an element of $(\mathbb{N} \cup \{*\})^n$, representing the set of tuples obtained replacing every occurrence of $*$ in the pattern by a natural number (occurrences of $*$ in a pattern will be called *freedoms*). Thus, the non-shaded regions may be represented by a multiset of patterns. For example, the non-shaded region of figure 1-b) is represented by

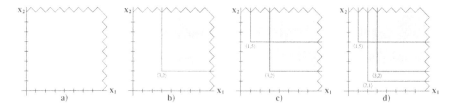

Fig. 1. Graphical idea of the measure.

$\{\!\{\langle 0,*\rangle, \langle 1,*\rangle, \langle 2,*\rangle, \langle *,0\rangle, \langle *,1\rangle\}\!\}$. We denote as $\mathcal{S}(\Pi)$ and $\mathcal{S}(\mathcal{P})$, the set of tuples represented by a pattern Π and by a multiset of patterns $\mathcal{P}$, respectively.

In every step, the new region is obtained from the previous one, by replacing some patterns by others. Given a new tuple T in the sequence, a pattern Π has to be replaced if there is some $T' \in \mathcal{S}(\Pi)$ divisible by T (we say in that case that Π is **reducible** by T). These reducible patterns are replaced by a new collection of patterns representing the new region obtained excluding the divisible tuples (we call these new patterns the **reductions** of Π with respect to T). Note that Π' is a reduction of Π with respect to T, if Π' is equal to Π except that one of the occurrences of $*$ in Π has been replaced by a natural number less than the number that appears in the same position in T. In the following table we present the patterns computed, for $k = 0, 1, 2, 3$, when f is the sequence of the example of figure 1. We also indicate the reducible patterns in each step.

k	Non-shaded regions	f_k	Reducible patterns
0	$\{\!\{\langle *,*\rangle\}\!\}$	$\langle 3,2\rangle$	$\langle *,*\rangle$
1	$\{\!\{\langle 0,*\rangle, \langle 1,*\rangle, \langle 2,*\rangle, \langle *,0\rangle, \langle *,1\rangle\}\!\}$	$\langle 1,5\rangle$	$\langle 1,*\rangle, \langle 2,*\rangle$
2	$\{\!\{\langle 0,*\rangle, \langle 1,0\rangle, \langle 1,1\rangle, \langle 1,2\rangle, \langle 1,3\rangle, \langle 1,4\rangle, \langle 2,0\rangle,$ $\langle 2,1\rangle, \langle 2,2\rangle, \langle 2,3\rangle, \langle 2,4\rangle, \langle *,0\rangle, \langle *,1\rangle\}\!\}$	$\langle 2,1\rangle$	$\langle 2,1\rangle, \langle 2,2\rangle, \langle 2,3\rangle,$ $\langle 2,4\rangle, \langle *,1\rangle$
3	$\{\!\{\langle 0,*\rangle, \langle 1,0\rangle, \langle 1,1\rangle, \langle 1,2\rangle, \langle 1,3\rangle, \langle 1,4\rangle, \langle 2,0\rangle,$ $\langle *,0\rangle, \langle 0,1\rangle, \langle 1,1\rangle\}\!\}$		

If we define the **dimension** of a pattern as its number of freedoms, then it is clear that every reducible pattern is replaced by a finite number of patterns with dimension strictly smaller. For example, the multiset of dimensions of the patterns representing the region of figure 1-b) is $\{\!\{1,1,1,1,1\}\!\}$ and the corresponding multiset for the region of figure 1-c) is $\{\!\{1,0,0,0,0,0,0,0,0,0,0,1,1\}\!\}$. In other words, every time the region is reduced, the multiset of the dimensions of the patterns representing the region decreases with respect to the multiset relation induced by the usual order between natural numbers. This multiset relation is known to be well-founded, and thus it is not possible to reduce the regions infinitely often, justifying Dickson's Lemma.

We now explain how we formalize these constructions in ACL2. A pattern will be represented as a list with the same length as the tuples. The function `member-tuple` implements the property $T \in \mathcal{S}(\Pi)$ (note that any occurrence in the pattern of an object that it is not a natural number stands for "$*$"):

DEFINITION:
$$\texttt{member-tuple}(T,\Pi) =$$
    if $\texttt{endp}(T)$ **then** $\texttt{endp}(\Pi)$
    elseif $\texttt{endp}(\Pi)$ **then** $\texttt{endp}(T)$
    elseif $\texttt{car}(\Pi) \in \mathbb{N}$ **then** $\texttt{car}(T) = \texttt{car}(\Pi) \wedge \texttt{member-tuple}(\texttt{cdr}(T),\texttt{cdr}(\Pi))$
    else $\texttt{member-tuple}(\texttt{cdr}(T),\texttt{cdr}(\Pi))$

Next, we present the definition of the function $\texttt{reductions}(\Pi, T)$ that computes the multiset[2] of reductions of a pattern Π with respect to a tuple T (assuming that Π is reducible by T). Let us recall that every reduction is obtained by replacing a freedom of Π by a natural number less than the one that appears in the same position in T:

DEFINITION:
$$\texttt{reductions}(\Pi,T) =$$
    if $\texttt{endp}(\Pi)$ **then** $\texttt{nil}$
    elseif $\texttt{car}(\Pi) \in \mathbb{N}$
        then $\texttt{cons-list-cdr}(\texttt{car}(\Pi), \texttt{reductions}(\texttt{cdr}(\Pi),\texttt{cdr}(T)))$
    else $\texttt{cons-list-car}(\texttt{natural-<-list}(\texttt{car}(T)), \texttt{cdr}(\Pi))$ @
        $\texttt{cons-list-cdr}(\texttt{car}(\Pi), \texttt{reductions}(\texttt{cdr}(\Pi),\texttt{cdr}(T)))$

where the symbol @ is the "append" operation between lists, the function $\texttt{natural-<-list}$ returns the list of natural numbers less than its argument (that is, $(\texttt{natural-<-list}\ n) = \texttt{'(0 1 ... } n{-}1))$ and the functions $\texttt{cons-list-car}$ and $\texttt{cons-list-cdr}$ behave schematically in the following way:

$$(\texttt{cons-list-car}\ \texttt{'}(x_1\ ...\ x_n)\ \texttt{'}l) = \texttt{'}((x_1\ .\ l)\ ...\ (x_n\ .\ l))$$

$$(\texttt{cons-list-cdr}\ \texttt{'}x\ \texttt{'}(l_1\ ...\ l_n)) = \texttt{'}((x\ .\ l_1)\ ...\ (x\ .\ l_n))$$

Given a multiset of patterns $\mathcal{P}$ and a tuple T, the function $\texttt{reduction-list}$ describes how the multiset of patterns $\mathcal{P}$ is reduced to a new multiset by the tuple T:

DEFINITION:
$$\texttt{reductions-list}(\mathcal{P},T) =$$
    if $\texttt{endp}(\mathcal{P})$ **then** $\mathcal{P}$
    elseif $\texttt{member-tuple}(T,\texttt{car}(\mathcal{P}))$ **then** $\texttt{reductions}(\texttt{car}(\mathcal{P}),T)$ @ $\texttt{cdr}(\mathcal{P})$
    else $\texttt{cons}(\texttt{car}(\mathcal{P}), \texttt{reductions-list}(\texttt{cdr}(\mathcal{P}),T))$

Note that the above function differs from the intuitive construction outlined above in two aspects. First, *only the first reducible pattern* is replaced by its reductions. Second, instead of looking for a pattern Π reducible by T, we check the stronger condition $T \in \mathcal{S}(\Pi)$. As we will see, both simplifications are sound[3].

---

[2] We will represent multisets as lists. Although this representation is not unique (the same multiset may be represented by different lists), it is adequate for our purposes.

[3] It is interesting to note that the soundness of both simplifications (which are not intuitive, especially the first one) makes for simpler proofs and were discovered from the interaction with the prover.

The function `reductions-tuple-list` iterates the reduction process over a finite sequence of tuples. It must be noticed that the list of tuples is provided in the reverse order:

DEFINITION:
    reductions-tuple-list($\mathcal{P}$,*T-lst*) =
        if endp(*T-lst*) then $\mathcal{P}$
        else reductions-list(reductions-tuple-list($\mathcal{P}$,cdr(*T-lst*)), car(*T-lst*))

The function `pattern-list-measure` computes the multiset of dimensions of a multiset of patterns (we omit here the definition of the function `dimension` which computes the number of freedoms in a pattern):

DEFINITION:
    pattern-list-measure($\mathcal{P}$) =
        if endp($\mathcal{P}$) then nil
        else cons(dimension(car($\mathcal{P}$)), pattern-list-measure(cdr($\mathcal{P}$)))

And finally, following the intuitive idea sketched above, we can associate a measure (a multiset of natural numbers) to every index k:

DEFINITION:
    dickson-indices-measure(k) =
        pattern-list-measure(
            reductions-tuple-list(list(initial-pattern(N))),
                                  initial-segment-f($k - 1$))

where the function `initial-pattern(N)` builds the initial pattern $\langle *, \ldots, * \rangle$ and the function `initial-segment-f`(k) builds the list of tuples (f_k ... f_1 f_0).

2.3   Termination Proof of `dickson-indices`

The last step in this formal proof is to define a well-founded relation and prove that the given measure decreases with respect to it in every recursive call of the function `dickson-indices`. We will define it as the relation induced by a well-founded relation on finite multisets of natural numbers. Intuitively, this relation is defined such that a smaller multiset can be obtained by removing a non-empty subset of elements, and adding elements which are smaller than some element removed. In [5], Dershowitz and Manna show that if the base relation is well-founded, then the relation induced on finite multisets is also well-founded.

As we said above, the only predefined well-founded relation in ACL2 is `e0-ord-<`, implementing the usual order between ordinals less than ε_0. The function `e0-ordinalp` recognizes those ACL2 objects representing such ordinals. If we want to define a new well-founded relation in ACL2, we have to explicitly provide a monotone ordinal function, and prove the corresponding order-preserving theorem (see [6] for details). Fortunately, we do not have to do this: we use the `defmul` tool. This tool, previously implemented and used by the authors in [13], automatically generates the definitions and prove the theorems needed to introduce in ACL2 the multiset relation induced by a given well-founded relation. In our case, we only need the following `defmul` call:

```
(defmul (e0-ord-< nil e0-ordinalp e0-ord-<-fn nil nil))
```

This automatically generates the definition of a function `mul-e0-ord-<`, implementing the multiset relation on finite multisets (lists) of ordinals induced by the relation `e0-ord-<`. And it also automatically proves the theorems needed to introduce this relation as a well-founded relation in ACL2. See details about the `defmul` syntax in [13]. For simplicity, in the following we denote `mul-e0-ord-<` as $<_{\varepsilon_0,\mathcal{M}}$.

We finally prove that the measure decreases with respect to $<_{\varepsilon_0,\mathcal{M}}$ in the recursive call of the function `dickson-indices`, hence justifying its termination. We now explain the main lemmas needed to show this result.

Note that if $T \in \mathcal{S}(\mathcal{P})$, then the multiset measure of `reduction-list`$(\mathcal{P}, T)$ is smaller than the measure of $\mathcal{P}$ with respect to $<_{\varepsilon_0,\mathcal{M}}$. This is established by the following theorem, where the property $T \in \mathcal{S}(\mathcal{P})$ is defined by the function `exists-pattern`, omitted here:

LEMMA: `reductions-list-reduces-pattern-list-measure`
   `exists-pattern`$(\mathcal{P},T)$
     $\rightarrow$ `pattern-list-measure(reductions-list`$(\mathcal{P},T))$
       $<_{\varepsilon_0,\mathcal{M}}$ `pattern-list-measure`$(\mathcal{P})$

This lemma is an easy consequence of the definition of $<_{\varepsilon_0,\mathcal{M}}$ and the fact that the replaced pattern has a bigger dimension than its reductions:

LEMMA: `reductions-property`
   $\Pi_1 \in$ `reductions`$(\Pi_2,T) \rightarrow$ `dimension`$(\Pi_1) <$ `dimension`(Π_2)

The following lemma establishes the main property of the function `reductions-tuple-list`. If a tuple T is in the set of tuples represented by a pattern multiset $\mathcal{P}$, then this tuple is still in the pattern multiset obtained after applying a sequence of reductions corresponding to a given sequence of tuples T-lst, provided that T is not divisible by any of the tuples of T-lst (this divisibility condition is checked by the function `divisible-tuple`, omitted here):

LEMMA: `exists-pattern-reductions-tuple-list`
   (`natural-listp`$(T) \wedge$ `natural-list-listp`$(T$-$lst)$
     $\wedge$ `exists-pattern`$(\mathcal{P},T) \wedge \neg$`divisible-tuple`$(T$-$lst,T)$)
     $\rightarrow$ `exists-pattern(reductions-tuple-list`$(\mathcal{P},T$-$lst),T)$

In addition, every tuple is in the initial multiset pattern:

LEMMA: `initial-pattern-exists-pattern`
   `len`$(T) = n \rightarrow$ `exists-pattern(list(initial-pattern`$(n)),T)$

As a consequence of the above two lemmas, if f_k is not divisible by any of $f_0 \ldots f_{k-1}$ (that is, the recursive case in the definition of `dickson-indices`), then there exists a pattern Π in the multiset of patterns generated in the k-th step such that $f_k \in \mathcal{S}(\Pi)$. So now we can use the lemma `reductions-list-reduces-pattern-list-measure` to conclude that the measure of the argument in the recursive call in `dickson-indices` decreases with respect to $<_{\varepsilon_0,\mathcal{M}}$. That is, we have the following theorem:

THEOREM: `dickson-indices-termination-property`
$k \in \mathbb{N} \wedge \neg$`get-tuple-<=-f`$(k,$`f`$(k))$
$\rightarrow$ `dickson-indices-measure`$(k+1) <_{\mathcal{M}}$ `dickson-indices-measure`(k)

This is exactly the proof obligation generated to show the termination of the function `dickson-indices`. Thus, its definition is admitted in the logic and then the theorem `dickson-lemma` presented in subsection 2.1 is easily proved.

3   Conclusions and Related Work

We have presented a formalization and proof of Dickson's Lemma in the ACL2 system. This is an essential preliminary step to obtain a formal termination proof of a Common Lisp implementation of Buchberger's algorithm [9]. We think that this is a good example of how a non-trivial result can be formalized in the first-order, quantifier-free logic of ACL2 (overriding its apparent lack of expressiveness). In fact, the automation of the proof is very simple: the hard part was to preconceive a proof of the result in the restricted ACL2 logic. It is worth pointing that after obtaining it, we realized that we had rediscovered a proof with similar arguments to some constructive proofs of Dickson's Lemma already present in the literature [10, 14].

There are several contributions related to the formalization of Dickson's Lemma using proof checkers. In [16] a formalization of Buchberger's Algorithm is presented in COQ, using a non-constructive proof of Dickson's Lemma developed in [12]. There is also a non-constructive development in Mizar [8] based on the book [2]. In [3] a particular case of Dickson's Lemma ($n = 2$) is constructively formalized in the system MINLOG. Another constructive approach is [4], in which a constructive proof of Dickson's Lemma is mechanized using open induction in the system AGDA. This proof is used to get a fully constructive proof of the existence of Gröbner bases in COQ [11]. A comparison with our work is difficult since the proof we formalize is substantially different and, more important, the ACL2 logic is less expressive than the logics of those systems. At the time of this writing, a new proof of Dickson's Lemma [15] was carried out in ACL2. In this proof, instead of using multisets, an explicit ordinal mapping is assigned to finite sequences of monomials, and proved to be strictly decreasing if no monomial divides a subsequent monomial.

To quantify the proof effort, it should be noted that only 20 definitions and 32 lemmas are needed in the proof, which gives an idea of the degree of automation of the proof and its simplicity. Of course, part of its simplicity comes from the use of the `multiset` book, which provides a proof of well-foundedness of the multiset relation induced by a well-founded relation. It is worth pointing the reuse of the `defmul` tool for generating multiset well-founded relations in ACL2: although it was originally developed to prove Newman's Lemma about abstract reductions [13], it was designed in a very general way such that it has turned out to be useful in other formalization tasks, being Dickson's Lemma a relevant example of this.

References

1. F. Baader and T. Nipkow. *Term Rewriting and All That.* Cambridge University Press, 1998.
2. T. Becker and V. Weispfenning. *Gröbner Bases: A Computational Approach to Commutative Algebra.* Springer–Verlag, 1998.
3. U. Berger, H. Schwichtenberg and M. Seisenberger. The Warshall Algorithm and Dickson's Lemma: Two Examples of Realistic Program Extraction. *Journal of Automated Reasoning* 26: 205–221, 2001.
4. T. Coquand and H. Persson. Gröbner Bases in Type Theory. In *Types for Proofs and Programs: Selected papers of TYPES'98*, LNCS 1657, pages 33–46. Springer–Verlag, 1999.
5. N. Dershowitz and Z. Manna. Proving Termination with Multiset Orderings. *Communications of the ACM* 22(8):465–476, 1979.
6. M. Kaufmann, P. Manolios, and J S. Moore. *Computer-Aided Reasoning: An Approach.* Kluwer Academic Publishers, 2000.
7. M. Kaufmann and J S. Moore. *ACL2 Version 2.7*, 2001. Homepage: `http://www.cs.utexas.edu/users/moore/acl2/`
8. G. Lee and P. Rudnicki. Dickson's Lemma. *Journal of Formalized Mathematics* 14, 2002.
9. I. Medina–Bulo, J.A. Alonso, F. Palomo. Polynomial algorithms in ACL2 (an approach to Buchberger algorithm). In *I Taller Iberoamericano sobre Deducción Automática e Inteligencia Artificial, IDEIA 2002* (in spanish), 2002. Available at `http://www.cs.us.es/ideia`
10. H. Perdry. Strong noetherianity: a new constructive proof of Hilbert's basis theorem. Available at `http://perdry.free.fr/StrongNoetherianity.ps`
11. H. Persson. *An Integrated Development of Buchberger's Algorithm in Coq.* Rapport de recherche de l'INRIA, n 4271, 2001.
12. L. Pottier. *Dixon's lemma*, 1996. Available at `ftp://ftp-sop.inria.fr/lemme/Loic.Pottier/MON/`
13. J.L. Ruiz–Reina, J.A. Alonso, M.J. Hidalgo, and F.J. Martín. Multiset Relations: a Tool for Proving Termination. In *Second ACL2 Workshop*, Technical Report TR-00-29, Computer Science Departament, University of Texas, 2000. Available at `http://www.cs.utexas.edu/users/moore/acl2/workshop-2000/`
14. S.G. Simpson. Ordinal numbers and the Hilbert basis theorem. *Journal of Symbolic Logic* 53(3): 961–974, 1988.
15. M. Sustyk. Proof of Dickson's Lemma Using the ACL2 Theorem Prover via an Explicit Ordinal Mapping. In *Fourth ACL2 Workshop*, 2003. Available at `http://www.cs.utexas.edu/users/moore/acl2/workshop-2003/`
16. L. Théry. A Machine-Checked Implementation of Buchberger's Algorithm. *Journal of Automated Reasoning* 26(2): 107-137, 2001.

Imperative Object-Based Calculi
in Co-inductive Type Theories

Alberto Ciaffaglione[1], Luigi Liquori[2], and Marino Miculan[1]

[1] DiMI, Università di Udine, Italy,
[ciaffagl,miculan]@dimi.uniud.it
[2] INRIA-LORIA, Nancy, France,
lliquori@loria.fr

Abstract. We discuss the formalization of Abadi and Cardelli's impς, a paradigmatic object-based calculus with types and side effects, in Co-Inductive Type Theories, such as the *Calculus of (Co)Inductive Constructions* (CC$^{(Co)Ind}$).
Instead of representing directly the original system "as it is", we reformulate its syntax and semantics bearing in mind the proof-theoretical features provided by the target metalanguage. On one hand, this methodology allows for a smoother implementation and treatment of the calculus in the metalanguage. On the other, it is possible to see the calculus from a new perspective, thus having the occasion to suggest original and cleaner presentations.
We give hence a new presentation of impς, exploiting *natural deduction semantics*, *(weak) higher-order abstract syntax*, and, for a significant fragment of the calculus, *coinductive* typing systems. This presentation is easier to use and implement than the original one, and the proofs of key metaproperties, *e.g.* subject reduction, are much simpler.
Although all proof developments have been carried out in the Coq system, the solutions we have devised in the encoding of and metareasoning on impς can be applied to other imperative calculi and proof environments with similar features.

Introduction

In recent years, much effort has been put in the formalization of class-based object-oriented languages. The Coq system [19] has been used for studying formally the JavaCard Virtual Machine and its platform [4], and for checking the behavior of a byte-code verifier for the JVM language [6]. PVS and Isabelle have been used for formalizing and certifying an executable bytecode verifier for a significant subset of the JVM [21], for reasoning on Java programs with Hoare-style logics [18] and on translations of coalgebraic specifications to programs in JavaCard [29] and C++ [28].

In spite of this large contribution on class-based languages, relatively little or no formal work exists for *object-based* ones, like *e.g.* Self and Obliq, where there is no notion of "class" and objects may act as prototypes. This is due mainly to the fact that object-based languages are less used in practice than class-based ones. However, the former are simpler and provide more primitive and flexible mechanisms, and can be used as intermediate level for implementing the latter. From a foundational point of view, indeed, most of the calculi introduced for the mathematical analysis of the object-oriented paradigm are object-based, as *e.g.* [1, 14]. Among the several calculi, Abadi and

M.Y. Vardi and A. Voronkov (Eds.): LPAR 2003, LNAI 2850, pp. 59–77, 2003.

Cardelli's impς [1] is particularly representative: it features objects, methods, cloning, dynamic lookup, method update, types, subtypes, and, last but not least, imperative features. This makes impς quite complex, both at the syntactic and at the semantic level. Beside the idiosyncrasies of functional languages with imperative features, the store model underlying impς allows for loops, thus making the typing system quite awkward. This level of complexity is reflected in developing metatheoretic properties; for instance, the fundamental *subject reduction* and *type soundness* are much harder to state and prove for impς than for traditional functional languages.

It is clear that this situation can benefit from the use of *proof assistants*, where the theory of an object system can be formally represented in some metalanguage, the proofs can be checked, and new, error-free proofs can be safely developed in interactive sessions. However, up to our knowledge, there is no formalization of an object-based calculus with side-effects like impς, yet. This is, in fact, the aim of our work.

In this paper, we represent and reason on both static and dynamic aspects of impς in a proof assistant based on type theory, *i.e.* Coq. To this end we will use Coq's specification language, the coinductive type theory $CC^{(Co)Ind}$, as a Logical Framework (LF). The encoding methodology forces us to spell out in full detail all aspects of the calculus, thus any problematic issues which are skipped on paper are identified and fixed. Moreover, we have the occasion to (re)formulate the object system, taking full advantage of the definition and proof-theoretical principles provided by the LF, whose perspective may suggest alternative, and cleaner, definitions of the same systems. In particular, most type theory-based LFs support *natural deduction* and *(weak) higher-order abstract syntax*, and some of them even *coinductive* datatypes and predicates, as in the case of $CC^{(Co)Ind}$.

Therefore, we reformulate the static and dynamic semantics of impς in the style of *Natural Deduction Semantics* (NDS) [7, 23] (the counterpart in Natural Deduction of Kahn's *Natural Semantics* [12, 20]) using weak higher-order abstract syntax. In this way, α-conversion and the handling of structures which obey a stack discipline (such as the *environments*), are fully delegated to the metalanguage, making judgments and proofs rather simpler than traditional ones.

Another key proof-theoretical innovation is the use of *coinductive* types and proof systems. This is motivated by the observation that the proof of the Subject Reduction in [1] is quite involved, mainly because the store may contain "pointer loops". Since loops have a non well-founded nature, usual inductive arguments cannot be applied and extra structures, the so-called *store types*, have to be introduced and dealt with. However, coinductive tools are seen nowadays as the canonical way for dealing with circular, non well-founded objects. Therefore, we elaborate a novel and original coinductive reformulation of the typing system for the fragment of impς without *method update* (which we denote by impς^-), thus getting rid of the extra structure of store types and making the proof of the Subject Reduction dramatically simpler. It is still an open question whether our coinductive approach can be extended to the full impς, which has been formalized, at the moment, using store types and related typing system (but still using HOAS and NDS). Due to lack of space, we discuss in this paper only the impς^- fragment; we refer to [10] for the treatment of the full impς.

Our effort is useful also from the point of view of LFs. The theoretical development of LFs and their implementation will benefit from complex case studies like the present one, where we test the applicability of advanced encoding methodologies. In this perspective, our contribution can be considered pioneering in combining the higher-order approach with coinductive proof systems in natural deduction style. The techniques we have developed in the encoding of and metareasoning on impς can be reused for other imperative calculi featuring similar issues.

Synopsis. Section 1 gives a brief account of impς. In Section 2 we focus on the fragment impς⁻, which is reformulated bearing in mind the proof-theoretical concepts provided by $CC^{(Co)Ind}$. The formalization in Coq of this system, and the formal proof of the Subject Reduction, are discussed in Sections 3 and 4, respectively. Conclusions and directions for future work are presented in Section 5. The Coq code is available at [11].

1   Abadi and Cardelli's impς Calculus

The impς-calculus is an imperative calculus of objects forming the kernel of the language Obliq [8]. The syntax of impς is the following:

$$Term : \ a,b ::= x \qquad\qquad\qquad \text{variable} \qquad a.l \qquad\qquad\qquad \text{method invocation}$$
$$[l_i = \varsigma(x_i)b_i]^{i\in I} \quad \text{object} \qquad a.l \leftarrow \varsigma(x)b \quad \text{method update}$$
$$clone(a) \qquad\qquad \text{cloning} \qquad let \ x = a \ in \ b \quad \text{local declaration}$$

Notice that *let* and ς bind x in b, and that usual conventions about α-conversion apply. We refer to [1, Ch.10,11] for an explanation of the intuitive meaning of these constructs.

Dynamic Semantics. The big-step operational semantics is expressed by a reduction relation relating a store σ, a stack S, a term a, a result v and another store σ', *i.e.* $\sigma \cdot S \vdash a \rightsquigarrow v \cdot \sigma'$. The intended meaning is that, with the store σ and the stack S, the term a reduces to a result v, yielding an updated store σ' and leaving the stack S unchanged in the process. The sorts involved in the reduction semantics are the following:

$$Loc : \ \iota \ \in \ \mathtt{Nat} \qquad \text{store location} \quad Stack : \ S ::= x_i \mapsto v_i{}^{i\in I} \qquad\qquad \text{stack}$$
$$Res : \ v ::= [l_i = \iota_i]^{i\in I} \ \text{result} \qquad\qquad Store : \ \sigma ::= \iota_i \mapsto \langle \varsigma(x_i)b_i, S_i \rangle^{i\in I} \ \text{store}$$

A *store* is a function mapping locations to *method closures*: closures (denoted by c) are pairs built of *methods* and *stacks*. Stacks are used for the reduction of the method bodies: they associate variables with *object results*. Results are sequences of pairs: method labels together with store locations, one location for each object method. The operational semantics needs two auxiliary judgments, namely $\sigma \vdash \diamond$, and $\sigma \cdot S \vdash \diamond$ (Figure 1), checking the well-formedness of stores and stacks, respectively. In the following, the notation $\iota_i \mapsto c_i{}^{i\in I}$ denotes the store that maps the locations ι_i to the closures c_i, for $i \in I$; the store $\sigma, \iota \mapsto c$ extends σ with c at ι (fresh) and $\sigma.\iota_j \leftarrow c$ denotes the result of replacing the content of the location ι_j of σ with c. Unless explicitly remarked, all the l_i, ι_i are distinct. The rules for the reduction judgment are in Figure 2.

$$\frac{}{\emptyset \vdash \diamond} \ (Store-\emptyset) \qquad \frac{\sigma \cdot S \vdash \diamond \quad \iota \notin \mathsf{Dom}(\sigma)}{\sigma, \iota \mapsto \langle \varsigma(x)b, S \rangle \vdash \diamond} \ (Store-\iota)$$

$$\frac{\sigma \vdash \diamond}{\sigma \cdot \emptyset \vdash \diamond} \ (Stack-\emptyset) \qquad \frac{\sigma \cdot S \vdash \diamond \quad \iota_i \in \mathsf{Dom}(\sigma) \quad x \notin \mathsf{Dom}(S) \quad \forall i \in I}{\sigma \cdot (S, x \mapsto [l_i = \iota_i]^{i \in I}) \vdash \diamond} \ (Stack-Var)$$

Fig. 1. Well-formedness for Store and Stack.

$$\frac{\sigma \cdot (S', x \mapsto v, S'') \vdash \diamond}{\sigma \cdot (S', x \mapsto v, S'') \vdash x \rightsquigarrow v \cdot \sigma} \ (Red-Var)$$

$$\frac{\sigma \cdot S \vdash a \rightsquigarrow v' \cdot \sigma' \quad \sigma' \cdot (S, x \mapsto v') \vdash b \rightsquigarrow v'' \cdot \sigma''}{\sigma \cdot S \vdash let\ x = a\ in\ b \rightsquigarrow v'' \cdot \sigma''} \ (Red-Let)$$

$$\frac{\sigma \cdot S \vdash \diamond \quad \iota_i \notin \mathsf{Dom}(\sigma) \quad \forall i \in I}{\sigma \cdot S \vdash [l_i = \varsigma(x_i)b_i]^{i \in I} \rightsquigarrow [l_i = \iota_i]^{i \in I} \cdot (\sigma, \iota_i \mapsto \langle \varsigma(x_i)b_i, S \rangle^{i \in I})} \ (Red-Obj)$$

$$\frac{\sigma \cdot S \vdash a \rightsquigarrow [l_i = \iota_i]^{i \in I} \cdot \sigma' \quad \iota_i \in \mathsf{Dom}(\sigma') \quad \iota'_i \notin \mathsf{Dom}(\sigma') \quad \forall i \in I}{\sigma \cdot S \vdash clone(a) \rightsquigarrow [l_i = \iota'_i]^{i \in I} \cdot (\sigma', \iota'_i \mapsto \sigma'(\iota_i)^{i \in I})} \ (Red-Clone)$$

$$\frac{\sigma'(\iota_j) = \langle \varsigma(x_j)b_j, S' \rangle \quad x_j \notin \mathsf{Dom}(S') \quad j \in I \quad \sigma \cdot S \vdash a \rightsquigarrow [l_i = \iota_i]^{i \in I} \cdot \sigma' \quad \sigma' \cdot (S', x_j \mapsto [l_i = \iota_i]^{i \in I}) \vdash b_j \rightsquigarrow v \cdot \sigma''}{\sigma \cdot S \vdash a.l_j \rightsquigarrow v \cdot \sigma''} \ (Red-Sel)$$

$$\frac{\sigma \cdot S \vdash a \rightsquigarrow [l_i = \iota_i]^{i \in I} \cdot \sigma' \quad \iota_j \in \mathsf{Dom}(\sigma') \quad j \in I}{\sigma \cdot S \vdash a.l_j \Leftarrow \varsigma(x)b \rightsquigarrow [l_i = \iota_i]^{i \in I} \cdot (\sigma'.\iota_j \Leftarrow \langle \varsigma(x)b, S \rangle)} \ (Red-Upd)$$

Fig. 2. Natural Operational Semantics for impς.

Static Semantics. The type system is first-order with subtyping. The only type constructor is the one for object types, *i.e.* $TType :\ A, B ::= [l_i : A_i]^{i \in I}$, so the only ground type is $[\ ]$. The typing environment E consists of a list of assumptions for variables, each of the form $x{:}A$. The type system is given by four judgments: well-formedness of type environment $E \vdash \diamond$, well-formedness of object types $E \vdash A$, subtyping $E \vdash A <: B$ and term typing $E \vdash a : A$. Rules for these judgments are collected in Figures 3 and 4. Notice that the subtype relation between object types induces the notion of *subsumption*: an object of a given type also belongs to any supertype of that type and can subsume objects in the supertype, because these have a more limited protocol. The rule $(Sub-Obj)$ allows a longer object type to be a subtype of a shorter one: $[l_i : A_i]^{i \in I \cup J} <: [l_i : B_i]^{i \in I}$ requires $A_i \equiv B_i$ for all $i \in I$; that is, object types are *invariant* (*i.e.* neither covariant nor contravariant) in their component types. This condition guarantees the soundness of the type discipline.

$$\frac{}{\emptyset \vdash \diamond}\ (Env-\emptyset)$$

$$\frac{E \vdash A \quad x \notin \mathrm{Dom}(E)}{E, x{:}A \vdash \diamond}\ (Env-Var)$$

$$\frac{E \vdash A_i \quad \forall i \in I}{E \vdash [l_i : A_i]^{i \in I}}\ (Type-Obj)$$

$$\frac{E \vdash A}{E \vdash A <: A}\ (Sub-Refl)$$

$$\frac{E \vdash A <: B \quad E \vdash B <: C}{E \vdash A <: C}\ (Sub-Trans)$$

$$\frac{E \vdash A_i \quad \forall i \in I \cup J}{E \vdash [l_i : A_i]^{i \in I \cup J} <: [l_i : A_i]^{i \in I}}\ (Sub-Obj)$$

Fig. 3. Auxiliary Typing judgments.

$$\frac{E \vdash a : A \quad E \vdash A <: B}{E \vdash a : B}\ (Val-Sub)$$

$$\frac{E', x{:}A, E'' \vdash \diamond}{E', x{:}A, E'' \vdash x : A}\ (Val-Var)$$

$$\frac{E, x_i{:}[l_i : A_i]^{i \in I} \vdash b_i : A_i \quad \forall i \in I}{E \vdash [l_i = \varsigma(x_i)b_i]^{i \in I} : [l_i : A_i]^{i \in I}}\ (Val-Obj)$$

$$\frac{E \vdash a : [l_i : A_i]^{i \in I} \quad j \in I}{E \vdash a.l_j : A_j}\ (Val-Sel)$$

$$\frac{E \vdash a : [l_i : A_i]^{i \in I}}{E \vdash clone(a) : [l_i : A_i]^{i \in I}}\ (Val-Clone)$$

$$\frac{E \vdash a : A \quad E, x{:}A \vdash b : B}{E \vdash let\ x = a\ in\ b : B}\ (Val-Let)$$

$$\frac{E \vdash a : [l_i : A_i]^{i \in I} \quad E, x{:}[l_i : A_i]^{i \in I} \vdash b : A_j \quad j \in I}{E \vdash a.l_j \leftarrow \varsigma(x)b : [l_i : A_i]^{i \in I}}\ (Val-Upd)$$

Fig. 4. Type Checker for impς.

Result and Store Typing. The typing of results is delicate, because results point to the store, and stores may contain loops: thus it is not possible to determine the type of a result examining its substructures recursively. *Store types* allow to type results independently of particular stores: this is possible because type-sound computations do not store results of different types in the same location. A store type Σ associates a *method type* to each store location. Method types have the form $[l_i : B_i]^{i \in I} \Rightarrow B_j$, where $[l_i : B_i]^{i \in I}$ is the type of self and B_j, such that $j \in I$, is the result type:

$$M ::= [l_i : B_i]^{i \in I} \Rightarrow B_j \ (j \in I) \quad \Sigma_1(\iota) \triangleq [l_i : B_i]^{i \in I} \text{ if } \Sigma(\iota) = [l_i : B_i]^{i \in I} \Rightarrow B_j$$

$$\Sigma ::= \iota_i \mapsto M_i^{i \in I} \qquad\qquad \Sigma_2(\iota) \triangleq B_j \qquad\quad \text{if } \Sigma(\iota) = [l_i : B_i]^{i \in I} \Rightarrow B_j$$

The system for store typing is given by five judgments: well-formedness of method types $M \models \diamond$ and store types $\Sigma \models \diamond$, result typing $\Sigma \models v : A$, store typing $\Sigma \models \sigma$, and stack typing $\Sigma \models S : E$, which are given in Figure 5. The intended meaning of the judgment $\Sigma \models v : A$ is to assign the type A to the result v looking at Σ, and the judgment $\Sigma \models \sigma$ ensures that the content of every store location of σ is given the type of the same location of Σ.

$$\frac{j \in I}{[l_i : B_i]^{i \in I} \Rightarrow B_j \models \diamond} \ (Meth{-}Type)$$

$$\frac{M_i \models \diamond \quad \forall i \in I}{\iota_i \mapsto M_i^{i \in I} \models \diamond} \ (Store{-}Type)$$

$$\frac{\Sigma \models \diamond \quad \Sigma_1(\iota_i) = [l_i : \Sigma_2(\iota_i)]^{i \in I} \quad \forall i \in I}{\Sigma \models [l_i = \iota_i]^{i \in I} : [l_i : \Sigma_2(\iota_i)]^{i \in I}} \ (Res)$$

$$\frac{\Sigma \models S_i : E_i \quad \forall i \in I \quad E_i, x_i{:}\Sigma_1(\iota_i) \vdash b_i : \Sigma_2(\iota_i)}{\Sigma \models \iota_i \mapsto \langle \varsigma(x_i)b_i, S_i \rangle^{i \in I}} \ (Store{-}Typing)$$

$$\frac{\Sigma \models \diamond}{\Sigma \models \emptyset : \emptyset} \ (Stack{-}\emptyset{-}Typ)$$

$$\frac{x \notin \mathsf{Dom}(S, E) \quad \Sigma \models S : E \quad \Sigma \models v : A}{\Sigma \models S, x \mapsto v : E, x{:}A} \ (Stack{-}Var{-}Typ)$$

Fig. 5. Extra judgments for Store Types.

Subject Reduction. An important property of impς is that every well-typed and not diverging term never yields the *message-not-found* runtime error. This is an immediate consequence of the Subject Reduction theorem (see [1] for a complete proof).

Definition 1 (Store Type Extension). *We say that $\Sigma' \geq \Sigma$ (Σ' is an extension of Σ) if and only if $\mathsf{Dom}(\Sigma) \subseteq \mathsf{Dom}(\Sigma')$, and for all $\iota \in \mathsf{Dom}(\Sigma)$: $\Sigma'(\iota) = \Sigma(\iota)$.*

Theorem 1 (Subject Reduction). *If $E \vdash a : A$, and $\sigma \cdot S \vdash a \rightsquigarrow v \cdot \sigma'$, and $\Sigma \models \sigma$, and $\mathsf{Dom}(\sigma) = \mathsf{Dom}(\Sigma)$, and $\Sigma \models S : E$, then there exist a type A', and a store type Σ', such that $A' <: A$, $\Sigma' \geq \Sigma$, $\Sigma' \models \sigma'$, $\mathsf{Dom}(\sigma') = \mathsf{Dom}(\Sigma')$, and $\Sigma' \models v : A'$.*

2 impς^- in Coinductive Natural Deduction Semantics

In this section, we focus on the fragment of impς without method update, denoted by impς^-. For this fragment, we elaborate an original, alternative presentation of static and dynamic semantics, taking advantage of $CC^{(Co)Ind}$, a type theory providing *natural deduction, higher-order abstract syntax* and *coinductive types*. This setting, which we call *Coinductive Natural Deduction Semantics*, leads to a very clean and compact system, allowing for an easier treatment of theoretical and metatheoretical results. The major changes of our reformulation concern the operational semantics, whereas the type system for terms needs only a minor revision; very delicate is the typing of results, which makes also use of coinductive principles.

Syntax. Following the higher-order abstract syntax paradigm [16, 25], we reduce all binders to the sole λ-abstraction. Therefore, from now on we write $let(a, \lambda x.b)$ for $let\ x = a\ in\ b$, and $\varsigma(\lambda x.b)$ for $\varsigma(x)b$, where $let : Term \times (Var \to Term) \to Term$, and $\varsigma : (Var \to Term) \to Term$. (We keep using the notation "$\varsigma(x)b$" as syntactic sugar). Usual conventions about α-conversion apply.

2.1   Dynamic Semantics

The key point in using the Natural Deduction Semantics (NDS) [7, 23] is that all stack-like structures (*e.g.* environments) are distributed in the hypotheses of proof derivations. Therefore, judgments and proofs we have to deal with become appreciably simpler.

The *term reduction* judgment of imp$_\varsigma$, $\sigma \cdot S \vdash a \leadsto v \cdot \sigma'$, is translated as $\Gamma \vdash eval(s, a, s', v)$; that is, we model the operational semantics by a predicate $eval$ defined on 4-tuples $eval \subseteq Store \times Term \times Store \times Res$. Γ is the *proof derivation context*, *i.e.* a set of assertions (of any judgment) which can be used as assumptions in the proof derivations. The intended meaning of the derivation $\Gamma \vdash eval(s, a, s', v)$ is that, starting with the store s and using the assumptions in Γ, the term a reduces to a result v, yielding an updated store s'. The rules for $eval$ are in Figure 6: as usual in Natural Deduction, rules are written in "vertical" notation, *i.e.* the hypotheses of a derivation $\Gamma \vdash \mathcal{J}$ are distributed on the leaves of the proof tree.

$$
\dfrac{
\begin{array}{c}
(x \mapsto v) \\
\vdots \\
eval(s', b(x), s'', v') \\
eval(s, a, s', v)
\end{array}
}{
eval(s, let(a, b), s'', v')
} \ (e\_let)
\qquad
\dfrac{
\begin{array}{cc}
\begin{array}{c}
(closed(x_i)) \\
\vdots \\
wrap(b_i, \overline{b}_i) \\
s'' \equiv (s, \iota_i \mapsto \lambda x_i.\overline{b}_i)^{i \in I}
\end{array}
&
\begin{array}{c}
\iota_i \notin \mathsf{Dom}(s) \\
\forall i \in I
\end{array}
\end{array}
}{
eval(s, [l_i = \varsigma(x_i)b_i]^{i \in I}, s'', [l_i = \iota_i]^{i \in I})
} \ (e\_obj)
$$

$$
\dfrac{
\begin{array}{cc}
\begin{array}{c}
(x \mapsto [l_i : \iota_i]^{i \in I}) \\
\vdots \\
eval_b(s', \overline{b}_j, s'', v) \\
eval(s, a, s', [l_i : \iota_i]^{i \in I})
\end{array}
&
\begin{array}{c}
j \in I \\
s'(\iota_j) = \lambda x.\overline{b}_j
\end{array}
\end{array}
}{
eval(s, a.l_j, s'', v)
} \ (e\_call)
\qquad
\dfrac{
\begin{array}{c}
\iota_i, \iota'_i \notin \mathsf{Dom}(s') \\
s'' \equiv s', \iota'_i \mapsto s'(\iota_i)^{i \in I} \\
eval(s, a, s', [l_i = \iota_i]^{i \in I}) \quad \forall i \in I
\end{array}
}{
eval(s, clone(a), s'', [l_i = \iota'_i]^{i \in I})
} \ (e\_clone)
$$

$$
\dfrac{x \mapsto v}{eval(s, x, s, v)} \ (e\_val)
\qquad
\dfrac{eval(s, a, s', v)}{eval_b(s, ground(a), s', v)} \ (e_b\_ground)
\qquad
\dfrac{
\begin{array}{c}
(closed(x_i)) \\
\vdots \\
closed(b_i) \quad \forall i \in I
\end{array}
}{
closed([l_i = \varsigma(x_i)b_i]^{i \in I})
} \ (c\_obj)
$$

$$
\dfrac{
\begin{array}{c}
(y \mapsto v) \\
\vdots \\
eval_b(s, \overline{b}, s', v')
\end{array}
}{
eval_b(s, bind(v, \lambda y.\overline{b}), s', v')
} \ (e_b\_bind)
\qquad
\dfrac{closed(a) \quad closed(b(x))}{closed(let(a, b))} \ (c\_let)
\qquad
\dfrac{
\begin{array}{c}
(closed(x)) \\
\vdots \\
closed(a)
\end{array}
}{
closed(clone(a))
} \ (c\_clone)
$$

$$
\dfrac{closed(a)}{closed(a.l)} \ (c\_call)
\qquad
\dfrac{closed(b)}{wrap(b, ground(b))} \ (w\_ground)
\qquad
\dfrac{
\begin{array}{cc}
\begin{array}{c}
(closed(z)) \\
\vdots \\
wrap(b\{z/y\}, \overline{b}\{z/y\})
\end{array}
&
\begin{array}{c}
z \ fresh \\
y \mapsto v
\end{array}
\end{array}
}{
wrap(b, bind(v, \lambda y.\overline{b}))
} \ (w\_bind)
$$

Fig. 6. Natural Deduction Dynamic Semantics for imp$_\varsigma^-$.

Notice that the stack S disappears in the judgment $eval$: its content is distributed in Γ, *i.e.* Γ contains enough assumptions to carry the association between variables and results. These bindings are created in the form of hypothetical premises local to sub-reductions, discharged in the spirit of natural deduction style—see *e.g.* rules (e_let) and (e_call). It is worth noticing that we do not need to introduce the well-formedness judgments for stores and stacks: these properties are automatically ensured by freshness conditions of *eigenvariables* in the natural deduction style.

A consequence of NDS is that closures cannot be pairs $\langle method, stack \rangle$, because there are no explicit stacks to put in anymore. Rather, we have to "calculate" closures by gathering from Γ the results associated to the free variables in the methods bodies. Closures *à la* Abadi and Cardelli $\langle \varsigma(x)b, S \rangle$ are translated as:

$$\lambda x.bind(v_1, \lambda y_1.bind(\dots bind(v_n, \lambda y_n.ground(b))\dots))$$

where the first (outmost) abstraction λx stands for $\varsigma(x)$, and the n remaining abstractions ($n \geq 0$) capture the free variables of b. Hence, $bind$ and $ground$ are the two constructors of a new syntactic sort, *i.e.*: $Body : \bar{b} ::= ground(b) \mid bind(v, \lambda x.\bar{b})$.

Closures are dealt with by two auxiliary judgments $wrap \subseteq Term \times Body$ and $eval_b \subseteq Store \times Body \times Store \times Res$. The judgment $wrap$ implements the formation of closure *bodies*, that is, terms where the only possibly free variable is the one corresponding to *self*. The intended meaning of $\Gamma \vdash wrap(b, \bar{b})$ is "$\bar{b}$ is a closure body obtained by binding all free variables in the term b to their respective results, which are in Γ." In order to keep track of the free variables in terms, we introduce a judgment $closed \subseteq Term$, whose formal meaning is $\Gamma \vdash closed(a) \iff$ for all $x \in \mathsf{FV}(a) : closed(x) \in \Gamma$. Intuitively, the rules of $wrap$ allow for successively binding the free variables appearing in the method body (w_bind), until it is "closed" (w_ground). Notice that the closures we get in this way are "optimized", because only variables which are really free in the body need to be bound in the closure.

Evaluation of closures takes place in the rule of method selection (e_call), in a context extended with the binding between a fresh variable (representing *self*) and the (implementation of) host object. Of course, all the local bindings of the closure have to be unraveled (*i.e.* assumed in the hypotheses) before the real evaluation of the body is performed; this unraveling is implemented by the auxiliary judgment $eval_b$, which can be seen as the dual of $wrap$ and is defined by mutual induction with $eval$. For lack of space, we cannot describe in detail all the rules of Figure 6; we refer to [9] for a complete discussion.

Adequacy. We prove now on paper that the presentation of the operational semantics of $imp\varsigma$ in NDS corresponds faithfully to the original one; see [9] for more details.

First, we establish the relationship between our heterogeneous context Γ and the environments S, E of the original setting, and between the two kinds of stores s and σ.

Definition 2 (Well-Formed Context). *A context Γ is well-formed if it can be partitioned as $\Gamma = \Gamma_{Res} \cup \Gamma_{TType} \cup \Gamma_{closed}$, where Γ_{Res} contains only formulae of the form $x \mapsto v$, and Γ_{TType} contains only formulae of the form $x \mapsto A$, and Γ_{closed} contains only formulae of the form $closed(x)$; moreover, Γ_{Res} and Γ_{TType} are functional (e.g., if $x \mapsto v, x \mapsto v' \in \Gamma_{Res}$, then $v \equiv v'$).*

Definition 3. *For Γ a context, S a stack, E a type environment, s, σ stores, we define:*

$$\Gamma \subseteq S \triangleq \forall x \mapsto v \in \Gamma.\, x \mapsto v \in S \qquad\qquad \Gamma \subseteq E \triangleq \forall x{:}A \in \Gamma.\, x{:}A \in E$$

$$S \subseteq \Gamma \triangleq \forall x \mapsto v \in S.\, x \mapsto v \in \Gamma \qquad\qquad E \subseteq \Gamma \triangleq \forall x{:}A \in E.\, x{:}A \in \Gamma$$

$$\gamma(S) \triangleq \{x \mapsto S(x) \mid x \in \mathsf{Dom}(S)\}$$

$$s \lesssim \sigma \triangleq \forall \iota_i \in \mathsf{Dom}(s).\, \gamma(S_i), closed(x_i) \vdash wrap(b_i, s(\iota_i)(x_i)),\ and\ \sigma(\iota_i) = \langle \varsigma(x_i)b_i, S_i \rangle$$

$$\sigma \lesssim s \triangleq \forall \iota_i \in \mathsf{Dom}(\sigma).\, \gamma(S_i), closed(x_i) \vdash wrap(b_i, s(\iota_i)(x_i)),\ and\ \sigma(\iota_i) = \langle \varsigma(x_i)b_i, S_i \rangle$$

In the following, for $\bar{b}$ a closure body, let us denote by $stack(\bar{b})$ the stack containing the bindings in $\bar{b}$, and by $body(\bar{b})$ the innermost body. These functions can be defined recursively on $\bar{b}$:

$$stack(ground(b)) = \emptyset \qquad stack(bind(v, \lambda x.\bar{b})) = stack(\bar{b}) \cup \{x \mapsto v\}$$

$$body(ground(b)) = b \qquad body(bind(v, \lambda x.\bar{b})) = body(\bar{b})$$

Theorem 2 (Adequacy of Dynamic Semantics). *Let Γ be well-formed, and $\sigma \cdot S \vdash \diamond$.*

1. *Let $\Gamma \subseteq S$, and $s \lesssim \sigma$.*
   (a) *If $\Gamma \vdash eval(s, a, s', v)$, then there exists σ' such that $\sigma \cdot S \vdash a \rightsquigarrow v \cdot \sigma'$, and $s' \lesssim \sigma'$;*
   (b) *If $\Gamma \vdash eval_b(s, \bar{b}, s', v)$, then there exists σ' such that $\sigma \cdot stack(\bar{b}) \vdash body(\bar{b}) \rightsquigarrow v \cdot \sigma'$, and $s' \lesssim \sigma'$.*
2. *Let $S \subseteq \Gamma$ and $\sigma \lesssim s$. If $\sigma \cdot S \vdash a \rightsquigarrow v \cdot \sigma'$, then there exists s' such that $\Gamma \vdash eval(s, a, s', v)$, and $\sigma' \lesssim s'$.*

Proof. (1) By mutual induction on the structure of the derivations $\Gamma \vdash eval(s, a, s', v)$ and $\Gamma \vdash eval_b(s, \bar{b}, s', v)$. (2) By structural induction on $\sigma \cdot S \vdash a \rightsquigarrow v \cdot \sigma'$. $\square$

2.2   Static Semantics

The typing system for terms is easily rendered in NDS: the *term typing* judgment $E \vdash a : A$ is transformed as $\Gamma \vdash type(a, A)$, where $type \subseteq Term \times TType$. The *well-formedness* of types and the *subtyping* are also recovered in this setting, respectively as $wt \subseteq TType$ and $sub \subseteq TType \times TType$. As for stacks, well-formedness of the (distributed) typing environment is ensured by the freshness of locally quantified variables.

As the stack S disappears from the reduction judgment, so the type environment E disappears from the typing judgment, thus simplifying the judgment itself and the formal proofs about it: hence the global context Γ contains, among other assertions, the bindings between (free) variables and object types. The rules for term typing and related judgments in NDS are given in Figure 7. They consist in only a light transformation of the original ones: just notice that in the rules (t_obj) and (t_let) we discharge a typing assumption on a locally-quantified (*i.e.* fresh) variable, and that the premise $wt(A)$ in the rule (t_var) ensures that only well-formed types can be used for typing terms.

$$\frac{wt(B_i) \quad \forall i \in I}{wt([l_i : B_i]^{i \in I})} \, (wt\_obj)$$

$$\frac{wt(A)}{sub(A, A)} \, (sub\_refl)$$

$$\frac{sub(A, B) \quad sub(B, C)}{sub(A, C)} \, (sub\_trans)$$

$$\frac{wt(B_i) \quad \forall i \in I \cup J}{sub([l_i : B_i]^{i \in I \cup J}, [l_i : B_i]^{i \in I})} \, (sub\_obj)$$

$$\frac{type(a, A) \quad sub(A, B)}{type(a, B)} \, (t\_sub)$$

$$\frac{type(a, [l_i : B_i]^{i \in I}) \quad j \in I}{type(a.l_j, B_j)} \, (t\_call)$$

$$\frac{wt(A) \quad x \mapsto A}{type(x, A)} \, (t\_var)$$

$$\frac{type(a, [l_i : B_i]^{i \in I})}{type(clone(a), [l_i : B_i]^{i \in I})} \, (t\_clone)$$

$$\frac{\begin{array}{c} (x_i \mapsto [l_i : B_i]^{i \in I}) \\ \vdots \\ type(b_i, B_i) \quad \forall i \in I \end{array}}{type([l_i = \varsigma(x_i)b_i]^{i \in I}, [l_i : B_i]^{i \in I})} \, (t\_obj)$$

$$\frac{\begin{array}{c} (x \mapsto A) \\ \vdots \\ type(a, A) \quad type((b\,x), B) \end{array}}{type(let(a, b), B)} \, (t\_let)$$

Fig. 7. Natural Deduction Static Semantics for $\mathsf{imp}\varsigma^-$.

Theorem 3 (Adequacy of Static Semantics). *Let Γ be well-formed, and E such that $E \vdash \diamond$.*

1. If $\Gamma \subseteq E$, and $\Gamma \vdash type(a, A)$, then $E \vdash a : A$;
2. If $E \subseteq \Gamma$, and $E \vdash a : A$, then $\Gamma \vdash type(a, A)$.

Proof. (1) By structural induction on the derivation of $\Gamma \vdash type(a, A)$.
(2) By structural induction on the derivation of $E \vdash a : A$.   □

2.3   Result Typing

In order to type results we need to type store locations, which, in turn, may contain other pointers to the store: thus, in this process potential loops may arise. A naïve system would chase pointers infinitely, unraveling non-wellfounded structures in the memory. The solution adopted in [1] (see Section 1) is to introduce yet another typing structure, *i.e. store types*, and further proof systems which assign to each location a type consistent with the content of the location. In proofs, store types have to be provided beforehand.

In this section, we propose here a different approach to result typing, using *coinduction* for dealing with non-wellfounded, circular data. This approach is quite successful for $\mathsf{imp}\varsigma^-$; it is still an open question whether there exists an adequate coinductive semantics (without store types) for the full $\mathsf{imp}\varsigma$.

For $\mathsf{imp}\varsigma^-$, the two original judgments of *result typing* $\Sigma \models v : A$ and *store typing* $\Sigma \models \sigma$ collapse into a unique judgment $\Gamma \vdash cores(s, v, A)$. More precisely, we introduce a (potentially) coinductive predicate $cores \subseteq Store \times Res \times TType$, and an inductive one $cotype_b \subseteq Store \times Body \times TType$, which are mutually recursive

$$\dfrac{\begin{array}{ccc} & & (x \mapsto A), (cores(s,v,A)) \\ v \equiv [l_i = \iota_i]^{i \in I} \quad A \equiv [l_i : B_i]^{i \in I} & & \vdots & \iota_i \in \mathsf{Dom}(s) \\ s(\iota_i) \equiv \lambda x_i.\bar{b}_i \quad wt([l_i : B_i]^{i \in I}) & & cotype_b(s, \bar{b}_i, B_i) & \forall i \in I \end{array}}{cores(s,v,A)} \ (t\_cores)$$

$$\dfrac{type(b,A)}{cotype_b(s, ground(b), A)} \ (t\_coground) \qquad \dfrac{cores(s,v,A) \quad cotype_b(s,\bar{b},B)}{cotype_b(s, bind(v, \lambda y.\bar{b}), B)} \ (t\_cobind)$$

with hypothesis $(y \mapsto A)$ above the t_cobind rule.

Fig. 8. Natural Deduction Result Typing for $\mathsf{imp}_\varsigma^{-}$.

defined. The intended meaning of the derivation of $\Gamma \vdash cores(s,v,A)$ is that the result v, containing pointers to the store s, has type A; similarly, $\Gamma \vdash cotype_b(s, \bar{b}, A)$ means that the body $\bar{b}$ in the store s has type A. The rules for these judgments are in Figure 8.

It is interesting to notice the way coinduction arises. The idea at the heart of the type system is simple and it can be caught by looking at rule (t_cores). In order to check whether a result v can be given a type A, we open all the results (if any) belonging to the pointed method closures. Then, we visit and type recursively the store until we reach a closure without free variables, whose body can be typed using the traditional $type$ judgment $(t\_coground)$. If the original result v is encountered in this process, then its type is the type A we started with (t_cobind), therefore the assertion we are proving has to be *assumed* in the hypotheses, hence the coinduction.

In conclusion, the typing system for results is very compact: we do not need store types (and all related machinery) anymore. And also, since stacks and type environments are already distributed in the proof contexts, we can dispense with the *stack typing* judgment. However, in stating and proving the Subject Reduction theorem, we will have to require that the types of the variables in the proof derivation context are consistent with the results associated to the same variables.

An example of coinductive proof is the following. We type the result $[l = 0]$ in the store (containing a loop) $s \triangleq \{0 \mapsto \lambda x.bind([l = 0], \lambda y.ground(y))\}$, or $\sigma \triangleq \{0 \mapsto \langle \varsigma(x)y, (y \mapsto [l = 0]) \rangle\}$ in the original notation of [1], as follows:

$$\dfrac{\dfrac{\dfrac{(y \mapsto [l : [\,]])_{(2)}}{type(y, [l : [\,]])} \ (t\_var) \quad sub([l : [\,]], [\,])}{\dfrac{type(y, [\,])}{cotype_b(s, ground(y), [\,])} \ (t\_coground)} \ (t\_sub)}{\dfrac{(cores(s, [l = 0], [l : [\,]]))_{(1)} \qquad \qquad (t\_cobind)\,(2)}{\dfrac{cotype_b(s, bind([l = 0], \lambda y.ground(y)), [\,])}{cores(s, [l = 0], [l : [\,]])} \ (t\_cores)\,(1)}}$$

Adequacy. Since we use coinductive proof systems, our perspective is quite different *w.r.t.* the original formulation of impς. However, we have the following result.

Theorem 4 (Adequacy of Result Typing). *Let Γ be a well-formed context.*

1. *For $s \lesssim \sigma$, if $\Gamma \vdash cores(s, v, A)$, then there exists Σ such that $\Sigma \models v : A$, and $\Sigma \models \sigma$.*
2. *For $\sigma \lesssim s$, if $\Sigma \models v : A$, and $\Sigma \models \sigma$, then $\Gamma \vdash cores(s, v, A)$.*

Proof. (1) (2) By inspection on the hypothetical derivations.   □

2.4   Subject Reduction

Due to the new presentation, for stating and proving the Subject Reduction we have just to require the coherence between types and results associated to the variables in the proof derivation context Γ. That is, given the store s: $\forall x, w, C.\ x \mapsto w, x{:}C \in \Gamma \Rightarrow \Gamma \vdash cores(s, w, C)$. This hypothesis corresponds to the *stack typing* judgment of [1], but our management, thanks to distributed stacks and environments, is easier. Finally, we obtain the following version of the Subject Reduction theorem, which is considerably simpler both to state and prove *w.r.t.* the original one.

Theorem 5 (Subject Reduction for impς^-). *Let Γ be a well-formed context. If $\Gamma \vdash type(a, A)$, and $\Gamma \vdash eval(s, a, t, v)$, and $\forall x, w, C.\ (x \mapsto w, x \mapsto C \in \Gamma) \Rightarrow \Gamma \vdash cores(s, w, C)$, then there exists a type A^+ such that $cores(t, v, A^+)$, and $sub(A^+, A)$.*

Proof. By structural induction on the derivation $\Gamma \vdash eval(s, a, t, v)$; see [10].   □

3   Formalization in CC$^{(Co)Ind}$

The formalization of our novel presentation of impς^- in the specification language of a proof assistant is still a complex task (although much simpler than formalizing the original system of [1]), because we have to face some subtle details which are left "implicit" on the paper. We can discuss here only some of the aspects of this development in CC$^{(Co)Ind}$, the specification language of Coq; see [9, 11] for further details.

Syntax. A well-known problem we have to address is the treatment of the *binders*, namely ς and *let*. Binders are difficult to deal with: we would like the metalanguage takes care of all the burden of α-conversion, substitutions, variable scope and so on. In recent years, several approaches have been proposed for the formal reasoning on structures with binders, essentially differing on the expressive power of the underlying metalanguage; see *e.g.* [16, 24–26] for more discussion.

Among the many possibilities, we have chosen the *second-order abstract syntax*, called also "weak HOAS" [17, 24]. In this approach, binding operators are represented by constructors of higher-order type [13, 24]. The main difference with respect to the full HOAS is that abstractions range over unstructured (*i.e.* non inductive) sets of *abstract variables*. In this way, α-conversion is automatically provided by the metalanguage, while substitution of terms for variables is not. This fits perfectly the needs for the encoding of imp$_\varsigma$, since the language is taken up-to α-equivalence, and there is no need of substitution in the semantics.

The signature of the weak HOAS-based encoding of the syntax is the following:

```
Parameter   Var : Set. Definition Lab := nat.
Inductive Term : Set := var : Var->Term |obj : Obj->Term
               |clone: Term->Term|call: Term->Lab->Term
               |let  : Term->(Var->Term)->Term
with Obj : Set := obj_nil : Obj
               | obj_cons: Lab->(Var->Term)->Obj->Obj.
Coercion var : Var >-> Term.
Inductive TType : Set := mk: (list (Lab * TType))->TType.
```

Notice that we use a separate type Var for variables: the only terms which can inhabit Var are the variables of the metalanguage. Thus α-equivalence on terms is immediately inherited from the metalanguage, still keeping induction and recursion principles. The constructor var is declared as a coercion, thus it may omitted in the following. An alternative definition of objects would use the lists of Coq library, but this choice does not allow for defining by recursion on terms some fundamental functions, essential for the rest of the formalization (such as, for example, the non-occurrence of variables "$\notin$").

Weak HOAS has well-known encoding methodologies [16, 24, 26]; therefore, the adequacy of the encoding *w.r.t.* the NDS presentation follows from standard arguments.

3.1 Dynamic Semantics

Due to lack of space, we discuss here only a selection of the datatypes necessary to represent the entities and operations for their manipulation, as required by the semantics. Locations and method names can be faithfully represented by natural numbers; this permits to define results and stacks:

```
Definition Loc := nat.Definition Res : Set := (list (Lab * Loc)).
Parameter stack : Var->Res.
```

The environmental information of the stack is represented as a function associating a result to each (declared) variable. This map is never defined effectively: (stack x)=v corresponds to $x \mapsto v$, which is discharged from the proof environment but never proved as a judgment. Correspondingly, assumptions about stack will be discharged in the rules in order to associate results to variables.

On the other hand, stores cannot be distributed in the proof environment: instead, they are lists of method closures, the i-th element of the list is the closure associated to ι_i. Closures are bodies abstracted with respect to the *self* variable, where bodies inhabit an inductive higher-order datatype:

```
Inductive Body : Set := ground : Term->Body
                     |bind   : Res->(Var->Body)->Body.
Definition Closure : Set := (Var->Body).
Definition Store   : Set := (list Closure).
```

Some functions are needed for handling lists, *e.g.* for merging lists of pairs into single lists, generating new results from objects and results, etc.; see [11] for the code.

Extra Notions and Judgments. For simplifying the representation of operational semantics and the proofs in Coq, we can formalize the predicate *closed*, which is used in the
formation of closures, as a function:

```
Parameter dummy : Var->Prop.
Fixpoint closed [t:Term] : Prop := Cases t of
    (var x) =>(dummy x)|(obj ml)=>(closed_obj ml)
  |(call a l)=>(closed a)|  (clone a)=>(closed a)
  |(let a b) =>(closed a)/\((x:Var)(dummy x)->(closed (b x)))
with closed_obj [ml:Obj] : Prop := Cases ml of
  (obj_nil) =>True|(obj_cons l m nl)=>
  (closed_obj nl)/\((x:Var)(dummy x)->(closed (m x))) end.
```

The intended behavior of this function, defined by mutual recursion on the structure
of terms and objects, is to reduce an assertion (closed a):Prop into a conjunction of similar assertions about simpler terms. The dummy is the usual workaround
for the negative occurrences of closed in the definition: dummy variables are just fill-
ins for holes, and must be considered as "closed". The proposition resulting from the
Simplification of a (closed a) goal is easily dealt with using the tactics provided
by Coq. In the same way, we define also the functions $notin : Var \to Term \to Prop$
and $fresh : Var \to Varlist \to Prop$, which capture the "freshness" of a variable in
a term and w.r.t. a list of variables, respectively (see [11]).

Finally, the judgment wrap is formalized via an inductive predicate:

```
Inductive wrap : Term->Body->Prop:=
  w_ground: (b:Term) (closed b)->(wrap b (ground b))
| w_bind   : (b:Var->Term; c:Var->Body; y:Var; v:Res; xl:Varlist)
             ((z:Var)(dummy z)/\(fresh z xl)->(wrap (b z)(c z)))->
             (stack y) = (v)->((z:Var)~(y=z)->(notin y(b z)))->
             (wrap (b y) (bind v c)).
```

In the rule w_bind, the premise ((z:Var)~(y=z)->(notin y (b z))) ensures
that b is a "good context" for y, *i.e.* y does not occur free in b. Thus, the replacement
$b\{z/y\}$ in the rule *(w_bind)* can be rendered simply as the application (b z).

Term Reduction. The semantics of Figure 6 is formalized by two inductive judgments:

```
Mutual Inductive eval: Store->Term->Store->Res->Prop := ...
         with eval_body: Store->Body->Store->Res->Prop := ...
```

Most of their rules are encoded straightforwardly; only notice that the rules for variables
and *let* illustrate how the proof derivation context is used to represent the stack:

```
e_var: (s:Store)(x:Var)(v:Res)  (stack x) = (v)->(eval s x s v)
e_let: (s,s',t:Store) (a:Term) (b:Var->Term) (v,w:Res)
       (eval s a s' v)->
       ((x:Var)(stack x)=(v)->(eval s' (b x) t w))->
       (eval s (let a b) t w)
```

The formalization of the rule *(e_obj)* is a good example of the kind of machinery
needed for manipulating objects, closures, stores and results:

```
e_obj: (s:Store) (ml:Obj) (cl:(list Closure)) (xl:Varlist)
  (scan (proj_meth_obj (ml))(cl)(xl)(distinct (proj_lab_obj ml)))
    -> (eval s (obj ml) (alloc s cl) (new_res_obj ml (size s)))
```

The function `alloc` simply appends the new list of closures to the old store. The function `new_res_obj` produces a new result, collecting method names of the given object and pairing them with new pointers to the store. The function `scan` builds the closures using `wrap` and returns a predicate, whose validity ensures that the object methods have distinct names.

The method selection uses the extra predicate `eval_body` for evaluating closures:

```
e_call : (s,s',t:Store) (a:Term) (v,w:Res) (c:Closure) (l:Lab)
         (eval s a s' v)->(In l (proj_lab_res v))->
         (store_nth (loc_in_res v l s') s') = (c)->
         ((x:Var) (stack x) = (v)->(eval_body s' (c x) t w))->
         (eval s (call a l) t w)
```

The evaluation of the body takes place in an environment where a local variable x denoting "self" is associated to (the value of) the receiver object itself. The predicate `eval_body` is defined straightforwardly.

3.2   Static Semantics

The encoding of the typing system for terms is not problematic. Like for stacks, we model the typing environment by means of a functional symbol, associating object types to variables:

```
Parameter typenv : Var->TType.
```

Term typing is defined by mutual induction with the typing of objects; note that we need to carry along the whole (object) type while we scan and type the methods of objects:

```
Mutual Inductive type : Term->TType->Prop :=
| t_sub : (a:Term) (A,B:TType)
          (type a A)->(subtype A B)->(type a B)
| t_obj : (ml:Obj) (A:TType)
          (type_obj A (obj ml) A)-> (type (obj ml) A)    ...
with type_obj : TType->Term->TType->Prop :=
  t_nil : (A:TType)
          (type_obj A (obj (obj_nil)) (mk (nil (Lab*TType))))
| t_cons: (A,B,C:TType; ... m:Var->Term; pl:(list (Lab*TType)))
          (type_obj C (obj ml) A)->(wftype B)->(wftype C)->
          ((x:Var) (typenv x) = (C)->(type (m x) B))->
          ~(In l (labels A))->(list_from_type A) = (pl)->
      (type_obj C (obj (obj_cons l m ml))(mk (cons (l,B) pl))).
```

where `subtype` represents the *sub* predicate. We omit here its encoding, which makes also use of an auxiliary predicate for permutation of lists representing object types.

3.3 Result Typing

The coinductive result typing system of Figure 8 is easily rendered in Coq by means of
two mutual coinductive predicates. We only point out that, in the encoding of cores,
we have to carry along the whole (result) type, as in the above typing of objects:

```
CoInductive cotype_body : Store->Body->TType->Prop :=
  t_ground: (s:Store) (b:Term) (A:TType)
            (type b A)->(cotype_body s (ground b) A)
| t_bind  : (s:Store) (b:Var->Body) (A,B:TType) (v:Res)
            (cores A s v A)->
            ((x:Var)(typenv x) = (A)->(cotype_body s (b x) B))->
            (cotype_body s (bind v b) B)
with cores : TType->Store->Res->TType->Prop :=
  t_void  : (A:TType) (s:Store)
            (cores A s (nil (Lab*Loc)) (mk (nil (Lab*TType))))
| t_step:   (A,B,C:TType) (s:Store) (v:Res) (i:Loc) (c:Closure)
            (l:Lab) (pl:(list (Lab*TType)))
            (cores C s v A)->(store_nth i s) = (c)-> ...
            ((x:Var) (typenv x) = (C)->(cotype_body s (c x) B))->
            (cores C s (cons (l,i) v) (mk (cons (l,B) pl))).
```

4   Metatheory in Coq

One of the main aims of the formalization presented above is to allow for the formal
development of important properties of impς. In this section we discuss briefly the
upmost important, yet delicate to prove, property of Subject Reduction. We have stated
Subject Reduction for impς⁻ as Theorem 5, which is formalized in Coq as follows:

```
Theorem SR : (s,t:Store) (a:Term) (v:Res)
         (eval s a t v)->(A:TType) (type a A)->
         ((x:Var; w:Res; C:TType)(stack x)=(w)/\(typenv x)=C->
                            (cores s w C))->
         (EX B:TType|(cores t v B)/\(sub B A)).
```

In order to prove the theorem, we have to address all the aspects concerning concrete
structures, such as stores, objects, object types, results, and so on: thus, many technical
lemmata about operational semantics, term and result typing have been formally proved.
It turns out that these lemmata are relatively compact and easy to prove. In particular,
we have carried out coinductive proofs for the cores predicate via the Cofix tactic;
that is, we can construct infinitely regressive proofs by using the thesis as hypothesis,
provided its application is guarded by introduction rules [15].

It is interesting to compare this development with that of the full impς, where store
types and result typing are encoded inductively, close to the original setting [9, 10]. Due
to the handling of store types, that encoding yields a formal development considerably
more involved. Nevertheless, we can reuse with a minimal effort some (or part) of
the proofs developed for the coinductive encoding, especially those not requiring an
explicit inspection on the structure of store types. This re-usability of proofs enlightens
the modularity of the present approach. At the same time, some properties concerning

linear structures (such as stores) become much more involved when we have to manage also store types. In this case we cannot neither reuse, nor follow the pattern, of the proofs developed for imp_ς^-. This points out that managing bulky linear structures explicitly in judgments is unwieldy. We can conclude that the delegation of stacks and typing environments to the proof context, and the use of coinduction for dealing with store loops, reduce considerably the length and complexity of proofs.

Another key aspect of our formalization is the use of (weak) higher-order abstract syntax. Nowadays there is a lot of research towards a satisfactory support for programming with and reasoning about datatypes in higher-order abstract syntax, whose discussion is out of the scope of this paper. In the present case, the expressive power of $CC^{(Co)Ind}$ reveals to be not enough. A general methodology for adding the required extra expressive power, known as the *Theory of Contexts* (ToC), is presented in [17, 26]. The gist is to assume a small set of axioms capturing some basic and natural properties of *(variable) names* and *term contexts*. These axioms allow for a smooth handling of schemata in HOAS, with a very low mathematical and logical overhead. Thus this work can be seen also as an extensive case study about the application of the Theory of Contexts, used here for the first time on an imperative object-oriented calculus.

The Theory of Contexts allows to create "fresh" variables, via the *unsaturation axiom:* "$\forall M. \exists x. x \notin M$". This axiom has been introduced in an untyped setting. In our case, we have to take into account also the informations associated to the variables, such as results and types. More precisely, we adopt the unsaturation axiom in two flavours. The first one corresponds to the case of using metavariables as *placeholders*:

```
Axiom unsat : (A:TType; xl:Varlist)
              (EX x|(fresh x xl)/\(dummy x)/\(typenv x)=A).
```

The second axiom reflects the use of metavariables for *variables* of the object language; we assume the existence of fresh names to be associated both to results and their type, provided they are consistent in a given store. This corresponds exactly to the stack typing judgment in [1]:

```
Axiom unsat_cores : (s:Store) (v:Res) (A:TType) (cores s v A)->
    (xl:Varlist)(EX x|(fresh x xl)/\(stack x)=v/\(typenv x)=A).
```

Both axioms can be validated in models similar to that of the original ToC.

5   Conclusions and Future Work

In this paper, we have studied the formal development of the theory of object-based calculi with types and side effects, such as imp_ς, in type-theory based proof assistants, such as Coq. Before encoding the syntax and semantics of the calculus, we have taken advantage of the features offered by coinductive type theories, such as $CC^{(Co)Ind}$. This perspective has suggested an original, and easier to deal with, presentation of the very same language, in the setting of *natural deduction semantics* (NDS) and *weak higher-order abstract syntax* (HOAS), and, for a significant fragment of imp_ς, *coinductive* typing systems. This reformulation is interesting *per se*; moreover the absence of explicit linear structures (environments and store types) in the judgments has a direct impact on the structure of proofs, thus allowing for a simpler and smoother treatment of complex (meta)properties. The complete system has been encoded in Coq, and the fundamental property of Subject Reduction formally proved.

To our knowledge, this is the first development of the theory of an object-based language with side effects, in Logical Frameworks. The closest work may be [22], where Abadi and Cardelli's *functional* object-based calculus $Ob_{1<:\mu}$ is encoded in Coq, using traditional first-order techniques and Natural Semantics specifications through the Centaur system. A logic for reasoning "on paper" about object-oriented programs with imperative semantics, aliasing and self-reference in objects, has been presented in [2].

Our experience leads us to affirm that the approach we have followed in the present work, using Coinductive Natural Deduction Semantics and HOAS with the Theory of Contexts, is particularly well-suited with respect to proof practice, also in the very challenging case of a calculus with objects, methods, cloning, dynamic lookup, types, subtypes, and imperative features. In particular, the use of coinduction seems to fit naturally the semantics of object calculi with side effects; therefore, the development of coinductive predicates and types in existing logical frameworks and proof environments should be pursued at a deeper extent.

Future Work. As a first step, we plan to experiment further with the formalization we have carried out so far. We will consider other (meta)properties of impς, beside the albeit fundamental Subject Reduction theorem. In particular, we can use the formalization for proving observational and behavioural equivalences of object programs.

Then, we plan to extend the development presented in this paper and in [10] to other object-based calculi, for instance those featuring *object extensions* [14], or *recursive types* [1]. The latter case could benefit again from coinductive types and predicates.

From a practical point of view, the formalization of impς can be used for the development of *certified* tools, such as interpreters, compilers and type-checking algorithms. Rather than *extracting* these tools from proofs, we plan to *certify* a given tool with respect to the formal semantics of the object calculus and the target machine. Some related results along this line regard the use of Coq and Isabelle for certifying compilers for an imperative language [5] and Java [27]. However, none of these works adopts higher-order abstract syntax for dealing with binders; we feel that the use of NDS and HOAS should simplify these advanced tasks in the case of languages with binders.

Acknowledgments

The authors are grateful to Yves Bertot, Joëlle Despeyroux, and Bernard Paul Serpette for fruitful discussions on earlier formalisations of impς.

References

1. M. Abadi and L. Cardelli. *A theory of objects*. Springer-Verlag, 1996.
2. M. Abadi and K. Leino. A logic of object-oriented programs. In *Proc. of TAPSOFT*, LNCS 1214. Springer-Verlag, 1997.
3. H. Barendregt and T. Nipkow, editors. *Proc. of TYPES*, LNCS 806. Springer-Verlag, 1994.
4. G. Barthe, P. Courtieu, G. Dufay, and S. M. de Sousa. Tool-assisted specification and verification of the JavaCard platform. In *Proc. of AMAST*, LNCS 2422, 2002.

5. Y. Bertot. A certified compiler for an imperative language. Technical Report INRIA, 1998.
6. Y. Bertot. Formalizing a JVML verifier for initialization in a theorem prover. In *Proc. of CAV*, LNCS 2102. Springer-Verlag, 2001.
7. R. Burstall and F. Honsell. Operational semantics in a natural deduction setting. In *Logical Frameworks*. Cambridge University Press, 1990.
8. L. Cardelli. Obliq: A Language with Distributed Scope. *Computing Systems*, 1995.
9. A. Ciaffaglione. *Certified reasoning on Real Numbers and Objects in Co-inductive Type Theory*. PhD thesis, Dipartimento di Matematica e Informatica, Università di Udine, Italy and LORIA-INPL, Nancy, France, 2003.
10. A. Ciaffaglione, L. Liquori, and M. Miculan. On the formalization of imperative object-based calculi in (co)inductive type theories. Technical Report INRIA, 2003.
11. A. Ciaffaglione, L. Liquori, and M. Miculan. The Web Appendix of this paper, 2003. `http://www.dimi.uniud.it/~ciaffagl/Objects/ Imp-covarsigma.tar.gz`.
12. J. Despeyroux. Proof of translation in natural semantics. In *Proc. of LICS 1986*. ACM, 1986.
13. J. Despeyroux, A. Felty, and A. Hirschowitz. Higher-order syntax in Coq. In *Proc. of TLCA*, LNCS 905. Springer-Verlag, 1995
14. K. Fisher, F. Honsell, and J. Mitchell. A lambda calculus of objects and method specialization. *Nordic Journal of Computing*, 1994.
15. E. Giménez. Codifying guarded recursion definitions with recursive schemes. In *Proc. of TYPES*, LNCS 996. Springer-Verlag, 1995
16. R. Harper, F. Honsell, and G. Plotkin. A framework for defining logics. *J. ACM*, 1993.
17. F. Honsell, M. Miculan, and I. Scagnetto. An axiomatic approach to metareasoning on systems in higher-order abstract syntax. In *Proc. of ICALP*, LNCS 2076. Springer-Verlag, 2001.
18. M. Huisman. *Reasoning about Java programs in higher order logic with PVS and Isabelle*. PhD thesis, Katholieke Universiteit Nijmegen, 2001.
19. INRIA. *The Coq Proof Assistant*, 2003. `http://coq.inria.fr/doc/main.html`.
20. G. Kahn. Natural Semantics. In *Proc. of TACS*, LNCS 247. Springer-Verlag, 1987.
21. G. Klein and T. Nipkow. Verified bytecode verifiers. *TCS 298(3)*, 2003.
22. O. Laurent. Sémantique Naturelle et Coq : vers la spécification et les preuves sur les langages à objets. Technical Report INRIA, 1997.
23. M. Miculan. The expressive power of structural operational semantics with explicit assumptions. In [3].
24. M. Miculan. *Encoding Logical Theories of Programs*. PhD thesis, Dipartimento di Informatica, Università di Pisa, 1997.
25. F. Pfenning and C. Elliott. Higher-order abstract syntax. In *Proc. of ACM SIGPLAN*, 1988.
26. I. Scagnetto. *Reasoning about Names In Higher-Order Abstract Syntax*. PhD thesis, Dipartimento di Matematica e Informatica, Università di Udine, 2002.
27. M. Strecker. Formal verification of a Java compiler in Isabelle. In *Proc. of CADE*, LNCS 2392. Springer-Verlag, 2002.
28. H. Tews. A case study in coalgebraic specification: memory management in the FIASCO microkernel. Technical report, TU Dresden, 2000.
29. J. van den Berg, B. Jacobs, and E. Poll. Formal specification and verification of JavaCard's application identifier class. In *Proc. of the JavaCard 2000 Workshop*, LNCS 2041, 2001.

Congruence Closure with Integer Offsets

Robert Nieuwenhuis[*] and Albert Oliveras[**]

Technical University of Catalonia,
Jordi Girona 1, 08034 Barcelona, Spain,
{roberto,oliveras}@lsi.upc.es

Abstract. Congruence closure algorithms for deduction in ground equational theories are ubiquitous in many (semi-)decision procedures used for verification and automated deduction. They are also frequently used in practical contexts where some interpreted function symbols are present. In particular, for the verification of pipelined microprocessors, in many cases it suffices to be able to deal with *integer offsets*, that is, instead of only having ground terms t built over free symbols, all (sub)terms can be of the form $t + k$ for arbitrary integer values k.

In this paper we first give a different very simple and clean formulation for the standard congruence closure algorithm which we believe is of interest on itself. It builds on ideas from the abstract algorithms of [Kap97, BT00], but it is easily shown to run in the best known time, $O(n \log n)$, like the classical algorithms [DST80, NO80, Sho84].

After that, we show how this algorithm can be smoothly extended to deal with integer offsets without increasing this asymptotic complexity.

1 Introduction

Many applications of verification and automated deduction benefit from (semi-)decision procedures for particular theories. For example, in circuit verification one can consider abstractions that forget about the meaning of certain interpreted functions, and then decide the satisfiability of formulae in the so-called logic of equality with uninterpreted functions (EUF) [BD94]. EUF formulae are boolean formulae over atoms that are (dis)equalities between terms without variables. For example, the EUF formula:

$$f(a, b) = f(c, d) \ \lor \ a \neq c \ \lor \ b \neq d$$

is a tautology, and

$$(\ f(f(a)) \neq b \lor f(f(f(b))) \neq b \ ) \ \land \ f(a) = a \ \land \ a = b$$

is unsatisfiable.

---

[*] Both authors partially supported by the Spanish CICYT project Maverish ref. TIC2001-2476-C03-01.

[**] Supported by a FPU grant, ref.AP2002-3533, from the Spanish Secretaría de Estado de Educación y Universidades.

M.Y. Vardi and A. Voronkov (Eds.): LPAR 2003, LNAI 2850, pp. 78–90, 2003.
© Springer-Verlag Berlin Heidelberg 2003

Deciding the satisfiablity of EUF formulae also has applications for proving satisfiability in first-order logic with equality: checking whether a model of cardinality k exists roughly amounts to instantiating in all possible ways with k new constants and deciding the satisfiability of the resulting ground EUF formula.

Due to the arbitrary boolean part of the formula, the EUF satisfiability problem is obviously NP-hard, and its membership in NP is also easily shown. Currrently, most implementations dealing with EUF and its extensions are based on translations into propositional SAT. However, we are working on a general procedure for EUF, and several extensions of it, without translating into SAT. Our algorithm is based on the Davis-Putnam-Logemann-Loveland (DPLL) procedure [DP60, DLL62], but where the information coming from the current interpretation is eagerly propagated by incremental constraint solvers. The idea is that these constraint solvers can be plugged in into a general $DPLL(X)$ scheme, very much in the flavour of the constraint logic programming scheme $CLP(X)$. In the case of EUF, which can be seen as $DPLL(=)$, the solver roughly amounts to a *congruence closure* procedure (extended for dealing with backtracking and disequalities), which finds the new equalities that follow from the given ones.

In this paper we concentrate on congruence closure for positive equations. Nowadays well-known congruence closure algorithms were already given in the early 1980s by Downey, Sethi, and Tarjan, [DST80] and also by Nelson and Oppen [NO80]; see also Shostak's method for the combination of decision procedures [Sho84]. However, for two main reasons, these early versions of congruence closure are not very convenient for our purposes.

First, they are formulated on graphs, and, in order to obtain the best known worst-case complexity bound, $O(n \ log \ n)$, rather involved manipulations are needed; for example, a transformation to graphs of outdegree 2 is applied, see [DST80]. Since our DPLL procedure will call the congruence closure module a large number of times, and since we will extend our procedure to richer logics, we prefer to replace this transformation by another cleaner one, at the formula representation level, and which is done *once and for all*, already on the input formula given to our $DPLL(=)$ procedure. Our key idea for this is to *Curryfy*, like in the implementation of functional languages; as far as we know, this had not been done before for congruence closure; as a result, there will be only one binary "apply" function symbol (denoted here by a dot $\cdot$) and constants. For example, Curryfying $f(a, g(b), b)$ gives $\cdot(\cdot(\cdot(f, a), \cdot(g, b)), b)$. This idea makes the algorithms surprisingly simple and clean and hence easier to extend and to reason about.

Second, like in the more abstract congruence closure approaches, such as the ones of [Kap97, BT00], we introduce new constant symbols c for giving names to non-constant subterms t; such t are then replaced everywhere by c and the equation $t = c$ is added. As we will see, then, in combination with Curryfication, one can obtain the same efficiency as in more sophisticated directed acyclic graph (DAG) implementations by appropriately indexing the new constants like c, which play the role of the pointers to the (shared) subterms like t in the DAG approaches. For example, we flatten the equation

$$\cdot(\cdot(\cdot(f,a),\cdot(g,b)),b) = b$$

by replacing it by

$$\{\ \cdot(f,a) = c,\ \ \cdot(g,b) = d,\ \ \cdot(c,d) = e,\ \ \cdot(e,b) = b\ \}$$

As a consequence of this transformation, which is again done once and for all on the initial problem that is input to our DPLL procedure, we can assume that our congruence closure module receives as input only equations between two constants or between a constant and a "·" applied to two constants[1].

Congruence closure algorithms are also frequently used in practical contexts where some interpreted function symbols are present. In particular, for the verification of pipelined and/or superscalar microprocessors, in many cases it suffices to be able to deal with *integer offsets*, that is, instead of only having ground terms t built over free symbols in the equations, all (sub)terms can be of the form $t + k$ for arbitrary integer values k. This has been done in the logic handled by Bryant et al. [BLS02], where predecessor and successor symbols occur.

The remainder of this paper is structured as follows. Section 2 introduces the basic notions and notations. After Section 3, where the two initial transformations are formalized, in Section 4 we give our extremely simple formulation of the congruence closure algorithm, and we prove its correctness and its $O(n\ log\ n)$ runtime and linear space requirements. In Section 5, we give evidence for an additional advantage of this clean algorithm, by showing that it can be extended in very a smooth way for dealing with integer offsets, while maintaining the same time and space requirements. Finally, in Section 6 we conclude and outline our plans for future work in this project.

2   Basic Notions and Notations

Let $\mathcal{F}$ be a (finite) set of function symbols with an arity function $arity\colon \mathcal{F} \to I\!\!N$. Function symbols f with $arity(f) = n$ are called n-ary symbols (when $n = 1$, one says *unary* and when $n = 2$, *binary*). If $arity(f) = 0$, then f is a *constant symbol*. The set of ground terms over $\mathcal{F}$, denoted by $\mathcal{T}(\mathcal{F})$, is the smallest set containing all constant symbols such that $f(t_1,\ldots,t_n)$ is in $\mathcal{T}(\mathcal{F})$ whenever $f \in \mathcal{F}$, $arity(f) = n$, and $t_1,\ldots,t_n \in \mathcal{T}(\mathcal{F})$.

By $|s|$ we denote the *size* (number of symbols) of a ground term s: we have $|a| = 1$ if a is a constant symbol and $|f(t_1,\ldots,t_n)| = 1 + |t_1| + \ldots + |t_n|$. The *depth* of a term s is denoted by $depth(s)$ and is defined: $depth(a) = 1$ if a is a constant symbol and $depth(f(t_1,\ldots,t_n)) = 1 + max(depth(t_1),\ldots,depth(t_n))$.

An *equivalence relation* is a reflexive, symmetric, and transitive binary relation. A relation $=$ on $T(\mathcal{F})$ is *monotonic* if $f(s_1,\ldots,s_n) = f(t_1,\ldots,t_n)$ whenever f is an n-ary function symbol in $\mathcal{F}$ and $s_i = t_i$ for all i in $1\ldots n$. A *congruence relation* is a monotonic equivalence relation.

---

[1] In fact, after this, the atoms in our EUF formula will be (dis)equalities between constants: all function symbols are hidden inside the congruence closure module.

A *ground equation* is an (unordered) pair of ground terms (s, t), denoted by $s = t$. Given a set of ground equations E built over $\mathcal{F}$, we denoted by E^* the congruence *generated* by E: the smallest congruence relation $=$ over $T(\mathcal{F})$ containing E. We sometimes write $E \models s = t$ to denote the fact that $s = t$ belongs to E^*, and if E' is a set of equations, we write $E \models E'$ to denote that $E \models s = t$ for all $s = t$ in E', and we write $E \equiv E'$ to denote that $E \models E'$ and $E' \models E$.

3 Initial Transformations

3.1 Transformation into Curry Terms

Consider a new signature $\mathcal{F}'$ obtained from the original $\mathcal{F}$ by introducing a new binary function symbol "$\cdot$", and converting all other symbols into constants. Then the *Curry form* of a term t in $T(\mathcal{F})$ is a term $Curry(t)$ in $T(\mathcal{F}')$ defined as follows:
$Curry(c) = c$, if c is a constant symbol, and
$Curry(f(t_1...t_n)) = \cdot(.... (\cdot(f, Curry(t_1)), Curry(t_2)),..., Curry(t_n))$
For example, the Curry form of $f(a, g(b), c)$ is $\cdot(\cdot(\cdot(f, a), \cdot(g, b)), c)$. Similarly, we consider the *Curry* transformation on equations, where $Curry(s = t)$ is $Curry(s) = Curry(t)$, and on sets of equations: $Curry(E) = \{ Curry(e) \mid e \in E \}$. We make the following simple observations:

Proposition 1. *Let t be a term. Then $|Curry(t)| \leq 2|t|$, i.e., the Curry transformations only produces a linear growth of the input.*

Proposition 2. *Let E be a set of ground equations over $\mathcal{F}$ and let $s = t$ be an equation over $\mathcal{F}$. Then $Curry(E) \models Curry(s = t)$ if, and only if, $E \models s = t$.*

3.2 The Flattening Transformation into Terms of Depth at Most 2

Consider the following transformation step on E:

$$E \Rightarrow E' \cup \{c = t\} \qquad \textit{(Constant introduction and replacement)}$$

where c is a new constant symbol not occurring anywhere in E and E' is obtained by replacing all occurrences of t in E by c. We have the following:

Proposition 3. *Let E_0 be a set of equations, let $s = t$ be an equation, (both built over $\mathcal{F}'$), and let E be obtained by applying zero or more constant introduction and replacement steps on E_0.*
Then $E_0 \models s = t$ if, and only if, $E \models s = t$.
Furthermore, if a and b are constants not occurring in E and in $s = t$, then $E \models s = t$ if, and only if, $E \cup \{s = a, t = b\} \models a = b$.
By applying a linear number of constant introduction and replacement steps to E_0 an E can be obtained such that all equations of E have a constant side, E has depth at most 2, and $|E| \leq 2|E_0|$.

4   Congruence Closure

In the following, (possibly primed or indexed) lowercase letters $a, b, c, d, \ldots$ denote constant symbols. The procedure receives as input a set of equations E of the form $a = b$ or of the form $\cdot(a, b) = c$, and we assume that no term $\cdot(a, b)$ occurs more than once in the input (i.e., after flattening no different constant names exist for the same term).

The procedure halts when it has computed the congruence generated by the input equations, after which it can output (in linear time) the list of congruence classes. It can also answer in constant time queries asking whether two terms (constants or terms $\cdot(a, b)$) belong to the same class. In fact, the procedure produces a convergent term rewrite system by which any term t rewrites into its unique normal form in time linear in $|t|$ (see Subsection 4.2); hence this allows one to decide in time $O(|s| + |t|)$ whether two arbitrary terms s and t belong to the same class (note that it is irrelevant whether s and t are built over the original signature or the Curryfied one, since the translation is linear too). This is possible without any post-processing because, unlike other congruence closure algorithms, our procedure does not rely on the well-known union-find data structure (by which equalities between constants cannot always be decided in constant time).

The procedure uses the following five simple data structures, which include the equivalence class representation, where (as usual) each class has a single distinguished *representative* constant:

1. *Pending Unions*: a list of pairs of constants yet to be merged.
2. The *Representative* table: an array indexed by constants, containing for each constant its current representative.
3. The *Class Lists*: for each representative, the list of all constants in its class.
4. The *Lookup Table*: for each input term $\cdot(a, b)$,
   $Lookup(Representative(a), Representative(b))$ returns in constant time a constant c such that $\cdot(a, b)$ is equivalent to c, and returns $\perp$ if there is no such c.
5. The *Use Lists*: for each representative a, the list of input equations $\cdot(b, c) = d$ such that a is the representative of b or c (or of both).

These data structures are initialized as expected: *Pending* contains the initial equations of the form $a = b$, and for each initial equation $\cdot(a, b) = c$, it belongs to $UseList(a)$ and to $UseList(b)$, and $Lookup(a, b)$ is c ($Lookup(a, b)$ is undefined for all other pairs (a, b)). *Representative* and *ClassList* contain all constants as their own representatives in one-element classes. In the following algorithm, a' denotes $Representative(a)$ for each constant a:

1. **While** *Pending* is non-empty **Do**
2.   Remove an equation $a = b$ from *Pending*
3.   **If** $a' \neq b'$ and, wlog., $|ClassList(a')| \leq |ClassList(b')|$ **Then**
4.   **For each** c in $ClassList(a')$ **Do**
5.   set *Representative*(c) to b' and add c to $ClassList(b')$
6.   **EndFor**
7.   **For each** $\cdot(c, d) = e$ in $UseList(a')$ **Do**
8.   **If** $Lookup(c', d')$ is some f and $f' \neq e'$ **Then**
9.   add $e' = f'$ to *Pending*
10.   **EndIf**
11.   set $Lookup(c', d')$ to e'
12.   add $\cdot(c, d) = e$ to $UseList(b')$
13.   **EndFor**
14.   **EndIf**
15. **EndWhile**

Example 1. Consider the following input and the set E_0 obtained after curryfying and flattening it:

$$
\left.
\begin{array}{c}
f(a) = g(b) \\
g(c) = h(f(c), g(a)) \\
b = c \\
f(c) = g(a) \\
h(d, d) = g(b) \\
g(a) = d
\end{array}
\right\}
\implies
\begin{bmatrix}
\cdot(f, a) = e_1 \\
\cdot(g, b) = e_2 \\
\cdot(g, c) = e_3 \\
\cdot(f, c) = e_4 \\
\cdot(h, e_4) = e_5 \\
\cdot(g, a) = e_6 \\
\cdot(e_5, e_6) = e_7 \\
\cdot(h, d) = e_8 \\
\cdot(e_8, d) = e_9
\end{bmatrix}
+
\begin{bmatrix}
e_1 = e_2 \\
e_3 = e_7 \\
b = c \\
e_4 = e_6 \\
e_9 = e_2 \\
e_6 = d
\end{bmatrix}
$$

The following eight iterations take place:

1. Let the first equation to be removed from *Pending* be $e_1 = e_2$. We set *Representative*(e_1) to e_2 (although since $|e_1| = |e_2| = 1$ we also had the reverse choice); since $UseList(e_1)$ is empty, we can go the next iteration.
2. Now the equation $e_3 = e_7$ is picked from *Pending*, and (again we can choose) set *Representative*(e_3) to e_7; $UseList(e_3)$ is also empty.
3. We pick $b = c$ from *Pending*, set *Representative*(b) to c, and now need to handle the single equation $\cdot(g, b) = e_2$ in $UseList(b)$: since $Lookup(g', b') = Lookup(g, c) = e_3$, and $e_3' = e_7$ and $e_2' = e_2$, the equation $e_7 = e_2$ is added to *Pending*; furthermore, $Lookup(g, c)$ is set to e_2, and $\cdot(g, b) = e_2$ is added to $UseList(c)$.
4. $e_7 = e_2$ is handled (here, *Pending* is a stack) and *Representative*(e_2) is set to e_7; $UseList(e_2) = \emptyset$.
5. Pick $e_4 = e_6$ and set *Representative*(e_4) to e_6; the only equation in $UseList(e_4)$ is $\cdot(h, e_4) = e_5$, which leads to no new equations.
6. Set *Representative*(e_9) to e_7.
7. Set *Representative*(d) to e_6; $UseList(d) = \{\cdot(h, d) = e_8, \cdot(e_8, d) = e_9\}$, from which, due to its first equation, $e_5 = e_8$ is added to *Pending*, because

$Lookup(h', d')$ is $Lookup(h, e_6) = e_5$ and e_5 and e_8 are distinct representatives.

8. Set $Representative(e_5)$ to e_8; $UseList(e_5) = \{\cdot(e_5, e_6) = e_7\}$, and, since $Lookup(e_5', e_6')$ is $Lookup(e_8, e_6) = e_9$, a new equality $e_7 = e_9$ follows, but it is discarded because $e_7' = e_9' = e_7$.

The final congruence (with representatives written in bold) is:

$\{\,\mathbf{a}\,\}$ $\{\,\mathbf{c} = b\,\}$ $\{\,\mathbf{f}\,\}$ $\{\,\mathbf{g}\,\}$ $\{\,\mathbf{h}\,\}$
$\{\,\mathbf{e_6} = e_4 = d = \cdot(g, a) = \cdot(f, c)\,\}$
$\{\,\mathbf{e_7} = e_1 = e_2 = e_3 = e_9 = \cdot(f, a) = \cdot(g, b) = \cdot(g, c) = \cdot(e_8, d) = \cdot(e_5, e_6)\,\}$
$\{\,\mathbf{e_8} = e_5 = \cdot(h, e_4) = \cdot(h, d)\, ;\}$ □

4.1 Runtime Analysis

Theorem 1. *The algorithm runs in $O(n \log n)$ time and in linear space.*

Proof. The proof is simple and quite standard. The *Lookup* table can be implemented by a hash table, or, if hashing is not considered appropriate, by a two-dimensional array[2]. The time spent for maintaining the *Representative* data structure that gives constant time access to representatives is amortized over the whole algorithm: the loop at lines 4,5,6 is executed $O(k \log k)$ times, where k (which is –usually much– smaller than the input size n) is the number of different constants, namely each time one of the k constants changes its representative (which cannot happen more than $\log k$ times, because the size of its class is at least doubled each time and is upper bounded by k). The same happens for the loop at lines 7-13: each one of the at most n input equations of the form $\cdot(c, d) = e$ is treated when c or d changes its representative (which, as before, cannot happen more than $\log k$ times). This in turn implies that $O(n \log k)$ new equations are added to *Pending* at line 9. Altogether, we obtain an $O(n \log n)$ runtime. Using hashing for the *Lookup* table, only linear space is used. Note that the $UseList(a')$ in line 7 is no longer needed and its space can be re-used (otherwise, this would require $O(n \log n)$ space).   □

4.2 Correctness

The aim of the algorithm is to compute the congruence generated by the input equations, in the following standard form:

Definition 1. *A set of equations E is in* standard *form if its equations are of the form $a = b$ or of the form $\cdot(a, b) = c$ whose (respective) left hand sides a and $\cdot(a, b)$ only occur once in E.*

---

[2] To avoid the quadratic initialization time of such a two-dimensional *Lookup* table, one can store in each $Lookup[a, b]$ an index k to an auxiliary array A, where $A[k]$ contains $\cdot(a, b) = c$, and with a counter max indicating that A contains correct (i.e., initialized) information for all $k < max$.

Intuitively, in such a standard E, the constants at the right hand sides and below the "·" symbols are all representatives of their respective classes. In fact, considering its equations (oriented from left to right) as rewrite rules, it is a convergent term rewrite system (see [DP01]); by rewriting with it, deciding whether an equation $s = t$ is in the congruence can be done in time $O(|s = t|)$.

Definition 2. *Let E_0 be a set of equations of the form $a = b$ or of the form $\cdot(a, b) = c$. A* standard congruence closure *for E_0 is a set of equations E in standard form such that $E_0 \equiv E$.*

In the following, again $a, b, c, \ldots$ denote constant symbols, and their primed versions $a', b', c', \ldots$ denote their current representatives. The set of input equations of the algorithm is denoted by E_0. For a given time line 1 of the algorithm is executed, we denote by $RepresentativeE$ the set of all non-trivial equations of the form $a = a'$ and of the form $\cdot(a', b') = c'$ where a, b and c are constants in E_0 and c is $Lookup(a', b')$.

We will prove that when our algorithm terminates, $RepresentativeE$ is a standard congruence closure for the input E_0.

Lemma 1. *Apart from the invariants of the data structures 2, 3, 4, and 5, the following are invariants of the main loop of our algorithm, i.e., they hold each time line 1. is executed:*

  Inv1: RepresentativeE is in standard form
  Inv2: $(RepresentativeE \cup Pending)^* = E_0^*$

Proof. Invariant *Inv1* always holds by definition of *RepresentativeE*. The invariants of the data structures 2, 3, 4, and 5, as well as invariant *Inv2* hold initially, by the assumptions on E_0. To see that they are also preserved by the loop, we check lines 2, 5, 9, 11, and 12, which are the only ones that modify the data structures, and show that the congruence $(RepresentativeE \cup Pending)^*$ is changed by no iteration: (i) each time an equation $a = b$ is removed from *Pending* (line 2.), line 5. ensures that this equality will belong to the next *RepresentativeE*, and also preserves the invariants of the data structures 2 and 3; (ii) all $e' = f'$ that are added to *Pending* (at line 9.) are in the previous $(RepresentativeE \cup Pending)^*$: if $e' \neq f$, this is because, say, c (the reasoning is the same for d) has changed its representative from a' to b', and $Lookup(a', d')$ and $Lookup(b', d')$ were congruent to e' and f' repectively in the previous $(RepresentativeE \cup Pending)^*$. (iii) lines 11 and 12 ensure that $Lookup(a', b')$ is defined for all input terms $\cdot(a, b)$ and that the use lists for each representative contain all needed equations, i.e., they preserve the representation invariants 3 and 4. □

Now the following result follows easily:

Theorem 2. *When the algorithm terminates, $RepresentativeE$ is a standard congruence closure for the input E_0.*

Proof. The algorithm terminates when *Pending* is empty. Then, since by invariant *Inv2* $(RepresentativeE \cup Pending)^* = E_0^*$, we have $RepresentativeE^* = E_0^*$; since by invariant *Inv1* $RepresentativeE$ is in standard form, $RepresentativeE$ is a standard congruence closure for the input E_0. □

5   Integer Offsets

In a recent paper by Bryant, Lahiri, and Seshia [BLS02] the logic of EUF is extended in several ways. In particular, in some of their formulae coming from the verification of pipelined microprocessors, the functions *successor (s)* and *predecessor (p)* appear, and all terms are interpreted as integers.

In this section we deal with (conjunctions of positive, as before) input equations built over free symbols and *successor* and *predecessor*. To denote a (sub)term t with k successor symbols $s(\ldots s(t)\ldots)$, we write $t + k$ and similarly write $t + k$ with negative k for $p(\ldots p(t)\ldots)$. This is why we speak of terms with *integer offsets*.

A difference with the standard congruence closure problem is that conjunctions of positive equations with integer offsets can be unsatisfiable:

Example 2. The set $\{\, f(a) = c,\ f(b) = c + 1,\ a = b \,\}$ is unsatisfiable.   □

However, in spite of this difference, we will show that one can still obtain the same time and space bounds as for the case with only free symbols. The main idea is to extend the notion of equivalence relation for dealing with *equivalences up to offsets*:

Example 3. Consider the three equations:

$$
\begin{array}{c}
a + 2 = b - 3 \\
b - 5 = c + 7 \\
c = d - 4
\end{array}
\quad
\begin{array}{c}
\text{which can equivalently} \\
\text{be written as:}
\end{array}
\quad
\begin{array}{c}
a = b - 5 \\
b = c + 12 \\
c = d - 4
\end{array}
$$

Here all four constants are equivalent up to some offset. If we take b as the representative of this class, we can write the other constants with their corresponding offsets with respect to the representative b in a class list:

$$\{\, \mathbf{b} = a + 5 = c + 12 = d + 8 \}$$

thus storing an infinite set of congruence classes, namely the ones represented by $\ldots, b - 1, b, b + 1, \ldots$ in finite space.   □

5.1   The Initial Transformations

The extension to integer offsets does not affect much the process of curryfication and flattening. Curryfication is only modified by imposing that for any term t and any integer k we have $Curry(t + k) = Curry(t) + k$ and flattening is not affected at all.

Example 4. The equation $f(a + 1, g(b + 2), b - 2) = b - 1$ in Curryfied form becomes:

$$\cdot(\cdot(\cdot(\cdot(f, a + 1), \cdot(g, b + 2)), b - 2) = b - 1$$

which is flattened into:

$$
\begin{array}{r}
\cdot(f, a + 1) = c \\
\cdot(g, b + 2) = d \\
\cdot(c, d) = e \\
\cdot(e, b - 2) = b - 1
\end{array}
$$

□

Note that, due to the fact that the first arguments of the "·" symbol do not represent full (sub)terms of the original input, after the transformation they will have no integer offsets.

Moreover, this property is preserved during the congruence closure process, because the congruence closure process can only make them equal to other such first-argument terms. This fact is illustrated by the following example.

Example 5. Consider the equations:

$$
\begin{array}{cccccc}
f(a,a,a) = c & & \cdot(\cdot(\cdot(f,a),a),a) = c & & \cdot(f,a) = f_1 & \cdot(f,b) = f_1' \\
f(b,b,b) = d & \xrightarrow{\text{Curry}} & \cdot(\cdot(\cdot(f,b),b),b) = d & \xrightarrow{\text{flat}} & \cdot(f_1,a) = f_2 & \cdot(f_1',b) = f_2' \\
a = b & & a = b & & \cdot(f_2,a) = c & \cdot(f_2',b) = d \\
& & & & a = b &
\end{array}
$$

Here f represents a non-existing 0-ary version of f, and f_1 represents a term $f(a)$ with a unary version of f, which of course also does not exist in the input equations; similarly, f_2 is $f(a,a)$ (a non-existing version of f with 2 arguments). The same happens for f_1' and f_2'. During the congruence closure process, when a is merged with b, the unary versions of f and f' get merged as well, and also the binary versions, as well as, finally, the 3-ary versions, represented by c and d. But note that it is impossible that f_i gets merged with f_j or with f_j', for $i \neq j$. Roughly speaking, there is a distinct sort for each arity.   □

Altogether, we can assume that no integer offsets will ever appear in the first argument of a "·" symbol.

5.2   The Algorithm for Integer Offsets

In the following, possibly subindexed k will represent concrete integers and $a, b, c, d, \ldots$ will be constants. The input for our procedure will be a set of equations E of the form $a = b + k$ or of the form $\cdot(a, b + k_b) = c + k_c$, and we again assume that no term $\cdot(a, b + k)$ occurs more than once in the input.

The procedure for dealing with integer offsets halts giving the congruence generated by E whenever E is satisfiable. When it is not, it returns *unsatisfiable*.

The data structures used in this case are nearly the same as in the previous section:

1. *Pending Unions*: a list of equalities of the form $a = b+k$ yet to be processed.
2. The *Representative* Table: an array indexed by constants, containing for each constant a, the pair (b, k) such that b is its representative constant, with $b = a+k$.
3. The *Class Lists*: for each representative, the list of all pairs (constant, offset) in its class, as in Example 3.
4. The *Lookup Table*: for each input term $\cdot(a, b+k_b)$, where $Representative(a) = (a', 0)$ and $Representative(b) = (b', k_{b'})$ (that is, b is $b' - k_{b'}$), the function $Lookup(a', b'+(k_b-k_{b'}))$ returns in constant time $c+k_c$ such that $\cdot(a, b+k_b)$ is equivalent to $c+k_c$, and returns $\perp$ if there is no such $c+k_c$.

5. The *Use Lists*: for each representative a, the list of input equations $\cdot(b, c+k_c) = d+k_d$ such that a is the representative of b or c (or of both).

The initialization is as adapted as expected from the case without offsets. In the following, for each constant a, as before we denote its representative constant by a', and now also we write $r(a+k_a)$ to denote the representative of such a sum, i.e., $r(a+k_a)$ is $a'+k_a-k$ if $Representative(a) = (a', k)$. The algorithm is as follows:

1. **While** *Pending* is non-empty **Do**
2.   Remove $a = b+k$ with representative $a' = b'+k_{b'}$ from *Pending*
3.   **If** $a' \neq b'$ and, wlog., $|ClassList(a')| \leq |ClassList(b')|$ **Then**
4.   **For each** $c+k_c$ in $ClassList(a')$ **Do**
5.   set $Representative(c)$ to $(b', k_c - k_{b'})$ and add it to $ClassList(b')$
6.   **EndFor**
7.   **For each** $\cdot(c, d+k_d) = e+k_e$ in $UseList(a')$ **Do**
8.   **If** $Lookup(c', r(d+k_d))$ is $f+k_f$ and $r(f+k_f) \neq r(e+k_e)$ **Then**
9.   add $e = f+(k_f - k_e)$ to *Pending*
10.   **EndIf**
11.   set $Lookup(c', r(d+k_d))$ to $r(e+k_e)$
12.   add $\cdot(c, d+k_d) = e+k_e$ to $UseList(b')$
13.   **EndFor**
14.   **ElseIf** $a' = b'$ and $k_{b'} \neq 0$
15.   return *unsatisfiable*
16.   **EndIf**
17. **EndWhile**

Theorem 3. *The algorithm for congruence closure with integer offsets runs in* $O(n \log n)$ *time and in linear space.*

Proof. The proof is analogous to the one of Theorem 1. In this case the *Lookup* table has to be implemented by a hash table, since the *Lookup* function now in fact has three arguments (constant, constant, offset), unless one could in advance determine the range of the offsets.   □

The notions of standard form and of standard congruence extend in the expected way to integer offsets, and the corresponding result, analogous to Theorem 2, follows along the same lines.

6   Conclusions

We have given a new congruence closure algorithm. Apart for being short, clean and simple, it combines the efficiency of the classical algorithms [DST80, NO80] [Sho84] with the elegance of the more modern abstract view, as expressed in the frameworks of [Kap97, BT00, BTV]. These frameworks for abstract congruence closure have led to new insights and new results for several problems in rewriting, but only provide sub-optimal (quadratic) time complexity results (although we have recently learned that the algorithm of [BT00] can be extended with less abstract and less simple control data in its inference rules in order to make it run in $O(n \ log \ n)$ time; in particular, this requires an on-the-fly ordering on constants that forces congruence classes to be merged in the right order; this is sketched in the journal version [BTV], to appear).

Possibly this work can be seen as a concrete implementation of some of these abstract approaches, but for which a tighter and simpler complexity analysis has become possible, essentially due to the initial Curryfication.

On the other hand, the existing algorithms for ground Knuth-Bendix completion (which implicitly also compute a congruence closure) are all rather involved, and moreover either quadratic, like [PSK96], or are based on the previous use of one of the classical congruence closure algorithms on graphs [Sny89].

We believe that our cleaner formulation of congruence closure will also be useful for improving its explanation and understanding, and for applications and extensions such as the ones we have mentioned. Regarding practical aspects, from our first experiments our algorithm appears to be fast, in spite of the fact that it is extremely easy to implement. We are currently working on the design and a first implementation of the whole $DPLL(=)$ procedure, including, of course, the congruence closure module, as well as on its extension to EUF with integer offsets. Further extensions to be studied include the presence of other interpreted symbols, like associative and/or commutative ones.

In the paper by Bryant, Lahiri, and Seshia [BLS02] the logic with integer offsets is also further extended with an ordering predicate $>$. But surprisingly, already when only positive atoms $s > t$ are added to the input E_0, deciding the satisfiability of such E_0, which we call here the *CC-Ineq problem* (for congruence closure with inequalities), becomes NP-complete:

Proposition 4. *The CC-Ineq problem is NP-complete.*

Proof. Here we only sketch NP-hardness. Given a graph $G = (V, E)$ where $V = \{a_1, \ldots, a_n\}$ and $E = \{(b_1, b'_1), \cdots, (b_m, b'_m)\}$ and an integer k, the following CC-Ineq formula F_G is satisfiable if and only if G is k-colorable:

$$G(c+1, c+1) = G(c+2, c+2) = \ldots = G(c+k, c+k) = true$$

$$
\begin{array}{ll}
c + k + 1 > f(a_1) > c & true > G(f(b_1), f(b'_1)) \\
c + k + 1 > f(a_2) > c & true > G(f(b_2), f(b'_2)) \\
\quad\vdots \qquad \vdots \qquad \vdots & \quad\vdots \qquad \vdots \\
c + k + 1 > f(a_n) > c & true > G(f(b_m), f(b'_m))
\end{array}
$$

Intuitively, f represents the colour of each vertex (k possibilites), and G is used to express that no two adjacent vertices will have the same colour.   □

References

[BD94]   J. R. Burch and D. L. Dill.   Automatic verification of pipelined micro-
           processor control. In *Proc. 6th International Computer Aided Verification
           Conference*, pages 68–80, 1994.

[BLS02]   R. Bryant, S. Lahiri, and S. Seshia. Modeling and verifying systems using
           a logic of counter arithmetic with lambda expressions and uninterpreted
           functions.   In E. Brinksma and K. G. Larsen, editors, *Procs. 14th Intl.
           Conference on Computer Aided Verification (CAV)*, volume 2404 of *Lecture
           Notes in Computer Science*. Springer-Verlag, July 27–31 2002.

[BT00]   Leo Bachmair and Ashish Tiwari. Abstract congruence closure and special-
           izations. In David McAllester, editor, *Conference on Automated Deduction,
           CADE '2000*, volume 1831 of *Lecture Notes in Artificial Intelligence*, pages
           64–78, Pittsburgh, PA, June 2000. Springer-Verlag.

[BTV]   Leo Bachmair, Ashish Tiwari, and Laurent Vigneron. Abstract congruence
           closure. *Journal of Automated Reasoning*. To appear.

[DLL62]   Martin Davis, George Logemann, and Donald Loveland. A machine program
           for theorem-proving. *Communications of the ACM*, 5(7):394–397, July 1962.

[DP60]   Martin Davis and Hilary Putnam. A computing procedure for quantification
           theory. *Journal of the ACM*, 7:201–215, 1960.

[DP01]   Nachum Dershowitz and David Plaisted. Rewriting. In J.A. Robinson and
           A. Voronkov, editors, *Handbook of Automated Reasoning*. Elsevier Science
           Publishers and MIT Press, 2001.

[DST80]   Peter J. Downey, Ravi Sethi, and Robert E. Tarjan.   Variations on the
           common subexpressions problem. *J. of the Association for Computing Ma-
           chinery*, 27(4):758–771, 1980.

[Kap97]   Deepak Kapur. Shostak's congruence closure as completion. In H. Comon,
           editor, *Proceedings of the 8th International Conference on Rewriting Tech-
           niques and Applications*, volume 1232 of *Lecture Notes in Computer Science*.
           Springer-Verlag, 1997.

[NO80]   Greg Nelson and Derek C. Oppen. Fast decision procedures bases on con-
           gruence closure. *Journal of the Association for Computing Machinery*,
           27(2):356–364, April 1980.

[PSK96]   David A. Plaisted and Andrea Sattler-Klein. Proof lengths for equational
           completion. *Information and Computation*, 125(2):154–170, 15 March 1996.

[Sho84]   Robert E. Shostak. Deciding combinations of theories. *Journal of the ACM*,
           31(1):1–12, January 1984.

[Sny89]   Wayne Snyder. An O(n log n) algorithm for generating reduced sets of
           ground rewrite rules equivalent to a set of ground equations E. In N. Der-
           showitz, editor, *Rewriting Techniques and Applications, 3th International
           Conference*, LNCS. Springer-Verlag, 1989.

A Machine-Verified Code Generator

Christoph Walther and Stephan Schweitzer

Fachgebiet Programmiermethodik, Technische Universität Darmstadt,
{chr.walther,schweitz}@informatik.tu-darmstadt.de

Abstract. We consider the machine-supported verification of a code generator computing machine code from WHILE-programs, i.e. abstract syntax trees which may be obtained by a parser from programs of an imperative programming language. We motivate the representation of states developed for the verification, which is crucial for success, as the interpretation of tree-structured WHILE-programs differs significantly in its operation from the interpretation of the linear machine code. This work has been developed for a course to demonstrate to the students the support gained by computer-aided verification in a central subject of computer science, boiled down to the classroom-level. We report about the insights obtained into the properties of machine code as well as the challenges and efforts encountered when verifying the correctness of the code generator. We also illustrate the performance of the ✓eriFun system that was used for this work.

1   Introduction

We develop the ✓eriFun system [1],[22], a semi-automated system for the verification of programs written in a functional programming language. One reason for this development originates from our experiences when teaching Formal Methods, Automated Reasoning, Semantics, Verification, and similar subjects. As the motivation of the students largely increases when they can gather *practical* experiences with the principles and methods taught, ✓eriFun has been developed as a small, highly portable system with an elaborated user interface and a simple base logic, which nevertheless allows the students to perform ambitious verification case studies within the restricted time frame of a course. The system has been used in practical courses at the graduate level, cf. [24], for proving e.g. the correctness of a first-order matching algorithm, the *RSA* public key encryption algorithm and the unsolvability of the *Halting Problem*, as well as recently in an undergraduate course about *Algorithms and Data Structures*, where more than 400 students took their first steps in computer-aided verification of simple statements about *Arithmetic* and *Linear Lists* and the verification of algorithms like *Insertion Sort* and *Mergesort*. ✓eriFun comes as a JAVA application which the students can run on their home PC (whatever platform it may use) after a 1 MB download to work with the system whenever they like to.

   This paper is concerned with the verification of a code generator for a simple imperative language. Work on verified code generators and compilers dates

M.Y. Vardi and A. Voronkov (Eds.): LPAR 2003, LNAI 2850, pp. 91–106, 2003.
© Springer-Verlag Berlin Heidelberg 2003

back more than 35 years [9]. With the development of elaborated logics and the evolving technology of theorem proving over the years, systems developed that provide a remarkable support for compiler verification as well. Various impressive projects have been carried out which demonstrate well the benefits of certain logical frameworks and their implementation by reasoning systems in this domain. Meanwhile a tremendous amount of literature exists, which excludes an exhaustive account. E.g., [8] presents a case study using the ELF language, [14] uses the HOL system to verify a compiler for an assembly language, [6] and [3] report on compiler verification projects for a subset of COMMONLISP using PVS, and [15] verifies a compiler for PROLOG with the KIV system. Much work also centers around the Boyer-Moore prover and its successors, e.g. [4], and in one of the largest projects the compilation of an imperative programming language via an assembly language down to machine code is verified, cf. [10], [11], [27].

However, the high performance of these systems also comes with the price of highly elaborated logics and complicated user interfaces, which makes their use difficult for teaching within the restricted time frame of a course (if it is not impossible at all). Furthermore, as almost all of the cited work is concerned with real programming languages and the bits-and-pieces coming with them, it is hard to work out the essential principles and problems from the presentations to demonstrate them in the classroom. And last but not least, it is also difficult (in particular for the students) to assess the effort needed when using a certain tool, as most of the papers do not provide appropriate statistics but refer to large proof scripts in an appendix or to be downloaded from the web for further investigation.

The work presented here was prepared (in addition to the material given in [18]) for a course about *Semantics and Program Verification* to illustrate the principles of state-based semantics and the practical use of formal semantics when developing compilers etc. However, the main focus is to demonstrate the support gained by computer-aided verification in a central subject of computer science education, boiled down to the classroom-level. The code generator computes machine code from abstract syntax trees as used in standard textbooks of formal semantics, e.g. [7], [13], [26]. We report about the insights obtained into the properties of machine code as well as the challenges and efforts encountered when verifying the correctness of this program. We also illustrate the performance of the √eriFun system that was used for this work.

2   WHILE – Programs

The language of WHILE-programs consists of conditional statements, *while*-loops, assignments, compound statements and statements for doing nothing, and is defined by the data structure WHILE.PROGRAM in Fig. 1. WHILE-programs represent *abstract syntax trees* which for instance are computed by a compiler from a program conforming to the concrete syntax of a programming language to be available for subsequent code generation, cf. e.g. [2]. The language of WHILE-programs uses program variables and expressions built with arithmetical and

```
structure VARIABLE <= VAR(ADR:nat)

structure EXPR <=
 EXPR0(e-op0:nullary.operator),EXPR1(e-op1:unary.operator,arg:EXPR),
 EXPR2(e-op2:binary.operator,arg1:EXPR,arg2:EXPR), VAR@(index:nat)

structure WHILE.PROGRAM <=
 SKIP, COMPOUND(LEFT:WHILE.PROGRAM,RIGHT:WHILE.PROGRAM),
 SET(CELL:VARIABLE,TERM:EXPR), WHILE(WCOND:EXPR,BODY:WHILE.PROGRAM),
 IF(ICOND:EXPR,THEN:WHILE.PROGRAM,ELSE:WHILE.PROGRAM)
```

Fig. 1. The languages of Expressions and WHILE-programs

logical operators, which are defined by further data structures, cf. Fig. 1. Following the standard approach for the definition of a (structural) operational semantics of WHILE-programs, e.g. [7], [13], [26], we start by providing an operational semantics for the expressions EXPR: Given a data structure memory which assigns natural numbers to VARIABLEs, we define a procedure function value(e:EXPR,m:memory):nat <= ... to compute the value of an expression wrt. the assignments in memory m and the semantics provided for the operators. Procedure value retrieves the number assigned to a program variable by memory m, and otherwise applies the operation corresponding to the expression's operator to the values of the expression's arguments computed recursively by value. For example, the computation of value(EXPR2(PLUS,e1,e2),m) yields call-PLUS(value(e1,m),value(e2,m)), where call-PLUS and similar procedures defining the semantics of the other operators are given elsewhere.

An operational semantics for WHILE-programs is given by the interpreter eval, which maps a program state and a WHILE-program to a program state, cf. Fig. 2. A program state is either the symbol timeout (denoting a non-terminating interpretation of a WHILE-program) or is a triple consisting of a counter loops, a memory store and a stack stack. The store holds the current variable assignments under which expressions are evaluated by value (when executing a WHILE-, SET- or IF-statement), and which is updated when executing a SET-statement. The rôle of counter loops is discussed in Sections 6 and 7. Also the stack is used for subsequent developments, cf. Section 3, and may be ignored here as eval does not consider this component of a triple at all.

3   Machine Programs

Our target machine consists of a program store, a random access memory, a stack and a program counter *pc*. Arithmetical and logical operations are performed by a subdevice of the target machine, called the *stack machine*. The stack machine may push some content of the memory onto the stack and performs arithmetical and logical operations by fetching operands from and returning results to the stack. The operation of the stack machine is controlled by so-called *stack pro-*

```
function eval(r:state, wp:WHILE.PROGRAM):state <=
if r=timeout
 then timeout
 else if wp=WHILE(WCOND(wp),BODY(wp))
       then if value(WCOND(wp),store(r))=0
             then if loops(r)=0
                   then timeout
                   else if pred(loops(r))≥loops(eval(S,BODY(wp)))
                         then eval(eval(S,BODY(wp)),wp)
                         else timeout
                         fi fi
             else r fi
       else if wp=SET(CELL(wp),TERM(wp))
             then triple(loops(r),
                          update(assoc(CELL(wp),value(TERM(wp),store(r))),
                                 store(r)),stack(r))
             else if wp=COMPOUND(LEFT(wp),RIGHT(wp))
                   then eval(eval(r,LEFT(wp)),RIGHT(wp))
                   else if wp=IF(ICOND(wp),THEN(wp),ELSE(wp))
                         then if value(ICOND(wp),store(r))=0
                               then eval(r,THEN(wp))
                               else eval(r,ELSE(wp))
                         fi
                   else r   fi fi fi fi fi
```
where S abbreviates `triple(pred(loops(r)),store(r),stack(r))`

Fig. 2. An interpreter `eval` for WHILE-programs

grams. The target machine provides an instruction EXEC which calls the stack machine to run the stack program provided by the parameter of EXEC.

Stack programs are finite sequences of PUSH-commands, defined by some data structure STACK.PROGRAM. An operational semantics for stack programs is given by a procedure `function run(sp:STACK.PROGRAM,s:Stack,m:memory):Stack <= ...` which interprets the commands of a stack program step by step: When executing PUSH.VAR(v, sp), the number assigned to program variable v by memory m is pushed onto the stack, and otherwise operands are fetched from and the result of the operation is pushed onto the stack. For instance, stack s is replaced by `push(call-PLUS(top(pop(s)),top(s)),pop(pop(s)))` when executing PUSH.OP2(PLUS, sp), where call-PLUS and the procedures defining the semantics of the other operators are the same like for value. Having executed a PUSH-command, run proceeds with the execution of the remaining stack program sp.

Besides the EXEC instruction, the target machine also provides a LOAD instruction to write the top-of-stack to a designated address of the memory, two

```
function exec(r:state, pc:nat, mp:MACHINE.PROGRAM):state <=
if r=timeout
 then timeout
 else if mp=VOID
        then r
        else if pc>size(end(mp))
          then r
          else if fetch(pc,mp)=LOAD(loc(fetch(pc,mp)))
                then exec(triple(loops(r),update(assoc(loc(fetch(pc,mp)),
                                                    top(stack(r))),
                              store(r)),pop(stack(r))),succ(pc),mp)
            else if fetch(pc,mp)=EXEC(prog(fetch(pc,mp)))
                then exec(triple(loops(r),store(r),run(prog(fetch(pc,mp))),
                              stack(r),store(r))),succ(pc),mp)
                else if fetch(pc,mp)=BRANCH-(displ.B-(fetch(pc,mp)))
                      then if top(stack(r))=0
                            then if succ(displ.B-(fetch(pc,mp)))>pc
                                  then r
                                  else if loops(r)=0
                                        then timeout
                                        else exec(triple(pred(loops(r)),
                                                store(r),pop(stack(r))),
                                            minus(pred(pc),
                                            displ.B-(fetch(pc,mp))),
                                            mp) fi fi
                            else exec(triple(loops(r),store(r),pop(stack(r))),
                                  succ(pc),mp) fi
                else if fetch(pc,mp)=JUMP+(displ.J+(fetch(pc,mp)))
                    then exec(r,succ(plus(pc,displ.J+(fetch(pc,mp)))),mp)
                    else if fetch(pc,mp)=NOOP then exec(r,succ(pc),mp) fi ...
```

Fig. 3. The interpreter exec for machine programs

unconditional jump instructions JUMP+ and JUMP- to move the *pc* forward or backward in the program store, two conditional jump instructions BRANCH+ and BRANCH- which are controlled by the top-of-stack, a HALT instruction which halts the target machine, and a NOOP instruction which does nothing (except incrementing the *pc*). The instruction set is formally defined by some data structure INSTRUCTION, and a MACHINE.PROGRAM is simply a linear list of instructions, where VOID denotes the empty program, **begin** yields the first instruction and **end** denotes the machine program obtained by removing the first instruction.

An operational semantics of machine programs is defined by procedure exec of Fig. 3 (where some instructions are omitted). This interpreter uses a procedure fetch to fetch the instruction to which the program counter *pc* points in the machine program `mp`. The interpreter `exec` returns the input state if called in state `timeout`, with an empty machine program, with a `HALT` instruction or if pc is not within the address space $[0, ..., size(mp) - 1]$ of the machine program `mp`, where `size(mp)` computes the number of instructions in `mp`.

4   Code Generation

We aim at defining a procedure `code` which generates a machine program from a `WHILE`-program such that both programs compute the same function. To do so, we start by generating stack programs from the expressions used in a `WHILE`-program. This is achieved by some procedure `postfix` which simply translates the tree-structure of expressions into the linear format of stack programs. E.g., the expression `EXPR2(EQ,VAR@(1),VAR@(2))` is translated by `postfix` to the stack program `PUSH.VAR(VAR(1),PUSH.VAR(VAR(2),PUSH.OP2(EQ,null)))`.

Using the stack code generation for expressions, procedure `code` of Fig. 4 defines the machine code generation for `WHILE`-programs in a straightforward recursive way, where the recursively computed code is embedded into machine instructions in order to translate the control structure of the statement under consideration. The correctness property for `code` is formally stated by

$$\text{lemma code\_is\_correct} <= \text{all wp:WHILE.PROGRAM, r:state} \atop \text{eval(r,wp)=exec(r,0,code(wp))} . \tag{1}$$

5   About ✔eriFun

We intend to prove (1) `code_is_correct` with ✔eriFun. In a typical session with the system, a user defines a program by stipulating the data structures and the procedures of the program, defines statements about these program elements and verifies these statements and the termination of the procedures.

✔eriFun consists of several automated routines for theorem proving and for the formation of hypotheses to support verification. It is designed as an interactive system, where, however, the automated routines substitute the human expert in striving for a proof until they fail. In such a case, the user may step in to guide the system for a continuation of the proof.

When called to prove a statement, the system computes a *prooftree*. An interaction, which may be required when the construction of the prooftree gets stuck, is to instruct the system

- to perform a case analysis, – to unfold a procedure call,
- to apply an equation,   – to use an induction axiom,
- to use an instance of a lemma or an induction hypothesis, or
- to insert, move or delete some hypothesis in the sequent of a proof-node.

For simplifying proof goals, a further set of so-called *computed* proof rules is provided. For example, the *Simplification* rule rewrites a goalterm using the

```
function code(wp:WHILE.PROGRAM):MACHINE.PROGRAM <=
if wp=SKIP
 then conc(NOOP,VOID)
 else if wp=IF(ICOND(wp),THEN(wp),ELSE(wp))
      then conc(EXEC(postfix(ICOND(wp))),
                conc(BRANCH+(succ(size(code(ELSE(wp))))),
                     append(code(ELSE(wp)),
                            conc(JUMP+(size(code(THEN(wp)))),
                                 code(THEN(wp))))))
      else if wp=WHILE(WCOND(wp),BODY(wp))
           then conc(JUMP+(size(code(BODY(wp)))),
                     append(code(BODY(wp)),
                            conc(EXEC(postfix(WCOND(wp))),
                                 conc(BRANCH-(size(code(BODY(wp)))),
                                      VOID))))
           else if wp=SET(CELL(wp),TERM(wp))
                then conc(EXEC(postfix(TERM(wp))),
                          conc(LOAD(CELL(wp)),VOID))
                else append(code(LEFT(wp)),code(RIGHT(wp)))
                fi fi fi fi
```

Fig. 4. Code generation for WHILE-programs

definitions of the data structures and the procedures, the hypotheses and the induction hypotheses of the proof-node sequent and the lemmas already verified. The other computed proof rules perform a similar rewrite, however with restricted performance. The computed proof rules are implemented by the *Symbolic Evaluator*, i.e. an automated theorem prover over which the ✓eriFun user has no control. ✓eriFun provides no control commands (except disabling induction hypotheses upon symbolic evaluation), thus leaving the proof rules as the only means to control the system's behavior. The symbolic evaluations and all proofs computed by the system may be inspected by the user.

Having applied a user suggested proof rule, the system takes over control again and tries to develop the prooftree further until it gets stuck once more etc. or it eventually succeeds. In addition, it may be necessary to formulate (and to prove) an auxiliary lemma (sometimes after providing a new definition) in order to complete the actual proof task.

✓eriFun demands that the termination of each procedure that is called in a statement be verified before a proof of the statement can be started. Therefore the system's automated termination analysis [16] is activated immediately after the definition of a recursively defined procedure. If the automated termination analysis fails, the user has to tell the system useful termination functions represented by (sequences of) so-called *measure terms*. Based on this hint, the system computes termination hypotheses that are sufficient for the procedure's termination and then need to be verified like any other statement.

An introduction into the use of the system is given in [20], a short survey is presented in [22], and a detailed account on the system's operation and its logical foundations can be found in [21].

6   A Machine Verification of code

Termination. ✓eriFun's automated termination analysis verifies termination of all procedures upon definition, except for eval and exec. The interpreter eval terminates because upon each recursive call either the size of the program decreases or otherwise remains unchanged (for the outer eval-call in the WHILE-case), but the loops-counter decreases. But the system is unable to recognize this argumentation by itself and must be provided with the pair of termination functions $\lambda wp.|wp|$, $\lambda r.loops(r)$, causing the system to prove termination by the lexicographic relation $(wp_1, r_1) >_{eval} (wp_2, r_2)$ iff $|wp_1| > |wp_2|$ or $|wp_1| = |wp_2|$ and $loops(r_1) > loops(r_2)$. Hence for the outer eval-call in the WHILE-case, the proof obligation loops(r)>loops(eval(S,body(wp))) is obtained, which is trivially verified as loops(r)$\neq$0 and (*) pred(loops(r))$\geq$loops(eval(S,body(wp))) must hold, cf. Fig. 2. Note that requirement (*) controlling the outer recursive call in the WHILE-case is always satisfied, as we may prove (*after* having verified eval's termination)

```
lemma eval_not_increases_loops <=
    all r:state, wp:WHILE.PROGRAM loops(r)≥loops(eval(r,wp))
```
(2)

expressing that eval never *increases* the loops-component of a state. However, when removing (*) from the definition of eval, ✓eriFun is unable to prove termination because the system verifies only *strong* termination of procedures. Roughly speaking, a terminating procedure terminates *strongly* iff termination can be proven without reasoning about the procedure's semantics, cf. [17] for a formal definition. Since one has to reason about the semantics of eval, viz. (2), for proving its termination if (*) is not provided, the system would fail to prove eval's termination.[1]

The interpreter exec terminates because with each *fetch&execute* cycle either the loops-component of the state decreases (in case of a back-leap BRANCH- or JUMP-) or otherwise stays even, but pc moves towards the end of the program, cf. Fig. 3. Here the system is unable to recognize this argumentation as well and needs to be provided with the pair of termination functions $\lambda r . loops(r)$, $\lambda mp, pc . |mp| - pc$.

---

[1] The need for terminating procedures is necessitated by the logic implemented by our system, while the failure to prove eval's termination without requirement (*) is a lack of our *implementation* only. This is because, as proved in [5], our approach for automated termination proofs [16] is also sound for procedures with *nested* recursions like eval. We learned how to transform a terminating procedure with nested recursions into a *strongly* terminating procedure from [12].

Correctness of `code`. Before considering (1) `code_is_correct`, the correctness of the procedure `postfix` has to be verified. Therefore we start with proving

$$
\begin{aligned}
&\texttt{lemma postfix\_is\_correct <= all e:EXPR, s:Stack, m:memory} \\
&\quad\texttt{top(run(postfix(e),s,m))=value(e,m)}
\end{aligned}
\tag{3}
$$

expressing that the value computed by `value` upon the evaluation of an expression `e` is obtained as top-of-stack after running the stack program returned by `postfix` when applied to expression `e`. The proof of (3) requires two auxiliary lemmas, one stating that stack programs can be executed step-by-step

$$
\begin{aligned}
&\texttt{lemma run\_extend <= all m:memory,s:Stack,sp1,sp2:STACK.PROGR} \\
&\quad\texttt{run(extend(sp1,sp2),s,m)=run(sp2,run(sp1,s,m),m)}
\end{aligned}
\tag{4}
$$

and the other one expressing that the execution of stack programs obtained by `postfix` does not affect the stack initially given to `run`, i.e.

$$
\begin{aligned}
&\texttt{lemma pop\_run\_postfix <= all e:EXPR, s:Stack, m:memory} \\
&\quad\texttt{pop(run(postfix(e),s,m))=s .}
\end{aligned}
\tag{5}
$$

All three lemmas have an automated proof and are frequently (and automatically) used in subsequent proofs.

The induction proof of (1) is based on `eval`'s recursion structure. Hence it develops into 3 base cases, viz. `wp` is a SKIP- or a SET-statement or `wp` is a WHILE-statement and `loops(r)`=0, and 3 step cases, viz. `wp` is a compound statement, `wp` is an IF-statement, or `wp` is a WHILE-statement and `loops(r)`≠0.

The base cases are proved easily. However, *Unfold Procedure* must be applied to `exec`-calls several times before *Simplification* (using (3) and (5)) succeeds. Of course, it is annoying to call interactively for *Unfold Procedure* quite often instead of only letting *Simplification* doing the job. The reason is that the unfold of procedure calls needs to be controlled heuristically upon *symbolic* evaluation, because otherwise unusable goalterms may result. ✓eriFun uses a heuristic which is based on a similarity measure between the well-founded relation used for an induction proof of a statement and the well-founded relations that have been used to prove the termination of the procedures involved in the statement, and only calls of procedures having a termination relation similar to the induction relation are automatically unfolded. This heuristic proved successful in almost all cases but may fail if a statement refers to procedures which differ significantly in their recursion structure, as `eval` and `exec` do in the present case. In the proof of (1), we must therefore call for *Unfold Procedure* not only in the base cases, but also in the step cases to instruct the system interactively to execute parts of the machine code in the goalterms symbolically.

Having proved the base cases, the system proceeds with the first step case (where `wp` is a compound statement) and simplifies the induction conclusion to

$$
\begin{aligned}
&\texttt{if(r=timeout,} \\
&\quad\texttt{true,} \\
&\quad\texttt{exec(exec(r,0,code(LEFT(wp))),0,code(RIGHT(wp)))} \\
&\quad\texttt{= exec(r,0,append(code(LEFT(wp)),code(RIGHT(wp)))))}
\end{aligned}
\tag{6}
$$

which we straightforwardly generalize to

$$\texttt{exec(exec(r,pc,mp1),0,mp2)} = \texttt{exec(r,pc,append(mp1,mp2))} \qquad (7)$$

in order to prove the subgoal (6) with this equation.

However, (7) does not hold. If the `pc` points to some instruction of `append(mp1,mp2)` but is not within the address space of `mp1`, equation (7) rewrites to `exec(r,0,mp2)=exec(r,pc,append(mp1,mp2))`, which obviously is false. We therefore demand `size(mp1)>pc`, but this restriction is not enough: Assume that `mp1` contains a `HALT` instruction and `exec(r,pc,mp1)` returns the state `r'` upon the execution of `HALT`. Then `r'` is also obtained when executing `append(mp1,mp2)`, and consequently equation (7) rewrites to `exec(r',0,mp2)=r'`. Hence we also demand `HALT.free(mp1)`, where procedure `HALT.free` returns `true` iff it is applied to a machine program free of `HALT` instructions. But even with this additional restriction equation (7) is still false. This time we assume that `mp1` contains some forward-leap instruction with a displacement pointing beyond the last instruction of `append(mp1,mp2)`. If this instruction is executed in a state `r'`, `exec` returns `r'` and equation (7) rewrites to `exec(r',0,mp2)=r'` again. We therefore demand `closed+(mp1)` as a further restriction, where procedure `closed+` returns `true` iff it is applied to a machine program `mp` such that `pc+d≤size(mp)-1` for each forward-leap instruction in `mp` with `fetch(pc,mp)=JUMP+(d)` or `fetch(pc,mp)=BRANCH+(d)`. We continue with our analysis and now assume that `mp2` contains some back-leap instruction with a displacement pointing beyond the first instruction of `mp2`. For instance, `mp1` may consist of one instruction `NOOP` only and `mp2` may consist of only one instruction `JUMP-(0)`. Then equation (7) rewrites to `r=timeout`, and a counter example is found again. We therefore demand `closed-(mp2)` as another restriction, where procedure `closed-` returns `true` iff it is applied to a machine program `mp` such that `pc≥d+1` for each back-leap instruction in `mp` with `fetch(pc,mp)=BRANCH-(d)` or `fetch(pc,mp)=JUMP-(d)`. But we also have to demand `closed-(mp1)`, as otherwise equation (7) may rewrite to `exec(r',0,mp2)=r'` again. We are done with this final restriction, and the required lemma reads as

```
lemma exec_stepwise <=
all pc:nat, mp1,mp2:MACHINE.PROGRAM, r:state
if(size(mp1)>pc,if(HALT.free(mp1),if(closed+(mp1),
   if(closed-(mp1),if(closed-(mp2),
      exec(exec(r,pc,mp1),0,mp2) = exec(r,pc,append(mp1,mp2)),
      true), ... , true) .
```
(8)

However, in order to prove subgoal (6) by lemma (8), it must be verified that all preconditions of (8) are satisfied for machine programs `mp1` and `mp2` computed by `code`. We therefore formulate the lemmas `code_is_closed-`, `code_is_closed+`, `size_code_not_zero` and `code_is_HALT.free` all of which are proved easily. Recognizing the lemmas just developed and verified, the system simplifies the induction conclusion of the first step case to `true`.

We continue in the verification of lemma (1) with the remaining step cases, which are concerned with the code generation for the IF- and the WHILE-statements (if loops(r)≠0). Here, too, a sequence of symbolic machine program executions followed by *Simplification* rewrites the goalterm to a subgoal, which then has to be generalized to a further lemma in order to complete the proof. For the WHILE-case, the lemma

```
lemma exec_repetition <=
all mp:MACHINE.PROGRAM, pc:nat, sp:STACK.PROGRAM, r:state
if(pc>size(mp),true,if(closed-(mp),if(closed+(mp),
  if(HALT.free(mp),
    exec(exec(r,pc,mp),size(mp),                            (9)
      append(mp,conc(EXEC(sp),conc(BRANCH-(size(mp)),VOID)))),
      =exec(r,pc,append(mp,conc(EXEC(sp),
                              conc(BRANCH-(size(mp)),VOID))))
  true), ... , true).
```

is speculated, and the IF-case requires the lemma

```
lemma exec_skip_program <=
all mp1,mp2:MACHINE.PROGRAM, r:state, pc:nat
if(closed-(mp2),                                            (10)
  exec(r,plus(size(mp1),pc),append(mp1,mp2))=exec(r,pc,mp2),
  true)
```

To avoid over-generalizations, the equations in (9) and (10) must be restricted to machine programs being closed-, closed+ and HALT.free, where these requirements have been recognized by the same careful analysis undertaken when developing lemma (8). Using these lemmas, each step case (and in turn the whole lemma (1) code_is_correct) is proved easily, see [23] for details.

7   Discussion

Viewed in retrospect, the *proofs* required to verify (1) code_is_correct were obtained without that much effort. However, theorem proving sometimes is like crossing an unknown terrain for climbing a hill. Viewing the way after reaching the top, it seems quite obvious how to get there directly, but being on the way one is faced with deadends and traps turning the whole event into a nightmare. In case of (1) code_is_correct, the crucial steps to success were (1) the "right" definition of the machine language's interpreter exec, (2) the "right" definition of a state, and (3) the invention of the key lemmas (8) exec_stepwise, (9) exec_repetition and (10) exec_skip_program as well as the key notions needed to formulate them.

Our first attempt was to define a state without the loops- and the stack-components, but to care for the termination of exec by limiting the total number of fetch-calls performed when executing a machine program. This means to use a definition like `function exec(r:state, pc:nat, mp: MACHINE.PROGRAM, cycles:nat):state <= ...`, were `cycles` is decremented in each recursive call of `exec` to enforce termination (and the treatment of the `stack` is ignored here for the moment). But this approach requires an additional procedure, say `get.cycles`, computing the minimum number of `cycles` needed to execute a machine program (if this execution does not result in `timeout`). This procedure `get.cycles` is required to formulate the correctness statement for `code`, as the number of loop-bodies of a WHILE-program `wp` evaluated by `eval` has to be related to the number of machine cycles needed to execute `code(wp)` by `exec`. Procedure `get.cycles` is easily obtained from the definition of `exec`, but with this procedure also a bunch of additional lemmas, in particular the `get.cycles`-versions of the key lemmas (8) – (10) need to be formulated and verified.[2]

Having followed this approach for some time, we gave up and started to work with another version of `exec`. This definition was based on the observation that the number of evaluated loop-bodies in a WHILE-program `wp` is exactly the number of BRANCH--calls performed upon the execution of `code(wp)`. We therefore got rid of `get.cycles` (and also, what is even more important, of all the lemmas coming with it) by (renaming `cycles` by `loops` and) decrementing `loops` only in the recursive `exec`-calls coming with a JUMP- or a BRANCH--instruction.

However, this approach has problems, too: This time another procedure, say `get.loops`, is required to rephrase the equation in (8) `exec_stepwise` for this version of `exec`, which then would read

```
exec(exec(r,pc,mp1,loops),
         0,mp2,minus(loops,get.loops(r,pc,mp1,loops)))       (11)
  = exec(r,pc,append(mp1,mp2),loops).
```

Here the procedure `get.loops` is needed to compute the number of `loops` *remaining* after the execution of `mp1` starting at `pc` in state `r`, hence this approach necessitates the same burden of additional lemmas as the `get.cycles` idea.

But fortunately, there is an easy remedy to this problem. We simply let `loops` become a component of a `state` rather than a formal parameter of `exec`, and then the need for an additional procedure `get.loops` disappears. As similar problems with the formulation of (8) arise if `exec` is provided with a formal parameter `s:stack`, also the `stack` becomes a component of a `state`, and this motivates our definitions of the data structure `state` and the procedure `exec`.

Having settled these definitions, the next problem was to formulate the key lemmas (8), (9) and (10). It is interesting to see that each lemma corresponds directly to a statement of the WHILE-language, viz. the compound-, the WHILE-, and the IF-statement. Whereas the control structure of WHILE-programs is easily captured by the notions of the *meta-language*, viz. functional composition, conditionals and recursion, cf. Fig. 2, the control structure of a machine program `mp` is encoded in the *data* (viz. `mp`) by the JUMP and BRANCH instructions, cf. Fig. 3.

---

[2] `get.cycles` corresponds to the `clock`-procedures used in [4], [10], [11], [27], causing similar problems there. However, `clock` can be used to reason about running times, and also for proof-technical reasons as Moore explains (personal communication).

This requires making the control structure of machine programs explicit in the meta-language, and this is achieved by the key lemmas, whose syntactical similarity with the recursive eval-calls (necessitated by the respective statements) is obvious. However, this was not obvious to us when we developed the proof of (1) code_is_correct, and most of the time was spent to analyze the system's outcome when it got stuck, to find out which properties of machine programs are required in order to get the proof through. Upon this work, the key notions of HALT.free, closed-, and closed+ machine programs were recognized, and the key lemmas were speculated step by step.

While the speculation of the key lemmas constituted the main challenge for us, the proofs of these lemmas constituted the main challenge for the system: By the rich case-structure of procedure exec, goalterms evolved which are so huge that the *Symbolic Evaluator* fails to process them within reasonable time. A remedy to this problem is to throw in interactively a case analysis (stipulating the kind of instructions fetch(pc,mp) may yield) which separates the goalterm into smaller pieces so that the theorem prover can cope with them.[3]

But still the system showed performance problems for another reason: For each key lemma, 8 induction hypotheses are available in the step case which separate into 66 clauses having 10–12 literals each. This creates a large search space for the *Symbolic Evaluator* and performance decreases significantly.[4] We therefore instructed the system to disable the induction hypotheses upon symbolic evaluation, and then the system went through the proofs (needing further advice from time to time).[5] Using this setting, ✓eriFun succeeded because after *Simplification* following the case analysis, the system picked up the right induction hypotheses with the *Use Lemma* rule, and a subsequent *Simplification* then proved the case. In addition, a bunch of "routine" lemmas had been created (expressing for example that HALT.free distributes over append, etc.), whose need, however, was immediately obvious from the system's outcome and whose proofs needed an interaction in very rare cases only.

Fig. 5 gives an account on ✓eriFun's automation degree measured in terms of prooftree edits.[6] For the whole case study, 13 data structures and 22 procedures were defined to formulate 56 lemmas, whose verification required 1038 prooftree edits in total, where only 186 of them had to be suggested interactively.

---

[3] This case study also revealed a shortcoming of ✓eriFun's object language, viz. not having *let*- and *case*-instructions available. We intend to remove this lack of the language in a future version of the system, as this would significantly improve the performance of the *Symbolic Evaluator*.

[4] The system uses a *lemma-filter* to throw out all clauses computed from verified lemmas which (heuristically) do not seem to contribute to a proof. However, induction hypotheses are not considered by this filter, because they are quite similar to the original statement, thus causing the lemma-filter to let them pass in almost all cases.

[5] As a matter of fact, we had never seen the need for disabling induction hypotheses before.

[6] The values are computed for ✓eriFun 2.6.1 under *Windows XP* running JAVA 1.4.1_01 on a 2.2 GHz *Pentium 4* PC. The 3 interactions to disable induction hypotheses are not listed in Fig. 5.

Statistics of while-code.vf

Program Elements	Sum	Symbolic Evaluation	
Data Structures	13	GMN	64750
Procedures	22	"exec_repetition"	1259
System Generated Proce...	16	SRA	823068
Verified Lemmas	56	SRA/GMN	12,7
System Generated Lemmas	14	SRA/sec	414,6
Total	121	Time [hh:mm:ss]	0:33:05

Proof Rules	Total	Interactive	%	Automated	%
Simplification	656	0	0	656	100
Weak Simplification	16	0	0	16	100
Normalization	0	0	0	0	0
Weak Normalization	0	0	0	0	0
Inconsistency	0	-	-	0	0
Case Analysis	58	58	100	-	-
Use Lemma	174	44	25,3	130	74,7
Unfold Procedure	74	74	100	-	-
Apply Equation	16	10	62,5	6	37,5
Induction	44	0	0	44	100
Insert Hypotheses	0	0	0	-	-
Move Hypothesis	0	0	0	-	-
Delete Hypotheses	0	0	0	0	0
Total	1038	186	17,9	852	82,1

Termination	Total	Interactive	%	Automated	%
Measure Terms	19	2	10,5	17	89,5

Fig. 5. Proof statistics obtained for the verification of the `code` generator

The *Symbolic Evaluator* computed proofs with a total number of 64750 rewrite steps within 33 minutes running time, where the longest subproof of 1259 steps had been created for lemma (9) `exec_repetition`.

The value for the automated calls of *Use Lemma* is unusually high as compared to other case studies performed with √eriFun, e.g. [19], [25], which is caused by the fact that the induction hypotheses had been disabled upon symbolic evaluation of the key lemmas so that *Use Lemma* could succeed following *Simplification*. Whereas the *Induction* rule performed perfectly here, the values for *Unfold Procedure* and for *Case Analysis* are unusually high, which reflects the need for frequent interactive calls for symbolic execution of machine programs when proving (1), and also reflects the separation into subcases needed for the proofs of the key lemmas.

In total, 82.1% of the required prooftree edits had been computed by machine, a number which (although it is not as good as the values encountered in other cases) we consider as good enough to provide significant support for computer-aided verification. With the key notions for machine programs and the key lemmas for the machine language interpreter, a clear and illuminating structure for the proof of the main statement evolved, which lacks formal clutter and therefore provides a useful base to illustrate the rôle of formal semantics and the benefits of computer-aided verification in the classroom.

Acknowledgement

We are grateful to Markus Aderhold for useful comments.

References

1. http://www.informatik.tu-darmstadt.de/pm/verifun/.
2. A. V. Aho, R. Sethi, and J. D. Ullmann. *Compilers: Principles, Techniques and Tools.* Addison-Wesley, New York, 1986.
3. A. Dold and V. Vialard. A mechanically verified compiling specification for a Lisp compiler. In R. Hariharan, M. Mukund, and V. Vinay, editors, *FST TCS 2001: Foundations of Software Technology and Theoretical Computer Sience*, volume 2245 of *Lect. Notes in Comp. Sc.*, pages 144–155, 2001.
4. A. D. Flatau. *A Verified Implementation of an Applicative Language with Dynamic Storage Allocation.* PhD. Thesis, Univ. of Texas, 1992.
5. J. Giesl. Termination of Nested and Mutually Recursive Algorithms. *Journal of Automated Reasoning*, 19:1–29, 1997.
6. W. Goerigk, A. Dold, T. Gaul, G. Goos, A. Heberle, H. von Henke, U. Hoffmann, H. Langmaack, and W. Zimmermann. Compiler correctness and implementation verification: The Verifix approach. In P. Fritzson, editor, *Proc. of the Poster Session of CC'96 - Intern. Conf. on Compiler Construction*, pages 65 – 73, 1996.
7. C. A. Gunter. *Semantics of Programming Languages — Structures and Techniques.* The MIT Press, Cambridge, 1992.
8. J. Hannan and F. Pfenning. Compiler verification in LF. In A. Scedrov, editor, *Proceedings of the Seventh Annual IEEE Symposium on Logic in Computer Science*, pages 407–418. IEEE Computer Society Press, 1992.
9. J. McCarthy and J. A. Painter. Correctness of a Compiler for Arithmetical Expressions. In J. T. Schwartz, editor, *Proc. on a Symp. in Applied Math., 19, Math. Aspects of Comp. Sc.* American Math. Society, 1967.
10. J. S. Moore. A Mechanically Verified Language Implementation. *Journal of Automated Reasoning*, 5(4):461–492, 1989.
11. J. S. Moore. *PITON - A Mechanically Verified Assembly-Level Language.* Kluwer Academic Publishers, Dordrecht, 1996.
12. J. S. Moore. An exercise in graph theory. In M. Kaufmann, P. Manolios, and J. S. Moore, editors, *Computer-Aided Reasoning: ACL2 Case Studies*, pages 41–74, Boston, MA., 2000. Kluwer Academic Press.
13. H. R. Nielson and F. Nielson. *Semantics with Applications.* John Wiley and Sons, New York, 1992.
14. P. Curzon. A verified compiler for a structured assembly language. In M. Archer, J.J. Joyce, K.N. Levitt, and P.J. Windley, editors, *International Workshop on Higher Order Logic Theorem Proving and its Applications*, pages 253–262, Davis, California, 1991. IEEE Computer Society Press.
15. G. Schellhorn and W. Ahrendt. The WAM case study: Verifying compiler correctness for Prolog with KIV. In W. Bibel and P. H. Schmidt, editors, *Automated Deduction: A Basis for Applications. Volume III, Applications.* Kluwer Academic Publishers, Dordrecht, 1998.
16. C. Walther. On Proving the Termination of Algorithms by Machine. *Artificial Intelligence*, 71(1):101–157, 1994.
17. C. Walther. Criteria for Termination. In S. Hölldobler, editor, *Intellectics and Computational Logic.* Kluwer Academic Publishers, Dordrecht, 2000.
18. C. Walther. *Semantik und Programmverifikation.* Teubner-Wiley, Leipzig, 2001.
19. C. Walther and S. Schweitzer. A Machine Supported Proof of the Unique Prime Factorization Theorem. Technical Report VFR 02/03, Programmiermethodik, Technische Universität Darmstadt, 2002.

20. C. Walther and S. Schweitzer. The √eriFun Tutorial. Technical Report VFR 02/04, Programmiermethodik, Technische Universität Darmstadt, 2002.

21. C. Walther and S. Schweitzer. √eriFun User Guide. Technical Report VFR 02/01, Programmiermethodik, Technische Universität Darmstadt, 2002.

22. C. Walther and S. Schweitzer. About √eriFun. In F. Baader, editor, *Proc. of the 19th Inter. Conf. on Automated Deduction (CADE-19)*, volume 2741 of *Lecture Notes in Artifical Intelligence*, pages 1–5, Miami, 2003. Springer-Verlag.

23. C. Walther and S. Schweitzer. A Machine-Verified Code Generator. Technical Report VFR 03/01, Programmiermethodik, Technische Universität Darmstadt, 2003.

24. C. Walther and S. Schweitzer. Verification in the Classroom. *To appear in Journal of Automated Reasoning - Special Issue on Automated Reasoning and Theorem Proving in Education*, pages 1–21, 2003.

25. C. Walther and S. Schweitzer. A Verification of Binary Search. In D. Hutter and W. Stephan, editors, *Mechanizing Mathematical Reasoning: Techniques, Tools and Applications*, volume 2605 of *LNAI*, pages 1–18. Springer-Verlag, 2003.

26. G. Winskel. *The Formal Semantics of Programming Languages*. The MIT Press, Cambridge, 1993.

27. W. D. Young. A Mechanically Verified Code Generator. *Journal of Automated Reasoning*, 5(4):493–518, 1989.

A Translation Characterizing
the Constructive Content of Classical Theories

Matthias Baaz and Christian G. Fermüller

Technische Universität Wien, A-1040 Vienna, Austria,
{baaz,chrisf}@logic.at

Abstract. A simple syntactical translation of theories and of existential formulas — $\mathcal{C}^\forall$ and $\mathcal{C}^\exists$, respectively — is described for which the following holds: For any classical theory T and all formulas $A(x)$,

$$T \vdash A(t) \text{ for some term } t \;\Leftrightarrow\; \mathcal{C}^\forall(T) \vdash \mathcal{C}^\exists(\exists x A(x)).$$

In other words, $\mathcal{C}^\forall(T)$ proves exactly those formulas $\mathcal{C}^\exists(\exists x A(x))$ for which T can prove $\exists x A(x)$ *constructively* and thus circumscribes the constructive fragment of T. The proof of the theorem is based on properties of the resolution calculus; which allows to extract a primitive recursive bound on the size of the witness term t, with respect to the size of a proof of $\mathcal{C}^\forall(T) \vdash \mathcal{C}^\exists(\exists x A(x))$. In fact, a generalization of the above statement, that takes into account a designation of certain function symbols as 'constructor symbols' is proved. Different types of examples are provided: Some formalize well known non-constructive arguments from mathematics, others illustrate the use of the theorem for characterizing classes of classical theories that are constructive with respect to certain types of existential formulas.

1 Introduction

It is natural to ask for proofs of existential statements $\exists x A$ to exhibit an object, which satisfies A: Such *constructive proofs* correspond to the first-glance meaning of 'there exists' (contrary to the discovered properties of classical semantics).

Logicians' traditional solution to this problem is to restrict the logic in some way, such that all existential statements that are provable are in fact realizable. (Switching from classical to intuitionistic logic is just one possible move of this kind.) The disadvantage of this approach however is that — while it might provide the desired properties for purely logical statements — there are usually T and $\exists x A(x)$ such that $T \vdash \exists x A(x)$ and $T \nvdash A(t)$ for all t in the restricted logic, but $T \vdash A(t)$ for some t in classical logic.

Remark 1. The following observation shows that no proper intermediary logic can capture (classical) constructive provability.

Let L be an intermediary first-order logic. (I.e., $\vdash_{\text{Int}} \subseteq \vdash_{\text{L}} \subseteq \vdash_{\text{Cl}}$, where the three $\vdash$-relations stand for provability in intuitionistic logic (Int), logic L, and classical logic (Cl), respectively.) We make the following modest assumptions:

M.Y. Vardi and A. Voronkov (Eds.): LPAR 2003, LNAI 2850, pp. 107–121, 2003.

(a) L is not classical: $\nvdash_L F \vee \neg F$, for some formula F,
(b) L is closed under substitution: $\Pi \vdash_L E$ implies $\Pi[^F_A] \vdash_L E[^F_A]$, for atomic A and arbitrary F,
(c) L is closed under cut: $\Pi \vdash_L E$ and $\{E\} \cup \Gamma \vdash_L G$ implies $\Pi \cup \Gamma \vdash_L G$.

We show that there exist theories T and formulas $\exists x A(x)$ such that

(1) $T \vdash_L \exists x A(x)$,
(2) $T \nvdash_L A(t)$ for all terms t, but
(3) $T \vdash_{Cl} A(t)$ for some term t.

Take $T = \{P(0) \vee P(1), (F \vee \neg F) \supset P(1)\}$.

ad (1): Since $P(0) \vee P(1) \vdash_{Int} \exists x P(x)$ we have also $T \vdash_L \exists x P(x)$.
ad (2): Suppose $T \vdash_L P(0)$. Then also $T \vdash_{Cl} P(0)$, which implies $T[^\perp_{P(0)} {}^\top_{P(1)}] \vdash_{Cl}$
$P(0)[^\perp_{P(0)} {}^\top_{P(1)}]$ and therefore $\vdash_{Cl} \perp$, contradiction.
Suppose $T \vdash_L P(1)$. Then $T[^\top_{P(0)} {}^{F \vee \neg F}_{P(1)}] \vdash_L P(0)[^\top_{P(0)} {}^{F \vee \neg F}_{P(1)}]$, which implies
$\{\top \vee (F \vee \neg F), (F \vee \neg F) \supset (F \vee \neg F)\} \vdash_L F \vee \neg F$. It follows $\vdash_L F \vee \neg F$,
since $\vdash_{Int} \top \vee (F \vee \neg F)$ and $\vdash_{Int} (F \vee \neg F) \supset (F \vee \neg F)$, and $\vdash_{Int} \subseteq \vdash_L$,
contradiction.
ad (3): Obviously $T \vdash_{Cl} P(1)$.

In contrast to the traditional approach mentioned above, we seek to specify the class of existential statements which are constructively provable from a given theory T in *classical* logic. I.e., instead of reformulating the logic, we reformulate T and the existential statement in question, using a straightforward translation $\mathcal{C}^\forall$ ($\mathcal{C}^\exists$) of theories (existential formulas) such that $\exists x A$ follows constructively from T iff $\mathcal{C}^\exists(\exists x A)$ follows from $\mathcal{C}^\forall(T)$. In fact, we proof a more general result, which takes into account that one might be interested be interested in the existence of witness terms for existential formulas that only use a restricted signature. The proof of the adequacy of the translations relies on an intrinsic connectivity property of the resolution calculus.

Remark 2. A translation with the indicated properties has already been formulated for *universal theories* and *purely existential* consequences in [1], and is here extended to arbitrary theories and arbitrary consequences. Furthermore we here generalize the basic result, as mentioned above, by parameterizing the translation with a subset of the signature. This allows for the characterization of constructivity with respect to designated function symbols. (Such restrictions are necessary if one is interested in the characterization of constructivity in logics, whose semantics are embeddable into classical first order logic, such as Kripke semantics based logics.) The formulation of this paper directly refers to resolution proofs and makes the results thereby more accessible to automated theorem proving.

One might ask whether it is not sufficient to just stick to the teratological statement 'to prove $\exists x A(x)$ constructively means to exhibit an object and to prove that A applies to this object'. However, the merit of our translation is that it allows to use *classical counter-models* to demonstrate that $\exists x A$ is not constructively provable from T.

We will also point out that there are classes of theories and existential formulas, which are invariant with respect to the introduced translation in the sense that the derivability of $\exists x A$ from T is equivalent to the derivability of $\mathcal{C}^{\exists}(\exists x A)$ from $\mathcal{C}^{\forall}(T)$; i.e., cases where no existential statement is provable only non-constructively. Furthermore, we show that there are theories T, such that the constructive provability of $\exists x A$ is undecidable in general, even if the classical provability is known. (In this context one should note that constructive provability might change it's decidability status for T if T is reformulated in a different language). The theory of Real Closed Fields will serve as prime example.

2   Concepts from Clause Logic

Since we declare interest in constructivity, it seems worth to emphasize that throughout this paper we only refer to ordinary *classical* (first-order) logic. In particular, by a constructive proof of $\exists x A(x)$ we do not mean a proof in intuitionistic logic or some other 'constructive logic', but a classical derivation that demonstrates some closed term t to be a witness ('realization') for $\exists x A(x)$, i.e., a classical proof of $A(t)$.

We assume familiarity with standard notions for (classical) first-order logic. We refer to classical logic without equality (as a logical constant). By a *theory* we mean any set of closed first-order formulas. We write $T \vdash F$ if the formula F follows from the set of formulas T. By the completeness of first-order logic we can read $T \vdash F$ as 'T proves F'.

For clause logic let us fix the following terminology. *Literals* are negated or unnegated atomic formulas, called *atoms*. A *clause* is a finite set of literals. It is called *ground* if no variables occur in it. The result $C\sigma$ of applying a substitution σ to a clause C, where σ maps each variable in C into a closed (i.e. variable free) term, is called a *ground instance* of C.[1]

We will have to refer to clausal forms of formulas and theories. To keep the paper self-contained and unambiguous we provide the following definitions. To translate an arbitrary closed first-order formula F into a corresponding finite set of clauses we first apply the following rewrite rules to sub-formulas of F as often as possible:

1. $A \supset B \longmapsto \neg A \vee B$
2. $\neg(A \vee B) \longmapsto (\neg A \wedge \neg B)$
3. $\neg(A \wedge B) \longmapsto (\neg A \vee \neg B)$
4. $\neg \exists x A(x) \longmapsto \forall x \neg A(x)$
5. $\neg \forall x A(x) \longmapsto \exists x \neg A(x)$

Next we apply Skolemization. We assume the variable names to be standardized apart; i.e., each quantifier occurrence binds a unique variable. Each occurrence of

---

[1] We always assume the presence of a constant symbols in the language to prevent the set of closed terms from being empty.

an existentially quantified variable x is replaced by a *Skolem term* $f(y_1, \ldots, y_n)$, where f is a new function symbol and where $y_1, \ldots, y_n$ are the variables bound by those universal quantifiers, in the scope of which we find $\exists x$. Skolemization renders all quantifier occurrences redundant; consequently they are deleted.

Finally we convert the remaining formula into conjunctive normal form by iteratively applying the laws of distributivity. By collecting the literals in a disjunction of the conjunctive normal form we obtain a clause. The set of all such clauses is called the *clause form* $\mathrm{cl}(F)$ of the original formula F. For a theory T, its *clause form* $\mathrm{cl}(T)$ is defined as $\bigcup_{F \in T} \mathrm{cl}(F)$.

Remark 3. Note that, by fixing a strategy in the application of rewrite rules and Skolemization steps, we may assume the clause form of a formula or theory to be unique. This fact is of no importance for the existence of resolution refutations, but will help to understand the proof of our main theorem (Theorem 2), below.

Proposition 1. *For any theory T and closed formula A: $T \vdash A$ iff $cl(T) \cup cl(\neg A)$ is unsatisfiable.*

Ground resolution is the following well known rule on ground clauses:

$$\frac{\{A\} \cup C \quad \{\neg A\} \cup D}{C \cup D}$$

where $C \cup D$ is called the *(ground) resolvent* of $\{A\} \cup C$ and $\{\neg A\} \cup D$.

A *ground refutation* of a set of clauses C is a rooted binary tree of clauses satisfying the following properties:

1. the root node consists in the empty clause
2. every leaf node is a ground instance of a clause in C
3. if C and D are the two successor nodes (clauses) of an internal node E, then E is a ground resolvent of C and D.

It is a well known fact (see, e.g., [8]) that ground resolution is sound and complete in the following sense:

Theorem 1. *A set of clauses C is unsatisfiable iff there exists a ground resolution refutation of C.*

3 A Simple Language Translation

In order to formulate our main theorem at an appropriate level of generality, we partition the signature into two parts. More exactly, we assume that some constant and function symbols from the signature are called *constructor symbols*. Terms built up from constructor symbols only are called *constructor terms*.[2] To

---

[2] A partition of the signature into constructor symbols and non-constructor symbols is quite common in different contexts in computer science. By labelling certain terms 'constructor terms' we do not want to imply any special semantic role beyond what is explicit in the statements of our results, below. If one is only interested in the existence of any term (not just constructor terms) as witness to existential formulas, it suffices to consider all constant and function symbols as constructor symbols.

prevent the set of constructor terms from being empty, we will assume that at least one constant is a constructor symbol.

To simplify notation we will consider constant symbols as 0-ary function symbols. Moreover, let Σ always denote the set of constructor symbols from now on. We define a language translation that adds a new argument position to each non-constructor symbol as well as to each predicate symbol. More exactly, we associate a new $n+1$-ary predicate symbol P^* with each n-ary predicate symbol P ($n \geq 1$) of the original language and a new $k+1$-ary predicate symbol f^* with each k-ary predicate symbol f ($k \geq 0$) that is not in Σ. We define

for function symbols f (of arity $n \geq 0$):

$$\gamma_\Sigma^{(x)}(f(t_1,\ldots,t_n)) = f(t_1,\ldots,t_n) \ \text{ if } f \in \Sigma$$

$$\gamma_\Sigma^{(x)}(f(t_1,\ldots,t_n)) = f^*(\gamma_\Sigma^{(x)}(t_1),\ldots,\gamma_\Sigma^{(x)}(t_n),x) \ \text{ if } f \notin \Sigma$$

for predicate symbols P (of arity $n \geq 1$):

$$\gamma_\Sigma^{(x)}(P(t_1,\ldots,t_n)) = P^*(t_1,\ldots,t_n,x)$$

for compound formulas:

$$\gamma_\Sigma^{(x)}(\neg A) = \neg\gamma_\Sigma^{(x)}(A)$$

$$\gamma_\Sigma^{(x)}(A \vee B) = \gamma_\Sigma^{(x)}(A) \vee \gamma_\Sigma^{(x)}(B)$$

$$\gamma_\Sigma^{(x)}(A \wedge B) = \gamma_\Sigma^{(x)}(A) \wedge \gamma_\Sigma^{(x)}(B)$$

$$\gamma_\Sigma^{(x)}(A \supset B) = \gamma_\Sigma^{(x)}(A) \supset \gamma_\Sigma^{(x)}(B)$$

$$\gamma_\Sigma^{(x)}(\forall y A) = \forall y \gamma_\Sigma^{(x)}(A)$$

$$\gamma_\Sigma^{(x)}(\exists y A) = \exists y \gamma_\Sigma^{(x)}(A)$$

The translation of a theory T is defined as

$$C_\Sigma^\forall(T) = \{\forall x \gamma_\Sigma^{(x)}(A) \mid A \in T\},$$

for some variable x, that does not occur in T.[3]

The existential formulas $\exists x A(x)$, for which we interested in constructive provability with respect to x, are translated as follows:

$$C_\Sigma^\exists(\exists x A(x)) = \exists x \gamma_\Sigma^{(x)}(A(x)).$$

---

[3] Obviously, $C_\Sigma^\forall(T)$ is unique up to the name of the variable bound by the outermost universal quantifiers.

Example 1. It is important to note that we refer to pure first order logic without equality as a predefined logical symbol. In other words, if we want to apply the translation $\mathcal{C}_\Sigma^\forall$ to theories with equality, we have to make the equality axioms explicit and translate them using a new ternary predicate symbol E^* associated to the binary predicate '='.

E.g., for the transitivity axiom tr

$$\forall u \forall v \forall w (u = v \wedge v = w) \supset u = w$$

we have

$$\gamma_\Sigma^{(x)}(tr) = \forall u \forall v \forall w (E^*(u, v, x) \wedge E^*(v, w, x)) \supset E^*(u, w, x).$$

Likewise, the substitutivity axiom $subP$ for a binary predicate symbol P

$$\forall u \forall v \forall y \forall z (P(u, v) \wedge u = y \wedge v = z) \supset P(y, z)$$

turns into

$$\gamma_\Sigma^{(x)}(subP) = \forall u \forall v \forall y \forall z (P^*(u, v, x) \wedge E^*(u, y, x) \wedge E^*(v, z, x)) \supset P^*(v, w, x).$$

Example 2. In Example 1 there was no need to refer to function symbols. In contrast, let $F = \exists x P(d, f(c, g(f(x, d))))$, where c, d are constants, g is unary function symbol and f is a binary function symbol. Moreover let $\Sigma = \{c, g\}$. Then $\mathcal{C}_\Sigma^\forall(\{F\}) = \{\forall y \exists x P^*(c^*(y), f^*(c^*(y), g(f^*(x, d^*(y), y))), y)\}$ and $\mathcal{C}_\Sigma^\exists(\{F\}) = \exists x P^*(c^*(x), f^*(c^*(x), g(f^*(x, d^*(x), x))), x)$.

4 $\mathcal{C}^\forall / \mathcal{C}^\exists$ Is Adequate

The proof of our main theorem, below, relies on the particular structure of ground resolution refutations of clause sets corresponding to statements of form $\mathcal{C}_\Sigma^\forall(T) \vdash \mathcal{C}_\Sigma^\exists(\exists x A(x))$. The central property needed is highlighted in the following technical lemma.

Lemma 1. *Let S be a set of clauses where all atoms are of form $P_i(t_1, \ldots, t_{m_i}, x)$ for a fixed variable x. For all substitutions σ, τ applied to clauses of S in a ground resolution refutation we have:*

(1) $\sigma(x) = \tau(x)$.
(2) If f is a function symbol such that all terms of form $f(t_1, \ldots, t_k)$ occurring in S contain x as one of its arguments, then we may assume that $\sigma(x)$ does not contain f.

Proof. Property (1): In order to be resolvable the last argument terms of the two resolved atoms have to be identical. By the particular form of the clauses in S this implies that all last argument positions of literals in the resolved clauses are filled by the same term. This property is clearly inherited to resolvents and therefore is fulfilled by all clauses of the refutation.

Property (2): If x *only* occurs in the last argument position of atoms in clauses from S that are instantiated in the ground refutation, then x can be instantiated by any (fixed) term t. In particular, we can assume that t does not contain f.

The non-trivial case arises if x occurs not only as the last argument of the resolved atoms. One then has to unify at least one pair of atoms of form

$$\langle P(\dots t[x] \dots, x), \ P(\dots t'[s] \dots, x) \rangle$$

where the indicated occurrence of s in the second atom has to be matched with the first indicated occurrence of x in the first atom. In this case $\sigma(x) = s\sigma$. Therefore — since unifiers are idempotent ('occurs check') — s cannot contain a subterm of form $f(\dots, x, \dots)$. $\square$

Theorem 2. *Let T be a first-order theory and let $A(x)$ be a first-order formula with x as only free variable, and let Σ be the constructor symbols:*

$$T \vdash A(t) \text{ for some constructor term } t \ \Leftrightarrow \ \mathcal{C}_\Sigma^\forall(T) \vdash \mathcal{C}_\Sigma^\exists(\exists x A(x)).$$

Proof. ($\Rightarrow$:)   Assume $T \vdash A(t)$. By Proposition 1, $\mathrm{cl}(T) \cup \mathrm{cl}(\neg A(t))$ is an unsatisfiable set of clauses. By the completeness of ground resolution (Theorem 1) there is a ground resolution refutation ρ of $\mathrm{cl}(T) \cup \mathrm{cl}(\neg A(t))$.

Clearly, if we replace every occurrence of an atom $P(t_1, \dots, t_n)$ in ρ by $P^*(t_1, \dots, t_n, t)$, we are still left with a ground resolution refutation. The same is true if we further replace any subterm of form $f(s_1, \dots, s_n)$ in ρ, by $f^*(s_1, \dots, s_n, t)$ if $f \in \Sigma$. We call the resulting ground resolution refutation ρ'. Note that the translation $\mathcal{C}^\forall$ preserves the logical structure of T and A. In $\mathrm{cl}(\mathcal{C}_\Sigma^\exists(\neg\exists x A(x))$ $= \mathrm{cl}(\forall x \gamma_\Sigma^{(x)}(\neg A(x)))$ all argument positions corresponding to x are filled by the same variable within a clause. Therefore ρ' demonstrates the unsatisfiability of $\mathrm{cl}(\mathcal{C}_\Sigma^\forall(T)) \cup \mathrm{cl}(\mathcal{C}_\Sigma^\exists(\neg\exists x A(x)))$. By Proposition 1 we conclude that $\mathcal{C}_\Sigma^\forall(T) \vdash \mathcal{C}_\Sigma^\exists(\exists x A(x))$.

($\Leftarrow$:)   Assume $\mathcal{C}_\Sigma^\forall(T) \vdash \mathcal{C}_\Sigma^\exists(\exists x A(x))$. Again, we consider the clausal version of this statement, i.e.: $\mathrm{cl}(\mathcal{C}_\Sigma^\forall(T)) \cup \mathrm{cl}(\neg\mathcal{C}_\Sigma^\exists(\exists x A(x)))$ is unsatisfiable. Remember that $\mathrm{cl}(\neg\mathcal{C}_\Sigma^\exists(\exists x A(x))) = \mathrm{cl}(\forall x \gamma_\Sigma^{(x)}(\neg A(x)))$. The clauses in $\mathrm{cl}(\mathcal{C}_\Sigma^\forall(T)) \cup$ $\mathrm{cl}(\forall x \gamma_\Sigma^{(x)}(\neg A(x)))$ are identical to the ones in $\mathrm{cl}(T) \cup \mathrm{cl}(\forall x \neg A(x))$ except for an additional last argument place in each atom and each subterm with a constructor symbol as leading symbol. This additional argument place is uniformly filled by the variable x. By Theorem 1 there is a ground resolution refutation ρ of $\mathrm{cl}(\mathcal{C}_\Sigma^\forall(T)) \cup \mathrm{cl}(\forall x \gamma_\Sigma^{(x)}(\neg A(x)))$. By part (1) of Lemma 1 we know that every substitution, that is applied to some clause in this set to obtain ρ, maps x into the same term — let's call it t. Observe that the outermost quantifier in $\mathcal{C}_\Sigma^\forall(T)$ as well as in $\neg\mathcal{C}_\Sigma^\exists(\exists x A(x)) = \forall x \gamma_\Sigma^{(x)}(\neg A(x))$ binds x. Therefore all Skolem terms in $\mathrm{cl}(\mathcal{C}_\Sigma^\forall(T)) \cup \mathrm{cl}(\forall x \gamma_\Sigma^{(x)}(A(x)))$ contain x as an argument. We conclude by part (2) of Lemma 1 that t does not contain Skolem functions; i.e., it is a term in the original language of T. For the same reason it follows that t can only be built up from constructor symbols, since $\gamma_\Sigma^{(x)}$ ensures that all terms containing non-constructor symbols also contain x. In other words: t is a constructor term.

We obtain a refutation of $\mathrm{cl}(T) \cup \mathrm{cl}(\neg A(t))$ from ρ, by simply deleting the last argument position in each atom and replacing each predicate symbol P^* by P. By the correctness of ground resolution and Proposition 1 this shows that $T \vdash A(t)$. $\square$

Remark 4. As pointed out by a referee to an earlier version of this paper, one may prove the theorem also by model theoretic arguments (at least in the case where all terms are constructor terms). However, below, we will show that our proof method allows to extract a primitive recursive bound for the size of witness terms. This seems only possible when referring to proof theoretic methods. The advantage of a model theoretic construction lies in the potential extension of the results to second order logic, which is beyond the limits of resolution and Herbrand's theorem.

Our formulation of Theorem 2 distinguishes between constructor terms and terms that may contain non-constructor symbols. This should not distract from the fact that the special case where we ask for the existence of *any* term as witness for an existential claim is already of considerable interest. In the following we will often drop the reference to constructor symbols and implicitly assume that *all* function symbols are treated as like constructor symbols: i.e., $\gamma_{\Sigma}^{(x)}(t)$, written now as $\gamma^{(x)}(t)$, is identical to t for all terms t, in this case.

We will say that T *proves* $\exists x A(x)$ *constructively (with respect to x)* if $T \vdash A(t)$ for some closed term t. Thus Theorem 2 can be re-phrased as: $\mathcal{C}^{\forall}(T)$ proves the translations of exactly those formulas $\exists x A(x)$, which T proves constructively.

Corollary 1. *Let T be a first-order theory and let $A(x)$ be a first-order formula with x as only free variable: let Σ be the constructor symbols:*

$$T \text{ proves } \exists x A(x) \text{ constructively} \;\Leftrightarrow\; \mathcal{C}^{\forall}(T) \vdash \mathcal{C}^{\exists}(\exists x A(x)).$$

Example 3. It may help the reader to check the theorem for the following, almost trivial case. Let $T = \{\forall y \exists z P(y, z)\}$. Assume the constant 0 to be in the language. Then T obviously proves $\exists x P(0, x)$, but *not constructively* so.

Indeed, $\gamma^{(x)}(\forall y \exists z P(y, z)) = \forall x \forall y \exists z P^*(y, z, x)$ — i.e., the only member of $\mathcal{C}^{\forall}(T)$ — does not imply $\mathcal{C}^{\exists}(\exists x P(0, x)) = \exists x P^*(0, x, x)$; just as Corollary 1 states.

Example 4. Let $T = \{\forall v \exists z P(v, p(s(v)))\}$, where $\Sigma = \{0, s\}$ (but p is a non-constructor symbol). T not only proves $\exists x P(0, x)$, but also $P(0, p(s(0)))$. However $p(s(0))$ is not a constructor term. Applying Theorem 2, we can check that no constructor term serves as witness for the existential claim by checking that $\mathcal{C}_{\Sigma}^{\forall}(T) \nvdash \mathcal{C}_{\Sigma}^{\exists}(\exists x P(0, x))$. Indeed, the only member of $\mathcal{C}_{\Sigma}^{\forall}(T)$ is $\forall x \gamma_{\Sigma}^{(x)}(\forall v \exists z P(v, p(s(v)))) = \forall x \forall v \exists z P^*(v, p^*(s(v), x), x)$; and this formula does not imply $\mathcal{C}_{\Sigma}^{\exists}(\exists x P(0, x)) = \exists x P^*(0, x, x)$.

If, however, we set $\Sigma = \{0, s, p\}$, then $p(s(0))$ is a constructor term. Now $\forall x \gamma_{\Sigma}^{(x)}(\forall v \exists z P(v, p(s(v)))) = \forall x \forall v \exists z P^*(v, p^*(s(v)), x)$ *does* imply $\mathcal{C}_{\Sigma}^{\exists}(\exists x P(0, x)) = \exists x P^*(0, x, x)$, in compliance with Theorem 2.

Example 5. For another simple example consider $T = \{\forall y P(1,y) \vee P(2,y)\}$. $\exists x \exists y P(x,y)$ follows from T but, again, no witness for x can be provided.

Indeed, it is easy to construct counterexamples to $\mathcal{C}^{\forall}(T) \vdash \mathcal{C}^{\exists}(\exists x \exists y P(x,y))$: Take $\{1,2\}$ as universe of discourse. Since

$$\mathcal{C}^{\forall}(T) = \{\forall x \forall y P^*(1,y,x) \vee P^*(2,y,x)\}$$

and

$$\gamma^{(x)}(\exists x \exists y P(x,y)) = \exists x \exists y P^*(x,y,x)$$

it suffices to set $P^*(1,1,1)$, $P^*(1,2,1)$, $P^*(2,1,2)$, as well as $P^*(2,2,2)$ *false*, but $P^*(k,l,m)$ *true* for all other combinations of $k,l,m \in \{1,2\}$.

On the other hand,

$$\gamma^{(x)}(\exists x \exists y \exists z P(x,y) \vee P(z,x)) = \exists x \exists y \exists z P^*(x,y,x) \vee P^*(z,x,x)$$

is derivable from $\mathcal{C}^{\forall}(T)$; and indeed, $T \vdash \exists y \exists z P(1,y) \vee P(z,1)$. I.e., the constant 1 is a witness, with respect to the first existential quantifier, for the truth of the formula $\exists x \exists y \exists z P(x,y) \vee P(z,x)$ in T. In other words T proves this formula constructively with respect to x.

A Paradigmatic Example

We analyze another simple, but famous example for non-constructivity (see, e.g., [7]) to illustrate possible applications of Theorem 2.

Claim. There are irrational numbers a,b such that a^b is rational.

Proof. Consider $\sqrt{2}^{\sqrt{2}}$. If $\sqrt{2}^{\sqrt{2}}$ is rational let $a = b = \sqrt{2}$. If $\sqrt{2}^{\sqrt{2}}$ is irrational let $a = \sqrt{2}^{\sqrt{2}}$ and $b = \sqrt{2}$, since then

$$a^b = \left(\sqrt{2}^{\sqrt{2}}\right)^{\sqrt{2}} = \sqrt{2}^{\sqrt{2}\cdot\sqrt{2}} = \sqrt{2}^2 = 2 \qquad \square$$

We formalize (the essence of) this argument using the constant $\sqrt{2}$, the function $\exp(x,y)$, written as x^y, and the predicate $R(x)$, representing 'rational'.

Let $T = \{\neg R(\sqrt{2}), R\left((\sqrt{2}^{\sqrt{2}})^{\sqrt{2}}\right)\}$. We have

$$T \vdash \exists x \exists y \neg R(x) \wedge \neg R(y) \wedge R(x^y)$$

$$\mathcal{C}_{\Sigma}^{\forall}(T) = \{\forall x \neg R^*(\sqrt{2},x), \forall x R^*\left((\sqrt{2}^{\sqrt{2}})^{\sqrt{2}},x\right)\}$$

$$\mathcal{C}_{\Sigma}^{\exists}(\exists x \exists y \neg R(x) \wedge \neg R(y) \wedge R(x^y)) = \exists x \exists y \neg R^*(x,x) \wedge \neg R^*(y,x) \wedge R^*(x^y,x)$$

We look for a structure $\mathcal{I} = \langle M, \bar{R}^*, \exp, \sqrt{2}\rangle$ that is a model for

$$\{\forall x \neg R^*(\sqrt{2},x), \forall x R^*\left((\sqrt{2}^{\sqrt{2}})^{\sqrt{2}},x\right), \forall x \forall y (R^*(x,x) \vee R^*(y,x) \vee \neg R^*(x^y,x))\}$$

and consequently a counterexample to

$$\mathcal{C}_{\Sigma}^{\forall}(T) \vdash \mathcal{C}_{\Sigma}^{\exists}(\exists x \exists y \neg R(x) \wedge \neg R(y) \wedge R(x^y))$$

$\mathcal{I}$ can be specified as the following term model:

- M is the set of terms constructed from $\sqrt{2}$ and $\exp(\cdot,\cdot)$
- $\bar{R}^*$ is given by:
  $(\sqrt{2}, v) \notin \bar{R}^*$ for all v,
  $(\sqrt{2}^{\sqrt{2}}, \sqrt{2}) \notin \bar{R}^*$, and
  $(u, v) \in \bar{R}^*$ else.

By Theorem 2 it follows that there is no term t such that

$$T \vdash \neg R(t) \wedge (\exists y \neg R(y) \wedge R(t^y)).$$

We invite the reader to check that T can be augmented by many more axioms about the field of real numbers without changing this fact.

5   A Bound on the Size of Witnessing Terms

By the *size* of a term we mean the number of symbols occurring in it. By the *logical complexity* of a formula or a sequent we mean the number of atomic subformulas occurring in it. By the *length* of a proof or a resolution refutation we mean the corresponding number of inference steps.

Theorem 2 (Corollary 1)[4] only states the existence of a witness term for $\exists x A(x)$ in the context of T, given a proof of $\mathcal{C}^\forall_\Sigma(T) \vdash \mathcal{C}^\exists_\Sigma(\exists x A(x))$. The proof in Section 4, however, indicates how a witness term can be extracted from such a given proof. We show this by proving a primitive recursive bound on the size of a witness term in terms of the size of a given proof of $\mathcal{C}^\forall_\Sigma(T) \vdash \mathcal{C}^\exists_\Sigma(\exists x A(x))$.[5] Without loss of generality we will assume that a proof of $\mathcal{C}^\forall_\Sigma(T) \vdash \mathcal{C}^\exists_\Sigma(\exists x A(x))$ is a derivation (from axiom sequents) of a sequent $\Gamma_1, \ldots, \Gamma_n \longrightarrow \mathcal{C}^\exists_\Sigma(\exists x A(x))$ in Gentzen's sequent calculus LK, where $\Gamma_i \in \mathcal{C}^\forall_\Sigma(T)$ for $i \in \{1, \ldots, n\}$. (For a details about LK see, e.g., [5].)

Theorem 3. *There exists a primitive recursive function ψ such that $T \vdash A(t)$ for a term t of size at most $\psi(l, m)$, where l is the size of a given proof of $\mathcal{C}^\forall(T) \vdash \mathcal{C}^\exists(\exists x A(x))$ and m is the logical complexity of the endsequent of this proof.*

Proof. (Sketch) A proof of $\mathcal{C}^\forall(T) \vdash \mathcal{C}^\exists(\exists x A(x))$ is an LK-derivation of a sequent $G_1, \ldots, G_n \longrightarrow F$, where $G_i \in \mathcal{C}^\forall(T)$, for $i \in \{1, \ldots, n\}$, and $F = \mathcal{C}^\exists(\exists x A(x))$.

We first Skolemize the derivation of $G_1, \ldots, G_n \longrightarrow F$. This means that the derivation is translated into one of $\mathrm{sk}(G_1), \ldots, \mathrm{sk}(G_n) \longrightarrow \mathrm{sk}(F)$, where $\mathrm{sk}(B)$ is the Skolemized form of B (i.e. all occurrences of variables bound by strong quantifier occurrences are replaced by appropriate Skolem terms). This transformation does not increase the length of the derivation. (Proof Skolemization

---

[4] From now on we treat all function symbols as 'constructor symbols' (i.e., as in Corollary 1). The generalization of the results to a partitioned signature is straightforward.

[5] Since we are not interested in optimal bounds, we essentially do not have to care about which underlying proof system is used or how exactly corresponding derivations are denoted.

is described in detail in [2].) Moreover — as also shown in [2] — we can transform the resulting derivation into one of $\text{sk}(G_1)^{pr}, \ldots, \text{sk}(G_n)^{pr} \longrightarrow \text{sk}(F)^{pr}$, where B^{pr} is the prenex normal form of B, thereby increasing the length of the derivation at most exponentially. Let us denote the LK-derivation obtained in this way σ.

Next, we transform σ into a derivation by σ' of the sequent

$$\text{clf}(\text{sk}(G_1)^{pr}), \ldots, \text{clf}(\text{sk}(G_n)^{pr}), \text{clf}(\neg \text{sk}(F)^{pr}) \longrightarrow , \tag{1}$$

where $\text{clf}(B)$ is the sequence of clauses in the clause form $\text{cl}(B)$ of B, if a clause is written as universal closure of the disjunction of its literals. This can be done as follows: For each G_i we join a derivation of the sequent $\text{clf}(\text{sk}(G_i)^{pr}) \longrightarrow \text{sk}(G_i)^{pr}$ to σ by cutting on $\text{sk}(G_i)^{pr}$. Similarly for F, after extending σ by introducing $\neg F$ on the left hand side the endsequent. The minimal length of cut-free derivations of $\text{clf}(B) \longrightarrow B$ is at most exponential in the logical complexity of B. (This follows from the fact that these derivations can be partitioned into a purely propositional part, followed by a sequence of universal quantifier introductions.) Therefore the length (and size) of σ' is exponentially bounded by the length (and size) of the original derivation of $G_1, \ldots, G_n \longrightarrow F$.

Next, we apply a standard cut-elimination procedure to obtain a cut-free sequent derivation σ^* of Σ. By [3], the length of σ^* is at most $\phi(k, m)$, where ϕ is some primitive recursive function, k is the length of σ', and m is the logical complexity of the endsequent of σ'.

Instances of formulas in sequent (1) are (up to the order of disjuncts) of form

$$\neg P_1 \vee \ldots \vee \neg P_\ell \vee P_{\ell+1} \vee \ldots \vee P_k,$$

where the P_i $(1 \leq i \leq k, k \geq 1)$ are atomic formulas. By the atomic sequent corresponding to such a formula we mean the sequent

$$P_1, \ldots, P_\ell \longrightarrow P_{\ell+1}, \ldots, P_k.$$

One can transform (see, e.g., [4]) a derivation (using atomic cuts) of form σ' into a derivation σ_ρ of the empty sequent from atomic sequents that correspond to instances of formulas in (1). The length of σ_ρ is polynomially bounded be the length of σ'. Clearly σ_ρ directly corresponds to a ground resolution refutation ρ of $\text{cl}(G_1) \cup \ldots \cup \text{cl}(G_n) \cup \text{cl}(\neg F)$.

According to the proof of Theorem 2, it remains to show that the size of terms occurring in a corresponding ground resolution refutation is appropriately bounded with respect to the length of the refutation and the size of terms in the input clauses. A ground resolution refutation ρ can be obtained from a non-ground, tree-like resolution refutation ρ' (where all clauses are renamed to be variable disjoint) of the same length by instantiating iteratively for each inference step all clauses with the most generalized unifiers used, and finally substituting the remaining variables by a constant. The terms in the co-domain of a most general unifier are at most exponentially bigger than the unified terms. Since, as seen above, the number of inference steps in ρ is bounded with respect to the length of the given proof of $\mathcal{C}^{\forall}(T) \vdash \mathcal{C}^{\exists}(\exists x A(x))$ and the logical complexity of its endsequent by a primitive recursive function, the claim follows. $\square$

6   More than One Existential Quantifier

So far, we have only considered constructivity with respect to a single existential quantifier. It is easy to generalize the definition of the translation to refer to whole a string of variables $x_1, \ldots, x_k$ instead.

We associate a new $n + k$-ary predicate symbol P^* with each n-ary predicate symbol P of the original language and define:

$$\gamma^{(x_1,\ldots,x_k)}(P(t_1,\ldots,t_n)) = P^*(t_1,\ldots,t_n,x_1,\ldots,x_k),$$

For compound formulas $\gamma^{(x_1,\ldots,x_k)}$ is defined exactly as $\gamma^{(x)}_\Sigma$, above.

The translation of a theory T with respect to new variables $x_1,\ldots,x_k$ is defined as

$$\mathcal{C}^{k\forall}(T) = \{\forall x_1 \ldots \forall x_k \gamma^{(x_1,\ldots,x_k)}(A) \mid A \in T\}.$$

The existentially quantified formulas $\exists x_1 \ldots \exists x_k A(x_1,\ldots,x_k)$ for which we interested in the existence of provable witnesses for $x_1,\ldots,x_k$, respectively, are translated as

$$\mathcal{C}^{k\exists}(\exists x_1 \ldots \exists x_k A(x_1,\ldots,x_k)) = \exists x_1 \ldots \exists x_k \gamma^{(x_1,\ldots,x_k)}(A(x_1,\ldots,x_k)).$$

Given these definitions, Theorem 2 can straightforwardly be generalized to the following form:

Corollary 2. *Let T be a theory and let $B = \exists x_1 \ldots \exists x_k A(x_1,\ldots,x_k)$, where $x_1,\ldots,x_k$ are the only free variables in A:*

$$T \vdash A(t_1,\ldots,t_k) \text{ for some closed terms } t_1,\ldots,t_k \Leftrightarrow \mathcal{C}^{k\forall}(T) \vdash \mathcal{C}^{k\exists}(B).$$

By T *proves* $\exists x_1 \ldots \exists x_k A(x_1,\ldots,x_k)$ *constructively (with respect to $x_1,\ldots,x_k$),* we mean $T \vdash A(t_1,\ldots,t_k)$ for some closed terms $t_1,\ldots,t_k$.

7   (Un)decidability of Constructive Provability

At the first glance one could think of the decision problem of constructive provability as the quest for an algorithm which correctly reports whether an existential formula is constructively provable or not. However, this is in contrast to mathematical practice, where usually some proof of an existential statement precedes the question for a constructive proof of it.

We therefore say *constructive provability is decidable for a theory T* (possibly with respect to some class $\mathcal{A}$ of formulas) if there exists an algorithm which expects a proof of $\exists x_1 \ldots \exists x_k A(x_1,\ldots,x_k)$ $(\in \mathcal{A})$ from the axioms T as input, and outputs 'yes' if T proves $\exists x_1 \ldots \exists x_k A(x_1,\ldots,x_k)$ also constructively, and outputs 'no' otherwise.

If it is algorithmically undecidable whether an existential formula is provable in a theory T, then also constructive provability will frequently be undecidable. In contrast, as the following example shows, there are large, natural classes of theories T, where T is undecidable in general, but for which constructive provability is trivially decidable, since, for all relevant A, $T \vdash \exists x A(x)$ implies $T \vdash A(t)$ for some term t.

Horn Theories

A *universal Horn theory* is a set of closed formulas of form

$$\forall x_1 \ldots \forall x_k (A_1 \wedge \ldots \wedge A_n) \supset B$$

or of form

$$\forall x_1 \ldots \forall x_k B,$$

where B and all A_i $(1 \leq i \leq n)$ are atoms. Of course, universal Horn theories are undecidable (even with respect to atomic formulas) in general.

Observe that all *equational theories* are universal Horn theories in equality-free logic: not only the equations themselves, but also all equality axioms are of the required form.

Clearly, universal Horn theories correspond to *(pure, negation-free) logic programs*, i.e., sets of definite Horn clauses.[6] It is well known (see, e.g, [9]) that for every pure logic program $\mathcal{P}$ certain resolution strategies compute an *answer substitution* σ for the variables in a *query* C, represented as clause of form $\{\neg A_1, \ldots, \neg A_n\}$, if the set of clauses $\{C\} \cup \mathcal{P}$ is unsatisfiable. Without loss of generality we can assume that σ maps the variables of C into *ground terms*.

Using the previously introduced terminology, this fact can equivalently be expressed as follows:

Proposition 2. *If a closed formula of form $\exists x_1 \ldots \exists x_k B_1 \wedge \ldots \wedge B_n$, where the B_i are atomic formulas, follows from a universal Horn theory T, then T proves $\exists x_1 \ldots \exists x_k B_1 \wedge \ldots \wedge B_n$ also constructively with respect to $x_1, \ldots, x_k$.*

Note that already the very simple Example 3, above, shows that it is essential for Proposition 2 to hold, that T is universal. Moreover, as Example 5 demonstrates, that Proposition 2 does not hold if T is (universal but) not Horn.

Theories of Real Closed Fields

We consider the following presentation RCF of real closed fields: The language contains the unary predicate symbol '> 0', the binary predicate symbol '$=$', the constants 0 and 1, the unary function symbol $-$, and the binary function symbols $+$ and $\times$.[7] Axioms for ordered real closed fields are:

1. Equality axioms
2. Axioms for a commutative field
3. Order axioms
4. The axiom

$$(\forall x)(\exists y)(x = y^2 \vee -x = y^2)$$

   asserting the existence of square roots

---

[6] A definite Horn clause is a clause in which exactly one of its literals is unnegated.
[7] As usual, we write st for $s \times t$ and s^n for $(s \times (\ldots \times s))$.

$$\underbrace{\qquad\qquad}_{n \text{ times}}$$

5. The infinite set of axioms

$$(\forall x_0)\ldots(\forall x_{2n})(\exists y)(x_0 + x_1 y + \cdots + x_{2n}y^{2n} + y^{2n+1} = 0$$

asserting the existence of a root for every polynomial of odd degree.

Observe that the language is such that all ground terms (i.e., variable free terms) denote integers. A *diophantic polynomial* $p(x_1, \ldots, x_k)$ is a term of form

$$t_0 + (t_1 x_{1_1}^{n_{1_1}} \cdots x_{1_m}^{n_{1_m}}) + \ldots + (t_k x_{k_1}^{n_{k_1}} \cdots x_{k_m}^{n_{k_m}})$$

where the t_i are ground terms, the x_{i_j} are variables $\in \{x_1, \ldots, x_k\}$, and the n_{i_j} are positive integers.

By a well known result of Tarski (see, e.g., [6]) RCF is decidable. In particular one can decide for all diophantic polynomials whether

$$RCF \vdash \exists x_1 \ldots \exists x_k p(x_1, \ldots, x_k) = 0.$$

But what about

$$\mathcal{C}^{k\forall}(RCF) \vdash \mathcal{C}^{k\exists}(\exists x_1 \ldots \exists x_k p(x_1, \ldots, x_k) = 0) ?$$

Since all ground terms denote (easily computable) integers, it follows directly from Matiyasevič's negative solution of Hilbert's Tenth Problem (see [10]) and Theorem 2 that this problem is undecidable. Since the undecidability of the existence of integer solutions holds also for classes of polynomials that always have roots in the real numbers[8], one also obtains the undecidability of constructive provability for RCF.

Observe that the undecidability of constructive provability for RCF depends on the language chosen to represent the theory of real closed fields. It is well known how a binary function symbol can be replaced by a ternary predicate. Let RCF^* by the reformulation of RCF where $\times$ and $+$ are replaced by predicates M and P, respectively. I.e., $u \times v = w$ ($u + v = w$) is now represented as $M(u, v, w)$ ($P(u, v, w)$). Since, for this language, all ground terms denote either 0, 1, or -1, one can algorithmically check whether RCF^* proves $\exists x_1 \ldots \exists x_k [p(x_1, \ldots, x_k) = 0]^*$ constructively, where $[p(x_1, \ldots, x_k) = 0]^*$ is the formula expressing $p(x_1, \ldots, x_k) = 0$ in the new language.

8   Conclusion

The method of proof used for the main result (Theorem 2) of this paper relies specifically on a strong connectivity property of ground resolution refutations. These resolution proofs can be considered as variants of Herbrand's Theorem, which is used in their justification. Herbrand's Theorem however does not enforce connectivity of the atoms of the Herbrand disjunction and can therefore not replace the reference to the resolution calculus as basis of the argument. To sum up, this paper is based on the frequently denied proof theoretic significance of the resolution calculus.

---

[8] Take, e.g., those $p(x_1, \ldots, x_k)$ in which the maximal number of variable occurrences in a summand with non-zero coefficient is odd.

References

1. Matthias Baaz. Note on a translation to characterize constructivity. *Proc. of the Steklov Institute 242* (Selected papers of the Novikov-conference), to appear.
2. Matthias Baaz and Alexander Leitsch. Cut normal forms and proof complexity. *Ann. Pure Appl. Logic*, pages 127–177, 1999.
3. Jan Krajíćek and Pawel Pudlák. The number of proof lines and the size of proofs in first-order logic. *Arch. Math. Logic* 27 (1988), pages 69–84.
4. Grigori Mints. Gentzen-type systems and Resolution Rule. Part II. *Logic Colloquium '90*. Lecture Notes in Logic 2, 1994, pages 163–190.
5. Gaisi Takeuti. *Proof Theory*. North Holland, 1987.
6. Alfred Tarski. *A Decision Method for Elementary Algebra and Geometry*. University of California Press, 1951.
7. A. Troelstra and D. van Dalen. *Constructivism in Mathematics, An Introduction*. Volume I. North Holland, 1988.
8. Alexander Leitsch. *The Resolution Calculus*. EATCS Texts in Theoretical Computer Science. Springer, 1997.
9. J.W. Lloyd. *Foundations of Logic Programming*. Springer, 1987.
10. Yuri Matjasevich. *Hilbert's Tenth Problem*. The MIT Press, Cambridge, London, 1993.

Extensions of Non-standard Inferences to Description Logics with Transitive Roles

Sebastian Brandt[1], Anni-Yasmin Turhan[1], and Ralf Küsters[2,*]

[1] Institute for Theoretical Computer Science, TU Dresden, Germany,
{brandt,turhan}@tcs.inf.tu-dresden.de
[2] Theoretical Computer Science, CAU Kiel, Germany,
kuesters@ti.informatik.uni-kiel.de

Abstract. Description Logics (DLs) are a family of knowledge representation formalisms used for terminological reasoning. They have a wide range of applications such as medical knowledge-bases, or the semantic web. Research on DLs has been focused on the development of sound and complete inference algorithms to decide satisfiability and subsumption for increasingly expressive DLs. Non-standard inferences are a group of relatively new inference services which provide reasoning support for the building, maintaining, and deployment of DL knowledge-bases. So far, non-standard inferences are not available for very expressive DLs. In this paper we present first results on non-standard inferences for DLs with transitive roles. As a basis, we give a structural characterization of subsumption for DLs where existential and value restrictions can be imposed on transitive roles. We propose sound and complete algorithms to compute the least common subsumer (lcs).

1 Introduction and Motivation

Description Logics (DLs) are a family of formalisms used to represent terminological knowledge of a given application domain in a structured and well-defined way. The basic notions of DLs are *concept-descriptions* and *roles*, representing unary predicates and binary relations, respectively. Atomic concepts and concept descriptions represent sets of individuals, whereas roles represent binary relations between individuals [5]. The main characteristic of a DL is the set of concept constructors by which complex concept descriptions can be built from atomic concepts and roles. In the present paper, we are concerned with the DL $\mathcal{FLE}^+$ which provides the constructors conjunction ($C \sqcap D$), existential restriction ($\exists r.C$), value restriction ($\forall r.C$), and the top concept ($\top$).

In $\mathcal{FLE}^+$, a role can be defined transitive. In this case it represents the transitive closure of a binary relation. Transitive roles appear naturally in many application domains, such as medicine and process engineering [1]. Consider, for instance, a machine that comprises several components each of which again consists of several devices. A natural way to represent such a machine by means of

---

* This work has been supported by the Deutsche Forschungsgemeinschaft, DFG Project BA 1122/4-3.

M.Y. Vardi and A. Voronkov (Eds.): LPAR 2003, LNAI 2850, pp. 122–136, 2003.

DLs would be to use some *has-part* role to reflect its compositional structure. It would be natural here to implicitly regard every part of a component also as a part of the whole. To this end, a DL with transitive roles is necessary.

Inference problems for DLs are divided into so-called standard and non-standard ones. Well known standard inference problems are satisfiability and subsumption of concept descriptions. These are well investigated for a great range of DLs. For many of them, sound and complete decision procedures could be devised and lower and upper bounds for the computational complexity have been found [12]. Many standard inference algorithms have been successfully extended to cope with transitive roles [13, 14] and are put into practice in state of the art DL Systems.

Prominent non-standard inferences are matching, the least common subsumer (lcs), the most specific concept (msc), and, more recently, approximation. Non-standard inferences resulted from the experience with real-world DL-knowledge bases (KBs), where standard inference algorithms sometimes did not suffice for building and maintaining purposes. For example, the problem of how to structure the application domain by means of concept definitions may not be clear at the beginning of the modeling task. Moreover, the expressive power of the DL under consideration sometimes makes it difficult to come up with a faithful formal definition of the concept originally intended. To alleviate these difficulties it is expedient to employ non-standard inferences [8].

The lcs was first mentioned as an inference problem for DLs in [11]. Given two concept descriptions A and B in a description logic $\mathcal{L}$, the lcs of A and B is defined as the least (w.r.t. subsumption) concept description in $\mathcal{L}$ subsuming A and B. It has been argued in [8] that the lcs facilitates a "bottom-up"-approach to the above mentioned modeling task: a domain expert can select a number of intuitively related concept descriptions already existent in a KB and use the lcs operation to automatically construct a new concept description representing the closest generalization of them.

Matching in DLs was first proposed in [7]. A matching problem (modulo subsumption) consists of a concept description C and a concept *pattern* D, i.e., a concept description with variables. Matching D against C means finding a substitution of variables in D by concept descriptions such that C is subsumed by the instantiated concept pattern D. Among other applications, matching can be employed for queries in KBs: a domain expert unable to specify uniquely the concept he is looking for in a KB can use a concept pattern to retrieve all those concepts in the KB for which a matcher exists. The structural constraints expressible by patterns exceed the capabilities of simple "wildcards" familiar from ordinary search engines [8].

Approximation was first mentioned as a new inference problem in [4]. The upper (lower) approximation of a concept description C_1 from a DL $\mathcal{L}_1$ is defined as the least (greatest) concept description in another DL $\mathcal{L}_2$ which subsumes (is subsumed by) C_1. Approximation can be used to make non-standard inferences accessible to more expressive DLs by transferring a given inference problem to a less expressive DL where at least an approximate solution can be computed.

Another application of approximation lies in user-friendly DL-systems offering a simplified frame-based view on KBs defined in a more expressive background DL [6]. Here approximation can be used to compute simple frame-based representations of otherwise overwhelmingly complicated concept descriptions.

In contrast to standard inference problems, comparatively little research exists on non-standard inferences in DLs with transitive roles [2]. If existential restrictions can be expressed in a DL then the inferences matching and approximation are defined by means of the lcs operation. This central role of the lcs for non-standard inferences has lead us to make this inference problem the first to be extended to $\mathcal{FLE}^+$. Experience with other DLs has shown that to find an lcs algorithm is the crucial step towards algorithms for other non-standard inferences such as matching and approximation. For this reason the lcs in $\mathcal{FLE}^+$ may be regarded as the foundation of several other non-standard inferences in $\mathcal{FLE}^+$. After introducing some basic notions and notation, our first step towards the lcs will be a characterization of subsumption for $\mathcal{FLE}^+$-concept descriptions by means of so-called *description graphs*. We shall see that for two $\mathcal{FLE}^+$-concept descriptions A and B, subsumption ($A \sqsubseteq B$) holds if and only if there exists a simulation relation from the description graph of B into the one of A. The lcs inference of A and B is then defined as the graph product of the respective description graphs.

As a result, we shall see that the lcs of a finite set of $\mathcal{FLE}^+$-concept descriptions always exists and is uniquely determined up to equivalence. Moreover, an effective algorithm for the computation of the lcs will be provided.

All technical details and relevant proofs can be found in our technical report [9]. Moreover, the problem of the lcs computation in two sublanguages of $\mathcal{FLE}^+$, namely $\mathcal{FL}_0^+$ and $\mathcal{EL}^+$, is also addressed in detail.

2   Preliminaries

DLs are based on the following sets of names: N_C is the set of concept names, and N_R is the set of non-transitive roles, and N_R^T is the set of transitive roles, where $N_R \cap N_R^T = \emptyset$. Concept descriptions are inductively defined starting from the set of concept names and use the concept constructors shown in Table 1. The DL $\mathcal{FLE}$ offers the top-concept, conjunction, existential, and value restrictions,

Table 1. Syntax and semantics of $\mathcal{FLE}^+$-concept descriptions.

Construct name	Syntax	Semantics
top-concept	$\top$	$\Delta_\mathcal{I}$
conjunction	$C \sqcap D$	$C^\mathcal{I} \cap D^\mathcal{I}$
existential restrictions	$\exists r.C$	$\{x \in \Delta_\mathcal{I} \mid \exists y : (x, y) \in r^\mathcal{I} \wedge y \in C^\mathcal{I}\}$
value restrictions	$\forall r.C$	$\{x \in \Delta_\mathcal{I} \mid \forall y : (x, y) \in r^\mathcal{I} \rightarrow y \in C^\mathcal{I}\}$
transitive roles	r^+	$\bigcup_{1 \leq n} (r^\mathcal{I})^n$

as displayed in Table 1. In $\mathcal{FLE}^+$, transitive roles can be used in existential and value restrictions.

As usual, the semantics of a concept description is defined in terms of an *interpretation* $\mathcal{I} = (\Delta, \cdot^I)$. The domain Δ of $\mathcal{I}$ is a non-empty set and the interpretation function $\cdot^I$ maps each concept name $A \in N_C$ to a set $A^I \subseteq \Delta$ and each role name $r \in N_R \cup N_R^T$ to a binary relation $r^I \subseteq \Delta \times \Delta$. The extension of $\cdot^I$ to arbitrary concept descriptions is defined inductively, as shown in the second column of Table 1. Note that all concept descriptions in the above mentioned DLs are satisfiable.

One of the most important traditional inference services provided by DL systems is computing the subsumption hierarchy. The concept description C is *subsumed* by the description D ($C \sqsubseteq D$) iff $C^I \subseteq D^I$ for all interpretations $\mathcal{I}$; C and D are *equivalent* ($C \equiv D$) iff $C \sqsubseteq D$ and $D \sqsubseteq C$.

In this paper we focus on the *non-standard inference* of computing the *least common subsumer (lcs)*.

Definition 1 (lcs). *Given $\mathcal{L}$-concept descriptions $C_1, \ldots, C_n$, for some description logic $\mathcal{L}$, the $\mathcal{L}$-concept description C is the* least common subsumer *(lcs) of $C_1, \ldots, C_n$ ($C = \mathsf{lcs}(C_1, \ldots, C_n)$ for short) iff (i) $C_i \sqsubseteq C$ for all $1 \leq i \leq n$, and (ii) C is the least concept description with this property, i.e., if C' satisfies $C_i \sqsubseteq C'$ for all $1 \leq i \leq n$, then $C \sqsubseteq C'$.*

The idea behind the lcs inference is to extract the commonalities of the input concepts. The lcs is uniquely determined up to equivalence. Therefore it is justified to speak about "the" lcs instead of "an" lcs.

3   Least Common Subsumer for $\mathcal{FLE}^+$

The lcs has already been investigated for sub-logics of $\mathcal{FLE}^+$. The work of Baader et al. [3, 4] investigates the computation of the lcs in $\mathcal{FLE}$ and its sublanguages.

As long as a sublanguage of $\mathcal{FLE}$ does not allow for both existential and value restrictions it is comparatively easy to adapt the existing lcs algorithms to transitive roles. In [9] this is done both for $\mathcal{FL}_0$, admitting only conjunction and value restrictions, as well as for $\mathcal{EL}$, where only conjunction and existential restrictions are admitted. For $\mathcal{EL}^+$, it is possible to translate a concept C into an equivalent one in $\mathcal{EL}$. Thus, all the additional restrictions imposed by transitive roles in C are made explicit. This simple approach, however, does not work for $\mathcal{FLE}^+$-concept descriptions, as the following example illustrates.

Example 1. Consider the $\mathcal{FLE}^+$-concept description $C_{\text{ex}} := (\forall r.\exists r.A) \sqcap \exists r.A$, where r is transitive. To explicitly satisfy the (transitive) value restriction, we need to propagate $\forall r.\exists r.A$ to the existential restriction. This yields $(\forall r.\exists r.A) \sqcap \exists r.(A \sqcap \exists r.A \sqcap \forall r.\exists r.A)$ which equals $(\forall r.\exists r.A) \sqcap \exists r.(A \sqcap C_{\text{ex}})$. Obviously, an attempt of exhaustive propagation would not terminate.

Hence, our first aim is to find a finite representation of $\mathcal{FLE}^+$-concept descriptions in which the transitivity of roles is made explicit. Such a representation is introduced by the following section.

3.1 Description Graphs

In this section we will not only introduce description graphs as a syntactic construct but also provide a model-theoretic semantics for them which makes it easier to examine the equivalence between a concept description and a description graphs directly.

Definition 2 (Description Graph). *Let $\mathcal{G} := (V, E, v_0, \ell_V, \ell_E)$ be a rooted, directed, and connected graph with labeling functions for vertices and edges. The labeling function ℓ_V assigns a set of concept descriptions to every vertex in V and ℓ_E assigns a label of the form Qr to every edge in E, where $Q \in \{\forall, \exists\}$ and $r \in N_R \cup N_R^T$. An edge labeled $\forall r$ is called* forall-edge, *an edge labeled $\exists r$* exists-edge. *If every vertex v in $\mathcal{G}$ has at most one outgoing forall-edge per role then it is called a* description graph.

For the sake of simplicity, we use the notation $(v\, Qr\, w) \in E$ to express that (i) $(v, w) \in E$ and (ii) $\ell_E(v, w) = \{Qr\}$. Note that description graphs can be cyclic. Like concept descriptions, description graphs are interpreted w.r.t. a model-theoretic semantics to be introduced next.

Definition 3 (Semantics of Description Graphs). *Let $\mathcal{G} := (V, E, v_0, \ell_V, \ell_E)$ be a description graph and let $\mathcal{I} := (\Delta, \cdot^{\mathcal{I}})$ be an interpretation. A mapping $\pi \colon V \to 2^{\Delta^{\mathcal{I}}} \setminus \emptyset$ is called a* model mapping *iff for all $v, w \in V$ it holds that:*

- $\pi(v) \subseteq C^{\mathcal{I}}$ for all $C \in \ell(v)$;
- *if $(v\, \exists r\, w) \in E$ for $r \in N_R$ and $x \in \pi(v)$ then there exists some $y \in \Delta^{\mathcal{I}}$ with $(x, y) \in r^{\mathcal{I}}$ and $y \in \pi(w)$;*
- *if $(v\, \exists r\, w) \in E$ for $r \in N_R^T$ and $x \in \pi(v)$ then there exists some $y \in \Delta^{\mathcal{I}}$ with $(x, y) \in (r^{\mathcal{I}})^+$ and $y \in \pi(w)$;*
- *if $(v\, \forall r\, w) \in E$ for $r \in N_R$ and $x \in \pi(v)$ then $(x, y) \in r^{\mathcal{I}}$ implies $y \in \pi(w)$.*

For a given $x \in \Delta^{\mathcal{I}}$, define $\mathcal{I}, x \models \mathcal{G}$ iff there is a model mapping π with $x \in \pi(v_0)$. The semantics of $\mathcal{G}$ w.r.t. $\mathcal{I}$ is defined as $\mathcal{G}^{\mathcal{I}} := \{x \in \Delta^{\mathcal{I}} \mid \mathcal{I}, x \models \mathcal{G}_C\}$.

There is a similarity between the semantics of description graphs and that of concept descriptions as defined in Section 2. A (transitive) $\exists r$-edge $(v\, \exists r\, w)$ like an existential restriction implies a corresponding r-edge (r-path) for all witnesses $x \in \pi(v)$ in the model. Similarly, every $\forall r$-edge $(v\, \forall r\, w)$ imposes restrictions on every witness in the model reachable via an r-edge from some $x \in \pi(v)$.

Regarded as a description graph the syntax tree of every $\mathcal{FLE}$-concept description C is equivalent to C. This, however, is not generally true of $\mathcal{FLE}^+$-concept descriptions. Moreover, there are description graphs for which no equivalent $\mathcal{FLE}^+$-concept description exists. Ultimately, however, we are interested in description graphs guaranteed to represent concept descriptions. To this end, we introduce six conditions to restrict description graphs further, leading to the notion of simple description graphs. As a prerequisite, we need to specify the notion of a simulation relation for description graphs.

Definition 4 (Simulation Relation). *For $i \in \{1, 2\}$, let $\mathcal{G}_i := (V_i, E_i, v_{0i}, \ell_{V_i}, \ell_{E_i})$ be description graphs. Then, $\mathcal{G}_2 \precsim \mathcal{G}_1$ iff there exists a relation $R \subseteq V_2 \times V_1$ with:*

1. $(v_{02}, v_{01}) \in R$
2. $\ell_V(v) \cap N_C \subseteq \ell_V(v') \cap N_C$ *for all* $(v, v') \in R$.
3. *If* $(v \, Q r \, w) \in E_2$ *and* $(v, v') \in R$ *then there exists a vertex* $w' \in V_1$ *such that* $(v' \, Q r \, w') \in E_1$ *and* $(w, w') \in R$.

For vertices $v_1 \in V_1$ *and* $v_2 \in V_2$, *denote by* $\mathcal{G}_2(v_2) \rightleftharpoons \mathcal{G}_1(v_1)$ *the fact that a simulation relation* R *exists between the subgraph of* $\mathcal{G}_2$ *reachable from* v_2 *and the subgraph of* $\mathcal{G}_1$ *reachable from* v_1. *In particular, this implies* $(v_2, v_1) \in R$.

Definition 5 (Simple Description Graph). *Let* $\mathcal{G} := (V, E, v_0, \ell_V, \ell_E)$ *be a description graph.* $\mathcal{G}$ *is a* simple description graph *iff the following properties hold.*

1. *W.r.t. a breadth-first search tree,* $\mathcal{G}$ *has no forall-forward edges and no cross edges. Every exists-forward edge only connects vertices connected by a path of exists-tree edges w.r.t. one transitive role.*
2. *If* $(v_0 \, Q_0 r_0 \, v_1 \ldots v_{n-1} \, Q_{n-1} r_{n-1} \, v_0)$ *is a cycle in* E *with pairwise distinct vertices then there exists one transitive role* r *with* $r_i = r$ *for all* i.
3. *If* $(v_0 \, Q_0 r \, v_1 \ldots v_{n-1} \, Q_{n-1} r \, v_0)$ *is a cycle in* E *with pairwise distinct vertices and* $r \in N_R^T$ *then* v_0 *has a* $\forall r$*-successor.*
4. *If* $\{(u \, \forall r \, v), (u \, \exists r \, w)\} \subseteq E$ *then* $\mathcal{G}(v) \rightleftharpoons \mathcal{G}(w)$. *If* $r \in N_R^T$ *then there exists a vertex* w' *such that* $(w \, \forall r \, w') \in E$ *and* $\mathcal{G}(v) \rightleftharpoons \mathcal{G}(w')$.
5. *If* $(u \, \forall r \, v) \in E$ *with* $r \in N_R^T$ *then there exists a vertex* v' *such that* $(v \, \forall r \, v') \in E$ *and* $\mathcal{G}(v) \rightleftharpoons \mathcal{G}(v')$.
6. *If* $B \in \ell_V(v)$ *then* $\mathcal{G}_B \rightleftharpoons \mathcal{G}(v)$ *for every vertex* $v \in V$.

The idea behind the above definition to is imitate the propagation of existential and value restrictions in the graph structure. For instance, Condition 4 ensures that no subgraph representing an existential restriction may be more general that a corresponding subgraph representing a value restriction. Hence, a value restriction must be propagated over all existential restrictions. Condition 5 similarly ensures that value restrictions over transitive roles are propagated to deeper role levels, as $\forall r.A$ implies $\forall r.(A \sqcap (\forall r.A))$ and so on. Conditions 2 and 3 ensure that cycles cannot occur arbitrarily. By means of Condition 6, complex concept descriptions are already represented in the structure of the description graph. The first condition excludes a number of irregularities which would make the proofs over description graphs more intricate.

The following lemma can be shown for all description graphs.

Lemma 1. *For description graphs* $\mathcal{G}$ *and* $\mathcal{H}$ *it holds that* $\mathcal{H} \rightleftharpoons \mathcal{G}$ *implies* $\mathcal{G} \sqsubseteq \mathcal{H}$.

Having defined syntax and semantics of description graphs in general the next step is to translate $\mathcal{FLE}^+$-concept descriptions into equivalent description graphs.

3.2 Translation of $\mathcal{FLE}^+$-Concept Descriptions into $\mathcal{FLE}^+$-Description Graphs

To show that every $\mathcal{FLE}^+$-concept description has a corresponding $\mathcal{FLE}^+$-description graph we devise a suitable translation function. As a technical prerequisite, we require a normal form for $\mathcal{FLE}$-concept descriptions, as introduced in [3]. The purpose of this normal form is merely to flatten conjunctions, to make the top-concept explicit, and to propagate value restrictions over existential restrictions. The problem of implicit information induced by transitive roles remains untouched here.

Definition 6 ($\mathcal{FLE}$ Normalization Rules). *Let E, F be two $\mathcal{FLE}^+$-concept descriptions and $r \in N_R \cup N_R^T$ a primitive role. The $\mathcal{FLE}$-normalization rules are defined as follows*

1)	$\forall r.\top \longrightarrow \top$	3)	$\forall r.E \sqcap \forall r.F \longrightarrow \forall r.(E \sqcap F)$
2)	$E \sqcap \top \longrightarrow E$	4)	$\forall r.E \sqcap \exists r.F \longrightarrow \forall r.E \sqcap \exists r.(E \sqcap F)$
		5)	$E \sqcap (F \sqcap G) \longrightarrow E \sqcap F \sqcap G.$

A concept description is in $\mathcal{FLE}$-normal form if the $\mathcal{FLE}$-normalization rules have been applied to it exhaustively.

Each of the above normalization rules preserve equivalence and should be read modulo commutativity of conjunction. It has been shown in [3] that exhaustive application of these rules may produce concept descriptions of size exponential in the size of the original. During the translation of an $\mathcal{FLE}^+$-concept description into an $\mathcal{FLE}^+$-description tree the $\mathcal{FLE}$-normalization rules need to be applied only to the out most role-level of the $\mathcal{FLE}^+$-concept at a time.

The following definition provides the framework of the translation of $\mathcal{FLE}^+$-concept descriptions into description graphs. For a given concept description C we start with an empty description graph $\mathcal{G}$ consisting only of a root vertex v_0 with C in its label. Then we exhaustively apply graph generation rules (defined in detail in Figure 1) producing new vertices and edges. In this process we distinguish three kinds of edges. The set $E^\mathcal{D}$ contains the edges of the underlying spanning tree, in E^+ are the forward-edges induced by transitivity, and in $E^\circlearrowleft$ are self-loops or edges that connect a vertex with an ancestor vertex in w.r.t. the spanning tree. As soon as no production rules are applicable, all non-atomic concept descriptions are removed from the label sets of $\mathcal{G}$ and the graph is returned.

For the actual definition, a shorthand notation needs to be introduced first. For a set $\{C_1, \ldots, C_n\}$ of $\mathcal{FLE}^+$-concept descriptions, let $\{C_1, \ldots, C_n\}^*$ denote the corresponding set in which (i) the $\mathcal{FLE}^+$ normalization rules defined above have been applied exhaustively on the top most role-level of every C_i and (ii) every C_i is split into its conjuncts. Observe that there is at most one value restriction per role r in $\{C_1, \ldots, C_n\}^*$.

Definition 7 ($\mathcal{FLE}^+$-Description Graph). *Let C be a $\mathcal{FLE}^+$-concept description. The $\mathcal{FLE}^+$-description graph $\mathcal{G}_C$ is obtained by the following procedure:*

1. *Initialize the sets $V := \{v_0\}$, $\ell_V = \ell_V(v_0) = \{C\}^*$, and $E := E^+ := E^\mathcal{D} := E^\circlearrowleft := \emptyset$.*
2. *Apply the $\mathcal{FLE}^+$-description graph generation rules from Figure 1 exhaustively to obtain $\mathcal{G}_C' := (V, E, v_0, \ell_V, \ell_E)$, where $E = E^\mathcal{D} \cup E^\circlearrowleft \cup E^+$.*
3. *Reduce the label sets of vertices: $\forall v \in V: \ell_V'(v) := \ell_V(v) \cap N_C$.*
4. *return $\mathcal{G}_C := (V, E, v_0, \ell_V', \ell_E)$.*

$\mathbf{R}_\exists$:   If $(\exists r.C') \in \ell_V(v)$, $(\forall r.C'') \notin \ell_V(v)$ for some C', C'', and
there is no $v'' \in V : (v, \exists r, v'') \in E^{\mathcal{D}} \cup E^{\circlearrowleft} \wedge \{C'\}^* = \ell_V(v'')$,
then if there is $v_i \in V : v_i$ appears in $\rho(v) \wedge \ell_V(v_i) = \{C'\}^*$,
then $E^{\circlearrowleft} := E^{\circlearrowleft} \cup \{(v, \exists r, v_i)\}$,
else $V := V \cup \{v'\}$, $E^{\mathcal{D}} := E^{\mathcal{D}} \cup \{(v, \exists r, v')\}$, $\ell_V(v') := \{C'\}^*$.

$\mathbf{R}_{\exists\forall}$:   If $r \in N_R$, and $\{(\exists r.C'), (\forall r.C'')\} \subseteq \ell_V(v)$ for some C', C'', and
there is no $v'' \in V : (v, \exists r, v'') \in E^{\mathcal{D}} \cup E^{\circlearrowleft} \wedge \{C'\}^* = \ell_V(v'')$,
then if there is $v_i \in V : v_i$ appears in $\rho(v) \wedge \ell_V(v_i) = \{C'\}^*$
then $E^{\circlearrowleft} := E^{\circlearrowleft} \cup \{(v, \exists r, v_i)\}$,
else $V := V \cup \{v'\}$, $E^{\mathcal{D}} := E^{\mathcal{D}} \cup \{(v, \exists r, v')\}$, $\ell_V(v') := \{C'\}^*$.

$\mathbf{R}_{\exists\forall+}$: If $r \in N_R^T$, and $\{(\exists r.C'), (\forall r.C'')\} \subseteq \ell_V(v)$ for some C', C'', and
there is no $v'' \in V : (v, \exists r, v'') \in E^{\mathcal{D}} \cup E^{\circlearrowleft} \wedge \{C', \forall r.C''\} = \ell_V(v'')$,
then if there is $v_i \in V : v_i$ appears in $\rho(v) \wedge \ell_V(v_i) = \{C', \forall r.C''\}^*$
then $E^{\circlearrowleft} := E^{\circlearrowleft} \cup \{(v, \exists r, v_i)\}$,
else $V := V \cup \{v'\}$, $E^{\mathcal{D}} := E^{\mathcal{D}} \cup \{(v, \exists r, v')\}$, $\ell_V(v') := \{C', \forall r.C''\}^*$.

$\mathbf{R}_\forall$:   If $r \in N_R$, and $(\forall r.C') \in \ell_V(v)$ for some C', and
there is no $v'' \in V : (v, \forall r, v'') \in E^{\mathcal{D}} \cup E^{\circlearrowleft}$
then if there is $v_i \in V : v_i$ appears in $\rho(v) \wedge \ell_V(v_i) = \{C'\}^*$
then $E^{\circlearrowleft} := E^{\circlearrowleft} \cup \{(v, \forall r, v_i)\}$,
else $V := V \cup \{v'\}$, $E^{\mathcal{D}} := E^{\mathcal{D}} \cup \{(v, \forall r, v')\}$, $\ell_V(v') := \{C'\}^*$.

$\mathbf{R}_{\forall+}$:   If $r \in N_R^T$, and $(\forall r.C') \in \ell_V(v)$ for some C', and
there is no $v'' \in V : (v, \forall r, v'') \in E^{\mathcal{D}} \cup E^{\circlearrowleft}$
then if there is $v_i \in V : v_i$ appears in $\rho(v) \wedge \ell_V(v_i) = \{C', \forall r.C'\}^*$
then $E^{\circlearrowleft} := E^{\circlearrowleft} \cup \{(v, \forall r, v_i)\}$,
else $V := V \cup \{v'\}$, $E^{\mathcal{D}} := E^{\mathcal{D}} \cup \{(v, \forall r, v')\}$, $\ell_V(v') := \{C', \forall r.C'\}^*$.

$\mathbf{R}_{E+}$:   If $r \in N_R^T$, and $\{(v, \exists r, v'), (v', \exists r, v'')\} \in E^{\mathcal{D}}$ and $(v, \exists r, v'') \notin E^+$
then $E^+ := E^+ \cup \{(v, \exists r, v'')\}$

Fig. 1. $\mathcal{FLE}^+$-Description Graph Generation Rules.

All non-atomic concept descriptions in the label sets of the vertices of $\mathcal{G}$ are discarded afterwards because their information (as we shall see) is then represented by the structure of the graph. It remains to define the generation rules used in Step 2 of the above definition.

Figure 1 shows the generation rules referred to in Definition 7. For every v, $\rho(v)$ denotes the (unique) path from v_0 to v w.r.t. tree edges. Intuitively, the idea of the rules is to use the concept descriptions occurring in the label set of a vertex v to extend the description graph "accordingly", i.e., if an existential restriction $\exists r.C$ occurs in $\ell_V(v)$ then a vertex w must be introduced (or probably only found) such that (i) w is connected to v by an exists-edge and (ii) a concept equivalent to C occurs in $\ell_V(w)$. Moreover, a value restriction $\forall r.D$ probably also occurring in $\ell_V(v)D$ must be propagated to $\ell(w)$.

Starting at a given vertex v, the rules $\mathbf{R}_\exists$, $\mathbf{R}_{\exists\forall}$, and $\mathbf{R}_{\exists\forall+}$ all produce new exists-edges, possibly to a newly generated vertex. $\mathbf{R}_\exists$ applies if only an existential restriction is present in $\ell_V(v)$, $\mathbf{R}_{\exists\forall}$ applies if an additional value restriction (w.r.t. the same non-transitive role) is present, and $\mathbf{R}_{\exists\forall+}$ covers the analogous transitive case. Similarly, $\mathbf{R}_\forall$ and $\mathbf{R}_{\forall+}$ address the case where only a value restriction (non-transitive or transitive) is present. Rule $\mathbf{R}_{\exists+}$ never introduces new vertices but only adds forward-edges over exists-paths w.r.t. one transitive role.

To avoid generating infinitely many new vertices, every generation rule has a *blocking condition*[1] testing for every vertex v whether or not a new vertex w can be avoided by a back edge to an already existing ancestor vertex u. This is the case if the ancestor u has the same label set as the new vertex w would get, i.e., $\ell_V(u) = \ell_V(w)$. The vertex u is regarded as ancestor of v iff u lies on a (the) tree-path from the root vertex to v. Note that the condition $\ell_V(u) = \ell_V(w)$ determines u uniquely and that $v = w$ is not excepted. The following example shows the corresponding $\mathcal{FLE}^+$-description graph of two simple $\mathcal{FLE}^+$-concepts.

Example 2. Let $C_{ex} := \exists r.(B \sqcap \exists r.B \sqcap \forall r.\exists r.B)$ and $D_{ex} := \exists r.(\exists r.B \sqcap \forall r.\exists r.B)$ for a transitive role r and an atomic concept B. The corresponding $\mathcal{FLE}^+$-description graphs are depicted in Figure 2. The figure also shows the normalized label sets of every vertex. Note that the non-atomic concept descriptions in the label sets are used only during the generation of the description graphs.

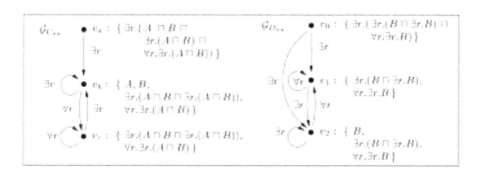

Fig. 2. $\mathcal{FLE}^+$-description graphs

It remains to be shown that the resulting $\mathcal{FLE}^+$-description graphs are in fact equivalent to the original concept descriptions. It is shown in [9] that the following theorem holds.

Lemma 2. *Let C be an $\mathcal{FLE}^+$-concept descriptions, then (1) $C \equiv \mathcal{G}_C$ and (2) $\mathcal{G}_C$ is a simple description graph.*

As a result, we know how to encode the information represented by $\mathcal{FLE}^+$-concept descriptions in $\mathcal{FLE}^+$-description graphs. Our next step is to find a way to translate description graphs back to concept descriptions.

---

[1] Blocking strategies originally have been introduced in the DL context in [10] for a tableaux-based satisfiability tester for expressive DLs.

3.3   Translation of Simple Description Graphs into $\mathcal{FLE}^+$-Concept Descriptions

It has already been mentioned in Section 3.1 that description graphs exist without an equivalent $\mathcal{FLE}^+$-concept description, see [9]. We shall see that it suffices to restrict our backward translation procedure to the class of simple description graphs introduced in the previous section.

For the backward translation procedure we may not rely on complex concept descriptions in the label sets of the graphs in question. On the contrary, the idea is to re-build complex concept descriptions in the label sets while preserving equivalence to the original description graph. This process is continued until the desired concept description occurs in the root label. Note that this strategy is just the reverse of the generation procedure of $\mathcal{FLE}^+$-description graphs, where the label of the root vertex generates the entire description graph.

To formalize the notion of re-building complex labels we devise an operation which modifies a given description graph by altering its label function. Intuitively, the function acc "accumulates" complex concept descriptions in the label sets of the vertices.

Definition 8. *Let $\mathcal{G} := (V, E, v_0, \ell_V, \ell_E)$ be a description graph and $|E| := n$. Then, $\mathrm{acc}(\mathcal{G}) := (V, E, v_0, \ell'_V, \ell_E)$ where ℓ'_V is defined as follows. For every $v \in V$,*

$$\ell'_V(v) := (\ell_V(v) \cap N_C) \cup \bigcup_{r \in N_R \cup N_R^T} \left(\bigcup_{(v\, \exists r\, w) \in E} \exists r. \bigsqcap \ell_V(w) \right.$$

$$\left. \cup \bigcup_{(v\, \forall r\, w) \in E} \left(\forall r. \bigsqcap (\ell_V(w) \setminus \{\forall r.\top\}) \sqcap \bigsqcap_{(w\, \exists r\, w') \in E} \exists r. \bigsqcap \ell_V(w') \right) \right).$$

Define $\mathrm{conc}(\mathcal{G}) := \bigsqcap \ell_V(v'_0)$, where v'_0 denotes the root vertex of $\mathrm{acc}^n(\mathcal{G})$.

For every vertex v, the modified label function ℓ'_V contains the same atomic labels as before but additionally has an existential restriction based on the label of every $\exists r$-successor of v. Forall-edges are treated similarly only that existential edges starting from vertices reachable by forall-edges are also taken into account. Observe that $\mathrm{acc}(\mathcal{G})$ is still a simple description graph.

To illustrate the effect of the function acc, consider the a simple description graph $\mathcal{G}$ with only one vertex v_0 with a label $\ell_V(v_0) = \{A\}$ and edges $E := \{(v_0, \exists r, v_0), (v_0 \,\forall r\, v_0)\}$. In the graph $\mathrm{acc}(\mathcal{G})$ the root vertex has the label $\{A, \exists r.A, \forall r.(A \sqcap \exists r.A)\}$. Applying acc again we obtain the root label of $\mathrm{acc}^2(\mathcal{G})$ which equals $\{A, \exists r.(A \sqcap \exists r.A \sqcap \forall r.(A \sqcap \exists r.A)), \forall r.(A \sqcap \exists r.A \sqcap \forall r.(A \sqcap \exists r.A) \sqcap \exists r.(A \sqcap \exists r.A \sqcap \forall r.(A \sqcap \exists r.A)))\}$.

It suffices to show that applying the function acc at most $|E|$ times produces a root label such that the conjunction of all contained concepts is equivalent to $\mathcal{G}$. Hence, we obtain the following theorem.

Theorem 1. *For every simple description graph $\mathcal{G} = (V, E, v_0, \ell_V, \ell_E)$ it holds that $\mathrm{conc}(\mathcal{G}) \equiv \mathcal{G}$.*

The idea of the proof is to show the equivalence $\mathrm{conc}(\mathcal{G}) \equiv \mathcal{G}$ in three steps. Firstly, we show for every $\mathcal{G}$ that a single application of acc preserves equivalence, i.e., $\mathcal{G} \equiv \mathrm{acc}(\mathcal{G})$. This immediately implies $\mathcal{G} \equiv \mathrm{acc}^{|E|}(\mathcal{G})$. Secondly, due to the semantics of description graphs it is also easy to see that every concept description in the root label of $\mathrm{acc}^{|E|}(\mathcal{G})$ subsumes $\mathrm{acc}^{|E|}(\mathcal{G})$. Hence, $\mathrm{acc}^{|E|}(\mathcal{G}) \sqsubseteq \mathrm{conc}(\mathcal{G})$. Thirdly, we can show that every model of $\mathrm{conc}(\mathcal{G})$ is also a model of $\mathrm{acc}^{|E|}(\mathcal{G})$. See [9] for the full proof.

Now the necessary means are provided to translate $\mathcal{FLE}^+$-concept descriptions (back and forth) into a representation where the transitivity of roles is made explicit. To define the lcs operation w.r.t. description graphs we first need a complete characterization of subsumption in this representation.

3.4 Characterization of Subsumption in $\mathcal{FLE}^+$

In this section, the description graphs introduced previously are used to characterize subsumption of $\mathcal{FLE}^+$-concept descriptions.

Theorem 2. *Let C, D be $\mathcal{FLE}^+$-concept descriptions, then $C \sqsubseteq D$ iff $\mathcal{G}_D \rightrightarrows \mathcal{G}_C$.*

To show the 'if'-direction, one can use a canonical model I_C of C obtained from $\mathcal{G}_C$ by renaming the labels of all edges $(v\,Q\,r\,w)$ in E_C to $(v\,r\,w)$. The fact that (i) I_C actually is a model of C and (ii) that by subsumption every model of C is also one of D can then be used to construct a simulation relation R. This is done iteratively while traversing $\mathcal{G}_D$ in depth-first order starting from the root vertex. See [9] for the full proof. However, the proof of the 'only if'-direction is easily obtained as a consequence of Lemma 2 and two results shown in the previous sections, namely Lemma 1 and Theorem 1. To illustrate the above result, we return to the example introduced in the previous section.

Example 3. Recall the concepts from Example 2. The only difference between C_{ex} and D_{ex} is the atomic concept B in the outermost existential restriction of C_{ex}. Hence, $C_{ex} \sqsubseteq D_{ex}$. It is easy to see that $R := \{(v_0, v_a), (v_1, v_c), (v_2, v_b)\}$ is in fact a simulation relation from $\mathcal{G}_{D_{ex}}$ into $\mathcal{G}_{C_{ex}}$. For all pairs it holds that the label set of the first vertex is a subset of that of the second one. Moreover, every edge starting from the first vertex can also be traveled from the second one, reaching again a pair in R. Note that this property does not hold without the transitive edge $(v_0\,\exists r\,v_2)$ in $\mathcal{G}_{D_{ex}}$.

3.5 Computation of the lcs in $\mathcal{FLE}^+$

With all the information captured in a $\mathcal{FLE}$-concept description made explicit by $\mathcal{FLE}^+$-description graphs the next step is to extract the commonalities of the description graphs. Similar to other approaches to computing the lcs [1, 4] the graph product is employed to this end. In a description graph $\mathcal{G}$ the *depth* of a vertex v is defined as the distance to the root vertex w.r.t. tree edges.

Definition 9 (Product of $\mathcal{FLE}^+$-Description Graphs). *The product $\mathcal{G}_C \times \mathcal{G}_D$ of two $\mathcal{FLE}^+$-description graphs $\mathcal{G}_A = (V_A, E_A, v_{0A}, \ell_{V_A}, \ell_{E_A})$ for $A \in \{C, D\}$*

is defined by induction on the depth of the $\mathcal{FLE}^+$-description graphs. The vertex (v_{0C}, v_{0D}) *labeled with* $\ell_{V_C}(v_{0C}) \cap \ell_{V_D}(v_{0D})$ *is the root vertex of* $\mathcal{G}_C \times \mathcal{G}_D$. *For each pair* $(v_C, v_D), v_C \in V_C, v_D \in V_D$ *s.t.* v_C *is a Qr-successor of* v_{0C} *in* $\mathcal{G}_C$ *and for* v_D *is a Qr-successor of* v_{0D} *in* $\mathcal{G}_D$, *we obtain a Qr-successor* (v_C, v_D) *of* (v_{0C}, v_{0D}) *in* $\mathcal{G}_C \times \mathcal{G}_D$. *The vertex* (v_C, v_D) *is the root vertex of the inductively defined product of* $\mathcal{G}_C \times \mathcal{G}_D$. *The graph* $\mathcal{H} = \mathcal{G}_C \times \mathcal{G}_D$ *is called the* product graph.

The resulting product graph $\mathcal{G}_C \times \mathcal{G}_D$ is rooted, connected, and directed. Since all vertices in $\mathcal{G}_C$ and $\mathcal{G}_D$ have at most one outgoing all-edge, every vertex in the product graph has at most one outgoing all-edge. Thus, product graphs are description graphs. Note that by construction of the product graph there trivially exists a simulation $Z : \mathcal{G}_C \times \mathcal{G}_D \rightleftarrows \mathcal{G}_C$ and between $Z' : \mathcal{G}_C \times \mathcal{G}_D \rightleftarrows \mathcal{G}_D$.

Example 4. Let us return to the concept descriptions C_{ex} and D_{ex} from Example 2. The product of their $\mathcal{FLE}^+$-description graphs is displayed in Figure 3. The edges between v_{b2} and v_{c1} are cross edges.

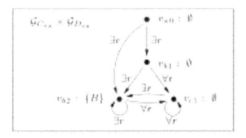

Fig. 3. Product Graph for $\mathcal{G}_{C_{\text{ex}}}$ and $\mathcal{G}_{D_{\text{ex}}}$

Once the product graph is obtained, we need to transform this representation into a $\mathcal{FLE}^+$-concept description. In order to apply the conc function introduced in Section 3, we have to check whether the obtained graph is a simple description graph. Unfortunately, this is not necessarily the case since the product graph may contain cross edges (w.r.t. a breadth-first spanning tree).

Cross edges violate Condition 1 from Definition 5. We therefore have to eliminate them before applying the function conc to read out a concept description from a product graph. The elimination of cross edges is performed by an unraveling function introduced in Definition 10. The idea is to introduce a new vertex in $\mathcal{G}'$ for each path over distinct vertices in the original graph starting from the root vertex and then transform every cross edge (v, w) into a new tree edge (v, w') by redirecting it to a copy of the subgraph reachable from w. For the formal definition, an auxiliary function eliminate-cross-edges is introduced first.

Definition 10 (Unravel-Function). *Let* $\mathcal{G} := (V, E, v_0, \ell_V, \ell_E)$ *be an* $\mathcal{FLE}$-*description graph. For every non-empty path* $p := (v_0 \ldots v_n)$ *in* V, *let* $\text{Tail}(p) := v_n$.

Denote by $p \cdot q$ the concatenation of two such paths. Let

$$\text{Final-Path}(\mathcal{G}) := \bigcup_{1 \leq i \leq |V|} \{(v_0 v_1 \ldots v_i) \in V^i \mid (v_j \, Qr \, v_{j+1}) \in E, v_j \neq v_k \text{ for } j \neq k\}.$$

Define the function eliminate-cross-edges *by*
eliminate-cross-edges$(\mathcal{G}) := (\text{Final-Path}(\mathcal{G}), E', \ell'_V, \ell'_E)$, *where*

$$E' := \{(\langle p \rangle, \langle p \cdot v \rangle) \in V' \times V' \mid (\text{Tail}(p) \, Qr \, v) \in E\} \cup$$
$$\{(\langle p \cdot v \cdot q \rangle, \langle p \cdot v \rangle) \in V' \times V' \mid (\text{Tail}(q) \, Qr \, v) \in E\}$$
$$\ell'_V(p) := \ell_V(\text{Tail}(p))$$
$$\ell'_E(p \, Qr \, q) := \ell_E(\text{Tail}(p) \, Qr \, \text{Tail}(q))$$

The set Final-Path$(\mathcal{G})$ contains vertices of the underlying spanning tree of $\mathcal{G}$. For a given input graph $\mathcal{G}$, the result unravel(G) is constructed in three steps: firstly, remove forward edges from $\mathcal{G}$; secondly, apply the function eliminate-cross-edges on the resulting graph, and; thirdly, augment the resulting graph by the transitive-closure over all exists-edges. It can be shown that the graph obtained by the function unravel is equivalent to the original one.

Lemma 3. *Let C, D be $\mathcal{FLE}^+$-concept descriptions, then, (1) unravel$(\mathcal{G}_C \times \mathcal{G}_D)$ $\rightleftharpoons \mathcal{G}_C \times \mathcal{G}_D$ and $\mathcal{G}_C \times \mathcal{G}_D \rightleftharpoons$ unravel$(\mathcal{G}_C \times \mathcal{G}_D)$ and (2) unravel$(\mathcal{G}_C \times \mathcal{G}_D) \rightleftharpoons \mathcal{G}_C$.*

The underlying idea of the proof of (1) in this Lemma is to construct a simulation by extending the identity relation on $\mathcal{G}_C \times \mathcal{G}_D$ to the desired simulations by mapping the copied parts of the unraveled graph obtained from the unravel function to (or from resp.) the same vertices as their originals. For the exact proof refer to [9]. In this Lemma (2) is an immediate consequence of (1), since there always exists a simulation $Z' \colon \mathcal{G}_C \times \mathcal{G}_D \rightleftharpoons \mathcal{G}_C$ and simulations are closed under concatenation.

Lemma 4. *Let C, D be $\mathcal{FLE}^+$-concept descriptions, then* unravel$(\mathcal{G}_C \times \mathcal{G}_D)$ *is a $\mathcal{FLE}^+$- description graph.*

Again, for the exact proof of this lemma refer to [9]. Since the graph obtained by the function unravel is a simple description graph, Theorem 1 is applicable and the concept description corresponding to the unraveled graph can be obtained by the conc function. We are now ready to prove the main theorem of this paper.

Theorem 3. *Let C, D be $\mathcal{FLE}^+$-concept descriptions then* conc$($unravel$(\mathcal{G}_C \times \mathcal{G}_D)) \equiv \text{lcs}(C, D)$.

Proof. Let $L = \text{conc}(\text{unravel}(\mathcal{G}_C \times \mathcal{G}_D))$. We have to show that (1) $C \sqsubseteq L$ and $D \sqsubseteq L$ and (2) if there exist another $\mathcal{FLE}^+$-concept E with $E \sqsubseteq L$, $C \sqsubseteq E$, and $D \sqsubseteq E$ then $L \sqsubseteq E$.
    Proof of (1): It is sufficient to show $C \sqsubseteq L$. Lemma 3 implies that there exists a simulation $Z \colon$ unravel$(\mathcal{G}_C \times \mathcal{G}_D) \rightleftharpoons \mathcal{G}_C$. Applying Lemma 4 to the unraveled graph and by the definition of $\mathcal{G}_C$ we know that unravel$(\mathcal{G}_C \times \mathcal{G}_D)$ and $\mathcal{G}_C$ are both

simple description graphs. Thus by Lemma 1 it holds that $\mathcal{G}_C \sqsubseteq \text{unravel}(\mathcal{G}_C \times \mathcal{G}_D)$. From Theorem 1 it follows that $\text{unravel}(\mathcal{G}_C \times \mathcal{G}_D) \equiv \text{conc}(\text{unravel}(\mathcal{G}_C \times \mathcal{G}_D))$ and since $\mathcal{G}_C$ is a $\mathcal{FLE}^+$-description graph Lemma 2 can be applied and we can conclude that $\mathcal{G}_C \equiv C \sqsubseteq \text{conc}(\text{unravel}(\mathcal{G}_C \times \mathcal{G}_D)) \equiv \text{unravel}(\mathcal{G}_C \times \mathcal{G}_D)$.

Proof of (2): By contradiction: assume $E \sqsubseteq L$, $C \sqsubseteq E$, $D \sqsubseteq E$ and $L \not\sqsubseteq E$. Let $\mathcal{G}_A := (V_A, E_A, v_0^A, \ell_V^A, \ell_E^A)$ where $A \in \{C, D, E, L\}$. From $C \sqsubseteq E$, $D \sqsubseteq E$ and Theorem 2 follows that there exist simulations $Z_C : \mathcal{G}_E \overset{\sim}{\rightsquigarrow} \mathcal{G}_C$ and $Z_D : \mathcal{G}_E \overset{\sim}{\rightsquigarrow} \mathcal{G}_D$. Thus it holds by definition of simulations: $\forall v \in V_E$:

- $\forall v_F \in V_F$: If $v_F \in Z_F(v)$ then $\ell_V^E(v) \subseteq \ell_V^F(v_F)$, and
- $\forall (v \, Q r \, w) \in E_E$ there exist $v_F, w_F \in V_F$ s.t. $\{v_F\} \in Z_F(v), \{w_F\} \in Z_F(w)$ and $(v_F \, Q r \, w_F) \in E_F$,

where $F \in \{C, D\}$. From the existence of both simulation relations and from Definition 9 follows that for all $v \in V_E$:

- If $v_C \in Z_C(v)$ and $v_D \in Z_D(v)$ for $v_C \in V_C, (v_C \, Q r \, w_C) \in E_C$ and for $v_D \in V_D, (v_D \, Q r \, w_D) \in E_D$ then there exist the vertices $\{(v_C, v_D), (w_C, w_D)\} \in V_{\mathcal{G}_C \times \mathcal{G}_D}$ and $((v_C, v_D) \, Q r \, (w_C, w_D)) \in E_{\mathcal{G}_C \times \mathcal{G}_D}$.
- Since $\ell_V^E(v) \subseteq \ell_V^C(v_C) \cup \ell_V^D(v_D) = \ell_V^{\mathcal{G}_C \times \mathcal{G}_D}((v_C, v_D))$

Thus there exists a simulation relation $Z_L : \mathcal{G}_E \overset{\sim}{\rightsquigarrow} \mathcal{G}_C \times \mathcal{G}_D$, where $Z_L(v) = \{(v'v'') \in V_{\mathcal{G}_C \times \mathcal{G}_D} \mid v' \in Z_C(v), v'' \in Z_D(v)\}$. By Lemma 3 there also must exist a simulation $Z_L' : \mathcal{G}_E \overset{\sim}{\rightsquigarrow} \text{unravel}(\mathcal{G}_C \times \mathcal{G}_D)$. Since $\mathcal{G}_E$ and $\text{unravel}(\mathcal{G}_C \times \mathcal{G}_D)$ are simple description graphs, Lemma 1 implies $\mathcal{G}_E \sqsubseteq \text{unravel}(\mathcal{G}_C \times \mathcal{G}_D)$. From this we obtain with Lemma 2 and Lemma 4, that $\mathcal{G}_E \equiv E \sqsubseteq \text{conc}(\text{unravel}(\mathcal{G}_C \times \mathcal{G}_D)) \equiv \text{unravel}(\mathcal{G}_C \times \mathcal{G}_D)$. This is a contradiction to our initial assumption. Thus we can conclude that $\text{conc}(\text{unravel}(\mathcal{G}_C \times \mathcal{G}_D)) \equiv \text{lcs}(C, D)$.

In case the n-ary lcs is to be computed from a set of concepts, the product of all corresponding $\mathcal{FLE}^+$-description graphs should be computed first and then the unravel and the conc function should be applied only once.

4   Conclusion and Outlook

We have introduced a sound and complete algorithm for the computation of the lcs in the DL $\mathcal{FLE}^+$. In particular, the lcs of a finite set of $\mathcal{FLE}^+$-concept descriptions always exists and is uniquely determined up to equivalence. As a key utility for the lcs computation we have proposed description graphs as a finite representation of $\mathcal{FLE}^+$-concept descriptions in which all restrictions additionally imposed by transitive roles are made explicit. The lcs could thus be defined by means of the graph product of the description graphs of the input concepts.

It is easy to see that the lcs algorithm can be optimized in several ways to produce smaller output concept descriptions. Firstly, the blocking conditions used to generate description graphs out of concept descriptions so far only allow for blocking w.r.t. ancestors. This might be replaced by a more general blocking strategy capable of blocking between arbitrary vertices. Secondly, it seems expedient to reduce redundancies possibly produced by the function conc. In particular, it is not always necessary to apply the acc-function once for every edge in the description graph. A thorough investigation of the computational complexity of the lcs computation in $\mathcal{FLE}^+$ remains future work. Nevertheless, already for then non-transitive language $\mathcal{FLE}$ it is known that the lcs may be exponentially large in the input size.

References

1. F. Baader. Least common subsumers, most specific concepts, and role-value-maps in a description logic with existential restrictions and terminological cycles. LTCS-Report LTCS-02-07, Chair f. Automata Theory, Inst. f. Theor. Comp. Sci. TU Dresden, Germany, 2002.
2. F. Baader and R. Küsters. Unification in a description logic with inconsistency and transitive closure of roles. In I. Horrocks and S. Tessaris, eds., *Proc. of the 2002 International Workshop on Description Logics*, Toulouse, France, 2002.
3. F. Baader, R. Küsters, and R. Molitor. Computing least common subsumers in description logics with existential restrictions. LTCS-Report LTCS-98-09, LuFG Theoretical Comp. Sci. RWTH Aachen, Germany, 1998.
4. F. Baader, R. Küsters, and R. Molitor. Computing least common subsumer in description logics with existential restrictions. In T. Dean, ed., *Proc. of IJCAI-99*, p. 96–101, Stockholm, Sweden, 1999. Morgan Kaufmann.
5. F. Baader and P. Narendran. Unification of concept terms in description logics. In H. Prade, ed., *Proc. of ECAI-98*, p. 331–335. John Wiley & Sons Ltd, 1998.
6. S. Bechhofer, I. Horrocks, C. Goble, and R. Stevens. OilEd: a Reason-able Ontology Editor for the Semantic Web. In *Proc of KI-01*.
7. A. Borgida and D. L. McGuinness. Asking queries about frames. In Luigia C. Aiello, John Doyle, and Stuart C. Shapiro, eds., *Proc. of KR-96*, p. 340–349, Cambridge, MA, 1996. Morgan Kaufmann.
8. S. Brandt and A.-Y. Turhan. Using non-standard inferences in description logics — what does it buy me? In *Proc. of KIDLWS'01*, nr 44 in CEUR-WS, Vienna, Austria, 2001. RWTH Aachen.
9. S. Brandt, A.-Y. Turhan, and R. Küsters. Foundations of non-standard inferences for description logics with transitive roles. LTCS-Report 03-02, Chair f. Automata Theory, Inst. f. Theor. Comp. Sci. TU Dresden, Germany, 2003.
10. Martin Buchheit, Francesco M. Donini, and Andrea Schaerf. Decidable reasoning in terminological knowledge representation systems. *Journal of Artificial Intelligence Research*, 1:109–138, 1993.
11. W. W. Cohen, A. Borgida, and H. Hirsh. Computing least common subsumers in description logics. In W. Swartout, ed., *Proc. of AAAI-92*, San Jose, CA, 1992. AAAI Press.
12. F. M. Donini, M. Lenzerini, D. Nardi, and A. Schaerf. Reasoning in description logics. In G. Brewka, ed., *Foundation of Knowledge Representation*. CSLI Publication, Cambridge University Press, 1996.
13. V. Haarslev and R. Möller. Expressive abox reasoning with number restrictions, role hierarchies, and transitively closed roles. In *Proc. of KR-00*, 2000.
14. I. Horrocks and U. Sattler. A description logic with transitive and inverse roles. *J. of Logic and Computation*, 9(3):385–410, 1999.

Extended Canonicity
of Certain Topological Properties of Set Spaces

Bernhard Heinemann

Fachbereich Informatik, FernUniversität in Hagen, 58084 Hagen, Germany,
Phone: + 49 2331 987 2714, Fax: + 49 2331 987 319,
Bernhard.Heinemann@fernuni-hagen.de

Abstract. This paper is about the question to what extent the addition of names (of points and sets) to the underlying language increases the expressive power of the modal logic of subset spaces. We ask, in particular, whether or not certain topological properties like separation or connectedness could become canonical then. Our answer is 'yes', if the system is enriched by two pairs of appropriate Gabbay–style rules.

Keywords: topological reasoning, modal logic of subset spaces, canonicity, rules in modal languages with names

1 Introduction

Recently, the *modal logic of subset spaces,* [4], has proved to be a useful tool for modelling both the interaction of knowledge and effort, and topological ideas related to that. Originating from [11], this logic appears as a *bi-modal* propositional system, comprising two unary connectives K representing *knowledge* and $\Box$ representing *effort in the course of time,* respectively.[1] To be a little more precise here, subset spaces are triples $(X, \mathcal{O}, V)$ consisting of a non-empty set X of points (or *states*), a set $\mathcal{O}$ of distinguished subsets of X (which can be viewed as *knowledge states,* changing in the course of time, of an agent), and a valuation V (determining the states where the atomic propositions are true). The operator K quantifies then across any knowledge state, and $\Box$ quantifies 'downward' across $\mathcal{O}$.

Abstracting away the knowledge context a *topological* scenario is left over. In fact, a subset space is, in particular, a space X equipped with a system $\mathcal{O}$ of subsets of X where 'closeness' is achieved by descending (via $\Box$) with respect to the set inclusion relation inside $\mathcal{O}$. Thus it is small wonder that one of the first issues of the modal logic of subset spaces was a characterization of the class of topological spaces, actually, by means of an appropriate axiom system; cf [6], where also the decidability of the resulting 'topologic' was proved.

---

[1] Concerning the basic idea of knowledge and its varied applications to computer science and AI the reader may consult the textbooks [5] and [10], which give comprehensive introductions to this field. As to the other modality, the effort operator might, e.g., model any knowledge acquisition procedure and, therefore, incorporate time into the system (though rather implicitly).

M.Y. Vardi and A. Voronkov (Eds.): LPAR 2003, LNAI 2850, pp. 137–151, 2003.

Subsequently, further classes of subset spaces have been investigated, in particular, such ones related to topology among them. The above outlined framework proved to be appropriate for, e.g., the classes of all *treelike, finite chain condition* and *intersection closed* spaces; cf [7], [8] and [12], respectively.

In contrast, some basic topological properties cannot, apparently, be dealt with purely modally, e.g., *separation* and *connectedness*. But strengthening the underlying language by introducing *names* of the original semantic ingredients, viz states and sets of states, respectively, we can get to grips with these notions. This enables us not only to express those properties adequately but also to prove their *canonicity*. In fact, the main results of the present paper state the *canonical completeness* of the modal logic of subset spaces with names and the correspondents to some fundamental topological concepts amalgamated.

As it stands, this paper is a theoretical one. However, the intended application of the logics studied here is obvious: they should serve the purpose that *formal topological reasoning,* which underlies diverse geometric reasoning tasks, gets firmly established.

The paper is organized as follows. The extension by names of the basic language of subset spaces is carried out in the next section. We also give there some examples what topological properties can be expressed. Section 3 contains the main contributions of this paper: an axiomatization of the modal logic of subset spaces with names, and the proofs of completeness and canonicity of the various topological notions. In order to succeed in that it is decisive that we add a pair of Gabbay–style rules for each class of names to our system.[2] In the final section, the advantage of our approach compared to that one using *hybrid logic* is emphasized (among other things); cf [9]. (A very readable introduction to the latter topic is [1]; see also [2], Sec. 7.3.)

2   Adding Names to the Language of Subset Spaces

In this section we extend the basic bi-modal language of subset spaces. Syntactically we add simply two sets of names. Each of those names receives either a unique state as denotation or a distinguished set of states.

Let PROP $= \{p, q, \ldots\}$ be a denumerable set of symbols called *proposition variables.* Moreover, let $N_{stat} = \{i, j, \ldots\}$ and $N_{sets} = \{A, B, \ldots\}$ be two further sets of symbols called *names of states* and *names of sets*, respectively. We assume that the sets PROP, N_{stat} and N_{sets} are pairwise disjoint. From the point of view of ordinary modal logic the elements of $N_{stat} \cup N_{sets}$ are treated like propositions.

We define the set $\mathfrak{F}$ of *well-formed formulas* over PROP $\cup N_{stat} \cup N_{sets}$ by the rule

$$\alpha ::= p \mid i \mid A \mid \neg\alpha \mid \alpha \wedge \beta \mid K\alpha \mid \Box\alpha.$$

That is, our language contains two boxes K and $\Box$. These modalities retain their semantics from the basic language of subset spaces.

---

[2] The term 'Gabbay–style' should remind one of the formal relationship to Gabbay's *irreflexivity rule;* cf [2], Sec. 4.7 and Notes to Ch. 4.

The missing boolean connectives $\top, \bot, \vee, \rightarrow, \leftrightarrow$ are treated as abbreviations, as needed. The duals of the modal operators K and $\square$ are denoted L and $\Diamond$, respectively.

We give meaning to formulas next. To begin with we have to define the domains where formulas are to be interpreted in. We let $\mathcal{P}(X)$ designate the powerset of a given set X.

Definition 1 (Subset Spaces with Names).

1. *A subset frame $(X, \mathcal{O})$ consists of a non-empty set X and a set $\mathcal{O} \subseteq \mathcal{P}(X)$ of subsets of X containing X.*
2. *Let $\mathcal{S} := (X, \mathcal{O})$ be a subset frame.*
   (a) The set of neighbourhood situations of $\mathcal{S}$ is the set

$$\mathcal{N} := \{x, U \mid x \in U \text{ and } U \in \mathcal{O}\}.$$

   (b) An $\mathcal{S}$–valuation is a mapping

$$V : \mathrm{PROP} \cup \mathrm{N}_{stat} \cup \mathrm{N}_{sets} \longrightarrow \mathcal{P}(X)$$

   such that
   – $V(i)$ is either $\emptyset$ or a singleton subset of X for every $i \in \mathrm{N}_{stat}$, and
   – $V(A) \in \mathcal{O}$ for every $A \in \mathrm{N}_{sets}$;
   if $V(i) \neq \emptyset$, then the unique element of $V(i)$ is called the denotation of i.
3. *A subset space with names (or, in short, an SSN) is a triple $(X, \mathcal{O}, V)$, where $\mathcal{S} := (X, \mathcal{O})$ is a subset frame and V an $\mathcal{S}$–valuation. We say that $\mathcal{M} := (X, \mathcal{O}, V)$ is based on $\mathcal{S}$.*

For a given SSN $\mathcal{M}$ we define now the relation of satisfaction, $\models_{\mathcal{M}}$, between neighbourhood situations of the underlying frame and formulas in $\mathfrak{F}$.

Definition 2 (Satisfaction and Validity).

1. *Let $\mathcal{M} := (X, \mathcal{O}, V)$ be an SSN based on $\mathcal{S} := (X, \mathcal{O})$, and x, U a neighbourhood situation of $\mathcal{S}$. Then*

$$
\begin{aligned}
x, U &\models_{\mathcal{M}} p &&:\Longleftrightarrow\; x \in V(p) \\
x, U &\models_{\mathcal{M}} i &&:\Longleftrightarrow\; x \in V(i) \\
x, U &\models_{\mathcal{M}} A &&:\Longleftrightarrow\; V(A) = U \\
x, U &\models_{\mathcal{M}} \neg\alpha &&:\Longleftrightarrow\; x, U \not\models_{\mathcal{M}} \alpha \\
x, U &\models_{\mathcal{M}} \alpha \wedge \beta &&:\Longleftrightarrow\; x, U \models_{\mathcal{M}} \alpha \text{ and } x, U \models_{\mathcal{M}} \beta \\
x, U &\models_{\mathcal{M}} K\alpha &&:\Longleftrightarrow\; y, U \models_{\mathcal{M}} \alpha \text{ for all } y \in U \\
x, U &\models_{\mathcal{M}} \square\alpha &&:\Longleftrightarrow\; \begin{cases} x, U' \models_{\mathcal{M}} \alpha \text{ for all } U' \in \mathcal{O} \\ \text{such that } x \in U' \subseteq U, \end{cases}
\end{aligned}
$$

for all $p \in \mathrm{PROP}$, $i \in \mathrm{N}_{stat}$, $A \in \mathrm{N}_{sets}$ and $\alpha, \beta \in \mathfrak{F}$. In case $x, U \models_{\mathcal{M}} \alpha$ is true we say that α holds in $\mathcal{M}$ at the neighbourhood situation x, U.

2. Let $\mathcal{M}$ be an SSN. A formula α is called valid in $\mathcal{M}$ iff it holds in $\mathcal{M}$ at every neighbourhood situation of the subset frame $\mathcal{M}$ is based on. (Manner of writing: $\mathcal{M} \models \alpha$.)

Note that the meaning of both proposition variables and names of states is regardless of neighbourhoods, thus stable with respect to $\square$.

Because of the second clause in Definition 2, a name $i \in N_{stat}$ reminds one of a nominal as known from hybrid logic; cf [1]. However, due to the two-component semantics we cannot specify a corresponding satisfaction operator $@_i$ accordingly. Therefore, our language cannot capture some of the particular features of the naming technique of hybrid logic.

What can be expressed in the extended language of subset spaces? — We give a couple of examples in the following definition and proposition, respectively.

Definition 3 (Special Types of Subset Frames). Let $\mathcal{S} = (X, \mathcal{O})$ be a subset frame. Then $\mathcal{S}$ is called

1. linear iff $\mathcal{O}$ is totally ordered by the set inclusion relation $\supseteq$,
2. separated iff for all $x, y \in X$ we have

$$x \neq y \Rightarrow \exists U_1, U_2 \in \mathcal{O} : (x \in U_1 \setminus U_2 \text{ and } y \in U_2 \setminus U_1),$$

3. connected iff for all $U, U_1, U_2 \in \mathcal{O}$ such that $U_1 \neq \emptyset \neq U_2$:

$$U = U_1 \cup U_2 \text{ implies } U_1 \cap U_2 \neq \emptyset.$$

Proposition 1. Let $\mathcal{S} = (X, \mathcal{O})$ be a subset frame. Then

1. $\mathcal{S}$ is linear iff for all SSNs $\mathcal{M}$ based on $\mathcal{S}$

$$\mathcal{M} \models K\square (i \to Lj) \vee K\square (j \to Li) \text{ for all } i, j \in N_{stat};$$

2. $\mathcal{S}$ is separated iff for all SSNs $\mathcal{M}$ based on $\mathcal{S}$

$$\mathcal{M} \models i \wedge L(j \wedge \neg i) \to \Diamond K\neg j \wedge K(j \to \Diamond K\neg i) \text{ for all } i, j \in N_{stat}.$$

3. $\mathcal{S}$ is connected iff for all SSNs $\mathcal{M}$ based on $\mathcal{S}$

$$\mathcal{M} \models K\Diamond(A \vee B) \to L(\Diamond A \wedge \Diamond B) \text{ for all } A, B \in N_{sets}.$$

Proof. We prove only 1. (The proofs of 2 and 3 can be done in a similar way.) First, let $\mathcal{S}$ be linear. Suppose that there are an SSN $\mathcal{M} = (X, \mathcal{O}, V)$ based on $\mathcal{S}$, a neighbourhood situation x, U of $\mathcal{S}$, and $i, j \in N_{stat}$ such that $x, U \not\models_{\mathcal{M}} K\square (i \to Lj) \vee K\square (j \to Li)$. Then, $x, U \models_{\mathcal{M}} L\Diamond (i \wedge K\neg j) \wedge L\Diamond (j \wedge K\neg i)$. It follows that there are $y, z \in U$ and $U_1, U_2 \in \mathcal{O}$ such that $y \in U_1 \subseteq U$, $z \in U_2 \subseteq U$ and $y, U_1 \models_{\mathcal{M}} i \wedge K\neg j$ and $z, U_2 \models_{\mathcal{M}} j \wedge K\neg i$. Consequently, $V(i) = \{y\}$ and $V(j) = \{z\}$ holds, in particular. Because of linearity we have $U_1 \subseteq U_2$ or $U_2 \subseteq U_1$. Let the first inclusion be valid (without loss of generality). That is, $y \in U_2$. But this contradicts $z, U_2 \models_{\mathcal{M}} K\neg i$. Thus the supposition is wrong; i.e., $\mathcal{M} \models K\square (i \to Lj) \vee K\square (j \to Li)$ for all SSNs $\mathcal{M}$ based on $\mathcal{S}$ and $i, j \in N_{stat}$, as desired. This shows the 'only if' direction.

Suppose on the other hand that $\mathcal{S} = (X, \mathcal{O})$ violates the linearity condition. Then there are $U_1, U_2 \in \mathcal{O}$ such that neither $U_1 \subseteq U_2$ holds nor $U_2 \subseteq U_1$. Thus there exist $y, z \in X$ such that $y \in U_1 \setminus U_2$ and $z \in U_2 \setminus U_1$. Now, fix any two distinct names $i, j \in \mathrm{N}_{stat}$, and let $V : \mathrm{PROP} \cup \mathrm{N}_{stat} \cup \mathrm{N}_{sets} \longrightarrow \mathcal{P}(X)$ be any $\mathcal{S}$–valuation satisfying $V(i) = \{y\}$ and $V(j) = \{z\}$. Define $\mathcal{M} := (X, \mathcal{O}, V)$. Then, $y, U_1 \models_{\mathcal{M}} i \wedge K\neg j$ and $z, U_2 \models_{\mathcal{M}} j \wedge K\neg i$. Taking any $x \in X$ we obtain $x, X \models_{\mathcal{M}} L\Diamond (i \wedge K\neg j) \wedge L\Diamond (j \wedge K\neg i)$. We conclude $x, X \not\models_{\mathcal{M}} K\Box (i \rightarrow Lj) \vee K\Box (j \rightarrow Li)$ from that. This shows the 'if' direction. Thus the first assertion of the proposition is proved.

It should be remarked that the separation condition from Definition 3.2 equals the (T 1)–Axiom for topological spaces. Moreover, the notion of connectedness from Definition 3.3 means that all non-empty sets $U \in \mathcal{O}$ are connected in the topological sense; cf [3], Ch. I, § 11, Sec. 1, Definition 2.

The reader has noticed that the above properties of subset spaces were specified using both names of states *and* sets. This is no accident, for both kinds of names are going to play their part in the completeness proof contained in the next section, and after that as well.

3   Extended Canonicity

We provide now an axiom system for subset spaces with names. Adding derivation rules gives us a system then which we call **SN**. We prove the soundness and *canonical* completeness of **SN** with respect to the class of all SSNs later on in this section. Finally, we characterize the respective classes of SSNs based on linear, separated and connected subset frames, too. (The term 'extended' in the heading refers to the use of names, and to the just indicated extensions of **SN** as well.)

The axiom schemata are arranged in two groups. First, the usual axioms for arbitrary subset spaces are listed.

1. All instances of propositional tautologies.
2. $K(\alpha \rightarrow \beta) \rightarrow (K\alpha \rightarrow K\beta)$
3. $K\alpha \rightarrow \alpha$
4. $K\alpha \rightarrow KK\alpha$
5. $L\alpha \rightarrow KL\alpha$
6. $(p \rightarrow \Box p) \wedge (\Diamond p \rightarrow p)$
7. $\Box (\alpha \rightarrow \beta) \rightarrow (\Box \alpha \rightarrow \Box \beta)$
8. $\Box \alpha \rightarrow \alpha$
9. $\Box \alpha \rightarrow \Box \Box \alpha$
10. $K\Box \alpha \rightarrow \Box K\alpha$,

where $p \in \mathrm{PROP}$ and $\alpha, \beta \in \mathfrak{F}$. We need not comment on these axioms here because this has been done elsewhere repeatedly; cf, eg, [11], [4] or [7].

The second group of axioms concerns names and is jointly responsible for canonicity of the subset space structure (along with a couple of new rules given below).

11. $(i \to \Box i) \wedge (\Diamond i \to i)$
12. $i \wedge \alpha \to K(i \to \alpha)$
13. $A \to KA$
14. $K\Box(A \wedge L\alpha \to L\beta) \vee K\Box(A \wedge L\beta \to L\alpha)$
15. $K(\Diamond B \to \Diamond A) \wedge L\Diamond B \to \Box(A \to L\Diamond B)$
16. $K\Diamond A \to A$,

where $i \in N_{stat}$, $A, B \in N_{sets}$ and $\alpha, \beta \in \mathfrak{F}$. Some comments on the axioms in this group are mandatory. Axiom 11 looks like Axiom 6, but is formulated for names of states instead of proposition variables. The schema 12 guarantees that every class of the equivalence relation induced by the operator K on the canonical model contains at most one element of the meaning of i there. Axiom 13 is formally similar to the first conjunct of Axiom 11, but names of states were replaced with names of sets, and $\Box$ and K were interchanged. (The analogue to the second conjunct of Axiom 11 is a theorem of the system to be defined immediately.) Axioms 14 – 16 are needed to ensure the uniqueness of the interpretation of a set name. Note that Axiom 14 looks quite similar to the correspondent to linearity given in Proposition 1.1.

Now we define the logical system **SN**. Apart from the common rules of proof of modal logic there are four additional ones concerning names.

Definition 4 (The Logic). *Let **SN** be the smallest set of formulas containing all of the above axiom schemata and closed under the following schemata of rules:*

$$(\text{MODUS PONENS}) \quad \frac{\alpha \to \beta, \alpha}{\beta}$$

$$(K\text{-NECESSITATION}) \quad \frac{\alpha}{K\alpha} \qquad (\Box\text{-NECESSITATION}) \quad \frac{\alpha}{\Box\alpha}$$

$$(\text{NAME}_{stat}) \quad \frac{j \to \beta}{\beta} \qquad (\text{NAME}_{sets}) \quad \frac{B \to \beta}{\beta}$$

$$(K\text{-ENRICHMENT}) \quad \frac{L\Diamond(i \wedge A \wedge L(j \wedge \alpha)) \to \beta}{L\Diamond(i \wedge A \wedge L\alpha) \to \beta}$$

$$(\Box\text{-ENRICHMENT}) \quad \frac{L\Diamond(i \wedge A \wedge \Diamond(B \wedge \alpha)) \to \beta}{L\Diamond(i \wedge A \wedge \Diamond\alpha) \to \beta},$$

where $\alpha, \beta \in \mathfrak{F}$, $i, j \in N_{stat}$, $A, B \in N_{sets}$, and j and B are, respectively, 'new' each time.

The reader can easily convince himself or herself that **SN** is *sound* with respect to SSNs.

Proposition 2. *Let $\mathcal{M}$ be any SSN. Then all of the above axioms are valid in $\mathcal{M}$. Moreover, each of the rules from Definition 4 preserves validity.*

Towards *completeness* some notations must be agreed on first. The canonical model of **SN** is designated

$$\mathcal{M}_{can} := \left(C, \{\xrightarrow{L}, \xrightarrow{\Diamond}\}, V_{can}\right).$$

To go into details about $\mathcal{M}_{\mathrm{can}}$,

- C is the set of all maximal **SN**–consistent sets of formulas,[3]
- $\xrightarrow{L}\; \subseteq C \times C$ is the accessibility relation of $\mathcal{M}_{\mathrm{can}}$ belonging to the connective K (this relation is defined by $s \xrightarrow{L} t : \Longleftrightarrow \{\alpha \mid K\alpha \in s\} \subseteq t$, for all $s, t \in C$),
- $\xrightarrow{\Diamond}$ is the (accordingly defined) accessibility relations of $\mathcal{M}_{\mathrm{can}}$ belonging to $\Box$, and
- V_{can} is the distinguished valuation of $\mathcal{M}_{\mathrm{can}}$ (defined by $V_{\mathrm{can}}(\sigma) := \{s \in C \mid \sigma \in s\}$, for all $\sigma \in \mathrm{PROP} \cup \mathrm{N}_{stat} \cup \mathrm{N}_{sets}$).

Axioms 1 – 5 and 7 – 10 from above force the following properties, which we are particularly interested in, of the accessibility relations $\xrightarrow{L}$ and $\xrightarrow{\Diamond}$ of the canonical model.

Proposition 3.   *1. The relation $\xrightarrow{L}$ is an equivalence.*

2. The relation $\xrightarrow{\Diamond}$ is reflexive and transitive.

3. For all $s, t, u \in C$ such that $s \xrightarrow{\Diamond} t \xrightarrow{L} u$ there exists $v \in C$ such that $s \xrightarrow{L} v \xrightarrow{\Diamond} u$ (or, in other words, $\xrightarrow{\Diamond} \circ \xrightarrow{L} \; \subseteq \; \xrightarrow{L} \circ \xrightarrow{\Diamond}$).

Proof. The first and the second assertion are well-known from basic modal logic. The third one was proved in [4], Proposition 2.2.

The property stated in Proposition 3.3 was introduced in [4] and called the *cross property* there. We are going to use this manner of speaking during the course of the present paper as well.

Let γ be a non-derivable formula. For completeness we have to realize the negation $\neg\gamma$ of γ. As $\{\neg\gamma\}$ is consistent, we take some maximal consistent set $\bar{s}$ containing $\neg\gamma$ for that purpose. Then, our first task is to *name* and *enrich* $\bar{s}$.

Definition 5 (Named and Enriched Maximal Consistent Sets). *A maximal consistent set s of formulas is called*

1. *named iff s contains some $i \in \mathrm{N}_{stat}$ and some $A \in \mathrm{N}_{sets}$ (in this case we say that the pair (i, A) is a name for s);*
2. *enriched iff*
   - *$L\Diamond(i \wedge A \wedge L\alpha) \in s$ implies $L\Diamond(i \wedge A \wedge L(j \wedge \alpha)) \in s$ for some $j \in \mathrm{N}_{stat}$ and*
   - *$L\Diamond(i \wedge A \wedge \Diamond\alpha) \in s$ implies $L\Diamond(i \wedge A \wedge \Diamond(B \wedge \alpha)) \in s$ for some $B \in \mathrm{N}_{sets}$.*

Let $\widetilde{\mathrm{N}}_{stat}$ and $\widetilde{\mathrm{N}}_{sets}$ be denumerable sets of *new* symbols and $\widetilde{\mathfrak{F}}$ the corresponding set of formulas. Then we have the following modified Lindenbaum Lemma.

Lemma 1. *Every maximal consistent set $s \subseteq \mathfrak{F}$ can be extended to a named and enriched maximal consistent set $\widetilde{s} \subseteq \widetilde{\mathfrak{F}}$.*

---

[3] We omit the prefix '**SN**' in the following.

Proof. Let a maximal consistent set s of formulas from $\mathfrak{F}$ be given. We first enumerate each of the sets $\tilde{N}_{stat}$ and $\tilde{N}_{sets}$.

1. We take the respective first symbol $j \in \tilde{N}_{stat}$ and $B \in \tilde{N}_{sets}$. Assume towards a contradiction that $s' := s \cup \{j, B\}$ is inconsistent. Then there are $n \in \mathbb{N}$ and $\alpha_1, \ldots, \alpha_n \in s_0$ such that $\{\alpha_1, \ldots, \alpha_n\} \cup \{j, B\}$ is inconsistent, too. Some propositional reasoning yields then $\Vdash j \to \neg(B \wedge \alpha_1 \wedge \ldots \wedge \alpha_n)$.[4] From this we get $\Vdash \neg(B \wedge \alpha_1 \wedge \ldots \wedge \alpha_n)$ by means of the rule (NAME$_{stat}$). Consequently, $\Vdash B \to \neg(\alpha_1 \wedge \ldots \wedge \alpha_n)$. Applying (NAME$_{sets}$) we obtain $\Vdash \neg(\alpha_1 \wedge \ldots \wedge \alpha_n)$ from that, contradicting the consistency of s_0. This shows that s' is consistent.

2. We want to enrich s' à la Lindenbaum. To this end we enumerate $\tilde{\mathfrak{F}}$; i.e., $\tilde{\mathfrak{F}} = \{\alpha_0, \alpha_1, \ldots\}$. We define inductively an ascending chain of sets of formulas in the following way. We let $s_0 := s'$. Now assume that s_m has already been defined, where $m \geq 0$. If $s_m \cup \{\alpha_m\}$ is inconsistent, then we let $s_{m+1} := s_m$. Otherwise we distinguish three cases:

    (a) if α_m is not of the form $L\Diamond(i \wedge A \wedge L\beta)$ or $L\Diamond(i \wedge A \wedge \Diamond\beta)$, then we let

    $$s_{m+1} := s_m \cup \{\alpha_m\};$$

    (b) if α_m is of the form $L\Diamond(i \wedge A \wedge L\beta)$, then we let

    $$s_{m+1} := s_m \cup \{\alpha_m, L\Diamond(i \wedge A \wedge L(j \wedge \beta))\},$$

    where j is the first element of $\tilde{N}_{stat}$ not yet processed;

    (c) if α_m is of the form $L\Diamond(i \wedge A \wedge \Diamond\beta)$, then we let

    $$s_{m+1} := s_m \cup \{\alpha_m, L\Diamond(i \wedge A \wedge \Diamond(B \wedge \beta))\},$$

    where B is the first element of $\tilde{N}_{sets}$ not yet processed.

    It turns out that s_m is consistent for all $m \in \mathbb{N}$. This was shown in item 1 of this lemma for the case $m = 0$. The induction step can be proved in a similar manner, using the rules (K–ENRICHMENT) and ($\Box$–ENRICHMENT), respectively. As a consequence we get that

$$\hat{s} := \bigcup_{m \in \mathbb{N}} s_m$$

is consistent as well. Therefore, there is a maximal consistent set $\tilde{s}$ such that $\hat{s} \subseteq \tilde{s}$. Due to our construction $\tilde{s}$ is obviously named and enriched, and $\tilde{s}$ contains s. This proves the lemma.

Now we let

$$\tilde{\mathcal{M}} := \left(\tilde{C}, \{ \xrightarrow{L}_{\sim}, \xrightarrow{\Diamond}_{\sim} \}, \tilde{V} \right)$$

be the canonical model of **SN** with respect to the extended language, and we take

$$C' := \left\{ s \in \tilde{C} \mid s \text{ is named and } (\tilde{s}, s) \in \xrightarrow{L}_{\sim} \circ \xrightarrow{\Diamond}_{\sim} \right\},$$

---

[4] We let $\Vdash$ designate **SN**–derivability.

where $\tilde{s}$ is any maximal consistent named and enriched set extending $\bar{s}$. Moreover, we consider the model

$$\mathcal{M}' := \left(C', \{\overset{L}{\longrightarrow}', \overset{\Diamond}{\longrightarrow}'\}, V'\right),$$

where $\overset{L}{\longrightarrow}'$, $\overset{\Diamond}{\longrightarrow}'$ and V' are the respective restrictions of $\overset{L}{\longrightarrow}$, $\overset{\Diamond}{\longrightarrow}$ and $\tilde{V}$ to C'. (For the sake of simplifying notation we omit the primes writing down the accessibility relations of $\mathcal{M}'$ in the following.) Then, first of all it should be mentioned that the properties stated in Proposition 3.1 and 3.2 remain valid for $\overset{L}{\longrightarrow}$ and $\overset{\Diamond}{\longrightarrow}$. But we can say much more about $\mathcal{M}'$ and, in particular, the accessibility relations of this model.

Lemma 2.   *1. Let $i \in \tilde{N}_{stat}$ and $A \in \tilde{N}_{sets}$. Then there is at most one $s \in C'$ such that (i, A) is a name for s.*
2. Let $s \in C'$ contain $L\alpha$ for some formula α. Then there exists $t \in C'$ such that $s \overset{L}{\longrightarrow} t$ and $\alpha \in t$.
3. Let $s \in C'$ contain $\Diamond\alpha$ for some formula α. Then there exists $t \in C'$ such that $s \overset{\Diamond}{\longrightarrow} t$ and $\alpha \in t$.
4. $\mathcal{M}'$ satisfies the cross property.

Proof.   1. Suppose first that there are $s, s' \in C'$ such that $A \in s \cap s'$ and not $s \overset{L}{\longrightarrow} s'$. Then there exist formulas $\alpha, \beta \in \mathfrak{F}$ such that $L\alpha \in s \setminus s'$ and $L\beta \in s' \setminus s$. It follows that $\neg L\beta \in s$ and $\neg L\alpha \in s'$. Letting $\tilde{s}$ be as above we get $L\Diamond(A \wedge L\alpha \wedge \neg L\beta) \wedge L\Diamond(A \wedge L\beta \wedge \neg L\alpha) \in \tilde{s}$ from that, according to the definition of C'. This contradicts Axiom 14. Therefore, $A \in s \cap s'$ implies $s \overset{L}{\longrightarrow} s'$. Now suppose that $i \in s \cap s'$, $s \overset{L}{\longrightarrow} s'$, but $s \neq s'$. Then there exists a formula $\alpha \in s \setminus s'$. We infer $\neg\alpha \in s'$ from that, hence we get $L(i \wedge \neg\alpha) \in s$. All in all we obtain $i \wedge \alpha \wedge L(i \wedge \neg\alpha) \in s$, contradicting Axiom 12. This shows that $s = s'$. Thus item 1 is proved.

2. Let $s \in C'$ contain $L\alpha$. As s is named, there exist $i \in \tilde{N}_{stat}$ and $A \in \tilde{N}_{sets}$ such that $i \wedge A \in s$. It follows that $L\Diamond(i \wedge A \wedge L\alpha) \in \tilde{s}$. But $\tilde{s}$ is enriched, thus $L\Diamond(i \wedge A \wedge L(j \wedge \alpha)) \in \tilde{s}$ for some $j \in \tilde{N}_{stat}$. Consequently, there is some point $s' \in \tilde{C}$ satisfying $(\tilde{s}, s') \in \overset{L}{\longrightarrow} \circ \overset{\Diamond}{\longrightarrow}$ and $i \wedge A \wedge L(j \wedge \alpha) \in s'$. Since $i \wedge A \in s'$ we have $s' \in C'$; moreover, $s = s'$ because of item 1. Due to the fact that $L(j \wedge \alpha) \in s$ there is a point $t \in \tilde{C}$ such that $s \overset{L}{\longrightarrow} t$ and $j \wedge \alpha \in t$. Because of Axiom 13, $A \in t$. Thus t is named. With the aid of the cross property for $\tilde{\mathcal{M}}$ and the transitivity of $\overset{L}{\longrightarrow}$ we obtain $t \in C'$. This proves item 2.

3. The proof is similar to that of 2, hence the corresponding details are omitted. Note, however, that the first conjunct of Axiom 11 has to be used instead of Axiom 13 now, and the transitivity of $\overset{\Diamond}{\longrightarrow}$ instead of that of $\overset{L}{\longrightarrow}$.

4. Assume that $s \overset{\Diamond}{\longrightarrow} t \overset{L}{\longrightarrow} u$ holds for $s, t, u \in C'$. There are $i \in \tilde{N}_{stat}$ and $A \in \tilde{N}_{sets}$ such that $i \wedge A \in u$. From this we get $\Diamond L(i \wedge A) \in s$. Axiom 10 implies now $L\Diamond(i \wedge A) \in s$. As above we conclude $L(j \wedge \Diamond(i \wedge A)) \in s$ from

that, for some $j \in \widetilde{N}_{stat}$. It follows that there exists some v that contains $j \wedge \Diamond(i \wedge A)$ and satisfies $s \xrightarrow{L}_{\sim} v$. As s is named, this is also true for v. Moreover, v is in fact an element of C' (which can be seen by means of the cross property for $\widetilde{\mathcal{M}}$, as above). Finally, $v \xrightarrow{\Diamond} u$ holds because (i, A) is a name for u. This proves the last assertion of the lemma.

We turn to the final steps enabling us to build an SSN on the model $\mathcal{M}'$. For every $s \in C'$ we let $[s] := \{t \in C' \mid s \xrightarrow{L} t\}$, and we define a binary relation $\preccurlyeq$ on the set $\mathcal{Q} := \{[s] \mid s \in C'\}$ by

$$[s] \preccurlyeq [t] : \Longleftrightarrow \text{ there are } s' \in [s], t' \in [t] \text{ satisfying } s' \xrightarrow{\Diamond} t', \text{ for all } s, t \in C'.$$

Assume that $[s] \preccurlyeq [t]$ holds. Then it cannot happen that there are $s' \in [s]$ and $t', t'' \in [t]$ such that $t' \neq t''$, $s' \xrightarrow{\Diamond} t'$ and $s' \xrightarrow{\Diamond} t''$, nor that there are $s', s'' \in [s]$ and $t' \in [t]$ such that $s' \neq s''$, $s' \xrightarrow{\Diamond} t'$ and $s'' \xrightarrow{\Diamond} t'$. We say in these cases that $\preccurlyeq$ is *functionally* and *injectively induced* by $\xrightarrow{\Diamond}$, respectively.

Lemma 3.   *1. The relation $\preccurlyeq$ is functionally induced by $\xrightarrow{\Diamond}$.*
2. The relation $\preccurlyeq$ is injectively induced by $\xrightarrow{\Diamond}$.

Proof.   1. Suppose that there are $s' \in [s]$ and $t', t'' \in [t]$ such that $s' \xrightarrow{\Diamond} t'$ and $s' \xrightarrow{\Diamond} t''$. Then, clearly, $t' \xrightarrow{L} t''$. Since every point of C' is named there exists some $i \in \widetilde{N}_{stat}$ contained in s'. With the aid of the first conjunct of Axiom 11 we conclude $i \in t'$ and $i \in t''$. Now Axiom 12 gives us $t' = t''$, as in the proof of Lemma 2.1. Thus $\preccurlyeq$ is functionally induced by $\xrightarrow{\Diamond}$.

2. Suppose that there are $s', s'' \in [s]$ and $t' \in [t]$ such that $s' \xrightarrow{\Diamond} t'$ and $s'' \xrightarrow{\Diamond} t'$. We utilize again that every point of C' is named and let $i \in \widetilde{N}_{stat}$ be contained in t' this time. Due to the second conjunct of Axiom 11 we obtain $i \in s'$ and $i \in s''$. Thus $s' = s''$, by Axiom 12. Therefore, $\preccurlyeq$ is also injectively induced by $\xrightarrow{\Diamond}$.

We are now in a position to define the desired structure falsifying the given non-derivable formula γ. We take $\widetilde{s}$ from above. That is, in particular, $\widetilde{s}$ extends $\bar{s} \ni \neg \gamma$. Then we let

- $X := [\widetilde{s}]$,
- $U_{[s]} := \{x \in X \mid \exists t \in [s] : x \xrightarrow{\Diamond} t\}$, where $s \in C'$ (that is, $[s] \in \mathcal{Q}$),
- $\mathcal{O} := \{U_{[s]} \mid [s] \in \mathcal{Q}\} \cup \{\emptyset\}$, and
- $V(\sigma) := \{x \in X \mid \exists t \in C' : (x \xrightarrow{\Diamond} t \text{ and } \sigma \in t)\}$, for all $\sigma \in \text{PROP} \cup N_{stat} \cup N_{sets}$.

It turns out that we have just defined a subset space with names, actually.

Proposition 4. $\mathcal{M} := (X, \mathcal{O}, V)$ *is an SSN such that, for all $[s], [t] \in \mathcal{Q}$,*

1. $U_{[t]} \subseteq U_{[s]}$ *implies* $[s] \preccurlyeq [t]$, *and*
2. $U_{[s]} = U_{[t]}$ *implies* $[s] = [t]$.

Proof. We first have to show that V is an $(X, \mathcal{O})$–valuation. Let $i \in \widetilde{N}_{stat}$. Then, due to Axiom 12 there is at most one $x \in X$ containing i. Thus $V(i)$ is either empty or a singleton subset of X. Now let $A \in \widetilde{N}_{sets}$ and assume that $V(A) \neq \emptyset$. Let $x \in V(A)$. Then there is some $t \in C'$ such that $x \xrightarrow{\diamond} t$ and $A \in t$. We claim that $V(A) = U_{[t]}$ holds. First, take any $x' \in V(A)$. According to the definition of V there is some $t' \in C'$ such that $x' \xrightarrow{\diamond} t'$ and $A \in t'$. Exploiting Axiom 14 as above yields $[t] = [t']$. Thus $x' \in U_{[t]}$. It follows that $V(A) \subseteq U_{[t]}$. On the other hand, let $x' \in U_{[t]}$. Then there exists some $t' \in [t]$ such that $x' \xrightarrow{\diamond} t'$. Moreover, $A \in t'$ holds because of Axiom 13. Therefore, $x' \in V(A)$. This shows that $U_{[t]} \subseteq V(A)$. All in all we get $V(A) = U_{[t]}$, as desired.

1. Next assume that $U_{[t]}$ is contained in $U_{[s]}$. Since both s and t are named, there are $A, B \in \widetilde{N}_{sets}$ such that $A \in s'$ for all $s' \in [s]$ and $B \in t'$ for all $t' \in [t]$. Thus our assumption gives us $K(\diamond B \to \diamond A) \in x$, where x is an arbitrarily chosen element of $U_{[s]}$. Since $L\diamond B \in x$ holds as well, we infer $\square (A \to L\diamond B) \in x$ from that with the aid of Axiom 15. That is, $L\diamond B \in x_s$. Therefore, there are $s' \in [s]$ and $t' \in C'$ such that $s' \xrightarrow{\diamond} t'$ and $B \in t'$, by the second and the third assertion of Lemma 2. Now $t' \in [t]$ can be concluded from that. Consequently, $[s] \preccurlyeq [t]$ holds, as desired.

2. Finally, let $U_{[s]} = U_{[t]}$ be valid, where $[s], [t] \in \mathcal{Q}$. Then $[s] \preccurlyeq [t]$ and $[t] \preccurlyeq [s]$, as follows from Proposition 4.1. Therefore, the cross property and Lemma 3 ensure that the relation $\xrightarrow{\diamond}$ restricted to $[s]$ in the domain and $[t]$ in the range is a (bijective) function. Let (i, A) be a name for t. Then we obtain $K\diamond A \in s$ from the left-totality of $\xrightarrow{\diamond}\big|_{[s] \times [t]}$. Axiom 16 implies now $A \in s$.

   That is, $s \xrightarrow{L} t$, which we wanted to verify.

We are about to prove an appropriate *Truth Lemma* for $\mathcal{M}$. According to Lemma 3.1, $\preccurlyeq$ is functionally induced by $\xrightarrow{\diamond}$. So, for every $x \in X$ and $[s] \in \mathcal{Q}$ there is at most one $\xrightarrow{\diamond}$ –successor of x contained in $[s]$. In case of existence (this is the case iff $x \in U_{[s]}$) we let x_s designate that element of $[s]$. Using this notation we state first

Lemma 4. *For all $[s], [t] \in \mathcal{Q}$ and $x \in X$ such that $x \in U_{[t]}$: if $[s] \preccurlyeq [t]$, then $x \in U_{[s]}$ and $x_s \xrightarrow{\diamond} x_t$.*

Proof. Let $[s] \preccurlyeq [t]$ and $x \in U_{[t]}$ be satisfied. Then there are $s_1 \in [s]$ and $t_1 \in [t]$ such that $s_1 \xrightarrow{\diamond} t_1$. Furthermore, there are $x' \in X$ and $s' \in [s]$ such that $x' \xrightarrow{\diamond} s'$, since $[s] \in \mathcal{Q}$. Applying the cross property repeatedly yields the existence of elements $x_1 \in X$ and $s'_1 \in [s]$ such that $x_1 \xrightarrow{\diamond} s'_1 \xrightarrow{\diamond} x_t$. Thus we have $x \xrightarrow{\diamond} x_t$ and $x_1 \xrightarrow{\diamond} x_t$. Because $\preccurlyeq$ is injectively induced by $\xrightarrow{\diamond}$ (Lemma 3.2) we infer $x = x_1$ from that. Consequently, $x \in U_{[s]}$, $s'_1 = x_s$, and $x_s \xrightarrow{\diamond} x_t$.

Now the desired Truth Lemma reads as follows.

Lemma 5. *For all $\alpha \in \widetilde{\mathfrak{F}}$, $x \in X$, and $[s] \in Q$ such that $x \in U_{[s]}$, we have*

$$x, U_{[s]} \models_{\mathcal{M}} \alpha \iff \alpha \in x_s.$$

Proof. The proof is by induction on the structure of α. We treat the basic and the non-boolean cases only.

Case $\alpha = p \in \mathrm{PROP}$: First, let $x, U_{[s]} \models_{\mathcal{M}} p$ be satisfied. Then $x \in V(i)$ by Definition 2.1. By the definition of V, there exists $t \in C'$ such that $x \overset{\diamond}{\longrightarrow} t$ and $p \in t$. It follows that $\diamond p \in x$. The second conjunct of Axiom 6 implies $p \in x$ then, and the first one $p \in x_s$ since $x \overset{\diamond}{\longrightarrow} x_s$. This shows that the left-to-right direction is true. – As to the converse, let $p \in x_s$. Then $p \in V(i)$ is immediate from the definition of V. But the latter implies $x, U_{[s]} \models_{\mathcal{M}} p$.

Case $\alpha = i \in \widetilde{\mathsf{N}}_{stat}$: This case is completely analogous to the previous one.

Case $\alpha = A \in \widetilde{\mathsf{N}}_{sets}$: We have $x, U_{[s]} \models_{\mathcal{M}} A \iff V(A) = U_{[s]}$ by Definition 2.1. As was shown in the first part of the proof of Proposition 4, $A \in x_s$ implies $V(A) = U_{[s]}$ since $x \overset{\diamond}{\longrightarrow} x_s$. – On the other hand, the same proof shows that if $V(A) \neq \emptyset$, then $V(A) = U_{[t]}$ for some $t \in C'$ containing A. Therefore, if $V(A) = U_{[s]}$, then $U_{[s]} = U_{[t]}$ holds. Now $[s] = [t]$ follows from Proposition 4.2. Hence we get $A \in x_s$.

Case $\alpha = K\beta$: Suppose that $x, U_{[s]} \not\models_{\mathcal{M}} K\beta$. Then there is some $y \in U_{[s]}$ such that $y, U_{[s]} \not\models_{\mathcal{M}} \beta$. It follows that $\beta \notin y_s$, by induction hypothesis. As $x_s \overset{L}{\longrightarrow} y_s$, the formula $K\beta$ is not contained in x_s. This proves the right-to-left direction. – Concerning the opposite one first note that $[s] = \{y_s \mid y \in U_{[s]}\}$. (The nontrivial inclusion '$\subseteq$' follows from the cross property.) Now, $x, U_{[s]} \models_{\mathcal{M}} K\beta$ implies $y, U_{[s]} \models_{\mathcal{M}} \beta$ for all $y \in U_{[s]}$. By induction hypothesis and the preceding note we get $\beta \in s'$ for all $s' \in [s]$. Lemma 2.2 guarantees $\beta \in t$ for all $t \in \widetilde{C}$ satisfying $s \overset{L}{\underset{\sim}{\longrightarrow}} t$. Consequently, $K\beta \in s$. This proves the left-to-right direction.

Case $\alpha = \Box\beta$: Let $x, U_{[s]} \models_{\mathcal{M}} \Box\beta$. Then, $x, U_{[t]} \models_{\mathcal{M}} \beta$ for all $[t] \in Q$ such that $x \in U_{[t]} \subseteq U_{[s]}$. From Proposition 4.1 we get $x, U_{[t]} \models_{\mathcal{M}} \beta$ for all $[t] \in Q$ satisfying $[s] \preccurlyeq [t]$ and $x \in U_{[t]}$. Due to the induction hypothesis, $\beta \in x_t$ for all such $[t]$. It follows that $\beta \in u$ for all $u \in C'$ satisfying $x_s \overset{\diamond}{\longrightarrow} u$ (for $[s] \preccurlyeq [u]$ and $x \in U_{[u]}$ is valid then). With the aid of Lemma 2.3, $\Box\beta \in x_s$ can be concluded from that. Therefore, the left-to-right direction is proved. – As to the other one suppose that $x, U_{[s]} \not\models_{\mathcal{M}} \Box\beta$. Then some $t \in C'$ is yielded as just a minute ago which satisfies $[s] \preccurlyeq [t]$, $x \in U_{[t]}$ and $\beta \notin x_t$. Since $x_s \overset{\diamond}{\longrightarrow} x_t$ holds because of Lemma 4, we get $\Box\beta \notin x_s$, as desired. This ends the proof of the Truth Lemma.

Next we apply Lemma 5 to the formula $\neg\gamma$, which is contained in $\widetilde{s} = \widetilde{s}_{\widetilde{s}}$ by construction. Then, restricting $\mathcal{M}$ to the language we started with we conclude that γ is falsified in an SSN of the right signature as well. We have, therefore, established the following theorem.

Theorem 1 (Completeness). *Every formula $\alpha \in \mathfrak{F}$ that is valid in all SSNs is contained in the logic* **SN**.

Concluding this section we are heading for *extended* completeness. That is, we want to have canonical completeness not only for the basic logic corresponding to the class of *all* SSNs, but also for logics corresponding to more special classes. We are particularly interested in SSNs based on linear, separated and connected subset frames, respectively;[5] see Definition 3.

Concerning linearity it turns out that the correspondent from Proposition 1.1 is not sufficient for our purposes. Instead, we have to specify by means of names of *sets*. An appropriate axiom schema is

17. $K\square\,(A \to L\lozenge B) \vee K\square\,(B \to L\lozenge A)\,,$

where $A, B \in \mathrm{N}_{sets}$. In fact, soundness with respect to linear SSNs is easy to see, and the following proposition holds, which gives us completeness. We keep the notations from above.

Proposition 5. *In the presence of Axiom 17, $(\mathcal{Q}, \preccurlyeq)$ is a linear order.*

Proof. Only dichotomy of the relation $\preccurlyeq$ has to be proved yet, since reflexivity follows from the reflexivity of $\overset{\lozenge}{\longrightarrow}$, transitivity from the cross property and the transitivity of $\overset{\lozenge}{\longrightarrow}$, and antisymmetry was established in the proof of Proposition 4.2. Suppose towards a contradiction that there are two classes $[s], [t] \in \mathcal{Q}$ which are incomparable with respect to $\preccurlyeq$. As s and t are named, there are $A, B \in \widetilde{\mathrm{N}}_{sets}$ such that $A \in s$ and $B \in t$. It follows that $L\lozenge B \notin s$ and $L\lozenge A \notin t$. Consequently, $L\lozenge(A \wedge \neg L\lozenge B) \wedge L\lozenge(B \wedge \neg L\lozenge A) \in \tilde{s}$. But this formula is the negation of an instance of Axiom 17. Thus we arrived at a contradiction. This shows that $\preccurlyeq$ is a dichotomous relation. Therefore, $(\mathcal{Q}, \preccurlyeq)$ is a linear order.

As an easy consequence of Proposition 5 we get

Corollary 1. **SN** $+ (17)$ *is sound and complete with respect to the class of linear SSNs.*

Proof. We have to show that the set $\{U_{[s]} \mid [s] \in \mathcal{Q}\}$ is totally ordered by the set inclusion relation $\supseteq$. First note that if $[s] \preccurlyeq [t]$, then $U_{[t]} \subseteq U_{[s]}$. This is immediate from Lemma 4. Thus if $U_{[s]} \not\supseteq U_{[t]}$, then $[s] \not\preccurlyeq [t]$. Hence $[t] \preccurlyeq [s]$ by Proposition 5. Now, applying Lemma 4 once more yields $U_{[t]} \supseteq U_{[s]}$.

In contrast, the correspondent to the separation property from Proposition 1.2 *is* strong enough to force this property on the canonical model. For convenience, we write down that schema once again here:

18. $i \wedge L(j \wedge \neg i) \to \lozenge K\neg j \wedge K(j \to \lozenge K\neg i),$

where $i, j \in \mathrm{N}_{stat}$. — We prove now

Proposition 6. **SN** $+ (18)$ *is sound and complete with respect to the class of separated SSNs.*

---

[5] For short, those SSNs are also called *linear, separated* and *connected*, respectively.

Proof. We have to show that $(X, \mathcal{O})$ is separated, where X and $\mathcal{O}$ are as above. So, let $x, y \in X$ be given and assume that $x \neq y$. As x and y are named, there are $i, j \in \tilde{\mathsf{N}}_{stat}$ such that $i \in x$ and $j \in y$. From $x \neq y$ we conclude $i \wedge L(j \wedge \neg i) \in x$. By means of Axiom 18 we obtain $\Diamond K \neg j \wedge K(j \rightarrow \Diamond K \neg i) \in x$ from that. Therefore, $\Diamond K \neg j \in x$ and $\Diamond K \neg i \in y$. It follows that there are $s, t \in C'$ such that $x \xrightarrow{\Diamond} s$, $y \xrightarrow{\Diamond} t$, $j \notin s'$ for all $s' \in [s]$ and $i \notin t'$ for all $t' \in [t]$. That is, $y \notin U_{[s]}$ and $x \notin U_{[t]}$. This shows that $(X, \mathcal{O})$ is separated.

At the end of this section we turn to connectedness. In order to obtain canonical completeness in this case, we have to modify the corresponding schema from Proposition 1 as well. To this end we let

19. $K(\Diamond C \leftrightarrow \Diamond(A \vee B)) \rightarrow L(\Diamond A \wedge \Diamond B)$,

where $A, B, C \in \mathsf{N}_{sets}$. Then we have

Proposition 7. $\mathbf{SN} + (19)$ *is sound and complete with respect to the class of connected SSNs.*

The proof of Proposition 7 can be done similarly to the proof of the previous propositions. Therefore, we omit the details.

It is not hard to convince oneself of the canonicity of further interesting (topological) properties of subset spaces; see, e.g., the examples mentioned in the introduction.

4   Concluding Remarks

In this paper we added names of states and sets, repectively, to the bi-modal language of subset spaces. We axiomatized the resulting logic of subset spaces with names. Integrating two pairs of new rules gave us a system, $\mathbf{SN}$, of which we proved soundness and 'canonical' completeness. We also considered a couple of topologically significant extensions of $\mathbf{SN}$.

Comparing our approach with hybrid logic was left over from the introduction. This is done briefly now. In order to respect on the one hand the semantics of the modal logic of subset spaces, on the other hand to integrate the hybrid naming technique without any restriction, it is necessary to interpret nominals by neighbourhood situations. By doing that one can really get to a rather expressive hybrid language, enabling one to deal satisfactorily with, e.g., linear structures.[6] However, naming neighbourhood situations means binding states to sets more closely than it is appropriate for many purposes. For instance, separation (depending rather on points than on sets in a sense; see Proposition 1.2) cannot be captured then. On the other hand, the framework developed in this paper seems to be the right formulation putting one in a position to act as flexible as possible.

---

[6] The desire to have logical control of linear subset spaces was our original motivation to extend the basic modal approach hybridly; cf [9].

There is something else we would like to say at the end: *effectivity proper-ties* of our logic have not been dealt with presently, but will be studied in a forthcoming paper.

References

1. Patrick Blackburn. Representation, Reasoning, and Relational Structures: a Hybrid Logic Manifesto. *Logic Journal of the IGPL*, 8:339–365, 2000.
2. Patrick Blackburn, Maarten de Rijke, and Yde Venema. *Modal Logic*, volume 53 of *Cambridge Tracts in Theoretical Computer Science*. Cambridge University Press, Cambridge, 2001.
3. Nicolas Bourbaki. *General Topology, Part 1*. Hermann, Paris, 1966.
4. Andrew Dabrowski, Lawrence S. Moss, and Rohit Parikh. Topological Reasoning and The Logic of Knowledge. *Annals of Pure and Applied Logic*, 78:73–110, 1996.
5. Ronald Fagin, Joseph Y. Halpern, Yoram Moses, and Moshe Y. Vardi. *Reasoning about Knowledge*. MIT Press, Cambridge, MA, 1995.
6. Konstantinos Georgatos. Knowledge Theoretic Properties of Topological Spaces. In M. Masuch and L. Pólos, editors, *Knowledge Representation and Uncertainty, Logic at Work*, volume 808 of *Lecture Notes in Computer Science*, pages 147–159. Springer, 1994.
7. Konstantinos Georgatos. Knowledge on Treelike Spaces. *Studia Logica*, 59:271–301, 1997.
8. Bernhard Heinemann. Topological Modal Logics Satisfying Finite Chain Conditions. *Notre Dame Journal of Formal Logic*, 39(3):406–421, 1998.
9. Bernhard Heinemann. Axiomatizing modal theories of subset spaces (an example of the power of hybrid logic). In *HyLo@LICS, 4th Workshop on Hybrid Logic, Proceedings*, pages 69–83, Copenhagen, Denmark, July 2002.
10. J.-J. Ch. Meyer and W. van der Hoek. *Epistemic Logic for AI and Computer Science*, volume 41 of *Cambridge Tracts in Theoretical Computer Science*. Cambridge University Press, Cambridge, 1995.
11. Lawrence S. Moss and Rohit Parikh. Topological Reasoning and The Logic of Knowledge. In Y. Moses, editor, *Proceedings of the 4th Conference on Theoretical Aspects of Reasoning about Knowledge (TARK 1992)*, pages 95–105, San Francisco, CA, 1992. Morgan Kaufmann.
12. M. Angela Weiss and Rohit Parikh. Completeness of Certain Bimodal Logics for Subset Spaces. *Studia Logica*, 71:1–30, 2002.

Algebraic and Model Theoretic Techniques for Fusion Decidability in Modal Logics

Silvio Ghilardi[1] and Luigi Santocanale[2,*]

[1] Dipartimento di Scienze dell'Informazione, Università degli Studi Di Milano,
ghilardi@dsi.unimi.it
[2] Laboratoire Bordelais de Recherche en Informatique, Université Bordeaux 1,
santocan@labri.fr

Abstract. We introduce a new method (derived from model theoretic general combination procedures in automated deduction) for proving fusion decidability in modal systems. We apply it to show fusion decidability in case not only the boolean connectives, but also a universal modality and nominals are shared symbols.

Introduction

The combination or fusion of two first order equational theories T_1 and T_2 – in the signatures Σ_1 and Σ_2, respectively – is the theory in the signature $\Sigma_1 \cup \Sigma_2$ having as axioms the set of equations $T_1 \cup T_2$. Among the transfer properties from the theories to their fusion, researchers have investigated when a positive answer to the decidability of uniform word problems for the two theories implies a positive answer to the decidability of uniform word problems for their fusion. In case Σ_1, Σ_2 are disjoint the positive answer has been known since [19], whereas in the general case the problem becomes undecidable (a simple undecidable example is supplied in [8]). Recently, a positive answer was independently obtained in [4, 8] in case the two theories share so-called 'constructors', however this rather natural hypothesis seems not to be applicable in the case of modal logics. On the other hand, rather strong fusion decidability transfer results for modal logics exist [2, 32], so a natural challenge arises: how to get them as instances of general combination methods in automated deduction?

In the area of combination problems in automated deduction another main technique consists on the so-called Nelson-Oppen combination procedure [17, 18, 27]. This procedure is also concerned with disjoint signatures, but it is not specifically tailored to uniform word problems and equational theories: it transfers in a general setting the decidability of the universal fragment to the combined theory, provided the input theories are only stably infinite, see below. Consequently, as pointed out in [3], the procedure can be useful for combined uniform word problems only in case the input theories have decidable universal fragments

* The second author acknowledges financial support from the European Commission through a Marie Curie Individual Fellowship. We thank V. Goranko for suggestions on an earlier version of this paper.

(which means, in case of modal logics, that global and not only local consequence relations should be decidable).

In [11, 12] a general algebraic and model theoretic framework is provided in order to extend the Nelson-Oppen combination procedure to non-disjoint signatures. The algorithm presented there relies on a skillful application of Robinson's joint consistency theorem in model theory [6]. In order to apply it the main ingredients are the following. (i) The shared theory $T_0 = T_1 \cap T_2$ should be locally finite: roughly speaking such a theory gives rise to a finite number of configurations to search for. (ii) The theory T_0 is completable, meaning that a model completion T_0^* of T_0 – see [6, 13, 21, 31] – exists. (iii) Every model of the theory T_i can be extended to a model whose T_0-reduct is a model of the completed theory T_0^*. This method is a real extension of the Nelson-Oppen combination procedure from disjoint to non disjoint signatures: indeed, for the Nelson-Oppen procedure to work, one needs that theories T_i are stably infinite, i.e. equivalently, that each model of T_i can be embedded into an infinite model of T_i. Considering that the theory of an infinite set is the model completion of the theory of pure equality, one realizes why the procedure of [11, 12] generalizes the Nelson-Oppen procedure. If, on the other hand, one considers that the theory of Boolean algebras – which is the theory shared by two distinct modal logics – is locally finite, that it has as model completion the theory of atomless Boolean algebras, and that every modal algebra in a given variety can be embedded into an atomless Boolean algebra in the same variety, one immediately recovers Wolter's result concerning fusion transfer of decidability of global consequence relation [32].

The main goal of this paper is to take advantage from the experience matured through [11, 12] to obtain an handy criterion on fusion decidability in modal logics with nominals and a universal modality. Nominals and the universal modality were introduced in modal logics in [5, 20] and further investigated in [10, 14]. Nominals can either be seen as (universally quantified) variables in axiomatization issues or as propositional constants, for instance in description logics (and in this paper too). In the latter sense, they provide a method to define atoms in a Boolean algebra and to code a small amount of predicative logic into the propositional setting. Many description logics [1] can be regarded as fragments of modal logics with nominals and a universal modality. An algorithm for fusion decidability in this setting can therefore be used to solve fusion decidability when dealing with knowledge representation systems.

With a similar aim of dealing with knowledge representation systems, fusion decidability results were partially extended from modal logics to description logics in [2]. Compared to this work, we emphasize here the algebraic perspective: we consider a logic as being determined by its syntax, its axioms, and by the standard inference rules; the logic is not determined by a class of frames and we avoid analyzing the completeness issue. The algebraic perspective makes it possible to specialize the general combined decidability algorithm of [11, 12] and to analyze with different tools the results obtained in [2]. A problem left open there was how to deal with description logics with non trivial use of the universal modality and of nominals. The setting we consider turns out to be quite comprehensive; for example, nominals and the universal modality are allowed in axioms: using a DL terminology, we allow an unrestricted use of individuals and of the universal modality in concept descriptions. We can also cover interesting examples of non trivial use of the universal modality – non trivial in that the universal modality is related to other modalities by specific axioms – that arise in computational logics. Among these logics are the logic of knowledge [16], the converse propositional dynamic logic [28], and the propositional μ-calculus with converse operators [29].

Our main result sounds as follows: we find a criterion on modal systems which ensures fusion decidability. More precisely, we call a modal system nominal closed if – roughly speaking – all the definable nominals are already explicitly named. The fusion of two decidable nominal closed modal systems is shown to be decidable.

The paper is structured as follows. In section 1 we formalize the algebraic setting of modal systems with nominals and present the main result about fusion decidability of modal systems. We discuss the concepts introduced with examples. In section 2 we present the model theoretic background and the extension of the Nelson-Oppen method. This method relies on the notion of model completion of the minimal modal system, which is the object of study of section 3. Finally, in section 4 we apply the method to fusion decidability of modal systems, therefore completing the proof of the main result.

1   Modal Systems with Nominals

Fix $k \geq 0$; by a k-nominals modal signature (or simply a modal signature, if k is understood) we mean a tuple $\Sigma M = \langle \mathcal{O}, \mu, N_1, \ldots, N_k \rangle$, where $\mathcal{O}$ is a set (called the set of of modal operators) and μ is an arity function associating with every $O \in \mathcal{O}$ a natural number $\mu(O) \geq 0$. We always assume that $\mathcal{O}$ contains a special operator $\Box_U$ (the universal modality) of arity 1. ΣM-formulas are built up in the usual way using countably many propositional variables $x, y, z, \ldots$, the propositional constants $N_1, \ldots, N_k$ (called the nominals), the Boolean connectives $\neg, \wedge, \vee, \top, \bot, \rightarrow, \leftrightarrow$, and the operators in $\mathcal{O}$. We use $\alpha, \beta \ldots$ as metavariables for formulas; $\Diamond_U \alpha$ abbreviates $\neg \Box_U \neg \alpha$. A k-nominals modal system L (or simply a modal system) based on ΣM is a set of formulas closed under uniform substitution and containing (at least) the basic axiom schemata below. We write $L \vdash \alpha$ in order to say that there is an L-deduction of α, where an L-deduction is a deduction using the axiom schemata for L and two inference rules: modus ponens and necessitation (from α infer $\Box_U \alpha$). The basic axiom schemata are all the propositional tautologies, the congruential axioms

$$\bigwedge_{i=1}^{n} \Box_U(\alpha_i \leftrightarrow \beta_i) \rightarrow (O(\alpha_1, \ldots, \alpha_n) \leftrightarrow O(\beta_1, \ldots, \beta_n)) \tag{1}$$

(we have one such axiom for every $O \in \mathcal{O}$ of arity n), the S5 axioms for $\Box_U$

$$\Box_U(\alpha \to \beta) \to (\Box_U \alpha \to \Box_U \beta) \qquad\qquad \Box_U \alpha \to \alpha$$
$$\Box_U \alpha \to \Box_U \Box_U \alpha \qquad\qquad\qquad \Diamond_U \alpha \to \Box_U \Diamond_U \alpha \,,$$

and the following axioms for nominals

$$\Diamond_U N_i \qquad\qquad \Diamond_U (N_i \wedge \alpha) \to \Box_U (N_i \to \alpha) \,. \qquad (2)$$

We say that a unary modal operator $\Box \in \mathcal{O}$ is normal if L contains the axiom schemata $\Box\top$ and $\Box(\alpha \to \beta) \to (\Box\alpha \to \Box\beta)$; if $\Box \in \mathcal{O}$ is normal, its necessitation rule follows from necessitation rule for $\Box_U$ and the remaining axiom schemata; also, the corresponding congruential axioms (1) can equivalently be replaced by the simpler axiom $\Box_U \alpha \to \Box\alpha$.

It is standard practice in propositional logic to associate a variety of algebras with a logic, see for example [9, §1.5]. In the case of a modal system L based on the modal signature ΣM, we can define *a first order equational theory* T_L as follows. The first order signature of T_L is obtained by adding to ΣM the Boolean operators $\neg, \wedge, \vee, \top, \bot, \to$.[1] The axioms of T_L contain for every $\alpha \in L$ a corresponding equation $\alpha = \top$ (here and in the following, we may treat ambiguously the metavariables $\alpha, \beta, \ldots$ as denoting propositional modal formulas and first order terms in the signature of T_L). Models of T_L form the variety V_L, called the variety of L-algebras. It should be clear (for general reasons) that *$L \vdash \alpha$ is equivalent to the fact that* $T_L \models \alpha = \top$. The problem $L \vdash \alpha$ is known as the *decidability problem* for the modal system L, whereas the problem $T_L \models \alpha = \top$ is known as the (uniform) *word problem* for V_L. Given the above mentioned equivalence, in this paper *we shall treat decidability problems for modal logics as word problems in universal algebra*, thus applying general combination methods from automated reasoning.

A main result of Universal Algebra – see for example [15] – is that every algebra can be embedded in a product of subdirectly irreducible algebras, i.e. of algebras having a minimal non trivial congruence. Consequently an equation fails in an arbitrary algebra if and only if it fails in a subdirectly irreducible one. By means of the congruential axioms (1) we can ensure a nice behaviour of congruences of an L-algebra $\mathcal{A}$: these bijectively correspond with $\Box_U$-closed filters of the algebra.[2] Using this information it is easily argued that: the finitely generated congruences are all principal and form a Boolean algebra; in the variety V_L subdirectly irreducible algebras coincide with *simple* algebras, i.e. the algebras with exactly one non trivial congruence; simple algebras are the models of the first order theory T_L^s obtained by adding to T_L the axioms $\bot \neq \top$ and $\forall x (x \neq \top \Rightarrow \Box_U x = \bot)$. Recall that an atom in a Boolean algebra is a minimal non-zero element. Observe then that if N is an element of a simple L-algebra $\mathcal{A}$,

---

[1] In order to avoid confusion, we shall use different symbols, like $\sim$ for negations, & for conjunctions, $\Rightarrow$ for implications, etc. when we denote connectives in first order logic (this is because $\neg, \wedge, \to, \ldots$ are used to form first order terms containing the operations of the signature of Boolean algebras).

[2] A filter $\Phi \subseteq \mathcal{A}$ is $\Box_U$-closed iff $a \in \Phi$ implies $\Box_U a \in \Phi$.

then the relations

$$\Diamond_U N = \top \qquad\qquad \Diamond_U (N \wedge x) \leq \Box_U (N \to x)$$

– that correspond to the axioms (2) – hold for N and for all $x \in \mathcal{A}$ iff N is an atom of $\mathcal{A}$.

1.1 Main Result

A modal system L is *nominal closed* if and only if, for every formula α, whenever

$$L \vdash \Diamond_U (\alpha \wedge x) \to \Box_U (\alpha \to x)$$

for a propositional variable x not occurring in α, then

$$L \vdash \Box_U (\alpha \to \bot) \vee \bigvee_{i=1}^{k} \Box_U (\alpha \to N_i) \,.$$

Roughly speaking, in a nominal-closed system, there are no hidden nominals, apart from $N_1, \ldots, N_k$ which are explicitly mentioned.

Let now L_1, L_2 be k-nominals modal systems over the signatures $\Sigma M_1, \Sigma M_2$ (notice that k is the same in both cases); assume also that $\Sigma M_1 \cap \Sigma M_2$ contains just the universal modality $\Box_U$ and the k-nominals $N_1, \ldots, N_k$. The *fusion* of L_1, L_2 is the modal system $L_1 \cup L_2$ over the signature $\Sigma M_1 \cup \Sigma M_2$. Our main result is a decidability transfer (to be proved in sections 2-4):

Theorem. *If L_1, L_2 are both decidable and nominal-closed, their fusion $L_1 \cup L_2$ is decidable too.*

We summarize here the variant of the Nelson-Oppen [17, 18] combination schema suggested by the proofs of Theorem 2.3, Lemma 4.1 and Theorem 4.4 of this paper:

Input: A $(\Sigma M_1 \cup \Sigma M_2)$- formula α.
Step 1. Apply successive variable abstractions of alien subterms to the literal $\alpha \neq \top$ in order to produce a set Γ_1 of pure T_{L_1}-literals and a set Γ_2 of pure T_{L_2}-literals, so that $\Gamma_1 \cup \Gamma_2$ is equisatisfiable with $\{\alpha \neq \top\}$.
Step 2. Guess a Boolean arrangement[3] Δ of the shared variables appearing both in Γ_1 and in Γ_2 and let $\Gamma'_1 = \Gamma_1 \cup \Delta$, $\Gamma'_2 = \Gamma_2 \cup \Delta$.
Step 3. Using the decision procedures for L_1, L_2, check whether

$$L_i \nvdash (\bigwedge_{\beta = \top \in \Gamma'_i} \Box_U \beta) \to (\bigvee_{\gamma \neq \top \in \Gamma'_i} \Box_U \gamma).$$

If this is the case for both $i = 1$ and $i = 2$, **return** '$L_1 \cup L_2 \nvdash \alpha$'. Otherwise, go back to Step 2.

---

[3] By a Boolean arrangement on a finite set $\{x_1, \ldots, x_n\}$ we mean a set of unit literals representing the diagram of a (necessarily finite) Boolean algebra generated by $x_1, \ldots, x_n$. A Boolean arrangement can be guessed by specifying which terms of the kind $\bigwedge_{i=1}^{n} \epsilon_i x_i$ are equal to $\top$ and which ones are not (here $\epsilon_i x_i$ is either x_i or $\neg x_i$).

Step 4. If this step is reached (namely if all Boolean arrangements in Step 2 have been unsuccessfully tried), **return** '$L_1 \cup L_2 \vdash \alpha$'.

As for complexity of this combined procedure, the same observations of [2] apply: since the purified problem can be produced in linear time and since the guess takes exponential space, the combined procedure may raise the complexity from polynomial to exponential space and from exponential time to double exponential time.[4]

1.2   Examples

Description Logics. Inclusion of nominals into modal systems makes it possible to translate terminologies and assertions of Description Logics into our framework – see also [24] for earlier considerations on description and modal logics. The following is a simple example: consider the terminology and assertion

$$\texttt{Mother} \equiv \texttt{Female} \sqcap \exists\texttt{hasChild}.\top \qquad \texttt{Mother(MARY)}.$$

It can be translated into a modal system (in our sense) with given propositional constants $P_{\texttt{Mother}}$, $P_{\texttt{Female}}$, one normal modal operator $\Diamond_{\texttt{hasChild}}$, and one nominal $N_{\texttt{MARY}}$. On the top of the axioms for nominals and modal operators, the modal system contains the axioms

$$P_{\texttt{Mother}} \leftrightarrow (P_{\texttt{Female}} \wedge \Diamond_{\texttt{hasChild}} \top) \qquad N_{\texttt{MARY}} \rightarrow P_{\texttt{Mother}}.$$

Many extensions of the core description logic $\mathcal{ALC}$ can also be algebraized within our modal systems. We list, among them, extensions with transitive roles [25], least or greatest fixed point semantics of cyclic terminologies [23], number restrictions [7], functional and inverse roles – which we are going to exemplify within example (e).

The Universal Modality in Computational Logics. The universal modality is also worth studying in its own since it arises in many contexts. For a finite set of modalities $\Box_\sigma$, $\sigma \in \Sigma$, define $\Box_U x$ as the greatest fixed point

$$\Box_U x = \nu_y.(x \wedge \bigwedge_{\sigma \in \Sigma} \Box_\sigma y). \tag{3}$$

That is, $\Box_U x$ is a fixed point of $f(y) = x \wedge \bigwedge_{\sigma \in \Sigma} \Box_\sigma y$ which is greater of any z such that $z \leq f(z)$. Usually, this modality satisfies the S4 axioms but not the S5 axiom, but there are interesting logics where the latter axiom holds too. In the logic of knowledge [16] the modality $\Box_\sigma$ represents the knowledge of the individual agent σ; usually this is an S5 modality. The common knowledge modality, which is defined as in (3), becomes an S5 modality too.

---

[4] Notice that the addition of the universal modality usually leads by itself to EXPTIME-complete decision problems (see [26]).

Another interesting example is the converse (test-free) PDL and its extension to the full propositional modal μ-calculus with converse modalities [28, 29]. In these logics there is a converse action $\bar{\sigma} \in \Sigma$ for each $\sigma \in \Sigma$, and the formulas

$$\Diamond_\sigma \Box_{\bar{\sigma}} x \to x \qquad\qquad x \to \Box_{\bar{\sigma}} \Diamond_\sigma x\,, \qquad\qquad (4)$$

expressing that $\Diamond_\sigma$ and $\Box_{\bar{\sigma}}$ is a residuated pair, are axioms. Again $\Box_U x$, defined as in (3), is easily seen to be a universal modality.

Considering the μ-calculus with converse modalities is appropriate in this context since this logic can be fully algebraized, see [23]. With the μ-calculus we can also exemplify the way non-normal operators arise: the interpretation of an arbitrary inductively defined μ-term gives rise to a non-normal modal operator satisfying the congruential axiom (1), see [22]; moreover such operator is uniquely determined by the original modalities $\Box_\sigma$ and therefore algebraically related to the universal modality $\Box_U$.

How to Check that a Modal System Is Nominal Closed. Apparently the property of a modal system L to be nominal closed is difficult to decide: one would expect to need a nice presentation of L such as a sequent calculus with good proof theoretic properties. This is not the case; the following Proposition gives an equivalent algebraic criterion which turns out to be very useful:

Proposition 1.1. *A system L is nominal closed if and only if for any simple L-algebra $\mathcal{A}$ and any atom $a \in \mathcal{A}$ distinct from the N_i, there is a simple L-algebra $\mathcal{B}$ and an L-algebra monomorphism $h : \mathcal{A} \longrightarrow \mathcal{B}$ such that $h(a)$ is not an atom.*

Later on, after Proposition 4.3, it will be evident why the Proposition holds.

(a) We apply Proposition 1.1 to a trivial modal system L. That is, we assume that L has no nominals and that the universal modality interacts with other operators (including itself) only through the congruential axioms (1). It is enough to consider the diagonal $\mathcal{A} \longrightarrow \mathcal{A} \times \mathcal{A}$ where the universal modality is defined on $\mathcal{A} \times \mathcal{A}$ in the unique possible way to obtain a simple algebra: $\Box_U z = \top$ if $z = \top$ and $\Box_U z = \bot$ otherwise. The operations $O \in \mathcal{O}$ are defined as usual in a product algebra. It is an exercise to verify that the congruential axioms hold. Finally, the image of an atom a is the pair (a, a) which is not anymore an atom since $(\bot, \bot) < (a, \bot) < (a, a)$. Thus we have proved: *a trivial modal system L is nominal closed*. This statement is analogous to [2, §25]. □

(b) We consider now the modal system L – introduced above – with one nominal N_{MARY}, propositional constants P_{Mother}, P_{Female}, and one normal modal operator $\Diamond_{\mathrm{hasChild}}$. We use Proposition 1.1 to show that this system is nominal closed.

Suppose that $\mathcal{A}$ is a simple L-algebra and that $a \neq N_{\mathrm{MARY}}$ is an atom of $\mathcal{A}$. Recall that the function $\phi : \mathcal{A} \longrightarrow 2$ defined by $\phi(x) = \top$ if and only if $a \leq x$ is morphism of Boolean algebras. Thus we define $h_a = \langle \mathrm{id}, \phi \rangle : \mathcal{A} \longrightarrow \mathcal{A} \times 2$ and put a structure of a simple L-algebra on $\mathcal{A} \times 2$ as follows: the universal modality is defined as in (a) while we define

$$P_{\mathrm{Female}} = (P_{\mathrm{Female}}, \phi(P_{\mathrm{Female}})) \qquad\qquad P_{\mathrm{Mother}} = (P_{\mathrm{Mother}}, \phi(P_{\mathrm{Mother}}))$$
$$N_{\mathrm{MARY}} = (N_{\mathrm{MARY}}, \phi(N_{\mathrm{MARY}})) \qquad \Diamond_{\mathrm{hasChild}}(x, y) = (\Diamond_{\mathrm{hasChild}} x, \phi(\Diamond_{\mathrm{hasChild}} x))\,.$$

By definition the extension h_a preserves the L-structure and therefore the relations on constants axiomatizing the system. It is readily seen that the operator $\Diamond_{\mathtt{hasChild}}$ on $\mathcal{A} \times 2$ is normal and that the constant $N_{\mathtt{MARY}}$ is an atom of $\mathcal{A} \times 2$. This follows since $\phi(N_{\mathtt{MARY}}) = \bot$, as a is an atom of $\mathcal{A}$ distinct from $N_{\mathtt{MARY}}$. $\square$

(c) There is an easy sufficient semantic criterion for modal systems L which are Kripke complete w.r.t. a class of frames – see a standard textbook on modal logic such as [9] for frame semantics. Say that a Kripke frame is simple iff the universal modality is interpreted by means of the total relation. In this case, *a modal system L which is complete w.r.t. a class $\mathcal{C}$ of simple Kripke frames is nominal closed provided for every simple frame F in the class $\mathcal{C}$ and each element $w \in F$ distinct from the interpretation of a nominal, there are a simple frame F' in the class $\mathcal{C}$ and a surjective p-morphism $f : F' \longrightarrow F$ such that the fiber $f^{-1}(w)$ contains at least two elements.* The criterion is easily seen to be sufficient by considering the contrapositive of the definition of a nominal closed system.

  Here is an application of this semantic criterion. Let L be a modal system containing nominals (and the universal modality) and normal modal operators $\Box_i$, $i = 1, \ldots, n$. The axioms of L are the ones for nominals and the universal modality and any combination of the axioms K, T, K4, B for the normal modal operators $\Box_i$. As a Kripke completeness theorem is available, we can apply the above semantic criterion. Argue as follows: let F be a frame for L and $w \in F$ be distinct from the interpretation of nominals; define F' to be $F + \{*\}$ and the function f by $f(v) = v$, for $v \in F$, $f(*) = w$. Define the relation R_i (corresponding to the normal operator $\Box_i$) as follows: $v_1 R_i v_2$ iff $f(v_1) R_i f(v_2)$. This proves that L is nominal closed.

(d) The same technique used in the previous example can be applied to show that the systems we met in the previous subsection are nominal closed, whenever a Kripke completeness theorem is available. For example, the standard filtration technique can be adapted to prove that the converse PDL with k nominals has the finite model property, hence it is complete with respect to the related class of simple Kripke frames. Using this technique is then easy to see that converse PDL with at least one nominal is nominal closed.

(e) Finally, we exhibit a modal system L that is not nominal closed. The modal system L has one nominal N_1 and contains a normal operator $\boxdot$ as well as its converse modality $\boxminus$: formulas analogous to those in (4) are axioms. The formula $\Diamond x \to \boxdot x$ is an axiom of L too. We first observe that: *if $\mathcal{A}$ is a simple L-algebra and a is an atom of $\mathcal{A}$, then either $\Diamond a = \bot$ or $\Diamond a$ is an atom.* For this, it is enough to show that the condition $\bot \leq x \leq \Diamond a$ implies either $\Diamond a \leq x$ or $x = \bot$, so let us assume this condition. If $a \wedge \boxminus x \neq \bot$, then $a \leq \boxminus x$, and therefore $\Diamond a \leq x$. If $a \wedge \boxminus x = \bot$, then $a \leq \neg \boxminus x = \Diamond \neg x \leq \boxminus \neg x$. It follows that $x \leq \Diamond a \leq \Diamond \boxminus \neg x \leq \neg x$, and therefore $x \leq \bot$. It is now easy to construct a simple L-algebra – by means of a Kripke frame – with the property that $\Diamond^n N_1$ is distinct from $\Diamond^m N_1$ if $n \neq m$. In particular we have a definable infinity of atoms: if $\Diamond^l N_1$ is distinct from the N_i, then it is not possible to embed such an algebra into an algebra where $\diamondsuit^l N_1$ is not an atom. This shows that the system is not nominal closed.[5]   □

2   Model Theory and Combination Problems

We are planning to adapt the extension of the Nelson-Oppen combined decision procedure outlined in [11, 12] to our fusion decidability transfer problem. To this aim, we need to recall some classical model-theoretic ingredients.

A *first order signature* Σ is a set of functions and predicate symbols (each of them endowed with the corresponding arity). We assume the binary equality predicate symbol $=$ to be always present in Σ. The signature obtained from Σ by the addition of a set of new constants ($=$ 0-ary function symbols) X is denoted by $\Sigma \cup X$ or by Σ^X. We have the usual notions of Σ-*term*, (full first order) -*formula*, -*atom*, -*literal*, -*clause*, etc.: e.g. atoms are just atomic formulas, literals are atoms and their negations, clauses are disjunctions of literals, etc. We use letters $\alpha, \beta, \dots$ for terms and letters $\phi, \psi, \dots$ for formulas. Terms, literals and clauses are called *ground* whenever free variables do not appear in them. *Sentences* are formulas without free variables. A Σ-*theory* T is a set of sentences (called the axioms of T) in the signature Σ; however when we write $T \subseteq T'$ for theories, we may mean not just set-theoretic inclusion but the fact that all the axioms for T are logical consequences of the axioms for T'.

From the semantic side, we have the standard notion of a Σ-*structure* $\mathcal{A}$: this is nothing but a support set endowed with an arity-matching interpretation of the predicate and function symbols from Σ. We shall notationally confuse, for the sake of simplicity, a structure with its support set. Truth of a Σ-formula in $\mathcal{A}$ is defined in any one of the standard ways; a Σ-structure $\mathcal{A}$ is a *model* of a Σ-theory T (in symbols $\mathcal{A} \models T$) iff all axioms of T are true in $\mathcal{A}$ (for models of a Σ-theory T we shall sometimes use the letters $\mathcal{M}, \mathcal{N}, \dots$ to distinguish them from arbitrary Σ-structures). If ϕ is a formula, $T \models \phi$ ('ϕ *is a logical consequence of* T') means that ϕ is true in any model of T. The *word problem* for T is the problem of deciding whether the universal closure of a Σ-atom is a logical consequence of T; similarly, the *clausal word problem* for T is the problem of deciding whether the universal closure of a Σ-clause is a logical consequence of T. A Σ-theory T is *complete* iff for every Σ-sentence ϕ, either ϕ or $\neg\phi$ is a logical consequence of T; T is *consistent* iff it has a model.

An *embedding* between two Σ-structures $\mathcal{A}$ and $\mathcal{B}$ is any map $f : \mathcal{A} \longrightarrow \mathcal{B}$ among the corresponding support sets satisfying the condition

$$(*) \qquad\qquad \mathcal{A} \models A \quad \text{iff} \quad \mathcal{B} \models A$$

for all $\Sigma^{\mathcal{A}}$ atoms A (here $\mathcal{A}$ is regarded as a $\Sigma^{\mathcal{A}}$-structure by interpreting each $a \in \mathcal{A}$ into itself and $\mathcal{B}$ is regarded as a $\Sigma^{\mathcal{A}}$-structure by interpreting each $a \in \mathcal{A}$

---

[5] A little warning: there might be 0-nominals modal systems which are not nominal-closed. Notice however that this may happen only in case the universal modality has a non-trivial interaction with the remaining modal operators, because of example (a).

into $f(a)$). In case $(*)$ holds for all first order formulas, the embedding is said to be *elementary*.

The *diagram* $\Delta(\mathcal{A})$ of a Σ-structure $\mathcal{A}$ is the set of ground $\Sigma^{\mathcal{A}}$-literals which are true in $\mathcal{A}$; the elementary diagram $\Delta^e(\mathcal{A})$ of a Σ-structure $\mathcal{A}$ is the set of $\Sigma^{\mathcal{A}}$-sentences which are true in $\mathcal{A}$. Robinson (elementary) diagram theorem [6] says that there is an (elementary) embedding between the Σ-structures $\mathcal{A}$ and $\mathcal{B}$ iff it is possible to expand $\mathcal{B}$ to a $\Sigma^{\mathcal{A}}$-structure in such a way that it becomes a model of the (elementary) diagram of $\mathcal{A}$. This theorem will be repeatedly used without explicit mention in the paper.

We shall need the well-known notion of a *model completion* of a theory; we take the definition from e.g. [30]. Let T be a Σ-theory and let $T^* \supseteq T$ be a further Σ-theory; we say that T^* is a model completion of T iff (i) every model of T has an embedding into a model of T^* and (ii) for every model $\mathcal{M}$ of T, we have that $T^* \cup \Delta(\mathcal{M})$ is a complete theory. The following Proposition gives an equivalent formulation in case T is universal and the signature is at most countable:

Proposition 2.1. *Let T be a universal Σ-theory (where Σ is at most countable) and let $T^* \supseteq T$ be a further Σ-theory such that every model of T has an embedding into a model of T^*. Then T^* is a model completion of T iff whenever $\mathcal{M}_1, \mathcal{M}_2$ are both at most countable models of T^* extending a common finitely generated substructure $\mathcal{A}$, then $\mathcal{M}_1$ and $\mathcal{M}_2$ are elementarily equivalent as $\Sigma \cup \mathcal{A}$-structures.*

Proof. One side is trivial (because $\mathcal{M}_1, \mathcal{M}_2$ are both models of $T^* \cup \Delta(\mathcal{A})$ and $\mathcal{A} \models T$, being T universal). For the other side, let $\mathcal{M}$ be a model of T and let $\phi(\underline{a})$ be a formula with parameters $\underline{a}$ from $\mathcal{M}$. Suppose that there are models $\mathcal{M}_1, \mathcal{M}_2$ of $T^* \cup \Delta(\mathcal{M})$ such that $\mathcal{M}_1 \models \phi(\underline{a})$ and $\mathcal{M}_2 \models \neg\phi(\underline{a})$. Let $\mathcal{A}$ be the substructure of $\mathcal{M}$ generated by $\underline{a}$; by downward Löwenheim-Skolem theorem, $\mathcal{M}_1, \mathcal{M}_2$ are elementarily equivalent as $\Sigma^{\underline{a}}$-structures to at most countable models $\mathcal{M}'_1, \mathcal{M}'_2$, respectively: this gives a contradiction. $\square$

It can be shown that a model completion T^* of a theory T is unique, in case it exists, see [6]. There are many classical examples of model completions from algebra [6]: the theory of algebraically closed fields is the model completion of the theory of fields, the theory of divisible torsion free abelian groups is the model completion of the theory of torsion free abelian groups, etc. An example which is more relevant for this paper is the following: the theory of atomless Boolean algebras is the model completion of the theory of Boolean algebras (for model completions arising in the algebra of logic, see the book [13]). Next, we give the definition of Σ_0-compatibility [11, 12]:

Definition 2.2. *Let T be a theory in the signature Σ and let T_0 be a universal theory in a subsignature $\Sigma_0 \subseteq \Sigma$. We say that T is T_0-compatible iff (i) $T_0 \subseteq T$; (ii) T_0 has a model-completion T_0^*; (iii) every model of T embeds into a model of $T \cup T_0^*$.*

We say that a Σ_0-universal theory T_0 is *locally finite* iff Σ_0 is finite and for every finite set $\underline{a}$ of new free constants, there are only finitely many $\Sigma^{\underline{a}}$-ground terms up to T_0-identity (let their number be $k_{T_0}(\underline{a})$). As we are mainly dealing with computational aspects, we consider part of the definition the further request that $k_{T_0}(\underline{a})$ is effectively computable from $\underline{a}$. Examples of locally finite theories important for this paper are the theory of Boolean algebras and of $S5$-(uni)modal algebras.

For our fusion decidability results, the main ingredient is the following theorem [11, 12]. The decision algorithm presented in the previous section is suggested from its proof which therefore is included.

Theorem 2.3. *Assume that T_1 is a Σ_1-theory and that T_2 is a Σ_2-theory which are both compatible with respect to a locally finite universal Σ_0-theory T_0 (where Σ_0 is $\Sigma_1 \cap \Sigma_2$). If the clausal word problem in both T_1, T_2 is decidable, so is the clausal word problem in $T_1 \cup T_2$.*

Proof. Let $\forall \underline{x} \ (\alpha_1 \neq \beta_1 \vee \cdots \vee \alpha_n \neq \beta_n \vee \alpha_1' = \beta_1' \vee \cdots \vee \alpha_m' = \beta_m')$ be the $\Sigma_1 \cup \Sigma_2$-clause we want to decide. Taking negation and skolemization, we need to test for $T_1 \cup T_2$-consistency the set of ground literals (here $\underline{b}$ are new constants)

$$\{\alpha_1(\underline{b}) = \beta_1(\underline{b}), \ldots, \alpha_n(\underline{b}) = \beta_n(\underline{b}), \alpha_1'(\underline{b}) \neq \beta_1'(\underline{b}), \ldots, \alpha_m'(\underline{b}) \neq \beta_m'(\underline{b})\}.$$

This set, call it Γ, can be purified: in fact we get equiconsistency if we replace in it a subterm γ with a new constant c and add the further equation $c = \gamma$. Doing that repeatedly, we finally get two sets of literals Γ_1, Γ_2 such that for a certain finite set $\underline{a}$ of new constants (including the $\underline{b}$'s) we have that: (a) Γ_1 is a set of $\Sigma_1^{\underline{a}}$-ground literals; (b) Γ_2 is a set of $\Sigma_2^{\underline{a}}$-ground literals; (c) $\Gamma_1 \cup \Gamma_2$ is $T_1 \cup T_2$-equiconsistent with Γ.

We shall show that $\Gamma_1 \cup \Gamma_2$ is $T_1 \cup T_2$-consistent iff there is a Σ_0-structure $\mathcal{A}$ such that: (i) $\mathcal{A}$ is generated by $\underline{a}$; (ii) $\Gamma_1 \cup \Delta(\mathcal{A})$ is T_1-consistent and (iii) $\Gamma_2 \cup \Delta(\mathcal{A})$ is T_2-consistent. This will prove the theorem since the input problem has been reduced to finitely many pairs of pure problems, which are solvable by hypothesis.[6]

One side is trivial; so suppose that there is $\mathcal{A}$ satisfying (i)-(ii)-(iii). This means that $T_1 \cup \Gamma_1 \cup \Delta(\mathcal{A})$ has a Σ_1-model $\mathcal{M}_1$ and that $T_2 \cup \Gamma_2 \cup \Delta(\mathcal{A})$ has a Σ_2-model $\mathcal{M}_2$: by T_0-compatibility, we can freely suppose that $\mathcal{M}_i \models T_0^*$ for $i = 1, 2$ (recall that truth of Γ_i, which is a set of ground literals, is preserved by superstructures). Also, we can rename elements in the supports so that $\mathcal{M}_1 \cap \mathcal{M}_2 = \mathcal{A}$. Now $T_0^* \cup \Delta(\mathcal{A})$ is a $\Sigma_0 \cup \mathcal{A}$-complete theory and $\Delta^e(\mathcal{M}_1), \Delta^e(\mathcal{M}_2)$ are both consistent extensions of its (in signatures $\Sigma_1 \cup \mathcal{M}_1$ and $\Sigma_2 \cup \mathcal{M}_2$ such that $(\Sigma_1 \cup \mathcal{M}_1) \cap (\Sigma_2 \cup \mathcal{M}_2) = \Sigma_0 \cup \mathcal{A})$. By Robinson joint consistency theorem [6], $\Delta^e(\mathcal{M}_1) \cup \Delta^e(\mathcal{M}_2)$ has a model which in particular is a $(\Sigma_1 \cup \Sigma_2)^{\underline{a}}$-model of $T_1 \cup \Gamma_1 \cup T_2 \cup \Gamma_2$, as desired. □

---

[6] Notice that Σ_0-structures satisfying (i)-(ii)-(iii) are finitely many and effectively computable: since T_0 is universal, they must be models of T_0, hence they cannot have more than $k_{T_0}(\underline{a})$ elements, because T_0 is locally finite.

3   The Model Completion of $T_{L_0}^s$

We call L_0 the minimum k-nominal modal system: it just contains the universal modality and the nominals $N_1, \ldots, N_k$; the basic axiom schemata of every k-nominal modal system (see section 1) are the only axiom schemata in L_0. In view of applying Theorem 2.3 to the fusion of modal systems, we need a better grasp on the model completion of $T_{L_0}^s$, the theory of simple L_0-algebras.

Definition 3.1. *A simple L_0-algebra $\mathcal{A}$ is said to be* quasi-atomless *if the only atoms of $\mathcal{A}$ are $N_1, \ldots, N_k$.*

Clearly, there are many first order formulas that axiomatize quasi-atomless L_0-algebras; among them

$$\forall y \, (\, y \neq \bot \, \& \, y \neq N_1 \, \& \cdots \& \, y \neq N_k \, \Rightarrow \, \exists x \, (\bot < x < y) \,). \qquad \text{(QA)}$$

We have that:

Theorem 3.2. *The theory $(T_{L_0}^s)^*$ of quasi-atomless simple L_0-algebras is the model completion of the theory $T_{L_0}^s$ of simple L_0-algebras.*

Using Proposition 2.1, the theorem is proved observing that:

Proposition 3.3. *(i) Every simple L_0-algebra can be embedded into a quasi-atomless simple L_0-algebra. (ii) Given a finite L_0-algebra $\mathcal{A}$ and two at most countable simple quasi-atomless extensions $\mathcal{B}, \mathcal{C}$ of $\mathcal{A}$, there is an isomorphism from $\mathcal{B}$ to $\mathcal{C}$ fixing $\mathcal{A}$.*

For lack of space, we only sketch the proof. The first statement (i) is proved using a tool introduced in section 1: given a simple L_0-algebra and an atom $a \in \mathcal{A}$ distinct from the N_i one produces a simple L_0-algebra on $\mathcal{A} \times 2$ and shows that the embedding h_a defined in example (b) is an homomorphism of L_0-algebras; starting from a simple L_0-algebra, one carefully iterates this construction producing an infinite chain: the inductive limit of this chain is the desired quasi-atomless simple L_0-algebra. The second statement (ii) is a consequence of:

Lemma 3.4. *Let $\mathcal{A}$ and $\mathcal{B}$ be two finite simple L_0-algebras, and let $\mathcal{C}$ be an infinite quasi-atomless L_0-algebras. Given monomorphisms $i : \mathcal{A} \longrightarrow \mathcal{C}$ and $j : \mathcal{A} \longrightarrow \mathcal{B}$, there exists a monomorphism $k : \mathcal{B} \longrightarrow \mathcal{C}$ such that $k \circ j = i$.*

This lemma – easily verified using Stone duality – allows to progressively construct the isomorphism of (ii) using back and forth.

4   Fusion Decidability for Modal Systems

We are now ready is to apply Theorem 2.3 to fusion decidability of modal systems.

Lemma 4.1. *If the modal system L is decidable, then so is the clausal word problem in T_L^s.*

Proof. A finite set $\{\alpha_1 = \top, \ldots, \alpha_n = \top, \beta_1 \neq \top, \ldots, \beta_m \neq \top\}$ of T_L^s-literals (containing additional free constants induced by the Skolemization of the universal closure of a T_L-clause) is satisfiable iff there is a simple algebra $\mathcal{A}$ such that $\mathcal{A} \models \Box_U \alpha_1 = \top, \ldots \mathcal{A} \models \Box_U \alpha_n = \top, \mathcal{A} \models \Box_U \beta_1 = \bot, \ldots, \Box_U \beta_m = \bot$ i.e. iff there is a simple algebra $\mathcal{A}$ such that

$$\mathcal{A} \models \Box_U \alpha_1 \wedge \cdots \wedge \Box_U \alpha_n \wedge \neg \Box_U \beta_1 \wedge \cdots \wedge \neg \Box_U \beta_m = \top.$$

As simple algebras coincide with subdirectly irreducible algebras in our variety, this simply means that the formula

$$\neg(\Box_U \alpha_1 \wedge \cdots \wedge \Box_U \alpha_n \wedge \neg \Box_U \beta_1 \wedge \cdots \wedge \neg \Box_U \beta_m)$$

is not a theorem of the system L (notice that this formula can denote either $\bot$ or $\top$ in any simple algebra). $\qquad\Box$

Lemma 4.2. *Suppose that L is nominal closed. Let $\mathcal{A}$ be a model of T_L^s and let a be an atom of $\mathcal{A}$ which is different from $N_1, \ldots, N_k$. Then it is possible to embed $\mathcal{A}$ into a model of T_L^s in which a is not an atom anymore.*

Proof. Let $\mathcal{F}(X)/\Phi$ be a presentation of $\mathcal{A}$ as a quotient of the free algebra $\mathcal{F}(X)$ divided by the $\Box_U$-closed filter Φ; suppose that a is (in this presentation) the equivalence class $[\alpha]$ of the term α. Take $y \notin X$ and consider the algebra $\mathcal{B}$ having $\mathcal{F}(X \cup \{y\})/\Psi$ as a presentation, where Ψ is the $\Box_U$-closed filter generated by the set of formulas $\Phi \cup \{\Diamond_U(\alpha \wedge y), \Diamond_U(\alpha \wedge \neg y)\}$. If we are able to show that Ψ does not contain $\bot$, then we are done, since if $\mathcal{C}$ is a simple quotient of $\mathcal{B}$ then the composite map $\mathcal{A} \longrightarrow \mathcal{B} \longrightarrow \mathcal{C}$ is injective – because $\mathcal{A}$ is simple – and the relations $\bot < [\alpha \wedge y] < [\alpha]$ hold in $\mathcal{C}$ by construction. Suppose therefore that Ψ contains $\bot$, then for some X-term β such that $[\Box_U \beta] \in \Phi$, we have $L \vdash \Box_U \beta \wedge \Diamond_U(\alpha \wedge y) \wedge \Diamond_U(\alpha \wedge \neg y) \to \bot$ and also, by the S5 axioms, $L \vdash \Diamond_U(\Box_U \beta \wedge \alpha \wedge y) \wedge \Diamond_U(\Box_U \beta \wedge \alpha \wedge \neg y) \to \bot$. By Boolean transformations, we get $L \vdash \Diamond_U(\Box_U \beta \wedge \alpha \wedge y) \to \Box_U(\Box_U \beta \wedge \alpha \to y)$. As L is nominal closed, we have $L \vdash \bigvee_{i=0}^{k} \Box_U(\Box_U \beta \wedge \alpha \to N_i)$ (where we take $N_0 = \bot$). If we read this relation within the simple algebra $\mathcal{A}$, we get $a = [\alpha] \leq N_i$ for some i, a contradiction. $\qquad\Box$

Proposition 4.3. T_L^s *is* $T_{L_0}^s$*-compatible iff L is nominal-closed.*

Proof. Suppose that L is nominal-closed. It is sufficient to repeatedly apply the previous Lemma: given a simple algebra $\mathcal{A}_0$, let $\{a_i\}_i$ be a well-ordering of the atoms of $\mathcal{A}_0$ different from $N_1, \ldots, N_k$. Define simple algebras $\mathcal{A}_0^i$ by transfinite induction by inserting new elements $\bot < b_i < a_i$; then take the union $\mathcal{A}_1 = \bigcup_i \mathcal{A}_0^i$ and repeat this construction ω-times (in order to eliminate also newly introduced atoms).

Suppose, vice-versa, that T_L^s is $T_{L_0}^s$-compatible and let α be such that $L \vdash \Diamond_U(\alpha \wedge x) \to \Box_U(\alpha \to x)$ holds for x not occurring in α. If $L \not\vdash \bigvee_{i=0}^{k} \Box_U(\alpha \to N_i)$, then there is a subdirectly irreducible (hence simple) algebra $\mathcal{A}$ such that $\mathcal{A} \not\models \bigvee_{i=0}^{k} \Box_U(\alpha(\underline{a}) \to N_i) \neq \top$, for some $\underline{a} \in \mathcal{A}$ (replacing the variables appearing in α). This means that $\alpha(\underline{a}) \neq \bot$ and that for all $i = 1, \ldots, k$, in $\mathcal{A}$ we have $\alpha(\underline{a}) \not\leq N_i$. By compatibility, we can embed $\mathcal{A}$ into a simple algebra $\mathcal{B}$ in which $\alpha(\underline{a})$ is not an atom. This means that in $\mathcal{B}$ there is b such that $\bot < b < \alpha(\underline{a})$: such b contradicts the fact that $L \vdash \Diamond_U(\alpha \wedge x) \to \Box_U(\alpha \to x)$ (just replace the propositional variables in α by $\underline{a}$ and x by b). □

We can now prove our main result:

Theorem 4.4. *Let L_1, L_2 be both nominal-closed. If L_1, L_2 are decidable, so is their fusion $L_1 \cup L_2$.*

Proof. By general reasons, $L_1 \cup L_2 \not\vdash \alpha$ iff there is a subdirectly irreducible (hence simple) algebra $\mathcal{A} \models T_{L_1} \cup T_{L_2}$ in which the equation $\alpha = \top$ fails. Hence it is sufficient to be able to solve word problems in $(T_{L_1} \cup T_{L_2})^s = T_{L_1}^s \cup T_{L_2}^s$: this is in fact the case, by Theorem 2.3, Lemma 4.1, Theorem 3.2 and Proposition 4.3. □

It is easily seen that T_0-compatibility is a modular property (see in any case Proposition 3.3 of [12]), hence it is an immediate corollary of Proposition 4.3 that if L_1, L_2 are both nominal closed, so is their fusion. We can consequently generalize the above results to:

Corollary 4.5. *If $L_1, \ldots, L_n$ are nominal closed and decidable, then their iterated fusion $L_1 \cup \ldots \cup L_n$ is also decidable.*

References

[1] F. Baader, D. Calvanese, D. McGuinness, D. Nardi, and P. Patel-Schneider, editors. *The Description Logic Handbook*. Cambridge University Press, 2002.

[2] F. Baader, C. Lutz, H. Sturm, and F. Wolter. Fusions of description logics and abstract description systems. *Journal of Artificial Intelligence Research (JAIR)*, 16:1–58, 2002.

[3] F. Baader and C. Tinelli. A new approach for combining decision procedures for the word problem, and its connection to the Nelson-Oppen combination method. In W. Mc Cune, editor, *Conference on Automated Deduction, CADE-14*, Lecture Notes in Computer Science 1249, pages 19–33. Springer, 1997.

[4] F. Baader and C. Tinelli. Deciding the word problem in the union of equational theories. *Information and Computation*, 178(2):346–390, 2002.

[5] R. A. Bull. An approach to tense logic. *Theoria*, 36:282–300, 1970.

[6] C. C. Chang and H. J. Keisler. *Model theory*, volume 73 of *Studies in Logic and the Foundations of Mathematics*. North-Holland Publishing Co., Amsterdam, third edition, 1990.

[7] M. Fattorosi-Barnaba and F. De Caro. Graded modalities. I. *Studia Logica*, 44(2):197–221, 1985.

[8] C. Fiorentini and S. Ghilardi. Combining word problems through rewriting in categories with products. *Theoretical Computer Science*, 294:103–149, 2003.

[9] D. Gabbay, A. Kurucz, F. Wolter, and M. Zakharyaschev. *Many-Dimensional Modal Logics: Theory and Applications*. Elsevier, 2003. In print.

[10] G. Gargov and V. Goranko. Modal logic with names. *J. Philos. Logic*, 22(6):607–636, 1993.

[11] S. Ghilardi. Quantifier elimination and provers integration. *Electronic Notes In Theoretical Computer Science (Proceedings of First Order Theorem Proving (FTP) '03)*, 2003.

[12] S. Ghilardi. Reasoners' cooperation and quantifier elimination. Technical Report 288-03, Dipartimento di Scienze dell'Informazione, Università degli Studi di Milano, March 2003.

[13] S. Ghilardi and M. Zawadowski. *Sheaves, Games, and Model Completions*. Trends in Logic. Kluwer Academic Publishers, 2002.

[14] V. Goranko and S. Passy. Using the universal modality: gains and questions. *J. Logic Comput.*, 2(1):5–30, 1992.

[15] G. Grätzer. *Universal algebra*. Springer-Verlag, New York, second edition, 1979.

[16] J. Y. Halpern. Reasoning about knowledge: a survey. In *Handbook of logic in artificial intelligence and logic programming, Vol. 4*, Oxford Sci. Publ., pages 1–34. Oxford Univ. Press, New York, 1995.

[17] G. Nelson. Complextity, convexity and combination of theories. *Theoretical Computer Science*, 12:291–302, 1980.

[18] G. Nelson and D. Oppen. Simplification by cooperating decision procedures. *ACM Transactions on Programming Languages and Systems*, 1(2):245–257, 1979.

[19] D. Pigozzi. The join of equational theories. *Colloq. Math.*, 30:15–25, 1974.

[20] A. N. Prior. Modality and quantification in S5. *J. Symb. Logic*, 21:60–62, 1956.

[21] A. Robinson. *Complete theories*. North-Holland Publishing Co., Amsterdam, second edition, 1977.

[22] L. Santocanale. Congruences of modal μ-algebras. In Z. Ésik and A. Ingólfsdóttir, editors, *FICS02*, volume NS-02-02 of *BRICS Notes Series*, pages 83–87, June 2002.

[23] L. Santocanale. On the equational definition of the least prefixed point. *Theoretical Computer Science*, 295(1-3):341–370, February 2003.

[24] K. Schild. From terminological logics to modal logics, 1991. Proceedings of the International Workshop on Terminological Logics, DFKI-D-91-13, 1991.

[25] K. Segerberg. A completeness theorem in the modal logic of programs. *Notices Amer. Math. Soc*, 24:A552, 1977. Abstract 77T-E69.

[26] E. Spaan. *Complexity of Modal Logics*. PhD thesis, Department of Mathematics and Computer Science, University of Amsterdam, The Nethertlands, 1993.

[27] C. Tinelli and Harandi M. A new correctness proof of the Nelson-Oppen combination procedure. In F. Baader and K. Schulz, editors, *Frontiers of Combining Systems, FROCOS'96*, number 3 in Applied Logic Series, pages 103–120. Kluwer Academic Publishers, 1996.

[28] M. Y. Vardi. The taming of converse: reasoning about two-way computations. In *Logics of programs (Brooklyn, N.Y., 1985)*, volume 193 of *Lecture Notes in Comput. Sci.*, pages 413–424. Springer, Berlin, 1985.

[29] M. Y. Vardi. Reasoning about the past with two-way automata. In K. G. Larsen, S. Skyum, and G. Winskel, editors, *Proceedings of ICALP'98*, volume 1443 of *Lecture Notes in Computer Science*, pages 628–640. Springer, 1998.

[30] W. H. Wheeler. Model-companions and definability in existentially complete structures. *Israel J. Math.*, 25(3-4):305–330, 1976.

[31] W. H. Wheeler. A characterization of companionable, universal theories. *J. Symbolic Logic*, 43(3):402–429, 1978.

[32] F. Wolter. Fusions of modal logics revisited. In *Advances in modal logic, Vol. 1 (Berlin, 1996)*, volume 87 of *CSLI Lecture Notes*, pages 361–379. CSLI Publ., Stanford, CA, 1998.

Improving Dependency Pairs

Jürgen Giesl, René Thiemann, Peter Schneider-Kamp, and Stephan Falke

LuFG Informatik II, RWTH Aachen, Ahornstr. 55, 52074 Aachen, Germany,
{giesl|thiemann}@informatik.rwth-aachen.de,
{nowonder|spf}@i2.informatik.rwth-aachen.de

Abstract. The dependency pair approach is one of the most powerful techniques for termination and innermost termination proofs of term rewrite systems (TRSs). For any TRS, it generates inequality constraints that have to be satisfied by weakly monotonic well-founded orders. We improve the dependency pair approach by considerably reducing the number of constraints produced for (innermost) termination proofs. Moreover, we extend transformation techniques to manipulate dependency pairs which simplify (innermost) termination proofs significantly. In order to fully automate the dependency pair approach, we show how transformation techniques and the search for suitable orders can be mechanized efficiently. We implemented our results in the automated termination prover AProVE and evaluated them on large collections of examples.

1 Introduction

Most traditional methods to prove termination of TRSs (automatically) use *simplification orders* [7, 24], where a term is greater than its proper subterms. However, there are numerous important TRSs which are not *simply terminating*, i.e., their termination cannot be shown by simplification orders. Therefore, the *dependency pair* approach [2, 11, 12] was developed which allows the application of simplification orders to non-simply terminating TRSs. In this way, the class of systems where termination is provable mechanically increases significantly.

Example 1. The following TRS from [2] is not simply terminating, since in the last quot-rule, the left-hand side is embedded in the right-hand side if y is instantiated with $s(x)$. Thus, classical approaches for automated termination proofs fail on this example, while it is easy to handle with dependency pairs.

$$minus(x, 0) \rightarrow x \qquad\qquad quot(0, s(y)) \rightarrow 0$$
$$minus(s(x), s(y)) \rightarrow minus(x, y) \qquad quot(s(x), s(y)) \rightarrow s(quot(minus(x, y), s(y)))$$

In Sect. 2, we recapitulate the dependency pair approach for termination and innermost termination proofs. Then we show that the approach can be improved significantly by reducing the constraints for termination (Sect. 3) and innermost termination (Sect. 4). Sect. 5 introduces new conditions for transforming dependency pairs in order to simplify (innermost) termination proofs further.

For automated (innermost) termination proofs, the constraints generated by the dependency pair approach are pre-processed by an *argument filtering* and

M.Y. Vardi and A. Voronkov (Eds.): LPAR 2003, LNAI 2850, pp. 167–182, 2003.
© Springer-Verlag Berlin Heidelberg 2003

afterwards, one tries to solve them by standard simplification orders. We present an algorithm to generate argument filterings in our improved dependency pair approach (Sect. 6) and discuss heuristics to increase efficiency in Sect. 7.

Our improvements and algorithms are implemented in our termination prover AProVE. We give empirical results which show that they are extremely successful in practice. Thus, our contributions are also very helpful for other tools based on dependency pairs ([1], CiME [6], TTT [16]) and we conjecture that they can also be used in other recent approaches for termination of TRSs [5, 10] which have several aspects in common with dependency pairs. Finally, dependency pairs can be combined with other termination techniques (e.g., in [25] we integrated dependency pairs and the *size-change principle* from termination analysis of functional [19] and logic programs [9]). Moreover, the system TALP [22] uses dependency pairs for termination proofs of logic programs. Thus, improving dependency pairs is also useful for termination analysis of other kinds of programming languages. All proofs and details on our experiments can be found in [13].

2   Dependency Pairs

We briefly present the *dependency pair* approach of Arts and Giesl and refer to [2, 11, 12] for refinements and motivations. We assume familiarity with term rewriting (see, e.g., [4]). For a TRS $\mathcal{R}$ over a signature $\mathcal{F}$, the *defined symbols* $\mathcal{D}$ are the root symbols of the left-hand sides of rules and the *constructors* are $\mathcal{C} = \mathcal{F} \setminus \mathcal{D}$. We restrict ourselves to finite signatures and TRSs. Let $\mathcal{F}^\sharp = \{f^\sharp \mid f \in \mathcal{D}\}$ be a set of *tuple symbols*, where $f^\sharp$ has the same arity as f and we often write F for $f^\sharp$, etc. If $t = g(t_1, \ldots, t_m)$ with $g \in \mathcal{D}$, we write $t^\sharp$ for $g^\sharp(t_1, \ldots, t_m)$.

Definition 2 (Dependency Pair). *If $l \to r \in \mathcal{R}$ and t is a subterm of r with defined root symbol, then the rewrite rule $l^\sharp \to t^\sharp$ is called a* dependency pair *of $\mathcal{R}$. The set of all dependency pairs of $\mathcal{R}$ is denoted by $DP(\mathcal{R})$.*

So the dependency pairs of the TRS in Ex. 1 are

$$\text{MINUS}(\text{s}(x), \text{s}(y)) \to \text{MINUS}(x, y) \ (1) \qquad \text{QUOT}(\text{s}(x), \text{s}(y)) \to \text{MINUS}(x, y) \ (2)$$

$$\text{QUOT}(\text{s}(x), \text{s}(y)) \to \text{QUOT}(\text{minus}(x, y), \text{s}(y)) \ (3)$$

To use dependency pairs for (innermost) termination proofs, we need the notion of (innermost) *chains*. We always assume that different occurrences of dependency pairs are variable disjoint and we always consider substitutions whose domains may be infinite. Here, $\xrightarrow{i}_{\mathcal{R}}$ denotes innermost reductions.

Definition 3 (R-Chain). *A sequence of dependency pairs $s_1 \to t_1, s_2 \to t_2, \ldots$ is an $\mathcal{R}$-chain if there exists a substitution σ such that $t_j \sigma \to_{\mathcal{R}}^* s_{j+1} \sigma$ for every two consecutive pairs $s_j \to t_j$ and $s_{j+1} \to t_{j+1}$ in the sequence. Such a chain is an innermost $\mathcal{R}$-chain if $t_j \sigma \xrightarrow{i}_{\mathcal{R}}^* s_{j+1} \sigma$ and if $s_j \sigma$ is a normal form for all j.*

Theorem 4 (Termination Criterion [2]). *$\mathcal{R}$ terminates iff there is no infinite chain. $\mathcal{R}$ is innermost terminating iff there is no infinite innermost chain.*

To estimate which dependency pairs may occur consecutively in (innermost) chains, one builds a so-called (innermost) *dependency graph* whose nodes are the dependency pairs and there is an arc from $v \to w$ to $s \to t$ iff $v \to w$, $s \to t$ is an (innermost) chain. In our example, the dependency graph and the innermost dependency graph have the arcs $(1) \Rightarrow (1)$, $(2) \Rightarrow (1)$, $(3) \Rightarrow (2)$, and $(3) \Rightarrow (3)$.

Since it is undecidable whether two dependency pairs form an (innermost) chain, we construct *estimated* graphs such that all cycles in the real graph are also cycles in the estimated graph. Let CAP(t) result from replacing all variables and all subterms of t that have a defined root symbol by different fresh variables. Here, multiple occurrences of the same variable are replaced by the same fresh variable, but multiple occurrences of the same subterm with defined root are replaced by pairwise different fresh variables. Let REN(t) result from replacing all occurrences of variables in t by different fresh variables (i.e., REN(t) is a linear term). For instance, CAP(QUOT(minus(x, y), s(y))) $=$ QUOT(z, s(y_1)), CAP(QUOT(x, x)) $=$ QUOT(x_1, x_1), and REN(QUOT(x, x)) $=$ QUOT(x_1, x_2). In the *estimated dependency graph*, there is an arc from $v \to w$ to $s \to t$ iff REN(CAP(w)) and s are unifiable. In the *estimated innermost dependency graph* there is an arc from $v \to w$ to $s \to t$ iff CAP$_v$(w) and s are unifiable by a most general unifier (mgu) μ such that $v\mu$ and $s\mu$ are in normal form. Here, CAP$_v$ is defined like CAP except that subterms with defined root that already occur in v are not replaced by new variables. In Ex. 1, the estimated dependency and the estimated innermost dependency graph are identical to the real dependency graph. For alternative approximations of dependency graphs see [15, 20].

A set $\mathcal{P} \neq \varnothing$ of dependency pairs is called a *cycle* if for any two pairs $v \to w$ and $s \to t$ in $\mathcal{P}$ there is a non-empty path from $v \to w$ to $s \to t$ in the graph which only traverses pairs from $\mathcal{P}$. In our example, we have the cycles $\mathcal{P}_1 = \{(1)\}$ and $\mathcal{P}_2 = \{(3)\}$. Since we only regard finite TRSs, any infinite (innermost) chain of dependency pairs corresponds to a cycle in the (innermost) dependency graph.

To show (innermost) termination, one proves absence of infinite (innermost) chains separately for every cycle. To this end, one generates sets of constraints which should be satisfied by a *reduction pair* $(\succsim, \succ)$ [18] consisting of a quasi-rewrite order $\succsim$ (i.e., $\succsim$ is reflexive, transitive, monotonic and stable (closed under contexts and substitutions)) and a stable well-founded order $\succ$ which is compatible with $\succsim$ (i.e., $\succsim \circ \succ \subseteq \succ$ and $\succ \circ \succsim \subseteq \succ$). Note that $\succ$ need not be monotonic. Essentially, the constraints for termination of a cycle $\mathcal{P}$ ensure that all rewrite rules and all dependency pairs in $\mathcal{P}$ are weakly decreasing (w.r.t. $\succsim$) and at least one dependency pair in $\mathcal{P}$ is strictly decreasing (w.r.t. $\succ$). For innermost termination, only the *usable rules* have to be weakly decreasing. In Ex. 1, the usable rules for $\mathcal{P}_1$ are empty and the usable rules for $\mathcal{P}_2$ are the minus-rules.

Definition 5 (Usable Rules). *For $f \in \mathcal{F}$, let $Rls(f) = \{l \to r \in \mathcal{R} | \text{root}(l) = f\}$. For any term, the usable rules are the smallest set of rules such that $\mathcal{U}(x) = \varnothing$ for $x \in \mathcal{V}$ and $\mathcal{U}(f(t_1, \ldots, t_n)) = Rls(f) \cup \bigcup_{l \to r \in Rls(f)} \mathcal{U}(r) \cup \bigcup_{j=1}^{n} \mathcal{U}(t_j)$. Moreover, for any set $\mathcal{P}$ of dependency pairs, we define $\mathcal{U}(\mathcal{P}) = \bigcup_{s \to t \in \mathcal{P}} \mathcal{U}(t)$.*

We want to use standard techniques to synthesize reduction pairs satisfying the constraints of the dependency pair approach. Most existing techniques generate monotonic *orders* $\succ$. However, we only need a monotonic *quasi-order* $\succsim$, whereas $\succ$ does not have to be monotonic. (This is often called "*weak* monotonicity".) For that reason, before synthesizing a suitable order, some of the arguments of function symbols can be eliminated (we use the notation of [18]).

Definition 6 (Argument Filtering). *An argument filtering π for a signature $\mathcal{F}$ maps every n-ary function symbol to an argument position $i \in \{1, \ldots, n\}$ or to a (possibly empty) list $[i_1, \ldots, i_m]$ of argument positions with $1 \leq i_1 < \ldots < i_m \leq n$. The signature $\mathcal{F}_\pi$ consists of all function symbols f such that $\pi(f) = [i_1, \ldots, i_m]$, where in $\mathcal{F}_\pi$ the arity of f is m. Every argument filtering π induces a mapping from $\mathcal{T}(\mathcal{F}, \mathcal{V})$ to $\mathcal{T}(\mathcal{F}_\pi, \mathcal{V})$, also denoted by π, which is defined as:*

$$\pi(t) = \begin{cases} t & \text{if } t \text{ is a variable} \\ \pi(t_i) & \text{if } t = f(t_1, \ldots, t_n) \text{ and } \pi(f) = i \\ f(\pi(t_{i_1}), \ldots, \pi(t_{i_m})) & \text{if } t = f(t_1, \ldots, t_n) \text{ and } \pi(f) = [i_1, \ldots, i_m] \end{cases}$$

An argument filtering with $\pi(f) = i$ for some $f \in \mathcal{F}$ is called collapsing.

Now the technique of automating dependency pairs can be formulated as follows. Here, we always use argument filterings for the signature $\mathcal{F} \cup \mathcal{F}^\sharp$.

Theorem 7 (Automating Dependency Pairs [2, 12]). *A TRS $\mathcal{R}$ is terminating iff for any cycle $\mathcal{P}$ of the (estimated) dependency graph, there is a reduction pair $(\succsim, \succ)$ and an argument filtering π such that both*

(a) $\pi(s) \succ \pi(t)$ *for one dependency pair $s \to t$ from $\mathcal{P}$ and*
    $\pi(s) \succsim \pi(t)$ *or $\pi(s) \succ \pi(t)$ for all other dependency pairs $s \to t$ from $\mathcal{P}$*
(b) $\pi(l) \succsim \pi(r)$ *for all $l \to r \in \mathcal{R}$*

$\mathcal{R}$ is innermost terminating if for any cycle $\mathcal{P}$ of the (estimated) innermost dependency graph, there is a reduction pair $(\succsim, \succ)$ and argument filtering π with

(c) $\pi(s) \succ \pi(t)$ *for one dependency pair $s \to t$ from $\mathcal{P}$ and*
    $\pi(s) \succsim \pi(t)$ *or $\pi(s) \succ \pi(t)$ for all other dependency pairs $s \to t$ from $\mathcal{P}$*
(d) $\pi(l) \succsim \pi(r)$ *for all $l \to r \in \mathcal{U}(\mathcal{P})$*

So in Ex. 1, we obtain the following constraints for termination. Here, $(\succsim_i, \succ_i)$ is the reduction pair and π_i is the argument filtering for cycle $\mathcal{P}_i$, where $i \in \{1, 2\}$.

$$\pi_1(\mathsf{MINUS}(\mathsf{s}(x), \mathsf{s}(y))) \succ_1 \pi_1(\mathsf{MINUS}(x, y)) \tag{4}$$

$$\pi_2(\mathsf{QUOT}(\mathsf{s}(x), \mathsf{s}(y))) \succ_2 \pi_2(\mathsf{QUOT}(\mathsf{minus}(x, y), \mathsf{s}(y))) \tag{5}$$

$$\pi_i(\mathsf{minus}(x, 0)) \succsim_i \pi_i(x) \tag{6}$$

$$\pi_i(\mathsf{minus}(\mathsf{s}(x), \mathsf{s}(y))) \succsim_i \pi_i(\mathsf{minus}(x, y)) \tag{7}$$

$$\pi_i(\mathsf{quot}(0, \mathsf{s}(y))) \succsim_i \pi_i(0) \tag{8}$$

$$\pi_i(\mathsf{quot}(\mathsf{s}(x), \mathsf{s}(y))) \succsim_i \pi_i(\mathsf{s}(\mathsf{quot}(\mathsf{minus}(x, y), \mathsf{s}(y)))) \tag{9}$$

The filtering $\pi_i(\mathsf{minus}) = [1]$ replaces all terms $\mathsf{minus}(t_1, t_2)$ by $\mathsf{minus}(t_1)$. With this filtering, (4)–(9) are satisfied by the lexicographic path order (LPO) with the precedence $\mathsf{quot} > \mathsf{s} > \mathsf{minus}$. Thus, termination of this TRS is proved.

For innermost termination, we only obtain the constraint (4) for the cycle $\mathcal{P}_1$, since it has no usable rules. For $\mathcal{P}_2$, the constraints (8) and (9) are not necessary, since the quot-rules are not usable for any right-hand side of a dependency pair. In general, the constraints for innermost termination are always a subset of the constraints for termination. Thus, for classes of TRSs where innermost termination already implies termination (e.g., non-overlapping TRSs) [14], one should always use the approach for innermost termination when proving termination.

As shown in [15], to implement Thm. 7, one does not compute all cycles, but only maximal cycles (*strongly connected components (SCCs)*) that are not contained in other cycles. When solving the constraints of Thm. 7 for an SCC, the strict constraint $\pi(s) \succ \pi(t)$ may be satisfied for *several* dependency pairs $s \to t$ in the SCC. Thus, subcycles of the SCC containing such a strictly decreasing dependency pair do not have to be considered anymore. So after solving the constraints for the initial SCCs, all strictly decreasing dependency pairs are removed and one now builds SCCs from the remaining dependency pairs, etc.

3   Improved Termination Proofs

Now the technique of Thm. 7 for termination proofs is improved. For automation, one usually uses a *quasi-simplification order* $\succsim$ (i.e., a monotonic, stable quasi-order with $f(\ldots t \ldots) \succsim t$ for any term t and symbol f). As observed in [21], then the constraints (a) and (b) of Thm. 7 even imply C_ε-termination of $\mathcal{R}$. A TRS $\mathcal{R}$ is C_ε-*terminating* iff $\mathcal{R} \cup \{c(x, y) \to x, c(x, y) \to y\}$ is terminating where c is a fresh function symbol not occurring in $\mathcal{R}$. Urban showed in [27] how to use dependency pairs for modular termination proofs of hierarchical combinations of C_ε-terminating TRSs. However in the results of [27], he did not integrate the consideration of cycles in (estimated) dependency graphs and required all dependency pairs to be strictly decreasing. Thm. 8 extends his modularity results by combining them with cycles. In this way, one obtains an improvement for termination proofs with dependency pairs which can be used for TRSs in general. The advantage is that the set of constraints (b) in Thm. 7 is reduced significantly.

The crucial idea of [27] is to consider the recursion hierarchy of function symbols. A function symbol f *depends on* the symbol h (denoted $f \geq_d h$) if $f = h$ or if there exists a symbol g such that g occurs in an f-rule and g depends on h. We define $>_d = \geq_d \setminus \leq_d$ and $\sim_d = \geq_d \cap \leq_d$. So $f \sim_d g$ means that f and g are mutually recursive. If $\mathcal{R} = \mathcal{R}_1 \uplus \ldots \uplus \mathcal{R}_n$ and $f \sim_d g$ iff $Rls(f) \cup Rls(g) \subseteq \mathcal{R}_i$, then we call $\mathcal{R}_1, \ldots, \mathcal{R}_n$ a *separation* of $\mathcal{R}$. Moreover, we extend $\geq_d$ to the sets $\mathcal{R}_i$ by defining $\mathcal{R}_i \geq_d \mathcal{R}_j$ iff $f \geq_d g$ for all f, g with $Rls(f) \subseteq \mathcal{R}_i$ and $Rls(g) \subseteq \mathcal{R}_j$. For any i, let $\mathcal{R}'_i$ denote the rules that $\mathcal{R}_i$ depends on, i.e., $\mathcal{R}'_i = \bigcup_{\mathcal{R}_i \geq_d \mathcal{R}_j} \mathcal{R}_j$.

Clearly, a cycle only consists of dependency pairs from one $\mathcal{R}_i$. Thus, in Thm. 7 we only have to regard cycles $\mathcal{P}$ with pairs from $DP(\mathcal{R}_i)$. However, to detect the cycles $\mathcal{P}$, we still have to regard the dependency graph of the whole TRS $\mathcal{R}$. The reason is that we consider $\mathcal{R}$-chains, not just $\mathcal{R}_i$- or $\mathcal{R}'_i$-chains.[1]

Thm. 8 states that instead of requiring $\pi(l) \succsim \pi(r)$ for all rules $l \to r$ of $\mathcal{R}$, it suffices to demand it only for rules that $\mathcal{R}_i$ depends on, i.e., for rules from $\mathcal{R}'_i$. So in the termination proof of Ex. 1, $\pi(l) \succsim \pi(r)$ does not have to be required for the quot-rules when regarding the cycle $\mathcal{P}_1 = \{\mathsf{MINUS}(\mathsf{s}(x), \mathsf{s}(y)) \to \mathsf{MINUS}(x, y)\}$. However, this improvement is sound only if $\succsim$ is a quasi-simplification order.[2]

Theorem 8 (Improved Termination Proofs with DPs). *Let* $\mathcal{R}_1, \ldots, \mathcal{R}_n$ *be a separation of* $\mathcal{R}$. $\mathcal{R}$ *is terminating if for all* $1 \leq i \leq n$ *and any cycle* $\mathcal{P}$ *of* $\mathcal{R}$'*s (estimated) dependency graph with* $\mathcal{P} \subseteq DP(\mathcal{R}_i)$, *there is a reduction pair* $(\succsim, \succ)$ *where* $\succsim$ *is a quasi-simplification order and an argument filtering* π *such that*

(a) $\pi(s) \succ \pi(t)$ *for one dependency pair* $s \to t$ *from* $\mathcal{P}$ *and*
       $\pi(s) \succsim \pi(t)$ *or* $\pi(s) \succ \pi(t)$ *for all other dependency pairs* $s \to t$ *from* $\mathcal{P}$
(b) $\pi(l) \succsim \pi(r)$ *for all* $l \to r \in \mathcal{R}'_i$

Example 9. This TRS of [23] shows that Thm. 8 not only increases efficiency, but also leads to a more powerful method. Here, $\mathsf{int}(\mathsf{s}^n(0), \mathsf{s}^m(0))$ computes $[\mathsf{s}^n(0), \mathsf{s}^{n+1}(0), \ldots, \mathsf{s}^m(0)]$, nil is the empty list, and cons represents list insertion.

$\mathsf{intlist}(\mathsf{nil}) \to \mathsf{nil}$	(10)	$\mathsf{intlist}(\mathsf{cons}(x, y)) \to \mathsf{cons}(\mathsf{s}(x), \mathsf{intlist}(y))$	(13)
$\mathsf{int}(\mathsf{s}(x), 0) \to \mathsf{nil}$	(11)	$\mathsf{int}(\mathsf{s}(x), \mathsf{s}(y)) \to \mathsf{intlist}(\mathsf{int}(x, y))$	(14)
$\mathsf{int}(0, 0) \to \mathsf{cons}(0, \mathsf{nil})$	(12)	$\mathsf{int}(0, \mathsf{s}(y)) \to \mathsf{cons}(0, \mathsf{int}(\mathsf{s}(0), \mathsf{s}(y)))$	(15)

The TRS is separated into the intlist-rules $\mathcal{R}_1$ and the int-rules $\mathcal{R}_2 >_d \mathcal{R}_1$. The constraints of Thm. 7 for termination of $\mathcal{P} = \{\mathsf{INTLIST}(\mathsf{cons}(x, y)) \to \mathsf{INTLIST}(y)\}$ cannot be solved with reduction pairs based on simplification orders. In contrast, by using Thm. 8, only $\mathcal{R}'_1 = \mathcal{R}_1$ must be weakly decreasing when examining $\mathcal{P}$. These constraints are satisfied by the embedding order using the argument filtering $\pi(\mathsf{cons}) = [2]$, $\pi(\mathsf{intlist}) = \pi(\mathsf{INTLIST}) = 1$, $\pi(\mathsf{s}) = [1]$.

The constraints from $\mathcal{R}_2$'s cycle and rules from $\mathcal{R}'_2 = \mathcal{R}_1 \cup \mathcal{R}_2$ can also be oriented (by LPO and a filtering with $\pi(\mathsf{cons}) = 1$, $\pi(\mathsf{INT}) = 2$). However, this part of the proof requires the consideration of cycles of the (estimated) dependency graph. The reason is that there is no argument filtering and simplification order where both dependency pairs of $\mathcal{R}_2$ are strictly decreasing. So if one only considers cycles or only uses Urbain's modularity result [27], then Ex. 9 fails with simplification orders. Instead, both refinements should be combined as in Thm. 8.

---

[1] To see this, consider Toyama's TRS [26] where $\mathcal{R}_1 = \mathcal{R}'_1 = \{\mathsf{f}(0, 1, x) \to \mathsf{f}(x, x, x)\}$ and $\mathcal{R}_2 = \mathcal{R}'_2 = \{\mathsf{g}(x, y) \to x, \mathsf{g}(x, y) \to y\}$. $\mathcal{R}'_1$'s and $\mathcal{R}'_2$'s dependency graphs are empty, whereas the dependency graph of $\mathcal{R} = \mathcal{R}_1 \cup \mathcal{R}_2$ has a cycle. Hence, if one only considers the graphs of $\mathcal{R}'_1$ and $\mathcal{R}'_2$, one could falsely prove termination.

[2] It suffices if $\succsim$ is extendable to $c(x, y) \succsim x, c(x, y) \succsim y$ and $(\succsim, \succ)$ is still a reduction pair.

4   Improved Innermost Termination Proofs

Innermost termination is easier to prove than termination: the innermost dependency graph has less arcs than the dependency graph and we only require $l \succsim r$ for *usable* instead of *all* rules. In Sect. 3 we showed that for termination, it suffices to require $l \succsim r$ only for rules of $\mathcal{R}'_i$ if the current cycle consists of $\mathcal{R}_i$-dependency pairs. Still, $\mathcal{R}'_i$ is a superset of the usable rules. Now we present an improvement of Thm. 7 for innermost termination to reduce the usable rules.

The idea is to apply the argument filtering first and to determine the usable rules afterwards. However, for collapsing argument filterings this destroys the soundness of the technique. Consider the non-innermost terminating TRS

$$\mathsf{f}(\mathsf{s}(x)) \to \mathsf{f}(\mathsf{double}(x)) \qquad \mathsf{double}(0) \to 0 \qquad \mathsf{double}(\mathsf{s}(x)) \to \mathsf{s}(\mathsf{s}(\mathsf{double}(x)))$$

In the cycle $\{\mathsf{F}(\mathsf{s}(x)) \to \mathsf{F}(\mathsf{double}(x))\}$, we could use the argument filtering $\pi(\mathsf{double}) = 1$ which results in $\{\mathsf{F}(\mathsf{s}(x)) \to \mathsf{F}(x)\}$. Since the filtered dependency pair contains no defined symbols, we would conclude that the cycle has no usable rules. Then, we could easily orient the only resulting constraint $\mathsf{F}(\mathsf{s}(x)) \succ \mathsf{F}(x)$ for this cycle and falsely prove innermost termination. Note that the elimination of double in the term $\mathsf{F}(\mathsf{double}(x))$ is not due to the outer function symbol F, but due to a collapsing argument filtering for double itself. For that reason a defined symbol like double may only be ignored if all its occurrences are in positions which are filtered away by the function symbols *above* them. Moreover, as in CAP$_v$, we build usable rules only from those subterms of right-hand sides of dependency pairs that do not occur in the corresponding left-hand side.

Definition 10 (Usable Rules w.r.t. Argument Filtering). *Let π be an argument filtering. For an n-ary symbol f, the set $RegPos_\pi(f)$ of regarded positions is $\{i\}$, if $\pi(f) = i$, and it is $\{i_1, \ldots, i_m\}$, if $\pi(f) = [i_1, \ldots, i_m]$. For a term, the* usable rules w.r.t. π *are the smallest set such that $\mathcal{U}(x, \pi) = \varnothing$ for $x \in \mathcal{V}$ and $\mathcal{U}(f(t_1, \ldots, t_n), \pi) = Rls(f) \cup \bigcup_{l \to r \in Rls(f)} \mathcal{U}(r, \pi) \cup \bigcup_{j \in RegPos_\pi(f)} \mathcal{U}(t_j, \pi)$. For a term s with $\mathcal{V}(t) \subseteq \mathcal{V}(s)$, let $\mathcal{U}_s(t, \pi) = \varnothing$ if t is a subterm of s. Otherwise, $\mathcal{U}_s(f(t_1, \ldots, t_n), \pi) = Rls(f) \cup \bigcup_{l \to r \in Rls(f)} \mathcal{U}(r, \pi) \cup \bigcup_{j \in RegPos_\pi(f)} \mathcal{U}_s(t_j, \pi)$. Moreover, for any set $\mathcal{P}$ of dependency pairs, let $\mathcal{U}(\mathcal{P}, \pi) = \bigcup_{s \to t \in \mathcal{P}} \mathcal{U}_s(t, \pi)$.*

Now we can refine the innermost termination technique of Thm. 7 (c) and (d) to the following one where the set of usable rules is reduced significantly.

Theorem 11 (Improved Innermost Termination with DPs). *$\mathcal{R}$ is innermost terminating if for any cycle $\mathcal{P}$ of the (estimated) innermost dependency graph, there is a reduction pair $(\succsim, \succ)$ and an argument filtering π such that*

(c) $\pi(s) \succ \pi(t)$ for one dependency pair $s \to t$ from $\mathcal{P}$ and
    $\pi(s) \succsim \pi(t)$ or $\pi(s) \succ \pi(t)$ for all other dependency pairs $s \to t$ from $\mathcal{P}$
(d) $\pi(l) \succsim \pi(r)$ for all $l \to r \in \mathcal{U}(\mathcal{P}, \pi)$

Example 12. This TRS of [17] for list reversal shows the advantages of Thm. 11.

$$\begin{array}{ll} \mathsf{rev}(\mathsf{nil}) \to \mathsf{nil} & \mathsf{rev}(\mathsf{cons}(x, l)) \to \mathsf{cons}(\mathsf{rev1}(x, l), \mathsf{rev2}(x, l)) \\ \mathsf{rev1}(x, \mathsf{nil}) \to x & \mathsf{rev1}(x, \mathsf{cons}(y, l)) \to \mathsf{rev1}(y, l) \\ \mathsf{rev2}(x, \mathsf{nil}) \to \mathsf{nil} & \mathsf{rev2}(x, \mathsf{cons}(y, l)) \to \mathsf{rev}(\mathsf{cons}(x, \mathsf{rev}(\mathsf{rev2}(y, l)))) \end{array}$$

For innermost termination with Thm. 7, from the cycle of the REV and REV2-dependency pairs, we get inequalities for the dependency pairs and $\pi(l) \succsim \pi(r)$ for all rules $l \to r$, since all rules are usable. But standard reduction pairs based on recursive path orders possibly with status (RPOS), Knuth-Bendix orders (KBO), or polynomial orders do not satisfy these constraints for any argument filtering. In contrast, with Thm. 11 and a filtering with $\pi(\mathsf{cons}) = [2], \pi(\mathsf{REV}) = \pi(\mathsf{rev}) = 1, \pi(\mathsf{REV2}) = \pi(\mathsf{rev2}) = 2$, we do not obtain any constraints from the rev1-rules, and all filtered constraints can be oriented by the embedding order.

Our experiments with the system AProVE show that Thm. 8 and 11 indeed improve upon Thm. 7 in practice by increasing power (in particular if reduction pairs are based on simple fast orders like the embedding order) and by reducing runtimes (in particular if reduction pairs are based on more complex orders).

5   Transforming Dependency Pairs

To increase the power of the dependency pair technique, a dependency pair may be transformed into several new pairs by *narrowing*, *rewriting*, and *instantiation* [2, 11]. A term t' is an $\mathcal{R}$-*narrowing of t with the mgu μ*, if a non-variable subterm $t|_p$ of t unifies with the left-hand side of a (variable-renamed) rule $l \to r \in \mathcal{R}$ with mgu μ, and $t' = t[r]_p \mu$. To distinguish the variants for termination and innermost termination, we speak of t- and *i-narrowing* resp. *-instantiation*.

Definition 13 (Transformations). *For a TRS $\mathcal{R}$ and a set $\mathcal{P}$ of pairs of terms*

- $\mathcal{P} \uplus \{s \to t\}$ *t-narrows to* $\mathcal{P} \uplus \{s\mu_1 \to t_1, \ldots, s\mu_n \to t_n\}$ *iff $t_1, \ldots, t_n$ are all $\mathcal{R}$-narrowings of t with the mgu's $\mu_1, \ldots, \mu_n$ and t does not unify with (variable-renamed) left-hand sides of pairs in $\mathcal{P}$. Moreover, t must be linear.*
- $\mathcal{P} \uplus \{s \to t\}$ *i-narrows to* $\mathcal{P} \uplus \{s\mu_1 \to t_1, \ldots, s\mu_n \to t_n\}$ *iff $t_1, \ldots, t_n$ are all $\mathcal{R}$-narrowings of t with the mgu's $\mu_1, \ldots, \mu_n$ such that $s\mu_i$ is in normal form. Moreover, for all $v \to w \in \mathcal{P}$ where t unifies with the (variable-renamed) left-hand side v by mgu μ, one of the terms $s\mu$ or $v\mu$ must not be in normal form.*
- $\mathcal{P} \uplus \{s \to t\}$ *rewrites to* $\mathcal{P} \uplus \{s \to t'\}$ *iff $\mathcal{U}(t|_p)$ is non-overlapping and $t \to_\mathcal{R} t'$, where p is the position of the redex.*
- $\mathcal{P} \uplus \{s \to t\}$ *is t-instantiated to*
  $\mathcal{P} \uplus \{s\mu \to t\mu \mid \mu = mgu(\mathrm{REN}(\mathrm{CAP}(w)), s), v \to w \in \mathcal{P}\}$.
- $\mathcal{P} \uplus \{s \to t\}$ *is i-instantiated to*
  $\mathcal{P} \uplus \{s\mu \to t\mu \mid \mu = mgu(\mathrm{CAP}_v(w), s), v \to w \in \mathcal{P}, s\mu, v\mu$ *are normal forms*$\}$.

Theorem 14 (Narrowing, Rewriting, Instantiation). *Let $DP(\mathcal{R})'$ result from $DP(\mathcal{R})$ by t-narrowing and t-instantiation (for termination) resp. by i-narrowing, rewriting, i-instantiation (for innermost termination). If the dependency pair constraints for (innermost) termination are satisfiable using $DP(\mathcal{R})'$, then $\mathcal{R}$ is (innermost) terminating. Moreover, if certain reduction pairs and argument filterings satisfy the constraints for $DP(\mathcal{R})$, then the same reduction pairs and argument filterings satisfy the constraints for $DP(\mathcal{R})'$. Here, we estimate (innermost) dependency graphs as in Sect. 2 when computing the constraints.*

By Thm. 14, these transformations never complicate termination proofs (but they may increase the number of constraints by producing similar constraints that can be solved by the same argument filterings and reduction pairs). On the other hand, the transformations are often crucial for the success of the proof.

Example 15. In this TRS [3], the minus-rules of Ex. 1 are extended with

$$
\begin{array}{ll}
\mathsf{le}(0, y) \to \mathsf{true} & \mathsf{quot}(x, \mathsf{s}(y)) \to \mathsf{if}(\mathsf{le}(\mathsf{s}(y), x), x, \mathsf{s}(y)) \\
\mathsf{le}(\mathsf{s}(x), 0) \to \mathsf{false} & \mathsf{if}(\mathsf{true}, x, y) \to \mathsf{s}(\mathsf{quot}(\mathsf{minus}(x, y), y)) \\
\mathsf{le}(\mathsf{s}(x), \mathsf{s}(y)) \to \mathsf{le}(x, y) & \mathsf{if}(\mathsf{false}, x, y) \to 0
\end{array}
$$

When trying to prove innermost termination, no simplification order satisfies the constraints of Thm. 11 for the following cycle.

$$\mathsf{QUOT}(x, \mathsf{s}(y)) \to \mathsf{IF}(\mathsf{le}(\mathsf{s}(y), x), x, \mathsf{s}(y)) \quad (16) \quad \mathsf{IF}(\mathsf{true}, x, y) \to \mathsf{QUOT}(\mathsf{minus}(x, y), y) \quad (17)$$

Intuitively, $x \succ \mathsf{minus}(x, y)$ only has to be satisfied if $\mathsf{le}(\mathsf{s}(y), x)$ reduces to true. This argumentation can be simulated using the above transformations. By i-narrowing, we perform a case analysis on how the le-term in (16) can be evaluated. In the first narrowing, x is instantiated by 0. This results in a pair $\mathsf{QUOT}(0, \mathsf{s}(y)) \to \mathsf{IF}(\mathsf{false}, 0, \mathsf{s}(y))$ which is not in a cycle. The other narrowing is

$$\mathsf{QUOT}(\mathsf{s}(x), \mathsf{s}(y)) \to \mathsf{IF}(\mathsf{le}(y, x), \mathsf{s}(x), \mathsf{s}(y)) \tag{18}$$

which forms a new cycle with (17). Now we perform i-instantiation of (17) and see that x and y must be of the form $\mathsf{s}(\ldots)$. So (17) is replaced by the new pair

$$\mathsf{IF}(\mathsf{true}, \mathsf{s}(x), \mathsf{s}(y)) \to \mathsf{QUOT}(\mathsf{minus}(\mathsf{s}(x), \mathsf{s}(y)), \mathsf{s}(y)) \tag{19}$$

that forms a cycle with (18). Finally, we do a rewriting step on (19) and obtain

$$\mathsf{IF}(\mathsf{true}, \mathsf{s}(x), \mathsf{s}(y)) \to \mathsf{QUOT}(\mathsf{minus}(x, y), \mathsf{s}(y)) \tag{20}$$

The constraints from the resulting cycle $\{(18), (20)\}$ (and from all other cycles) can be solved by $\pi(\mathsf{minus}) = \pi(\mathsf{QUOT}) = 1$, $\pi(\mathsf{IF}) = 2$, and the embedding order.

For innermost termination, Def. 13 and Thm. 14 extend the results of [2, 11] by permitting these transformations for a larger set of TRSs. In [11], narrowing a pair $s \to t$ was not permitted if t unifies with the left-hand side of some dependency pair. Rewriting dependency pairs was only allowed if all usable rules for the current cycle were non-overlapping. Finally, when instantiating dependency pairs, in contrast to [11] one can now use CAP$_v$. Moreover, for both instantiation and narrowing of dependency pairs, now one only has to consider instantiations which turn left-hand sides of dependency pairs into normal forms.

The crucial problem is that these transformations may be applied infinitely many times. Therefore, we have developed restricted *safe* transformations which are guaranteed to terminate. Our experiments on the collections of examples from [3, 8, 23] show that whenever the proof succeeds using narrowing, rewriting, and instantiation, then applying these safe transformations is sufficient.

A narrowing or instantiation step is *safe* if it reduces the number of pairs in cycles of the estimated (innermost) dependency graph. For a set of pairs $\mathcal{P}$, SCC($\mathcal{P}$) denotes the set of maximal cycles built from pairs of $\mathcal{P}$. Then, the transformation is safe if $\Sigma_{\mathcal{S} \in \mathrm{SCC}(\mathcal{P})} |\mathcal{S}|$ decreases. Moreover, it is also considered safe if by the transformation step, all descendants of some original dependency pair disappear from cycles. For every pair $s \to t$, $o(s \to t)$ denotes the original dependency pair whose repeated transformation led to $s \to t$. Now a transformation is also safe if $\{o(s \to t) \mid s \to t \in \bigcup_{\mathcal{S} \in \mathrm{SCC}(\mathcal{P})} \mathcal{S}\}$ decreases.

As an example, let $\mathcal{R} = \{f(a) \to g(b), g(x) \to f(x)\}$. The estimated dependency graph has the cycle $\{F(a) \to G(b), G(x) \to F(x)\}$. Instantiation transforms the second pair into $G(b) \to F(b)$. Now there is no cycle anymore and thus, this instantiation step is safe. Finally for each pair, one single narrowing and instantiation step which does not satisfy the above requirements is also considered safe. Hence, the narrowing and instantiation steps in Ex. 15 were safe as well.

As for termination, in innermost termination proofs we also benefit from considering the recursion hierarchy. So if $\mathcal{R}_1, \ldots, \mathcal{R}_n$ is a separation of the TRS $\mathcal{R}$ and $\mathcal{R}_i >_d \mathcal{R}_j$, then we show absence of innermost $\mathcal{R}$-chains built from $DP(\mathcal{R}_j)$ before dealing with $DP(\mathcal{R}_i)$. Now innermost rewriting a dependency pair $F(\ldots) \to \ldots$ is *safe* if it is performed with rules that do not depend on f (i.e., with g-rules where $g <_d f$). The reason is that innermost termination of g is already verified when proving innermost termination of f. So in Ex. 15, when proving innermost termination of the QUOT-cycle, we may assume innermost termination of minus and thus, the rewrite step from (19) to (20) was safe.

Definition 16 (Safe Transformations). *Let $\mathcal{Q}$ result from a set $\mathcal{P}$ of pairs of terms by transforming $s \to t \in \mathcal{P}$ as in Def. 13. The transformation is safe if*

(1) $s \to t$ *was transformed by narrowing or instantiation and*
- $\Sigma_{\mathcal{S} \in \mathrm{SCC}(\mathcal{P})} |\mathcal{S}| > \Sigma_{\mathcal{S} \in \mathrm{SCC}(\mathcal{Q})} |\mathcal{S}|$, *or*
- $\{o(s \to t) \mid s \to t \in \bigcup_{\mathcal{S} \in \mathrm{SCC}(\mathcal{P})} \mathcal{S}\} \supsetneq \{o(s \to t) \mid s \to t \in \bigcup_{\mathcal{S} \in \mathrm{SCC}(\mathcal{Q})} \mathcal{S}\}$

(2) $s \to t$ *was transformed by innermost rewriting with the rule $l \to r$ and* $\mathrm{root}(l) <_d f$ *where $f^\sharp = \mathrm{root}(s)$*

(3) $s \to t$ *was transformed by narrowing and all previous steps which transformed $o(s \to t)$ to $s \to t$ were not narrowing steps*

(4) $s \to t$ *was transformed by instantiation and all previous steps which transformed $o(s \to t)$ to $s \to t$ were not instantiation steps*

Theorem 17 (Termination). *Let $\mathcal{R}$ have the separation $\mathcal{R}_1, \ldots, \mathcal{R}_n$ and $\mathcal{P} \subseteq DP(\mathcal{R}_i)$. If there are no infinite innermost $\mathcal{R}$-chains from $DP(\mathcal{R}_j)$ for all $\mathcal{R}_j <_d \mathcal{R}_i$, then any repeated application of safe transformations on $\mathcal{P}$ terminates.*

After each transformation, the current cycle or SCC of the estimated (innermost) dependency graph is re-computed. For this re-computation, one only has to regard the former neighbors of the transformed pair in the old graph. Only former neighbors may have arcs to or from the new pairs resulting from the transformation. Regarding neighbors in the graphs also suffices when performing the unifications required for narrowing and instantiation. In this way, the transformations can be performed efficiently. Recall that one always regards SCCs first and then, one builds new SCCs from the remaining pairs which were not strictly decreasing (Sect. 2) [15]. Of course, these pairs may already have been transformed during the (innermost) termination proof of the SCC. So this approach has the advantage that one never repeats transformations for the same dependency pairs.

6 Computing Argument Filterings

In the dependency pair approach, we may apply an argument filtering π before orienting constraints with reduction pairs. Since there are exponentially many argument filterings, we now show how to search for suitable filterings efficiently. For every cycle $\mathcal{P}$, we compute small sets $\Pi^t(\mathcal{P})$ and $\Pi^i(\mathcal{P})$ containing all filterings which could possibly satisfy the constraints for termination or innermost termination, respectively. A corresponding algorithm was presented in [15] for termination proofs w.r.t. Thm. 7. We now develop such an algorithm for the improved dependency pair approach from Thm. 8 and 11. In particular for Thm. 11, the algorithm is considerably more involved since the set of constraints depends on the argument filtering used. Moreover, instead of treating constraints separately as in [15], we process them according to an efficient depth-first strategy.

Let $\mathcal{RP}$ be a class of reduction pairs (e.g., $\mathcal{RP}$ may contain all LPOs with arbitrary precedences). For any set of dependency pairs $\mathcal{P}$, $\Pi(\mathcal{P})$ denotes the set of all argument filterings where at least one dependency pair in $\mathcal{P}$ is strictly decreasing and the remaining ones are weakly decreasing w.r.t. some reduction pair in $\mathcal{RP}$. When referring to "dependency pairs", we also permit pairs resulting from dependency pairs by narrowing, rewriting, or instantiation. We use the approach of [15] to consider partial argument filterings, i.e., filterings which are only defined on a subset of the signature. For example, in a term $f(g(x), y)$, if $\pi(f) = [2]$, then we do not have to determine $\pi(g)$, since all occurrences of g are filtered away. Thus, we leave argument filterings as undefined as possible and permit the application of π to a term t if π is defined on all function symbols needed. For two (partial) argument filterings, we define $\pi \sqsubseteq \pi'$ iff $DOM(\pi) \subseteq DOM(\pi')$ and $\pi(f) = \pi'(f)$ for all $f \in DOM(\pi)$. Then $\Pi(\mathcal{P})$ should only contain $\sqsubseteq$-minimal elements, i.e., if $\pi' \in \Pi(\mathcal{P})$, then $\Pi(\mathcal{P})$ does not contain any $\pi \sqsubset \pi'$.

We now define a superset $\Pi^t(\mathcal{P})$ of all argument filterings where the constraints (a) and (b) for termination of the cycle $\mathcal{P}$ are satisfied by some reduction pair of $\mathcal{RP}$. So only these argument filterings have to be regarded when automating Thm. 8. To this end, we have to *extend* partial argument filterings.

Definition 18 (*Ex_f, $\Pi^t(\mathcal{P})$*). *For $f \in \mathcal{D}$, $Ex_f(\pi)$ consists of all $\sqsubseteq$-minimal argument filterings π' such that $\pi \sqsubseteq \pi'$ and such that there is a $(\succsim, \succ) \in \mathcal{RP}$ with $\pi'(l) \succsim \pi'(r)$ for all $l \to r \in Rls(f)$. For a set Π of filterings, let $Ex_f(\Pi) = \bigcup_{\pi \in \Pi} Ex_f(\pi)$. If $\mathcal{P}$ originates from $DP(\mathcal{R}_i)$ by t-narrowing and t-instantiation and $\{f_1, ..., f_k\}$ are $\mathcal{R}_i'$s defined symbols, then $\Pi^t(\mathcal{P}) = Ex_{f_k}(...Ex_{f_1}(\Pi(\mathcal{P}))...)$.*

We compute $\Pi^t(\mathcal{P})$ by depth-first search. So we start with a $\pi \in \Pi(\mathcal{P})$ and extend it to a minimal π' such that the f_1-rules are weakly decreasing. Then π' is extended such that the f_2-rules are weakly decreasing, etc. Here, f_1 is considered before f_2 if $f_1 >_d f_2$. When we have $\Pi^t(\mathcal{P})$'s first element π_1, we check whether Constraints (a) and (b) of Thm. 8 are satisfiable with π_1. In case of success, we do not compute further elements of $\Pi^t(\mathcal{P})$. Otherwise, we determine $\Pi^t(\mathcal{P})$'s next element, etc. The advantage of this approach is that $\Pi(\mathcal{P})$ is usually small, since it only contains argument filterings that satisfy a *strict* inequality.

For innermost termination, the set of constraints to be satisfied depends on the argument filtering used. If $f \geq_d g$, then when orienting the rules of f, we do not necessarily have to orient the rules of g as well, since all occurrences of g in f-rules may have been deleted by the argument filtering, cf. Thm. 11.

We extend $\mathcal{R}egPos_\pi$ to *partial* argument filterings by defining $\mathcal{R}egPos_\pi(f) = \varnothing$ for all $f \notin DOM(\pi)$. Now $\mathcal{U}(\mathcal{P}, \pi)$ is also defined for partial filterings by simply disregarding all subterms of function symbols where π is not defined. For a partial argument filtering π, whenever $Rls(f)$ is included in the usable rules $\mathcal{U}(\mathcal{P}, \pi)$ for the cycle $\mathcal{P}$, we use a relation "$\vdash_\mathcal{P}$" to extend π in order to make the f-rules weakly decreasing. We label each argument filtering by the set of those function symbols whose rules are already guaranteed to be weakly decreasing.

Definition 19 ($\vdash_\mathcal{P}$, $\Pi^i(\mathcal{P})$). *Each argument filtering π is labelled with a set $\mathcal{G} \subseteq \mathcal{D}$ and we denote a labelled argument filtering by $\pi_\mathcal{G}$. For sets of labelled argument filterings, we define a relation "$\vdash_\mathcal{P}$": $\Pi \uplus \{\pi_\mathcal{G}\} \vdash_\mathcal{P} \Pi \cup \{\pi'_{\mathcal{G} \cup \{f\}} \mid \pi' \in Ex_f(\pi)\}$, if $f \in \mathcal{D} \setminus \mathcal{G}$ and $Rls(f) \subseteq \mathcal{U}(\mathcal{P}, \pi)$. Note that $\vdash_\mathcal{P}$ is confluent and well founded, since the labellings increase in every $\vdash_\mathcal{P}$-step. Let $Nf_{\vdash_\mathcal{P}}(\Pi)$ denote the normal form of Π w.r.t. $\vdash_\mathcal{P}$. Then we define $\Pi^i(\mathcal{P}) = Nf_{\vdash_\mathcal{P}}(\{\pi_\varnothing \mid \pi \in \Pi(\mathcal{P})\})$.*

To compute $\Pi^i(\mathcal{P})$, we again start with a $\pi \in \Pi(\mathcal{P})$. If $Rls(f) \subseteq \mathcal{U}(\mathcal{P}, \pi)$, then π is extended to make f's rules weakly decreasing. If by this extension, the rules for g become usable, then we have to extend with Ex_g afterwards, etc.

Thm. 20 states that by $\Pi^t(\mathcal{P})$ (resp. $\Pi^i(\mathcal{P})$), one indeed obtains all argument filterings which could possibly solve the dependency pair constraints. In this way the set of argument filterings is reduced dramatically and thus, efficiency is increased. For example, for a TRS from [3, Ex. 3.11] computing quicksort, $\Pi^t(\mathcal{P})$ reduces the number of argument filterings from more than 26 million to 3734 and with $\Pi^i(\mathcal{P})$ we obtain a reduction from more than 1.4 million to 783.

Theorem 20. *Let $\mathcal{P}$ be a cycle. If the constraints (a) and (b) of Thm. 8 for termination are satisfied for some reduction pair from $\mathcal{RP}$ and argument filtering π', then $\pi \sqsubseteq \pi'$ for some $\pi \in \Pi^t(\mathcal{P})$. If the constraints (c) and (d) of Thm. 11 for innermost termination are satisfied for some reduction pair from $\mathcal{RP}$ and argument filtering π', then $\pi \sqsubseteq \pi'$ for some $\pi \in \Pi^i(\mathcal{P})$.*

The technique of this section can be extended by storing both argument filterings and corresponding parameters of the order in the sets $\Pi(\mathcal{P})$ and $Ex_f(\ldots)$. For example, if $\mathcal{RP}$ is the set of all LPOs, then $\Pi(\mathcal{P})$ would now contain all (minimal) pairs of argument filterings π and precedences such that $\pi(s) \succ_{lpo} \pi(t)$ resp. $\pi(s) \succsim_{lpo} \pi(t)$ holds for $s \to t \in \mathcal{P}$. When extending argument filterings, one would also have to extend the corresponding precedence. Of course, such an extension is only permitted if the extended precedence is still irreflexive (and hence, well founded). Then, $\Pi^t(\mathcal{P})$ (resp. $\Pi^i(\mathcal{P})$) is non-empty iff the constraints for (innermost) termination are satisfiable for $\mathcal{P}$. Thus, after computing $\Pi^t(\mathcal{P})$ resp. $\Pi^i(\mathcal{P})$, no further checking of orders and constraints is necessary anymore. This variant is particularly suitable for orders with few parameters like LPO.

7 Heuristics

Now we present heuristics to improve the efficiency of the approach. They concern the search for argument filterings (Sect. 7.1) and for base orders (Sect. 7.2, 7.3). In contrast to the improvements of the preceding sections, these heuristics affect the power of the method, i.e., there exist examples whose (innermost) termination can no longer be proved when following the heuristics.

7.1 Type Inference for Argument Filterings

In natural examples, termination of a function is usually due to the decrease of arguments of the *same type*. Of course, this type may be different for the different functions in a TRS. So we use a type inference algorithm to transform a TRS into a sorted TRS (i.e., a TRS with rules $l \rightarrow r$ where l and r are well-typed terms of same type). As a good heuristic to reduce the set of possible argument filterings further, one can require that for every symbol f, either no argument position is eliminated or all non-eliminated argument positions are of the same type. Our experiments show that all examples in the collections of [3, 8, 23] that can be solved using LPO as a base order can still be solved when using this heuristic.

7.2 Embedding Order for Dependency Pairs

To increase efficiency in our depth-first algorithm of Sect. 6, a successful heuristic is to only use the embedding order when orienting the constraints $\pi(s) \succ \pi(t)$ and $\pi(s) \succsim \pi(t)$ for dependency pairs $s \rightarrow t$. Only for constraints $\pi(l) \succsim \pi(r)$ for rules $l \rightarrow r$, one may apply more complex quasi-orders. The advantage is that now $\Pi(\mathcal{P})$ is much smaller. Our experiments show that due to the improvements in Sect. 3 and 4, this heuristic succeeds for more than 96 % of those examples of [3, 8, 23] where a full LPO was successful, while reducing runtimes by 58 %.

7.3 Bottom-Up Heuristic

To determine argument filterings in Sect. 6, we start with the dependency pairs and treat the constraints for rules afterwards, where f-rules are considered before g-rules if $f >_d g$. In contrast, now we suggest a bottom-up approach which starts with determining an argument filtering for constructors and then moves upwards through the recursion hierarchy where g is treated before f if $f >_d g$. While in Sect. 6, we determined *sets* of argument filterings, now we only determine one single argument filtering, even if several ones are possible. To obtain an efficient technique, no backtracking takes place, i.e., if at some point one selects the "wrong" argument filtering, then the proof can fail.

More precisely, we first guess an argument filtering π which is only defined for constructors. For every n-ary constructor c we define $\pi(c) = [1, \ldots, n]$ or we let π filter away all argument of c that do not have the same type as c's result. Afterwards, for every function symbol f, we try to extend π on f such that $\pi(l) \succsim \pi(r)$ for all f-rules $l \to r$. We consider functions according to the recursion hierarchy $>_d$. So when extending π on f, π is already defined on all $g <_d f$. Among the extensions of π which permit an orientation of the f-rules, we choose $\pi(f)$ such that it eliminates as many arguments of f as possible. If we are not able to orient the rules of f, then we mark f as not orientable. Finally, the filtering is extended to the tuple symbols by trying to orient the dependency pairs as well (where at least one dependency pair must be strictly decreasing).

In termination proofs, if $f \in \mathcal{R}_j$ is not orientable, then all symbols in $\mathcal{R}_i \geq_d \mathcal{R}_j$ as well as all dependency pairs resulting from $\mathcal{R}_i \geq_d \mathcal{R}_j$ are also not orientable. In innermost termination proofs, if f is not orientable, then a symbol that depends on f can still be orientable if one can extend the argument filtering in such a way that all occurrences of f in its rules are eliminated. Similarly, dependency pairs can still be orientable if the argument filtering eliminates all occurrences of f. Thus, here the bottom-up approach has the advantage that we already know that certain argument positions must be eliminated when extending the argument filtering to new function symbols.

This algorithm can also be modified by determining both the argument filtering and the reduction pair step by step. For example, a successful option is to use linear polynomial orders with coefficients 0 and 1. The bottom-up algorithm reduces the search space enormously. The number of TRSs from [3, 8, 23] where the bottom-up algorithm succeeds is 94 % of the number achieved by the full dependency pair approach with LPO, but runtime is reduced to less than 18 %.

8   Conclusion and Implementation in the System AProVE

We presented improvements of the dependency pair approach which significantly reduce the sets of constraints $\pi(l) \succsim \pi(r)$ for termination and innermost termination proofs. Moreover, we extended the applicability of dependency pair transformations and developed a criterion to ensure that their application is terminating without compromising the power of the approach in almost all examples. To implement the approach, we gave an algorithm for computing argument filterings which is tailored to the improvements presented before. Finally, we developed heuristics to increase efficiency which proved successful in large case studies.

We implemented these results in the system AProVE (Automated Program Verification Environment), available at http://www-i2.informatik.rwth-aachen. de/AProVE. The tool is written in Java and proofs can be performed both in a fully automated or in an interactive mode via a graphical user interface. To combine the heuristics of Sect. 7, for every SCC $\mathcal{P}$, AProVE offers the following combination algorithm which uses the heuristics as a pre-processing step and only calls the full dependency pair approach for cycles where the heuristics fail:

1. Safe transformations with Cases (1) and (2) of Def. 16
2. Bottom-up heuristic of Sect. 7.3
3. Heuristics of Sect. 7.1 and Sect. 7.2 with LPO as base order
4. Remaining safe transformations according to Def. 16.
   If at least one transformation was applied, go back to 1.
5. Full dependency pair approach with RPO as base order

When the constraints for the SCC are solved, the algorithm is called recursively with the SCCs of those remaining pairs which were only weakly decreasing. We tested the combination algorithm on the collections of [3, 8, 23] (108 TRSs for termination, 151 TRSs for innermost termination). Our system succeeded on 96.6 % of the innermost termination examples (including all of [3]) and on 93.5 % of the examples for termination. The automated proof for the whole collection took 80 seconds for innermost termination and 27 seconds for termination. These results indicate that the contributions of the paper are indeed very useful in practice.

References

1. T. Arts. System description: The dependency pair method. In *Proc. 11th RTA*, LNCS 1833, pages 261–264, 2000.
2. T. Arts and J. Giesl. Termination of term rewriting using dependency pairs. *Theoretical Computer Science*, 236:133–178, 2000.
3. T. Arts and J. Giesl. A collection of examples for termination of term rewriting using dependency pairs. Technical Report AIB-2001-09[3], RWTH Aachen, 2001.
4. F. Baader and T. Nipkow. *Term Rewriting and All That*. Cambr. Univ. Pr., 1998.
5. C. Borralleras, M. Ferreira, and A. Rubio. Complete monotonic semantic path orderings. In *Proc. 17th CADE*, LNAI 1831, pages 346–364, 2000.
6. E. Contejean, C. Marché, B. Monate, and X. Urbain. Cime version 2, 2000. Available from `http://cime.lri.fr`.
7. N. Dershowitz. Termination of rewriting. *J. Symbolic Comp.*, 3:69–116, 1987.
8. N. Dershowitz. 33 examples of termination. In *Proc. French Spring School of Theoretical Computer Science*, LNCS 909, pages 16–26, 1995.
9. N. Dershowitz, N. Lindenstrauss, Y. Sagiv, and A. Serebrenik. A general framework for automatic termination analysis of logic programs. *Applicable Algebra in Engineering, Communication and Computing*, 12(1,2):117–156, 2001.
10. O. Fissore, I. Gnaedig, and H. Kirchner. **Cariboo**: An induction based proof tool for termination with strategies. In *Proc. 4th PPDP*, pages 62–73. ACM, 2002.
11. J. Giesl and T. Arts. Verification of Erlang processes by dependency pairs. *Appl. Algebra in Engineering, Communication and Computing*, 12(1,2):39–72, 2001.
12. J. Giesl, T. Arts, and E. Ohlebusch. Modular termination proofs for rewriting using dependency pairs. *Journal of Symbolic Computation*, 34(1):21–58, 2002.
13. J. Giesl, R. Thiemann, P. Schneider-Kamp, and S. Falke. Improving dependency pairs. Technical Report AIB-2003-04[3], RWTH Aachen, Germany, 2003.
14. B. Gramlich. On proving termination by innermost termination. In *Proc. 7th RTA*, LNCS 1103, pages 97–107, 1996.

---

[3] Available from `http://aib.informatik.rwth-aachen.de`

15. N. Hirokawa and A. Middeldorp. Automating the dependency pair method. In *Proc. 19th CADE*, LNAI 2741, 2003.
16. N. Hirokawa and A. Middeldorp. Tsukuba termination tool. In *Proc. 14th RTA*, LNCS 2706, pages 311–320, 2003.
17. G. Huet and J.-M. Hullot. Proofs by induction in equational theories with constructors. *Journal of Computer and System Sciences*, 25:239–299, 1982.
18. K. Kusakari, M. Nakamura, and Y. Toyama. Argument filtering transformation. In *Proc. 1st PPDP*, LNCS 1702, pages 48–62, 1999.
19. C. S. Lee, N. D. Jones, and A. M. Ben-Amram. The size-change principle for program termination. In *Proc. POPL '01*, pages 81–92, 2001.
20. A. Middeldorp. Approximating dependency graphs using tree automata techniques. In *Proc. IJCAR 2001*, LNAI 2083, pages 593–610, 2001.
21. E. Ohlebusch. Hierarchical termination revisited. *IPL*, 84(4):207–214, 2002.
22. E. Ohlebusch, C. Claves, and C. Marché. TALP: A tool for the termination analysis of logic programs. In *Proc. 11th RTA*, LNCS 1833, pages 270–273, 2000.
23. J. Steinbach. Automatic termination proofs with transformation orderings. In *Proc. 6th RTA*, LNCS 914, pages 11–25, 1995. Full version appeared as Technical Report SR-92-23, Universität Kaiserslautern, Germany.
24. J. Steinbach. Simplification orderings: History of results. *Fund. I.*, 24:47–87, 1995.
25. R. Thiemann and J. Giesl. Size-change termination for term rewriting. In *Proc. 14th RTA*, LNCS 2706, pages 264–278, 2003.
26. Y. Toyama. Counterexamples to the termination for the direct sum of term rewriting systems. *Information Processing Letters*, 25:141–143, 1987.
27. X. Urbain. Automated incremental termination proofs for hierarchically defined term rewriting systems. In *Proc. IJCAR 2001*, LNAI 2083, pages 485–498, 2001.

On Closure under Complementation
of Equational Tree Automata for Theories Extending AC[*]

Kumar Neeraj Verma

LSV/CNRS UMR 8643 & INRIA Futurs projet SECSI & ENS Cachan, France,
verma@lsv.ens-cachan.fr

Abstract. We study the problem of closure under complementation of languages accepted by one-way and two-way tree automata modulo equational theories. We deal with the equational theories of commutative monoids (ACU), idempotent commutative monoids ($ACUI$), Abelian groups ($ACUM$), and the theories of exclusive-or ($ACUX$), generalized exclusive-or ($ACUX_n$), and distributive minus symbol ($ACUD$). While the one-way automata for all these theories are known to be closed under intersection, the situation is strikingly different for complementation. We show that one-way ACU and $ACUD$ automata are closed under complementation, but one-way $ACUX$, $ACUX_n$, $ACUM$ and $ACUI$ automata are not. The same results hold for the two-way automata, except for the theory $ACUI$, as the two-way automata modulo all these theories except $ACUI$ are known to be as expressive as the one-way automata. The question of closure under intersection and complementation of two-way $ACUI$ automata is open.

1 Introduction

Tree automata [2, 4] enjoy many good properties: emptiness is decidable, the class of languages accepted is closed under Boolean operations notably. *Two-way* tree automata extend ordinary tree automata (call them *one-way* tree automata to distinguish them from two-way tree automata) by allowing transitions that not only construct terms, as in one-way automata, but also destruct terms (see [2], Chapter 7, *Alternating Tree Automata*). More specifically, one-way automata have transitions of the form "if terms $t_1, ..., t_n$ are accepted at states $q_1, ..., q_n$ then term $f(t_1, ..., t_n)$ is accepted at state q". The new transitions allowed in two-way automata are of the form "if term $f(t_1, ..., t_n)$ is accepted at state q and terms $t_{i_1}, ..., t_{i_k}$ are accepted at states $q'_1, ..., q'_k$ then term t_i is accepted at state q'" where $1 \leq i, i_1, ..., i_k \leq n$. Two-way tree automata are more conveniently represented by the so called *definite clauses* of first order logic which provide a uniform mechanism for representing various kinds of transitions, like *alternation* ("if term t is accepted at states q_1 and q_2 then t is accepted at state q"), transitions with equality constraints between subterms, etc. Two-way tree automata can be effectively reduced to one-way tree automata. As a result they also enjoy the good properties of decidability of emptiness and closure under Boolean operations.

---

[*] Partially supported by the ACI "cryptologie" PSI-Robuste, ACI VERNAM, the RNTL project EVA and the ACI jeunes chercheurs "Sécurité informatique, protocoles cryptographiques et détection d'intrusions".

M.Y. Vardi and A. Voronkov (Eds.): LPAR 2003, LNAI 2850, pp. 183–197, 2003.
© Springer-Verlag Berlin Heidelberg 2003

In spite of having the same expressiveness as one-way automata, two-way automata are sometimes more convenient to work with because of the new kinds of transitions. An important area in which two-way tree automata have recently been applied is verification of cryptographic protocols [6, 11], where terms are used to represent messages and tree languages to represent sets of messages known to an intruder. The transitions of two-way tree automata allow us to model the ability of the intruder to encrypt and decrypt messages. This approach works fine when the cryptographic primitives are assumed to be perfect, in which case the messages are the members of the free term algebra. However often complex cryptographic primitives have additional algebraic properties, which need to be modeled using equational theories. The theory of associativity and commutativity, and its extensions like the theories of exclusive-or and Abelian groups are some examples that occur often. As an example the original version of the Bull's recursive authentication protocol presented in [14] was formally proved correct using the assumption of perfect cryptographic primitives. However this protocol uses the exclusive-or operation for encryption. By taking into account the properties of the exclusive-or operation, an attack against this protocol was found in [15]. Also protocols like the group Diffie-Hellman protocol [16], use algebraic properties of modular exponentiation [3]. This motivates exploring variants of tree automata which take into account equational properties of the function symbols.

Several notions of tree automata accepting terms modulo equational theories have been proposed recently [9, 12, 18], which extend the tree automata concept. The notions of one-way and two-way *equational tree automata* have been studied extensively in [18] which deals with several variants of the equational theory ACU of an associative, commutative operator $+$ with unit 0. It shows the decidability of emptiness and closure under intersection of the one-way automata for all these theories, as well as the equivalence between two-way and one-way automata for most of these theories. However the problem of closure under complementation has been left open. In this paper we examine this question.

More specifically, we study one-way and two-way equational tree automata, modulo the theory ACU and several of its extensions. The theory ACU of an associative-commutative symbol $+$ with unit 0 consists of the three axioms:

(A) $x + (y + z) = (x + y) + z$
(C) $x + y = y + x$
(U) $x + 0 = x$

The extensions of ACU that we deal with are obtained by adding one of the following axioms to the base theory ACU:

(X) $x + x = 0$ (xor axiom)
(X_n) $\underbrace{x + \ldots + x}_{n \text{ times}} = 0$ (generalization of xor axiom, where $n \geq 2$)
(M) $x + (-x) = 0$ (minus axiom)
(D) $-(x + y) = (-x) + (-y)$, $-(-x) = x$, $-0 = 0$ (distributivity of '$-$' symbol)
(I) $x + x = x$ (idempotence)

where $-$ is an additional unary symbol. We name a theory by the names of its axioms; e.g., $ACUM$ is the theory of Abelian groups and $ACUX$ the theory of xor. Note that

D is implied by $ACUM$, so $ACUD$ is a (strictly) weaker theory than $ACUM$. The theories dealt with in this paper are ACU, $ACUX$, $ACUX_n$, $ACUD$, $ACUM$ and $ACUI$.

We show that modulo ACU and $ACUD$ the one-way automata are closed under complementation. On the other hand, modulo $ACUI$, $ACUM$ (Abelian groups), $ACUX$ (the theory of xor) and $ACUX_n$, the one-way automata are not closed under complementation. Except for the theory $ACUI$, the same results hold for two-way tree automata. The case of two-way $ACUI$ automata is open. An interesting pattern visible here is the coincidence between closure under complementation of the one-way equational tree automata and the linearity of the equational theory involved. These results on complementation are in sharp contrast to the results on intersection.

Plan. After some material on related work, we define our one-way and two-way equational tree automata in Section 2, recalling some important results, notably connections of ACU automata with semilinear sets. These results are used in Section 3 to show closure under complementation of (one-way and two-way) ACU automata. The (one-way and two-way) $ACUX$ and $ACUX_n$ automata are not closed under complementation, as shown in Section 4. To deal with the $ACUD$ and Abelian groups case, we first generalize the results of Section 1 on ACU automata to the $ACUD$ case in Section 5. These are then used to show closure under complementation of (one-way and two-way) $ACUD$ automata in Section 6. The results and proofs in the Abelian groups case ($ACUM$) are exactly as in the $ACUX$ case, as we argue in Section 7. Lastly we show that the one-way $ACUI$ automata are not closed under complementation in Section 8, leaving open the question for two-way $ACUI$ automata. We conclude in Section 9.

Related Work. Tree automata modulo AC have been considered several times, though not all these notions coincide. Lugiez [9] considers one-way AC tree automata which have additional sort restrictions, but are also extended with a rich constraints language. Recent work by Lugiez [10] extends it to include equality and counting constraints, providing a rich framework that includes most known proposals for *one-way* AC tree automata with decidable emptiness problems. The resulting class of automata is also shown to be closed under Boolean operations. This framework is however incomparable to ours: while Lugiez's automata accommodate equality tests naturally, our two-way automata cannot avoid undecidability in the presence of equality constraints [7, 18].

Ohsaki [12, 13] considers a larger framework of (one-way) $\mathcal{E}$ tree automata, where $\mathcal{E}$ is an equational theory. Ohsaki's *regular* $\mathcal{E}$ automata coincide with our one-way $\mathcal{E}$ tree automata when $\mathcal{E}$ is linear (like AC, ACU), but this does *not* hold in theories like $ACUX$, $ACUM$, $ACUI$. For example, in Ohsaki's case, with transition rules $a \to q$, $b \to q$ and $0 \to q'$, and with the theory $ACUX$, we have $a + b \to^* q'$, meaning $a + b$ is accepted at q'. In our case, with the corresponding clauses $q(a)$, $q(b)$ and $q'(0)$, and with the theory $ACUX$, $a + b$ is not accepted at q'. For arbitrary $\mathcal{E}$ we do not know the relation between our automata and Ohsaki's automata, and the two notions appear rather dissimilar. One of the key differences is that while we extend the traditional correspondence between tree automata and logic programs from the non-equational case to the equational case, Ohaski's automata do not preserve this correspondence, as they mix equality on terms with equality on states, as illustrated by the above example.

While we consider tree automata as logic programs and extend them by adding equational theories, there has also been much work on *equational logic programs* [8] as such, which are logic programs in which the special equality predicate also appears, so that the equational theory can be coded in the logic program itself. In this context, complementation of equational tree automata corresponds to negation in equational logic programs. However our equational tree automata differ in that the equality symbol does not occur in the logic programs, and we separately consider an equational theory in which the equality predicate occurs. Moreover the author is not aware of any work on finding decision procedures or closure properties for subclasses of equational logic programs, especially for the ones corresponding to our automata.

The notion of *two-way* equational tree automata has been studied by Goubault-Larrecq and the author [7, 18] for the theory AC and its variants. Note that the specific theories $ACUX$, $ACUM$, etc., that we consider have traditionally not been considered in the framework of (one-way) tree automata; they give rise to specific technical problems and solutions. The notion of alternating two-way AC tree automata is treated in detail in [7], which also considers some additional push clause formats which are not relevant in this paper. Finally we have found that closure under Boolean operations has also been shown for the *multiset automata* of Colcombet [1], which correspond to the subclass of our one-way ACU automata in which all symbols other than $+, 0$ are unary, and were introduced for studying process rewrite systems.

To avoid confusion we clarify that the "two-way automata" of [17] are an entirely different notion from ours.

2   Two-Way $\mathcal{E}$-Tree Automata

Fix a signature Σ of function symbols, each coming with a fixed arity, and let $\mathcal{E}$ be an equational theory, inducing a congruence $=_\mathcal{E}$ on the terms built from Σ. We will use clauses of first order logic as a general means of representing various classes of automata. A *definite clause* is an implication of the form: $P(t) \Leftarrow P_1(t_1) \wedge ... \wedge P_n(t_n)$ (1) where $P, P_1, ..., P_n$ are predicates and $t, t_1, ..., t_n$ are terms built from Σ and variables. Given a finite set $\mathcal{C}$ of such definite clauses we define *derivations* of ground atoms using the following two rules:

$$\frac{P_1(t_1\sigma)...P_n(t_n\sigma)}{P(t\sigma)} \text{if } P(t) \Leftarrow P_1(t_1) \wedge ... \wedge P_n(t_n) \in \mathcal{C} \qquad \frac{P(s)}{P(t)} \text{if } s =_\mathcal{E} t$$

where σ is a ground substitution. Thus a derivation is a tree-like structure, which should not be confused with the trees which are the terms built from Σ. Accordingly, a *sub-derivation* of a derivation δ is a subtree of δ. The *last step* of a derivation δ refers to the step at the root of δ. The connection of definite clauses with automata is as follows: predicates are states, finite sets of definite clauses are automata, and an atom $P(t)$ is derivable using $\mathcal{C}$, iff the term t is *accepted* at state P in the automaton $\mathcal{C}$. The derivations using $\mathcal{C}$ are sometimes called *runs* of the automaton $\mathcal{C}$.

It is also easy to see that the set of derivable atoms is exactly the least Herbrand model of the set of clauses modulo $\mathcal{E}$.

The language $\mathcal{L}_P(\mathcal{C}/\mathcal{E})$ is the set of terms t such that $P(t)$ is derivable. When $\mathcal{E}$ is the empty theory, we shall call it $\mathcal{L}_P(\mathcal{C})$. If in addition some state P_f is specified as being *final* then the language *accepted* by $\mathcal{C}$ is $\mathcal{L}(\mathcal{C}/\mathcal{E}) = \mathcal{L}_{P_f}(\mathcal{C}/\mathcal{E})$. Also, given a language L and an equational theory $\mathcal{E}$, $\mathcal{E}(\mathcal{L})$ denotes the set of terms t such that $t =_{\mathcal{E}} s$ for some $s \in \mathcal{L}$.

We define *one-way automata* as consisting of clauses:

$$P(f(x_1, ..., x_n)) \Leftarrow P_1(x_1) \wedge ... \wedge P_n(x_n) \quad (2)$$

$$P(x) \Leftarrow P_1(x) \quad (3)$$

which we shall call *pop clauses* and *epsilon clauses* respectively. In (2), the variables $x_1, ..., x_n$ are distinct.

These automata (without equations) are exactly the classical tree automata usually described in the literature. It may be helpful to read the pop clause as: "if terms $x_1,...,x_n$ are accepted at states $P_1,...,P_n$ respectively, then $f(x_1, ..., x_n)$ is accepted at P". This is usually denoted by the rewrite rule $f(P_1, ..., P_n) \to P$. The epsilon clause corresponds to the rewrite rule $P_1 \to P$. We have the following easy result:

Lemma 1 ([18]). *For any one-way automaton $\mathcal{C}$ and equational theory $\mathcal{E}$, $\mathcal{L}_P(\mathcal{C}/\mathcal{E}) = \mathcal{E}(\mathcal{L}_P(\mathcal{C}))$. In particular emptiness of one-way $\mathcal{E}$ tree-automata is decidable.*

For Ohsaki's regular $\mathcal{E}$ tree automata, this result holds if $\mathcal{E}$ is linear, but not in general. A counter-example is the automaton modulo $ACUX$ given in Section 1.

Since we are dealing with theories extending ACU, we assume that Σ contains symbols $+$, 0 and in presence of equations D or M the symbol $-$. Note that we don't consider the case of Σ containing several $+$ (resp. $-$, 0) symbols. Symbols in $\Sigma_f = \Sigma \setminus \{+, -, 0\}$, are called *free*. Free symbols of zero arity are called *constants*. Terms of the form $f(t_1, ..., t_n)$ where f is free are called *functional terms*. Accordingly the pop clauses in our automata are of the following form:

$$P(x + y) \Leftarrow P_1(x) \wedge P_2(y) \quad (4) \qquad P(a)\text{where } a \text{ is a constant} \quad (6)$$

$$P(0) \quad (5) \qquad P(-x) \Leftarrow P_1(x) \quad (7)$$

$$P(f(x_1, ..., x_n)) \Leftarrow P_1(x_1) \wedge ... \wedge P_n(x_n), f \text{ being free} \quad (8)$$

Clauses (6) are special cases of clauses (8).

One-way ACU (resp. $ACUI$, $ACUX$, $ACUX_n$) automata are sets of clauses (3), (4–6) and (8); one-way $ACUM$ and $ACUD$ automata in addition contain clauses (7).

We define two-way automata by adding the following kind of clauses

$$Q(x_i) \Leftarrow P(f(x_1, ..., x_n)) \wedge Q_1(x_{i_1}) \wedge ... \wedge Q_k(x_{i_k}), \quad (9)$$

$$f \text{ being free}, i \in \{1, ..., n\} \setminus \{i_1, ..., i_k\}, 1 \le i_1 < ... < i_k \le n$$

called *push clauses*, to one-way automata (the variables $x_1, ..., x_n$ are distinct.) Hence *two-way* automata are sets of clauses (3) and (4–9)—with the proviso that (7) is only included when $- \in \Sigma$. The side-conditions "$i \in \{1, ..., n\} \setminus \{i_1, ..., i_k\}, 1 \le i_1 < ... < i_k \le n$" have been introduced in clause (9) to avoid undecidability problems. This is discussed in [18], which also argues that removing the side-condition "f being free" from clause (9) has no impact in the case of theories $ACUX$ and $ACUM$ but is problematic in the case of other theories like ACU and $ACUD$. Hence, while the expression "two-way automata" is normally used in a general sense, without the restrictions imposed by the side-conditions in clause (9), however in the rest of this paper, this expression will be used in the specialized sense defined above. *Constant-only* automata are one-way automata which contain clauses (6) instead of the general clauses (8) (the only free symbols in the signature are constants.) Given a one-way or two-way automaton $\mathcal{C}$, we define $\mathcal{C}_{eq}$ to be the part of $\mathcal{C}$ with clauses (3), (4), (5) and (7) (the equational part), and $\mathcal{C}_{free}$ is the remaining part.

Example 1. Consider a signature having constants a and b, a unary symbol f and a binary symbol g. Define two-way automaton $\mathcal{A}$ modulo $ACUX$ to consist of the clauses

(i) $P_1(a)$
(ii) $P_2(b)$
(iii) $P_3(f(x)) \Leftarrow P_2(x)$
(iv) $P_4(0)$
(v) $P_5(g(x,y)) \Leftarrow P_4(x) \wedge P_3(y)$

(vi) $P_6(x+y) \Leftarrow P_1(x) \wedge P_3(y)$
(vii) $P_7(x+y) \Leftarrow P_6(x) \wedge P_1(y)$
(viii)$P_8(x) \Leftarrow P_5(g(x,y)) \wedge P_7(y)$
(ix) $P_9(x+y) \Leftarrow P_8(x) \wedge P_1(y)$

Then the following is an example of a derivation in the automaton. At each step, the clause applied or the equational rewriting used is indicated on the right side.

$$
\cfrac{
  \cfrac{
    \cfrac{\cfrac{}{P_4(0)}\ (iv) \quad \cfrac{\cfrac{}{P_2(b)}\ (ii)}{P_3(f(b))}\ (iii)}{P_5(g(0,f(b)))}\ (v)
    \qquad
    \cfrac{
      \cfrac{\cfrac{}{P_1(a)}\ (i) \quad \cfrac{\cfrac{}{P_2(b)}\ (ii)}{P_3(f(b))}\ (iii)}{P_6(a+f(b))}\ (vi) \quad \cfrac{}{P_1(a)}\ (i)
    }{\cfrac{P_7(((a+f(b))+a))}{P_7(f(b))}\ (\mathrm{ACUX})}\ (vii)
  }{P_8(0)}\ (viii)
  \qquad
  \cfrac{}{P_1(a)}\ (i)
}{\cfrac{P_9(0+a)}{P_9(a)}\ (\mathrm{ACUX})}\ (ix)
$$

The languages accepted by all our one-way or two-way automata are trivially closed under union. It has been shown in [18] that the one-way automata for all these theories (ACU, $ACUD$, $ACUX$, $ACUX_n$, $ACUM$, $ACUI$) are closed under intersection. There it is also shown that two-way automata are as expressive as one-way automata, for all these theories, except $ACUI$ for which the problem is currently open. The emptiness test for one-way automata has already been dealt with (Lemma 1). In this paper, we shall concentrate on closure under complementation of these automata. Note also that closure under intersection and decidability of emptiness imply decidability of membership of one-way equational tree automata for all theories considered in this paper since, using Lemma 1, for any theory $\mathcal{E}$ and term t, the language $\mathcal{E}(\{t\})$ is easily recognized by a one-way $\mathcal{E}$ tree automaton.

First we recall some important results on constant-only ACU automata. Let the constants in our signature be $a_1, ..., a_p$. Modulo ACU, the ground terms are of the form $\sum_{i=1}^{p} n_i a_i$ with $n_i \in \mathbb{N}$: equivalently p-tuples of natural numbers. Recall that a *linear set* is a set of the form $\{\nu + n_1\nu_1 + ... + n_k\nu_k \mid n_1, ..., n_k \in \mathbb{N}\}$ for some $\nu, \nu_1, ..., \nu_k \in \mathbb{N}^p$. A *semilinear set* is a finite union of linear sets. The semilinear sets

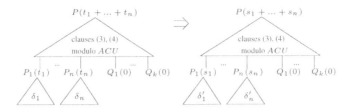

Fig. 1. Reuse of ACU derivations

are exactly the sets definable in Presburger arithmetic [5]. In particular they are closed under union, intersection, complementation and projection. Then we have:

Lemma 2 ([18]). *Constant-only ACU automata accept exactly semilinear sets.*

To prepare ourselves, we need another special property of ACU automata which allows us to 'reuse' parts of derivations. This will be required very often in the paper.

Lemma 3 ([18]). *Let $\mathcal{E}$ be any set of equations containing ACU. Consider a derivation δ of an atom $P(t)$ modulo $\mathcal{E}$. Let $\delta_1, ..., \delta_n$ be non-overlapping subderivations of δ such that outside the δ_i's, the only equations used are ACU and the set S of clauses used contains only clauses of kind (3), (4) and (5) (see Figure 1, noting that the derivation trees are shown with the root at the top.) Suppose the conclusions of $\delta_1, ..., \delta_n$ are $P_1(t_1), ..., P_n(t_n)$. Then*

1. $t =_{ACU} t_1 + ... + t_n$
2. *If there are derivations $\delta'_1, ..., \delta'_n$ of atoms $P_1(s_1), ..., P_n(s_n)$ modulo $\mathcal{E}$ then there is a derivation δ' of $P(s_1 + ... + s_n)$ modulo $\mathcal{E}$, containing δ'_i's as subderivations, such that outside the δ'_i's, the only equations used are ACU, and all clauses used belong to S.*

The following definition gives one way of computing such δ_i's and $P_i(t_i)$'s:

Definition 1. *Consider a derivation δ of an atom $P(t)$ in a one-way automaton modulo ACU. Let $\delta_1, ..., \delta_n$ be the set of maximal subderivations of δ in which the last step used is an application of clause (8) (or clause (6)). Suppose the conclusions of $\delta_1, ..., \delta_n$ are $P_1(t_1), ..., P_n(t_n)$ (in which case $t_1, ..., t_n$ must be functional.) Then we will say that the (unordered) list of atoms $P_1(t_1), ..., P_n(t_n)$ is the functional support of the derivation δ. (From Lemma 3 we have $t =_{ACU} t_1 + ... + t_n$.)*

3   Complementation of ACU Automata

Let $\mathcal{C}$ be a one-way ACU automaton with predicates from some finite set $\mathbb{P}$. We introduce new predicate symbols $\check{S}$ and $\widehat{S}$ for each $S \subseteq \mathbb{P}$ and constants a_S for each $S \subseteq \mathbb{P}$. We intend $\check{S}$ to accept terms accepted at all the predicates in S but nowhere else. $\widehat{S}$ is intended to accept the functional terms accepted at $\check{S}$.

Define automaton $\mathcal{C}_{eq}^* = \mathcal{C}_{eq} \cup \{P(a_S) \mid P \in S\}$. The idea in defining $\mathcal{C}_{eq}$ is to compute all possible derivations using the clauses of the equational part. The constant a_S acts as abstraction for the terms accepted at $\widehat{S}$ for $S \subseteq \mathbb{P}$.

From Lemma 2, $\mathcal{L}_P(\mathcal{C}_{eq}^*/ACU)$ is a semilinear set for every $P \in \mathbb{P}$. Given $S \subseteq \mathbb{P}$, define $\mathcal{L}^S = \bigcap_{P \in S} \mathcal{L}_P(\mathcal{C}_{eq}^*/ACU) \setminus \bigcup_{P \in \mathbb{P} \setminus S} \mathcal{L}_P(\mathcal{C}_{eq}^*/ACU)$. This is a semilinear set. By Lemma 2, we can construct a constant-only automaton $\mathcal{C}_S$ with final state F_S such that $\mathcal{L}(\mathcal{C}_S/ACU) = \mathcal{L}^S$. We assume that automata $\mathcal{C}_S$'s are built from mutually disjoint sets of (fresh) states.

Define automaton $\mathcal{C}^\dagger$ to consist of the following clauses:

- for each $S \subseteq \mathbb{P}$ the clause $\breve{S}(x) \Leftarrow F_S(x)$.
- clauses (3), (4) and (5) (but not (6)) from each $\mathcal{C}_S$.
- for each clause $R(a_S)$ in some $\mathcal{C}_S$, the clause $R(x) \Leftarrow \widehat{S}(x)$.
- for each free function symbol f of arity n, and each $S_1, ..., S_n \subseteq \mathbb{P}$, the clause $\widehat{S}(f(x_1, ..., x_n)) \Leftarrow \breve{S}_1(x_1) \wedge ... \wedge \breve{S}_n(x_n)$ where $S = \{P \mid \exists P_1 \in S_1.\exists...\exists P_n \in S_n.P(f(x_1, ..., x_n)) \Leftarrow P_1(x_1) \wedge ... \wedge P_n(x_n) \in \mathcal{C}_{free}\}$.

This construction plays the role of the usual determinization procedure in standard tree automata. Note that it is however more complex because of the ACU symbol. We have the following result:

Lemma 4. *For any $S \subseteq \mathbb{P}$ and any term t, $\breve{S}(t)$ is derivable in $\mathcal{C}^\dagger$ modulo ACU iff $S = \{P \in \mathbb{P} \mid P(t)\text{is derivable in } \mathcal{C}\text{modulo } ACU\}$.*

Proof. By induction on the size of t. Let $t =_{ACU} t_1 + ... + t_n (n \geq 0)$ where for $1 \leq i \leq n, t_i = f_i(t_i^1, ..., t_i^{k_i})$, for some free f_i. Let $S = \{P \in \mathbb{P} \mid P(t)\text{is derivable in } \mathcal{C}\}$. First we show that *(a)* $\breve{S}(t)$ is derivable in $\mathcal{C}^\dagger$ modulo ACU; then we show that *(b)* if $\breve{S}'(t)$ is derivable in $\mathcal{C}^\dagger$ modulo ACU for some $S' \subseteq \mathbb{P}$ then $S' = S$.

Proof of (a). For $1 \leq i \leq n, 1 \leq j \leq k_i$ let $S_i^j = \{Q \mid Q(t_i^j)\text{is derivable in } \mathcal{C}$ modulo $ACU\}$. By induction hypothesis $\breve{S}_i^j(t_i^j)$ is derivable in $\mathcal{C}^\dagger$ modulo ACU. For $1 \leq i \leq n$ let $S_i = \{Q \mid \exists Q^1 \in S_i^1.\exists...\exists Q^{k_i} \in S_i^{k_i}.Q(f_i(x_1, ..., x_{k_i})) \Leftarrow Q^1(x_i) \wedge ...\wedge Q^{k_i}(x_{k_i}) \in \mathcal{C}\}$. Then the clause $\widehat{S}_i(f_i(x_1, ..., x_{k_i})) \Leftarrow \breve{S}_i^1(x_1) \wedge...\wedge \breve{S}_i^{k_i}(x_{k_i}) \in \mathcal{C}^\dagger$. So $\widehat{S}_i(t_i)$ is derivable in $\mathcal{C}^\dagger$ modulo ACU for $1 \leq i \leq n$.

For each $P \in S$, the derivation of $P(t)$ has a functional support of the form $Q_1^P(t_1)$, ..., $Q_n^P(t_n)$. For $P \in S, 1 \leq i \leq n$, the derivation of $Q_i^P(t_i)$ uses at the last step, a clause $Q_i^P(f_i(x_1, ..., x_{k_i})) \Leftarrow Q_i^{P,1}(x_1) \wedge ... \wedge Q_i^{P,k_i}(x_{k_i})$ and derivations of $Q_i^{P,j}(t_i^j)(1 \leq j \leq k_i)$. Then $Q_i^{P,j} \in S_i^j$ for $P \in S, 1 \leq i \leq n, 1 \leq j \leq k_i$. Hence $Q_i^P \in S_i$. By Lemma 3, (*) $P(a_{S_1} + ... + a_{S_n})$ is derivable in $\mathcal{C}_{eq}^*$ modulo ACU for each $P \in S$.

(**)If $P \in \mathbb{P}\setminus S$ then $a_{S_1} + ... + a_{S_n} \notin \mathcal{L}_P(\mathcal{C}_{eq}^*/\widehat{ACU})$. Otherwise the corresponding derivation would have a functional support of the form $Q_1(a_{S_1}), ..., Q_n(a_{S_n})$ where $Q_i \in S_i$ for $1 \leq i \leq n$. Then by construction of $S_i, Q_i(t_i)$ would be derivable for $1 \leq i \leq n$. Then by Lemma 3, $P(t_1 + ... + t_n)$ would be derivable in $\mathcal{C}$ modulo ACU. Hence we would have a derivation of $P(t)$ in $\mathcal{C}$ modulo ACU which contradicts the definition of S.

Combining (*) and (**), $a_{S_1} + ... + a_{S_n} \in \mathcal{L}^S$. The derivation of $F_S(a_{S_1} + ... + a_{S_n})$ in $\mathcal{C}_S$ modulo ACU has a functional support of the form $R_1(a_{S_1}), ..., R_n(a_{S_n})$. Then

$R_i(t_i)$ is derivable in $\mathcal{C}^\dagger$ modulo ACU using the clause $R_i(x) \Leftarrow \widehat{S}_i(x)$ for $1 \leq i \leq n$. Hence by Lemma 3 we get a derivation of $F_S(t_1 + ... + t_n)$ in $\mathcal{C}^\dagger$ modulo ACU. Finally we use the clause $\breve{S}(x) \Leftarrow F_S(x)$ to get a derivation of $\breve{S}(t_1 + ... + t_n)$, i.e. of $\breve{S}(t)$. This proves *(a)*.

Proof of (b). Now suppose $S' \subseteq \mathbb{P}$ such that $\breve{S}'(t)$ is derivable in $\mathcal{C}^\dagger$ modulo ACU. We show that $S' = S$. The derivation of $\breve{S}'(t)$ uses at the last step a derivation of $F_{S'}(t)$. From the construction of $\mathcal{C}^\dagger$, the latter derivation has a functional support of the form $\widehat{S_1'}(t_1), ..., \widehat{S_n'}(t_n)$ and the clauses used immediately above the derivation of $\widehat{S_i'}(t_i)$ are of the form $R_i'(x) \Leftarrow \widehat{S_i'}(x)$ corresponding to the clause $R_i'(a_{S_i'})$ of $\mathcal{C}_{S'}$. Also the clauses used above the clauses $R_i'(x) \Leftarrow \widehat{S_i'}(x)$ are from $\mathcal{C}_{S'}$. Then by Lemma 3, $F_{S'}(a_{S_1'} + ... + a_{S_n'})$ is derivable in $\mathcal{C}_{S'}$ modulo ACU. For $1 \leq i \leq n$ the derivation of $\widehat{S_i'}(t_i)$ uses at the last step a clause of the form $\widehat{S_i'}(f_i(x_1, ..., x_{k_i})) \Leftarrow \breve{S}_i''^1(x_1) \wedge ... \wedge \breve{S}_i''^{k_i}(x_{k_i}) \in \mathcal{C}^\dagger$ and derivations of $\breve{S}_i''^j(t_i^j)(1 \leq j \leq k_i)$. Then by induction hypothesis $S_i''^j = S_i^j$. Then by definition of $\mathcal{C}^\dagger$, $S_i' = S_i$. Hence $a_{S_1} + ... + a_{S_n} \in \mathcal{L}_{S'}$. We have already seen that $a_{S_1} + ... + a_{S_n} \in \mathcal{L}^S$. Since the $\mathcal{L}^S$'s are mutually disjoint, so $S' = S$.   □

As a consequence we obtain:

Theorem 1. *One-way ACU automata are closed under complementation.*

Proof. Let $\mathcal{C}$ be a one-way ACU automaton with predicates from $\mathbb{P}$ and with final state F. Define automaton $\mathcal{C}^\dagger$ as above. Pick a new predicate $F^\dagger$. Add to $\mathcal{C}^\dagger$ the clauses $F^\dagger(x) \Leftarrow \breve{S}(x)$ for every $S \subseteq \mathbb{P}, F \notin S$. Call this new automaton $\mathcal{C}^\ddagger$. Then by Lemma 4, $t \in \mathcal{L}_{F^\dagger}(\mathcal{C}^\ddagger / ACU)$ iff for some $S \subseteq \mathbb{P}, F \notin S$ we have $t \in \mathcal{L}_{\breve{S}}(\mathcal{C}^\dagger / ACU)$, iff $F \notin \{P \in \mathbb{P} \mid t \in \mathcal{L}_P(\mathcal{C}/ACU)\}$ iff $t \notin \mathcal{L}_F(\mathcal{C}/ACU)$. Hence $F^\ddagger$ accepts the complement of the language accepted by F.   □

Since two-way ACU automata have the same expressiveness [18] as one-way ACU automata, we also have:

Theorem 2. *Two-way ACU automata are closed under complementation.*

The idea of using constants as abstractions for the functional terms accepted at certain states, and the correspondence between constant-only ACU automata and Presburger definability, have already been used in [18] to show closure under intersection of various classes of automata. This may give the impression that the arguments for closure under complementation are similar to the ones for intersection. There are indeed some common ideas, which led the author to conjecture that one-way tree automata modulo all theories considered here are closed under complementation. However it was surprisingly found that while these ideas work for showing closure under intersection of the one-way automata modulo all theories under consideration, they don't work for showing closure under complementation of the one-way automata modulo the theories $ACUX$, $ACUX_n$, $ACUM$ and $ACUI$. We will show that the latter are not closed under complementation. Unlike in the case of intersection, our results show a strong correlation between closure under complementation of one-way equational tree automata and the linearity of the equational theory involved, at least as far as the theories dealt with in this paper are concerned.

4   Counter-Example for $ACUX$ and $ACUX_n$ Automata

Contrary to the ACU case, $ACUX$ automata are not closed under complementation, as we show in this section. The result generalizes to the $ACUX_n$ case for $n \geq 2$, i.e. we can show that one-way or two-way $ACUX_n$ automata are not closed under complementation for any $n \geq 2$. (We get the $ACUX$ case by making $n = 2$.) To show this fix some $n \geq 2$. Define languages $\mathcal{L}_1 = \{f^{k_1}(a) + ... + f^{k_n}(a) \mid k_1, ..., k_n \geq 0\}$ (assuming a signature that has at least a unary symbol f and a constant a) and $\mathcal{L}_2 = \{0\}$. Let us clarify that we are considering languages modulo $ACUX_n$, so that, for example, when we write $\{0\}$, we actually mean the language $\{t \mid t =_{ACUX_n} 0\}$. Similar remarks hold for other theories considered later. Then $\mathcal{L}_1 \setminus \mathcal{L}_2 = \{f^{k_1}(a) + ... + f^{k_n}(a) \mid k_1, ..., k_n \geq 0$ and for some $1 \leq i, j \leq n, i \neq j$ and $k_i \neq k_j\}$. $\mathcal{L}_1$ and $\mathcal{L}_2$ are clearly accepted by one-way $ACUX_n$ automata. However $\mathcal{L}_1 \setminus \mathcal{L}_2$ is not:

Lemma 5. *The language $\mathcal{L} = \{f^{k_1}(a) + ... + f^{k_n}(a) \mid k_1, ..., k_n \geq 0$ and for some $1 \leq i, j \leq n, i \neq j$ and $k_i \neq k_j\}$ is not accepted by any one-way $ACUX_n$ automaton.*

Proof. Assume on the contrary that there is a one-way automaton $\mathcal{C}$ with final state P which modulo $ACUX_n$ accepts $\mathcal{L}$. Let $\mathbb{P}$ be the set of predicates in $\mathcal{C}$. For each $p \geq 0$ define $S_p = \{Q \in \mathbb{P} \mid Q(f^p(a))$ is derivable in $\mathcal{C}$ modulo $ACUX_n\}$. Since $\mathbb{P}$ is finite, it has finitely many subsets. Hence we have some $p \neq q$ such that $S_p = S_q$. Since $p \neq q$, the term $f^p(a) + \sum_{i=1}^{n-1} f^q(a) \in \mathcal{L}$. From Lemma 1, we have some $t =_{ACUX_n} f^p(a) + \sum_{i=1}^{n-1} f^q(a)$ such that $P(t)$ is derivable in $\mathcal{C}$ modulo ACU. We have $t =_{ACU} t_1 + t_2 + ... + t_n + u_1^1 + ... + u_1^n + ... + u_k^1 + ... + u_k^n (k \geq 0)$ such that t_j and u_i^j are functional for $1 \leq i \leq k, 1 \leq j \leq n, t_1 =_{ACUX_n} f^p(a), t_j =_{ACUX_n} f^q(a)$ for $2 \leq j \leq n$, and $u_i^j =_{ACUX_n} u_i^{j'}$ for $1 \leq i \leq k, 1 \leq j, j' \leq n$. The derivation of $P(t)$ has functional support of the form $I_1(t_1), I_2(t_2), ..., I_n(t_n), I_1^1(u_1^1), ..., I_1^n(u_1^n)$, $..., I_k^1(u_k^1), ..., I_k^n(u_k^n)$. Then $I_1 \in S_p$ and $I_2, ..., I_n \in S_q$. However $S_p = S_q$, hence $I_2, ..., I_n \in S_p$. Thus $I_1(f^p(a)), I_2(f^p(a)), ..., I_n(f^p(a))$ are derivable in $\mathcal{C}$ modulo $ACUX_n$. By Lemma 3, $P(\sum_{i=1}^n f^p(a) + u_1^1 + ... + u_1^n + ... + u_k^1 + ... + u_k^n)$ (or $P(0)$) is derivable in $\mathcal{C}$ modulo $ACUX_n$ leading to contradiction.   □

Since $\mathcal{L}_1 \setminus \mathcal{L}_2 = \mathcal{L}_1 \cap \complement(\mathcal{L}_2)$ where $\complement(\mathcal{L}')$ denotes the complement of $\mathcal{L}'$, we have:

Theorem 3. *One-way $ACUX_n$ automata are not closed under complementation for any $n \geq 2$. This holds for one-way $ACUX$ automata in particular.*

The key idea, also used in the further counter-examples, is that in presence of non-linear equations like X, doing complementation involves putting disequality constraints on subterms, which is beyond the power of our automata.

Again, since two-way $ACUX_n$ automata have the same expressiveness [18] as one-way $ACUX_n$ automata, we get:

Theorem 4. *Two-way $ACUX_n$ automata are not closed under complementation for any $n \geq 2$. This holds for one-way $ACUX$ automata in particular.*

We remark that the situation is different for the theory $ACUX_n$ when $n = 1$. In this case the axiom $x = 0$ means that every term is equal to 0. Trivially the automata are closed under intersection and complementation. This is clearly not an interesting case.

5   Constant-Only $ACUD$ Automata and Reuse of $ACUD$ Derivations

In this section we generalize Lemmas 2 and 3 to the $ACUD$ case. These will be useful in dealing with the $ACUD$ and $ACUM$ automata.

First we consider constant only $ACUD$ automata. Recall that Σ_f is the set of constants in our signature. Let $\overline{\Sigma}_f$ be a set of fresh constants $\{\overline{a} \mid a \in \Sigma_f\}$. Terms built from $\Sigma_f \cup \{+, -, 0\}$ modulo $ACUD$ are of the form $a_1 + \dots + a_m - b_1 - \dots - b_n$ ($m, n \geq 0$) while those built from $\Sigma_f \cup \overline{\Sigma}_f \cup \{+, 0\}$ modulo ACU are of the form $a_1 + \dots + a_m + \overline{b_1} + \dots + \overline{b_n}$ ($m, n \geq 0$). Hence there is a natural 1-1 correspondence between terms (languages) on $\Sigma_f \cup \{+, -, 0\}$ modulo $ACUD$ and terms (languages) on $\Sigma \cup \overline{\Sigma}_f \cup \{+, 0\}$ modulo ACU. Then modulo this correspondence of languages:

Lemma 6 ([18]). *The language accepted by a constant-only $ACUD$ automata with constants from Σ_f is a semilinear set with constants from $\Sigma_f \cup \overline{\Sigma}_f$. Conversely, a semilinear set with constants from $\Sigma_f \cup \overline{\Sigma}_f$ can be represented as accepted by a constant-only $ACUD$ automaton with constants from Σ_f.*

Also we have the following generalization of Lemma 3 to the $ACUD$ case.

Lemma 7. *Let $\mathcal{E}$ be any set of equations implying $ACUD$. Consider a derivation δ of an atom $P(t)$ modulo $\mathcal{E}$. Let $\delta_1, \dots, \delta_n$ be non-overlapping subderivations of δ such that outside the δ_i's, the only equations used are $ACUD$ and the set S of clauses used contains only clauses of kind (3), (4), (5) and (7). Suppose the conclusions of $\delta_1, \dots, \delta_n$ are $P_1(t_1), \dots, P_n(t_n)$. Then*

1. *$t =_{ACUD} \pm_1 t_1 \pm_2 \dots \pm_n t_n$ for some $\pm_1, \dots, \pm_n \in \{+, -\}$. ($+t_1$ means t_1.)*
2. *If there are derivations $\delta'_1, \dots, \delta'_n$ of atoms $P_1(s_1), \dots, P_n(s_n)$ modulo $\mathcal{E}$ then there is a derivation δ' of $P(\pm_1 s_1 \pm_2 \dots \pm_n s_n)$ (the $\pm_i$'s here are the same as above) modulo $\mathcal{E}$, containing δ'_i's as subderivations, such that outside the δ'_i's, the only equations used are $ACUD$, and all clauses used belong to S.*

Finally the notion of functional support is generalized to $ACUD$ derivations.

Definition 2. *Consider a derivation δ of an atom $P(t)$ in a one-way automaton modulo $ACUD$. Let $\delta_1, \dots, \delta_n$ be the set of maximal subderivations of δ in which the last step used is an application of clause (8) (or clause (6)). Suppose the conclusions of $\delta_1, \dots, \delta_n$ are $P_1(t_1), \dots, P_n(t_n)$ (in which case $t_1, \dots, t_n$ must be functional.) Then we will say that the (unordered) list of atoms $P_1(t_1), \dots, P_n(t_n)$ is the functional support of the derivation δ. (From Lemma 7, t must be of the form $\pm_1 t_1 \pm_2 \dots \pm_n t_n$.)*

6   Complementation of $ACUD$ Automata

In the $ACUD$ case the situation is similar to the ACU case: the automata are closed under complementation. The arguments being similar to the ACU case, we give the full construction with a sketch of the proof.

Let $\mathcal{C}$ be a one-way $ACUD$ automaton with predicates from $\mathbb{P}$. Introduce predicate symbols $\check{S}$ and $\widehat{S}$ for each $S \subseteq \mathbb{P}$, and sets of constants $A = \{a_S \mid S \subseteq \mathbb{P}\}$ and

$\overline{A} = \{\overline{a_S} \mid S \subseteq \mathbb{P}\}$. Define automaton $\mathcal{C}^*_{eq} = \mathcal{C}_{eq} \cup \{P(a_S) \mid P \in S\}$. From Lemma 6, for each P, $\mathcal{L}_P(\mathcal{C}^*_{eq}/ACUD)$ is a semilinear set on constants from $A \cup \overline{A}$. Given $S \subseteq \mathbb{P}$, define $\mathcal{L}^S = \bigcap_{P \in S} \mathcal{L}_P(\mathcal{C}^*_{eq}/ACUD) \setminus \bigcup_{P \in \mathbb{P} \setminus S} \mathcal{L}_P(\mathcal{C}^*_{eq}/ACUD)$. This is a semilinear set on constants from $A \cup \overline{A}$. By Lemma 6 we can construct a constant-only $ACUD$ automaton $\mathcal{C}_S$, using constants from A, and with final state F_S such that $\mathcal{L}(\mathcal{C}_S/ACUD) = \mathcal{L}^S$. We assume that automata $\mathcal{C}_S$'s are all built from mutually disjoint sets of (fresh) predicates.

Define automaton $\mathcal{C}^\dagger$ to consist of the following clauses:

- for each $S \subseteq \mathbb{P}$ the clause $\check{S}(x) \Leftarrow F_S(x)$.
- clauses (3), (4), (5) and (7) (but not (6)) from each $\mathcal{C}_S$.
- for each clause $R(a_S)$ in some $\mathcal{C}_S$, the clause $R(x) \Leftarrow \widehat{S}(x)$.
- for each free functional symbol f of arity n, and each $S_1, ..., S_n \subseteq \mathbb{P}$, the clause $\widehat{S}(f(x_1, ..., x_n)) \Leftarrow \check{S}_1(x_1) \wedge ... \wedge \check{S}_n(x_n)$ where $S = \{P \mid \exists P_1 \in S_1.\exists...\exists P_n \in S_n.P(f(x_1, ..., x_n)) \Leftarrow P_1(x_1) \wedge ... \wedge P_n(x_n) \in \mathcal{C}_{free}\}$.

Lemma 8. *For any $S \subseteq \mathbb{P}$ and any term t, $\check{S}(t)$ is derivable in $\mathcal{C}^\dagger$ modulo $ACUD$ iff $S = \{P \in \mathbb{P} \mid P(t)$ is derivable in $\mathcal{C}$ modulo $ACUD\}$.*

Proof. By induction on the size of t. Let $t =_{ACUD} s_1 + ... + s_m - t_1 - ... - t_n (m, n \geq 0)$ where for $1 \leq i \leq m$ $s_i = f_i(s^1_i, ..., s^{k_i}_i)$ for some free f_i, and for $1 \leq i \leq n$ $t_i = g_i(t^1_i, ..., t^{l_i}_i)$ for some free g_i. Let $S = \{P \in \mathbb{P} \mid P(t)$ is derivable in $\mathcal{C}\}$. First we show that *(a)* $\check{S}(t)$ is derivable in $\mathcal{C}^\dagger$ modulo $ACUD$; then we show that *(b)* if $\check{S}'(t)$ is derivable in $\mathcal{C}^\dagger$ modulo $ACUD$ for $S' \subseteq \mathbb{P}$ then $S' = S$.

Proof of (a). For $1 \leq i \leq m, 1 \leq j \leq k_i$ let $S^j_i = \{Q \mid Q(s^j_i)$ is derivable in $\mathcal{C}$ modulo $ACUD\}$. By induction hypothesis $\check{S}^j_i(s^j_i)$ is derivable in $\mathcal{C}^\dagger$ modulo $ACUD$. For $1 \leq i \leq n, 1 \leq j \leq l_i$ let $T^j_i = \{Q \mid Q(t^j_i)$ is derivable in $\mathcal{C}$ modulo $ACUD\}$. Then by induction hypothesis $\check{T}^j_i(t^j_i)$ is derivable in $\mathcal{C}^\dagger$ modulo $ACUD$. For $1 \leq i \leq m$ let $S_i = \{Q \mid \exists Q^1 \in S^1_i.\exists...\exists Q^{k_i} \in S^{k_i}_i.Q(f_i(x_1, ..., x_{k_i})) \Leftarrow Q^1(x_i) \wedge ... \wedge Q^{k_i}(x_{k_i}) \in \mathcal{C}\}$. Then the clause $\widehat{S}_i(f_i(x_1, ..., x_{k_i})) \Leftarrow S^1_i(x_1) \wedge ... \wedge S^{k_i}_i(x_{k_i}) \in \mathcal{C}^\dagger$. So $\widehat{S}_i(s_i)$ is derivable in $\mathcal{C}^\dagger$ for $1 \leq i \leq n$. Similarly for $1 \leq i \leq m$ let $T_i = \{Q \mid \exists Q^1 \in T^1_i.\exists...\exists Q^{l_i} \in T^{l_i}_i.Q(g_i(x_1, ..., x_{l_i})) \Leftarrow Q^1(x_i) \wedge ... \wedge Q^{l_i}(x_{l_i}) \in \mathcal{C}\}$. Then the clause $\widehat{T}_i(g_i(x_1, ..., x_{l_i})) \Leftarrow T^1_i(x_1) \wedge ... \wedge T^{l_i}_i(x_{l_i}) \in \mathcal{C}^\dagger$. So $\widehat{T}_i(t_i)$ is derivable in $\mathcal{C}^\dagger$ for $1 \leq i \leq n$.

Arguing as in the ACU case, but using Lemma 7 instead of Lemma 3 we show that $P(a_{S_1} + ... + a_{S_m} - a_{T_1} - ... - a_{T_n})$ is derivable in $\mathcal{C}^*_{eq}$ modulo $ACUD$ for each $P \in S$. Also we show that if $P \in \mathbb{P} \setminus S$ then $a_{S_1} + ... + a_{S_m} - a_{T_1} - ... - a_{T_n} \notin \mathcal{L}_P(\mathcal{C}^*_{eq}/ACUD)$.

Hence $a_{S_1} + ... + a_{S_m} - a_{T_1} - ... - a_{T_n} \in \mathcal{L}^S$. The derivation of $F_S(a_{S_1} + ... + a_{S_m} - a_{T_1} - ... - a_{T_n})$ in $\mathcal{C}$ modulo $ACUD$ has a functional support of the form $R_1(a_{S_1}), ..., R_m(a_{S_m}), R'_1(a_{T_1}), ..., R'_n(a_{T_n})$. As in the ACU case we use Lemma 7 to get a derivation of $F_S(s_1 + ... + s_m - t_1 - ... - t_n)$ in $\mathcal{C}^\dagger$ modulo $ACUD$. Finally we use the clause $\check{S}(x) \Leftarrow F_S(x)$ to get a derivation of $\check{S}(s_1 + ... + s_m - t_1 - ... - t_n)$, i.e. of $\check{S}(t)$. This proves *(a)*.

Proof of (b). Now suppose $S' \subseteq \mathbb{P}$ such that $\check{S}'(t)$ is derivable in $\mathcal{C}^\dagger$ modulo $ACUD$. We show that $S' = S$. The derivation of $\check{S}'(t)$ uses at the last step a derivation of $F_{S'}(t)$.

The latter derivation has a functional support of the form $\widehat{S'_1}(s_1), ..., \widehat{S'_m}(s_m), \widehat{T'_1}(t_1), ...,$ $\widehat{T'_n}(t_n)$. Arguing as in the ACU case, we use Lemma 7 to show that $F_{S'}(a_{S'_1} + ... + a_{S'_m} - a_{T'_1} - ... - a_{T'_n})$ is derivable in $\mathcal{C}_{S'}$ modulo $ACUD$. For $1 \leq i \leq m$ the derivation of $\widehat{S'_i}(s_i)$ uses at the last step, a clause $\widehat{S'_i}(f_i(x_1, ..., x_{k_i})) \Leftarrow S'^1_i(x_1) \wedge ... \wedge S'^{k_i}_i(x_{k_i}) \in \mathcal{C}^\dagger$ and derivations of $S'^j_i(s^j_i)(1 \leq j \leq k_i)$. By induction hypothesis $S'^j_i = S^j_i$. By definition of $\mathcal{C}^\dagger$, $S'_i = S_i$. Similarly for $1 \leq i \leq n$, $T'_i = T_i$. Hence $a_{S_1} + ... + a_{S_m} - a_{T_1} - ... - a_{T_n} \in \mathcal{L}_{S'}$. We have already seen that $a_{S_1} + ... + a_{S_m} - a_{T_1} - ... - a_{T_n} \in \mathcal{L}^S$. Since the $\mathcal{L}^S$'s are mutually disjoint, we have $S' = S$. $\qquad \square$

Then as in the ACU case, and using the fact that two-way $ACUD$ automata have the same expressiveness [18] as one-way $ACUD$ automata, we conclude:

Theorem 5. *One-way $ACUD$ automata are closed under complementation. Also two-way $ACUD$ automata are closed under complementation.*

7   Counter-Example for $ACUM$ Automata

The $ACUM$ (Abelian groups theory) case is similar to the $ACUX$ case. Define languages $\mathcal{L}_1 = \{f^n(a) - f^m(a) \mid n, m \geq 0\}$, $\mathcal{L}_2 = \{0\}$. Then $\mathcal{L}_1 \setminus \mathcal{L}_2 = \{f^n(a) - f^m(a) \mid n, m \geq 0$ and $n \neq m\}$ is not accepted by any one-way $ACUM$ automaton:

Lemma 9. *The language $L = \{f^n(a) - f^m(a) \mid n, m \geq 0$ and $n \neq m\}$ is not accepted by any one-way $ACUM$ automaton.*

Proof. The proof is similar to that of Lemma 5, the difference being that we need the $ACUD$ case (Lemma 7) instead of the ACU case (Lemma 3). Assume on the contrary that there is a one-way automaton $\mathcal{C}$ with final state P which modulo $ACUM$ accepts $\mathcal{L}$. Let $\mathbb{P}$ be the set of predicates in $\mathbb{C}$. For each $n \geq 0$ define $S_n = \{Q \in \mathbb{P} \mid Q(f^n(a))$ is derivable in $\mathcal{C}$ modulo $ACUM\}$. Then we have some $n \neq m$ such that $S_n = S_m$. Then $f^n(a) - f^m(a) \in \mathcal{L}$. We have some $t =_{ACUM} f^n(a) - f^m(a)$ such that $P(t)$ is derivable in $\mathcal{C}$ modulo $ACUD$. $t =_{ACUD} t_1 - t_2 + u_1 - v_1 + ... + u_k - v_k(k \geq 0)$ such that t_1 and t_2 are functional, $t_1 =_{ACUM} f^n(a)$, $t_2 =_{ACUM} f^m(a)$, u_i, v_i are functional and $u_i =_{ACUM} v_i$ for $1 \leq i \leq k$. The derivation of $P(t)$ has functional support of the form $I(t_1), J(t_2), I_1(u_1), J_1(v_1), ..., I_k(u_k), J_k(v_k)$. As before, $I(f^n(a))$ and $J(f^n(a))$ are derivable in $\mathcal{C}$ modulo $ACUM$. Then by Lemma 7, $P(f^n(a) - f^n(a) + u_1 - v_1 + ... + u_k - v_k)$ (or $P(0)$) is derivable in $\mathcal{C}$ modulo $ACUM$ leading to contradiction. $\qquad \square$

Since one-way $ACUM$ automata are closed [18] under intersection and are as expressive [18] as two-way $ACUM$ automata, we have as for the $ACUX$ case:

Theorem 6. *One-way $ACUM$ automata are not closed under complementation. Neither are two-way $ACUM$ automata closed under complementation.*

8   Counter-Example for $ACUI$ Automata

We now show that one-way $ACUI$ automata are not closed under complementation either. Define languages $\mathcal{L}_1 = \{f^n(a) + f^m(a) \mid n, m \geq 0\}$ and $\mathcal{L}_2 = \{f^n(a) \mid n \geq 0\}$. We have $\mathcal{L}_1 \setminus \mathcal{L}_2 = \{f^n(a) + f^m(a) \mid n, m \geq 0$ and $n \neq m\}$.

Lemma 10. *The language* $\mathcal{L} = \{f^n(a) + f^m(a) \mid n, m \geq 0 \text{ and } n \neq m\}$ *is not accepted by any one-way ACUI automaton.*

Proof. Assume on the contrary that there is a one-way automaton $\mathcal{C}$ with final state P which accepts $\mathcal{L}$. Let $\mathbb{P}$ be the set of predicates in $\mathcal{C}$. For each $n \geq 0$ define $S_n = \{Q \in \mathbb{P} \mid Q(f^n(a)) \text{ is derivable in } \mathcal{C} \text{ modulo } ACUI\}$. We must have some $n \neq m$ such that $S_n = S_m$. Then $f^n(a) + f^m(a) \in \mathcal{L}$. From Lemma 1, we must have some $t =_{ACUI} f^n(a) + f^m(a)$ such that $P(t)$ is derivable in $\mathcal{C}$ modulo ACU. t must be of the form $s_1 + ... + s_p + t_1 + ... + t_q (p, q \geq 1)$ such that for $1 \leq i \leq p, 1 \leq j \leq q$, s_i and t_j are functional, $s_i =_{ACUI} f^n(a)$ and $t_j =_{ACUI} f^m(a)$. Then arguing as in the $ACUX_n$ case, we get a derivation of $P(\sum_{i=1}^{p+q} f^n(a))$ (or $P(f^n(a))$) modulo $ACUI$ leading to contradiction. □

Since one-way $ACUI$ automata are closed [18] under intersection we have:

Theorem 7. *One-way ACUI automata are not closed under complementation.*

However this does not answer whether two-way $ACUI$ automata are closed under complementation since the question of equivalence between two-way and one-way $ACUI$ automata is currently open [18]. Closure under intersection of two-way $ACUI$ automata is also left open in [18], but it is mentioned that the two-way $ACUI$ automata are powerful enough to encode alternation. This suggests that this case is difficult, because adding alternation to one-way automata is already known to produce undecidability in the case of theories $ACU, ACUD, ACUM$, while in the case of theories $ACUX, ACUX, ACUI$ the question is open.

9   Conclusion

We have studied the problem of closure under complementation of one-way and two-way tree automata modulo the equational theories ACU (associativity, commutativity, unit), $ACUD$ (ACU with a distributive '$-$' symbol), $ACUM$ (Abelian groups), $ACUX$ (exclusive-or), $ACUX_n$ (generalized exclusive-or), and $ACUI$ (ACU with idempotence.)

We have shown that for the theories ACU and $ACUD$, the one-way and two-way automata are closed under complementation. For the theories $ACUM, ACUX$ and $ACUX_n$, we have shown that neither one-way nor two-way automata are closed under complementation. In the case of $ACUI$, while the one-way automata are not closed under complementation, the question in open for two-way automata. An interesting pattern visible here is the coincidence between closure under complementation of the one-way automata and the linearity of the equational theory.

These results are in sharp contrast with the results on closure under intersection. The one-way automata for all the above theories are known to be closed under intersection. Also, the two-way automata for all theories except $ACUI$ are known to be closed under intersection. (The question is open for two-way $ACUI$ automata.)

The results about the two-way automata are obtained by reducing them to one-way automata. The equivalence between one-way and two-way $ACUI$ automata is however open. A positive answer would also mean that two-way $ACUI$ automata are closed under intersection but not under complementation.

Acknowledgements

I thank Jean Goubault-Larrecq for discussions and suggestions, as well as the anonymous referees for helpful comments.

References

1. T. Colcombet. Rewriting in the partial algebra of typed terms modulo AC. In *Electronic Notes in Theoretical Computer Science*, volume 68. Elsevier Science Publishers, 2002.
2. H. Comon, M. Dauchet, R. Gilleron, F. Jacquemard, D. Lugiez, S. Tison, and M. Tommasi. Tree automata techniques and applications. www.grappa.univ-lille3.fr/tata, 1997.
3. W. Diffie and M. Hellman. New directions in cryptography. *IEEE Transactions on Information Theory*, IT-22(6):644–654, 1976.
4. F. Gécseg and M. Steinby. Tree languages. In G. Rozenberg and A. Salomaa, editors, *Handbook of Formal Languages*, volume 3, pages 1–68. Springer Verlag, 1997.
5. S. Ginsburg and E. H. Spanier. Semigroups, Presburger formulas and languages. *Pacific Journal of Mathematics*, 16(2):285–296, 1966.
6. J. Goubault-Larrecq. A method for automatic cryptographic protocol verification. In *FMPPTA'2000, 15th IPDPS Workshops*, pages 977–984. Springer-Verlag LNCS 1800, 2000.
7. J. Goubault-Larrecq and K. N. Verma. Alternating two-way AC-tree automata. In preparation.
8. M. Hanus. The integration of functions into logic programming: From theory to practice. *Journal of Logic Programming*, 19 & 20:583–628, 1994.
9. D. Lugiez. A good class of tree automata. Application to inductive theorem proving. In *ICALP'98*, pages 409–420. Springer-Verlag LNCS 1443, 1998.
10. D. Lugiez. Counting and equality constraints for multitree automata. In *FOSSACS'03*, pages 328–342. Springer-Verlag LNCS 2620, 2003.
11. D. Monniaux. Abstracting cryptographic protocols with tree automata. In *SAS'99*, pages 149–163. Springer-Verlag LNCS 1694, 1999.
12. H. Ohsaki. Beyond regularity: Equational tree automata for associative and commutative theories. In *CSL'01*, pages 539–553. Springer-Verlag LNCS 2142, 2001.
13. H. Ohsaki and T. Takai. Decidability and closure properties of equational tree languages. In *RTA'02*, pages 114–128. Springer-Verlag LNCS 2378, 2002.
14. L. C. Paulson. Mechanized proofs for a recursive authentication protocol. In *10th IEEE Computer Security Foundations Workshop*, pages 84–95, 1997.
15. P. Ryan and S. Schneider. An attack on a recursive authentication protocol: A cautionary tale. *Information Processing Letters*, 65(1):7–10, 1998.
16. M. Steiner, G. Tsudik, and M. Waidner. Key agreement in dynamic peer groups. *IEEE Transactions on Parallel and Distributed Systems*, 11(8):769–780, 2000.
17. M. Y. Vardi. Reasoning about the past with two-way automata. In *ICALP'98*, pages 628–641. Springer Verlag LNCS 1443, 1998.
18. K. N. Verma. Two-way equational tree automata for AC-like theories: Decidability and closure properties. In *RTA'03*, pages 180–196. Springer Verlag LNCS 2706, 2003.

Completeness of E-Unification
with Eager Variable Elimination

Barbara Morawska

Theoretical Computer Science, TU Dresden, D-01062 Dresden, Germany,
`morawska@tcs.inf.tu-dresden.de`

Abstract. The paper contains a proof of completeness of a goal-directed
inference system for general E-unification with eager Variable Elimination. The proof is based on a careful analysis of a concept of ground,
equational proof. The theory of equational proofs is developed in the first
part. Solving variables in a goal is then shown to be reflected in defined
transformations of an equational proof. The termination of these transformations proves termination of inferences with eager Variable Elimination.

1 Introduction

E-unification is concerned with finding a set of solutions for a given equation
in a given equational theory E. The problem of E-unification arises in many
areas of computer science like formal verification, theorem proving and logic
programming. In general the E-unification problem, i.e. the problem of finding
a set of solutions for a given equation in a non-empty equational theory E
is undecidable, unlike in the case of the syntactic unification problem, i.e. in
the case of searching for a solution for an equation in the context of the empty
equational theory. Nevertheless, the E-unification problem is semi-decidable and
there are complete algorithms for solving it.

Goal-directed algorithms for E-unification are based on the idea of transforming goal equations into a solved form which will allow easily to define a
solution. Such an inference system was presented first in [2], and is displayed
here in a different notation in Figure 1. Consider the rule Variable Elimination
in this set of inference rules. If applied to an equation of the form $x \approx v$ in the
goal, it will eliminate x from all other equations in the goal and thus solve the
equation $x \approx v$.[1] The Variable Elimination is forced to be applied eagerly here,
because there is no other rule to deal with equations of the form $x \approx v$, where x
is not a variable in v.

There was no proof up to now that this system of inferences (Figure 1,
page 199) is complete for E-unification. It is complete, when we allow other
rules to apply to an equation $x \approx v$, but then Variable Elimination cannot be
applied eagerly. The problem was first discovered and called *the Eager Variable
Elimination Problem* by Gallier and Snyder in [2].

---

[1] Formal definition of a solved equation is in the section 6.

M.Y. Vardi and A. Voronkov (Eds.): LPAR 2003, LNAI 2850, pp. 198–212, 2003.

Decomposition

$$\frac{\{f(s_1, \cdots, s_n) \approx f(t_1, \cdots, t_n)\} \cup G}{\{s_1 \approx t_1, \cdots, s_n \approx t_n\} \cup G}$$

where $f(s_1, \cdots, s_n) \approx f(t_1, \cdots, t_n)$ is selected in the goal.

Mutate

$$\frac{\{u \approx f(v_1, \cdots, v_n)\} \cup G}{\{u \approx s, t_1 \approx v_1, \cdots, t_n \approx v_n\} \cup G}$$

where $u \approx f(v_1, \cdots, v_n)$ is selected in the goal, and $s \approx f(t_1, \cdots, t_n) \in E$.[a]

Variable Mutate

$$\frac{\{u \approx f(v_1, \cdots, v_n)\} \cup G}{\{u \approx s, x \approx f(v_1, \cdots, v_n)\} \cup G}$$

where $s \approx x \in E$, x is a variable, and $u \approx f(v_1, \cdots, v_n)$ is selected in the goal.

Variable Decomposition (for cycle)

$$\frac{\{x \approx f(t_1, \cdots, t_n)\} \cup G}{\{x \approx f(x_1, \cdots, x_n)\} \cup (\{x_1 \approx t_1, \cdots, x_n \approx t_n\} \cup G)[x \mapsto f(x_1, \cdots, x_n)]}$$

where x is a variable, $x \approx f(t_1, \cdots, t_n)$ is selected in the goal,
$x \in Var(f(t_1, \cdots, t_n))$.

Variable Elimination

$$\frac{\{x \approx v\} \cup G}{\{x \approx v\} \cup G[x \mapsto v]}$$

where $x \notin Var(v)$.

Orient

$$\frac{\{t \approx x\} \cup G}{\{x \approx t\} \cup G}$$

where x is a variable.
and t is not a variable.

Trivial

$$\frac{\{x \approx x\} \cup G}{G}$$

where $x \approx x$ is selected in the goal.

---

[a] We assume that E is closed under symmetry.

Fig. 1. E-Unification with eager Variable Elimination

Eager Variable Elimination is justified in the context of syntactic unification (the empty equational theory) because it decreases the number of unsolved variables in the goal, while preserving a set of solutions. The number of unsolved variables is not increased by any other rule and hence we may be sure that the inferences will terminate.

In the context of E-unification we must use another rule called here Mutate.[2] Notice that we have here conflicting results of applications of Mutate and Variable Elimination to the goal: Variable Elimination decreases the number of unsolved variables in the goal, but Mutate increases this number, and while Mutate decreases the length of a ground proof of an instance of a goal, Variable Elimination may increase this length.

In [3] Gallier and Snyder proved completeness of their system without eager Variable Elimination. In [5] the authors stated that Mutate (*replacement*) and eager Variable Elimination (*merging*) do not preserve the form of the proof.

In this paper we prove that Variable Elimination may be applied eagerly without destroying the completeness of the E-unification procedure. The fact that Variable Elimination can be applied eagerly decreases non-determinism in the inherently non-deterministic general E-unification algorithms. It may reduce redundancy of inferences and limit the search space for a solution to a given equation. This was pointed out e.g. in [7], [6], [4].

The main idea in the proof of completeness of our inference rules (Figure 1), is to consider a ground equational proof for a goal. Most of this paper is concerned with a description of a theory of equational ground proofs (definitions in Section 3) and a construction of new equational proof which reflects effects of eager Variable Elimination (Section 4). We present then the concept of *paths* in an equational proof (Section 5) and this enables us to define a measure of a goal and prove the result by induction on this measure (Section 6).

2   Preliminaries

We use standard definitions as in [1].

We will consider equations of the form $s \approx t$, where s and t are terms. Please note that throughout this paper these equations are considered to be oriented, so that $s \approx t$ is a different equation than $t \approx s$. Let E be a set of equations, and $u \approx v$ be an equation, then we write $E \models u \approx v$ (or $u =_E v$) if $u \approx v$ is true in any model containing E. We call E an equational theory, and assume that E is closed under symmetry. A goal (E-unification problem) is usually denoted by G and it is a set of equations. $E \models G$ means that $E \models e$ for all e in G.

We will be considering ground terms as ground objects that may or may not have the same syntactic form. In other words we will be concerned with the occurrences of the terms more than their values. A term may be identified by its address in a proof sequence and a position of it as a subterm in a term in the proof. Hence the equality sign between ground terms is treated in a special way. If u, v are ground terms, by $u = v$, u is understood to be an object identical with v, whereas when syntactic equality is sufficient, it will be denoted by $u == v$. Syntactic inequality will be denoted by $u \neq= v$. The difference between identity and syntactic identity is that the first involves *objects* and the second involves *names*.

---

[2] In [3] this rule is called *Root Rewriting*. The name *Mutate* came from [5], where it was used for E-unification in Syntactic Theories.

We can say that a variable x points to its occurrences in a term u, where each of these occurrences under some ground substitution γ, is identical with some subterm of $u\gamma$ at a position α ($x\gamma = u\gamma|_\alpha$). Different occurrences of the same variables are different objects, though they have the same syntactic form (each one is of the form $x\gamma$). In order to distinguish between different occurrences of the same variable, we will use superscript numbers, usually numbering the occurrences from left to right in order of their appearances in an equational proof. Hence $x\gamma^1$ and $x\gamma^2$ are different occurrences of x in a proof.

Sometimes we will want to state that some subterm has a form (or value) of $x\gamma$, but is not identical to $x\gamma$ (hence is not pointed to by a variable x). This will be indicated by quote marks. Hence $w["x\gamma"]_\alpha$ is different from $w[x\gamma]_\alpha$ since in the second term $x\gamma$ actually occurs at position α, while in the first one there is only a subterm that has the value of $x\gamma$.

If γ is a ground substitution, γ_x means the restriction of this substitution to a variable x. Hence if $\gamma = [x \mapsto a, y \mapsto b, z \mapsto c]$, $\gamma_x = [x \mapsto a]$.

3   Equational Proofs

Given an equational theory E, we define an equational proof as a pair (Π, γ) such that Π is a series of ground terms and γ is a ground substitution.

Definition 1. *(Equational Proof).*
Let E be a set of equations. An equational proof of an equation $u \approx v$ is a pair (Π, γ) where $\Pi = (w_1, w_2, \ldots, w_n)$ is series of ground terms from T_{Σ_E}, called proof sequence, such that: 1. $u\gamma = w_1$, $v\gamma = w_n$,
2. for each pair (w_i, w_{i+1}) for $1 \leq i \leq (n-1)$, there is an equation $s \approx t \in E$ and a matcher ρ, such that there is a subterm $w_i|_\alpha$ of w_i and a subterm $w_{i+1}|_\alpha$ of w_{i+1}, and $w_i|_\alpha = s\rho$, $w_{i+1}|_\alpha = t\rho$.

We can write the equational proof as:

$$u\gamma = w_1 \approx_{[\alpha_1, s_1 \approx t_1, \rho_1]} w_2 \approx_{[\alpha_2, s_2 \approx t_2, \rho_2]} \cdots \approx_{[\alpha_{n-1}, s_{n-1} \approx t_{n-1}, \rho_{n-1}]} w_n = v\gamma$$

where $[\alpha_i, s_i \approx t_i, \rho_i]$ indicates at what position α_i is the matching subterm, which equation from E was used ($s_i \approx t_i$), and how the variables in this equation were substituted (ρ). Each w_i in the above sequence is called a term in the proof, as distinct from any proper subterms of w_i, which are not counted as terms in the proof. We will sometimes use the notation borrowed from that for arrays, and $\Pi[i]$ will mean the i'th term in Π.

Since every matcher at each step uses a renamed version of an equation from E, the domain of the matcher is disjoint from the domain of γ and the domains of matchers at all other steps in the proof, we extend γ to γ' such that: $\gamma' = \gamma \cup \rho_1 \cup \ldots \cup \rho_n$. From now on we will assume that γ is an extended version of itself.

In order to be able to identify new variables introduced by a possible application of Variable Decomposition (Figure 1), we have to extend γ even more.[3] A general extension of γ will add variables for each subterm of a term v if $\gamma_x = [x \mapsto v]$. We call these new variables *subterm variables*.

Definition 2. *(General Extension of γ).*
Let γ be a ground substitution. A general extension of γ, $ex(\gamma)$, is defined recursively as follows:
1. *if $\gamma_x = [x \mapsto v]$ and $|v| = 1$ (v is a constant), then $ex(\gamma_x) = \gamma_x$,*
2. *if $\gamma_x = [x \mapsto f(v_1, \ldots, v_n)]$, and $n \geq 1$, then let $\gamma_{y_i} = [y_i \mapsto v_i]$, for $1 \leq i \leq n$, and $ex(\gamma_x) = \gamma_x \cup ex(\gamma_{y_1}) \cup \cdots \cup ex(\gamma_{y_n})$,*
3. *$ex(\gamma) = \bigcup_{x \in Dom(\gamma)} ex(\gamma_x)$*

From now on we will consider γ in (Π, γ) as a general extension of itself. We have 3 kinds of variables in $Dom(\gamma)$: the *goal* variables, i.e. the variables in $Var(u \approx v)$; the *system* variables, i.e. if there is a step $\Pi[i] \approx_{[\alpha_i, s_i \approx t_i, \gamma]} \Pi[i+1]$ in (Π, γ), then the variables in $Var(s_i \approx t_i)$ are called *system variables*; the *subterm* variables in $\Pi[i]$, for each $\Pi[i]$ in the proof, i.e. variables that are introduced by general extension of γ. We will see that each variable occurrence starts or ends some subproof in an equational proof. In order to define this subproof, we will use a notion of *orientation* of a variable occurrence defined as follows:

Definition 3. *(Orientation of Variable Occurrences).*
Let (Π, γ) be an equational proof and $x \in Dom(\gamma)$.
1. *If $x\gamma$ is a system variable occurrence in $\Pi[i] \approx_{[\alpha_i, s_i \approx t_i, \gamma]} \Pi[i+1]$ and $x\gamma = \Pi[i]|_\alpha$ for some position α, then $x\gamma$ has left orientation. If $x\gamma = \Pi[i+1]|_\alpha$, then $x\gamma$ has right orientation.*
2. *if $x\gamma$ is a goal variable occurrence in $\Pi[1]$ ($x\gamma = \Pi[1]|_\alpha$), then $x\gamma$ has right orientation, and if $x\gamma = \Pi[n]|_\alpha$, where $\Pi[n]$ is the last term in the proof, then $x\gamma$ has left orientation.*
3. *if $x\gamma$ is a subterm variable, hence $x\gamma = y\gamma|_\alpha$, then $x\gamma$ has the same orientation as $y\gamma$.*

3.1   Part of Equational Proof and Subproof

Now we define subproofs in an equational proof as proofs embedded at some position in *parts* of this proof.

Definition 4. *(Part of Proof for Depth α).*
Let (Π, γ) be an equational proof:

$$w_1 \approx_{[\alpha_1, s_1 \approx t_1, \gamma]} w_2 \approx_{[\alpha_2, s_2 \approx t_2, \gamma]} \cdots \approx_{[\alpha_{n-1}, s_{n-1} \approx t_{n-1}, \gamma]} w_n.$$

Let α be one of $\alpha_1, \ldots, \alpha_{n-1}$, which are the positions at which the steps in the proof are performed. A part of the proof (Π, γ) for depth α is a sequence:

---

[3] The following definition is similar to the definition of general extension of a substitution in [3]. It was introduced there with a similar purpose: to accommodate the Variable Decomposition rule.

$\Pi[i] \approx_{[\alpha_i, s_i \approx t_i, \gamma]} \cdots \approx_{[\alpha_{i+j-1}, s_{i+j-1} \approx t_{i+j-1}, \gamma]} \Pi[i+j]$, *such that for* $i \leq k \leq j-1$, $\alpha_k \geq \alpha$ *or* $\alpha_k \| \alpha$.

Hence in a part of a proof all steps are performed at a position α, lower or at parallel positions. If $j = 0$, the part of the proof is composed of one term only. Now we define a subproof in an equational proof as a sequence of subterms of terms in a part of the original proof.

Definition 5. *(Subproof).*
Let (Π, γ) *be an equational proof. Let* $\Pi[i] \approx_{[\alpha_i, s'_1 \approx t'_1, \gamma]} \cdots \approx_{[\alpha_{i+k-1}, s'_{i+k-1} \approx t'_{i+k-1}, \gamma]}$
$\Pi[i+k]$ *be a part of the proof* (Π, γ) *for depth* α, *and let* α_n *be a such that* $\alpha \leq \alpha_n$.
Then a pair (Σ, γ), *where* Σ *is a sequence of terms (called* subproof sequence*):*
$\Pi[i]|_{\alpha_n}, \Pi[i+1]|_{\alpha_n}, \ldots, \Pi[i+k]|_{\alpha_n}$ *is called a subproof of* (Π, γ).

In the next sections, we want to be able to use a copy of a subproof in creating new proofs. In this copy only some variables, called *internal variables*, will be renamed.

Definition 6. *(Internal/External Variables in a Subproof).*
Let (Π, γ) *be an equational proof and* $(\Sigma_{w \approx w'}, \gamma)$ *a subproof in* (Π, γ). *If there is a step in* $(\Sigma_{w \approx w'}, \gamma)$: $w_i \approx_{[\alpha, s \approx t, \gamma]} w_{i+1}$, $y \in Var(s \approx t)$, y *is called an internal variable in* $(\Sigma_{w \approx w'}, \gamma)$. *If* y *has occurrences in* $(\Sigma_{w \approx w'}, \gamma)$, *but is not internal variable in this subproof, it is called an external variable in* $(\Sigma_{w \approx w'}, \gamma)$.

Definition 7. *(Renaming of a Subproof).*
Let (Π, γ) *be an equational proof and* $(\Sigma_{w \approx w'}, \gamma)$ *a subproof in* (Π, γ). $(\Sigma'_{w \approx w'}, \gamma')$
is a renaming of $(\Sigma_{w \approx w'}, \gamma)$ *if* $(\Sigma'_{w \approx w'}, \gamma')$ *is exactly like* $(\Sigma_{w \approx w'}, \gamma)$, *with all internal variables renamed.*

Example 1. Let $E := \{ffx \approx fgx\}$ and $(\Pi, \gamma) = fgfa \approx_{[\epsilon, ffx_1 \approx fgx_1, [x_1 \mapsto fa]]}$
$fffa \approx_{[<1>, ffx_2 \approx fgx_2, [x_2 \mapsto a]]} ffga \approx_{[\epsilon, ffx_3 \approx fgx_3, [x_3 \mapsto ga]]} fgga$.
   Obviously, (Π, γ) is its own subproof. We have also one more subproof:
$ffa \approx_{[\epsilon, ffx_2 \approx fgx_2, [x_2 \mapsto a]]} fga$, where $ffa = \Pi[2]|_{<1>}$. A renaming of this subproof would have the following form: $ffa \approx_{[\epsilon, ffx_4 \approx fgx_4, [x_4 \mapsto a]]} fga$, where x_4 is a new variable.

Further analysis of subproofs and their normal forms may be found in the long version of the paper [8].

3.2   Embedding a Proof into a Term and Contracting

We will use two operations on equational proofs: embedding and contracting. Embedding a proof into a term is a way to construct a proof from a given subproof.

Definition 8. *(Embedding of a Proof).*
If w *is a ground term,* (Π, γ) *is a proof of the form:*

$$w_1 \approx_{[\alpha_1, s_1 \approx t_1, \gamma]} w_2 \approx_{[\alpha_2, s_2 \approx t_2, \gamma]} \cdots \approx_{[\alpha_{n-1}, s_{n-1} \approx t_{n-1}, \gamma]} w_n$$

*and there is a position β in w such that $w|_\beta == w_1$, then there is a proof (Π', γ)
of the form:* $w[w_1]_\beta \approx_{[\beta\alpha_1, s_1 \approx t_1, \gamma]} w[w_2]_\beta \approx_{[\beta\alpha_2, s_2 \approx t_2, \gamma]} \cdots \approx_{[\beta\alpha_{n-1}, s_{n-1} \approx t_{n-1}, \gamma]}$
$w[w_n]_\beta$ *We say that (Π', γ) is the* **embedding of the proof** (Π, γ) **in the
term** w.

We can attach a proof to a given equational proof (Π, γ) by embedding it
into the last term of (Π, γ), if the conditions of the definition are met. If (Π, γ)
is a proof such that it is composed from (Σ_1, γ_1) and (Σ_2, γ_2) by embedding
(Σ_2, γ_2) into the last term of (Σ_1, γ_1), we say that (Π, γ) is a *composition* of
(Σ_1, γ_1) and (Σ_2, γ_2).
A simple procedure (called **contraction**) of cutting out loops out of subproof
sequences in a proof sequence, allows us to obtain a non-redundant proof from
any redundant one:[4]

Definition 9. *(Non-redundant Equational Proof).*
*An equational proof Π is non-redundant if there are no two terms $\Pi[i]$ and
$\Pi[j]$ such that $i \neq j$ and $\Pi[i] == \Pi[j]$, and all proper subproofs of Π are
non-redundant.*

3.3   Associated Subproofs, Associated Terms and a Hierarchy of Variable Occurrences

In this section, for each occurrence of a variable x in $Dom(\gamma)$, we define a
ground term associated with this occurrence. An associated term in the proof is
a subterm which can be linked to an occurrence of $x\gamma$ by a subproof in a given
equational proof. If $x \approx v$ is an equation in our goal G, and $E \models G\gamma$, then $v\gamma$
is a term associated with $x\gamma$. First, we define ground subproofs associated with
each occurrence of x in an equational proof.

Definition 10. *(Subproof Associated with an Occurrence of a Variable).*
*Let (Π, γ) be an equational proof, $x \in Dom(\gamma)$ and $x\gamma$ is an occurrence of x in
(Π, γ).*

1. *If $x\gamma$ has a left orientation and $x\gamma = \Pi[i]|_\alpha$, then there is the longest subproof*

$$\Pi[i-k]|_\alpha \approx \cdots \approx \Pi[i]|_\alpha$$

   We reverse the order of the terms in this subproof:

$$\Pi[i]|_\alpha \approx \cdots \approx \Pi[i-k]|_\alpha$$

   and we call this subproof **a subproof associated with this** $x\gamma$. *We say
   that the subproof associated with $x\gamma$ is left-oriented.*

---

[4] In the case of proofs in normal form, it is enough to require that there are no
identical terms in the proof, to show that it is non-redundant. The definition of
normal form for a proof is in the long version of the paper [8].

2. If $x\gamma$ has right orientation and $x\gamma = \Pi[i]|_\alpha$, then there is the longest subproof

$$\Pi[i+1]|_\alpha \approx \cdots \approx \Pi[i+l]|_\alpha$$

We call this subproof **a subproof associated with this** $x\gamma$ and we say that it is right-oriented.

Notice that if (Π, γ) is an equational proof of $u\gamma \approx v\gamma$, then the external variables in this proof are only variables in $Var(u)$ and $Var(v)$. By the definition of subproofs associated with variable occurrences, if $(\Sigma_{x\gamma\approx v}, \gamma)$ is such a subproof, external variables in this subproof have their occurrences only in $x\gamma$ (x and its subterm variables are external variables in this subproof) and v. The external variable occurrences in v have opposite orientation to that of $x\gamma$. We will sometimes indicate an orientation of an occurrence of a variable by an arrow, like in $\overrightarrow{x}\gamma$, which denotes an occurrence of x with right orientation. Similarly, if (Σ, γ) is a subproof in (Π, γ), $(\overrightarrow{\Sigma}, \gamma)$ indicates that this subproof has right orientation.

Definition 11. *(Term Associated with an Occurrence of x).*
Let (Π, γ) be an equational proof, $x \in Dom(\gamma)$ and $x\gamma$ is an occurrence of x in (Π, γ). Let a subproof $(\Sigma_{x\gamma\approx v}, \gamma)$ be a subproof associated with $x\gamma$, then we define a term associated with $x\gamma$, $ass(x\gamma)$, in the following way:

1. if no occurrence of x appears in v, then $ass(x\gamma) = v$,
2. if an occurrence of x appears in v, then
   (a) if there is a step at the root in $(\Sigma_{x\gamma\approx v}, \gamma)$, we will choose the rightmost such step: $w_i \approx_{[\epsilon, s_i \approx t_i, \gamma]} w_{i+1}$ and define $ass(x\gamma) = w_i$,
   (b) if there is no step at the root in $(\Sigma_{x\gamma\approx v}, \gamma)$, we define $ass(x\gamma) = x\gamma$.

If $x \approx w$ is an equation in a goal, where $x \notin Var(w)$, we know that there is a ground proof of $x\gamma \approx w\gamma$, and $w\gamma = ass(x\gamma)$. In this situation, we will show how to construct an equational proof of the goal with the ground substitution changed to γ', such that $\gamma'_x = [x \mapsto w\gamma]$.

There is a hierarchy among occurrences of the variables of an equational proof. In order to display it, we construct a graph G_Π with occurrences of variables in a given equational proof as nodes and arrows as follows:

1. for each variable x in $Dom(\gamma)$ and for each occurrence $x\gamma$ of this variable, if for any $y \in Dom(\gamma)$, $(\Sigma_{x\gamma\approx w[y\gamma]}, \gamma)$ is a subproof of a proof associated with $x\gamma$ and w is not empty, draw an arrow from $x\gamma$ to $y\gamma$;

2. for each variable x in $Dom(\gamma)$ and for each occurrence $x\gamma$ of this variable, if for any $y \in Dom(\gamma)$, $(\Sigma_{x\gamma\approx y\gamma}, \gamma)$ is a subproof of a proof associated with $x\gamma$:

2.1 if $(\Sigma_{y\gamma\approx x\gamma}, \gamma)$ is a subproof of a proof associated with $y\gamma$, then non-deterministically decide the direction of an arrow between $x\gamma$ and $y\gamma$;

2.2 if $(\Sigma_{y\gamma\approx x\gamma}, \gamma)$ is not a subproof associated with $y\gamma$, then draw an arrow from $x\gamma$ to $y\gamma$.

The graph G_Π, for an equational proof helps us to recognize/decide the parent/child relation. If $x\gamma$ is a node in G_Π and there is an arrow $x\gamma \to y\gamma$, then $x\gamma$ is called a parent of $y\gamma$ and $y\gamma$ is a child of $x\gamma$.

This relation is in some cases determined by the structure of the proof (we cannot discover new variables in the transformation of the goal before solving/eliminating some other variables first), or it is decided by the selection rule and orientation of an equation of the form $x \approx y$. The *maximal* nodes in the graph are just those occurrences of variables that are discovered in the goal and may be selected for eager Variable Elimination. A set of maximal nodes in G_{Π}, M, is the set containing all nodes which have no parents in G_{Π}. We will see that if $x \approx v$ is an equation in a goal G, and $E \models G\gamma$, then there is a subproof $(\Sigma_{x\gamma\approx v\gamma}, \gamma)$ in an equational proof (Π, γ) of $G\gamma$ and $x\gamma$ is a maximal node in the graph G_{Π} for the proof.

4   Solving Variables in an Equational Proof

The following construction explains what happens with an equational proof of a goal, if an equation of the type $x \approx t$ is selected for eager Variable Elimination. Notice that in this construction we declare which variables in $Dom(\gamma)$ are solved or unsolved. In the justification of the completeness of the inference system with eager Variable Elimination we start with the equational proof of an instance of a goal with all variables unsolved. Variable Elimination reflects solving variables in a ground equational proof.

Let (Π, γ) be an equational proof with the proof sequence:

$$\Pi = (w_1 \approx_{[\alpha_1, s_1 \approx t_1, \gamma]} w_2 \approx_{[\alpha_2, s_2 \approx t_2, \gamma]} \cdots \approx_{[\alpha_{n-1}, s_{n-1} \approx t_{n-1}, \gamma]} w_n)$$

and γ be an extended ground substitution.

Let $U = \{x_1, \ldots, x_n\}$ be a set of variables called "unsolved" in (Π, γ), G_{Π} be the graph for (Π, γ) constructed only with respect to unsolved variables (hence we treat all other variables as non-existent in (Π, γ)).

Let $x \in U$ and $x\gamma$ be a maximal node in G_{Π} and let $ass(x\gamma) = v$.

There is a subproof $(\Sigma_{x\gamma\approx v}, \gamma)$ in (Π, γ), let $(\Sigma'_{x\gamma\approx v}, \gamma')$ be a renaming of this subproof.[5]

If x has no occurrences in v, create a new proof (Π^*, γ^*) that is exactly as (Π, γ) with the proof sequence modified in the following way:

1. **Extension**
   Whenever $x\gamma = w_i|_\alpha$ and hence $w_i = w_i[x\gamma]$, and
   (a) $x\gamma$ has right orientation, replace w_i (the i'th step in (Π, γ)), by the sequence of steps:

   $$w_i[v]_\alpha \approx (\Sigma'_{v\approx \text{``}x\gamma\text{''}}) \approx w_i[\text{``}x\gamma\text{''}]_\alpha$$

   where $(\Sigma'_{v\approx \text{``}x\gamma\text{''}})$ means a renaming of $(\Sigma_{\text{``}x\gamma\text{''}\approx v}, \gamma)$ reversed and embedded in w_i at position α leftwards. Note that the renamings of internal occurrences of variables and new occurrences of external variables in the renaming of $(\Sigma_{\text{``}x\gamma\text{''}\approx v}, \gamma)$ have reversed orientation in the new proof.

---

[5] If x has no occurrences in v, $(\Sigma_{x\gamma\approx v}, \gamma)$ is a subproof associated with $x\gamma$.

(b) $x\gamma$ has left orientation, replace w_i (the i'th step in (Π, γ)) by the sequence of steps:

$$w_i[``x\gamma"]_\alpha \approx (\Sigma'_{``x\gamma"\approx v}) \approx w_i[v]_\alpha$$

where $(\Sigma'_{``x\gamma"\approx v})$ means a renaming of $(\Sigma_{``x\gamma"\approx v}, \gamma)$ embedded in w_i at position α rightwards. The renamings of internal occurrences of variables and new occurrences of external variables in $(\Sigma'_{``x\gamma"\approx v})$ preserve their orientation in the new proof.

2. **Standard Contraction**

   For each occurrence of an unsolved variable y in (Π, γ), if $(\Sigma_{y\gamma\approx s}, \gamma)$ is a proper associated subproof of this occurrence in (Π, γ) and there is a subproof sequence: $\Sigma_{s\approx``y\gamma"} \Sigma_{``y\gamma"\approx s}$ in the proof sequence Π^* after extension, contract the subproof sequence to a one-element sequence, s;

   The substitution γ^* is defined as follows:

$\gamma_x^* = [x \mapsto v]$,

if $y\gamma|_\alpha = x\gamma$, and $y \notin U$, then $\gamma_y^* = [y \mapsto y\gamma[x\gamma^*]_\alpha]$,

if $z \notin Dom(\gamma)$, z is a renaming of a variable $z' \in Dom(\gamma)$, that appeared in some $(\Sigma'_{x\gamma\approx v}, \gamma')$, then $\gamma_z^* = [z \mapsto z'\gamma]$,

for any other variable, $\gamma^* = \gamma$;

   If x has occurrences in v, then $(\Pi^*, \gamma^*) = (\Pi, \gamma)$.

Mark Variables

*Mark variable x **solved** in (Π^*, γ^*). If x has no occurrences in v, mark also all subterm variables of x as **solved** New variables in $Dom(\gamma^*)$, which did not appear in $Dom(\gamma)$ are marked as unsolved.*

If a proof (Π^*, γ^*) is obtained from (Π, γ) in this way, then we say that (Π^*, γ^*) is generated from (Π, γ) by substitution $[x \mapsto v]$, written $(\Pi, \gamma) \overset{[x\mapsto v]}{\to} (\Pi^*, \gamma^*)$. As a corollary to this construction we notice that:

Corollary 1. *If $(\Pi, \gamma) \overset{[x\mapsto v]}{\to} (\Pi', \gamma')$ and $y \in Dom(\gamma')$, then for each occurrence $y\gamma'$ in (Π', γ'), either*

1. *$y \in Dom(\gamma)$ and $y\gamma'$ is an occurrence of this variable identical with an occurrence in (Π, γ), ($y\gamma'$ is in the part of (Π', γ') not affected by extension and contraction), or*
2. *$y \in Dom(\gamma)$ and $y\gamma'$ is a new occurrence of y, introduced in the effect of extending (Π, γ) with $(\Sigma_{x\gamma\approx v}, \gamma)$, (there was an occurrence $y\gamma^k$ of an external variable y in $(\Sigma_{x\gamma\approx v}, \gamma)$ which generated new occurrences in all places the copy of this subproof was used and not contracted), or*
3. *$y \notin Dom(\gamma)$, (y is a new variable) then $y\gamma'$ may be identified as a renamed version of a variable $y' \in Dom(\gamma)$, where y' was an inner variable in $(\Sigma_{x\gamma\approx v}, \gamma)$.*

Example 2. Let an equational proof be:

$$f(a, g(b, b)) \approx_{[<1>, a\approx b, []]} f(b, g(b, b)) \approx_{[\epsilon, f(x, g(x,x))\approx c, [x\mapsto b]]} c$$

Then the subproof associated with $\overset{\leftarrow}{x\gamma}^{1}$ is $b \approx a$. Notice the left orientation of all occurrences of x in this case. We want to solve x in the proof with $x \mapsto a$. Hence we will use $b \approx a$ for the extension at each occurrence of x.

$$f(a, g(b, b)) \approx_{[<1>, a \approx b, []]} f(b, g(b, b)) \approx_{[<1>, b \approx a, []]} f(a, g(b, b))$$
$$\approx_{[<2>, b \approx a, []]} f(a, g(a, b)) \approx_{[<3>, b \approx a, []]} f(a, g(a, a))$$
$$\approx_{[\epsilon, f(x, g(x, x)) \approx c, [x \mapsto a]]} C$$

Standard contraction will shorten the proof to:

$$f(a, g(b, b)) \approx_{[<2>, b \approx a, []]} f(a, g(a, b)) \approx_{[<3>, b \approx a, []]} f(a, g(a, a))$$
$$\approx_{[\epsilon, f(x, g(x, x)) \approx c, [x \mapsto a]]} C$$

Notice that we have a new assignment for x, but now we will treat x as solved.

5 Paths in Equational Proof

A concept of path is a generalization of an associated subproof for an occurrence of a variable. A path is a subproof starting with some variable occurrence, constructed in such a way that it reflects the form of an associated subproof for this variable occurrence assuming that all other variables *involved* in the path were solved first. In order to restrict the definition of a path in a proof (Π, γ), we have to take into consideration solved and unsolved occurrences of variables in $Dom(\gamma)$. We have to remember where the solved variables had their occurrences at the time they were being solved.

Since in this section we will deal with compositions of subproofs, in order to simplify notation, we will identify a subproof with its subproof sequence.

Definition 12. *(Path Starting with a Variable Occurrence and Variable Occurrence Involved in a Subproof).*
Let (Π, γ) be an equational proof, U a set of unsolved variables in $Dom(\gamma)$, $x \in U$ and $x\gamma$ a given variable occurrence in (Π, γ). A path in (Π, γ) starting with $x\gamma$ is a composition of subproofs, $\Sigma_1 \ldots \Sigma_n$, defined in a recursive way:

1. *if y is a solved variable and $\Sigma_{v_1 \approx "y\gamma'^i"} \Sigma_{"y\gamma'^k" \approx v_2}$ is a subproof in (Π, γ), then $y\gamma'^k$ is an occurrence of a solved variable involved in this subproof;*
2. *if $\Sigma_{x\gamma \approx v}$ is an associated subproof for $x\gamma$, $\Sigma_{x\gamma \approx v}$ is a path starting with $x\gamma$ and $x\gamma$ is involved in this path;*
3. *if $y\gamma$ is a parent of $x\gamma$, then $\Sigma_{y\gamma \approx w[x\gamma]}$ is a path starting with $y\gamma$ and $y\gamma$ is involved in this path.*
4. *(a) if $\Sigma_1, \ldots, \Sigma_n$ is a path in (Π, γ) starting with $x_1\gamma$ and $\Sigma_n = \Sigma_{x_n\gamma \approx v[x_{n+1}\gamma^k]}$, and if x_{n+1} is an external variable in $\Sigma_{x_n\gamma \approx v[x_{n+1}\gamma^k]}$ and $\Sigma'_1, \ldots, \Sigma'_m$ is a path in (Π, γ) starting with $x_{n+1}\gamma^i$, and if no variable occurrence that is involved in the first part is involved in the second, and vice versa then the composition $\Sigma_1 \ldots \Sigma_n \Sigma'_1 \ldots \Sigma'_m$ is also a path in (Π, γ) starting with $x_1\gamma$ and all variables involved in the first and second path are involved in the new path;*

(b) if $\Sigma_1, \ldots, \Sigma_n$ is a path in (Π, γ) starting with $x_1\gamma$ and $\Sigma_n = \Sigma_{x_n\gamma \approx y\gamma|_\alpha}$, and $\Sigma_{y\gamma^k|_\alpha \approx s}$ is a subproof in (Π, γ) and if no variable occurrence that is involved in $\Sigma_1, \ldots, \Sigma_n$ is involved in $\Sigma_{y\gamma^k|_\alpha \approx s}$, and vice versa then $\Sigma_1, \ldots, \Sigma_n, \Sigma_{y\gamma^k|_\alpha \approx s}$ is also a path in (Π, γ) starting with $x_1\gamma$ and all variable occurrences involved in $\Sigma_1, \ldots, \Sigma_n$, in $\Sigma_{y\gamma^k|_\alpha \approx s}$ and $y\gamma^k$ are involved in the new path;

5. if Π_l is a path or a subproof in a path, then any composition $\overleftarrow{\Pi_l}\overrightarrow{\Pi_l}$ in the path is contracted in an obvious way to one element (part of) path.

Notice that an occurrence of a variable is involved in a path if it is a *beginning* of a subpath. An occurrence of a variable that appears at the end of a path is not necessarily involved in this path. An occurrence of a variable that is involved in a path is an entry point to some subpath of this path.

Example 3. For example, let our goal be: $G = \{x \approx a, z \approx hx, z \approx c\}$ and an equational theory: $E = \{b \approx a, b \approx fga, hfy \approx c\}$, then the proof (Π, γ) may be:

$$x\gamma^1 \qquad\qquad x\gamma^2$$
$$\downarrow \qquad\qquad\qquad \downarrow$$
$$\{b \;\approx_{[\epsilon, b\approx a, []]} a, \; hb, \; hb \approx_{[<1>, b\approx fga, []]} hfga \approx_{[\epsilon, hfy\approx c, [y \mapsto ga]]} c\}$$
$$\uparrow \quad\quad \uparrow$$
$$z\gamma^1 \;\; z\gamma^2$$

1. An example of a path starting with $x\gamma^2$ would be: $\Sigma_{x\gamma^2 \approx z\gamma^1|_{<1>}}\Sigma_{z\gamma^2|_{<1>} \approx fy\gamma}$.
2. An example of a path starting with $z\gamma^1$ is: $\Sigma_{z\gamma^1 \approx h(x\gamma^2)}\Sigma_{x\gamma^1 \approx a}$.

We will prove that if $(\Pi, \gamma) \xrightarrow{[x \mapsto v]} (\Pi', \gamma')$, for an unsolved variable x in $Dom(\gamma)$, then each path in (Π', γ') starting with an unsolved variable in (Π', γ') is identical to a path in (Π, γ) (up to renaming). Hence any new paths will be renamings of the original ones. In order to show that the process of solving variables in (Π, γ) will terminate, we will use a multiset of lengths of paths as a measure, and show that it is decreasing.

Lemma 1. *Let (Π, γ) be an equational proof, $U \subset Dom(\gamma)$ be a set of unsolved variables in (Π, γ), $(\Pi, \gamma) \xrightarrow{[x \mapsto v]} (\Pi', \gamma')$, and U' be a set of unsolved variables in (Π', γ').*

Each path in (Π', γ') starting with a variable occurrence of a variable in U' is identical (up to renaming of some variables) to a path in (Π, γ) starting with a variable occurrence of a variable in U.

If there are many paths in (Π', γ'), which are renamings of one and the same path in (Π, γ), then they are strictly shorter than a path in (Π, γ), starting with a variable occurrence of a variable which is solved in (Π', γ').

Proof. The proof of this lemma is based on the fact that each path starting with an occurrence of an unsolved variable in (Π, γ) is finite. Hence we can use induction on the lengths of paths.

Let $(\Pi, \gamma) \overset{[x \mapsto v]}{\to} (\Pi', \gamma')$, where $\Sigma_{x\gamma^i \approx v}$ was used in construction of (Π', γ'), and $\Sigma_1 \ldots \Sigma_n$ is a path in (Π', γ') starting with $y_1\gamma$. We can assume that x does not occur in v, because otherwise $ass(x\gamma) = x\gamma$ and then (Π', γ') is identical to (Π, γ) with the only difference that x is solved and does not appear in U'.

We have to consider different cases connected with the possible ways the path $\Sigma_1 \ldots \Sigma_n$ was constructed in (Π', γ'). The full proof and examples are in the long version of the paper [8].

Here, as an example, we will see the first of the cases considered there, namely when $\Sigma_1 \ldots \Sigma_n$ is a path starting with $y_1\gamma$ by Definition 12.2. Hence $\Sigma_1 \ldots \Sigma_n$ is a subproof associated with $y_1\gamma$ in (Π', γ'). The only case, when such a subproof was not a path in (Π, γ) would be if the composition of shorter paths was prevented by the condition that an occurrence of a variable may be involved only once in a path. Hence $\Sigma_1 \ldots \Sigma_n$ would have to be composed from two shorter paths: $\Sigma_{y\gamma' \approx t["x\gamma^k"]}$ and $\Sigma_{"x\gamma^{i"} \approx v}$ and in both of them an occurrence of a variable z is involved. Since $\Sigma_{x\gamma^i \approx v}$ is an associated proof for $x\gamma^i$, the occurrence of z would have to be an occurrence of a solved variable. The both paths would have to be of the following forms: $\Sigma_{y_1'\gamma \approx s["z\gamma^{k"}]}\Sigma_{"z\gamma^{i"} \approx t[x\gamma^i]}$, $\Sigma_{x\gamma^i \approx v["z\gamma^{*k"}]}\Sigma_{"z\gamma^{*i"}} \approx t[x\gamma]$. Hence v contains occurrence of x contrary to our assumption.

Corollary 2. *Let (Π, γ) be an equational proof, $U \subset Dom(\gamma)$ a set of unsolved variables in (Π, γ), The process of solving (Π, γ) will terminate.*

Proof. If $(\Pi, \gamma) \overset{[x \mapsto v]}{\to} (\Pi', \gamma')$, and U' a set of unsolved variables in (Π', γ'), the multiset of lengths of paths in (Π', γ') is smaller than the multiset of lengths of paths in (Π, γ).

6   Result

We prove completeness of the inference rules presented in Figure 1.

Namely, we prove that in any equational theory E, a given goal G such that $E \models G\sigma$, may be transformed by applications of rules in Figure 1 applied to equations which are not *solved*, into a *solved form* with which we can define an E-unifier more general than σ. The solved form of an equation and of a goal is defined in the following way.

Definition 13. *(Solved Equation and Solved Goal).*
Let G be a set of equations. An equation $x \approx t \in G$ is in a solved form, if x is a variable, $x \notin Var(t)$ and $x \notin Var(G\backslash\{x \approx t\})$.
G is in a solved form if all equations in G are in solved form.

If G is in the solved form, then we define a substitution $\theta_G = [x_1 \mapsto t_1, \ldots, x_n \mapsto t_n]$. Obviously, θ_G is the most general unifier of G.

If G is a set of goal equations, an inference performed on G with one of the rules of Figure 1 is denoted by $G \to G'$, where G' is the result of this inference. The transitive, reflexive closure of $\to$ is written as $\overset{*}{\to}$.

In order to prove completeness, we will need the measure of a goal G, of which we will show that it may be decreased by application of an inference rule if G is E-unifiable and not in solved form.

Definition 14. *(Measure for an Equational Proof).*
Let (Π, γ) be an equational proof and $U \subset Dom(\gamma)$ be a set of unsolved variables in (Π, γ). The measure $M(\Pi, \gamma)$ is a multiset of the lengths of paths starting with occurrences of variables in U.

Definition 15. *(Measure of a Goal).*
Let E be an equational theory, and G, an unsolved part of a goal G', such that there is a ground substitution γ, for which $E \models G'\gamma$ and hence there is an equational proof (Π', γ') of $G'\gamma$ and its subproof, (Π, γ), which is a proof of $G\gamma$, and all variables in $Var(G)$ are unsolved in (Π', γ').

The measure of G' with respect to (Π', γ') is a 4-tuple (m, n, o, p), where $m = M(\Pi, \gamma)$, n is the length of Π, o is the size of terms in $G\gamma$, p is the number of equations in G, of the form $t \approx x$, where x is a variable and t is not a variable.

Measures for different goals are compared with respect to lexicographic order.

Theorem 1. *Let E be a set of equations, such that $E \models G\gamma$ for some ground substitution γ. Then there is H a set of equations in the solved form, such that $G \overset{*}{\to} H$ and $\theta_H[Var(G)] \leq_E \gamma$.*

Proof. If G is already in the solved form, then $\theta_G \leq_E \gamma$.

If G is not in solved form, then there is an unsolved part of G, G', such that $u \approx v \in G'$, if $u \approx v$ is not in solved form. Assume that $u \approx v$ was selected for an inference. If $E \models G\gamma$, there must be an equational proof (Π, γ) of $G'\gamma$. We will call it an actual proof of $G\gamma$. If $u\gamma \approx v\gamma \in G\gamma$, then there must be a subproof in (Π, γ), of this ground equation and $u\gamma$, $v\gamma$ are the extreme terms in this subproof. We can also assume that all solved variables in G are solved in (Π, γ) and all unsolved variables in G are unsolved in (Π, γ). Hence there is a graph G_Π for all unsolved variables in (Π, γ). As we have seen, there are sometimes choices in constructing G_Π. The choices reflect the selection function, but in any case, we can always choose such G_Π that if $x \approx v$ is selected for an inference, $x\gamma$ is a maximal node in G_Π.

The full proof which uses induction on the measure of a goal, is in the long version of the paper [8]. Here we will see only the case for eager Variable Elimination.

Assume that $x \approx v$ was selected for an inference and $x \notin Var(v)$. Then $E \models x\gamma \approx v\gamma$ and there is a subproof $(\Sigma_{x\gamma \approx v\gamma}, \gamma)$ in the proof (Π, γ) such that $x\gamma$ and $v\gamma$ are extreme terms of $(\Sigma_{x\gamma \approx v\gamma}, \gamma)$. If x is unsolved in the goal G, x is also unsolved in (Π, γ). Hence we know that $v\gamma = ass(x)$ and $(\Pi, \gamma) \overset{[x \mapsto v\gamma]}{\to} (\Pi', \gamma')$. $M(\Pi, \gamma) > M(\Pi', \gamma')$.

Since $E \models G\gamma$, also $E \models G\gamma'$ and (Π', γ') is the proof of $G\gamma'$. We change the actual equational proof to (Π', γ') and take it as the basis of completeness argument of further inferences. Since $x\gamma' = v\gamma'$, $E \models G[x \mapsto v]\gamma'$.

Let (m, n, o, p) be the measure of the goal before Variable Elimination and (m', n', o', p') after Variable Elimination. $m' < m$ after Variable Elimination, hence we can use induction hypothesis for the new goal. Notice also that after Variable Elimination, for each $u' \approx v'$ in G' there is a subproof in (Π', γ') such that $u'\gamma'$ and $v'\gamma'$ are the extreme terms in this subproof. If $u' \approx v'[x]$ was in G', then after Variable Elimination, $u' \approx v'[v]$ in G' and obviously (because of extension) there is a subproof $(\Sigma_{u'\gamma' \approx v'[v]\gamma'}, \gamma')$ in (Π', γ').

7   Conclusion

E-unification procedures are inherently non-deterministic, because there are usually many ways to apply inferences to goal equations and many possibilities of solving a goal. It means that a search space for a solution may be very extensive. Any restrictions of this non-determinism that we may justify are therefore welcome as restrictions of this search space. Eager Variable Elimination means that the rule should be applied whenever an equation $x \approx v$ is selected and x does not appear in v. In this case, we would not try to apply other rules to this equation. On the other hand, we may see that the ground equational proof of an instance of a goal, may be made longer by Variable Elimination. This means that we will have to do more Mutate inferences in order to reach solution. One can think about some *memoization* techniques to detect and reduce such possible overhead.

We think that the proof of completeness of eager Variable Elimination opens some possibilities of finding new classes of equational theories defined syntactically, for which E-unification problem may be proved solvable and tractable.

References

1. F. Baader and T. Nipkow. *Term Rewriting and All That.* Cambridge, 1998.
2. J. Gallier and W. Snyder. A general complete E-unification procedure. In *RTA 2*, ed. P. Lescanne, LNCS Vol. 256, 216-227, 1987.
3. J. Gallier and W. Snyder. Complete sets of transformations for general E-unification. In *TCS*, Vol. 67, 203-260, 1989.
4. S, Hölldobler. Foundations of Equational Logic Programming. *Lecture Notes in Artificial Intelligence*, Vol. 353, Springer, Berlin, 1989.
5. C. Kirchner and H. Kirchner. *Rewriting, Solving, Proving.* http://www.loria.fr/~ckirchne/ , 2000.
6. A. Martelli, C. Moiso and G. F. Rossi. Lazy Unification Algorithms for Canonical Rewrite Systems. In *Resolution of Equations in Algebraic Structures*, eds. H. Aït-Kaci and M. Nivat, Vol. II of Rewriting Techniques, 258-282, Academic Press, 1989.
7. A. Martelli, G. F. Rossi and C. Moiso. An Algorithm for Unification in Equational Theories. In *Proc. 1986 Symposium on Logic Programming*, 180-186, 1986.
8. B. Morawska. Completeness of *E*-unification with eager Variable Elimination. LTCS-Report (03-03), See http://lat.inf.tu-dresden.de/research/reports.html.

Computable Numberings

Serikzhan Badaev

Kazakh National University, Almaty 480078, Kazakhstan,
badaev@kazsu.kz

In the computability theory, various situations naturally lead to the study of classes of constructive objects. An examination of the algorithmic properties of classes of constructive objects fares best with the techniques and notions of the theory of computable numberings. The idea of using such numberings goes back to Gödel, who applied a computable numbering of formulas for embedding the metatheory of number theory into the theory of numbers.

The next steps toward applying computable numberings, in treating the class of partial computable functions, was taken by A.Turing and S.C.Kleene. They constructed an universal Turing machine and an universal partial computable function which both have great significance in the development of the theory of algorithms and computer science. It allows one to derive the basic recursion theorems and may be thought of as the starting point of the theory of computable numberings.

The study of computable numberings of the family $\mathcal{F}$ of all unary partial computable functions was initiated by H.Rogers. He brought into consideration the class $\mathrm{Com}\,(\mathcal{F})$ of all possible computable numberings of $\mathcal{F}$ and a reducibility relation $\leqslant$ amongst them, which determined a preordering on that class. Factorization with respect to an equivalence relation $\equiv$, induced by the preordering, made it possible to construct a partially ordered set $\mathcal{R}(\mathcal{F}) = \langle \mathrm{Com}\,(\mathcal{F})/\equiv, \leqslant \rangle$, which forms an upper semilattice.

In the mid of 90-th, S.Goncharov and A.Sorbi offered a general approach for studying families of objects which admit a constructive description in a formal language with Gödel numbering of the formulas. This approach allows one to unify in a very natural way various notions of computability for different families of constructive objects. Derived notion of Rogers semilattice introduced similar to $\mathcal{R}(\mathcal{F})$ permits to find algebraic interconnections between different processes of computation of a family and is usually treated as its complexity in whole.

We consider mainly problems related to the algebraic properties (cardinality, distributivity property, extremal elements, ideals, intervals, minimal covers) and elementary properties (i.e., first order properties in the language with operation of supremum) of Rogers semilattices of computable numberings for the families of sets from different levels of arithmetical and Ershov's hierarchies. Besides, we suggest also our point of view to some known approaches to the notion of computable numbering of the elements of topological spaces. The results we intend to talk about were obtained in the previous three years mostly by S.Badaev, S.Goncharov, A.Sorbi[1], and S.Lempp.

---

[1] Researches of these three authors on computables numberings were partially supported by grants INTAS-97-139 and INTAS-00-499.

M.Y. Vardi and A. Voronkov (Eds.): LPAR 2003, LNAI 2850, p. 213, 2003.

Handling Equality in Monodic Temporal Resolution

Boris Konev[1,*], Anatoli Degtyarev[2], and Michael Fisher[1]

[1] Department of Computer Science, University of Liverpool, Liverpool L69 7ZF, U.K.,
{B.Konev, M.Fisher}@csc.liv.ac.uk
[2] Department of Computer Science, King's College London, Strand, London WC2R 2LS, U.K.,
anatoli@dcs.kcl.ac.uk

Abstract. First-order temporal logic is a concise and powerful notation, with many potential applications in both Computer Science and Artificial Intelligence. While the full logic is highly complex, recent work on monodic first-order temporal logics has identified important enumerable and even decidable fragments including the guarded fragment with equality. In this paper, we specialise the monodic resolution method to the guarded monodic fragment with equality and first-order temporal logic over expanding domains. We introduce novel resolution calculi that can be applied to formulae in the normal form associated with the clausal resolution method, and state correctness and completeness results.

1 Introduction

First-order temporal logic (FOTL) is a powerful notation with many applications in formal methods. Unfortunately, this power leads to high complexity, most notably the lack of recursive axiomatisations for general FOTL. Recently, significant work has been carried out in defining *monodic* FOTL, a class of logics retaining finite axiomatisation, with both tableau and resolution systems being under development [3, 12]. However, until now, little work has been carried out concerning monodic FOTL with equality and *no* practical proof technique for such logics has been proposed. In real applications of formal specification, the notion of equality plays a key role and so, in this paper, we extend and adapt our clausal resolution approach, which has already been successfully applied to a variety of monodic logics, to the case of monodic FOTL with equality. In particular, we develop a decision procedure for the guarded monodic fragment of FOTL with equality over constant and expanding domains; decidability of this fragment has been established in [9]. However, decidability was given there using model-theoretic techniques, and practical proof techniques were not considered. In this paper we address the problem of producing a practical proof technique for this class of logic through extension of the clausal resolution method for monodic temporal logics. A complete temporal resolution calculus for the monodic temporal fragment *without equality* for the constant domain case has been presented in [3]. The expanding domain case has been announced in [11] and proved in a technical report [4]. Finally, we also point to a *fine-grained* superposition calculus for the monodic guarded fragment with equality interpreted over expanding domains. This suggests adapting our previous work on fine-grained temporal resolution [11] and combining this with (parts of) the superposition calculus for the (first-order) guarded fragment with equality given in [7].

---

* On leave from Steklov Institute of Mathematics at St.Petersburg

M.Y. Vardi and A. Voronkov (Eds.): LPAR 2003, LNAI 2850, pp. 214–228, 2003.

2   First-Order Temporal Logic

First-Order (discrete linear time) Temporal Logic, FOTL, is an extension of classical first-order logic with operators that deal with a linear and discrete model of time (isomorphic to $\mathbb{N}$, and the most commonly used model of time). The first-order function-free temporal language is constructed in a standard way [6, 10] from: *predicate symbols* $P_0, P_1, \ldots$, each of which is of some fixed arity (null-ary predicate symbols are called *propositions*); *equality*, denoted by the symbol $\approx$[1]; *individual variables* $x_0, x_1, \ldots$; *individual constants* $c_0, c_1, \ldots$; *Boolean operators* $\wedge$, $\neg$, $\vee$, $\Rightarrow$, $\equiv$, **true** ('true'), **false** ('false'); *quantifiers* $\forall$ and $\exists$; together with *unary temporal operators*, such as[2] $\Box$ ('always in the future'), $\Diamond$ ('sometime in the future'), and $\bigcirc$ ('at the next moment').

Formulae in FOTL are interpreted in *first-order temporal structures* of the form $\mathfrak{M} = \langle D_n, I_n \rangle$, $n \in \mathbb{N}$, where every D_n is a non-empty set such that whenever $n < m$, $D_n \subseteq D_m$, and I_n is an interpretation of predicate and constant symbols over D_n. We require that the interpretation of constants is *rigid*. Thus, for every constant c and all moments of time $i, j \geq 0$, we have $I_i(c) = I_j(c)$. The interpretation of $\approx$ is fixed as the identity on every D_n. The interpretation of predicate symbols is flexible. A *(variable) assignment* $\mathfrak{a}$ is a function from the set of individual variables to $\cup_{n \in \mathbb{N}} D_n$. (This definition implies that variable assignments are also rigid.) We denote the set of all assignments by $\mathfrak{V}$.

For every moment of time n, there is a corresponding *first-order* structure, $\mathfrak{M}_n = \langle D_n, I_n \rangle$; the corresponding set of variable assignments $\mathfrak{V}_n$ is a subset of the set of all assignments, $\mathfrak{V}_n = \{ \mathfrak{a} \in \mathfrak{V} \mid \mathfrak{a}(x) \in D_n$ for every variable $x \}$; clearly, $\mathfrak{V}_n \subseteq \mathfrak{V}_m$ if $n < m$. Intuitively, FOTL formulae are interpreted in sequences of *worlds*, $\mathfrak{M}_0, \mathfrak{M}_1, \ldots$ with truth values in different worlds being connected via temporal operators.

The *truth* relation $\mathfrak{M}_n \models^{\mathfrak{a}} \phi$ in a structure $\mathfrak{M}$, *only for those assignments* $\mathfrak{a}$ *that satisfy the condition* $\mathfrak{a} \in \mathfrak{V}_n$, is defined inductively in the usual way under the following understanding of temporal operators:

$$\mathfrak{M}_n \models^{\mathfrak{a}} \bigcirc \phi \text{ iff } \mathfrak{M}_{n+1} \models^{\mathfrak{a}} \phi;$$
$$\mathfrak{M}_n \models^{\mathfrak{a}} \Diamond \phi \text{ iff there exists } m \geq n \text{ such that } \mathfrak{M}_m \models^{\mathfrak{a}} \phi;$$
$$\mathfrak{M}_n \models^{\mathfrak{a}} \Box \phi \text{ iff for all } m \geq n, \mathfrak{M}_m \models^{\mathfrak{a}} \phi.$$

$\mathfrak{M}$ is a *model* for a formula ϕ (or ϕ is *true* in $\mathfrak{M}$) if there exists an assignment $\mathfrak{a}$ such that $\mathfrak{M}_0 \models^{\mathfrak{a}} \phi$. A formula is *satisfiable* if it has a model. A formula is *valid* if it is true in any temporal structure under any assignment.

The models introduced above are known as *models with expanding domains*. Another important class of models consists of *models with constant domains* in which the class of first-order temporal structures, where FOTL formulae are interpreted, is restricted to structures $\mathfrak{M} = \langle D_n, I_n \rangle$, $n \in \mathbb{N}$, such that $D_i = D_j$ for all $i, j \in \mathbb{N}$. The notions of truth and validity are defined similarly to the expanding domain case. It is known [14] that satisfiability over expanding domains can be reduced to satisfiability over constant domains.

---

[1] We are using the symbol $\approx$ for equality in the object language in order to avoid confusion with the symbol $=$ for equality in the meta language.

[2] W.r.t. satisfiability, the binary temporal operators U ('until') and W ('weak until') can be represented using the unary temporal operators [2, 6] with a linear growth in the size of a formula.

Example 1. The formula $\forall x P(x) \wedge \Box(\forall x P(x) \Rightarrow \bigcirc \forall x P(x)) \wedge \Diamond \exists x \neg P(x)$ is unsatisfiable over both expanding and constant domains; the formula $\forall x P(x) \wedge \Box(\forall x(P(x) \Rightarrow \bigcirc P(x))) \wedge \Diamond \exists x \neg P(x)$ is unsatisfiable over constant domains but has a model with an expanding domain.

This logic is complex. It is known that even "small" fragments of FOTL, such as the *two-variable monadic* fragment (all predicates are unary), are not recursively enumerable [10, 13]. However, the set of valid *monodic* formulae *without equality* is known to be finitely axiomatisable [15].

Definition 1 (Monodic Fragment). *An* FOTL*-formula ϕ is called* monodic *if any sub-formulae of the form $\mathcal{T}\psi$, where $\mathcal{T}$ is one of $\bigcirc$, $\Box$, $\Diamond$ (or $\psi_1 \mathcal{T} \psi_2$, where $\mathcal{T}$ is one of U, W), contains at most one free variable.*

The addition of either equality or function symbols to the monodic fragment leads to the loss of recursive enumerability [15]. Moreover, it was proved in [5] that the *two variable monadic monodic fragment with equality* is not recursively enumerable. However, in [9] it was shown that the guarded monodic fragment with equality is decidable[3].

Definition 2 (Guarded Monodic Fragment with Equality). *The formulae of the* guarded monodic fragment MGF *are inductively defined as follows:*

1. *If A is an atom (which can be non-equational, of the form $P(t_1, \ldots, t_n)$ an equation, of the form $s \approx t$, as well as a logical constant, **true** or **false**), then A is in* MGF, *where $t_1, \ldots, t_n, s, t$ are constants or variables.*
2. MGF *is closed under boolean combinations.*
3. *If $\phi \in$ MGF and G is an atom (possibly equation), for which every free variable of ϕ is among the arguments of G, then $\forall \overline{x}(G \Rightarrow \phi) \in$ MGF and $\exists \overline{x}(G \wedge \phi) \in$ MGF, for every sequence $\overline{x}$ of variables. The atom G is called a* guard.
4. *If $\phi(x) \in$ MGF and $\phi(x)$ contains at most one free variable, then $\bigcirc\phi(x) \in$ MGF, $\Box\phi(x) \in$ MGF, and $\Diamond\phi(x) \in$ MGF.*
5. *If $\phi(x) \in$ MGF and $\phi(x)$ contains exactly one free variable x, then $\forall x \phi(x)$ and $\exists x \phi(x)$ are in* MGF.

Note 1. Although the standard definition of the guarded fragment (see, for example, [7]) does not contain item 5, its addition does not extend the notion of the guarded fragment: we can always choose $x \approx x$ as the guard for $\forall x$ and $\exists x$.

3   Divided Separated Normal Form (DSNF)

Definition 3. *A temporal step clause is a formula either of the form $l \Rightarrow \bigcirc m$, where l and m are propositional literals, or $(L(x) \Rightarrow \bigcirc M(x))$, where $L(x)$ and $M(x)$ are unary literals. We call a clause of the the first type an (original)* ground *step clause, and of the second type an (original)* non-ground *step clause.*

---

[3] All cases considered in [5] included formulae of the form $\Box \forall x \forall y ((P(x) \wedge P(y)) \supset x \approx y)$ or similar non-guarded formulae.

Definition 4. *A monodic temporal problem in Divided Separated Normal Form (DSNF) is a quadruple $\langle \mathcal{U}, \mathcal{I}, \mathcal{S}, \mathcal{E} \rangle$, where*

1. *the universal part, $\mathcal{U}$, is a finite set of arbitrary closed first-order formulae;*
2. *the initial part, $\mathcal{I}$, is, again, a finite set of arbitrary closed first-order formulae;*
3. *the step part, $\mathcal{S}$, is a finite set of original (ground and non-ground) temporal step clauses; and*
4. *the eventuality part, $\mathcal{E}$, is a finite set of eventuality clauses of the form $\lozenge L(x)$ (a* non-ground *eventuality clause) and $\lozenge l$ (a* ground *eventuality clause), where l is a propositional literal and $L(x)$ is a unary non-ground literal.*

For a temporal problem, P, $\mathrm{const}(\mathsf{P})$ denotes the set of constants occurring in P.

Note that, in a monodic temporal problem, we disallow two different temporal step clauses with the same left-hand sides. We also disallow occurrences of equality in the step and eventuality parts. These requirements can be easily guaranteed by renaming.

In what follows, we will not distinguish between a finite set of formulae $\mathcal{X}$ and the conjunction $\bigwedge \mathcal{X}$ of formulae within the set. With each monodic temporal problem, we associate the formula $\mathcal{I} \wedge \Box\mathcal{U} \wedge \Box\forall x\mathcal{S} \wedge \Box\forall x\mathcal{E}$. Now, when we talk about particular properties of a temporal problem (e.g., satisfiability, validity, logical consequences etc) we mean properties of the associated formula.

Arbitrary monodic FOTL-formulae can be transformed into DSNF in a satisfiability equivalence preserving way using a renaming technique replacing non-atomic subformulae with new propositions and removing all occurrences of the U and W operators [3, 6]. If the given formula is a guarded monodic formula, then all parts of DSNF (and the associated formula) are guarded monodic formulae. In this case, we call the result of the transformation a *guarded monodic problem*.

4   Calculi

In this section we present two resolution calculi, $\mathfrak{I}_c$ and $\mathfrak{I}_e$, for guarded monodic problems (including equality). These calculi are very similar, but $\mathfrak{I}_c$ is complete for problems featuring constant domains, while $\mathfrak{I}_e$ is complete for those involving expanding domains. These resolution calculi are based on those introduced in [3] for problems *without* equality. Thus, the work described in this section extends previous calculi to allow consideration of equality in guarded monodic problems.

We begin with a number of important definitions.

Definition 5 (Equational Augmentation). *Let P be a temporal problem. Its (equational) augmentation is the set $\mathrm{aug}_=(\mathsf{P})$ of step clauses. For every constant $c \in \mathrm{const}(\mathsf{P})$, the following clauses are in $\mathrm{aug}_=(\mathsf{P})$.*

$$(x \approx c) \Rightarrow \bigcirc(x \approx c), \tag{1}$$
$$(x \not\approx c) \Rightarrow \bigcirc(x \not\approx c). \tag{2}$$

Note that clauses originating from such augmentation are the only step clauses that contain equality.

Definition 6 (Derived/E-Derived Step Clauses). *Let P be a monodic temporal problem, and let*

$$L_{i_1}(x) \Rightarrow \bigcirc M_{i_1}(x), \ldots, L_{i_k}(x) \Rightarrow \bigcirc M_{i_k}(x) \tag{3}$$

be a subset of the set of its original non-ground step clauses, or *clauses from* $\mathrm{aug}_=(P)$. *Then formulae of the form*

$$\exists x (L_{i_1}(x) \wedge \ldots \wedge L_{i_k}(x)) \Rightarrow \bigcirc \exists x (M_{i_1}(x) \wedge \ldots \wedge M_{i_k}(x)), \tag{4}$$

$$\forall x (L_{i_1}(x) \vee \ldots \vee L_{i_k}(x)) \Rightarrow \bigcirc \forall x (M_{i_1}(x) \vee \ldots \vee M_{i_k}(x)) \tag{5}$$

are called derived *step clauses. Formulae of the form (4) are called* e-derived *step clauses.*

Note that formulae of the form (4) are logical consequences of (3) in the *expanding domain* case; while formulae of the form (4) *and* (5) are logical consequences of (3) in the *constant domain* case. As Example 1 shows, (5) is not a logical consequence of (3) in the expanding domain case.

Definition 7 (Merged Derived/E-Derived Step Clauses). *Let* $\{\Phi_1 \Rightarrow \bigcirc \Psi_1, \ldots, \Phi_n \Rightarrow \bigcirc \Psi_n\}$ *be a set of derived (e-derived) step clauses or original ground step clauses. Then* $\bigwedge_{i=1}^{n} \Phi_i \Rightarrow \bigcirc \bigwedge_{i=1}^{n} \Psi_i$ *is called a* merged derived (merged e-derived) *step clause.*

Note 2. In [3], where no equality was considered, instead augmenting a problem with clauses of the form (1) and (2), we defined another derived step clause

$$L(c) \Rightarrow \bigcirc M(c), \tag{6}$$

where $c \in \mathrm{const}(P)$. Note that this clause is equivalent to an e-derived step clause

$$\exists x (L(x) \wedge x \approx c) \Rightarrow \bigcirc \exists x (M(x) \wedge x \approx c).$$

Definition 8 (Full Merged/E-Merged Step Clauses). *Let* $\mathcal{A} \Rightarrow \bigcirc \mathcal{B}$ *be a merged derived (merged e-derived) step clause,* $L_1(x) \Rightarrow \bigcirc M_1(x), \ldots, L_k(x) \Rightarrow \bigcirc M_k(x)$ *be original step clauses or step clauses from* $\mathrm{aug}_=(P)$, *and* $A(x) \stackrel{\mathrm{def}}{=} \bigwedge_{i=1}^{k} L_i(x)$, $B(x) \stackrel{\mathrm{def}}{=} \bigwedge_{i=1}^{k} M_i(x)$. *Then* $\forall x (\mathcal{A} \wedge A(x) \Rightarrow \bigcirc (\mathcal{B} \wedge B(x)))$ *is called a* full merged step clause *(full e-merged step clause, resp.). In the case* $k = 0$, *the conjunctions* $A(x)$, $B(x)$ *are empty, i.e., their truth value is* **true**, *and the merged step clause is just a merged derived step clause.*

We now present two calculi, $\mathfrak{I}_c$ and $\mathfrak{I}_e$, aimed at the constant and expanding domain cases, respectively. The inference rules of these calculi coincide; the only difference is in the merging operation. The calculus $\mathfrak{I}_c$ utilises merged derived and full merged step clauses; whereas $\mathfrak{I}_e$ utilises merged e-derived and full e-merged step clauses.

Inference Rules. In what follows, $\mathcal{A} \Rightarrow \bigcirc \mathcal{B}$ and $\mathcal{A}_i \Rightarrow \bigcirc \mathcal{B}_i$ denote merged derived (e-derived) step clauses, $\forall x(\mathcal{A}(x) \Rightarrow \bigcirc(\mathcal{B}(x)))$ and $\forall x(\mathcal{A}_i(x) \Rightarrow \bigcirc(\mathcal{B}_i(x)))$ denote full merged (e-merged) step clauses, and $\mathcal{U}$ denotes the (current) universal part of the problem. Thus, $\phi \models \psi$ means that ψ is a (first-order) logical consequence of ϕ.

- *Step Resolution Rule w.r.t.* $\mathcal{U}$: $\dfrac{\mathcal{A} \Rightarrow \bigcirc \mathcal{B}}{\neg \mathcal{A}}$ $(\bigcirc^{\mathcal{U}}_{res})$, where $\mathcal{U} \cup \{\mathcal{B}\} \models \perp$.
- *Initial Termination Rule w.r.t.* $\mathcal{U}$:   The contradiction $\perp$ is derived and the derivation is (successfully) terminated if $\mathcal{U} \cup \mathcal{I} \models \perp$.
- *Eventuality Resolution Rule w.r.t.* $\mathcal{U}$:

$$\frac{\forall x(\mathcal{A}_1(x) \Rightarrow \bigcirc(\mathcal{B}_1(x))) \ldots \forall x(\mathcal{A}_n(x) \Rightarrow \bigcirc(\mathcal{B}_n(x)))   \quad \Diamond L(x)}{\forall x \bigwedge_{i=1}^{n} \neg \mathcal{A}_i(x)} \ (\Diamond^{\mathcal{U}}_{res}),$$

where $\Diamond L(x) \in \mathcal{E}$ and $\forall x(\mathcal{A}_i(x) \Rightarrow \bigcirc \mathcal{B}_i(x))$ are full merged (full e-merged) step clauses such that for all $i \in \{1, \ldots, n\}$, the *loop* side conditions $\forall x(\mathcal{U} \wedge \mathcal{B}_i(x) \Rightarrow \neg L(x))$ and $\forall x(\mathcal{U} \wedge \mathcal{B}_i(x) \Rightarrow \bigvee_{j=1}^{n} (\mathcal{A}_j(x)))$ are both valid first-order formulae.
- *Eventuality Termination Rule w.r.t.* $\mathcal{U}$: The contradiction is derived and the derivation is (successfully) terminated if $\mathcal{U} \models \forall x \neg L(x)$, where $\Diamond L(x) \in \mathcal{E}$.
- *Ground Eventuality Resolution w.r.t.* $\mathcal{U}$ and *Ground Eventuality Termination w.r.t.* $\mathcal{U}$: These rules repeat the eventuality resolution and eventuality termination rules with the only difference that *ground eventualities* and merged *derived step clauses* are used instead of non-ground eventualities and full merged step clauses.

A *derivation* is a sequence of universal parts, $\mathcal{U} = \mathcal{U}_0 \subseteq \mathcal{U}_1 \subseteq \mathcal{U}_2 \subseteq \ldots$, extended little by little by the conclusions of the inference rules. Successful termination means that the given problem is unsatisfiable. The $\mathcal{I}$, $\mathcal{S}$ and $\mathcal{E}$ parts of the temporal problem are not changed in a derivation.

Example 2. Let us consider an unsatisfiable (over both constant and expanding domains) temporal problem given by

$$\mathcal{I} = \{i1. \ \exists x(x \not\approx c)\}, \mathcal{U} = \begin{cases} u1. \ \exists x(P(x)), \\ u2. \ \forall x(x \not\approx c \wedge \exists y \neg P(y) \Rightarrow Q(x)) \end{cases},$$

$$\mathcal{E} = \{e1. \ \Diamond \neg Q(x)\}, \quad \mathcal{S} = \{s1. \ P(x) \Rightarrow \bigcirc \neg P(x)\}$$

and apply temporal resolution to this. First, we produce the following e-derived step clause from $s1$:

$$d1. \ \exists y P(y) \Rightarrow \bigcirc \exists y \neg P(y).$$

Then, we merge $d1$ and $(x \not\approx c \Rightarrow \bigcirc(x \not\approx c))$ from $\text{aug}_{=}(P)$ to give

$$m1. \ \forall x(\exists y P(y) \wedge x \not\approx c \Rightarrow \bigcirc(\exists y \neg P(y) \wedge x \not\approx c)).$$

It can be immediately checked that the following formulae are valid

$$\forall x((\mathcal{U} \wedge \exists y \neg P(y) \wedge x \not\approx c) \Rightarrow Q(x)) \qquad (\text{see } u2),$$
$$\forall x((\mathcal{U} \wedge \exists y \neg P(y) \wedge x \not\approx c) \Rightarrow (\exists y P(y) \wedge x \not\approx c)) \qquad (\text{see } u1),$$

that is, the loop side conditions are valid for $m1$. We apply the eventuality resolution rule to $e1$ and $m1$ and derive a new universal clause

$$u3.\ (\forall y \neg P(y) \vee \forall x(x \approx c))$$

which contradicts clauses $u1$ and $i1$ (consequently, the initial termination rule is applied).

Correctness of the presented calculi is straightforward.

Theorem 1. *The rules of $\mathfrak{I}_c$ and $\mathfrak{I}_e$ preserve satisfiability over constant and expanding domains, respectively.*

Proof. Considering models, it follows that the temporal resolution rules preserve satisfiability. Consider, for example, the step resolution rule. Let $\mathcal{A} \Rightarrow \bigcirc \mathcal{B}$ be a merged derived clause and assume that $\mathfrak{M}_0 \models^{\mathfrak{a}} \Box(\mathcal{A} \Rightarrow \bigcirc \mathcal{B})$, but for some $i \geq 0$, $\mathfrak{M}_i \not\models^{\mathfrak{a}} \neg \mathcal{A}$. Then $\mathfrak{M}_{i+1} \models^{\mathfrak{a}} \mathcal{B}$ in contradiction with the side condition of the rule. $\qquad \Box$

We formulate now completeness results and prove them in Section 5, which is entirely devoted to this issue.

Theorem 2. *If a guarded monodic temporal problem with equality P is unsatisfiable over constant domains, then there exists a successfully terminating derivation in $\mathfrak{I}_c$ from P.*

Theorem 3. *If a guarded monodic temporal problem with equality P is unsatisfiable over expanding domains, then there exists a successfully terminating derivation in $\mathfrak{I}_e$ from P.*

The calculi are complete in the sense that they provides us with a decision procedure when side conditions checks are decidable and with a semi-decision procedure else.

Corollary 1. *Satisfiability of the guarded monodic temporal fragment with equality is decidable by temporal resolution.*

Proof. Since there are only finitely many different merged clauses, there are only finitely many different conclusions by the rules of temporal resolution. Now it suffices to note that these side conditions are expressed by first-order guarded formulae with equality (mind our "extended" definition of the guarded fragment, Note 1), and the first-order guarded fragment with equality is decidable [1, 8]. $\qquad \Box$

A complete temporal resolution calculus for the monodic temporal fragment *without equality* for the constant domain case has been presented in [3]. The expanding domain case has been announced in [11] and proved in a technical report [4]. We show that the calculi $\mathfrak{I}_c$ and $\mathfrak{I}_e$, that slightly differ from the calculi used in [3] and [4], are complete for these cases. We briefly discuss the difference between the calculi in Section 5.3.

Theorem 4. *Let an arbitrary monodic temporal problem without equality P be unsatisfiable over constant domains. Then there exists a successfully terminating derivation in $\mathfrak{I}_c$ from P.*

Theorem 5. *Let an arbitrary monodic temporal problem without equality P be unsatisfiable over expanding domains. Then there exists a successfully terminating derivation in $\mathfrak{I}_e$ from P.*

5   Completeness of Temporal Resolution

The proof of theorems 2 and 3, as well as of theorems 4 and 5, can be obtained by a modification of the corresponding proof of completeness for the constant domain case without equality (see [3], Theorem 2). In short, the proof in [3] proceeds by building a graph associated with a monodic temporal problem, then showing that there is a correspondence between properties of the graph and of the problem, and that all relevant properties are captured by the rules of the proof system. Therefore, if the problem is unsatisfiable, eventually our rules will discover it.

The outlined proof relies on the theorem on existence of a model (see [3], Theorem 3). In Section 5.1 we prove the theorem on existence of a model, Theorem 6, for the constant domain guarded monodic fragment with equality; in Section 5.2 we refine this reasoning for the expanding domain case; and in Section 5.3 we show that the proofs of sections 5.1 and 5.2 can be transfered to arbitrary monodic fragments without equality. It can be seen that the proof of completeness given in [3] holds for all these cases of the theorem on existence of a model considered in sections 5.1–5.3.

5.1   Guarded Monodic Fragment with Equality over Constant Domains

Let $\mathsf{P} = \langle \mathcal{U}, \mathcal{I}, \mathcal{S}, \mathcal{E} \rangle$ be a guarded monodic temporal problem with equality. Let $\{P_1(x), \ldots, P_N(x)\}$ and $\{p_1, \ldots, p_n\}$, $N, n \geq 0$, be the sets of all (monadic) predicates (including "predicates" of the form $x \approx c$ for every constant $c \in \mathrm{const}(\mathsf{P})$) and all propositions, respectively, occurring in $\mathcal{S} \cup \mathcal{E} \cup \mathrm{aug}_=(\mathsf{P})$.

A *predicate colour* γ is a set of unary literals such that for every $P_i(x) \in \{P_1(x), \ldots, P_N(x)\}$, either $P_i(x)$ or $\neg P_i(x)$ belongs to γ. A predicate colour is called *constant* if $x \approx c \in \gamma$ for some $c \in \mathrm{const}(\mathsf{P})$. A *propositional colour* θ is a sequence of propositional literals such that for every $p_i \in \{p_1, \ldots, p_n\}$, either p_i or $\neg p_i$ belongs to θ. Let Γ be a set of predicate colours. A couple (Γ, θ) is called a *colour scheme* for P. Since P only determines the signature, we may omit P when speaking of colour schemes.

For every colour scheme $\mathcal{C} = \langle \Gamma, \theta \rangle$ let us construct the formulae $\mathcal{F}_\mathcal{C}$, $\mathcal{A}_\mathcal{C}$, $\mathcal{B}_\mathcal{C}$ in the following way. For every $\gamma \in \Gamma$ and for every θ, introduce the conjunctions:

$$F_\gamma(x) = \bigwedge_{L(x) \in \gamma} L(x); \quad F_\theta = \bigwedge_{l \in \theta} l.$$

Let

$$A_\gamma(x) = \bigwedge \{L(x) \mid L(x) \Rightarrow \bigcirc M(x) \in \mathcal{S} \cup \mathrm{aug}_=(\mathsf{P}), \ L(x) \in \gamma\},$$

$$B_\gamma(x) = \bigwedge \{M(x) \mid L(x) \Rightarrow \bigcirc M(x) \in \mathcal{S} \cup \mathrm{aug}_=(\mathsf{P}), \ L(x) \in \gamma\},$$

$$A_\theta = \bigwedge \{l \mid l \Rightarrow \bigcirc m \in \mathcal{S}, \ l \in \theta\},$$

$$B_\theta = \bigwedge \{m \mid l \Rightarrow \bigcirc m \in \mathcal{S}, \ l \in \theta\}.$$

Now $\mathcal{A}_\mathcal{C}$, $\mathcal{B}_\mathcal{C}$, and $\mathcal{F}_\mathcal{C}$ are of the following forms:

$$\mathcal{A}_\mathcal{C} = \bigwedge_{\gamma \in \Gamma} \exists x A_\gamma(x) \wedge A_\theta \wedge \forall x \bigvee_{\gamma \in \Gamma} A_\gamma(x),$$

$$\mathcal{B}_\mathcal{C} = \bigwedge_{\gamma \in \Gamma} \exists x B_\gamma(x) \wedge B_\theta \wedge \forall x \bigvee_{\gamma \in \Gamma} B_\gamma(x),$$

$$\mathcal{F}_\mathcal{C} = \bigwedge_{\gamma \in \Gamma} \exists x F_\gamma(x) \wedge F_\theta \wedge \forall x \bigvee_{\gamma \in \Gamma} F_\gamma(x).$$

We can consider the formula $\mathcal{F}_\mathcal{C}$ as a "categorical" formula specification of the quotient structure given by a colour scheme. In turn, the formula $\mathcal{A}_\mathcal{C}$ represents the part of this specification which is "responsible" just for "transferring" requirements from the current world (quotient structure) to its immediate successors, and $\mathcal{B}_\mathcal{C}$ represents the result of this transferal.

Definition 9 (Canonical Merged Derived Step Clauses). *Let P be a first-order temporal problem, and $\mathcal{C}$ be a colour scheme for P. Then the clause*

$$(\mathcal{A}_\mathcal{C} \Rightarrow \bigcirc \mathcal{B}_\mathcal{C}),$$

is called a canonical merged derived step clause *for P (including the* degenerate *clause* **true** $\Rightarrow \bigcirc$**true***). If a conjunction $A_\gamma(x)$, $\gamma \in \Gamma$, is empty, that is its truth value is* **true***, then the formula $\forall x \bigvee_{\gamma \in \Gamma} A_\gamma(x)$ (or $\forall x \bigvee_{\gamma \in \Gamma} B_\gamma(x)$) disappears from $\mathcal{A}_\mathcal{C}$ (or from $\mathcal{B}_\mathcal{C}$ respectively). In the propositional case, the clause $(\mathcal{A}_\mathcal{C} \Rightarrow \bigcirc \mathcal{B}_\mathcal{C})$ reduces to $(A_\theta \Rightarrow \bigcirc B_\theta)$.*

Definition 10 (Canonical Merged Step Clause). *Let $\mathcal{C}$ be a colour scheme, $\mathcal{A}_\mathcal{C} \Rightarrow \bigcirc \mathcal{B}_\mathcal{C}$ be a canonical merged derived step clause, and $\gamma \in \mathcal{C}$.*

$$\forall x(\mathcal{A}_\mathcal{C} \wedge A_\gamma(x) \Rightarrow \bigcirc(\mathcal{B}_\mathcal{C} \wedge B_\gamma(x)))$$

is called a canonical merged step clause*. If the truth value of the conjunctions $A_\gamma(x)$, $B_\gamma(x)$ is* **true***, then the canonical merged step clause is just a canonical merged derived step clause. Here, $\gamma \in \mathcal{C}$ abbreviates $\gamma \in \Gamma$, where $\mathcal{C} = (\Gamma, \theta)$.*

Now, given a temporal problem $P = \langle \mathcal{U}, \mathcal{I}, \mathcal{S}, \mathcal{E} \rangle$ we define a finite directed graph G as follows. Every vertex of G is a colour scheme $\mathcal{C}$ for P such that $\mathcal{U} \cup \mathcal{F}_\mathcal{C}$ is satisfiable. For each vertex $\mathcal{C} = (\Gamma, \theta)$, there is an edge in G to $\mathcal{C}' = (\Gamma', \theta')$, if $\mathcal{U} \wedge \mathcal{F}_{\mathcal{C}'} \wedge \mathcal{B}_\mathcal{C}$ is satisfiable. They are the only edges originating from $\mathcal{C}$.

A vertex $\mathcal{C}$ is designated as an *initial* vertex of G if $\mathcal{I} \wedge \mathcal{U} \wedge \mathcal{F}_\mathcal{C}$ is satisfiable.

The *behaviour graph H* of P is the subgraph of G induced by the set of all vertices reachable from the initial vertices.

Definition 11 (Path; Path Segment). *A path, π, through a behaviour graph, H, is a function from $\mathbb{N}$ to the vertices of the graph such that for any $i \geq 0$ there is an edge $\langle \pi(i), \pi(i+1) \rangle$ in H. In the similar way, we define a* path segment *as a function from $[m,n]$, $m < n$, to the vertices of H with the same property.*

Lemma 1. *Let $P_1 = \langle \mathcal{U}_1, \mathcal{I}, \mathcal{S}, \mathcal{E} \rangle$ and $P_2 = \langle \mathcal{U}_2, \mathcal{I}, \mathcal{S}, \mathcal{E} \rangle$ be two problems such that $\mathcal{U}_1 \subseteq \mathcal{U}_2$. Then the behaviour graph of P_2 is a subgraph of the behaviour graph of P_1.*

Definition 12 (Suitability). *For* $\mathcal{C} = (\Gamma, \theta)$ *and* $\mathcal{C}' = (\Gamma', \theta')$, *let* $(\mathcal{C}, \mathcal{C}')$ *be an ordered pair of colour schemes for a temporal problem* P. *An ordered pair of predicate colours* (γ, γ') *where* $\gamma \in \Gamma$, $\gamma' \in \Gamma'$ *is called* suitable *if the formula* $\mathcal{U} \wedge \exists x (F_{\gamma'}(x) \wedge B_{\gamma}(x))$ *is satisfiable. Similarly, an ordered pair of propositional colours* (θ, θ') *is suitable if* $\mathcal{U} \wedge F_{\theta'} \wedge B_{\theta}$ *is satisfiable.*

Note that the satisfiability of $\exists x (F_{\gamma'}(x) \wedge B_{\gamma}(x))$ implies $\models \forall x (F_{\gamma'}(x) \Rightarrow B_{\gamma}(x))$ as the conjunction $F_{\gamma'}(x)$ contains a valuation at x of *all* predicates occurring in $B_{\gamma}(x)$.

Note 3. If an ordered pair (γ, γ') is suitable then for every constant $c \in \text{const}(\mathsf{P})$ we have $x \approx c \in \gamma$ iff $x \approx c \in \gamma'$. It implies that if $x \approx c \in \gamma$, then there exist not more than one γ' and not more than one γ'' such that the pairs (γ, γ') and (γ'', γ) are suitable.

Lemma 2. *Let* H *be the behaviour graph for the problem* $\mathsf{P} = \langle \mathcal{U}, \mathcal{I}, \mathcal{S}, \mathcal{E} \rangle$ *with an edge from a vertex* $\mathcal{C} = (\Gamma, \theta)$ *to a vertex* $\mathcal{C}' = (\Gamma', \theta')$. *Then*

1. *for every* $\gamma \in \Gamma$ *there exists a* $\gamma' \in \Gamma'$ *such that the pair* (γ, γ') *is suitable;*
2. *for every* $\gamma' \in \Gamma'$ *there exists a* $\gamma \in \Gamma$ *such that the pair* (γ, γ') *is suitable;*
3. *the pair of propositional colours* (θ, θ') *is suitable;*

Definition 13 (Run/E-Run). *Let* π *be a path through a behaviour graph* H *of a temporal problem* P, *and* $\pi(i) = (\Gamma_i, \theta_i)$. *By a* run *in* π *we mean a function* $r(n)$ *from* $\mathbb{N}$ *to* $\bigcup_{i \in \mathbb{N}} \Gamma_i$ *such that for every* $n \in \mathbb{N}$, $r(n) \in \Gamma_n$ *and the pair* $(r(n), r(n+1))$ *is suitable. In a similar way, we define a* run segment *as a function from* $[m, n]$, $m < n$, *to* $\bigcup_{i \in \mathbb{N}} \Gamma_i$ *with the same property.*

A run r *is called an* e-run *if for all* $i \geq 0$ *and for every non-ground eventuality* $\Diamond L(x) \in \mathcal{E}$ *there exists* $j > i$ *such that* $L(x) \in r(j)$.

Let π *be a path, the set of all runs in* π *is denoted by* $\mathcal{R}(\pi)$, *and the set of all e-runs in* π *is denoted by* $\mathcal{R}_e(\pi)$. *If* π *is clear, we may omit it.*

A run r is called a *constant run* if $x \approx c \in r(i)$ for some $i \geq 0$. Note that if a run is constant and $x \approx c \in r(i)$ for some $i \geq 0$, then $x \approx c \in r(j)$ for all $j \in \mathbb{N}$. If, for two runs r and r', a constant c, and some $i \geq 0$ we have $x \approx c \in r(i)$ and $x \approx c \in r'(i)$, then $r = r'$.

Let $\rho_{\mathcal{C}}$ be a mapping from $\text{const}(\mathsf{P})$ to Γ such that $x \approx c \in \rho_{\mathcal{C}}(c)$. Then the function defined as $r_c(n) = \rho_{\mathcal{C}_n}(c)$ is the unique constant run "containing" c.

Theorem 6 (Existence of a Model). *Let* $\mathsf{P} = \langle \mathcal{U}, \mathcal{I}, \mathcal{S}, \mathcal{E} \rangle$ *be a temporal problem. Let* H *be the behaviour graph of* P. *If both the set of initial vertices of* H *is non-empty and the following conditions hold*

1. *For every vertex* $\mathcal{C} = (\Gamma, \theta)$, *predicate colour* $\gamma \in \Gamma$, *and non-ground eventuality* $\Diamond L(x) \in \mathcal{E}$, *there exist a vertex* $\mathcal{C}' = (\Gamma, \theta)$ *and a predicate colour* $\gamma' \in \Gamma'$ *such that* $((\mathcal{C}, \gamma) \rightarrow^+ (\mathcal{C}', \gamma') \wedge L(x) \in \gamma')$;
2. *For every vertex* $\mathcal{C} = (\Gamma, \theta)$ *and ground eventuality* $\Diamond l \in \mathcal{E}$ *there exist a vertex* $\mathcal{C}' = (\Gamma, \theta)$ *such that* $(\mathcal{C} \rightarrow^+ \mathcal{C}' \wedge l \in \theta')$;

then P has a model.[4] *Here $(\mathcal{C},\gamma) \to^+ (\mathcal{C}',\gamma')$ denotes that there exists a path π from $\mathcal{C}$ to $\mathcal{C}'$ such that γ and γ' belong to a run in π; $\mathcal{C} \to^+ \mathcal{C}'$ denotes that there exists a path from $\mathcal{C}$ to $\mathcal{C}'$.*

Proof. The proof relies on the following lemma, whose proof was given in [3].

Lemma 3. *Under the conditions of Theorem 6, there exists a path π through H where:*

(a) $\pi(0)$ is an initial vertex of H;
(b) for every colour scheme $\mathcal{C} = \pi(i)$, $i \geq 0$, and every ground eventuality literal $\Diamond l \in \mathcal{E}$ there exists a colour scheme $\mathcal{C}' = \pi(j)$, $j > i$, such that $l \in \theta'$;
(c) for every colour scheme $\mathcal{C} = \pi(i)$, $i \geq 0$, and every predicate colour γ from the colour scheme there exists an e-run $r \in \mathcal{R}_e(\pi)$ such that $r(i) = \gamma$; and
(d) for every constant $c \in \mathrm{const}(P)$, the function $r_c(n)$ defined by $r_c(n) = \rho_{\mathcal{C}_n}(c)$ is an e-run in π.

Let $\pi = \mathcal{C}_0,\ldots,\mathcal{C}_n,\ldots$ be a path through H defined by Lemma 3. Let $\mathcal{G}_0 = \mathcal{I} \cup \{\mathcal{F}_{\mathcal{C}_0}\}$ and $\mathcal{G}_n = \mathcal{F}_{\mathcal{C}_n} \wedge \mathcal{B}_{\mathcal{C}_{n-1}}$ for $n \geq 1$. According to the definition of a behaviour graph, the set $\mathcal{U} \cup \{\mathcal{G}_n\}$ is satisfiable for every $n \geq 0$.

Now, Lemma 8 from [9], that captures properties of the guarded fragment, can be reformulated as follows.

Lemma 4. *Let κ be a cardinal, $\kappa \geq \aleph_0$. For every $n \geq 0$, there exists a model $\mathfrak{M}_n = \langle D, I_n \rangle$ of $\mathcal{U} \cup \{\mathcal{G}_n\}$ such that for every $\gamma \in \Gamma_n$ the set $\{a \in D \mid \mathfrak{M}_n \models F_\gamma(a)\}$ is of cardinality 1 if γ is a constant colour and of cardinality κ otherwise.*

Following [2, 9, 10] take a cardinal $\kappa \geq \aleph_0$ exceeding the cardinality of the set $\mathcal{R}_e$. Let r be a run in $\mathcal{R}_e$. We define the set D_r as $\{\langle r, 0\rangle\}$ if r is a constant run and as $\{\langle r, \xi\rangle \mid \xi < \kappa\}$ otherwise.

Let us define a domain $D = \bigcup_{r \in \mathcal{R}_e} D_r$. For every $n \in \mathbb{N}$ we have $D = \bigcup_{\gamma \in \Gamma_n} D_{(n,\gamma)}$, where $D_{(n,\gamma)} = \{\langle r, \xi\rangle \in D \mid r(n) = \gamma\} = \bigcup_{r \in \mathcal{R}_e,\, r(n)=\gamma} D_r$. Then $|D_{(n,\gamma)}| = 1$ if γ is a constant colour and $|D_{(n,\gamma)}| = \kappa$ otherwise.

Hence, by Lemma 4, for every $n \in \mathbb{N}$ there exists a structure $\mathfrak{M}_n = \langle D, I_n\rangle$ satisfying $\mathcal{U} \cup \{\mathcal{G}_n\}$ such that $D_{(n,\gamma)} = \{\langle r, \xi\rangle \in D \mid \mathfrak{M}_n \models F_\gamma(\langle r, \xi\rangle)\}$. Moreover, $c^{I_n} = \langle r_c, 0\rangle$ for every constant $c \in \mathrm{const}(P)$. A potential first order temporal model is $\mathfrak{M} = \langle D, I\rangle$, where $I(n) = I_n$ for all $n \in \mathbb{N}$. To be convinced of this we have to check validity of the step and eventuality clauses. (Recall that satisfiability of $\mathcal{I}$ in $\mathfrak{M}_0$ is implied by satisfiability of $\mathcal{G}_0$ in $\mathfrak{M}_0$.)

Let $\Box \forall x (L_i(x) \Rightarrow \bigcirc M_i(x))$ be an arbitrary step clause; we show that it is true in $\mathfrak{M}$. Namely, we show that for every $n \geq 0$ and every $\langle r, \xi\rangle \in D$, if $\mathfrak{M}_n \models L_i(\langle r, \xi\rangle)$ then

---

[4] Following [3], in the original version of this paper, Theorem 6 contained one more condition: for every vertex $\mathcal{C} = (\Gamma, \theta)$, non-ground eventuality $L(x) \in \mathcal{E}$, and constant $c \in \mathrm{const}(P)$ there exists a vertex $\mathcal{C}' = (\Gamma, \theta)$ such that $(\mathcal{C} \to^+ \mathcal{C}' \wedge L(x) \in \rho_{\mathcal{C}'}(c))$. This condition was essential for the completeness of the calculus without equality presented in [3], and it led to the introduction of so called *constant flooding*, see [3]. However, one of the referees noticed that, under definitions of this paper (after including equality into consideration), condition (1) already implies the additional condition leading to the obsolescence of constant flooding.

$\mathfrak{M}_{n+1} \models M_i(\langle r,\xi \rangle)$. Suppose $r(n) = \gamma \in \Gamma_n$ and $r(n+1) = \gamma' \in \Gamma'$, where (γ, γ') is a suitable pair in accordance with the definition of a run. It follows that $\langle r,\xi \rangle \in D_{(n,\gamma)}$ and $\langle r,\xi \rangle \in D_{(n+1,\gamma')}$, in other words $\mathfrak{M}_n \models F_\gamma(\langle r,\xi \rangle)$ and $\mathfrak{M}_{n+1} \models F_{\gamma'}(\langle r,\xi \rangle)$. Since $\mathfrak{M}_n \models L_i(\langle r,\xi \rangle)$ then $L_i(x) \in \gamma$. It follows that $M_i(x)$ is a conjunctive member of $B_\gamma(x)$. Since the pair (γ, γ') is suitable, it follows that the conjunction $\exists x(F_{\gamma'}(x) \wedge B_\gamma(x))$ is satisfiable and, moreover, $\models \forall x(F_{\gamma'}(x) \Rightarrow B_\gamma(x))$. Together with $\mathfrak{M}_{n+1} \models F_{\gamma'}(\langle r,\xi \rangle)$ this implies that $\mathfrak{M}_{n+1} \models M_i(\langle r,\xi \rangle)$.

Let $(\Box \forall x)\Diamond L(x)$ be an arbitrary eventuality clause. We show that for every $n \geq 0$ and every $\langle r,\xi \rangle \in D$, $r \in \mathcal{R}_e, \xi < \kappa$, there exists $m > n$ such that $\mathfrak{M}_m \models L(\langle r,\xi \rangle)$. Since r is an e-run, there exists $\mathcal{C}' = \pi(m)$ for some $m > n$ such that $r(m) = \gamma' \in \Gamma'$ and $L(x) \in \gamma'$. It follows that $\langle r,\xi \rangle \in D_{(m,\gamma')}$, that is $\mathfrak{M}_m \models F_{\gamma'}(\langle r,\xi \rangle)$. In particular, $\mathfrak{M}_m \models L(\langle r,\xi \rangle)$.

Propositional step and eventuality clauses are treated in a similar way. $\Box$

5.2   Guarded Monodic Fragment with Equality over Expanding Domains

We here outline how to modify the proof of Theorem 6 for the case of expanding domains. All the definitions and properties from the previous section are transfered here with the following exceptions.

Now, the universally quantified part does not contribute either to $\mathcal{A}$ or $\mathcal{B}$:

$$\mathcal{A}_\mathcal{C} = \bigwedge_{\gamma \in \Gamma} \exists x A_\gamma(x) \wedge A_\theta, \quad \mathcal{B}_\mathcal{C} = \bigwedge_{\gamma \in \Gamma} \exists x B_\gamma(x) \wedge B_\theta.$$

This change affects the suitability of predicate colours.

Lemma 5 (Analog of Lemma 2). *Let H be the behaviour graph for the problem $P = \langle \mathcal{U}, \mathcal{I}, \mathcal{S}, \mathcal{E} \rangle$ with an edge from a vertex $\mathcal{C} = (\Gamma, \theta)$ to a vertex $\mathcal{C}' = (\Gamma', \theta')$. Then*

1. for every $\gamma \in \Gamma$ there exists a $\gamma' \in \Gamma'$ such that the pair (γ, γ') is suitable;
3. the pair of propositional colours (θ, θ') is suitable;

Note that the missing condition (2) of Lemma 2 does not hold in the expanding domain case. However, under the conditions of Lemma 5, if $\gamma' \in \Gamma'$ contains $x \approx c$, there always exists a $\gamma \in \Gamma$ such that the pair (γ, γ') is suitable.

Since for a non-constant predicate colour γ there may not exist a colour γ' such that the pair (γ', γ) is suitable, the notion of a run is reformulated.

Definition 14 (Non-constant Run). *Let π be a path through a behaviour graph H of a temporal problem P. By a non-constant run in π we mean a function $r(n)$ mapping its domain, $dom(r) = \{n \in \mathbb{N} \mid n \geq n_0\}$ for some $n_0 \in \mathbb{N}$, to $\bigcup_{i \in \mathbb{N}} \Gamma_i$ such that for every $n \in dom(r)$, $r(n) \in \Gamma_n$, $r(n)$ is not a constant predicate colour, and the pair $(r(n), r(n+1))$ is suitable. (Constant runs are defined as in the constant domain case.)*

5.3   Monodic Fragment without Equality

Note that the only place where the proof of Theorem 6, given in Section 5.1, and its counterpart for the expanding domain case, given in Section 5.2, need the problem to be guarded is Lemma 4. If a monodic temporal problem P *does not* contain equality, Lemma 4 holds regardless the problem being guarded or not.

Consider the constant domain case (similar reasoning takes place for the expanding domain case). Let $\mathcal{U} \cup \{\mathcal{G}_n\}$ be satisfiable, and let $\mathfrak{M}_n$ be its model. Let $\mathcal{C}_n = (\Gamma_n, \theta_n)$. For a constant $c \in \mathrm{const}(\mathsf{P})$, let us define Γ_c to be $\{\gamma \in \Gamma_n \mid x \approx c \in \gamma\}$; the set Γ_c is a singleton. Let Γ'_n be obtained by eliminating all equations and disequations from Γ_n. Let us define now the formula $\mathcal{F}'_{\mathcal{C}_n}$ as

$$\bigwedge_{\gamma \in \Gamma'_n} \exists x F_\gamma(x) \wedge \bigwedge_{c \in \mathrm{const}(\mathsf{P}), \gamma \in \Gamma_c} F_\gamma(c) \wedge F_{\theta_n} \wedge \forall x \bigvee_{\gamma \in \Gamma'_n} F_\gamma(x).$$

Analogously, we define the formulae $\mathcal{B}'_{\mathcal{C}_n}$ and $\mathcal{G}'_n = \mathcal{F}'_{\mathcal{C}_n} \wedge \mathcal{B}'_{\mathcal{C}_{n-1}}$. It is not hard to see that since $\mathcal{U} \cup \{\mathcal{G}_n\}$ is satisfiable, $\mathcal{U} \cup \{\mathcal{G}'_n\}$ is satisfiable. As $\mathcal{U} \cup \{\mathcal{G}'_n\}$ does not contain equality, from classical model theory, there exists a model $\mathfrak{M}'_n = \langle D', I'_n \rangle$ of $\mathcal{U} \cup \{\mathcal{G}'_n\}$ such that for every $\gamma \in \Gamma'_n$ the set $D'_{(n,\gamma')} = \{a \in D' \mid \mathfrak{M}'_n \models F_\gamma(a)\}$ is of cardinality κ, and for all $c_1, c_2 \in \mathrm{const}(\mathsf{P})$, $I'_n(c_1) = I'_n(c_2)$ iff $I_n(c_1) = I_n(c_2)$. Note that $\mathfrak{M}_n$ is a model for $\mathcal{U} \cup \{\mathcal{G}_n\}$. Obviously, a constant predicate colour γ is true on a single element of the domain D; disequations such as $x \not\approx c$ exclude only finitely many elements.

As already mentioned in Section 4, Note 2, instead of extending P with step clauses of the form (1) and (2), we could consider derived step clauses of the form (6). Completeness of the resulting calculus for the constant domain case has been presented in [3]. Completeness for the expanding domain case can be obtained by combining the proof technique from [3] with the previous section.

6   Fine-Grained Temporal Superposition

The main drawback of the calculi introduced in Section 4 is that the notion of a merged step clause is quite involved and the search for appropriate merging of simpler clauses is computationally hard. Finding *sets* of such full merged step clauses needed for the temporal resolution rule is even more difficult.

This problem has been tackled for the expanding domain case without equality in [11]. The expanding domain case is simpler firstly because merged e-derived step clauses are simpler (formulae of the form (5) do not contribute to them) and, secondly, because conclusions of all inference rules of $\mathfrak{I}_e$ are first-order clauses. We have introduced in [11] a calculus where the inference rules of $\mathfrak{I}_e$ were refined into smaller steps, more suitable for effective implementation. We have also shown that the search for premises for the eventuality resolution rule can be implemented by means of a search algorithm based on step resolution. We called the resulting calculus *fine-grained resolution*.

In the same way as we have used first-order resolution to obtain a complete fine-grained resolution calculus for the expanding domain monodic fragment without equality, we can use first-order superposition to obtain a *fine-grained superposition* calculus for the expanding domain *guarded* monodic fragment *with equality*. In order to do that, we apply ideas from [11] to a first-order superposition decision procedure for the guarded fragment with equality given in [7]. Fine-grained superposition takes as input an augmented temporal problem transformed in clausal form: the universal and initial parts are clausified, as if there is no connection with temporal logic at all.

In contrast to $\mathfrak{I}_e$ which generates only universal formulae, fine-grained superposition might generate initial, universal, or step clauses of the form $C \Rightarrow \bigcirc D$, where C is a *conjunction* of propositional literals and unary literals of the form $L(x)$, $x \approx c$, or $x \not\approx c$; and ground formulae of the form $L(c)$, where $L(x)$, is a unary literal and c is a constant occurring in the originally given problem; D is a *disjunction* of arbitrary literals.

Following [11], we allow only the right-hand side of step clauses to be involved in an inference rule and impose a restriction on mgus. For example, the *step paramodulation* rule will take the following form:

$$\frac{C_1 \Rightarrow \bigcirc(D_1 \vee L[s]) \quad C_2 \Rightarrow \bigcirc(D_2 \vee t \approx u)}{(C_1 \wedge C_2)\sigma \Rightarrow \bigcirc(D_1 \vee D_2 \vee L[u])\sigma} \quad \text{and} \quad \frac{C_1 \Rightarrow \bigcirc(D_1 \vee L[s]) \quad D_2 \vee t \approx u}{C_1\sigma \Rightarrow \bigcirc(D_1 \vee D_2 \vee L[u])\sigma},$$

where $C_1 \Rightarrow \bigcirc(D_1 \vee L[s])$ and $C_2 \Rightarrow \bigcirc(D_2 \vee t \approx u)$ are step clauses, $D_2 \vee t \approx u$ is a universal clause, σ is an mgu of s and t *such that σ does not map variables from C_1 or C_2 (or just from C_1) into a Skolem constant or a Skolem functional term*. This restriction justifies skolemisation: Skolem constants and functions do not "sneak" in the left-hand side of step clauses, and, hence, Skolem constants from different moments of time do not interact.

Other rules of fine-grained superposition can be obtained in a similar way from the rules of the calculus given in [7]. Correctness and completeness of the resulting calculus for the expanding domain guarded monodic fragment with equality can be proved just as the corresponding properties of fine-grained resolution has been proved in [11].

Example 3. Consider a guarded monodic temporal problem, P, unsatisfiable over expanding domains:

$$\mathcal{I} = \{i1.\ c \not\approx d\}, \quad \mathcal{U} = \{u1.\ \forall x(\neg P(x) \vee x \approx c)\}$$
$$\mathcal{S} = \{s1.\ \textbf{true} \Rightarrow \bigcirc P(d)\}, \quad \mathcal{E} = \emptyset.$$

Although this problem is not in DSNF, it can be easily reduced to DSNF by renaming; however, such a reduction would complicate understanding.

First, we give a "course-grained" refutation. The right-hand side of a merged e-derived step clause

$$m1.\ \exists x(x \approx d \wedge x \not\approx c) \Rightarrow \bigcirc \exists x(x \approx d \wedge x \not\approx c \wedge P(d))$$

contradicts to the universal part, and, by the step resolution rule, we conclude $\forall x(x \not\approx d \vee x \approx c)$ which contradicts the initial part.

We show now how fine-grained superposition helps us to find the required merged e-derived step clause $m1$. We need the following step clauses from $\text{aug}_=(\mathsf{P})$:

$$a1.\ y \not\approx d \Rightarrow \bigcirc y \not\approx d \quad \text{and} \quad a2.\ x \approx c \Rightarrow \bigcirc x \approx c.$$

We now derive:
$$
\begin{array}{lll}
s2.\ \textbf{true} & \Rightarrow \bigcirc d \approx c & \text{(resolution } u1 \text{ and } s1\text{)} \\
s3.\ y \not\approx d & \Rightarrow \bigcirc y \not\approx c & \text{(paramodulation } s2 \text{ and } a1\text{)} \\
s4.\ y \not\approx d \wedge x \approx c & \Rightarrow \bigcirc x \not\approx y & \text{(paramodulation } s3 \text{ and } a2\text{)} \\
s5.\ x \not\approx d \wedge x \approx c & \Rightarrow \bigcirc \textbf{false} & \text{(reflexivity resolution } s4\text{)}
\end{array}
$$

We convert the step clause $s5$ into the universal clause $u2.\ x \approx d \vee x \not\approx c$ and resolve with $i1$ giving $i2.\ c \not\approx c$. Finally, we derive an empty clause by reflexivity resolution.

7   Concluding Remarks

In this paper we have considered the basis for mechanising the extension of monodic FOTL by equality. In particular, we have presented resolution calculi for the guarded monodic fragment with equality over both constant and expanding domains. Provided that there exists a first-order decision procedure for side conditions of all inference rules, then these calculi provide the basis for decision procedures. As indicated in section 6, a more practical approach is being developed (for the expanding domain case) based on fine-grained superposition for the guarded monodic fragment. Extension and implementation of this approach represents much of our future work. Finally, we acknowledge support from EPSRC via research grant GR/L87491 and thank the (anonymous) referees of the LPAR conference for their helpful and insightful comments.

References

1. H. Andréka, I. Németi, and J. van Benthem. Modal languages and bounded fragments of predicate logic. *Journal of Philosophical Logic*, 27(3):217–274, 1998.
2. A. Degtyarev and M. Fisher. Towards first-order temporal resolution. In *KI 2001, Proceedings*, volume 2174 of *LNCS*, pages 18–32. Springer, 2001.
3. A. Degtyarev, M. Fisher, and B. Konev. Monodic temporal resolution. In *Proc. CADE-19, to appear*, LNAI. Springer, 2003. Available as Technical report ULCS-03-001 from http://www.csc.liv.ac.uk/research/.
4. A. Degtyarev, M. Fisher, and B. Konev. Monodic temporal resolution: the expanding domain case. Technical Report ULCS-03-004, University of Liverpool, Department of Computer Science, 2003. http://www.csc.liv.ac.uk/research/.
5. A. Degtyarev, M. Fisher, and A. Lisitsa. Equality and Monodic First-Order Temporal Logic. *Studia Logica*, 72:147–156, 2002.
6. M. Fisher. A normal form for temporal logics and its applications in theorem proving and execution. *J. Logic and Computation*, 7(4):429–456, 1997.
7. H. Ganzinger and H. De Nivelle. A superposition decision procedure for the guarded fragment with equality. In *Proc. 14th IEEE Symposium on Logic in Computer Science*, pages 295–305, 1999.
8. E. Grädel. On the restraining power of guards. *J. Symbolic Logic*, 64:1719–1742, 1999.
9. I. Hodkinson. Monodic packed fragment with equality is decidable. *Studia Logica*, 72:185–197, 2002.
10. I. Hodkinson, F. Wolter, and M. Zakharyaschev. Decidable fragments of first-order temporal logics. *Annals of Pure and Applied Logic*, 106:85–134, 2000.
11. B. Konev, A. Degtyarev, C. Dixon, M. Fisher, and U. Hustadt. Towards the implementation of first-order temporal resolution: the expanding domain case. In *Proceedings TIME-ICTL'03*, To appear. Available from http://www.csc.liv.ac.uk/research/.
12. R. Kontchakov, C. Lutz, F. Wolter, and M. Zakharyaschev. Temporalising tableaux. *Studia Logica*, to appear.
13. S. Merz. Decidability and incompleteness results for first-order temporal logic of linear time. *J. Applied Non-Classical Logics*, 2:139–156, 1992.
14. F. Wolter and M. Zakharyaschev. Decidable fragments of first-order modal logics. *J. Symbolic Logic*, 66:1415–1438, 2001.
15. F. Wolter and M. Zakharyaschev. Axiomatizing the monodic fragment of first-order temporal logic. *Annals of Pure and Applied logic*, 118:133–145, 2002.

Once upon a Time in the West
Determinacy, Definability, and Complexity of Path Games[*]

Dietmar Berwanger[1], Erich Grädel[1], and Stephan Kreutzer[2]

[1] Aachen University
[2] University of Edinburgh

Abstract. We study determinacy, definability and complexity issues of path games on finite and infinite graphs.

Compared to the usual format of infinite games on graphs (such as Gale-Stewart games) we consider here a different variant where the players select in each move a path of arbitrary finite length, rather than just an edge. The outcome of a play is an infinite path, the winning condition hence is a set of infinite paths, possibly given by a formula from S1S, LTL, or first-order logic. Such games have a long tradition in descriptive set theory (in the form of Banach-Mazur games) and have recently been shown to have interesting application for planning in nondeterministic domains.

It turns out that path games behave quite differently than classical graph games. For instance, path games with Muller conditions always admit positional winning strategies which are computable in polynomial time. With any logic on infinite paths (defining a winning condition) we can associate a logic on graphs, defining the winning regions of the associated path games. We explore the relationships between these logics. For instance, the winning regions of path games with an S1S-winning condition are definable in the modal mu-calculus. Further, if the winning condition is first-order (on paths), then the winning regions are definable in monadic path logic, or, for a large class of games, even in first-order logic. As a consequence, winning regions of LTL path games are definable in CTL*.

1 Introduction

The Story. Once upon a time, two players set out on an infinite ride through the west. More often than not, they had quite different ideas on where to go, but for reasons that have by now been forgotten they were forced to stay together – as long as they were both alive. They agreed on the rule that each player can determine on every second day, where the ride should go. Of course the riders could go only a finite distance every day; but a day's ride might well lead back to the location where it started in the morning, or where it started a day ago.

---

[*] This research has been partially supported by the European Community Research Training Network "Games and Automata for Synthesis and Validation" (GAMES)

M.Y. Vardi and A. Voronkov (Eds.): LPAR 2003, LNAI 2850, pp. 229–243, 2003.

Hence, one of the players began by choosing the first day's ride: he indicated a finite, non-empty path p_1 from the starting point v; on the second day his opponent selected the next stretch of way, extending p_1 to a finite path $p_1 q_1$; then it was again the turn of the first player to extend the path to $p_1 q_1 p_2$ and so on. After ω days, an infinite ride is completed and it is time for payoff. There were variants of this game where, after a designated number of days, one of the players would be eliminated (these things happened in the west) and the other was to complete the game by himself for the remaining ω days (a very lonesome ride, indeed).

From Descriptive Set Theory to Planning in Nondeterministic Domains. Path games arise also in other contexts than the wild west. They have been studied in descriptive set theory, in the form of *Banach-Mazur games* (see [5, Chapter 6] or [6, Chapter 8.H]). In their original variant (see [7, pp. 113–117], the winning condition is a set W of real numbers; in the first move, one of the players selects an interval d_1 on the real line, then his opponent chooses an interval $d_2 \subset d_1$, then the first player selects a further refinement $d_3 \subset d_2$ and so on. The first player wins if the intersection $\bigcap_{n \in \omega} d_n$ of all intervals contains a point of W, otherwise his opponent wins. This game is essentially equivalent to a path game on the infinite binary tree T^2 or the ω-branching tree T^ω. An important issue in descriptive set theory is determinacy: to characterise the winning conditions W such that one of the two players has a winning strategy for the associated game. This is closely related to topological properties of W (see Section 3).

In a quite different setting, Pistore and Vardi [9] have used path games for task planning in nondeterministic domains. In their scenario, the desired infinite behaviour is specified by formulae in linear temporal logic LTL, and it is assumed that the outcome of actions may be nondeterministic; hence a plan does not have only one possible execution path, but an execution tree. Between weak planning (some possible execution path satisfies the specification) and strong planning (all possible outcomes are consistent with the specification) there is a spectrum of intermediate cases such as strong cyclic planning: every possible partial execution of the plan can be extended to an execution reaching the desired goal. In this context, planning can be modelled by a game between a friendly player E and a hostile player A selecting the outcomes of nondeterministic actions. The game is played on the execution tree of the plan, and the question is whether the friendly player E has a strategy to ensure that the outcome (a path through the execution tree) satisfies the given LTL-specification. In contrast to the path games arising in descriptive set theory, the main interest here are path games with finite alternations between players. For instance, strong cyclic planning corresponds to a AE^ω-game where a single move by A is followed by actions of E. Also the relevant questions are quite different: Rather than determinacy (which is clear for winning conditions in LTL) algorithmic issues play the central role. Pistore and Vardi show that the planning problems in this context can be solved by automata-based methods in 2EXPTIME.

Outline of This Paper. Here we consider path games in a general, abstract setting, but with emphasis on definability and complexity issues. In Section 2 we describe path games and discuss their basic structure. In Section 3 we review the classical results on determinacy of Banach-Mazur games. We then study in Section 4 path games that are positionally determined, i.e., admit winning strategies that only depend on the current position, not on the history of the play. In Section 5 we investigate definability issues. We are interested in the question how the logical complexity of defining a winning condition (a property of infinite paths) is related to the logical complexity of defining who wins the associated game (a property of game graphs). In particular, we will see that the winner of path games with LTL winning conditions is definable in CTL*.

2   Path Games and Their Values

Path games are a class of zero-sum infinite two-player games with complete information, where moves of players consist of selecting and extending finite paths through a graph. The players will be called Ego and Alter (in short E and A). All plays are infinite, and there is a payoff function P, defining for each play a real number. The goal of Ego is to maximise the payoff while Alter wants to minimise it.

A strategy for a player is a function, assigning to every initial segment of a play a next move. Given a strategy f for Ego and a strategy g for Alter in a game $\mathcal{G}$, we write $f\hat{\ }g$ for the unique play defined by f and g, and $P(f\hat{\ }g)$ for its payoff. The values of a game $\mathcal{G}$, from the point of view of Ego and Alter, respectively, are

$$e(\mathcal{G}) := \max_f \min_g P(f\hat{\ }g) \quad \text{and} \quad a(\mathcal{G}) := \min_g \max_f P(f\hat{\ }g).$$

A game is *determined* if $e(\mathcal{G}) = a(\mathcal{G})$. In the case of win-or-lose games, where the payoff of any play is either 0 or 1, this amounts to saying that one of the two players has a winning strategy. For two games $\mathcal{G}$ and $\mathcal{H}$ we write $\mathcal{G} \preceq \mathcal{H}$ if $e(\mathcal{G}) \leq e(\mathcal{H})$ and $a(\mathcal{G}) \leq a(\mathcal{H})$. Finally, $\mathcal{G} \equiv \mathcal{H}$ if $\mathcal{G} \preceq \mathcal{H}$ and $\mathcal{H} \preceq \mathcal{G}$.

Let $G = (V, F, v)$ be an arena (the west), consisting of a directed graph (V, F) without terminal nodes, a distinguished start node v, and let $P : V^\omega \to \mathbb{R}$ be a payoff function that assigns a real number to each infinite path through the graph.

We denote a move where Ego selects a finite path of length ≥ 1 by E and an ω-sequence of such moves by E^ω; for Alter we use corresponding notation A and A^ω. Hence, for any arena G and payoff function P we have the following games.

- $(EA)^\omega(G, P)$ and $(AE)^\omega(G, P)$ are the path games with infinite alternation of finite path moves.
- $(EA)^k E^\omega(G, P)$ and $A(EA)^k E^\omega(G, P)$, for arbitrary $k \in \mathbb{N}$, are the games ending with an infinite path extension by Ego.
- $(AE)^k A^\omega(G, P)$ and $E(AE)^k A^\omega(G, P)$ are the games where Alter chooses the final infinite lonesome ride.

All these games together form the collection Path(G, P) of *path games*. (Obviously two consecutive finite path moves by the same players correspond to a single move, so there is no need for prefixes containing EE or AA.)

It turns out that this infinite collection of games collapses to a finite lattice of just eight different games. This has been observed independently by Pistore and Vardi [9].

Theorem 1. *For every arena G and every payoff function P, we have*

$$E^\omega(G, P) \succeq EAE^\omega(G, P) \succeq AE^\omega(G, P)$$

$$\curlyvee| \qquad\qquad\qquad \curlyvee|$$

$$(EA)^\omega(G, P) \succeq (AE)^\omega(G, P)$$

$$\curlyvee| \qquad\qquad\qquad \curlyvee|$$

$$EA^\omega(G, P) \succeq AEA^\omega(G, P) \succeq A^\omega(G, P)$$

Further, every path game $\mathcal{H} \in \text{Path}(G, P)$ is equivalent to one of these eight games.

Proof. The comparison relations in the diagram follow by trivial arguments. We just illustrate them for one case. To show that $\mathcal{G} \succeq \mathcal{H}$ for $\mathcal{G} = EAE^\omega(G, P)$ and $\mathcal{H} = (EA)^\omega(G, P)$, consider first an optimal strategy f of Ego in $\mathcal{H}$, with $e(\mathcal{H}) = \min_g P(f\hat{\,}g)$. Ego can use this strategy also for $\mathcal{G}$: he just plays as if he would play $\mathcal{G}$, making an arbitrary move whenever it would be A's turn in $\mathcal{H}$. Any play in $\mathcal{G}$ that is consistent with this strategy, is also a play in $\mathcal{H}$ that is consistent with f, and therefore has payoff at least $e(\mathcal{H})$. Hence $e(\mathcal{G}) \geq e(\mathcal{H})$. Second, consider an optimal strategy g of Alter in $\mathcal{G}$, with $a(\mathcal{G}) = \max_f P(f\hat{\,}g)$. In $\mathcal{H} = (EA)^\omega(G, P)$, Alter answers the first move of E as prescribed by g, and moves arbitrarily in all further moves. Again, every play that can be produced against this strategy is also a play of $\mathcal{G}$ that is consistent with g, and therefore has payoff at most $a(\mathcal{G})$. Hence $a(\mathcal{G}) \geq a(\mathcal{H})$. In all other cases the arguments are analogous.

To see that any other path game over G is equivalent to one of those displayed, it suffices to show that

(1) $(EA)^k E^\omega(G, P) \equiv EAE^\omega(G, P)$, for all $k \geq 1$, and
(2) $A(EA)^k E^\omega(G, P) \equiv AE^\omega(G, P)$, for all $k \geq 0$.

By duality, we can then infer the following equivalences: $(AE)^k A^\omega(G, P) \equiv AEA^\omega(G, P)$ for $k \geq 1$ and $E(AE)^k A^\omega(G, P) \equiv EA^\omega(G, P)$ for all $k \geq 0$.

The equivalences (1) and (2) follow with similar reasoning as above. Ego can modify a strategy f for $EAE^\omega(G, P)$ to a strategy for $(EA)^k E^\omega(G, P)$. He chooses the first move according to f and makes arbitrary moves the next $k - 1$ times; he then considers the entire $A(EA)^{k-1}$-sequence of moves, which were played after his first move, as one single move of A in $EAE^\omega(G, P)$ and completes the play again according to f. The resulting play of $(EA)^k E^\omega(G, P)$ is a consistent play with f in $EAE^\omega(G, P)$. Conversely a strategy of Ego for $(EA)^k E^\omega$ also works if his opponent lets Ego move for him in all moves after the first one, i.e., in the game $EAE^\omega(G, P)$. This proves that the e-values of the two games coincide. All other equalities are treated in a similar way.   □

The question arises whether the eight games displayed in the diagram are really different or whether they can be collapsed further. The answer depends on the game graph and the payoff function, but for each comparison $\succeq$ in the diagram we find simple cases where it is strict. Indeed, standard winning conditions $W \subseteq \{0,1\}^\omega$ (defining the payoff function $P(\pi) = 1$ if $\pi \in W$, and $P(\pi) = 0$ otherwise) show that the eight games in the diagram are distinct on appropriate game graphs. Let us consider here the completely connected graph with two nodes 0 and 1.

If the winning condition requires some initial segment ("our journey will start with a ride through the desert") then Ego wins the path games where he moves first and loses those where Alter moves first. Thus, starting conditions separate the left half of the diagram from the right one.

Games with reachability conditions ("some day, there will be the showdown") and safety conditions ("no day without a visit to the saloon") separate games in which only one player moves, i.e. with prefix E^ω or A^ω respectively, from the other ones.

A game with a Büchi condition ("again and again someone will play the harmonica") is won by Ego if he has infinite control and lost if he only has a finite number of finite moves (prefix ending with A^ω). Similarly, Co-Büchi conditions ("some day, he will ride alone toward the sunset and never come back") separate the games which are controlled by Ego from some time onwards (with prefix ending in E^ω) from the others.

3   Determinacy

From now on we consider win-or-lose games, with a winning condition given by a set of plays W. Player E wins the path game if the resulting infinite path belongs to W, otherwise Player A wins.

The topological properties of winning conditions W implying that the associated path games are determined are known from descriptive set theory. We just recall the basic topological notions and the results. In the following section, we will proceed to the issue of *positional determinacy*, i.e. to the question which path games admit winning strategies that only depend on the current position, not on the history of the play.

Note that path games with only finite alternations between the two players are trivially determined, for whatever winning condition; hence we restrict attention to path games with prefix $(EA)^\omega$ or $(AE)^\omega$, and by duality, it suffices to consider $(EA)^\omega$. By unravelling the game graph to a tree, we can embed any game $(EA)^\omega(G, W)$ in a Banach-Mazur game over the ω-branching tree T^ω. The determinacy of Banach-Mazur games is closely related to the Baire property, a notion that arose from topological classifications due to René Baire.

Topology. We consider the space B^ω of infinite sequences over a set B, endowed with the topology whose basic open sets are $O(x) := x \cdot B^\omega$, for $x \in B^*$. A set $L \subseteq B^\omega$ is *open* if it is a union of sets $O(x)$, i.e., if $L = W \cdot B^\omega$ for some $W \subseteq B^*$. A tree $T \subseteq B^*$ is a set of finite words that is closed under prefixes. It is easily seen that $L \subseteq B^\omega$ is *closed* (i.e., the complement of an open set) if L is the set of infinite branches of some tree $T \subseteq B^*$, denoted $L = [T]$. This topological space is called *Cantor space* in case $B = \{0, 1\}$, and *Baire space* in case $B = \omega$.

The class of *Borel sets* is the closure of the open sets under countable union and complementation. Borel sets form a natural hierarchy of classes Σ_η^0 for $1 \leq \eta < \omega_1$, whose first levels are

$$\Sigma_1^0 \quad \text{(or } G) : \quad \text{the open sets}$$
$$\Pi_1^0 \quad \text{(or } F) : \quad \text{the closed sets}$$
$$\Sigma_2^0 \quad \text{(or } F_\sigma) : \quad \text{countable unions of closed sets}$$
$$\Pi_2^0 \quad \text{(or } G_\delta) : \quad \text{countable intersections of open sets}$$

In general, Π_η^0 contains the complements of the Σ_η^0-sets, $\Sigma_{\eta+1}^0$ is the class of countable unions of Π_η^0-sets, and $\Sigma_\lambda^0 = \bigcup_{\eta < \lambda} \Sigma_\eta^0$ for limit ordinals λ.

We recall that a set X in a topological space is *nowhere dense* if its closure does not contain a non-empty open set. A set is *meager* if it is a union of countably many nowhere dense sets and it has the *Baire property* if its symmetric difference with some open set is meager. In particular, every Borel set has the Baire property.

We are now ready to formulate the Theorem of Banach and Mazur (see e.g. [5, 6]). To keep in line with our general notation for path games we write $(EA)^\omega(T^\omega, W)$ for the Banach-Mazur game on the ω-branching tree with winning condition W.

Theorem 2 (Banach-Mazur). *(1) Player A has a winning strategy for the game $(EA)^\omega(T^\omega, W)$ if, and only if, W is meager.*

(2) Player E has a winning strategy for $(EA)^\omega(T^\omega, W)$ if, and only if, there exists a finite word $x \in \omega^*$ such that $x \cdot \omega^\omega \setminus W$ is meager (i.e., W is co-meager in some basic open set).

As a consequence, it can be shown that for any class $\Gamma \subseteq \mathcal{P}(\omega^\omega)$ that is closed under complement and under union with open sets, all games $(EA)^\omega(T^\omega, W)$ with $W \in \Gamma$ are determined if, and only if, all sets in Γ have the Baire property. Since Borel sets have the Baire property, it follows that Banach-Mazur games are determined for Borel winning conditions. (Via a coding argument, this can also been easily derived form Martin's Theorem, saying that Gale-Stewart games with Borel winning conditions are determined.)

Standard winning conditions used in applications (in particular the winning conditions that can be described in S1S) are contained in very low levels of the Borel hierarchy. Hence all path games of this form are determined.

4 Positional Determinacy

In general, winning strategies can be very complicated. However, there are interesting classes of games that are determined via relatively simple winning strategies. Of particular interest are *positional* (also called *memoryless*) strategies which only depend on the current position, not on the history of the play. On a game graph $G = (V, F)$ a positional strategy has the form $f : V \to V^*$ assigning to every move v a finite path from v through G.

To start, we present a simple example of a path game, that is determined, but does not admit a positional strategy.

Example 3. Let G_2 be the completely connected directed graph with nodes 0 and 1, and let the winning condition for Ego be the set of infinite sequences with infinitely many initial segments that contain more ones than zeros. Clearly, Ego has a winning strategy for $(EA)^\omega(G, W)$, but not a positional one.

Note that this winning condition is on the $\boldsymbol{\Pi}_2$-level of the Borel hierarchy. It has been pointed out by Jacques Duparc, that this is the lowest level with such an example.

Proposition 4. *If Ego has a winning strategy for a path game $(EA)^\omega(G, W)$ with $W \in \boldsymbol{\Sigma}_2^0$, then he also has a positional winning strategy.*

Proof. Let $G = (V, F)$ be the game graph. Since W is a countable union of closed sets, we have $W = \bigcup_{n<\omega}[T_n]$ where each $T_n \subseteq V^*$ is a tree. Further, let f be any (non-positional) winning strategy for Ego. We claim that, in fact, Ego can win with one move.

We construct this move by induction. Let x_1 be the initial path chosen by Ego according to f. Let $i \geq 1$ and suppose that we have already constructed a finite path $x_i \notin \bigcup_{n<i} T_n$. If $x_i y \in T_i$ for all finite y, then all infinite plays extending x_i remain in W, hence Ego wins with the initial move $w = x_i$. Otherwise choose some y_i such that $x_i y_i \notin T_i$, and suppose that Alter prolongs the play from x_i to $x_i y_i$. Let $x_{i+1} := f(x_i y_i)$ the result of the next move of Ego, according to his winning strategy f.

If this process did not terminate, then it would produce an infinite play that is consistent with f and won by Alter. Since f is a winning strategy for Ego, this is impossible. Hence there exists some $m < \omega$ such that $x_m y \in T_m$ for all y. Thus, if Ego moves to x_m in his opening move, then he wins, no matter how the play proceeds afterwards. In particular, Ego wins with a positional strategy. $\square$

While many important winning conditions are outside $\boldsymbol{\Sigma}_2^0$, they may well be Boolean combinations of $\boldsymbol{\Sigma}_2^0$-sets. For instance, this is the case for parity conditions, Muller conditions, and more generally, S1S-definable winning conditions. In the classical framework of infinite games on graphs (where moves are along edges rather than paths) it is well-known that parity games admit positional winning strategies, whereas there are simple games with Muller conditions that require strategies with some memory. We will see that for path games, the class of winning conditions admitting positional winning strategies is much larger than for classical graph games.

Let $G = (V, F)$ be a game graph with a colouring $\lambda : V \to C$ of the nodes with a finite number of colours. The winning condition is given by an ω-regular set $W \subseteq C^\omega$ which is defined by a formula in some appropriate logic over infinite paths. In the most general case, we have S1S-formulae (i.e. MSO-formulae on infinite paths with vocabulary $\{<\} \cup \{P_c : c \in C\}$) but we will also consider weaker formalisms like first-order logic or, equivalently, LTL.

Muller and Parity Conditions. As we mentioned before, typical examples of winning conditions for which strategies require memory on single-step games are Muller conditions. Such a condition is specified by a family $\mathcal{F} \subseteq 2^C$ of winning sets; a play is winning if the set of colours seen infinitely often belongs to $\mathcal{F}$.

Proposition 5. *All Muller path games* $(EA)^\omega(G, \mathcal{F})$ *and* $(AE)^\omega(G, \mathcal{F})$ *admit positional winning strategies.*

Proof. We will write $w \geq v$ to denote that position w is reachable from position v. For every position $v \in V$, let $C(v)$ be the set of colours reachable from v, that is, $C(v) := \{\lambda(w) : w \geq v\}$. Obviously, $C(w) \subseteq C(v)$ whenever $w \geq v$. In case $C(w) = C(v)$ for all $w \geq v$, we call v a *stable* position. Note that from every $u \in V$ some stable position is reachable. Further, if v is stable, then every reachable position $w \geq v$ is stable as well.

We claim that Ego has a winning strategy in $(EA)^\omega(G, \mathcal{F})$ iff there is a stable position v that is reachable from the initial position v_0, so that $C(v) \in \mathcal{F}$.

To see this, let us assume that there is such a stable position v with $C(v) \in \mathcal{F}$. Then, for every $u \geq v$, we choose a path p from u so that, when moving along p, each colour of $C(u) = C(v)$ is visited at least once, and set $f(u) := p$. In case v_0 is not reachable from v, we assign $f(v_0)$ to some path that leads from v_0 to v. Now f is a positional winning strategy for Ego in $(EA)^\omega(G, \mathcal{F})$, because, after the first move, no colours other then those in $C(v)$ are seen. Moreover, every colour in $C(v)$ is visited at each move of Ego, hence, infinitely often.

Conversely, if for every stable position v reachable from v_0 we have $C(v) \notin \mathcal{F}$, we can construct a winning strategy for Alter in a similar way. □

Note that in a finite arena all positions of a strongly connected component that is terminal, i.e., with no outgoing edges, are stable. Thus, the above characterisation translates as follows: Ego wins the game iff there is a terminal component whose set of colours belongs to $\mathcal{F}$. Obviously this can be established in linear time w.r.t. the size of the arena and the description of $\mathcal{F}$.

Corollary 6. *On a finite arena* G, *path games with a Muller winning condition* $\mathcal{F}$ *can be solved in time* $O(|G| \cdot |\mathcal{F}|)$.

We remark that solving single-step graph games with Muller winning condition is PSPACE-complete. We are not aware of any reference where this is stated explicitly, but it is not too difficult to derive this from the analysis presented in [1].

A special case of the Muller condition is the parity condition. Given an arena $G = (V, F)$ with positions coloured by a priority function $\Omega : V \to \mathbb{N}$ of finite range, this condition requires that the least priority seen infinitely often on a play is even. It turns out that path games with parity conditions are positionally determined for any game prefix. (By Theorem 1 we can restrict attention to the eight prefixes $E^\omega, A^\omega, AE^\omega, EA^\omega, EAE^\omega, AEA^\omega, (EA)^\omega$, and $(AE)^\omega$.)

Proposition 7. *Every parity path game* $\gamma(G, \text{parity})$ *is determined via a positional winning strategy.*

General S1S-**Winning Conditions.** In the following, we will use parity games as an instrument to investigate path games with winning conditions specified in the monadic second-order logic of paths, S1S. It is well known that every S1S-definable class of infinite words can be recognised by a deterministic parity automaton (see e.g. [2]). For words over the set of colours C, such an automaton has the form $\mathcal{A} = (Q, C, q_0, \delta, \Omega)$, where Q is a finite set of states, q_0 the initial state, $\delta : Q \times C \to Q$ a deterministic transition function, and $\Omega : Q \to \mathbb{N}$ a priority function. Given an input word, a run of $\mathcal{A}$ starts at the first word position in state q_0; if, at the current position v the automaton is in state q, it proceeds to the next position assuming the state $\delta(q, \lambda(v))$. The input is accepted if the least priority of a state occurring infinitely often in the run is even.

Via a reduction to parity games, we will first show that S1S-games admit finite-memory (or, automatic) strategies. By refining these, we will then establish strategies that are independent of the memory state, that is, positional.

Proposition 8. *For any winning condition* $\psi \in$ S1S *and any game prefix* γ, *the path games* $\gamma(G, \psi)$ *admit finite-memory winning strategies.*

Proof. Let $\mathcal{A} = (Q, C, q_0, \delta, \Omega)$ be an automaton that recognises the set of words defined by ψ. Given an arena $G = (V, E)$ with starting position v_0, we define the *synchronised product* $G \times \mathcal{A}$ to be the arena with positions $V \times Q$, edges from (v, q) to (v', q') whenever $(v, v') \in E$ and $\delta(q, \lambda(v)) = q'$, and designated starting position (v_0, q_0). We will use two sets of colours for $G \times \mathcal{A}$: one inherited from G, $\lambda(v, q) := \lambda(v)$, and the other one inherited from $\mathcal{A}$, $\Omega(v, q) := \Omega(q)$. When referring to a specific colouring we write, respectively, $G \times \mathcal{A}\!\restriction_\lambda$ and $G \times \mathcal{A}\!\restriction_\Omega$. Between the games on G and $G \times \mathcal{A}$ we can observe a strong relationship.

(1) For every prefix γ, a play starting from position (v_0, q_0) is winning in $\gamma(G \times \mathcal{A}\!\restriction_\lambda, \psi)$ if, and only if, it is winning in $\gamma(G \times \mathcal{A}\!\restriction_\Omega, \text{parity})$.
(2) The arenas G, v_0 and $G \times \mathcal{A}\!\restriction_\lambda, (v_0, q_0)$ are bisimilar.

The first assertion follows from the meaning of the automaton $\mathcal{A}$, and entails a strategical equivalence between the two games: Any winning strategy in $\gamma(G \times \mathcal{A}\!\restriction_\Omega, \text{parity})$ is also a winning strategy in $\gamma(G \times \mathcal{A}\!\restriction_\lambda, \psi)$ and vice versa. By Proposition 7, there always exists a positional winning strategy for the former game and, hence, for the latter one as well.

The second statement holds because $\mathcal{A}$ is deterministic. It implies that every winning strategy for a path game $\gamma(G, \psi)$ starting from position v_0 is also a winning strategy for the game $\gamma(G \times \mathcal{A}, \psi)$ starting from (v_0, q_0). Conversely, every winning strategy f for the latter game induces a winning strategy f' for the former one, namely $f'(v, s) := f((v, q'), s)$ where $q' := \delta(q_0, s)$ is the state reached by the automaton after processing the word s. Since f can be chosen to be positional, we obtain a winning strategy f' on $\gamma(G, \psi)$ that does not depend on the entire history, but only on a finite memory, namely the set of states Q. □

Note that the finite-memory strategy f' constructed above does not yet need to be positional, since a position v in G has several copies (v, q) in $G \times \mathcal{A}$ at which the prescriptions of f may differ. In order to obtain a state-independent winning strategy for $\gamma(G, \psi)$ we will unify, for each node $v \in V$, the prescriptions $f(v, q)$ for those position (v, q) which are reachable in a play of according to f.

Theorem 9. *For any winning condition $\psi \in \mathrm{S1S}$, the games $(EA)^\omega(G, \psi)$ and $(AE)^\omega(G, \psi)$ admit positional winning strategies.*

Proof. Let us assume that Ego wins the game $(EA)^\omega(G, \psi)$ starting from position v_0. We will base our argumentation on the game $(EA)^\omega(G \times \mathcal{A}, \psi)$, where Ego has a positional winning strategy f.

For any $v \in V$, we denote by $Q_f(v)$ the set of states q so that the position (v, q) can be reached from position (v_0, q_0) in a play according to f:

$$Q_f(v) := \{\delta(q_0, s) : s \text{ prolongs } f(v_0, q_0) \text{ and leads to } v\}.$$

Let $\{q_1, q_2, \dots, q_n\}$ be an enumeration of $Q_f(v)$, in which the initial state q_0 is taken first, in case it belongs to $Q_f(v)$. We construct a path associated to v along the following steps. First, set $p_1 := f(v, q_1)$; for $1 < i \le n$, let (v', q') be the node reached after playing the path $p_1 \cdot p_2 \cdots p_{i-1}$ from position (v, q_i) and set $p_i := f(v', q')$. Finally, let $f'(v)$ be the concatenation of $p_1, p_2, \dots, p_n$.

Now, consider a play on $(EA)^\omega(G \times \mathcal{A}, \psi)$ in which Ego chooses the path $f'(v)$ at any node $(v, q) \in V \times Q$. This way, the play will start with $f(q_0, v_0)$. Further, at any position (v, q) at which Ego moves, the prescription $f'(v)$ contains some segment of the form $(v', q') \cdot f(v', q')$. In other words, every move of Ego has some "good part" which would also have been produced by f at the position (v', q'). But this means that the play cannot be distinguished, post-hoc, from a play where Ego always moved according to the strategy f while all the "bad parts" were produced by Alter. Accordingly, Ego wins every play of $(EA)^\omega(G \times \mathcal{A}, \psi)$ starting from (q_0, v_0).

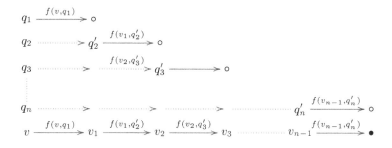

Fig. 1. Merging strategies at node v

This proves that f' is a positional strategy for Ego in the game $(EA)^\omega(G \times \mathcal{A}, \psi)$. Since the values do not depend on the second component, f' induces a positional strategy for Ego in $(EA)^\omega(G, \psi)$.

The same construction works for the case $(AE)^\omega(G, \psi)$, if we take instead of $Q_f(v)$ the set $Q(v) := \{\delta(q_0, s) : s \text{ is a path from } v_0 \text{ to } v\}$. $\square$

The above proof relies upon the fact that the players always take turns. If we consider games where the players alternate only finitely many times, the situation changes. Intuitively, a winning strategy of the solitaire player eventually forms an infinite path which may not be broken apart into finite pieces to serve as a positional strategy.

Proposition 10. *For any prefix γ with finitely many alternations between the players, there are arenas G and winning conditions $\psi \in \text{S1S}$ so that no positional strategy is winning in the game $\gamma(G, \psi)$.*

Proof. Consider, for instance, the arena G_2 from Example 3 and a winning condition $\psi \in \text{S1S}$ that requires the number of zeroes occurring in a play to be odd. When starting from position 1, Ego obviously has winning strategies for each of the games $E^\omega(G, \psi)$, $AE^\omega(G, \psi)$, and $EAE^\omega(G, \psi)$, but no positional ones. $\square$

Nevertheless, these games are positionally determined for one of the players. Indeed, if a player wins a game $\gamma(G, \psi)$ finally controlled by his opponent, he always has a positional winning strategy. This is trivial when $\gamma \in \{E^\omega, A^\omega, AE^\omega, EA^\omega\}$; for the remaining cases EAE^ω and AEA^ω a positional strategy can be constructed as in the proof of Theorem 9.

Finally we consider winning conditions that do not depend on initial segments. We say that ψ is a *future*-formula, if, for any ω-word π and any finite words x and y, we have $x\pi \models \psi$ if, and only if, $y\pi \models \psi$.

Theorem 11. *For any winning condition $\psi \in \text{S1S}$ specified by a future-formula and every prefix γ, the games $\gamma(G, \psi)$ admit a positional winning strategies.*

Proof. The core of our argument consists in showing that, given a solitaire game $E^\omega(G, \psi)$, Ego has a uniform positional winning strategy that works for all starting positions in his winning region W.

We again consider the game $E^\omega(G \times \mathcal{A}\!\restriction_\Omega, \text{parity})$ (as in the proof of Theorem 9). When playing solitaire, path games do not differ from single-step games, and it is well known that parity games admit winning strategies that are uniform on the entire winning region. Let f be such a strategy. We use f to define a positional strategy f' for $\exists^\omega(G, \psi)$ as follows. Starting from any winning position (v_0, q_0) in $E^\omega(G \times \mathcal{A}\!\restriction_\Omega, \text{parity})$, let $(v_n, q_n)_{n < \omega}$ be the unique play according to f. There are two cases. If the play visits only finitely many different positions, we have $(v_i, q_i) = (v_j, q_j)$ for some i, j and set $f'(v_0) := v_0, v_1, \ldots, v_i$ and $f'(v_i) := v_{i+1}, \ldots, v_j$ (overwriting $f'(v_0)$ if $v_i = v_0$). Otherwise, there are infinitely many positions (v_j, q_j) where v_j is fresh, in the sense that $v_j \neq v_i$ for all $i < j$. In that case, we assign to each fresh position v_j the path $f'(v_j) := v_{j+1}, \ldots, v_k$ which leads to the next fresh position v_k in the play. Next, for every node v where f' is still undefined but from which a position $v' \in \text{dom}(f')$ is reachable in G, we choose a path t from v to v' and set $f'(v) := t$. After this, if $\text{dom}(f')$ does not yet contain the entire winning region W of Ego, we take a new starting position $(v'_0, q_0) \in W$ with $v'_0 \in V \setminus \text{dom}(f')$, and proceed as above, through a possibly transfinite number of stages, until f' is defined on all nodes in W.

We claim that f' is a winning strategy on W. Consider any play π' in $E^\omega(G, \psi)$ that starts at some $v \in W$ and that is consistent with f'. By the construction of f' there exists a play π in the arena $G \times \mathcal{A}$, consistent with f, such that the projection of π to G differs from π' only by an initial segment. Now π is a winning play for Ego in $E^\omega(G \times \mathcal{A} \restriction \Omega, \text{parity})$ and therefore also for $\exists^\omega(G \times \mathcal{A} \restriction \lambda, \psi)$ (see item (1) in the proof of Theorem 9). By item (2), and since ψ is a future condition this implies that π' is winning for Ego in the game $E^\omega(G, \psi)$.

The case AE^ω follows now immediately since Ego wins $AE^\omega(G, \psi)$ if all positions v reachable from v_0 are in his winning region. For the case EAE^ω, let g be a winning strategy for Ego. If $g(v_0)$ leads to a position v from which v_0 is again reachable, then f' (constructed above for $E^\omega(G, \psi)$ is a winning strategy also for $EAE^\omega(G, \psi)$. Otherwise, we may change f' for the initial position by $f'(v_0) := g(v_0)$ to obtain a positional winning strategy. The other cases follow by duality.   □

5   Definability

We now study the question in what logics (MSO, μ-calculus, FO, CTL*, ...) winning positions of path games with ω-regular winning conditions can be defined. Given any formula φ from a logic on infinite paths (like S1S or LTL) and a quantifier prefix γ for path games, we define the game formula $\gamma.\varphi$, to be evaluated over game graphs, with the meaning that

$$G \models \gamma.\varphi \iff \text{Player } E \text{ wins the path game } \gamma(G, \varphi).$$

Note that the operation $\varphi \mapsto \gamma.\varphi$ maps a formula over infinite paths to a formula over graphs. Given a logic L over infinite paths, and a prefix γ, let $\gamma.L := \{\gamma.\varphi : \varphi \in L\}$. As usual we write $L \leq L'$ to denote that every formula in the logic L is equivalent to some formula from the logic L'.

Our main definability result can be stated as follows.

Theorem 12. *For any game prefix γ,*

(1) $\gamma.\text{S1S} \leq L_\mu$
(2) $\gamma.\text{LTL} \equiv \gamma.\text{FO} \leq \text{CTL}^*$.

Obviously, the properties expressed by formulae $\gamma.\varphi$ are invariant under bisimulation. This has two relevant consequences:

(a) We can restrict attention to trees (obtained for instance by unravelling the given game graph from the start node).
(b) It suffices to show that, on trees, γ. S1S $\leq$ MSO, and γ. FO $\leq$ MPL where MPL is *monadic path logic*, i.e., monadic second-order logic where second-order quantification is restricted to infinite paths.

Indeed, it has been proved by Janin and Walukiewicz [4] that every bisimulation-invariant class of trees that is MSO-definable is also definable in the modal μ-calculus. Similarly, it is known from results by Hafer and Thomas [3] and by Moller and Rabinovitch [8], that every bisimulation invariant property of trees expressible in MPL is also expressible in CTL*.

Proposition 13. *On trees, $(EA)^\omega$. S1S $\leq$ MSO and $(AE)^\omega$. S1S $\leq$ MSO.*

Proof. Let $x \leq y$ denote that y is reachable from x. A strategy for Player E in a game $(EA)^\omega(T,W)$ on a tree $T = (V,F)$ is a partial function $f : V \to V$, such that $w < f(w)$ for every w; it is winning if every infinite path through T containing $f(\varepsilon), y_1, f(y_1), y_2, f(y_2)\ldots$, where $f(y_i) < y_{i+1}$ for all i, satisfies W. An equivalent description can be given in terms of the set $X = f(V)$. A set $X \subseteq V$ defines a winning strategy for Player E in the game $(EA)^\omega(T,W)$ if

(1) $(\forall x \in X)\forall y(x < y \to (\exists z \in X)(y < z))$
(2) every path hitting X infinitely often is in W (i.e. is winning for Player E)
(3) X is non-empty.

Clearly these conditions are expressible in MSO. For the game $(AE)^\omega(G,W)$ we only have to replace (3) by the condition that the start node v is contained in X. □

Proposition 14. *Let γ be a game prefix with a bounded number of alternations between E and A. Then γ. S1S $\leq$ MSO and γ. FO $\leq$ MPL.*

Proof. Every move is represented by a path quantification; by relativizing the formula φ that defines the winning condition to the infinite path produced by the players, we obtain an MSO-formula expressing that Player E has a winning strategy for the game given by γ and φ. If φ a first-order formula over paths, then the entire formula remains in MPL. □

The most interesting case concerns winning conditions defined in first-order logic (or equivalently, LTL). In our proof, we will use a normal form for first-order logic on infinite paths (with $<$) that has been established by Thomas [10]. Recall that a first-order formula $\varphi(\overline{x})$ is *bounded* if it only contains bounded quantifiers of form $(\exists y \leq x_i)$ or $(\forall y \leq x_i)$.

Proposition 15. *On infinite paths, every first-order formula is equivalent to a formula of the form*

$$\bigvee_i \left(\exists x(\forall y \geq x)\varphi_i \wedge \forall y(\exists z \geq y)\vartheta_i \right)$$

where φ_i and ϑ_i are bounded.

Theorem 16. *On trees,* $(EA)^\omega.\text{FO} \leq \text{FO}$ *and* $(AE)^\omega.\text{FO} \leq \text{FO}$.

Proof. Let $\psi = \bigvee_i \left(\exists x (\forall y \geq x) \varphi_i \wedge \forall y (\exists z \geq y) \vartheta_i \right)$ be a first-order formula on infinite paths describing a winning condition. We claim that, on trees, $(EA)^\omega \psi$ is equivalent to the first-order formula

$$\psi^* := (\exists p_1)(\forall p_2 \geq p_1)(\exists p_3 \geq p_2) \bigvee_{i \in I} \psi_i^{(b)} \quad \text{where}$$

$$\psi_i^{(b)} := (\exists x \leq p_1)(\forall y . x \leq y \leq p_2)\varphi_i \wedge (\forall y \leq p_2)(\exists z . y \leq z \leq p_3)\vartheta_i.$$

Let $T = (V, E)$ and suppose first that Alter has a winning strategy for the game $(EA)^\omega(T, \psi)$. We prove that $T \models \neg\psi^*$. To see this we have to define an appropriate Skolem function $g : p_1 \mapsto p_2$ such that for all $p_3 \geq p_2$ and all $i \in I$

$$T \models \neg\psi_i^{(b)}(p_1, p_2, p_3).$$

Fix any p_1 which we can consider as the first move of Ego in the game $(EA)^\omega(T, \psi)$ and any play P (i.e., any infinite path through T) that prolongs this move and that is consistent with Alter's winning strategy. Since Alter wins, we have that $P \models \neg\psi$. Hence there exists some $J \subseteq I$ such that

$$P \models \bigwedge_{i \in J} \forall x (\exists y \geq x) \neg\varphi_i \wedge \bigwedge_{i \in I - J} \exists y (\forall z \geq y) \neg\vartheta_i.$$

To put it differently, there exist

- for every $i \in J$ and every $a \in P$ a witness $h_i(a) \in P$ such that $P \models \neg\varphi_i(a, h_i(a))$, and
- for every $i \in I - J$ an element b_i such that $P \models (\forall z \geq b_i) \neg\vartheta_i(b_i, z)$.

Now set

$$p_2 := \max(\{h_i(a) : a \leq p_1, i \in J\} \cup \{b_i : i \in I - J\}).$$

For any p_3 we now obviously have that $T \models \neg\psi_i^{(b)}(p_1, p_2, p_3)$.

For the converse, let $f : V \to V$ be a winning strategy for Ego in the game $(EA)^\omega(T, \psi)$. We claim that $T \models \psi^*$. Toward a contradiction, suppose that $T \models \neg\psi^*$. Hence there exists a Skolem function $g : V \to V$ assigning to each p_1 an appropriate $p_2 \geq p_1$ such that $T \models \neg\psi_i^{(b)}(p_1, p_2, p_3)$ for all $p_3 \geq p_2$ and all $i \in I$. We can view g as a strategy for Alter in the game $(EA)^\omega(T, \psi)$. If Ego plays according to f and Alter plays according to g, then the resulting infinite play $f\,\hat{}\,g = q_1 q_2 q_3 \ldots$ satisfies ψ (because f is a winning strategy). Hence there exists some $i \in I$ such that

$$f\,\hat{}\,g \models \exists x (\forall y \geq x) \varphi_i \wedge \forall y (\exists z \geq y) \vartheta_i.$$

Let a be a witness for x so that $f\,\hat{}\,g \models (\forall y \geq a)\varphi_i(a, y)$. Choose the minimal odd k, such that $a \leq q_k$, and set $p_1 := q_k$. Then $q_{k+1} = g(q_k) = g(p_1) = p_2$. Since $f\,\hat{}\,g \models \forall y (\exists z \geq y)\vartheta_i(y, z)$, we have, in particular, for every $b \leq p_2$ a witness

$h(b) \geq b$ on $f \hat{\ } g$ such that $f \hat{\ } g \models \vartheta_i(b, h(b))$. Choose $p_3 = \max\{h(b) : b \leq p_2\}$ It follows that $f \hat{\ } g \models \psi_i^{(b)}(p_1, p_2, p_3)$. Since $\psi_i^{(b)}$ is bounded, its evaluation on T is equivalent to its evaluation on $f \hat{\ } g$. Hence we have shown that there exists p_1 such that for $p_2 = g(p_1)$, given by the Skolem function g, we can find a p_3 with $T \models \psi_i^{(b)}(p_1, p_2, p_3)$. But this contradicts the assumption that g is an appropriate Skolem function for $\neg\psi^*$.

We have shown that whenever Ego has a winning strategy for $(EA)^\omega(T, \psi)$ then $T \models \psi^*$ and whenever Alter has a winning strategy, then $T \models \neg\psi^*$. By contraposition and determinacy, the reverse implications also hold. For games of form $(AE)^\omega(T, \psi)$ the arguments are analogous. □

Theorem 12 is implied by Propositions 13, Proposition 14, and Theorem 16.

Acknowledgement

We are grateful to Jacques Duparc for information on descriptive set theory and for pointing out Proposition 4 to us.

References

[1] S. DZIEMBOWSKI, M. JURDZIŃSKI, AND I. WALUKIEWICZ, *How much memory is needed to win infinite games?*, in Proceedings of 12th Annual IEEE Symposium on Logic in Computer Science (LICS 97), 1997, pp. 99–110.

[2] E. GRÄDEL, W. THOMAS, AND T. WILKE, eds., *Automata, Logics, and Infinite Games*, Lecture Notes in Computer Science Nr. 2500, Springer, 2002.

[3] T. HAFER AND W. THOMAS, *Computation tree logic CTL* and path quantifiers in the monadic theory of the binary tree*, in Automata, Languages and Programming, 14th International Colloquium, ICALP87, Lecture Notes in Computer Science Nr. 267, Springer, 1987, pp. 269–279.

[4] D. JANIN AND I. WALUKIEWICZ, *On the expressive completeness of the propositional mu-calculus with respect to monadic second order logic*, in Proceedings of 7th International Conference on Concurrency Theory CONCUR '96, no. 1119 in Lecture Notes in Computer Science, Springer-Verlag, 1996, pp. 263–277.

[5] A. KANAMORI, *The Higher Infinite*, Springer, 1991.

[6] A. KECHRIS, *Classical Descriptive Set Theory*, Springer, 1995.

[7] R. MAULDIN, ed., *The Scottish Book. Mathematics from the Scottish Café*, Birkhäuser, 1981.

[8] F. MOLLER AND A. RABINOVITCH, *Counting on CTL*: On the expressive power of monadic path logic*, Information and Computation, (2003). To appear.

[9] M. PISTORE AND M. VARDI, *The planning spectrum — one, two, three, infinity*, in Proc. 18th IEEE Symp. on Logic in Computer Science, 2003.

[10] W. THOMAS, *A combinatorial approach to the theory of omega-automata*, Information and Control, 48 (1981), pp. 261–283.

Ordered Diagnosis

Davy Van Nieuwenborgh* and Dirk Vermeir**

Dept. of Computer Science, Vrije Universiteit Brussel, VUB,
{dvnieuwe,dvermeir}@vub.ac.be

Abstract. We propose to regard a diagnostic system as an ordered logic theory, i.e. a partially ordered set of clauses where smaller rules carry more preference. This view leads to a hierarchy of the form *observations < system description < fault model*, between the various knowledge sources. It turns out that the semantics for ordered logic programming nicely fits this intuition: if the observations contradict the normal system behavior, then the semantics will provide an explanation from the fault rules. The above model can be refined, without adding additional machinery, to support e.g. problems where there is a clear preference among possible explanations or where the system model itself has a complex structure. Interestingly, these extensions do not increase the complexity of the relevance or necessity decision problems. Finally, the mapping to ordered logic programs also provides a convenient implementation vehicle.

1 Introduction

Diagnostic reasoning involves finding explanations, i.e. sets of causes, that explain certain observations. The topic has received a great deal of attention over the years, with important applications, e.g. in medicine [29].

There are two main approaches to the theory of model-based diagnosis[1].

In *consistency-based* diagnosis [25], one uses a model of the normal structure and behavior of the system under consideration. This model is typically formulated in terms of components and their relationship where, roughly, a proposition p asserts that a component p is functioning correctly. Rules such as $e \leftarrow p, q$ can be used to assert that the effect e will occur if both p and q are in working order. An observation that does not conform to the normal predicted behavior then leads to an inconsistency. E.g. the observation $\neg e$ is inconsistent with the assumption that p and q are both true (functioning correctly). Finding an explanation involves removing this inconsistency by withdrawing some assumptions on the correct functioning of some components. In the above example, both $\{\neg p\}$ ("p is faulty") and both $\{\neg q\}$ ("q is faulty") are acceptable explanations of the observation $\neg e$, as is $\{\neg p, \neg q\}$. The approach has been applied in several areas such as fault finding in electronic circuits [5].

* Supported by the FWO
** This work was partially funded by the Information Society Technologies programme of the European Commission, Future and Emerging Technologies under the IST-2001-37004 WASP project

[1] Other approaches that have been proposed in the literature include e.g. the set-covering theory of diagnosis [24] or hypothetico-deductive diagnosis [20].

M.Y. Vardi and A. Voronkov (Eds.): LPAR 2003, LNAI 2850, pp. 244–258, 2003.
© Springer-Verlag Berlin Heidelberg 2003

If an explicit *fault model* of the system is available, *abductive* reasoning can be used to perform diagnosis [3, 21]. Rules in the fault model specify cause-effect relationships that govern abnormal behavior. E.g. a rule such as *fever ← flu* asserts that the fever might be caused by flu. An explanation then consists of a set of causes that, when combined with the fault model, are sufficient to entail the observations.

In this paper, we formalize both of the above approaches in terms of ordered logic programs [33], i.e. partially ordered sets of rules, by providing a translation that, given a diagnostic problem D, constructs an ordered program $L(D)$ such that the explanations for D correspond exactly to the preferred answer sets of $L(D)$. Roughly, this is achieved by structuring $L(D)$ as shown below where rules in lower levels are smaller (more preferred) than rules in higher levels.

Intuitively, when faced with inconsistencies between the rules making up an ordered program, the semantics of [33] extends the usual answer set semantics of [19] by producing preferred answer sets that satisfy as many rules as possible, giving priority to the satisfaction of more preferred rules, possibly at the expense of defeating less preferred ones.

In $L(D)$, an observation o is typically represented by a most preferred rule of the form $o \leftarrow not(o)$, which, although it cannot be used to justify o, can only be satisfied by answer sets containing o. The overall effect is then that a preferred answer set will explain all observations, and satisfy as much as possible of the normal behavior rules, with minimal recourse to the fault model, in order to motivate the observations. An explanation can then be retrieved by selecting the "cause" literals from the answer set.

Not all explanations are equally convincing. E.g. when troubleshooting a circuit, an explanation $\{\neg c_1, \neg c_2\}$, asserting that both of the components c_1 and c_2 are broken, would be unlikely if the more parsimonious $\{\neg c_1\}$ were also an explanation. Thus it has been argued [7, 8, 21, 25] that minimal explanations are to be preferred, where one usually considers the subset ordering, or, possibly, the cardinality ordering, among alternative explanations.

We extend the above approach by allowing an arbitrary partial order structure on the set of causes that may occur in explanations. This partial order may reflect e.g. the likelihood that a cause actually occurs, the expense associated with verifying/removing the cause or any other preference criterion. One then prefers explanations that are minimal w.r.t. a partial order induced by the one on causes. The approach depicted in Figure 1 can be adapted such that $L(D)$ reflects the order on the causes and, moreover, the preferred answer sets of $L(D)$ correspond with preferred explanations.

We also consider diagnostic problems where the system model itself has a preference structure, which introduces another natural preference relation on explanations. E.g. laws are often ordered w.r.t. legal precedence. An abductive problem that uses such a system model would prefer explanations that are based on laws with higher precedence. We

| *fault model rules* |
| *normal model rules* |
| *observation rules* |

Fig. 1.

show that such problems can also be mapped to ordered programs where the preferred answer sets correspond to preferred explanations.

The remainder of this paper is organized as follows: Section 2 presents a brief overview of consistency-based and abductive diagnosis. In Section 3, these approaches are generalized to allow for a partial order relation on the possible causes, which induces a preference relation on the explanations. We present an algorithm to transform such an ordered diagnostic system into an ordered extended logic program. Diagnostic problems with ordered system descriptions are considered in Section 4. Some complexity results are presented in Section 5. Section 6 discusses the relationships with other approaches. Conclusions and directions for further research are stated in Section 7. All proofs can be found in the appendix.

2   Classical Diagnosis

We use simple logic programs, i.e. programs containing only classical negation, to describe the system behavior of a diagnostic problem.

We use the following basic definitions and notation. A *literal* is an *atom* a or a negated atom $\neg a$. For a set of literals X we use $\neg X$ to denote $\{\neg p \mid p \in X\}$, where $\neg(\neg a) \equiv a$. Also, X^+ denotes the positive part of X, i.e. $X^+ = \{a \in X \mid a \text{ is an atom}\}$. The *Herbrand base* of X, denoted $\mathcal{B}_X$, contains all atoms appearing in X, i.e. $\mathcal{B}_X = (X \cup \neg X)^+$. A set I of literals is *consistent* if $I \cap \neg I = \emptyset$. Furthermore, I is *total* w.r.t. a set of atoms J iff $J \subseteq I \cup \neg I$.

A *rule* is of the form $a \leftarrow \beta$, where $\{a\} \cup \beta$ is a finite set of literals. A countable set of rules P is called a *simple program*. The *Herbrand base* $\mathcal{B}_P$ of P contains all atoms appearing in P. For a simple program P we use $P^\star$ to denote the unique minimal[30] model of the positive logic program consisting of the rules in P, where negative literals $\neg a$ are considered as fresh atoms. This operator is monotonic, i.e. if $R \subseteq Q$ then $R^\star \subseteq Q^\star$. Then, P is *consistent* iff $P^\star$ is consistent. A consistent set of literals $S \subseteq \mathcal{B}_P \cup \neg \mathcal{B}_P$ is an *answer set* of P iff $P^\star = S$.

First recall the general framework of consistency-based diagnoses [25].

Definition 1. *A **C-diagnostic system** is a triple $S = (T, C, O)$, where T is a simple program describing the normal system behavior, C is the set of possible **causes**, i.e. negated atoms, each representing a malfunctioning component, and O is a set of **observation** literals.*

*A **hypothesis** for S is a set of causes. A hypothesis $H \subseteq C$ is a **C-explanation** or **C-diagnosis** for S iff $T \cup \{x \leftarrow \mid x \in H \cup \neg(C \setminus H) \cup O\}$ is consistent.*

Thus rules in T are of the form $a \leftarrow c_1, c_2$ with c_1 and c_2 corresponding to components that are in working order. Causes such as $\neg c_1$ express that c_1 is faulty. For an explanation H, components not in H are assumed to be working correctly, as witnessed by the $\neg(C \setminus H)$ construction in the definition.

Example 1. Consider the C-diagnostic system $S = (T, C, O)$, with $T = \{light \leftarrow power, bulb\}$, $C = \{\neg power, \neg bulb\}$ and $O = \{\neg light\}$. The system model asserts that if power is available and the bulb is OK, then light should be observed. The observation $\neg light$ has three explanations: $H_1 = \{\neg power\}$, $H_2 = \{\neg bulb\}$ and $H_3 = \{\neg power, \neg bulb\}$.

The abductive framework captures diagnostic reasoning using a system model that describes abnormal system behavior [3, 4, 9, 17, 21–23]. We use the definition from [28], which is based on the belief set semantics from [13].

Definition 2. *An **A-diagnostic system** is a triple $S = (T, C, O)$, where T is a simple program describing the abnormal behavior of the system, C is a set of literals representing the possible causes in the system, and O is a set of literals containing the observations.*

*Any subset $H \subseteq C$ is called a **hypothesis** for S. A hypothesis H is an **A-explanation** or **A-diagnosis** for S iff there is answer set Q for $T \cup \{x \leftarrow | \ x \in H\}$ such that $O \subseteq Q$ and $H = Q \cap C$.*

Thus, while an explanation in a C-diagnostic system prevents the derivation of $\neg o$ for some observable o, in an abductive system, the explanation is used to actually derive o.

Example 2. Suppose the screen of your computer is working unreliably, i.e. $O = \{unreliable\_screen\}$, which may be caused by any of the causes in $C = \{broken\_lcd, broken\_adapter, cable\_problem, broken\_cooler\}$. The fault model T describes how these causes can affect the system.

$$heating \leftarrow broken\_cooler$$
$$no\_screen \leftarrow broken\_lcd$$
$$no\_screen \leftarrow cable\_problem$$
$$no\_screen \leftarrow broken\_adapter$$
$$unreliable\_adapter \leftarrow heating$$
$$unreliable\_screen \leftarrow cable\_problem$$
$$unreliable\_screen \leftarrow broken\_adapter$$
$$unreliable\_screen \leftarrow unreliable\_adapter$$

E.g., a broken cooler causes a heating problem that makes the graphics adapter behave unreliably which, in turn, affects the screen performance. Alternatively, a cable problem or a broken LCD may also cause screen problems.

Some of the A-explanations for $unreliable\_screen$ are $H_1 = \{broken\_cooler\}$, $H_2 = \{cable\_problem\}$, $H_3 = \{broken\_adapter\}$, $H_4 = \{cable\_problem, broken\_cooler\}$ and $H_5 = \{broken\_cooler, broken\_lcd\}$.

Note that H_4 in Example 2 is likely to be redundant since $H_4 = H_2 \cup H_1$, i.e. the observations can be explained using a subset of the causes in H_4.

In general, we assume that sets of causes may carry a preference order. Preferred explanations then correspond to explanations that are minimal with respect to this order.

Definition 3. *Let $S = (T, C, O)$ be a diagnostic system, with $\leq$ a partial order relation on 2^C. An explanation of S is called $\leq$-**preferred** iff it is minimal w.r.t. $\leq$.*

Often, $\leq$ is taken as the subset order although cardinality order is also used (e.g. if all components in a circuit are equally likely to fail, cardinality-preferred explanations are more likely). In Example 1, both H_1 and H_2 are $\sqsubseteq$-preferred explanations, which are also cardinality preferred. In Example 2, H_1, H_2 and H_3 are $\sqsubseteq$-preferred explanations.

Definition 2, which follows [15, 16], differs from the definition in [9] which does not require the $H = Q \cap C$ condition. This influences the set of explanations, as illustrated in the following example.

Example 3. Consider the A-diagnostic system $S = (T, C, O)$ with T containing *air_in_fuel_pump* $\leftarrow$ *out_of_diesel* and *car_does_not_start* $\leftarrow$ *out_of_diesel*, $C = \{out\_of\_diesel, air\_in\_fuel\_pump\}$ and $O = \{car\_does\_not\_start\}$.

The semantics of [9] yields $\{out\_of\_diesel\}$ as a $\sqsubseteq$-preferred explanation while $\{out\_of\_diesel, air\_in\_fuel\_pump\}$ is $\sqsubseteq$-preferred according to Definition 2. Thus, [9] returns the "root cause" of the problem, leaving out side effects. On the other hand, Definition 2's solution includes the side effects, which is useful in this example, as just refueling diesel will not completely fix the problem: one also must ventilate the fuel pump.

One may wonder whether a C-diagnostic system could be easily converted to an equivalent abductive one by simply replacing "normal behavior" rules $a \leftarrow \alpha$ by "fault model" rules $\neg a \leftarrow \neg \beta$ where β is a minimal set of literals such that $\beta \cap \alpha \neq \emptyset$ for each a-rule $a \leftarrow \alpha$. This may, however, not produce all explanations warranted by the consistency-based system. E.g. if the C-system contains just $a \leftarrow b, c$, $c \leftarrow d$ and $e \leftarrow d$, the above construction would yield the "abductive rules" $\neg a \leftarrow \neg b$, $\neg a \leftarrow \neg c$, $\neg c \leftarrow \neg d$ and $\neg e \leftarrow \neg d$. For the observations $\{\neg a, \neg e\}$ and set of causes $\{\neg b, \neg c, \neg d\}$, the original consistency based system yields both $\{\neg b, \neg d\}$ and $\{\neg c, \neg d\}$ as $\sqsubseteq$-preferred explanations, while the abductive variant only supports $\{\neg c, \neg d\}$.

3   Ordered Diagnosis

Often, causes are themselves partially ordered according to some preference. E.g. in Example 1 it may be much more likely that the bulb is broken than that the power is off, or the reverse (depending on where one is located).

In an ordered diagnostic system, explanations are ordered according to the partial order induced by the order on causes.

Definition 4. *An **ordered diagnostic system** is a tuple $D = (S, <)$, where S is either a C- or A-diagnostic system $S = (T, C, O)$ and $<$ is a strict[2] partial order relation on the elements in C. When S is a C-diagnostic system (A-diagnostic system), we call D a C-ordered diagnostic system (A-ordered diagnostic system respectively). The explanations of D are the explanations of S.*

For explanations H_1 and H_2, $H_1 \sqsubseteq H_2$ iff $\forall c \in H_1 \setminus H_2 \cdot \exists c' \in H_2 \setminus H_1 \cdot c < c'$.

Intuitively, H_1 is preferred over H_2 if any cause c_1 from H_1 but not in H_2 is "covered" by a "less preferred" cause $c_2 > c_1$ in H_2 but not in H_1. It can be shown that $\sqsubseteq$ is a partial order, provided that the inverse of $<$ is well-founded, see Lemma 1 in [32].

---

[2] A strict partial order $<$ on a set X is a binary relation on X that is antisymmetric, anti-reflexive and transitive.

Example 4. If $\neg bulb < \neg power.$ in Example 1, then $H_2 \sqsubseteq H_1$ because $H_2 \setminus H_1 = \{\neg bulb\}, H_1 \setminus H_2 = \{\neg power\}$ and $\neg bulb < \neg power.$ Consequently, H_2 is $\sqsubseteq$-preferred.

Example 5. Extend Example 2 to an ordered diagnostic system $D = (S, <)$ with $cable\_problem < broken\_adapter$, $cable\_problem < broken\_lcd$, $broken\_cooler < broken\_adapter$, $broken\_cooler < broken\_lcd$. It follows that the explanations $H_1 = \{broken\_cooler\}$ and $H_2 = \{cable\_problem\}$ are both $\sqsubseteq$-preferred.

Each $\sqsubseteq$-preferred explanation is also $\subseteq$-preferred.

Theorem 1. *Let $D = (S, <)$ be an ordered diagnostic system. Every $\sqsubseteq$-preferred explanation H of D is a $\subseteq$-preferred explanation of S.*

If the order on the causes is empty, $\sqsubseteq$-preference reduces to $\subseteq$-preference.

Theorem 2. *Let S be a diagnostic system, either C or A. Then, all $\subseteq$-preferred explanations of S coincide with the preferred explanations of $D = (S, \emptyset)$.*

We will show that the $\sqsubseteq$-preferred explanations (and, by Theorem 2, also the $\subseteq$-preferred explanations) of an ordered diagnostic system D can be retrieved from the preferred answer sets of an extended ordered logic program (EOLP) $L(D)$ that can be constructed from D.

First, we review the definition and semantics of EOLPs [31].

An *extended literal* is a literal or a *naf-literal* of the form $not(l)$ where l is a literal. The latter form denotes negation as failure. We use l^- to denote the literal underlying the extended literal l. An extended literal l is true w.r.t. an interpretation I, denoted $I \models l$ if $l \in I$ in case l is ordinary, or $I \not\models a$ if $l = not(a)$ for some ordinary literal a. As usual, $I \models X$ for some set of (extended) literals l iff $\forall l \in X \cdot I \models l$.

An *extended rule* is a rule of the form $\alpha \leftarrow \beta$ where $\alpha \cup \beta$ is a finite set of extended literals and $|\alpha| \leq 1$. An extended rule $r = \alpha \leftarrow \beta$ is *satisfied* by I, denoted $I \models r$, if $I \models \alpha$, $\alpha \neq \emptyset$, whenever $I \models \beta$, i.e. if r is *applicable* ($I \models \beta$), then it must be *applied* ($I \models \alpha \cup \beta$).

A countable set of extended rules is called an *extended logic program* (ELP). For an ELP P and an interpretation I we use $P_I \subseteq P$ to denote the *reduct* of P w.r.t. I, i.e. $P_I = \{r \in P \mid I \models r\}$. We also define the *GL-reduct* for P w.r.t. I, denoted P^I, as the program consisting of those rules $\alpha \setminus not(\alpha^-) \leftarrow (\beta \setminus not(\beta^-))$ where $\alpha \leftarrow \beta$ is in P, $I \models not(\beta^-)$ and $I \models \alpha^-$. Note that all rules in P^I are free from negation as failure, i.e. P^I is a simple program. An interpretation I is then an *answer set* of P iff I is an answer set of the reduct P^I. An extended rule $r = \alpha \leftarrow \beta$ is *defeated* w.r.t. P and I iff there exists an applied *competing rule* $r' = \alpha' \leftarrow \beta'$ such that $\{\alpha, \alpha'\}$ is inconsistent. An *extended answer set* for P is any interpretation I such that I is an answer set of P_I and each unsatisfied rule in $P \setminus P_I$ is defeated.

An *extended ordered logic program* (EOLP) is a pair $(R, <)$ where R is an ELP and $<$ is a well-founded strict partial order on the rules in R. Intuitively, $r_1 < r_2$ indicates that r_1 is more preferred than r_2. In the examples we will often represent the order implicitly using the format

$$\frac{\cdots}{\dfrac{R_2}{\dfrac{R_1}{R_0}}}$$

where each R_i, $i \geq 0$, represents a set of rules, indicating that all rules below a line are more preferred than any of the rules above the line, i.e. $\forall i \geq 0 \cdot \forall r_i \in R_i, r_{i+1} \in R_{i+1} \cdot r_i < r_{i+1}$ or $\forall i \geq 0 \cdot R_i < R_{i+1}$ for short.

Let $P = \langle R, < \rangle$ be an EOLP. For subsets R_1 and R_2 of R we define $R_1 \preceq R_2$ iff $\forall r_2 \in R_2 \backslash R_1 \cdot \exists r_1 \in R_1 \backslash R_2 \cdot r_1 < r_2$. We write $R_1 \prec R_2$ just when $R_1 \preceq R_2$ and $R_1 \neq R_2$. For M_1, M_2 extended answer sets of R, we define $M_1 \preceq M_2$ iff $R_{M_1} \preceq R_{M_2}$. As usual, $M_1 \prec M_2$ iff $M_1 \preceq M_2$ and $M_1 \neq M_2$. An *answer set* for an EOLP P is any extended answer set of R. An answer set for P is called *preferred* if it is minimal w.r.t. $\preceq$. An answer set is called *proper* if it satisfies all minimal (according to $<$) rules in R.

Let $D = (S, <)$ with $S = (T, C, O)$ be an ordered diagnostic system. We construct an EOLP $L(D)$ which is such that the proper preferred answer sets of $L(D)$ represent the $\sqsubseteq$-preferred explanations of D, i.e. for any proper preferred answer set M of $L(D)$, $M \cap C$ is a preferred explanation and the other way around.

The construction of $L(D)$ follows the intuition sketched in Section 1.

- The bottom component R_b of $L(D)$, whose rules will always be satisfied, consists of the system description T and a set of "constraint" rules R_o that enforce the observations, without providing a justification for them. If D is an A-system, each observation o should be derived from an explanation while for a C-system, it suffices to be consistent with O, i.e. to prevent the derivation of $\neg o$. Therefore, constraint rules for A-systems will have the form $o \leftarrow not(o)$, $o \in O$, while for C-systems, rules of the form $o \leftarrow \neg o$ will be used.
- On top of the bottom component, we put a component R_n with rules that simulate the normal behavior of the system. To this end, R_n contains, for each cause $c \in C$, a rule r_c asserting that this cause is not valid. For an A-system, this can be achieved by defining r_c as $not(c) \leftarrow$ thus ensuring that the semantics will prefer answer sets that maximize false causes. For a C-system, Definition 1 demands that the negation of any cause not in the explanation holds, hence r_c will be of the form $\neg c \leftarrow$. To take into account the preference relation between causes, we order the rules in R_n such that the EOLP semantics, when confronted with the necessity to defeat either r_c or $r_{c'}$, it will defeat r_c if $c < c'$. Thus, it suffices to have $r_{c'} < r_c$, i.e. the order on R_n is the reverse of the order on C.
- The topmost component $R_a > R_n$ introduces the possibility of abnormal behavior. For each $c \in C$, R_a contains a rule $c \leftarrow$ that provides a justification, if necessary, for c. Note that all rule in R_a have a stronger competitor in R_n.

Intuitively, if no causes are necessary to explain the observations, any proper preferred answer set will satisfy all rules in $R_b \cup R_n$, defeating all rules in R_a. If, however, the observations cannot be explained without assuming some causes, the semantics will, in order to satisfy the rule in R_o, call upon rules in R_a to introduce them.

The following definition formalizes the above construction.

Definition 5. *Let $D = (S, <)$ be an ordered diagnostic system, with $S = (T, C, O)$ either a C- or A-diagnostic system. The EOLP version of D, denoted $L(D)$, is defined by $L(D) = \langle R_a \cup R_n \cup T \cup R_o, (R_o \cup T) < R_n^< < R_a \rangle$, where $R_a = \{c \leftarrow | c \in C\}$, $R_n = \{\phi(c) \leftarrow | c \in C\}$ and $R_o = \{o \leftarrow \phi(o) \mid o \in O\}$, with $\phi(l) = \neg l$ if S is a C-diagnostic system and $\phi(l) = not(l)$ if S is an A-diagnostic system. Furthermore, $R_n^<$ stands for $\phi(c_1) \leftarrow < \phi(c_2) \leftarrow$ with $c_1, c_2 \in C$ iff $c_2 < c_1$.*

Example 6. The program corresponding to the abductive ordered diagnostic system from Example 5 is shown below.

$$
\begin{array}{r}
broken\_adapter \leftarrow \\
broken\_lcd \leftarrow \\
cable\_problem \leftarrow \\
broken\_cooler \leftarrow \\
\hline
not(cable\_problem) \leftarrow \\
not(broken\_cooler) \leftarrow \\
\hline
not(broken\_adapter) \leftarrow \\
not(broken\_lcd) \leftarrow \\
\hline
heating \leftarrow broken\_cooler \\
no\_screen \leftarrow broken\_adapter \\
no\_screen \leftarrow broken\_lcd \\
no\_screen \leftarrow cable\_problem \\
unreliable\_screen \leftarrow broken\_adapter \\
unreliable\_screen \leftarrow unreliable\_adapter \\
unreliable\_adapter \leftarrow cable\_problem \\
unreliable\_adapter \leftarrow heating \\
unreliable\_screen \leftarrow not(unreliable\_screen)
\end{array}
$$

This program has two proper preferred answer sets: $N_1 = \{broken\_cooler, heating, unreliable\_adapter, unreliable\_screen\}$, corresponding with the preferred explanation $H_3 = N_1 \cap C$, and $N_2 = \{cable\_problem, unreliable\_adapter\}$, corresponding with the preferred explanation $H_2 = N_2 \cap C$.

Example 7. The program corresponding with the ordered C-diagnostic system of Example 4 is shown below.

$$
\begin{array}{c}
\neg power \leftarrow \quad \neg bulb \leftarrow \\
\hline
bulb \leftarrow \\
\hline
power \leftarrow \\
\hline
light \leftarrow power, bulb \\
\neg light \leftarrow light
\end{array}
$$

This program has only one proper preferred answer set $N = \{power, \neg bulb\}$, corresponding to the single preferred explanation $H_2 = N \cap C$.

In general, we have the following correspondence.

Theorem 3. *Let* $D = (S, <)$ *be an ordered diagnostic system with* $S = (T, C, O)$ *either a C- or A-diagnostic system. Then, H is a preferred explanation for D iff there is a proper preferred answer set N of* $L(D)$ *such that* $H = N \cap C$.

We illustrate the usefulness of the approach with a (simplified) example from software configuration management.

The goal of the installation (of a Linux system) is the availability of a set of packages. These will be considered as observables in an abductive diagnostic system where the system model contains rules and constraints representing inter-package dependencies and incompatibilities. Causes correspond to installation instructions for particular (versions of) packages.

Consequently, a preferred explanation will provide an "optimal" list of detailed install instructions that are necessary to achieve the objective.

Example 8. In the example, the goal is to have KDE installed as well as a music program called bpmdj. The owner being a version freak, the most recent version of a package is to be preferred but installing two versions of the same package should be avoided if possible.

Below we show the EOLP representation of the corresponding A-diagnostic program where a system model rule such as $bpmdj(1) \leftarrow install\_bpmdj(1), qt(2)$ asserts that bpmdj depends on qt(2).

$$install\_qt(2) \leftarrow$$
$$install\_qt(3) \leftarrow$$
$$install\_kde(3) \leftarrow$$
$$\underline{install\_bpmdj(1) \leftarrow}$$
$$\underline{not(install\_qt(3)) \leftarrow}$$
$$not(install\_qt(2)) \leftarrow$$
$$not(install\_kde(3)) \leftarrow$$
$$\underline{not(install\_bpmdj(1)) \leftarrow}$$
$$qt(2) \leftarrow install\_qt(2)$$
$$qt(3) \leftarrow install\_qt(3)$$
$$kde(3) \leftarrow install\_kde(3), qt(X)$$
$$bpmdj(1) \leftarrow install\_bpmdj(1), qt(2)$$
$$kde(3) \leftarrow not(kde(3))$$
$$bpmdj(1) \leftarrow not(bpmdj(1))$$

There is a single preferred explanation $E = \{install\_kde(3), install\_qt(2), install\_bpmdj(1)\}$, corresponding with the only proper preferred answer set $E \cup \{kde(3), qt(2), bpmdj(1)\}$. From the solution, it appears that a less recent version of qt is preferred because bpmdj compiles only with version 2 (not with 3) and kde can work with both version 2 and 3, making it unnecessary to install both qt(2) and qt(3).

4   Diagnosing Ordered Systems

In this section, we consider problems where the system model is itself an ordered program. Naturally, in such a case, one would prefer explanations that maximally satisfy the system model, in particular more preferred rules should only be defeated as a last resort.

Definition 6. *A **diagnostic ordered system** is a triple $D = (P, C, O)$, where $P = \langle R, <_R \rangle$ is an OLP[3] describing either the normal behavior (consistency-based) or the*

---

[3] An OLP is an EOLP without negation as failure in the rules, i.e. R is a simple logic program, see [33].

abnormal behavior (abductive) of the system. Further, C is either a set of negated atoms in the case of consistency based diagnosis or a set of literals in the case of abductive diagnosis, representing the possible causes in the system; and O is a set of literals containing the observations.

*A **hypothesis** is any subset $H \subseteq C$.*

- *If D is consistency-based, a hypothesis H is an **explanation** iff there exists an extended answer set Q of $R \cup \{h \leftarrow | \ h \in H \cup \neg(C \setminus H)\}$, such that $Q \cup O$ is consistent and $H = Q \cap C$.*
- *If D is abductive, a hypothesis H is an **explanation** iff there exists an extended answer set Q for $R \cup \{h \leftarrow | \ h \in H\} \cup \{not(h) \leftarrow | \ h \in C \setminus H\}$, such that $O \subseteq Q$ and $H = Q \cap C$.*

For an explanation H, we use $R_{H,Q}$ to denote the set $R_Q \subseteq R$, i.e. the reduct of R w.r.t. the extended answer set Q.

Note that there may be several extended answer sets Q, and associated reducts R_Q, to justify an explanation H.

Example 9. Consider the abductive diagnostic ordered system $D = (P, C, O)$ representing the trial of shooting incidents, where P is depicted below and $C = \{shoot, dead, unarmed, threatened\}$.

$$
\begin{array}{ll}
r_1 : & guilty \leftarrow shoot, dead \\
r_2 : & self\_defense \leftarrow threatened \\
\hline
r_3 : & \neg guilty \leftarrow shoot, dead, self\_defense \\
r_4 : & \neg self\_defense \leftarrow shoot, unarmed
\end{array}
$$

The preferred rules r_3 and r_4 state that one cannot be found guilty if one acted out of self defense and that self defense cannot be invoked if one shot an unarmed person. The more general rules r_1 and r_2 present the default treatment for a fatal shooting and a possible cause (having been threatened by the victim) for self defense.

Assuming that the facts of the case (i.e. the observations) are $F = \{shoot, dead, threatened\}$, the latter claimed by the defendant, a lawyer eager to obtain a conviction will search for an optimal explanation of $O = F \cup \{guilty\}$.

D has two explanations for O, namely $H_1 = \{shoot, dead, threatened\}$, corresponding to the answer set $Q_1 = O \cup \{self\_defense\}$ and $H_2 = H_1 \cup \{unarmed\}$ corresponding to both $Q_2 = O \cup \{unarmed, \neg self\_defense\}$ and $Q_2' = O \cup \{unarmed, self\_defense\}$. The corresponding sets of satisfied rules w.r.t. these explanations are $R_{H_1,Q_1} = P \setminus \{r_3\}$, $R_{H_2,Q_2} = P \setminus \{r_2\}$ and $R_{H_2,Q_2'} = P \setminus \{r_3, r_4\}$.

The preference order among explanations is based on the $\preceq$ order among the corresponding sets of satisfied rules.

Definition 7. *Let D be a diagnostic ordered system with R_{H_1,Q_1} and R_{H_2,Q_2}[4] sets of rules corresponding with the explanations H_1 and H_2. Then, R_{H_1,Q_1} is preferred upon*

---

[4] We abuse notation by considering $R_{H,Q}$ as a tagged set, such that $R_{H',Q'}$ may not be the same as $R_{H,Q}$ although, as sets of rules, $R_{H,Q} = R_{H',Q'}$.

R_{H_2,Q_2}, denoted $R_{H_1,Q_1} \sqsubseteq R_{H_2,Q_2}$ iff $\begin{cases} H_1 \subset H_2 & \text{if } R_{H_1,Q_1} = R_{H_2,Q_2} \text{,} \\ R_{H_1,Q_1} \prec R_{H_2,Q_2} & \text{otherwise .} \end{cases}$

An explanation H is **preferred** iff it corresponds to a minimal (w.r.t. $\sqsubseteq$) $R_{H,Q}$.

Note that the special clause for $R_{H_1,Q_1} = R_{H_2,Q_2}$ is necessary, e.g. when both Q_1 and Q_2 satisfy all rules in R. In such a case, the smaller (w.r.t. $\subseteq$) explanation is preferred.

Example 10. In Example 9, $R_{H_2,Q_2} = P \setminus \{r_2\}$ is the unique minimal (w.r.t. $\sqsubseteq$). Therefore, the lawyer should attempt to establish *unarmed* in order to obtain a conviction.

Using a similar intuition as in Definition 5, we can construct an EOLP program $L(D)$ that has exactly the $\sqsubseteq$-preferred explanations of a diagnostic ordered system as proper preferred answer sets.

Definition 8. Let $D = (P = (R, <_R), C, O)$ be a diagnostic ordered system. The EOLP version $L(D)$ of D is defined by $L(D) = \langle R_a \cup R_n \cup R \cup R_o, R_o <<_r < R_n < R_a \rangle$, where $R_a = \{c \leftarrow \mid c \in C\}$, $R_n = \{\phi(c) \leftarrow \mid c \in C\}$ and $R_o = \{o \leftarrow \phi(o) \mid o \in O\}$, with $\phi(l) = \neg l$ if P is consistency based and $\phi(l) = not(l)$ if P is abductive.

Example 11. The EOLP corresponding with the system from Example 9 is shown below.

$$
\begin{array}{c}
dead \leftarrow \\
shoot \leftarrow \\
unarmed \leftarrow \\
threatened \leftarrow \\
\hline
not(dead) \leftarrow \\
not(shoot) \leftarrow \\
not(unarmed) \leftarrow \\
not(threatened) \leftarrow \\
\hline
guilty \leftarrow shoot, dead \\
self\_defense \leftarrow threatened \\
\neg guilty \leftarrow shoot, dead, self\_defense \\
\neg self\_defense \leftarrow shoot, unarmed \\
\hline
shoot \leftarrow not(shoot) \\
dead \leftarrow not(dead) \\
guilty \leftarrow not(guilty) \\
threatened \leftarrow not(threatened)
\end{array}
$$

The only preferred answer set is $Q = \{guilty, shoot, dead, unarmed, \neg self\_defense, threatened\}$, corresponding with the unique preferred explanation H_2.

In general we have the following correspondence.

Theorem 4. Let $D = (P, C, O)$ be a diagnostic ordered system. Then, H is a preferred explanation for D iff $H = M \cap C$. for some proper preferred answer set M of $L(D)$.

5   Complexity of Ordered Diagnosis

In the context of complexity for diagnostic systems [9, 28], the properties consistency, relevance and necessity are of natural interest, where consistency means deciding if there exists a preferred explanation, relevance and necessity refer to checking whether a given cause c is contained in some, resp. all, preferred explanation(s).

The availability of a transformation to EOLP's, suggests that ordered diagnostic reasoning resides in the same level of complexity[5].

Obviously, checking whether a hypothesis H is an explanation for an ordered diagnostic system D can be done in polynomial time. Thus, checking whether H is *not* a preferred explanation is in NP, i.e. guess a hypothesis H' such that $H' \sqsubseteq H$, which can be done in polynomial time, and verify if it is an explanation. Now, finding a preferred explanation H can be done by an NP algorithm that guesses H and uses an NP oracle to verify that it is not the case that H is not a preferred explanation. Hence, the following theorem.

Theorem 5. *Let $D = (S, <)$ be an ordered diagnostic system, with $S = (T, C, O)$ either a C- or A-diagnostic system. Deciding the problem of consistency for D is in NP. Deciding the problem of relevance, for a given cause $c \in C$, for D is in Σ_2^P, while deciding necessity for c is in Π_2^P.*

Showing that relevance (necessity) is also Σ_2^P-hard (Π_2^P-hard), can be done by a reduction to the known Σ_2^P problem of deciding whether a quantified boolean formula $\phi = \exists x_1, \ldots, x_n \cdot \forall y_1, \ldots, y_m \cdot F$ is valid, where we may assume that $F = \vee_{c \in C} c$ with each c a conjunction of literals over $X \cup Y$ with $X = \{x_1, \ldots, x_n\}$ and $Y = \{y_1, \ldots, y_m\}$ ($n, m > 0$). The construction is inspired by a similar result for abductive diagnosis under $\subseteq$-preferredness in [9], illustrating that the preferred explanation semantics does not involve any computational overhead w.r.t. classical diagnostic frameworks. Together with Theorem 5, this yields.

Theorem 6. *Let $D = (S, <)$ be an ordered diagnostic system, with $S = (T, C, O)$ either a C- or A-diagnostic system and let $c \in C$ be a cause. Deciding the problem of relevance for D and c is Σ_2^P-complete and deciding the problem of necessity for D and c is Π_2^P-complete.*

Similar results can be obtained for diagnostic ordered systems (Section 4).

Theorem 7. *Let $D = (P, C, O)$ with $P = (R, <_R)$ be a diagnostic ordered system. Deciding the problem of consistency for D is in NP. Deciding the problem of relevance, for a given cause $c \in C$, for D is Σ_2^P-complete, while deciding necessity for c is Π_2^P-complete.*

6 Relationships to Other Approaches

Consistency-based diagnosis was proposed by [25], and extended in [6]. Definition 1 of C-diagnostic reasoning closely mirrors the original definition from [25], except that the notion of hypothesis in this paper contains only "malfunctioning" components, while the original definition considers total subsets of $C \cup \neg C$, i.e. also the correctly working components are mentioned.

---

[5] The results in this section hold for both C- and A-ordered diagnostic reasoning.

A number of different characterizations of abductive diagnosis exist, both in the context of logic and logic programming, e.g. [3, 4, 9, 10, 17, 21, 22]. Earlier formalizations of abductive diagnosis used first order logic, while [17] introduced an abductive framework in the context of logic programming. Later, generalized stable models [11] were introduced as an extension of the stable model semantics [14] to handle abductive reasoning. Independently, [13] formalized a similar idea, called the belief set semantics, providing an abductive reasoning formalism for systems containing disjunction, negation as failure and classical negation. In [15, 16] this semantics was used to formalize abductive extended disjunctive programs. Another formalization of abduction for logic programming was given in [9], using definitions closer to ones used in first order logic approaches. Example 3 illustrates the difference between [9] and [15, 16].

Subset minimality has been recognized from the start [25] as a desirable property for explanations, along with other preference criteria such as single-error diagnosis, accepting only explanations containing a single cause, and minimality w.r.t. cardinality.

[8] mentions a possible formalization of preferred explanations for a linearly prioritized set of causes in the context of abduction for classical logic. The more general preference relation on explanations of Definition 4 reduces to the one used in [8], for the case where the underlying partial order on causes is linear.

Although a variety of proposals exist for extending logic programs with some kind of preference relation [1, 2, 18, 27, 33, 34], we are not aware of any prior work on abduction for such ordered programs (Section 4). In fact, many of these systems do not lend themselves to an approach along the lines of this paper. E.g. proposals such as [1], that select preferred answer sets from the collection of answer sets of the unordered version of the program, cannot deal with contradictions as appear e.g. in Example 9. On the other hand, several formalisms, e.g. [18], while similar to OLP, allow a rule to be defeated only by a better rule with opposite head. This prevents rules modeling normal behavior from being defeated by less-preferred opposite rules that may be needed to explain an abnormal observation, a feature of OLP that supports a natural and intuitive representation for abductive problems, see e.g. Example 7.

Reducing abduction to model computation has been done before, e.g. [26, 28] provide a different method for transforming abductive logic programs into disjunctive logic programs, using the possible model semantics, but only for the subset-preferred case. Section 3 can be regarded as an extension to more general preference relations. Moreover, our approach does not need disjunction to obtain the simulation as it relies on a single mechanism (order) to simulate both abduction and minimality.

7 Conclusions and Direction for Further Research

We have extended diagnostic reasoning to systems involving preference, in either the description or the set of causes. Since such reasoning can be simulated using EOLP, which is equivalent to OLP (i.e. programs without negation as failure) [31], an implementation of OLP[6], e.g. using the algorithms described in [33], can be envisaged to perform diagnostic reasoning.

---

[6] A prototype system exists, computing preferred answer sets for EOLPs.

The approach to preference in diagnostic reasoning can also be extended, e.g. by combining both preference on causes and in the system model.

The proposed diagnostic framework could also be useful to refine the concept of therapy from [12], where one tries to suppress some of the undesired observations by repairing (a subset of) the possible causes. This results in an iterative process of diagnosing the system, repairing some of the causes, called a treatment, and checking if the undesired observations have disappeared, in which case the therapy is finished. In an ordered diagnostic system (see Definition 4), it seems reasonable to let the choice of causes to repair depend on the preference order. E.g., if the order represents (repair) cost, only minimal elements of the explanation would be selected.

References

1. Gerhard Brewka and Thomas Eiter. Preferred answer sets for extended logic programs. *Artificial Intelligence*, 109(1-2):297–356, April 1999.
2. Francesco Buccafurri, Wolfgang Faber, and Nicola Leone. Disjunctive logic programs with inheritance. In Danny De Schreye, editor, *Logic Programming: The 1999 International Conference*, pages 79–93, Las Cruces, New Mexico, December 1999. MIT Press.
3. L. Console and P. Torasso. A spectrum of logical definitions of model-based diagnosis. *Computational Intelligence*, 7(3):133–141, 1991.
4. P.T. Cox and T. Pietrzykowski. General diagnosis by abductive inference. In *Proceedings of the IEEE Symposium on Logic Programming*, pages 183–189, 1987.
5. J. De Kleer. Local methods for localizing faults in electronic circuits. *MIT AI Memo*, (394).
6. J. De Kleer, A. K. Mackworth, and R. Reiter. Characterizing diagnoses and systems. *Artificial Intelligence*, 52:197–222, 1992.
7. Thomas Eiter, Wolfgang Faber, Nicola Leone, and Gerald Pfeifer. The diagnosis frontend of the dlv system. *AI Communications*, 12(1-2):99–111, 1999.
8. Thomas Eiter and Georg Gottlob. The complexity of logic-based abduction. *Journal of the Association for Computing Machinery*, 42(1):3–42, 1995.
9. Thomas Eiter, Georg Gottlob, and Nicola Leone. Abduction from logic programs: Semantics and complexity. *Theoretical Computer Science*, 189(1-2):129–177, 1997.
10. Thomas Eiter, Georg Gottlob, and Nicola Leone. Semantics and complexity for abduction from default logic. *Artificial Intelligence*, 90(1-2):177–222, 1997.
11. K. Eshghi and R.A. Kowalski. Abduction compared with negation by failure. In *Proceedings of the 6th International Conference on Logic Programming*, pages 234–254. MIT Press, 1989.
12. Gerhard Friedrich, Georg Gottlob, and Wolfgang Nejdl. Hypothesis classification, abductive diagnosis and therapy. In *Expert Systems in Engineering*, volume 462 of *Lecture Notes in Computer Science*, pages 69–78. Springer, 1990.
13. Michael Gelfond. Epistemic approach to formalization of commonsense reasoning. Technical report, University of Texas at El Paso, 1991. Technical Report TR-91-2.
14. Michael Gelfond and Vladimir Lifschitz. The stable model semantics for logic programming. In *Logic Programming, Proceedings of the Fifth International Conference and Symposium*, pages 1070–1080, Seattle, Washington, August 1988. The MIT Press.
15. Katsumi Inoue and Chiaki Sakama. Transforming abductive logic programs to disjunctive programs. In *Proceedings of the 10th International Conference on Logic Programming*, pages 335–353. MIT Press, 1993.
16. Katsumi Inoue and Chiaki Sakama. A fixpoint characterization of abductive logic programs. *Journal of Logic Programming*, 27(2):107.136, May 1996.

17. A. C. Kakas, R. A. Kowalski, and F. Toni. Abductive logic programming. *Journal of Logic and Computation*, 2(6):719–770, 1992.

18. Els Laenens and Dirk Vermeir. Assumption-free semantics for ordered logic programs: On the relationship between well-founded and stable partial models. *Journal of Logic and Computation*, 2(2):133–172, 1992.

19. Vladimir Lifschitz. Answer set programming and plan generation. *Journal of Artificial Intelligence*, 138(1-2):39–54, 2002.

20. F.J. Macartney. Diagnostic logic. *Logic in Medicine*, 1988.

21. Y. Peng and J. Reggia. Abductive inference models for diagnostic problem solving. *Symbolic Computation - Artificial Intelligence*, 1990.

22. D. Poole. Explanation and prediction: An architecture for default and abductive reasoning. *Computational Intelligence*, 5(1):97–110, 1989.

23. C. Preist, K. Eshghi, and B. Bertolino. Consistency-based and abductive diagnosis as generalized stable models. *Annals of Mathematics and Artificial Intelligence*, 11:51–74, 1994.

24. J.A. Reggia, D.S. Nau, and Y. Wang. Diagnostic expert systems based on a set covering model. *International Journal of Man Machine Studies*, (19):437–460, 1983.

25. Raymond Reiter. A theory of diagnosis from first principles. *Artificial Intelligence*, 32(1):57–95, 1987.

26. Chiaki Sakama and Katsumi Inoue. On the equivalence between disjunctive and abductive logic programs. In Pascal Van Hentenryck, editor, *Logic Programming, Proceedings of the Eleventh International Conference on Logic Programming*, pages 489–503, Santa Margherita Ligure, Italy, June 1994. MIT Press.

27. Chiaki Sakama and Katsumi Inoue. Representing priorities in logic programs. In Michael J. Maher, editor, *Proceedings of the 1996 Joint International Conference and Syposium on Logic Programming*, pages 82–96, Bonn, September 1996. MIT Press.

28. Chiaki Sakama and Katsumi Inoue. Abductive logic programming and disjunctive logic programming: their relationship and transferability. *The Journal of Logic Programming*, 44(1-3):71–96, 2000.

29. E.H. Shortliffe. Computer-based medical consultations: Mycin. 1976.

30. M. H. van Emden and R. A. Kowalski. The semantics of predicate logic as a programming language. *Journal of the Association for Computing Machinery*, 23(4):733–742, 1976.

31. Davy Van Nieuwenborgh and Dirk Vermeir. Order and negation as failure. Accepted.

32. Davy Van Nieuwenborgh and Dirk Vermeir. Ordered diagnosis. Technical report, Vrije Universiteit Brussel, Dept. of Computer Science, 2003.

33. Davy Van Nieuwenborgh and Dirk Vermeir. Preferred answer sets for ordered logic programs. In *European Workshop, JELIA 2002*, volume 2424 of *Lecture Notes in Artificial Intelligence*, pages 432–443, Cosenza, Italy, September 2002. Springer Verlag.

34. Kewen Wang, Lizhu Zhou, and Fangzhen Lin. Alternating fixpoint theory for logic programs with priority. In *CL*, volume 1861 of *Lecture Notes in Computer Science*, pages 164–178, London, UK, July 2000. Springer.

Computing Preferred Answer Sets
in Answer Set Programming

Toshiko Wakaki[1], Katsumi Inoue[2], Chiaki Sakama[3], and Katsumi Nitta[4]

[1] Shibaura Institute of Technology
Department of Electronic Information Systems,
307 Fukasaku, Minuma-ku, Saitama-City, Saitama 337–8570 Japan,
twakaki@sic.shibaura-it.ac.jp
[2] Kobe University,
Department of Electrical and Electronics Engineering,
Rokkodai, Nada, Kobe 657–8501 Japan,
inoue@eedept.kobe-u.ac.jp
[3] Wakayama University,
Center for Information Science,
930 Sakaedani, Wakayama 640–8510, Japan,
sakama@sys.wakayama-u.ac.jp
[4] Tokyo Institute of Technology,
Department of Computational Intelligence and Systems Science,
4259 Nagatsuta, Midori-ku, Yokohama 226–8502, Japan,
nitta@dis.titech.ac.jp

Abstract. Prioritized logic programs (PLPs) have a mechanism of representing priority knowledge in logic programs. The declarative semantics of a PLP is given as preferred answer sets which are used for representing nonmonotonic reasoning as well as preference abduction. From the computational viewpoint, however, its implementation issues have little been studied and no sound procedure is known for computing preferred answer sets of PLPs. In this paper, we present a sound and complete procedure to compute all preferred answer sets of a PLP in answer set programming. The procedure is based on a program transformation from a PLP to a logic program and is realized on top of any procedure for answer set programming. The proposed technique also extends PLPs to handle dynamic preference and we address its application to legal reasoning.

1 Introduction

A framework of *prioritized logic programs* [18] (PLPs) introduces explicit representation of priorities between literals and negation-as-failure formulas to logic programs. A PLP is defined as a pair (P, Φ), where P is a (nonmonotonic) logic program and Φ is a set of priorities between literals and negation-as-failure formulas in the language. The semantics of PLP is given as *preferred answer sets* which are defined as the answer sets of P that are selected with respect to the priorities in Φ. It was shown that PLPs can realize various frameworks of nonmonotonic reasoning such as default reasoning [16], prioritized circumscription [13, 14] as well as preference abduction [12].

M.Y. Vardi and A. Voronkov (Eds.): LPAR 2003, LNAI 2850, pp. 259–273, 2003.

To realize prioritized reasoning in logic programming, there are several different frameworks and implementation techniques such as ordered logic programs [5], Logic Programs with Ordered Disjunctions [1], ordered default theories [4] and and preferred answer sets of extended logic programs [2]. As for the procedure of PLPs, on the other hand, Sakama and Inoue [18] provided a naive procedure for computing preferred answer sets of a PLP, but the procedure is applicable to a limited class of PLPs and it is turned unsound.

In this paper, we present a more efficient procedure to compute all preferred answer sets for a PLP in answer set programming (ASP) and show soundness and completeness theorems for the procedure. Our procedure is based on a *generate-and-test algorithm* and uses the technique of *meta-programming*. The basic idea of our approach is to translate a PLP (P, Φ) and any answer set S of a program P, into a single logic program $T[P, \Phi, S]$ whose answer sets represent answer sets of P preferable to S. More precisely, if $T[P, \Phi, S]$ is consistent, answer sets of P preferable to S can be obtained from the respective answer sets of $T[P, \Phi, S]$; otherwise we can conclude that such S is a "strictly" preferred answer set of (P, Φ). Thanks to our theorems, our procedure can compute all preferred answer sets of a given PLP, making use of preferences generated from such a translated logic program $T[P, \Phi, S]$ to decide whether an answer set S of P is preferred or not. Thus, our procedure can be easily implemented using answer set solvers (ASP solvers) such as *dlv* [6], *smodels* [15] and *MGTP* [10]. Moreover, we show that our approach can accommodate dynamic preferences [3] in addition to the original static ones which widen the class of PLPs and further increase their expressiveness.

The structure of the paper is as follows. In Section 2, we review some definitions and notation related to PLPs. In Section 3, we present two theorems and our sound and complete procedure of computing preferred answer sets. In Section 4, we give a brief discussion on applying our approach to a legal reasoning example. Section 5 provides some comparisons with related works and concluding remarks.

2   Preliminaries

We review some definitions and notations about PLP [17, 18].

2.1   General Extended Disjunctive Logic Programs

A *general extended disjunctive logic program* (GEDP) [11] is a set of rules of the form:

$$L_1 \mid \cdots \mid L_k \mid not\, L_{k+1} \mid not\, L_l \leftarrow L_{l+1}, \ldots, L_m, not\, L_{m+1}, \ldots, not\, L_n,$$
(1)

where $n \geq m \geq l \geq k \geq 0$, each L_i is a literal, that is either an atom A or its negation $\neg A$, and " $\mid$ " represents a disjunction. The left-hand side of $\leftarrow$ is the *head* and the right-hand side of $\leftarrow$ is the *body* of the rule. The rule with the empty head is called an *integrity constraint*. A rule with variables stands for the set of its ground instances (i.e. ground rules).

The semantics of a GEDP P is given by the *answer sets* [7, 11] as follows.

Definition 1. Let Lit_P be a set of all ground literals in the language of P.

First, let P be a *not*-free GEDP (i.e., for each rule $k = l, m = n$). Then, $S \subseteq Lit_P$ is an *answer set* of P if S is a minimal set satisfying the conditions:

1. For each ground rule $L_1 \mid \cdots \mid L_l \leftarrow L_{l+1}, \ldots, L_m$ in P, if $\{L_{l+1}, \ldots, L_m\} \subseteq S$, then $L_i \in S$ for some i ($1 \leq i \leq l$); In particular, for each integrity constraint $\leftarrow L_1, \ldots, L_m$ in P, $\{L_1, \ldots, L_m\} \not\subseteq S$ holds;
2. If S contains a pair of complementary literals, then $S = Lit_P$.

Second, let P be any GEDP and $S \subseteq Lit_P$. The *reduct* of P by S is a *not*-free GEDP P^S obtained as follows:

   A rule $L_1 \mid \cdots \mid L_l \leftarrow L_{l+1}, \ldots, L_m$ is in P^S
   iff there is a ground rule of the form (1) from P such that
$$\{L_{k+1}, \ldots, L_l\} \subseteq S \text{ and } \{L_{m+1}, \ldots, L_n\} \cap S = \emptyset.$$

For P^S, its answer sets have already been defined. Then, S is an answer set of P if S is an answer set of P^S.

An answer set is *consistent* if it is not Lit_P. The answer set Lit_P is said *contradictory*. A GEDP is *consistent* if it has a consistent answer set; otherwise, the program is *inconsistent*.

2.2   Prioritized Logic Programs

Given a GEDP P and the set of ground literals Lit_P, let $\mathcal{L}_P^*$ be the set defined as $Lit_P \cup \{not L \mid L \in Lit_P\}$. A prioritized logic program (PLP) is defined as follows.

Definition 2 (Priorities between Literals). A reflexive and transitive relation $\preceq$ is defined on $\mathcal{L}_P^*$. For any element e_1 and e_2 from $\mathcal{L}_P^*$, $e_1 \preceq e_2$ is called a *priority*, and we say e_2 *has a higher priority than* e_1. We write $e_1 \prec e_2$ if $e_1 \preceq e_2$ and $e_2 \not\preceq e_1$, and say e_2 *has a strictly higher priority than* e_1. A nonground priority stands for the set of its ground instances. That is, for tuples $\mathbf{x}$ and $\mathbf{y}$ of variables, $e_1(\mathbf{x}) \preceq e_2(\mathbf{y})$ stands for any priority $e_1(\mathbf{t}) \preceq e_2(\mathbf{s})$ for any instance $\mathbf{t}$ of $\mathbf{x}$ and instance $\mathbf{s}$ of $\mathbf{y}$.

Definition 3 (Prioritized Logic Programs: PLPs). A *prioritized logic program* (PLP) is defined as a pair (P, Φ), where P is a GEDP and Φ is a set of priorities on $\mathcal{L}_P^*$.

The declarative semantics of PLP is given by preferred answer sets as follows.

Definition 4 (Preferences between Answer Sets). Given a PLP (P, Φ), the preference relation $\sqsubseteq$ on answer sets of P is defined as follows: Let S_1 and S_2 be two answer sets of P. Then, S_2 is *preferable* to S_1 with respect to Φ, written as $S_1 \sqsubseteq S_2$, if for some element $e_2 \in S_2 \setminus S_1$,

(i) there is an element $e_1 \in S_1 \setminus S_2$ such that $e_1 \preceq e_2$, and (ii) there is no element $e_3 \in S_1 \setminus S_2$ such that $e_2 \prec e_3$.

Besides, the relation $\sqsubseteq$ on answer sets is also defined as reflexive and transitive. We write $S_1 \sqsubset S_2$ if $S_1 \sqsubseteq S_2$ and $S_2 \not\sqsubseteq S_1$. Hereafter, each $S_1 \sqsubseteq S_2$ is called *preference*.

Definition 5 (Preferred Answer Sets). An answer set S of P is called a *preferred answer set* (or *p-answer set*, for short) of P (with respect to Φ) if $S \sqsubseteq S'$ implies $S' \sqsubseteq S$ for any answer set S' of P.

Example 1.   Let (P, Φ) be the PLP such that

$$P: \quad p \leftarrow not\ q, \qquad\qquad \Phi: \quad p \preceq not\ q,$$
$$q \leftarrow not\ p,$$

where P has two answer sets $\{p\}$ and $\{q\}$. Of these, $\{q\}$ becomes the unique preferred answer set of (P, Φ).

Generally, NAF formulas in Φ are eliminated without changing the meaning of a PLP [18]. In the above example, a PLP (P, Φ) is transformed to the semantically equivalent (P', Φ') such that $P' = P \cup \{p' \leftarrow not\ p\}$, $\Phi' = \Phi \cup \{p \preceq p'\}$. As a result, (P', Φ') has the unique p-answer set $\{p',\ q\}$ which coincides with $\{q\}$ with respect to literals from Lit_P.

Then, without loss of generality in the following sections we consider a PLP (P, Φ) in which Φ contains no NAF formula.

3   Computing Preferred Answer Sets

Throughout this section, we introduce a sound and complete procedure for computing preferred answer sets of PLPs. In this section, we consider a ground PLP, i.e., a PLP (P, Φ) such that P is a ground GEDP and Φ is a set of priorities over ground literals.

3.1   Translation for Preference Generation

As is mentioned in the introduction, our procedure of computing preferred answer sets of a PLP is regarded as a *generate-and-test algorithm*, which constructs a logic program $T[P, \Phi, S]$ translated from both a given PLP (P, Φ) and any answer set S of a program P in order to generate preferences between answer sets of P in answer set programming.

First, we encode a given answer set S and another answer set S' of P in the single answer set of a program $T[P, \Phi, S]$, which is used for judging whether S' is preferable to S. To this end, we use *renaming of literals* such that each literal $L \in Lit_P$ in S is renamed by the newly introduced literal L^* respectively. This technique symbolically enables us to embed one answer set $S \subseteq Lit_P$ as a set S^* of renamed literals L^*, together with another one $S' \subseteq Lit_P$ in the same answer set E of $T[P, \Phi, S]$.

Second, to compare a literal $c \in S$ and another literal $d \in S'$ according to (i) and (ii) of Definition 4, we use *meta-programming* techniques. That is, to compare literals, a new ground term L_t is introduced for every literal $L \in Lit_P$. Note that both a literal $L \in Lit_P$ and its renamed literal L^* mentioned above are expressed using the same ground term L_t introduced for the corresponding literal L.

Third, we provide predicate symbols m_1 and m_2 such that, for the term c_t which corresponds to some literal $c \in Lit_P$ as well as its renamed literal c^*, $m_1(c_t)$ means $c \in S$ for a given answer set S, while $m_2(c_t)$ means $c \in S'$ for any answer set S' of P.

In the following, we define two sets, Lit_P^* and $\mathcal{C}$ where Lit_P^* is a set of renamed literals L^*s and $\mathcal{C}$ is a set of newly introduced ground terms L_ts mentioned above. Due to the restriction of answer set programming, we suppose that Lit_P is finite, and ground terms L_ts in $\mathcal{C}$ are individual constants which have no function symbols.

Definition 6. Lit_P^* and $\mathcal{C}$ are defined as follows.

$$Lit_P^* \overset{def}{=} \{L^* | L \in Lit_P\}$$

$$\mathcal{C} \overset{def}{=} \{L_t | L \in Lit_P\}$$

Next we define $T[P, \Phi, S]$ which is a *meta-program* constructed using a PLP (P, Φ) and an answer set S.

Definition 7. Given a PLP (P, Φ) and an answer set S of P, $T[P, \Phi, S]$ is the GEDP defined as:

$$T[P, \Phi, S] \overset{def}{=} P \cup \Gamma \cup \Pi,$$

where Γ is the set of *domain dependent* rules constructed from Φ and S as follows,

1. $L^* \leftarrow,$ for each $L \in S,$
    where each $L^* \in Lit_P^*$ is a renamed literal corresponding to $L \in S$ respectively,

2. $\preceq (a_t, b_t) \leftarrow,$ for any $a \preceq b \in \Phi$
    where $a_t, b_t \in \mathcal{C}$ are respective ground terms expressing literals $a, b \in Lit_P,$

3. $m_1(L_t) \leftarrow L^*,$ $m_2(L_t) \leftarrow L,$
    for every $L \in Lit_P$, its renamed literal $L^* \in Lit_P^*$ and a ground term $L_t \in \mathcal{C}$ expressing a literal $L,$

and Π is the set of *domain independent* rules as follows:

4. $\preceq (x, x) \leftarrow,$

5. $\preceq (x, z) \leftarrow \preceq (x, y), \; \preceq (y, z),$

6. $\prec (x, y) \leftarrow \preceq (x, y), \; not \preceq (y, x),$

7. $gr_1(x, y) \leftarrow m_1(x), \; \preceq (x, y), \; m_2(y), not \; m_2(x), \; not \; m_1(y),$

8. $gr_2(y, z) \leftarrow m_2(y), \; \prec (y, z), \; m_1(z), not \; m_1(y), \; not \; m_2(z),$

9. $attacked(y) \leftarrow gr_2(y, z),$

10. $defeated(x) \leftarrow gr_1(x, y), \; not \; attacked(y),$

11. $better \leftarrow defeated(x),$

12. $\leftarrow not \; better.$

Remark 1. $\preceq$ and $\prec$ in the above rules are predicate symbols.

Remark 2. The rule 2 enables us to express rules of P and priorities in Φ in the same logic program. The rule 4 and the rule 5 represent the reflexive and transitive laws of $\preceq$ respectively. The rule 5 and the rule 6 calculate the closure of the priority relation $\preceq$ and that of the strict priority relation $\prec$ respectively. Rules $7 \sim 10$ compute preference between S and another answer set of P according to (i) and (ii) of Definition 4. Thus, the rule 10 means that $defeated(x)$ is true if there exists some answer set S' of P such that, for an element $x \in S \setminus S'$, there exists some element $y \in S' \setminus S$ which has a higher priority than a element x and any element $z \in S \setminus S'$ does not have a strictly higher priority than y. Rule 11 means that $better$ is true if $defeated(x)$ is true for such $x \in S \setminus S'$.

Example 2. Let (P, Φ) be the PLP such that

$P:$ $\quad p \mid q \leftarrow,$

$\quad\quad q \mid r \leftarrow .$

$\Phi:$ $\quad p \preceq q, \; q \preceq r.$

P has two answer sets $S_1 = \{p, r\}$ and $S_2 = \{q\}$. With respect to the answer set S_1, $T[P, \Phi, S_1] = P \cup \Gamma_1 \cup \Pi$, is constructed with the following Γ_1,

$\Gamma_1 : \; p^* \leftarrow, \quad r^* \leftarrow, \quad \preceq (p_t, q_t) \leftarrow, \quad \preceq (q_t, r_t) \leftarrow,$

$\quad m_1(p_t) \leftarrow p^*, \quad m_1(q_t) \leftarrow q^*, \quad m_1(r_t) \leftarrow r^*,$

$\quad m_1(np_t) \leftarrow \neg p^*, \quad m_1(nq_t) \leftarrow \neg q^*, \quad m_1(nr_t) \leftarrow \neg r^*,$

$\quad m_2(p_t) \leftarrow p, \quad m_2(q_t) \leftarrow q, \quad m_2(r_t) \leftarrow r,$

$\quad m_2(np_t) \leftarrow \neg p, \quad m_2(nq_t) \leftarrow \neg q, \quad m_2(nr_t) \leftarrow \neg r.$

where $Lit_P = \{p, q, r, \neg p, \neg q, \neg r\}, \quad Lit_P^* = \{p^*, q^*, r^*, \neg p^*, \neg q^*, \neg r^*\},$
$C = \{p_t, q_t, r_t, np_t, nq_t, nr_t\}.$

Now, we define two kinds of preferred answer sets and show two theorems with respect to $T[P, \Phi, S]$, which guarantee the *soundness* and *completeness* of our transformation to compute all preferred answer sets of (P, Φ).

Definition 8 (Tie-Preferred, and Strictly Preferred Answer Set). A preferred answer set S of a PLP (P, Φ) is called *tie-preferred* if there is another preferred answer set S' of (P, Φ) such that $S \sqsubseteq S'$ and $S' \sqsubseteq S$. S is called *strictly preferred* if $S \not\sqsubseteq S'$ for any preferred answer set S'.

Theorem 1 (Soundness/Completeness of the Transformation). *Let* $T[P, \Phi, S]$ *be a GEDP constructed from a PLP (P, Φ) and an answer set S of P. Then if* $T[P, \Phi, S]$ *is consistent,* $S' \stackrel{def}{=} E \cap Lit_P$ *is another answer set of P such that* $S \sqsubseteq S'$ *for any answer set E of* $T[P, \Phi, S]$. *Conversely, if there is another answer set S' of P such that $S \sqsubseteq S'$, then* $T[P, \Phi, S]$ *is consistent.*

Proof: See Appendix.

Theorem 2. *Let* $T[P, \Phi, S]$ *be a GEDP constructed from a PLP (P, Φ) and an answer set S of P. Then,* $T[P, \Phi, S]$ *is inconsistent if and only if S is a strictly preferred answer set of (P, Φ).*

Proof: See Appendix.

Example 3.   Consider the PLP (P, Φ) in Example 2. According to Theorem 2, we can conclude that $S_1 = \{p, r\}$ is a strictly preferred answer set of (P, Φ) since $T[P, \Phi, S_1]$ is inconsistent. By contrast, for $S_2 = \{q\}$,

$$T[P, \Phi, S_2] = P \cup \Gamma_2 \cup \Pi$$
$$where \ \Gamma_2 = \Gamma_1 \setminus \{p^* \leftarrow, r^* \leftarrow\} \cup \{q^* \leftarrow\},$$

becomes consistent and has only one answer set E such that $E \cap Lit_P = \{p, r\}$, i.e. S_1. Thus we can obtain preference such that $S_2 \sqsubseteq S_1$ according to Theorem 1.

Example 4.   Let (P, Φ) be the PLP such that

$$P: \quad p \leftarrow not \ q,$$
$$q \leftarrow not \ p,$$
$$r \leftarrow p, \quad \neg s \leftarrow q.$$
$$\Phi: \quad p \preceq q, \ \neg s \preceq r. \qquad where \ Lit_P = \{p, q, r, s, \neg p, \neg q, \neg r, \neg s\}$$

P has two answer sets $S_1 = \{p, r\}$ and $S_2 = \{q, \neg s\}$.
With respect to $S_1 = \{p, r\}$, $T[P, \Phi, S_1] = P \cup \Gamma_1 \cup \Pi$ has rules of Γ_1 as follows:

$$\Gamma_1: p^* \leftarrow, \quad r^* \leftarrow, \quad \preceq (p_t, q_t) \leftarrow, \quad \preceq (ns_t, r_t) \leftarrow,$$
$$m_1(p_t) \leftarrow p^*, \quad m_1(q_t) \leftarrow q^*, \quad m_1(r_t) \leftarrow r^*, \quad m_1(s_t) \leftarrow s^*,$$
$$m_1(np_t) \leftarrow \neg p^*, \quad m_1(nq_t) \leftarrow \neg q^*, \quad m_1(nr_t) \leftarrow \neg r^*, \quad m_1(ns_t) \leftarrow \neg s^*,$$
$$m_2(p_t) \leftarrow p, \quad m_2(q_t) \leftarrow q, \quad m_2(r_t) \leftarrow r, \quad m_2(s_t) \leftarrow s,$$
$$m_1(np_t) \leftarrow \neg p, \quad m_1(nq_t) \leftarrow \neg q, \quad m_1(nr_t) \leftarrow \neg r, \quad m_1(ns_t) \leftarrow \neg s.$$

where $Lit_P^* = \{p^*, q^*, r^*, s^*, \neg p^*, \neg q^*, \neg r^*, \neg s^*\}, \mathcal{C} = \{p_t, q_t, r_t, s_t, np_t, nq_t, nr_t, ns_t\}$. In this case, $T[P, \Phi, S_1]$ is consistent and has only one answer set E_1 such that $E_1 \cap Lit_P = \{q, \neg s\}$, i.e. S_2. Similarly, for S_2, $T[P, \Phi, S_2]$ is consistent and has only

Table 1. A set Ψ of rules

$\sqsubseteq (x, x) \leftarrow as(x),$
$\sqsubseteq (x, z) \leftarrow \sqsubseteq (x, y), \ \sqsubseteq (y, z),$
$\sqsubset (x, y) \leftarrow \sqsubseteq (x, y), \ not \sqsubseteq (y, x),$
$worse(x) \leftarrow \sqsubset (x, y),$
$p\text{-}as(x) \leftarrow as(x), \ not \ worse(x).$

one answer set E_2 such that $E_2 \cap Lit_P=\{p, r\}$, i.e. S_1. As a result, preferences such that $S_1 \sqsubseteq S_2$ and $S_2 \sqsubseteq S_1$ are obtained according to Theorem 1. Thus according to Definition 8, we can decide that both S_1 and S_2 are tie-preferred answer sets.

3.2   A Procedure of Computing Preferred Answer Sets

We introduce a procedure *CompPAS* which computes all preferred answer sets of a PLP (P, Φ) based on Theorem 1 as follows. The procedure *CompPAS* uses a translated program $T[P, \Phi, S]$ to generate preferences with respect to a given answer set S. In addition, it uses a program Ψ shown in Table.1, to find all preferred answer sets of (P, Φ) from preferences generated by $T[P, \Phi, S]$.

Moreover, every answer set S of P is assigned a newly introduced individual constant s called an *answer set ID* respectively. Now, the procedure is as follows.

Procedure 1. $CompPAS(P, \Phi, \Delta)$

Input: a PLP (P, Φ)
Output: the set Δ of all preferred answer sets of (P, Φ)

In the following, AS is the set of answer sets of P, S and S' are answer sets of P, Ω is the set of answer set IDs, Δ is a set of preferred answer sets and Σ is a set of preferences which is initially the empty set $\emptyset$.

1. Compute the set AS of all answer sets of P.
2. If Φ is the empty set $\emptyset$,
   (a) then $\Delta := AS$, return Δ.
   (b) otherwise,
        i. let Ω be a set of answer set IDs such that $|\Omega| = |AS|$ [1],
        ii. for each answer set $S \in AS$, assign the corresponding answer set ID.
3. If $T[P, \Phi, S]$ is consistent for any answer set $S \in AS$ whose answer set ID is s, do from (a) to (c) for each answer set E of $T[P, \Phi, S]$.
   (a) put $S' := E \cap Lit_P$,
   (b) find the answer set ID $s' \in \Omega$ for S' where $S' \in AS$ by Theorem 1,
   (c) put $\Sigma := \Sigma \cup \{\sqsubseteq (s, s') \leftarrow\}$.

---

[1] For any set A, $|A|$ denotes the cardinality of A.

4. Compute an answer set U of the following logic program,

$$\Psi \cup \Sigma \cup \{as(s) \leftarrow |s \in \Omega\}$$

where Ψ is a set of rules shown in Table 1.

5. Return Δ which is given by

$\Delta = \{S \in AS \mid S$ is an answer set whose answer set ID s satisfies
$\qquad p\text{-}as(s) \in U\}.$

Remark 3. $\sqsubseteq$ and $\sqsubset$ are predicate symbols denoting preference relations defined in Definition 4 .

Remark 4. $as(s)$ and $p\text{-}as(s)$ represent that there exists some answer set of P whose answer set ID is s, and there exists some preferred answer set of (P, Φ) whose answer set ID is s, respectively.

Example 5.   Let (P, Φ) be the PLP such that

P: $p \leftarrow not\ q, not\ r,$
$\qquad q \leftarrow not\ p, not\ r,$
$\qquad r \leftarrow not\ p, not\ q,$
$\qquad s \leftarrow q.$

Φ: $p \preceq q,\ q \preceq p,\ s \preceq r.$

Here Lit_P, Lit_P^* and $\mathcal{C}$ are the same as those of Example 4. Preferred answer sets of this (P, Φ) can be computed using Procedure 1 as follows. P has three answer sets such as $S_1 = \{p\}$, $S_2 = \{q, s\}$, and $S_3 = \{r\}$, whose answer set IDs are s_1, s_2 and s_3, respectively. Then, in step 3, since $T[P, \Phi, S]$ is inconsistent only for $S = S_3$,

$$\Sigma = \{\sqsubseteq (s_1, s_2) \leftarrow,\ \sqsubseteq (s_2, s_1) \leftarrow,\ \sqsubseteq (s_2, s_3) \leftarrow\}$$

is obtained from preferences which are $S_1 \sqsubseteq S_2$ generated by $T[P, \Phi, S_1]$ as well as $S_2 \sqsubseteq S_1$, $S_2 \sqsubseteq S_3$ by $T[P, \Phi, S_2]$. In step 5, $\Delta = \{\{r\}\}$ is returned, since $p\text{-}as(s_3) \in U$, $p\text{-}as(s_1) \notin U$, $p\text{-}as(s_2) \notin U$ for an answer set U of a program: $\Psi \cup \Sigma \cup \{as(s_1) \leftarrow, as(s_2) \leftarrow, as(s_3) \leftarrow\}$. Thus, using the procedure, we can obtain the result that only $\{r\}$ is a preferred answer set of (P, Φ). [2]

Example 6. Let us compute the tie-preferred answer sets of the PLP in Example 4 using Procedure 1. Suppose that in step 2 of the procedure, s_1 and s_2 are assigned to answers sets $S_1 = \{p, r\}$ and $S_2 = \{q, \neg s\}$ as their IDs respectively.

In step 3, Σ is obtained as $\{\sqsubseteq (s_1, s_2) \leftarrow,\ \sqsubseteq (s_2, s_1) \leftarrow\}$ wrt preferences $S_1 \sqsubseteq S_2$ and $S_2 \sqsubseteq S_1$ shown in Example 4. Thus, in step 4, we obtain $p\text{-}as(s_1) \in U$ and $p\text{-}as(s_2) \in U$ for the answer set U of $\Psi \cup \Sigma \cup \{as(s_1) \leftarrow, as(s_2) \leftarrow\}$.

Therefore, we can decide both $\{p, r\}$ and $\{q, \neg s\}$ as preferred answer sets of (P, Φ) using our procedure.

---

[2] Sakama and Inoue's procedure for selecting p-answer sets [18] computes both $\{p\}$ and $\{r\}$ as preferred answer sets of this (P, Φ). So, their procedure is not sound.

4 Application to Legal Reasoning

We discuss an application of our approach to a legal reasoning example with dynamic preferences. Our procedure can accommodate dynamic preferences [3] by extending the framework of PLPs though the original PLPs are limited to the static ones. It is based on the result that, both Theorem1 and Theorem2 also hold, even if priorities with preconditions exist in Φ, by expressing them with rules of a stratified logic program whose heads are literals of $\preceq$ instead of rules without body for rule 2 in $T[P, \Phi, S_1]$.

The legal problem [9] is as follows. The domain knowledge is about *the person's ship* and *laws of the Uniform Commercial Code (UCC)* and *the Ship Mortgage Act (SMA)*, which are expressed by a set P of the following rules,

$$
\begin{array}{lll}
P: & perfected \leftarrow posses, not\ ab1, & (UCC) \\
& \neg perfected \leftarrow ship, \neg filstate, not\ ab2, & (SMA) \\
& posses \leftarrow, \quad ship \leftarrow, \quad \neg filstate \leftarrow, \\
& ab1|not\ ab1 \leftarrow, \quad ab2|not\ ab2 \leftarrow, \quad \leftarrow ab1, ab2, \\
& ucc \leftarrow not\ ab1, \quad sma \leftarrow not\ ab2.
\end{array}
$$

Since the two laws are in conflict with one another, they lead to two answer sets S_1 and S_2 of P as follows.

$$
\begin{aligned}
S_1 &= \{perfected, posses, ship, \neg filstate, ab2, ucc\}. \\
S_2 &= \{\neg perfected, posses, ship, \neg filstate, ab1, sma\}.
\end{aligned}
$$

Now, there are two well-known legal principles for resolving such conflict between laws as follows.

The principle of Lex Posterior gives precedence newer laws, and the principle of Lex Superior gives precedence to laws supported by the higher authority. In our case, UCC is newer than the SMA, and the SMA has higher authority since it is a federal law.

The above knowledge is described as a set Φ_1 which consists of priorities with preconditions. Then, we can represent it as a following stratified logic program, which corresponds to the extended rule 2 of Γ in Definition 7 as follows. [3]

$$
\begin{array}{lll}
\Phi_1: & moreRecent(ucc_t, sma_t) \leftarrow, \\
& fed(sma_t) \leftarrow, \quad state(ucc_t) \leftarrow, \\
& lp(Y, X) \leftarrow moreRecent(X, Y), \\
& ls(Y, X) \leftarrow fed(X), state(Y), \\
& \preceq (Y, X) \leftarrow lp(Y, X), not\ conf_1(X, Y), & (LP) \\
& \preceq (Y, X) \leftarrow ls(Y, X), not\ conf_1(X, Y), & (LS)
\end{array}
$$

---

[3] Precisely speaking, Φ_1 for a PLP (P, Φ_1) is a stratified logic program where terms occuring in Φ_1 are members of $\mathcal{C}$, and each rule from Φ containing variables stands for the set of all its ground instances such that any variable is replaced by any ground term from $\mathcal{C}$.

where $conf_1$ is a predicate symbol denoting *conflict resolution* for the conflict between the legal principles with respect to laws X and Y. In this case of (P, Φ_1), $T[P, \Phi_1, S_1]$ has only one answer set E_1 such that $E_1 \cap Lit_P = S_2$, and $T[P, \Phi_1, S_2]$ has only one answer set E_2 such that $E_2 \cap Lit_P = S_1$. These lead to $S_1 \sqsubseteq S_2$ and $S_2 \sqsubseteq S_1$. As a result, we obtain two *tie-preferred* answer sets S_1 and S_2 of this PLP due to the conflict between two legal principles, i.e. Lex Posterior and Lex Superior.

Next, suppose we have a new preference information such that Lex Superior has a higher priority than Lex Posterior as follows.

$$LexPosterior(X, Y) \preceq LexSuperior(U, V).$$

In our framework, such an additional *meta-priority* can be expressed by a tie-breaking rule (2) as follows.

$$conf_1(Y, X) \leftarrow lp(X, Y), ls(Y, X), not \ conf_2(X, Y), \tag{2}$$

where $conf_2$ denotes the conflict resolution for one level higher priorities than that of $conf_1$. Then, this case is expressed by a PLP (P, Φ_2) where $T[P, \Phi_2, S_2]$ is inconsistent. Thus we obtain the result that S_2 is a *strictly preferred* answer set of (P, Φ_2), but S_1 is not preferred in similar way. Therefore, $\neg perfected$ is determined.

5 Related Works and Conclusion

In this paper, we present a sound and complete procedure to compute all preferred answer sets of a given PLP based on answer set programming. Moreover, we introduce the capability of representing not only static preference but also dynamic one by slightly extending the framework of PLPs. With respect to complexity, our procedure calls the ASP solver polynomial order times. We are now going to implement our procedure by using *dlv* and C++.

In the following, we compare our approach with related works in the aspects of the methodology, preference representation and complexity.
(1) Sakama and Inoue's naive procedure
Sakama and Inoue [18] firstly provided the procedure for selecting preferred answer sets of a PLP. Their procedure computes all answer sets and then finds preferred answer sets by means of comparing all answer sets pairwise with respect to the "strict" priority relation $\prec$ obtained from Φ. According to their Theorem 4.1 in [18], they claim that their procedure is sound, and completeness of the procedure also holds if preferred answer sets of a given PLP are *cycle-free*. But Example 5 of this paper shows that their procedure is not sound. To fix the problem, it is necessary to use the pre-order priority relation $\preceq$ which is reflexive and transitive instead of using irreflexive "strict" priority relation $\prec$ from Φ. With this consideration, their procedure can compute the correct preferred answer set of Example 5. However, even if their procedure is corrected to become sound in this way, there still exists such a problem in the corrected procedure that it cannot find any tie-preferred answer set but only compute strictly preferred answer sets.

By contrast, without comparing all answer sets pairwise, our procedure *CompPAS* can obtain all strictly preferred answer sets immediately by checking the inconsistency of $T[P, \Phi, S]$ for each answer set of P in step 3. In addition, our procedure can find any strictly preferred answer set as well as any tie-preferred answer of a given PLP in step 4 and step 5 of *CompPAS* based on Theorem 1. Furthermore, in our approach, both P and Φ are represented in the same logic program $T[P, \Phi, S]$, it enables us to handle dynamic preferences in PLP though it is originally limited to the static ones.

(2) Delgrande and Schaub's approach

Delgrande and Schaub proposed the framework of a *ordered logic program* [5]. It is represented by an extended logic program in which rules are named by terms and preferences among rules are given by a set of preference atoms representing preference relations over a set of rule names. According to their methodology, each preference between rules is specified as a strict partial order and preferred answer sets of an ordered logic program Π are obtained as answer sets of a standard extended logic program which is translated from Π by preserving the order. This feature is a little similar to our case that the strictly preferred answer set of PLP can be decided directly when our translated program $T[P, \Phi, S]$ is inconsistent. However, in our case, tie-preferred answer sets can be also found after such translation, since priorities are represented by a pre-order relation $\preceq$. The complexity of our approach (see Lemma 4.4 in [18]) lies in the one level higher of the polynomial hierarchy than theirs. With respect to dynamic preferences, their framework can treat them as well as ours.

(3) Brewka, Niemelä and Syrjänen's approach

Brewka et al.[1] proposed *logic programs with ordered disjunction(LPODs)*. According to their approach, an ordered disjunction appears in the head of a rule which enables to represent knowledge above preference. Their implementation is based on two normal logic programs, a generator and a tester in order to compute preferred answer sets efficiently. Our procedure also consists of a generator which generates answer sets in step 1, and a tester which checks whether each answer set is preferred or not in step 4 using the preferences generated in step 3.

References

1. G. Brewka, I. Niemelä and T. Syrjänen: Implementing Ordered Disjunction Using Answer Set Solvers for Normal Programs, *Proc. 8th European Conference on Logics in Artificial Intelligence (JELIA'02), LNAI 2424*, Springer (2002) 445-455.
2. G. Brewka and T. Eiter: Preferred Answer Sets for Extended Logic Programs, *Artificial Intelligence* **109** (1999) 297-356.
3. G. Brewka: Well-founded Semantics for Extended Logic Programs with Dynamic Preferences, *Journal of Artificial Intelligence Research 4* (1996) 19-36.
4. J. P. Delgrande and T. Schaub T: Expressing Preferences in Default Logic, *Artificial Intelligence* **123** (2000) 41-87.
5. J. P. Delgrande, T. Schaub and H. Tompits: A Framework for Compiling Preferences in Logic Programs, Theory and Practice of Logic Programming 3(2) (2003) 129-187.

6. T. Eiter, N. Leone, C. Mateis, G. Pfeifer, F. Scarcello: A deductive system for nonmonotonic reasoning, *Proc. LPNMR-97, LNCS 1265*, Springer (1997) 364-375.
7. M. Gelfond and V. Lifschitz: Classical Negation in Logic Programs and Disjunctive Databases. *New Generation Computing 9* (1991) 365-385.
8. Gelfond, M. and Lifschitz, V.: Compiling Circumscriptive Theories into Logic Programs, *Proc. AAA1-88*, 455-459. Extended version in: *Proc. 2nd Int. Workshop on Nonmonotonic Reasoning*, LNAI 346 (1988) 74-99.
9. T. F. Gorden: The Pleadings Game: An Artifical Intelligence Model of Procedural Justice. *Ph.D. thesis, TU Darmstadt* (1993).
10. K. Inoue, M. Koshimura and R. Hasegawa: Embedding negation as failure into a model generation theorem prover, *In: Deepak Kapur, editor, Proceedings of the Eleventh International Conference on Automated Deduction, LNAI 607*, Springer (1992) 400-415.
11. K. Inoue and C. Sakama: On Positive Occurrences of Negation as Failure. *Proc. KR'94* (1994) 293-304.
12. K. Inoue and C. Sakama: Abducing Priorities to Derive Intended Conclusions *Proc. Sixteenth International Joint Conference on Artificial Intelligence* (1999) 44-49.
13. V. Lifschitz: Computing Circumscription. *Proc. IJCAI-85* (1985) 121-127.
14. J. McCarthy: Applications of Circumscription to Formalizing Commonsense Knowledge. *Artificial Intelligence* **28** (1986) 89-116.
15. I. Niemelä and P. Simons: Smodels: An implementation of the stable model and well-founded semantics for normal logic programs. *Proc. the Fourth International Conference on Logic Programming and Nonmonotonic Reasoning*, Springer-Verlag, (1997) 420-429.
16. D. Poole: A Logical framework for default reasoning, *Artificial Intelligence* **36** (1988) 27-47.
17. C. Sakama and K. Inoue: Representing Priorities in Logic Programs. *Proc. Joint International Conference and Symposium on Logic Programming* (1996) 82-96.
18. C. Sakama and K. Inoue: Prioritized logic programming and its application to commonsense reasoning, *Artificial Intelligence 123* (2000) 185-222.

Appendix: Proofs of Theorems

Proof of Theorem 1

Proof: ($\Longrightarrow$) Since $T[P, \Phi, S] = P \cup \Gamma \cup \Pi$ is consistent, it holds that *better* $\in E$ for any answer set E of $T[P, \Phi, S]$, and E is also an answer set of $T[P, \Phi, S] \setminus \{\leftarrow$ *not better*$\}$. Now, it is easily shown that E should be an augmented answer set of P which not only includes an answer set of P but also has ground head literals of the rules from $\Gamma \cup \Pi \setminus \{\leftarrow$ *not better*$\}$. Thus $S' = E \cap Lit_P$ should be an answer set of P. According to the rule 1, it is obvious that $S^* = E \cap Lit_P^*$ is a renamed answer set of a given answer set S such that each $L^* \in S^*$ is a renamed literal wrt $L \in S$. Then, according to rule 3,

$$m_1(c_t) \in E \quad \text{iff} \quad c^* \in S^* \quad (\text{i.e. } c \in S)$$

$$m_2(d_t) \in E \quad \text{iff} \quad d \in S' \overset{def}{=} E \cap Lit_P$$

where $c_t \in \mathcal{C}$ wrt c and $d_t \in \mathcal{C}$ wrt d. Let Φ^* be a closure of Φ. Due to rules 2, 4 and 5, it holds that,

$$\preceq (a_t, b_t) \in E \quad \text{iff} \quad a \preceq b \in \Phi^*$$

In addition, let Ψ^* be a closure of strict priorities defined as follows:

$$\Psi^* \stackrel{def}{=} \{a \prec b \mid a \preceq b \in \Phi^* \wedge b \preceq a \notin \Phi^*\}$$

Then, according to rule 6, it holds that,

$$\prec (a_t, b_t) \in E \quad \text{iff} \quad a \prec b \in \Psi^*.$$

Now, according to rules 7 ∼ 11, it holds that,

$better \in E$ for any answer set E of $T[P, \Phi, S]$

iff $defeated(c_t) \in E$ for $\exists c_t$

iff $gr_1(c_t, d_t) \in E \wedge attacked(d_t) \notin E$ for $\exists c_t \exists d_t$

iff for $\exists c_t$ s.t. $m_1(c_t) \in E \wedge m_2(c_t) \notin E$ and

$\exists d_t$ s.t. $m_2(d_t) \in E \wedge m_1(d_t) \notin E$,

$\preceq (c_t, d_t) \in E \wedge \prec (d_t, e_t) \notin E$

for $\forall e_t$ s.t. $m_1(e_t) \in E \wedge m_2(e_t) \notin E$

iff for $\exists c \in S \setminus S'$, $\exists d \in S' \setminus S$ such that $c \preceq d \in \Phi^*$,

there is no $e \in S \setminus S'$ such that $d \prec e \in \Psi^*$

iff $S \sqsubseteq S'$ where $S' \stackrel{def}{=} E \cap Lit_P$ and $S \neq S'$

($\Longleftarrow$) Suppose that there is another answer set S' of P such that $S \sqsubseteq S'$. Then, $S \sqsubseteq S'$ should be derived in a way of either case 1. or 2. as follows.

1. $S \sqsubseteq S'$ is directly decided only using priorities in Φ^*.

2. $S \sqsubseteq S'$ is not directly decided using priorities in Φ^*, but is indirectly decided via the transitive law as follows.
   For some other answer set U of P, the following (a) and (b) should be satisfied:
   (a) $S \sqsubseteq U$ is directly decided using priorities in Φ^*.
   (b) $U \sqsubseteq S'$ is decided inductively in a way of either case 1. or case 2..

   Then $S \sqsubseteq S'$ is transitively derived from $S \sqsubseteq U$ and $U \sqsubseteq S'$ according to (a) and (b).

Thus, in the case of either 1. or 2., there exists some answer set V of P which is directly decided to be preferable to S due to priorities in Φ^*. Then, according to Definition 4, there exists some element $d \in V \setminus S$ such that

(i) there is an element $c \in S \setminus V$ such that $c \preceq d$, and

(ii) there is no element $e \in S \setminus V$ such that $d \prec e$.

So, due to the existence of such an element $d \in V \setminus S$, it is easily shown that for such another answer set V of P, $\{L \leftarrow \mid L \in V\} \cup \Gamma \cup \Pi$ becomes consistent.

Therefore, $T[P, \Phi, S] \stackrel{def}{=} P \cup \Gamma \cup \Pi$ also becomes consistent.   □

Proof of Theorem 2

Proof: ($\Longrightarrow$) The contrapositive is proved. That is, in the following, we prove that if S is not a strictly preferred answer set of (P, Φ); $T[P, \Phi, S]$ is consistent.

Suppose that S is not a strictly preferred answer set of (P, Φ). Then S is either (i) a tie-preferred answer set, or (ii) not a preferred answer set. In case of (i), there exists some preferred answer set S' of (P, Φ) such that $S \sqsubseteq S'$ and $S' \sqsubseteq S$ where $S' \neq S$ according to Definition 8. In case of (ii), since S is not a preferred answer set of (P, Φ), there should exist some answer set S' of P such that $S \sqsubseteq S'$ and $S' \not\sqsubseteq S$ according to Definition 5. Thus in both cases, there exists another preferred answer set S' of P such that $S \sqsubseteq S'$. As a result, we can conclude that $T[P, \Phi, S]$ is consistent according to the proof of $\Leftarrow$ part of Theorem 1.

($\Longleftarrow$) Suppose that S is a strictly preferred answer set of (P, Φ). In the following, assuming that $T[P, \Phi, S]$ is consistent, we show that the contradiction is derived.

Since $T[P, \Phi, S]$ is consistent according to the assumption, $S' = E \cap Lit_P$ should be another answer set of P such that,

$$S \sqsubseteq S' \tag{3}$$

for any answer set E of $T[P, \Phi, S]$ according to the proof of $\Rightarrow$ part of Theorem 1. Then $S \sqsubseteq S'$ for a preferred answer set S of (P, Φ) leads to $S' \sqsubseteq S$ due to Definitions 5. Thus $S' \overset{def}{=} E \cap Lit_P$ should be also another preferred answer set of (P, Φ). On the other hand, since S is a strictly preferred answer set of (P, Φ), it holds that,

$$S \not\sqsubseteq S'' \tag{4}$$

for any preferred answer set S'' such that $S \neq S''$ according to Definition 8, which contradicts (3). □

A Syntax-Based Approach to Reasoning about Actions and Events*

Quoc Bao Vo[1], Abhaya Nayak[2], and Norman Foo[3]

[1] FR Informatik, Universität des Saarlandes,
66041 Saarbrücken, Germany,
bao@ags.uni-sb.de
[2] Department of Computing, Division of Information and Communication Sciences,
Macquarie University,
Sydney, NSW 2109, Australia,
abhaya@ics.mq.edu.au
[3] School of Computer Science and Engineering, University of New South Wales,
Sydney, NSW 2052, Australia,
norman@cse.unsw.edu.au

Abstract. In this paper, we introduce an alternative approach to reasoning about action. The approach provides a solution to the frame and the ramification problem in a uniform manner. The approach involves keeping a (syntax-based) model of the world that is updated when actions are performed. The approach is similar to the STRIPS system in which formulas are deleted and added as effects of an action. The approach however does not suffer from STRIPS' limitations in expressivity.

1 Introduction

Reasoning about action has been one of the classic areas of artificial intelligence (AI) research (see [10]). One of the main goals for research in the area is a good formalism to capture rational behaviour and common sense for automated agents. Other implications reach as far as database applications, e.g. database update operators, or system and control theories. As the foundation towards achieving rational behaviours, such a formalism should play a major role in planning. As such, a major problem identified by researchers in the area has been the motivation for the invention of one of the most successful and influential planners, *viz.* the STRIPS system [1].

Researchers in the community have since then searched for a good solution to their infamous problems, e.g. the frame, the qualification and the ramification problem. Many kinds of logic have been invented including several versions of Situation Calculus, Event Calculus, Dynamic Logic, Action languages, etc. Most of them rest on the same base: the frame problem is inherent for any kind of logical axiomatisation. Thus, for any logical approach to reasoning about action

---

* This work was performed when the first author was at the School of Computer Science and Engineering, University of New South Wales.

M.Y. Vardi and A. Voronkov (Eds.): LPAR 2003, LNAI 2850, pp. 274–288, 2003.

to be successful, a good axiomatisation must be discovered. Such an axiomatisation should overcome or at least get around the frame problem. To most people, this could be accomplished through adding a set of axioms, or an axiom, to some base formalisation. Such axioms are called the *frame axioms*. Depending on the underlying logics, these axioms can be realised as propositional, first-order, or even second-order axioms (e.g. in Situation Calculus, or Event Calculus), or as inference rules (e.g. in default logic, logic programming.) These usually result in a quite complex representation of the domain under consideration and normally incur a great deal of computation.

Alternatively, a number of researchers have employed the operational semantics of actions and causation to compute the effects of actions. These are well known as the state based formalisms. In particular, a transition system or an automaton will be introduced to capture the dynamics of the system under consideration. By maintaining the set of states that are compatible with its knowledge, the agent can reason about the resulting states after performing an action. The problems with this approach include: the size of the state space can be huge, it may involve checking a large number of states if the agent's knowledge is very incomplete, and the problem of expanding the language vocabulary to incorporate new concepts.

As a result, researchers in the planning community have been getting frustrated with the complexity of the formalisms provided by the reasoning about action community. Few have used these formalisations as the foundation for their planners. Instead, many of them have still used the thirty year old STRIPS systems at the heart of their planners.

In this paper we introduce a STRIPS-like representation and computation machinery. The agent represents what it believes as a set of sentences. The underlying logic which can be monotonic or non-monotonic tells the agent what can be derived from a given theory. The task of reasoning about actions is carried out through a STRIPS-like mechanism by removing certain formulas from the current theory before adding the updated information to form the updated theory. The process is provably correct relative to a state-based representation. With this simplicity, this hopefully provides people in the planning community with a representation and reasoning machinery to serve as the basis for an efficient planner. On the other hand, we don't have to sacrifice the expressiveness in representation which has been suffered in STRIPS.

The rest of the paper is organised as follows. Some logical preliminaries are presented in the next section. Then in Section 3 we will discuss our solution to the frame problem, through which our formalisation for reasoning about action is also fully exposed. As our approach is based on a formalisation of (partial) state update, it shares many commonalities with formalisms which are based on transition systems. We thus show the connection from our approach to one such formalism, *viz.* the action language $\mathcal{A}$, in Section 4. Section 5 discusses how the ramification problem is straightforwardly dealt with in our framework. Section 6 concludes the paper with a discussion about the related works and a summary about the framework described in this paper. All the proofs of the results presented in the paper are presented in the full paper and can also be found in [12].

2 Logical Preliminaries

We shall be dealing with the finite propositional language $\mathcal{L}_0$ consisting of the well formed formulas (wffs) over an alphabet $\mathbf{P} = \{p, q, r, \ldots\}$ of propositional letters. We assume the availability of the logical constants $\wedge, \vee, \neg, \mathbf{false}, \mathbf{true}$ while the other connectives, e.g. $\supset, \equiv$, will be considered as shorthands of more elaborate expressions. $L, L_1, \ldots$ denote literals. Clauses are disjunctions of literals. We will also interchangeably express clauses as sets of literals. Thus, $L_2 \vee L_5 \vee L_6 = \{L_2, L_5, L_6\} = \{L_2\} \cup \{L_5, L_6\} = L_2 \vee \{L_5, L_6\}$. $\varphi, \psi, \chi, \ldots$ denote clauses and formulas.

The following convention is also assumed throughout: If L is a literal, then by $|L|$ we denote its affirmative component, i.e. $|p| = |\neg p| = p$ where $p \in \mathbf{P}$. We are now introducing several notions to be used in the rest of the paper.

(*atm*) We denote by $atm(\varphi)$ the set of atoms occurring in the formula φ. For example, $atm(\neg p \vee (p \wedge q)) = \{p, q\}$, $atm(\mathbf{false}) = atm(\mathbf{true}) = \emptyset$.

(*theory*) Given the language $\mathcal{L}_0$, we define a *theory* to be a finite set of clauses. We can also treat a theory as a formula by taking the conjunction of its clauses.

(*partial interpretation*) Let $S \subseteq \mathbf{P}$ be given. A *partial interpretation* I over S is a function from S to $\{\mathbf{false}, \mathbf{true}\}$. We sometimes represent a partial interpretation I as a set of literals whose atoms are members of S such that for each $p \in S$, (i) $p \in I$ iff $I(p) = \mathbf{true}$ and (i) $\neg p \in I$ iff $I(p) = \mathbf{false}$.

(*state*) A *state* is a partial interpretation over $\mathbf{P}$. We denote by $Mod(\varphi)$ the set of all states that satisfy the formula φ.

3 A Simple Solution to the Frame Problem

3.1 Intuition

Given a set of formulas modelling the agent's beliefs about the dynamic world, the agent wants to reason about the outcome of an event e.[1] If the agent is to represent the domain as a set of logical formulas, the problem of axiomatizing the effects of an event becomes an interesting issue. A theorem prover can only show that an action of picking up a box does not change the color of that box, does not change the position of the house, and neither does it create a nuclear war, etc. if these (non) effects are explicitly axiomatized in the action description. This is well known as the frame problem. The most sought after approach to this problem has been to augment the core axiomatization with the so-called frame axioms to allow the theorem prover to arrive at the conclusions about unchanged fluents after an action. This has led to solutions, e.g. by Reiter [11],

---

[1] We consider actions as a special case of events. Accordingly, the execution of an action corresponds to an occurrence of the corresponding event.

Lin and Shoham [8], etc. Another approach is to accomplish the task of reasoning about the interesting actions using a special procedure coupled with a suitable data structure for representing the action descriptions. This has been the core of the STRIPS planner [1]. In this approach, each state of the world is expressed as a set of formulas. An event transforms the world from one state to another. The agent is normally given the initial state. To discover which state the world would become after an occurrence of an event E in a state σ, the agent uses the event description of E. An event description consists of a precondition which is a formula, and an add list and a delete list which are sets of formulas. If the precondition is satisfied in σ, the next state will be the result of removing all formulas in the delete list from σ and then adding all formulas in the add list to the resulting set of formulas. Lifschitz [6] has shown that this approach only works under severe restrictions, i.e. when the formulas allowed to represent the states, and the add and the delete lists are members of a set of specially designed formulas. For instance, only atomic formulas will be allowed.

While we enjoy the simplicity of the STRIPS approach, we are annoyed by the restrictions on its expressivity which would severely limit the actions the agent wants to represent. However, a simple modification to this approach can lead to a good solution to the frame problem without sacrificing the simplicity behind the STRIPS approach. Informally, we represent an event with its precondition and postcondition which are arbitrary formulas. There may even be multiple event descriptions for a single event depending on their preconditions. A world state will be represented as a finite set of arbitrary formulas, called a *theory*. All formulas will be normalised in CNF. Thus we may interchangeably use a set of clauses to refer to a formula or a finite set of formulas.

Now, let an event E be performed in a state σ. If the precondition of E is satisfied in σ, we would like to delete several clauses in σ before adding the post condition of E into the resulting set of clauses. Which clauses should we delete from σ? Under some conditions, the answer is as simple as: If Δ is the set of atoms of the postcondition then just delete all clauses whose sets of atoms have non-empty intersection with Δ. Intuitively, every atom which occurs in the postcondition of the event E potentially holds the value dictated in the postcondition of E, at least in one of the possible next states in case there are disjunctions in the postcondition of E. Thus the clauses in σ that contain those atoms should not be considered worth believing in the next state. In fact the only case when such a clause, called c, still maintains its status in the next state is when there exists some clause c' such that $c' \subseteq c$ and c' is derivable from the postcondition. In that case, even though c is deleted from σ in the first place, it will be restored in the next state as it is contained in the postcondition of event E. We remark that the reason for c to be in the next state is not because it is worth retaining from the previous state but rather because it is in the post condition of the event E.

To briefly summarise, our formalism centers around a syntactical approach to systematic detection of *relevant* formulas (with respect to a particular action or event) in the current state. Such relevant formulas must be removed from the theory representing the current state before the postconditions of the action/event are to be added to obtain the next state of the world. The set of atoms Δ discussed above provides the connection between the postconditions of the action or event with the "relevant" formulas from the theory representing the current state. We ignore the domain constraints, i.e. formulas that hold in all states, for now. We'll show how our framework is extended to deal with indirect effects and domain constraints later.

For example, $\sigma = \{s, t, r, p \vee q\}$, and $pre(a) = \textbf{true}$ and $post(E) = \{p \vee r\}$ then the next state $\sigma' = (\sigma \setminus \{r, p \vee q\}) \cup \{p \vee r\} = \{s, t, p \vee r\}$. There are possible next states in which r does not hold and the other in which $p \vee q$ does not hold.

Is there a condition for this approach to work correctly? Yes, there is one such condition. The following example shows just that. Assume that $\sigma = \{p, \neg p \vee q\}$ and $pre(E) = p$ and $post(E) = \{p\}$ then following the above approach, the next state $\sigma' = \{p\}$. However, intuitively we should have $\rho = \{p, q\}$ as the next state. The lesson learnt from this example is that the clause $c = \{q\}$ is a logical consequence of σ which happens to be independent of the postcondition of E. However, as it isn't too hard to find such independent clauses, a small modification on the above would do the trick. Now we proceed to formalizing this informal idea.

3.2   Formalization

In the following, we will make extensive use of the notation Δ as a set of propositional letters to which we have informally referred in the preceding sub-section. Intuitively, Δ consists of the atoms that occur in the postconditions of the action or event under consideration and provides the connection to the "relevant" formulas in the theory representing the current state of the world.

Definition 1. Let $\Delta \subseteq \mathbf{P}$ be given. We say that $\varphi \in \mathcal{L}_0$ is Δ-independent iff $atm(\varphi) \cap \Delta = \emptyset$.

Given a theory $T \subseteq \mathcal{L}_0$, $ind_\Delta(T)$ denotes the set of all Δ-independent members of T.

Definition 2. Let $\Delta \subseteq \mathbf{P}$ be given and Φ a set of formulas, a formula φ is a Δ-independent consequence of Φ iff
(i) $\Phi \models \varphi$, and
(ii) φ is Δ-independent.

The following definition specifies how independent consequences of a set of clauses are computed.

Let $\Delta \subseteq \mathbf{P}$ be given and T a set of clauses. Define:

- $T_0 = T$; and
- for $i \geq 0$: $T_{i+1} = T_i \cup \{\varphi_1 \vee \varphi_2 :$ there exists $p \in \Delta$ such that $p \vee \varphi_1, \neg p \vee \varphi_2 \in T_i\}$.

Then, $res_\Delta(T) \overset{def}{=} \bigcup_{i=0}^{\infty} T_i$.

Intuitively, $res_\Delta(T)$ represents the closure under **res**olution of the theory T with respect to the propositional letters from Δ.

Fact 1. *Let a theory T be given. For all $\Delta \subseteq \mathbf{P}$, $T \models res_\Delta(T)$.*

Theorem 1. *Given a set of atoms Δ and a theory T, a clause φ is an independent consequence of T with respect to Δ iff $ind_\Delta(res_\Delta(T)) \models \varphi$.*

Example 1. Let $T = \{p \vee q \vee r, \neg p \vee t, \neg r \vee s, \neg s \vee \neg t\}$ and $\Delta = \{p, r\}$.
Then $T_0 = T = \{p \vee q \vee r, \neg p \vee t, \neg r \vee s, \neg s \vee \neg t\}$,
$T_1 = T_0 \cup \{q \vee r \vee t, p \vee q \vee s\}$, and
$T_2 = T_1 \cup \{q \vee s \vee t\} = \{p \vee q \vee r, \neg p \vee t, \neg r \vee s, \neg s \vee \neg t, q \vee r \vee t, p \vee q \vee s, q \vee s \vee t\} = res_\Delta(T)$.

Now we can proceed to eliminating all clauses that contains atoms from Δ without losing the independent consequences (wrt Δ) in T. However, the above computational procedure for res_Δ may not be very computationally appealing as we potentially may have to enumerate through a number of unwanted clauses. The following more efficient procedure would guarantee a better computation in case Δ is finite which is the interesting case since we don't want to take into consideration actions or events that cause infinitely many effects to the world.

Let $\Delta = \{p_1, \ldots, p_n\}$ be given and T a theory. Define:

- $D_0 = \emptyset$; and
- for $i \geq 0$, let $\Theta_i = \bigcup_{j=1}^{i}\{c \in T \; : \; p_j \in atm(c)\}$:

$$D_{i+1} = \left\{\varphi_1 \vee \varphi_2 : p_{i+1} \vee \varphi_1, \neg p_{i+1} \vee \varphi_2 \in (T \setminus \Theta_i) \cup \left(\bigcup_{j=1}^{i} D_j\right)\right\}.$$

Then, $res'_\Delta(T) \stackrel{def}{=} T \cup \bigcup_{i=0}^{n} D_i$.

It is easy to see that the atoms in Δ will then be dealt with one at a time and the above procedure never re-visits an atom it has previously dealt with. The remaining problem is to show that res'_Δ will produce exactly what will be produced by res_Δ. The following proposition guarantees that this is the case.

Proposition 1. *Given a set of atoms Δ and a theory T,*

$$Cn(ind_\Delta(res_\Delta(T))) = Cn(ind_\Delta(res'_\Delta(T))).$$

Definition 3. An *event description* is a pair $\langle pre, post \rangle$ of formulas expressed in CNF (or, alternatively, as sets of clauses.)

Definition 4. A *dynamic domain* $\mathcal{D} = \langle Evt, ED \rangle$ consists of a set of events Evt and a function ED from Evt to the power-set of the set of event descriptions.

For instance, $ED(toggle\_switch) = \{\langle \neg on, on \rangle, \langle on, \neg on \rangle\}$.
Before we formally define the function to produce the next state in much the same way as we presented in the previous sub-section, an example may help to discover another problematic case.

Example 2. Consider a dynamic domain $\mathcal{D} = \langle Evt, ED \rangle$ where $Evt = \{E\}$ and $ED(E) = \{\langle q, \neg p \rangle\}$. We start with an initial theory $\sigma_0 = \{p\}$ and apply the event E in this state. Consider two possible initial worlds: $w_1 = \{pq\}$ and $w_2 = \{p\bar{q}\}$. From w_1 the resulting state would be $\{\bar{p}q\}$ and from w_2, $\{p\bar{q}\}$. However, starting with the theory σ_0, the resulting theory containing p will be derived from our framework. This is, of course, unintuitive. This is because we treat the case that $\sigma \not\models pre(E)$ in the same way as $\sigma \models \neg pre(E)$.[2] Basically, we have to distinguish three cases: (i) $\sigma \models pre(E)$, (ii) $\sigma \models \neg pre(E)$, and (iii) $\sigma \not\models pre(E)$ and $\sigma \not\models \neg pre(E)$.

To deal with the above problem, we introduce the notion of extension of a theory. The key to our solution is to distinguish theories that share the same base theory but are different on some special formulas. For instance, in the above example, we want to consider theories that share the same base theory $\sigma_0 = \{p\}$, but are different on the formula q. This is very similar to the consideration of the possible models of a theory. However, we don't have to take into account all possible models as the irrelevant features will be ignored. This is the computational advantage of our approach.

Definition 5. Let T be a theory and Φ a set of formulas. T is *complete* wrt Φ iff for each $\varphi \in \Phi$, either $T \models \varphi$ or $T \models \neg\varphi$.

Definition 6. Let T be a theory. A set of theories $\Sigma = \{\sigma_1, \ldots, \sigma_n\}$ is an *extension of* T (or T-*extension*) iff T is logically equivalent to $\bigvee_{i=1}^{n} \sigma_i$.

Now, the intention is to come up with the T-extension whose members are complete wrt a given set of formulas Φ. This will be done with the following definition:

Definition 7. (i) given a formula φ, we denote by $cnf(\varphi)$ the CNF of φ which is a set of clauses whose conjunction is equivalent to φ,

(ii) given a theory σ and a formula φ,[3]

$$ext(\sigma, \varphi) = \begin{cases} \{\sigma\} & \text{if } \sigma \models \varphi \text{ or } \sigma \models \neg\varphi, \\ \{\sigma \cup cnf(\varphi), \sigma \cup cnf(\neg\varphi)\} & \text{otherwise} \end{cases}$$

(iii) given a set of theories Σ and a formula φ,

$$ext(\Sigma, \varphi) = \bigcup_{\sigma \in \Sigma} ext(\sigma, \varphi)$$

(iv) given a set of theories Σ,
(iv.a)

$$ext(\Sigma, \emptyset) = \Sigma$$

---

[2] We informally make use of the notation $pre(E)$ to represent the pre-condition(s) of the event E. This notation and its counterpart $post(E)$ will be formally introduced in Definition 8 below.

[3] Recall that σ is a set of clauses.

(iv.b) and let $\Phi = \{\varphi_1, \ldots, \varphi_m\}$ be a set of formulas,

$$ext(\Sigma, \Phi) = ext(ext(\Sigma, \{\varphi_1, \ldots, \varphi_{m-1}\}), \varphi_m)$$

Strictly speaking, item (iv) in the above definition is a consequence of (i)-(iii) since the finite set of formulas $\Phi = \{\varphi_1, \ldots, \varphi_m\}$ can be equivalently represented as the conjunction $\varphi_1, \wedge \ldots \wedge \varphi_m$. However, these two representations certainly come with different computational consequences. For instance, consider the theory $\sigma = \{q, \neg q \vee a\}$ and the set $\Phi = \{a, b\}$. Then, $ext(\sigma, \Phi) = \{\{q, \neg q \vee a, b\}, \{q, \neg q \vee a, \neg b\}\}$ whereas, $ext(\sigma, a \wedge b) = \{\{q, \neg q \vee a, a, b\}, \{q, \neg q \vee a, \neg a \vee \neg b\}\}$. These two different representations also incur different time complexity at step (ii) in the above definition for the number of (CNF) normalizations and satisfiability checkings as well as the complexity of the involved formulas are different. Whereas step (iv) produces a clear advantage with respect to space complexity, it is not so clear whether it enjoys an advantage with respect to the time complexity of the computation carried out at step (ii).

Proposition 2. *Let T be a theory and $\Phi = \{\varphi_1, \ldots, \varphi_m\}$ a finite set of formulas,*

(i) $ext(T, \Phi)$ is a T-extension, and
(ii) for each theory $\sigma \in ext(T, \Phi)$, σ is complete wrt Φ.
(iii) different orders of applying $\varphi_1, \ldots, \varphi_m$ in general result in syntactically different sets of theories $ext(T, \Phi)$. However, they are logically equivalent.

Now, the intention is clear. Start from a theory that may not have a clear stand on every precondition of an event $E \in Evt$, we create a set of theories that is equivalent to the original theory. We introduce some syntactical sugar for convenience. Let $E \in Evt$ be an event with the description $ED(E) = \{\langle pre_1, post_1 \rangle, \ldots, \langle pre_n, post_n \rangle\}$, we denote by $pre(E)$ the set $\{pre_1, \ldots, pre_n\}$ and by $post(E)$ the set $\{post_1, \ldots, post_n\}$. In the following definition, we will abuse the notation by overloading the functions pre and $post$:

Definition 8. Let $E \in Evt$ be an event and σ a theory, we define:

1. $pre(E, \sigma) \stackrel{def}{=} \{c : \text{there exists } \varphi \in pre(E) \text{ such that } \sigma \models \varphi \text{ and } c \in \varphi\}$
2. $post(E, \sigma) \stackrel{def}{=} \{c : \text{there exists } \langle \varphi, \psi \rangle \in ED(E) \text{ such that } \sigma \models \varphi \text{ and } c \in \psi\}$.

Recall from Definition 3 that φ and ψ in the above definition are CNF-formulas which are expressed as sets of clauses.

When $pre(E)$ or $post(E)$ consists of a single element, we will omit the set notation to simplify the presentation. For instance, the action of picking a box (in the blocks world domain) can be described as follows: $E = pick$, $pre(pick) = free(hand) \wedge clear(block)$ and $post(pick) = inhand(block)$.

Definition 9. Given an event $E \in Evt$ and a theory σ which is complete wrt $pre(E)$, the *application* of E to σ is defined as follows:

$$result(\sigma, E) = \{c \in res_\Delta(\sigma) : atm(c) \cap \Delta = \emptyset\} \cup post(E, \sigma)$$

where $\Delta = atm(post(E, \sigma))$.

The above definition is extended to an arbitrary theory T in a straightforward way:

Given an event $E \in Evt$ and a theory T, the *application* of E to T is defined as follows:

$$result(T, E) = \bigcup_{\sigma \in ext(T, pre(E))} result(\sigma, E)$$

One distinguished feature of our approach is its ability to handle actions or events with disjunctive effects, i.e. non-deterministic actions. This is a clear advantage compared to approaches in belief update research (e.g. Winslett's [13] possible model approach, or PMA) and reasoning about action research (e.g. McCain and Turner's [9] framework) that are based on the principle of minimal change. We consider an example to illustrate this advantage.

Example 3. [4] The only action in this domain is throwing a chip onto a chess board with black and white squares (i.e., *throw*). The event description of *throw* is as follows: $pre(throw) = chip\_in\_hand$ and $post(throw) = (chip\_in\_white \vee chip\_in\_black) \wedge \neg chip\_in\_hand$. The fluents $chip\_in\_white$ (resp. $chip\_in\_black$) indicate that, when the chip is on the chess board, it is in a white (resp. black) square. Consider also the following initial state $\sigma_0 = \{chip\_in\_hand, \neg chip\_in\_white, \neg chip\_in\_black\}$. Using Winslett's PMA or McCain and Turner's minimal change approach we have the result:

$(\neg chip\_in\_hand \wedge chip\_in\_white \wedge \neg chip\_in\_black) \vee$
$(\neg chip\_in\_hand \wedge \neg chip\_in\_white \wedge chip\_in\_black)$,

which says that the chip must be in exactly one of the squares, either black or white, but not both. This is clearly unintuitive.

On the other hand, $res_\Delta(\sigma_0, throw) = \{\} \cup post(throw)$, i.e. firstly, the fluents $chip\_in\_hand, chip\_in\_white$ and $chip\_in\_black$ are removed from σ_0 since they all occur in the postcondition of *throw* and then the CNF of $post(throw)$ is added to form the next state. In other words, $res_\Delta(\sigma_0, throw) = \{chip\_in\_white \vee chip\_in\_black, \neg chip\_in\_hand\}$. In this approach, the chip is no longer in hand and can now be in a white square or in a black square or occupy both black and white squares.

One issue with our approach is due to the syntax-sensitivity with respect to the postcondition of the actions. For instance, $\neg p \vee p$ and **true** are logically equivalent but the resulting states as computed by the function $result$ defined above may be different on these two postconditions. We note that $atm(\neg p \vee p) = \{p\}$ while $atm(\textbf{true}) = \emptyset$. The common approach to avoid syntax-sensitivity is to eliminate the redundant atoms from a formula by reducing it to an equivalent one without that redundant atom. This process is known to be coNP-complete. However, such a redundancy may be intended as part of the action description. In other words, a process of eliminating the redundant atoms may not be desirable and it could be better that the framework would be sensitive to different syntaxes.

---

[4] This example was suggested by Ray Reiter and discussed in [5].

Example 4. Given the following event description of flipping a coin: $pre(flip) =$ **true** and $post(flip) = head \vee \neg head$. This is of course very different from having $post(flip) =$ **true**, especially if the initial state is $\sigma_0 = \{head\}$. This is because the set Δ of atoms used to determine the connection between the postcondition of the event $flip$ and the theory representing the next state contains the atom $head$ in the former and is empty in the latter. As a consequence, $res_\Delta(\sigma_0, flip) = \{head \vee \neg head\}$ when $post(flip) = head \vee \neg head$ and $res_\Delta(\sigma_0, flip) = \{head\}$ when $post(flip) =$ **true**. In other words, the former would be preferred over the latter.

Therefore, the syntax-sensitivity of our approach should be considered as a feature rather than a problem.

3.3   Technical Results

One might worry that there are clauses that should be removed from σ but would not be removed by the above definition (i.e. removing too few) or there are ones that should not be removed but would be removed by our definition (i.e. removing too many). The following theorem will assure that that will not be the case.

We first introduce the computation which is based on some complete description of the world. This is well-known through state-based formalisms of reasoning about action, e.g. Lin and Shoham's [8] epistemological completeness, Gelfond and Lifschitz's [2, 3] transition systems.

Let us ignore the ramification problem for now by assuming that no domain constraints are present in the domain of interest. The idea of this solution to the frame problem is similar to those in which the number of changed fluents is minimised. However, as explained above, all fluents that occur in the postcondition of an event will be subject to change. This is similar to the so-called non-inertial fluents introduced by Gelfond and Lifschitz [3]. We believe that this provides a better treatment as fluents are not required to be strictly non-inertial throughout but they can be non-inertial relative to some events while remaining inertial relative to the rest.

Before considering the resulting states by performing an event E in a state σ, we consider the issue of updating a state σ with a set of literals, or a partial interpretation, I.

Definition 10. Let ω be a state and S a set of atoms. Given a partial interpretation I over S, we define

$$updated(\omega, I)(p) = \begin{cases} I(p) \text{ if } p \in S, \\ \omega(p) \text{ otherwise} \end{cases}$$

In order to deal with the (direct) effects of an event E, we will enumerate all the possible partial interpretations that can be the effects of E in the state ω. Then the set of possible resulting states will be the updated states from ω relative to those partial interpretations.

Given a state w and an event $E \in Evt$, we denote by $TA(E, w)$ the set of all possible partial interpretations for the set of atoms $atm(post(E, w))$ that satisfy $post(E, w)$, i.e. if $\tau \in TA(E, w)$ then $\tau \models post(E, w)$.

For instance, given $post(E, w) = (p \vee q) \wedge (p \vee r) \wedge (q \vee r)$, then $TA(E, w) = \{\{p, q, r\}, \{p, q, \neg r\}, \{p, \neg q, r\}, \{\neg p, q, r\}\}$.

We can then introduce $nextState$ of a given state w for an event $E \in Evt$:

$$nextState(w, E) = \{updated(w, \tau) : \tau \in TA(E, w)\}.$$

Theorem 2. *Let $\mathcal{D} = (Evt, ED)$ be a dynamic domain. Given a theory T and an event $E \in Evt$, $Mod(result(T, E)) = \bigcup_{w \in Mod(T)} nextState(w, E)$.*

Example 5. We illustrate our approach with the classic example Yale Shooting Problem (YSP) [4]: Consider a dynamic domain $\mathcal{D} = \langle Evt, ED \rangle$ where $Evt = \{load, wait, shoot\}$ and

$pre(load) = \mathbf{true}$	$post(load) = loaded$
$pre(wait) = \mathbf{true}$	$post(wait) = \mathbf{true}$
$pre(shoot) = loaded$	$post(shoot) = \neg alive$

We start with an initial theory $\sigma_0 = \{\}$ and want to reason about the state of the world after applying the sequence of actions $load; wait; shoot$ in this state.

After performing the action $load$, the computed theory for the resulting state will be $\sigma_1 = \{loaded\}$. Note that $\sigma_0 \models pre(load)$.

Then, after performing the action $wait$, the computed theory for the resulting state will be $\sigma_2 = \{loaded\}$.

Then, after performing the action $shoot$, the computed theory for the resulting state will be $\sigma_3 = \{loaded, \neg alive\}$. Note that $\sigma_2 \models pre(shoot)$.

The above example shows the simplicity of this approach to the problem of reasoning about action. This also looks a very natural way to represent and reason about the effects of actions.

Consider a small modification to the postcondition of the action $shoot$. Assume that $post(shoot) = \{\neg alive, loaded \vee \neg loaded\}$. The idea of this description is of course that the gun can possibly get unloaded after the action $shoot$ in case, say, there is only one bullet left in the cartridge. In other words, the agent may not know whether the gun is still loaded after performing the action $shoot$. It's easy to see that the computed theory for the state of the world after performing the action $shoot$ from the state represented by σ_2 gives us: $\sigma_3' = \{loaded \vee \neg loaded, \neg alive\}$, which is a desirable outcome.

4   The Relationship with Action Language $\mathcal{A}$

Why is the above notion of $nextState$ of any interest to us at all? We will show that, in the special case of non-redundant postconditions of deterministic events, there is an equivalent translation from a dynamic domain to an action description in the action language $\mathcal{A}$ [3], and vice versa.

Recall that in the action language $\mathcal{A}$ ([3]),
(i) an $\mathcal{A}$-*proposition* is an expression of the form

$$A \textbf{ causes } L \textbf{ if } F$$

where A is an action name, L a literal and F a conjunction of literals (possibly empty),
(ii) an $\mathcal{A}$-*action description* is a set of propositions.

Translation from Dynamic Domains to $\mathcal{A}$-Action Descriptions: For each event $E \in Evt$: for each event description $\langle pre, post \rangle \in ED(E)$, as E is deterministic $post$ can be written as a conjunction of literals: $post = l_1 \wedge \ldots \wedge l_k$ and we just simply add the following $\mathcal{A}$-propositions to the $\mathcal{A}$-action description: $E \textbf{ causes } l_i \textbf{ if } pre$ (for $i = 1, \ldots, k$).

The following corollary is immediate from Theorem 2:

Corollary 1. *Let a deterministic dynamic domain $\mathcal{D} = (Evt, ED)$ be given. If D is an $\mathcal{A}$-action description obtained from $\mathcal{D}$ by the above translation and $\langle S, V, R \rangle$ is the transition system described by D then, for any theory T and any event $E \in Evt$, $\langle s, E, s' \rangle \in R$ if and only if $s' \in result(T, E)$ provided s is a model of T.*

Translation from $\mathcal{A}$-Action Descriptions to Dynamic Domains: For each action A:
(i) we add A to the set of events Evt and assign the empty set to $ED(A)$,
(ii) for each $\mathcal{A}$-propositions $A \textbf{ causes } L \textbf{ if } F$, we add the following event description to $ED(A)$: $\langle cnf(F), L \rangle$, where $cnf(F)$ is the conjunctive normal form of the formula F.

Corollary 2. *Let D be a (propositional) $\mathcal{A}$-action description over the action signature $\langle \{\textbf{false}, \textbf{true}\}, \textbf{F}, \textbf{A} \rangle$ and the transition system $\langle S, V, R \rangle$ be described by D (see [3] for the definitions of these concepts). If $\mathcal{D} = (Evt, ED)$ is the dynamic domain obtained by the above translation then for any $s \in S$ and $A \in \textbf{A}$,*
$$Mod(result(s, A)) = \{s' \in S \mid \langle s, A, s' \rangle \in R\}.$$

5   The Ramification Problem

So far we have not taken into consideration the indirect effects as well as the issues related to domain constraints. Lin ([7]) and McCain and Turner ([9]) have pointed out that domain constraints represented as formulas may not be sufficient to express the relationships between fluents of the domain. The missing information as largely recognised by researchers is the direction in which the fluents influence each others. For instance, killing the turkey causes it to stop walking but it is not the case that making a turkey walk causes it to be alive. We represent the set of such causal relationships as a special kind of event. One can actually call them natural events after all. In this way, we can uniformly treat ramifications as events that occur right after the occurrence of the main event but possibly in some unknown order.

We will assume that the set of events Evt is extended so that it includes a countable set of ramification rules Ram. As every indirect effect can be associated with a distinct ramification rule, for each $r \in Ram$, $ED(r)$ is a singleton. Therefore, we will abuse the notation sometimes by writing $pre(r)$ and $post(r)$ instead.

Definition 11. A theory σ is *stable* iff there does not exists any ramification rule $r \in Ram$ such that $\sigma \models pre(r)$ and $\sigma \not\models post(r)$.

Definition 12. A ramification rule $r \in Ram$ is *applicable* in a theory σ iff $\sigma \models pre(r)$.

A sequence $sr = \langle r_1, \dots, r_n \rangle$ of ramification rules is applicable to a theory σ iff there exists a sequence of theories $\langle \sigma_0, \dots, \sigma_n \rangle$ such that the following conditions hold:
1. $\sigma = \sigma_0$,
2. r_i (for $i = 1, \dots, n$) is applicable in σ_{i-1},
3. $\sigma_i \in result(\sigma_{i-1}, r_i)$.

A sequence of ramification rules $sr = \langle r_1, \dots, r_n \rangle$ which is applicable to a theory σ produces a possible next state iff all possible n-th states are stable.

Alternatively, instead of listing all the possible sequence of ramification rules, the agent may care only about what fluents would hold after the occurrence of some event e. In that case, many sequences of ramification rules may bring about the same eventual effects. The agent could effectively take into account the possible resulting theories. Such theories will be called reachable theories.

Definition 13. Given a theory τ, a theory σ is *reachable* from τ iff there exists a sequence of ramification rules which is applicable in σ such that τ is logically derivable from the resulting theory. Formally,

$\sigma_0 = \tau$

$\sigma_{i+1} = \{\varsigma : \text{there exist } r \in Ram \text{ and } \omega \in \sigma_i \text{ such that } \varsigma \in result(\omega, r)\}.$

6 Related Works

In the context of belief update and revision, Marianne Winslett ([13]) introduces a framework for theory update. Winslett's framework is similar to the approach presented in this paper on several accounts:

(i) First, her framework is also sensitive to the syntax of the formulas to be updated to the current theory. These are the consequences of the so-called *observations* by Winslett with the pre-requisites of the updating formulas being incorporated to the observations. The formulas that are brought forward from the old theory to the updated theory are those that don't contain any ground atom (or are not unifiable to a predicate) that is present in the observation.

(ii) The computation for the update operation is performed directly on the theories instead of over the set of models of the theory as has been done by most belief revision and update frameworks.

On the other hand, while Winslett's framework operates on first-order theories, our framework only operates on the propositional level. However, Winslett allows only ground formulas for the updating formulas. Therefore, Winslett's framework is a bit more general than the framework presented in this paper. An extension of our framework to allow the first-order setting accepted by Winslett is straightforward.

One issue with Winslett's formalism is the generation of new atoms. As the update operation is carried out, the so-called *history* atoms are generated to guarantee that the formulas to be got rid off will not be thrown away altogether but will still be kept in the form of the same formula but in regard to the historic atoms whose truth values are potentially changed during the course of the update operation. This way, Winslett guarantees that the formulas that provide information about the irrelevant atoms (relative to the on-going update) will not be missed out. This is what our framework achieves by carrying out the resolution step in the update operation presented above.

In the worst case, Winslett's framework increases the size of the language used to represent the knowledge base (or, data base) in exponential space as each atom may require a new history atom to be added to the language for each update. Moreover, as all formulas are kept during the update, either in the original form or as a historic formula, the size of the theory is strictly monotonically increased with each update. Thus, in terms of space complexity, our formalism is much more economical than Winslett's framework.

Furthermore, comparing to related model-based approaches which do not increase the language of representation such as McCain and Turner's [9] or Zhang and Foo's [14], our approach also avoids generating all possible world models which is exponential in the number of fluents. Instead, we only account for a fluent when it is necessary to determine whether our current theory about the world entails that proposition, i.e. in order to determine the applicability of the event/action. Certainly, in the worst case when the preconditions of a (very unusual) action require that every proposition be checked then the notion of theory extension presented in the present paper collapses to the set of all possible world models and thus suffers the same complexity as existing model-based approaches to reasoning about action and belief update.

For a more detailed exposition on the problems of reasoning about action and belief update (including the infamous *qualification problem*) as well as a comprehensive and uniform formalism for representation of and reasoning about dynamic domains, the reader is referred to [12]. The framework proposed in that dissertation provides answers to the questions about explicit time representation, non-deterministic actions with delayed effects, etc. as well as a uniform solution to the frame, the qualification and the ramification problems.

7   Concluding Remarks

In this paper we have described an approach to several problems of reasoning about action, namely the frame and the ramification problems. The approach is attractive in the way new states are computed. By treating ramifications as natural events, a uniform treatment for general actions and indirect effects can be achieved. The approach provides a machinery for general problem solvers that are required to function in dynamic domains.

The approach developed here is in some sense a formalised extension of the STRIPS system. It's similar to STRIPS in the way new information is updated to a current theory. Thus, it retains the conceptual simplicity of STRIPS. On the other hand, as arbitrary propositional theories are accepted and represented, it provides a significant improvement in the expressivity of STRIPS.

References

1. R. Fikes and N. J. Nilsson. STRIPS: A new approach to the application of theorem proving to problem solving. *Artificial Intelligence Journal*, 2(3/4):189–208, 1971.
2. M. Gelfond and V. Lifschitz. Representing action and change by logic programs. *Journal of Logic Programming*, 17:301–321, 1993.
3. M. Gelfond and V. Lifschitz. Action languages. *Electronic Transactions on AI*, 3(16), 1998.
4. S. Hanks and D. McDermott. Non-monotonic logic and temporal projection. *Artificial Intelligence Journal*, 33(3):379–412, 1987.
5. N. G. Kartha and V. Lifschitz. Actions with indirect effects. In *Principles of Knowledge Representation and Reasoning*, pages 341–350. Morgan Kaufmann, 1994.
6. V. Lifschitz. On the semantics of strips. In Georgeff and Lansky, editors, *Reasoning about Actions and Plans*. Morgan Kauffman, Los Altos, 1987.
7. F. Lin. Embracing causality in specifying the indirect effects of actions. In *International Joint Conference on Artificial Intelligence*, 1995.
8. F. Lin and Y. Shoham. Provably correct theories of action. *Journal of the ACM*, 42(2):293–320, 1995.
9. N. McCain and H. Turner. A causal theory of ramifications and qualifications. In *International Joint Conference on Artificial Intelligence*, 1995.
10. J. McCarthy and P. Hayes. Some philosophical problems from the standpoint of artificial intelligence. In D. Michie and B. Meltzer, editors, *Machine Intelligence 4*. Edinburgh University Press, 1969.
11. R. Reiter. The frame problem in the situation calculus: A simple solution (sometimes) and a completeness result for goal regression. In V. Lifschitz, editor, *AI and Mathematical Theory of Computation: Papers in Honor of John McCarthy*, pages 418–420. Academic Press, 1991.
12. Q. B. Vo. *Meta-constructs and Their Roles in Common Sense Reasoning*. PhD thesis, School of Computer Science and Engineering, University of New South Wales, 2002.
13. M. Winslett. Reasoning about action using a possible model approach. In *National Conference on Artificial Intelligence*, pages 89–93, 1988.
14. Y. Zhang and N. Y. Foo. Updating knowledge bases with disjunctive information. In *National Conference on Artificial Intelligence*, pages 562–568, 1996.

Minimizing Automata on Infinite Words

Thomas Wilke[*]

Christian-Albrechts University, 24098 Kiel, Germany,
wilke@ti.informatik.uni-kiel.de

Büchi automata (non-deterministic automata on infinite words with a simple acceptance condition) play a central rôle in model checking when properties are specified in temporal logic and state spaces are represented explicitly. Model checking then amounts to a graph search in a product of a transition system with a Büchi automaton that represents the specification. From a practical perspective it is therefore important to have procedures at hand which minimize the automata involved if possible. As computing—even approximating—minimum-state automata is PSPACE-hard, heuristics are applied. In the talk, a technique that is frequently used in current heuristics is presented: state-space reductions via simulation relations.

The main idea is to identify states that are structurally equivalent in the sense that they "simulate" each other. In order for a notion of "simulation" to be useful, it needs to meet certain criteria: it should preserve language containment, that is, if a word is accepted starting from one state, then it should be accepted from each state that simulates that state; it should preserve branching time properties (in a similar sense); passing from the given automaton to the quotient which identifies mutually similar states should preserve the recognized language; the simulation relation should be computable efficiently; it should be as coarse as possible to yield a small quotient. In the talk, various notions of simulation are discussed with respect to these issues.

Technically, most simulation relations are phrased in game-theoretic terms. This is a very elegant and suggestive way of describing simulation relations and at the same time the starting point for the design of efficient algorithms for computing them: the question whether two states mutually simulate each other becomes a question about who wins (has a winning strategy) in which game, and in order to answer this one can deploy algorithms from the theory of infinite games. The talk explains this.

As stated above, minimizing Büchi automata is important in explicit state-space model checking. The concrete problem one has to solve is to produce a small Büchi automaton for a given property in linear temporal logic. In a straightforward approach, one first translates the formula into some possibly large Büchi automaton and then uses heuristics to minimize this automaton. In the talk, it is explained how minimization by simulation quotienting for alternating automata can avoid the explicit construction of the intermediate automaton.

[*] The author acknowledges the EU contribution under the IST-FET programme.

M.Y. Vardi and A. Voronkov (Eds.): LPAR 2003, LNAI 2850, p. 289, 2003.
© Springer-Verlag Berlin Heidelberg 2003

Gandy's Theorem for Abstract Structures without the Equality Test[*]

Margarita Korovina[1,2]

[1] BRICS, Department of Computer Science, University of Aarhus,
Ny Munkegade, DK-8000 Aarhus C, Denmark,
[2] A.P. Ershov Institute of Informatics Systems, Lavrent'ev ave., 6, 630090,
Novosibirsk, Russia
korovina@brics.dk
http://www.brics.dk/~korovina

Abstract. In this paper we present a study of definability properties of fixed points of effective operators over astract structures without the equality test. We prove that Gandy's theorem holds for abstract structures without the equality test. This provides a useful tool for dealing with inductive definitions using Σ-formulas over continuous data types.

1 Introduction

Study of computability properties of continuous objects such as reals, real-valued functions and functionals is one of the fundamental areas of Computer Science motivated by applications from Engineering; where the vast majority of objects are of a continuous nature. The classical theory of computation, which works with discrete structures, is not suitable for formalisation of computations that operate on real-valued data. This theory is well established, whereas the theory of computation on continuous data is still in its infancy. This has resulted in many different nonequivalent approaches to computability of continuous objects [4, 5, 9, 10, 12, 14, 17, 20, 21, 24, 27].

One of the most promising approaches is based on the notion of definability, where continuous objects and computational processes involving these objects can be defined using finite formulas in suitable abstract structures. Let us mention some of the beneficial features of this approach which differ from other approaches to computability.

- It does not depend on representations of elements of structures.
- It is flexible: sometimes we can change the language of the structure to obtain appropriate computability properties.
- We can employ model theory to study computability.
- Formulas can be seen as a suitable finite representation of the relations they define.

[*] This research was partially supported by the Danish Natural Science Research Council, Grant no. 21-02-0474, RFFI-DFG Grant no. 01-01-04003 and Grant Scientific School-2112.2003.1.

M.Y. Vardi and A. Voronkov (Eds.): LPAR 2003, LNAI 2850, pp. 290–301, 2003.

One of the most interesting and practically important types of definability is Σ-definability. The concept of Σ-definability is closely related to the generalised computability on abstract structures [1, 11, 23, 25], in particular on the real numbers [20, 21, 25]. Notions of Σ-definable sets or relations generalise those of computable enumerable sets of natural numbers, and play a leading role in the specification theory that is used in the higher order computation theory on abstract structures.

One of the most fundamental theorems in the area is Gandy's theorem which states that the least fixed point of any positive Σ-operator is Σ-definable. This theorem allows us to treat inductive definitions using Σ-formulas. The role of inductive definability as a basic principle of general computability is discussed in [15, 22]. It is worth noting that for finite structures the least fixed points of definable operators give an important and well studied logical characterisation of complexity classes [8, 16, 26]. For infinite structures fixed point logics are also studied e.g. [7].

Gandy's theorem was first proven for abstract structures with the equality test (see [1, 11, 27]). In many cases it is natural to consider structures in the language without equality. For example, in all effective approaches to exact real number computation via concrete representations [12, 14, 24], the equality test is undecidable. This is not surprising, because infinite amount of information must be checked in order to decide that two given numbers are equal.

Until now there has been no Gandy-type theorem known for such structures. Let us note that in all known proofs of Gandy's theorem so far, it is the case that even when the definition of a Σ-operator does not involve equality, the resulting Σ-formula usually does. In this paper we show that it is possible to overcome this problem. In particular we show that Gandy's theorem holds for the set of hereditarily finite sets over abstract structures without the equality test. As a useful corollary we obtain Gandy's theorem for the set of hereditarily finite sets over structures without the equality test such as the real numbers and functionals of higher types over the reals. This gives us new tools for inverstigation of properties of computability on continuous data types.

The structure of this paper is as follows. In Section 2 we introduce basic notations and definitions. We provide the background information necessary to understand the main results. Section 3 presents Gandy's theorem for structures without the equality test. In Section 4 we give an application of our result to the real numbers without the equality test. We conclude with a discussion of future work.

2   Background

We start by introducing basic notations and definitions. Let us consider an abstract structure A in a finite language σ_0 without the equality test.

In order to do any kind of computation or to develop a computability theory one has to work within a structure rich enough for information to be coded and stored. For this purpose we extend the structure A by the set of hereditarily finite sets $\mathrm{HF}(A)$.

The idea that the hereditarily finite sets over A form a natural domain for computation is quite classical and is developed in detail in [1, 11].

Note that such or very similar extensions of structures with equality are used in the theory of abstract state machines [2, 3] and in query languages for hierarchic databases [6].

We will construct the set of hereditarily finite sets over the model without equality. This structure permits us to define the natural numbers, and to code and store information via formulas.

We construct the set of hereditarily finite sets, $\mathrm{HF}(A)$, as follows:

1. $\mathrm{HF}_0(A) \rightleftharpoons A$,
2. $\mathrm{HF}_{n+1}(A) \rightleftharpoons \mathcal{P}_\omega(\mathrm{HF}_n(A)) \cup \mathrm{HF}_n(A)$, where $n \in \omega$ and for every set B, $\mathcal{P}_\omega(B)$ is the set of all finite subsets of B.
3. $\mathrm{HF}(A) \rightleftharpoons \bigcup_{n \in \omega} \mathrm{HF}_n(A)$.

We define $\mathbf{HF}(A)$ as the following model:

$$\mathbf{HF}(A) \rightleftharpoons \langle \mathrm{HF}(A), U, S, \sigma_0, \emptyset, \in \rangle \rightleftharpoons \langle \mathrm{HF}(A), \sigma \rangle,$$

where the constant $\emptyset$ stands for the empty set, the binary predicate symbol $\in$ has the set-theoretic interpretation. Also we add predicates symbols U for urelements (elements from A) and S for sets. Let us denote $S(\mathrm{HF}(A)) \rightleftharpoons \mathrm{HF}(A) \setminus A$.

The natural numbers $0, 1, \ldots$ are identified with the (finite) ordinals in $\mathbf{HF}(A)$ i.e. $\emptyset, \{\emptyset, \{\emptyset\}\}, \ldots$, so in particular, $n + 1 = n \cup \{n\}$ and the set ω is a subset of $\mathrm{HF}(A)$.

We use variables subject to the following conventions:

$r, r_1, \ldots$ range over A (urelements),

$x, y, z, s, w, f, g, \ldots$ range over $S(\mathrm{HF}(A))$ (sets),

$n, m, l, \ldots$ range over ω (natural numbers) and

$a, b, c \ldots$ range over $\mathrm{HF}(A)$.

We use the same letters as for variables to denote elements from the corresponding structures and $\bar{r}$ to denote $r_1, \ldots, r_m$.

The notions of a term and an atomic formula are given in the standard manner.

The set of Δ_0-formulas is the closure of the set of atomic formulas under $\wedge, \vee, \neg$, and bounded quantifiers $(\exists a \in s)$ and $(\forall a \in s)$, where $(\exists a \in s)$ Ψ denotes $\exists a(a \in s \wedge \Psi)$ and $(\forall a \in s)$ Ψ denotes $\forall a(a \in s \rightarrow \Psi)$.

The set of Σ-formulas is the closure of the set of Δ_0 formulas under $\wedge, \vee$, $(\exists a \in s)$, $(\forall a \in s)$, and $\exists$.

We assume that predicates from the language σ_0 can occur only positively in our formulas.

We are interested in Σ-definability of sets on A^n which can be considered as generalisation of recursive enumerability. The analogy of Σ-definable and recursive enumerable sets is based on the following fact. Consider the structure $\mathbf{HF} = \langle \mathrm{HF}(\emptyset), \in \rangle$ with the hereditarily finite sets over $\emptyset$ as its universe and membership as its only relation. In $\mathbf{HF}$ the Σ-definable sets are exactly the recursively enumerable sets.

The notion of Σ-definability has a natural meaning also in the structure $\mathbf{HF}(A)$.

Definition 1.   *1. A relation $B \subseteq \mathrm{HF}(A)^n$ is Δ_0 (Σ)-definable, if there exists a Δ_0 (Σ)-formula $\Phi(\bar{a})$ such that*

$$\bar{b} \in B \leftrightarrow \mathbf{HF}(A) \models \Phi(\bar{b}).$$

2. A function $f : \mathrm{HF}(A)^n \to \mathrm{HF}(A)^m$ is Δ_0 (Σ)-definable, if there exists a Δ_0 (Σ)-formula $\Phi(\bar{c}, \bar{d})$ such that

$$f(\bar{a}) = \bar{b} \leftrightarrow \mathbf{HF}(A) \models \Phi(\bar{a}, \bar{b}).$$

Note that the sets A and ω are Δ_0-definable. This fact makes $\mathbf{HF}(A)$ a suitable domain for studying subsets of A^n and operators of the type

$$\Gamma : \mathcal{P}(A^n) \to \mathcal{P}(A^n).$$

In the following lemma we introduce some Δ_0-definable and Σ-definable predicates that we will use later.

Lemma 1.   *1. The predicates $R(a) \rightleftharpoons a \in A$, $S(a) \rightleftharpoons a$ is a set, and $n \in \omega$ are Δ_0-definable.*
2. The following predicates are Δ_0-definable: $x = y$, $x = y \cap z$, $x = y \cup z$, $x =< y, z >$, $x = y \setminus z$ (recall that all variables x, y, z range over sets).
3. A function $f : \omega^n \to \omega^m$ is computable if and only if it is Σ-definable.
4. Let $Fun(g)$ mean that g is a finite function i.e.

$$g = \{\langle x, y \rangle \,|\, \text{for every } x \text{ there exists a unique } y \}$$

then the predicate $Fun(g)$ is Δ_0-definable.
5. If $\mathbf{HF}(A) \models Fun(g)$ then the domain of g, denoted by δ_g, is Δ_0-definable.

PROOF.   Proofs of all properties are straightforward except (3) which can be found in [11]. □

For finite functions $Fun(f)$ let us denote $f(x) = y$ if $\langle x, y \rangle \in f$.

The following proposition states that we have full collection on $\mathbf{HF}(A)$.

Proposition 1.   *(Collection.) For every formula Φ the following claim holds. If $\mathbf{HF}(A) \models (\forall a \in x) \exists b \Phi(a, b)$ then there is a set z such that*

$$\mathbf{HF}(A) \models (\forall a \in x) \, (\exists b \in z) \, \Phi(a, b) \ and$$
$$\mathbf{HF}(A) \models (\forall b \in z) \, (\exists a \in x) \, \Phi(a, b).$$

PROOF.   The claim follows from the definition of $\mathbf{HF}(A)$. Indeed, if $x \in \mathrm{HF}(A)$ consists of k elements $a_1, \ldots, a_k$ and for each of these a_i there is an b_i such that $\Phi(a_i, b_i)$ holds. Then all $b_1, \ldots, b_k$ occur in $\mathrm{HF}_n(A)$ for some n, hence $\{b_1, \ldots, b_k\} \in \mathrm{HF}_{n+1}(A)$. □

3   The Least Fixed Points of Effective Operators

Now we recall the notion of Σ-operator and prove Gandy's theorem for structures without the equality test.

Let $\Phi(a_1, \ldots, a_n, P)$ be a Σ-formula where P occurs positively in Φ and the arity of P is equal to n.

We think of Φ as defining a Σ-operator

$$\Gamma : \mathcal{P}(\mathrm{HF}(A)^n) \to \mathcal{P}(\mathrm{HF}(A)^n)$$

given by

$$\Gamma(Q) = \{\bar{a}| \, (\mathbf{HF}(A), Q) \models \Phi(\bar{a}, P)\},$$

where for every set B, $\mathcal{P}(B)$ is the set of all subsets of B.

Since the predicate symbol P occurs only positively we have that the corresponding operator Γ is monotone i.e. for any sets from $A \subseteq B$ follows $\Gamma(A) \subseteq \Gamma(B)$.

By monotonicity, the operator Γ has the least (w.r.t. inclusion) fixed point which can be described as follows.

We start from the empty set and apply operator Γ until we reach the fixed point:

$$\Gamma^0 = \emptyset, \quad \Gamma^{n+1} = \Gamma(\Gamma^n), \quad \Gamma^\gamma = \cup_{n<\gamma} \Gamma^n, \tag{1}$$

where γ is a limit ordinal.

One can easily check that the sets Γ^n form an increasing chain of sets: $\Gamma^0 \subseteq \Gamma^1 \subseteq \ldots$. By set-theoretical reasons, there exists the least ordinal γ such that $\Gamma(\Gamma^\gamma) = \Gamma^\gamma$. This Γ^γ is the least fixed point of the given operator Γ.

In order to study the least fixed points of arbitrary Σ-operators (without the equality test), we first consider Σ-operators of the type

$$\Gamma : \mathcal{P}(S(\mathrm{HF}(A))^n) \to \mathcal{P}(S(\mathrm{HF}(A))^n).$$

Then we will show how the least fixed points of arbitrary Σ-operators can be constructed using the least fixed points of such operators. Note that, as $S(\mathrm{HF}(A))$ is closed under pairing, $S(\mathrm{HF}(A))^n \subseteq S(\mathrm{HF}(A))$ for $n > 0$. Moreover, $S(\mathrm{HF}(A))^n$ is a Σ-definable subset of $\mathrm{HF}(A)$. So, without loss of generality we can consider the case $n = 1$.

Let us formulate some properties of Σ-operators which we will use below. The following proposition states that each element from the value of a Σ-operator on a Σ-set can be obtained as an element of the value of this operator on a finite subset of the set.

Proposition 2. *If Q is a Σ-definable subset of $S(\mathrm{HF}(A))$ and $w \in \Gamma(Q)$ then there exists $p \in S(\mathrm{HF}(A))$ such that $p \subseteq Q$ and $w \in \Gamma(p)$.*

PROOF.   We prove the proposition for the more general case where we allow parameters from $S(\mathrm{HF}(A))$ to occur into the formula defining our operator.

Let $\Phi(\bar{b}, x, P)$ be a Σ-formula defining our operator Γ, where $\bar{b} = b_1, \ldots, b_n$ are parameters from $S(HF(A))$. And let Q be a Σ-definable subset of $S(HF(A))$

and $w \in \Gamma(Q)$. We need to prove that there exists $p \in S(HF(A))$ such that $p \subseteq Q$ and $w \in \Gamma(p)$.

We prove the claim by induction on the structure of Φ.

If $\Phi(\bar{b}, x, P) \rightleftharpoons P(x)$ and $(\mathbf{HF}(A), Q) \models P(w)$ then the set $p \rightleftharpoons \{w\}$ is a required one.

If Φ is an atomic formula which does not contain P then the set $p \rightleftharpoons \emptyset$ is a required one.

For the induction step let us consider all possible cases.

1. Suppose $\Phi(\bar{b}, x, P) \rightleftharpoons (\forall a \in b_j) \Psi(a, \bar{b}, x, P)$ and

$$(\mathbf{HF}(A), Q) \models (\forall a \in b_j) \Psi(a, \bar{b}, w, P).$$

By induction hypothesis,

$$(\mathbf{HF}(A),\ Q\ ) \models (\forall a \in b_j) \exists s \left(\Psi(a, \bar{b}, w, P)\right)_{t \in s}^{P(t)} \wedge s \subseteq Q.$$

Using Proposition 1, we find an element q such that

$$(\mathbf{HF}(A), Q) \models (\forall a \in b_j)(\exists s \in q)\left(\left(\Psi(a, \bar{b}, w, P)\right)_{t \in s}^{P(t)} \wedge s \subseteq Q\right) \wedge$$
$$(\forall s \in q)(\exists a \in b_j)\left(\left(\Psi(a, \bar{b}, w, P)\right)_{t \in s}^{P(t)} \wedge s \subseteq Q\right).$$

Let $p \rightleftharpoons \cup q$.

By definition, for all $a \in b_j$ there exists $s \subseteq p$ such that

$$(\mathbf{HF}(A), s) \models \left(\Psi(a, \bar{b}, w, P)\right)_{t \in s}^{P(t)}.$$

So we have

$$(\mathbf{HF}(A), p) \models \Psi(a, \bar{b}, w, P) \text{ for all } a \in b_j.$$

In other words,

$$(\mathbf{HF}(A), p) \models (\forall a \in b_j) \Psi(a, \bar{b}, x, P).$$

By construction the set p is a required one.

2. The case $\Phi(\bar{b}, x, P) \rightleftharpoons (\exists a \in b_j) \Psi(a, \bar{b}, x, P)$ is similar to the case above.

3. Suppose $\Phi(\bar{b}, x, P) \rightleftharpoons \exists a \Psi(a, \bar{b}, x, P)$ and

$$(\mathbf{HF}(A), Q) \models \Psi(b', \bar{b}, w, P).$$

By induction hypothesis, there exists $p_0 \subseteq Q$ such that $p_0 \in S(\mathrm{HF}(A))$ and

$$(\mathbf{HF}(A), p_0) \models \Psi(b', \bar{b}, w, P).$$

The set $p \rightleftharpoons p_0$ is a required one.

4. Suppose $\Phi(\bar{b}, x, P) \rightleftharpoons \Psi_1(\bar{b}, x, P) \wedge \Psi_2(\bar{b}, x, P)$ and

$$(\mathbf{HF}(A), Q) \models \Psi_1(\bar{b}, w, P) \wedge \Psi_2(\bar{b}, w, P).$$

By induction hypothesis, there exist $p_1 \subseteq Q$ and $p_2 \subseteq Q$ such that $p_1 \in S(\mathrm{HF}(A))$, $p_2 \in S(\mathrm{HF}(A))$ and

$$(\mathbf{HF}(A), p_1) \models \Psi_1(\bar{b}, w, P)$$

and

$$(\mathbf{HF}(A), p_2) \models \Psi_2(\bar{b}, w, P).$$

The set $p \rightleftharpoons p_1 \cup p_2$ is a required one.

5. The case $\Phi(\bar{b}, x, P) \rightleftharpoons \Psi_1(\bar{b}, x, P) \vee \Psi_2(\bar{b}, x, P)$ is similar to the case above.
□

Proposition 3. *Let* $\Gamma : \mathcal{P}(S(\mathrm{HF}(A))) \rightarrow \mathcal{P}(S(\mathrm{HF}(A)))$ *be a* Σ-*operator. The relation* $x \in \Gamma(y)$ *is* Σ-*definable.*

PROOF.   Let $\Phi(z, P)$ be a Σ-formula which defines the operator Γ. Suppose $x \in \Gamma(y)$. By definition,

$$x \in \{z \mid (\mathbf{HF}(A), y) \models \Phi(z, P)\}.$$

It means that

$$(\mathbf{HF}(A), y) \models \Phi(x, P).$$

So we have

$$(\mathbf{HF}(A)) \models (\Phi(x, P))_{t \in y}^{P(t)}.$$

It is easy to see that the relation $x \in \Gamma(y)$ is defined by Σ-formula $\Phi(x, P)_{t \in y}^{P(t)}$.
□

Now we are ready to prove Gandy's theorem for Σ-operators of the type

$$\Gamma : \mathcal{P}(S(\mathrm{HF}(A))) \rightarrow \mathcal{P}(S(\mathrm{HF}(A))).$$

Theorem 1. *Let* $\Gamma : \mathcal{P}(S(\mathrm{HF}(A))) \rightarrow \mathcal{P}(S(\mathrm{HF}(A)))$ *be a* Σ-*definable operator. Then the least fixed-point of* Γ *is* Σ-*definable and and the least ordinal such that* $\Gamma(\Gamma^\gamma) = \Gamma^\gamma$ *is less or equal to* ω.

PROOF.   We will prove that the least fixed point of the operator Γ is Γ^ω, where Γ^ω is defined as follows: $\Gamma^0 = \emptyset$, $\Gamma^n = \Gamma(\Gamma^{n-1})$ for a finite ordinal n, and $\Gamma^\omega = \bigcup_{m < \omega} \Gamma^m$.

Let us show Σ-definability of Γ^n for every finite ordinal n. For this purpose we introduce the following family of finite functions:

$$X_0 = \langle \emptyset, \emptyset \rangle,$$
$$X_n = \{f \mid Fun(f) \text{ and } \delta_f = n + 1, f(0) = \emptyset,$$
$$f \text{ is monotonic and for any } m \leq n$$
$$\text{the following is true:} f(m) \subseteq \bigcup_{l < m} \Gamma(f(l))\}$$

where $n > 0$.

From the definitions X_n and Γ it follows that X_n is Σ-definable for all $n \in \omega$, moreover there exists a Σ-formula $\psi(n, x)$ such that

$$\mathbf{HF}(A) \models \psi(n, x) \leftrightarrow x \in X_n.$$

Below we will use the following useful properties of the families X_n:

1. Let w be a finite subset of X_n. Let us define $f^*(m) \rightleftharpoons \bigcup_{f \in w} f(m)$ for all $m \leq n$. Then $f^* \in X_n$.
2. If $f \in X_n$ and $m \leq n$. Then $f \upharpoonright (m+1) \in X_m$.
3. Let $f \in X_m$ and $m \leq n$.
   Define a function
   $$f^*(l) = \begin{cases} f(l), & \text{if } l \leq m \\ f(m), & \text{if } m < l \leq n. \end{cases}$$
   Then $f^* \in X_n$.
4. Let $f \in X_n$ and $b \in \Gamma(f(m))$ where $m \leq n$.
   Define a function
   $$f^*(l) = \begin{cases} f(l), & \text{if } l \leq n \\ \{b\}, & \text{if } l = n + 1. \end{cases}$$
   Then $f^* \in X_{n+1}$.

Using these properties let us show that:

$$x \in \Gamma^n \text{ iff } \mathbf{HF}(A) \models \exists f \, (f \in X_n \wedge x \in f(n)) \tag{2}$$

by induction on n. For $n = 0$ we have $\Gamma^n = \emptyset$ and therefore (2) holds.

Assume that (2) holds for n let us prove that (2) holds for $n + 1$.

To prove from left to right let us consider an element $x \in \Gamma^{n+1} = \Gamma(\Gamma^n)$. By induction hypothesis we have that $x_1 \in \Gamma^n$ iff $\exists g \, (g \in X_n \wedge x_1 \in g(n))$. So the set Γ^n is Σ-definable. By Proposition 2 it follows that there exists $y \in S(\mathbf{HF}(A))$ such that $y \subseteq \Gamma^n$ and $x \in \Gamma(y)$.

By induction hypothesis and the condition $y \subseteq \Gamma^n$,

$$\mathbf{HF}(A) \models (\forall z \in y) \exists g \, (g \in X_n \wedge z \in g(n)).$$

Using Proposition 1, we find an element w such that

$$\mathbf{HF}(A) \models (\forall z \in y) \, (\exists g \in w) \, (g \in X_n \wedge z \in g(n)) \wedge$$
$$(\forall g \in w) \, (\exists z \in y) \, (g \in X_n \wedge z \in g(n)).$$

Starting from the finite subset $w \subseteq X_n$, we define the function g_0 as follows:

$$g_0(l) = \bigcup_{g \in w} g(l), \; l \leq n.$$

By Property (1) of X_n which is mentioned above, $g_0 \in X_n$. It is easy to check the following inclusion $y \subseteq g_0(n)$. Indeed, if $z \in y$ then there exists $g \in w$ such that $z \in g(n) \subseteq g_0(n)$.

Define a function

$$f(l) = \begin{cases} g_0(l), & \text{if } l \leq n \\ \{x\}, & \text{if } l = n + 1. \end{cases}$$

From Property (4) of X_n follows that $f \in X_{n+1}$ and moreover $x \in f(n+1)$ holds by the definition of f. So f is a required one.

To prove from right to left let us suppose there exists f such that

$$(f \in X_{n+1} \wedge x \in f(n+1)).$$

By the definition of X_{n+1}, $x \in \Gamma(f(m))$ for some $m \leq n$.

Let us check the inclusion : $f(m) \subseteq \Gamma^m$. For this purpose we consider $f_1 = f \restriction (m+1)$. From Property (2) of X_m follows that $f_1 \in X_m$. So, for all $y \in f_1(m)$ we have $\mathbf{HF}(A) \models \exists f (f \in X_m \wedge y \in f(m))$. By induction it means that $f_1(m) = f(m) \subseteq \Gamma^m$.

The operator Γ is monotone, so we have

$$x \in \Gamma(f(m)) \subseteq \Gamma(\Gamma^m) \subseteq \bigcup_{m < n+1} \Gamma(\Gamma^m) = \Gamma^{n+1}.$$

Thus we have proven that Γ^n is Σ-definable for all $n \in \omega$. Consequently,

$$x \in \Gamma^\omega \leftrightarrow \exists n \exists f (f \in X_n \wedge x \in f(n)) \tag{3}$$

is Σ-definable.

To check that Γ^ω is a fixed point i.e. $\Gamma(\Gamma^\omega) \subseteq \Gamma^\omega$ let us consider $x \in \Gamma(\Gamma^\omega)$. From (3) it follows that Γ^ω is Σ-definable. From Proposition 2 it follows that there exists $y \in S(\mathbf{HF}(A))$ such that $y \subseteq \Gamma^\omega$ and $x \in \Gamma(y)$. It is easy to check that $y \subseteq \Gamma^m$ for some $m \in \omega$. From this we have that $x \in \Gamma(\Gamma^m) \subseteq \Gamma^\omega$. By monotonicity of Γ, the set Γ^ω is the least fixed point. So the least fixed point of the operator Γ is Σ-definable. $\square$

Now we consider arbitrary Σ-operators on the structure A without the equality test.

Theorem 2. *Let* $\Gamma : \mathcal{P}(\mathbf{HF}(A)^n) \to \mathcal{P}(\mathbf{HF}(A)^n)$ *be an arbitrary Σ-operator. Then the least fixed-point of Γ is Σ-definable and the least ordinal such that $\Gamma(\Gamma^\gamma) = \Gamma^\gamma$ is less or equal to ω.*

PROOF. For simplicity of notation, we will give the construction only for the case $n = 1$, since the main ideas are already contained here. Let $\Phi(r, P)$ define the operator Γ. We construct a new Σ-operator $F : \mathcal{P}(S(\mathbf{HF}(A))) \to \mathcal{P}(S(\mathbf{HF}(A)))$ such that

$$r \in \Gamma^n \longleftrightarrow \exists x (x \in F^n \wedge r \in x).$$

For this purpose we define the following formula with a new unary predicate symbol Q:

$$\Psi(x, Q) = (\forall r \in x)(\Phi(r, P))^{P(t)}_{\exists y Q(y) \wedge t \in y}.$$

It is easy to see that Ψ induces a Σ-operator F given by

$$F(D) = \{x | (\mathbf{HF}(A), D) \models \Psi(x, Q)\}.$$

Let us show that

$$r \in \Gamma^n \leftrightarrow \exists x (x \in F^n \wedge r \in x) \tag{4}$$

by induction on n. For $n = 0$ we have $\Gamma^n = F^n = \emptyset$ and therefore (4) holds.

Assume that (4) holds for n let us prove that (4) holds for $n + 1$. In other words we need to prove that

$$(\mathbf{HF}(A), \Gamma^n) \models \Phi(r, P) \leftrightarrow$$
$$(\mathbf{HF}(A), F^n) \models \exists x \left(r \in x \wedge (\forall r' \in x) \, (\Phi(r', P))^{P(t)}_{\exists y Q(y) \wedge t \in y} \right).$$

Since the first formula does not contain Q and the second formula does not contain P it is sufficient to consider one structure $(\mathbf{HF}(A), \Gamma^n, F^n)$ and prove that

$$(\mathbf{HF}(A), \Gamma^n, F^n) \models \Phi(r, P) \leftrightarrow$$
$$(\mathbf{HF}(A), \Gamma^n, F^n) \models \exists x \left(r \in x \wedge (\forall r' \in x) \, (\Phi(r', P))^{P(t)}_{\exists y Q(y) \wedge t \in y} \right).$$

To prove from left to right let us consider $r \in \mathbf{HF}(A)$ such that

$$(\mathbf{HF}(A), \Gamma^n, F^n) \models \Phi(r, P).$$

Consider the formula $(\Phi(r, P))^{P(t)}_{\exists y Q(y) \wedge t \in y}$ then by induction hypothesis we have that

$$(\mathbf{HF}(A), \Gamma^n, F^n) \models \forall r' \, (P(r') \leftrightarrow \exists x (x \in Q \wedge r' \in x) \,) \tag{5}$$

and therefore (by replacement lemma) we have

$$(\mathbf{HF}(A), \Gamma^n, F^n) \models (\Phi(r, P))^{P(t)}_{\exists y Q(y) \wedge t \in y}.$$

Now it is easy to check that

$$(\mathbf{HF}(A), \Gamma^n, F^n) \models \exists x \left(r \in x \wedge (\forall r' \in x) \, (\Phi(r', P))^{P(t)}_{\exists y Q(y) \wedge t \in y} \right)$$

taking $x = \{r\}$.

To prove from right to left let us consider $r \in \mathbf{HF}(A)$ such that

$$(\mathbf{HF}(A), \Gamma^n, F^n) \models \exists x \left(r \in x \wedge (\forall r' \in x) \, (\Phi(r', P))^{P(t)}_{\exists y Q(y) \wedge t \in y} \right).$$

From this we have that

$$(\mathbf{HF}(A), \Gamma^n, F^n) \models (\Phi(r, P))^{P(t)}_{\exists y Q(y) \wedge t \in y}$$

and from (5) (by replacement lemma) we obtain that

$$(\mathbf{HF}(A), \Gamma^n, F^n) \models \Phi(r, P).$$

Now from Theorem 1 it follows that the least fixed point of the operator F is Σ-definable and therefore the the least fixed point of the operator Γ is also Σ-definable. $\square$

4   The Least Fixed Points of Effective Operators over the Real Numbers without the Equality Test

In this section we consider the standard structure of the real numbers

$$\langle \mathbb{R}, 0, 1, +, \cdot, < \rangle,$$

denoted also by $\mathbb{R}$, where $+$, $\cdot$ and $-$ are regarded as the usual arithmetic operations on the reals. We use the language of strictly ordered rings, so the predicate $<$ occurs positively in formulas. This allows us to consider Σ-definability as generalisation of computable enumerability. Indeed, in all effective approaches to exact real number computation via concrete representations, we need only finite amount of information in order to show that one given number is less than another one. The following is an immediate corollary of Theorem 2.

Corollary 1. *Let* $\Gamma : \mathcal{P}(\mathrm{HF}(\mathbb{R})^n) \to \mathcal{P}(\mathrm{HF}(\mathbb{R})^n)$ *be an arbitrary Σ–operator. Then the least fixed-point of Γ is Σ-definable.*

5   Future Work

In this paper we have proved Gandy's theorem for the set of hereditarily finite sets over abstract structures without the equality test. In the case of the real numbers without the equality test, Gandy's theorem, together with Engeler's Lemma for Σ-definability reveals algorithmic aspects of Σ-definability (recently proved in [18, 19]). We have proved that a relation over the real numbers is Σ-definable if and only if it is definable by a disjunction of a recursively enumerable set of quantifier free formulas. In this respect the following direction of research is of special interest: to propose and study reasonable requirements on the universe and the language of an abstract structure without the equality test under which the similar characterisation can be obtained.

References

1. J. Barwise. *Admissible sets and Structures*. Springer Verlag, Berlin, 1975.
2. A. Blass and Y. Gurevich. Background, reserve and Gandy machines. In *Proc. of CSL'2000*, volume 1862 of *Lecture Notes in Computer Science*, pages 1–17, 2000.
3. A. Blass, Y. Gurevich, and S. Shelah. Choiceless polynomial time. *Annals of Pure and Applied Logic*, 100:141–187, 1999.
4. L. Blum, F. Cucker, M. Shub, and S. Smale. *Complexity and Real Computation*. Springer Verlag, Berlin, 1996.
5. V. Brattka and P. Hertling. Topological properties of real number representations. *Theoretical Computer Science*, 284(2):1–17, 2002.
6. E. Dahlhaus and J. A. Makowsky. Query languages for hierarchic databases. *Information and Computation*, 101:1–32, 1992.
7. A. Davar and Y. Gurevich. Fixed-point logics. *BSL*, 8(1):65–88, 2002.
8. H. Ebbinghaus and J. Flum. *Finite Model Theory*. Springer Verlag, Berlin, 1999.

9. A. Edalat and M. Escardo. Integration in Real PCF. In *Proc. of 11th Annual IEEE Symposium on Logic in Computer Science*, pages 382–393, 1996.
10. A. Edalat and A. Lieutie. Domain theory and differential calculus (function of one variable. In *Proc. IEEE Conference on Logic in Computer Science (LICS)*, pages 277–298, 2002.
11. Yu. L. Ershov. *Definability and computability*. Plenum, New-York, 1996.
12. H. Friedman and K. Ko. Computational complexity of real functions. *Theoretical Computer Science*, 20:323–352, 1992.
13. R. Gandy. Inductive definitions. In J. E. Fenstad and P. D. Hinman, editors, *Generalized Recursion Theory*, pages 265–300. North-Holland, Amsterdam, 1974.
14. A. Grzegorczyk. On the definitions of computable real continuous function. *Fundamenta Mathematik*, 44:61–71, 1957.
15. P. G. Hinman. Recursion on abstract structure. In E. R. Griffor, editor, *Handbook of Computability Theory*, pages 317–359. Elsevier, Amsterdam-Tokyo, 1999.
16. N. Immerman. *Descriptive Complexity*. Springer Verlag, New-York, 1999.
17. Ulrich Kohlenbach. Proof theory and computational analysis. *Electronic Notes in Theoretical Computer Science*, 13, 1998.
18. M. Korovina. Computational aspects of Σ-definability over the real numbers without the equality test. In *Proc. of CSL'03*, Lecture Notes in Computer Science, 2003.
19. M. Korovina. Fixed points on the reals numbers without the equality test. *Electronic Notes in Theoretical Computer Science*, 66(1), 2002.
20. M. Korovina and O. Kudinov. Characteristic properties of majorant-computability over the reals. In *Proc. of CSL'98*, volume 1584 of *Lecture Notes in Computer Science*, pages 188–204, 1999.
21. M. Korovina and O. Kudinov. Some properties of majorant-computability. In M. Arslanov and S.Lempp, editors, *Recursion Theory and Complexity", Proceedings of the Kazan-97 Workshop, July 14-19*, volume 2, pages 97–115. de Gruyter Series in Logic and its Applications, Berlin - New York, 1999.
22. Y. N. Moschovakis. Abstract first order computability I, II. *Transactions of the American Mathematical Society*, 138:427–504, 1969.
23. Y. N. Moschovakis. *Elementary Induction on Abstract Structures*, volume 77 of *Studies in Logic and the Foundations of Mathematics*. North-Holland, 1974.
24. M. B. Pour-El and J. I. Richards. *Computability in Analysis and Physics*. Springer Verlag, Berlin, 1988.
25. J. V. Tucker and J. I. Zucker. Computable functions and semicomputable sets on many-sorted algebras. In T. S. E. Maibaum S. Abramsky, D. M. Gabbay, editor, *Handbook of Logic in Computer Science*, volume 5, pages 397–525. Oxford University Press, Oxford, 2000.
26. M. Vardi. The complexity of relational query languages. In *Proc. of the 14th ACM Symposium on the Theory of Computing*, pages 37–146, 1982.
27. Klaus Weihrauch. *Computable Analysis*. Springer Verlag, Berlin, 2000.

Efficient SAT Engines for Concise Logics: Accelerating Proof Search for Zero-One Linear Constraint Systems

Martin Fränzle[1] and Christian Herde[2]

[1] Informatics and Mathematical Modelling, The Technical University of Denmark,
Richard Petersens Plads, Bldg. 322, DK-2800 Kgs. Lyngby, Denmark,
Phone/Fax: +45-4525 7512/+45-4593 0074,
mf@imm.dtu.dk

[2] Department of Computer Science, Carl-von-Ossietzky Universität Oldenburg,
P.O. Box 2503, D-26111 Oldenburg, Germany,
Phone/Fax: +49-441-798-2160/+49-441-798-2145,
Christian.Herde@Informatik.Uni-Oldenburg.De

Abstract. We investigate the problem of generalizing acceleration techniques as found in recent satisfiability engines for conjunctive normal forms (CNFs) to linear constraint systems over the Booleans. The rationale behind this research is that rewriting the propositional formulae occurring in e.g. bounded model checking (BMC) [5] to CNF requires a blowup in either the formula size (worst-case exponential) or in the number of propositional variables (linear, thus yielding a worst-case exponential blow-up of the search space). We demonstrate that acceleration techniques like observation lists and lazy clause evaluation [14] as well as the more traditional non-chronological backtracking and learning techniques generalize smoothly to Davis-Putnam-like resolution procedures for the very concise propositional logic of linear constraint systems over the Booleans. Despite the more expressive input language, the performance of our prototype implementation comes surprisingly close to that of state-of-the-art CNF-SAT engines like ZChaff [14]. First experiments with bounded model-construction problems show that the overhead in the satisfiability engine that can be attributed to the richer input language is often amortized by the conciseness gained in the propositional encoding of the BMC problem.

Keywords: Satisfiability; non-clausal propositional logic; zero-one linear constraint systems; proof search; acceleration techniques

1 Introduction

As many verification and design automation problems concerning finite state hardware and software systems can be expressed as satisfiability problems for propositional logics, there is a growing demand for efficient satisfiability checkers for such logics. Application domains include combinational and sequential

M.Y. Vardi and A. Voronkov (Eds.): LPAR 2003, LNAI 2850, pp. 302–316, 2003.

equivalence checking for circuits, test pattern generation, FPGA routing, and bounded model-checking, i.e. the verification of a temporal property on a finite unraveling of a transition system [5]. As these are enabling technologies for tackling the complexity of ever larger circuits and ever more refined embedded software, and as furthermore even the size of the propositional formulae derived from current devices is prohibitive, this has sparked much research on enhancing satisfiability checkers and on generating more compact propositional encodings of the problem statements.

Concerning the performance of propositional satisfiability (SAT) checkers, the most dramatic improvements have recently been accomplished on SAT solvers for conjunctive normal forms (CNFs) that implement variants of the Davis-Putnam-Loveland-Logemann (DPLL) procedure [7]. As in the classical DPLL procedure, the main algorithmic ingredients of these solvers are unit propagation and backtrack search. These have, however, been enhanced by heuristics for finding a suitable traversal sequence through the backtrack-search tree, as well as by refined algorithms and data structures for pruning the search tree and for accelerating unit propagation. Considerable search-tree pruning has been achieved through non-chronological backtracking [9, 13, 14, 20] and conflict-driven learning [13, 14, 20], sometimes combined with random restart [3, 14]. Unit propagation is sped up through dedicated data structures [20, 21] and through lazy clause evaluation [14], which delays re-evaluation of the truth value of any clause that is definitely non-unit.

While these techniques actually yield a dramatic speedup in practice, now tackling instances with hundreds of thousands of propositions, which would have been completely impractical a decade ago, they still reach their limits for state-of-the-art verification problems derived from high-level design models (e.g., Statemate models [10]) of embedded software. Such models easily yield CNFs with millions of propositional variables under bounded model checking, even if BDD-based Boolean-function minimization is applied to the transition relation in a preprocessing step [11]. While some of this complexity is inherent to the verification task, another part can be attributed to the low expressiveness of conjunctive normal forms. Rewriting arbitrary propositional formulae to CNF yields a worst-case exponential blowup in formula size if the number of propositional variables is to be preserved. To avoid this, all practical verification environments take advantage of satisfiability-preserving transformations that yield linear-size encodings through introduction of a linear number of auxiliary variables [15, 17, 18]. The price for introducing a linear number of auxiliary variables is, however, a worst-case exponential blow-up in the size of the backtrack-search tree.

Yet, it has been observed that both causes of blow-up can often be avoided, as the DPLL procedure generalizes smoothly to zero-one linear constraint systems (the constraint parts of zero-one linear programs) [1, 4, 19]. Zero-one linear constraint systems are expressive enough to facilitate a linear-size encoding of, e.g., gate-level netlists without use of auxiliary variables. Following the seminal work of Barth, who generalized the basic DPLL procedure [4], Whittemore, Kim, and Sakallah tried to follow up the advances in the algorithmics of CNF

SAT solvers by adapting GRASP's conflict analysis and learning to zero-one linear constraint systems [19], and recently Aloul, Ramani, Markov, and Sakallah ported CHAFF's lazy clause evaluation to this setting [1]. Yet, they simply mimicked CHAFF's lazy evaluation scheme such that their type of lazy clause evaluation is confined to the pure CNF part of the problem, i.e. applies only to those clauses that are disjunctive. As all other clauses are evaluated eagerly, and as clause re-evaluation is known to account for the major part of a DPLL-based SAT solver [14], this is far from optimal. In this paper, we will show that it is possible and effective to generalize lazy clause evaluation to arbitrary linear constraints under a zero-one interpretation. A similar method has come to our knowledge after submission of this report: Chai and Kuehlmann have independently designed and implemented closely related techniques [6].

We will provide a brief introduction to zero-one linear constraint systems in Section 2 and to the state of the art in CNF SAT in Section 3. Section 4 explains the algorithms and data structures underlying our SAT solver for zero-one linear constraint systems, which incorporates generalized DPLL, conflict-driven learning, and lazy clause evaluation for general linear constraint clauses. Section 5, finally, provides benchmark results.

2   Zero-One Linear Constraint Systems

Given the fact that CNF encoding of formulae is often substantially more complex — either wrt. formula size or wrt. number of auxiliary propositional variables — than encoding in more general classes of propositional formulae, we take advantage of propositional formulae in conjunctive clause form that have a much more liberal notion of clause. In this class, called *zero-one linear constraint systems (ZOLCS)* or *linear pseudo-Boolean constraint systems* [4], formulae are conjunctions of linear threshold clauses. A *linear threshold clause* is of the form

$$a_1x_1 + a_2x_2 + \ldots a_nx_n \geq k \ ,$$

where the x_i are *literals*, i.e. positive or negated *propositional variables*, the a_i are natural numbers, called the *weights* of the individual literals, and $k \in \mathbf{N}$ is the *threshold*.

Given a Boolean valuation of the propositional variables, a threshold clause is satisfied iff its left hand side evaluates to a value exceeding the threshold when the truth values `false` and `true` are identified with 0 and 1, respectively. I.e.,

$$5a + 3\overline{b} + 3c + 1d \geq 7 \ ,$$

where $\overline{b}$ denotes the negation of b, is satisfied by the valuation

$$a \mapsto \mathtt{false}, b \mapsto \mathtt{false}, c \mapsto \mathtt{true}, d \mapsto \mathtt{true} \ ,$$

yet is not satisfied by the valuation

$$a \mapsto \mathtt{true}, b \mapsto \mathtt{true}, c \mapsto \mathtt{false}, d \mapsto \mathtt{true} \ .$$

Threshold clauses can represent a wide class of monotonic Boolean functions, e.g. $1a + 1b + 1\bar{c} + 1d \geq 1$ is equivalent to $a \vee b \vee \bar{c} \vee d$, $1a + 1b + 1\bar{c} + 1d \geq 4$ is equivalent to $a \wedge b \wedge \bar{c} \wedge d$, and $1a + 1b + 3\bar{c} + 1d \geq 3$ is equivalent to $c \implies (a \wedge b \wedge d)$. Consequently, zero-one linear constraint systems can be exponentially more concise than CNF: a CNF expressing that at least n out of k variables should be true requires $\binom{n}{k}$ clauses of length n each, i.e. is of size $O\left(\binom{n}{k}n\right)$, whereas the corresponding ZOLCS has size linear in k and logarithmic in n.

Formally, the syntax of zero-one linear constraint systems is

$$formula ::= \{clause \wedge\}^* clause$$
$$clause ::= linear\_term \geq threshold$$
$$linear\_term ::= \{weight\ literal +\}^* weight\ literal$$
$$weight ::\in \mathbf{N}$$
$$literal ::= var \mid \overline{var}$$
$$var ::\in V$$
$$threshold ::\in \mathbf{N}$$

where V is a countable set of propositional variable names. In accordance with the correspondence of certain linear threshold clauses to standard Boolean connectives, we say that a zero-one linear constraint system ϕ is *in CNF form* iff all the weights and all the thresholds occurring in ϕ are equal to 1.

ZOLCS' are interpreted over Boolean *valuations* $\sigma : V \xrightarrow{\text{total}} \mathbf{B}$ of the propositional variables. We say that σ *satisfies* ϕ, denoted $\sigma \models \phi$, iff σ satisfies all clauses of ϕ. σ satisfies a clause $a_1 x_1 + a_2 x_2 + \ldots a_n x_n \geq k$ iff $a_1 \chi_\sigma(x_1) + a_2 \chi_\sigma(x_2) + \ldots a_n \chi_\sigma(x_n) \geq k$, where

$$\chi_\sigma(x) = \begin{cases} 0 \text{ if } x \in V \text{ and } \sigma(x) = \texttt{false}, \\ 1 \text{ if } x \in V \text{ and } \sigma(x) = \texttt{true}, \\ 1 \text{ if } x \equiv \bar{y} \text{ for some } y \in V \text{ and } \sigma(y) = \texttt{false}, \\ 0 \text{ if } x \equiv \bar{y} \text{ for some } y \in V \text{ and } \sigma(y) = \texttt{true}. \end{cases}$$

When solving ZOLCS satisfiability problems with Davis-Putnam-like procedures, we will build valuations incrementally such that we have to reason about *partial valuations* $\rho : V \xrightarrow{\text{part.}} \mathbf{B}$ of the propositional variables. We say that a variable $v \in V$ is *unassigned in* ρ iff $v \notin dom(\rho)$. A partial valuation ρ is called *consistent for a formula* ϕ iff there exists a total extension $\sigma : V \xrightarrow{\text{total}} \mathbf{B}$ of ρ that satisfies ϕ. Otherwise, we call ρ *inconsistent for* ϕ. Furthermore, a partial valuation ρ is said to *satisfy* ϕ iff all its total extensions satisfy ϕ. As this definition of satisfaction agrees with the previous one on total valuations, we will use the same notation $\rho \models \phi$ for satisfaction by partial and by total valuations.

3   State of the Art in Clausal SAT

Many modern implementations of complete satisfiability-search procedures are enhancements of the Davis-Putnam-Loveland-Logemann recursive search procedure [7].Given a CNF ϕ and a partial valuation ρ, which is empty at the start, the DPLL procedure incrementally extends ρ until either $\rho \models \phi$ holds or ρ turns out to be inconsistent for ϕ, in which case another extension is tried through back-tracking. Extensions are constructed by either logical deduction based on *unit resolution* or by so-called *decision steps*, which entail selecting an unassigned variable and "blindly" assigning a truth-value to it. The DPLL procedure alternates between these two extension strategies, thereby using unit resolution whenever possible:

> $\mathrm{DPLL}(\phi, \rho)$:
>> $\mathrm{DEDUCE}(\phi, \rho)$ % Unit resolution
>> **if** ϕ contains conflicting clause **then return**
>> **if** no free variables left **then exit_with**(ρ)
>> $b := \mathrm{SELECT\_UNASSIGNED\_VARIABLE}(\phi)$ % Decision step:
>> $v := \mathrm{ONE\_OF}\ \{\texttt{true}, \texttt{false}\}$
>> $\mathrm{DPLL}(\phi, \rho \cup \{b \mapsto v\})$ %   Blind assignment,
>> $\mathrm{DPLL}(\phi, \rho \cup \{b \mapsto \neg v\})$ %   reversed upon backtrack

Unit resolution, as implemented by DEDUCE, checks for occurrence of so-called *unit clauses* and extends the current partial valuation by their implications. A clause "is unit" iff all its literals, except for exactly one unassigned literal, are set to false. To satisfy the CNF ϕ, the unassigned literal has to be assigned true. That assignment is thus said to be *propagated* by the unit clause. Such propagation is iterated until no further unit clauses exist.

> $\mathrm{DEDUCE}(\phi, \rho)$:
>> **while** unit-clause (x) exists in ϕ
>>> **if** $x \equiv b$ for some $b \in V$ **then** $\rho := \rho \cup \{b \mapsto \texttt{true}\}$
>>> **if** $x \equiv \bar{b}$ for some $b \in V$ **then** $\rho := \rho \cup \{b \mapsto \texttt{false}\}$

Deduction may yield a *conflicting clause* which has all its literals assigned false, indicating a dead end in search. Backtracking then backs up to the most recently assigned decision variable which has not yet been tried both ways, flips its truth-value, and resumes the search. If no such decision variable exists then ϕ is unsatisfiable. If, on the other hand, all variables of ϕ can be assigned without a conflict, a satisfying valuation has been found.

Being based on this recursive search procedure, actual implementations refine the above scheme by using different strategies for selecting the variable and the truth-value to be used at a decision step. See [12] for a detailed review of the impact of different decision strategies on the solving process. Furthermore, state-of-the-art SAT solvers enhance the basic procedure through various algorithmic modifications.

3.1   Conflict Analysis and Conflict-Driven Learning

Like all pure backtracking algorithms, the DPLL proceduresuffers from thrashing, i.e. repeated failure due to the same reason. To overcome this problem, sufficiently general reasons for the conflict encountered have to be deduced and stored for future guidance of the search procedure. The standard scheme traces the reason back to a small (ideally minimal) number of assignments that triggered the particular conflict, and stores this reason by adding the negation of that assignment as a clause — termed *conflict clause* — to the clause database.

Such reasons can be inferred from cuts in the propagation graph. The *propagation graph* is a directed graph recording the causal relationship between individual variable assignments performed. It is obtained through relating, for each propagation performed, the propagated literal to the previously assigned literals in the corresponding unit clause. A cut in this graph constitutes a reason for all assignments occurring later in the graph. A more general reason, i.e. a reason mentioning fewer literals, for an individual assignment can be derived by taking just those elements of a cut that actually have a path to that particular assignment. Using this technique, reasons for the assignments constituting a conflict can be inferred. The reason is, however, not unique, as different cuts can be used. The interested reader is referred to Zhang et al. [22], who examine several heuristics for deriving one or more conflict clauses from the propagation graph.

3.2 Backjumping

In addition to learning conflict clauses, the result of the conflict diagnosis can also be used to accelerate backtracking: instead of just backtracking to the most recent decision step, the algorithm may immediately undo all decisions up to the latest assignment to a variable occurring in the identified conflict clause, as later decisions do not affect the conflict. Because of this non-sequential way of backing up through the levels of the search tree, this technique is referred to as *backjumping*.

3.3 Restarts

Another enhancement which can be applied in presence of conflict-driven learning is *(random) restarts*. Restarts abort an ongoing search, discard the partial valuation which has been constructed so far, and resume solvingfrom an empty valuation while retaining the learned conflict clauses. This technique is intended to prevent the search from getting lost in non-relevant regions of the search space which might have been entered by early decisions. The restarted solver will not simply repeat its previous run due to the learned conflict clauses, which guide the solver to different parts of the search space. Note, however, that some care has to be taken to preserve completeness of the search process [2], e.g. by limiting the number of restarts.

3.4 Lazy Clause Evaluation

Concerning performance of DPLL-like procedures, probably the most important improvement in recent years can be attributed to a novel implementation of unit propagation, introduced with the ZChaff sat solver [14]. Unit propagation in general accounts for the major fraction of solver run-time.

Previous implementations of unit propagation identified unit clauses by visiting, after each assignment, *all* clauses containing the literal falsified by that assignment, as such clauses might have become unit. The key idea of the enhanced algorithm is to watch only two literals in each clause, and not to visit the clause when any other literal is assigned as the two watched literals provide evidence of its non-unitness. If an assignment, however, sets a watched literal to false, then this triggers a visit of the respective clause to evaluate its state. The algorithm then tries to replace the watched literal that has been assigned false with another unassigned or true literal occurring in the clause. If it succeeds then it has constructed a new witness for non-unitness of the clause. Otherwise, the clause has become unit and the unassigned one of the watched literals is the one to be propagated.

This technique, often called *lazy clause evaluation*, has been shown to achieve significant performance gains, especially on hard SAT instances [14].

4   Accelerated Proof Search for ZOLCS Satisfiability

We will now generalize DPLL and its recent enhancements, in particular lazy clause evaluation, to zero-one linear constraint systems. To simplify the exposition we assume in the following that each threshold clause is rewritten after each assignment according to the following simplification rules:

- A literal which has been set to false is removed from the lefthand side of the clause as it cannot contribute to its satisfaction any longer. For example, after assigning $b \mapsto \mathtt{true}$, the clause $1a + 1\bar{b} + 1\bar{c} \geq 2$ is written as $1a + 1\bar{c} \geq 2$.
- A literal which has become true is also removed from the clause, however with its weight subtracted from the threshold of that clause. For example, after assigning $b \mapsto \mathtt{false}$ the clause $1a + 1\bar{b} + 1\bar{c} \geq 2$ is written as $1a + 1\bar{c} \geq 1$.

Consequently, all literals appearing in clauses are yet unassigned, and indices range over unassigned literals only.

4.1   DPLL on Threshold Clauses

Since the seminal work of Barth [4] it is well-known that the basic DPLL procedure can easily be generalized to zero-one linear constraint systems through modification of the deduction procedure.

As before, the objective of the deduction routine is to detect propagating clauses and to perform the corresponding assignments. A threshold clause $\sum a_i x_i \geq k$ propagates a literal x_j iff setting this literal to false would make the clause unsatisfiable, i.e. iff $(\sum a_i) - a_j < k$.

In contrast to a CNF clause, a general threshold clause can propagate several literals simultaneously. As an example consider the clause

$$5a + 3\bar{b} + 3c + 1d + 1e \geq 7$$

which propagates $\bar{b}$ and c immediately after setting a to false. Carrying out the assignments $b \mapsto \texttt{false}$ and $c \mapsto \texttt{true}$ reduces the clause to

$$1d + 1e \geq 1$$

which shows that, as opposed to CNF-SAT, a threshold clause is not necessarily satisfied after propagation.

We refer to a threshold clause which propagates at least one literal as a *propagating clause*. With this notion, corresponding to the notion of a unit clause in CNF-SAT, we can formulate the generalized DEDUCE procedure for ZOLCS as follows:

DEDUCE(ϕ, ρ):
    while propagating clause $\mathcal{C}$ exists in ϕ
        for each literal x propagated by $\mathcal{C}$
            if $x \equiv b$ for some $b \in V$ **then** $\rho := \rho \cup \{b \mapsto \texttt{true}\}$
            if $x \equiv \bar{b}$ for some $b \in V$ **then** $\rho := \rho \cup \{b \mapsto \texttt{false}\}$

Observe that a propagating clause propagates at least the literal with the largest weight appearing in that clause. If this is not unique due to several literals with the same largest weight, then all those literals are propagated.

This can be demonstrated by the following argument: Let x_p be the (not necessarily unique) literal with the largest weight appearing in a clause $\sum a_i x_i \geq k$. Suppose that some literal x_q with $q \neq p$ is propagated by that clause. Then $(\sum a_i) - a_q < k$ holds due to the propagation rule given above. However, since $c_p \geq c_q$, also $(\sum a_i) - a_p < k$ holds, i.e. x_p is propagated, too.

4.2   Generalization of Lazy Clause Evaluation

While the generalization of the DPLL procedure to ZOLCS has already been proposed by Barth [4], its acceleration through lazy clause evaluation for arbitrary threshold clauses is a novel contribution.[1] To apply lazy clause evaluation to threshold clauses we have to determine a subset of unassigned literals from each clause such that watching these literals is sufficient for detecting change of clause state from normal to propagating. Obviously, we are looking for minimal sets with this property in order to avoid unnecessary clause visits.

To this end, we arrange the literals of each clause with respect to their weights, such that the literal with the largest weight is the leftmost one. Then we read the clause from left to right and select the literals to be watched as follows:

1) The leftmost literal is selected.
2) The following literals are selected until the sum of their weights, not including the weight of the leftmost literal, is greater than or equal to the threshold of the clause.

---

[1] Aloul et al.'s incorporation of CHAFF's lazy clause evaluation into ZOLCS solving [1] provides lazy clause evaluation for CNF clauses only.

In the example clause below, the literals selected by the aforementioned rules have been marked with grey boxes:

$$4a + 3b + 2c + 1d + 1e + 1f + 1g \quad \geq \quad 5$$

The set of literals chosen to be watched by these rules fulfills the requirements stated above:

a) Assignments which do not affect the watched literals will never make the clause unsatisfiable as the literals selected by rule 2) are by themselves sufficient to ensure satisfiability.

   Furthermore, no such assignment will turn the clause into a propagating one. To see this, assume that an assignment to an unwatched literal *does* cause the propagation of some literals. Then, as shown before, the watched literal with the largest weight, selected by rule 1), is among those implications. However, according to the propagation rule from section 4.1, this literal is *not* propagated because the remaining watched literals, selected by rule 2), ensure satisfiability of the clause.

   Consequently, a visit of the clause is unnecessary upon assignments affecting unwatched literals only.

b) If, on the other hand, an assignment sets a watched literal to false, the corresponding clause may become a propagating one. Hence, such assignments trigger an evaluation of the clause. However, the set of watched literals guarantees that the clause is satisfiable upon visit as any single literal can be assigned while preserving satisfiability of the clause: if the literal with the largest weight is set to false then the watched literals selected by rule 2) still guarantee satisfiability. If a literal selected according to rule 2) is set to false, the literal selected by rule 1) can compensate for it as its weight is greater than or equal to the one of the literal which has been assigned.

c) The chosen literals form a minimal subset with these properties as we start selecting from the largest weight towards the smallest.

If a watched literal of a clause is assigned false, our algorithm tries to reestablish a set of literals which is in accordance to rules 1) and 2). This requires the search for a minimal set of literals which are either unassigned or true and whose weights sum up to a value that at least equals that of the watched literal which has been assigned false. If such a set exists then it is added to the set of watched literals to replace the one which has dropped out. If no such set exists then this indicates that the clause has become a propagating one. The resulting propagations are determined by application of the propagation rule from section 4.1.

In our implementation, we decided to continue observing those watched literals which have been assigned true as well as those which have been set to false but cannot be replaced by new observations, instead of really removing them from the observation set. Clearly, these observations will not trigger any clause evaluation as long as the corresponding variables keep their values, s.t. there is no need to really remove them. The desired side-effect is, however, that upon *un*assignment of the corresponding variables, these observations are implicitly reactivated. This form of *lazy reactivation* ensures that after backtracking, an appropriate set of literals is watched in each clause. As this is achieved without any computational burden, the time spent on backtracking is linear in the number of unassignments that have to be performed, just as in CNF-SAT. The price to be paid is, however, that after backtracking the observation set of a clause may no longer be minimal, because a single watched literal, which after backtracking is unassigned again, might have previously been replaced by several literals with smaller weights. In principle we could re-establish a minimal set of watched literals by recording the changes in the observation sets triggered by each decision and undoing these changes when backtracking. Yet, this would make backtracking much more expensive and, furthermore, we would abandon the advantage that reassigning a variable shortly after unassigning it – due to the nature of tree-search algorithms a quite frequent case – is usually faster than its previous assignment, as thereafter it is only watched in a small subset of clauses.

Consider again the clause from the previous example. The figure below illustrates the changes of its state and its set of watched literals when successively setting g, c and b to false, then unassigning all variables.

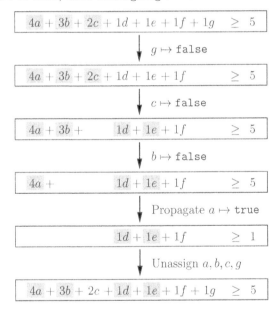

4.3   Generalization of Learning

Just as in CNF-SAT, conflict-driven learning in our solver for ZOLCS is based on an analysis of the propagation graph as described in section **3.1**. For sake of efficiency, the propagation graph is, exactly as e.g. in the ZChaff solver, only maintained implicitly during the search by annotating each variable assigned by propagation with a pointer to its propagating clause, but it is not constructed explicitly until a conflict is really encountered.

To construct the propagation graph, the conflict diagnosis procedure has to determine, for each propagation involved in the conflict, a subset of literals of the corresponding propagating clause whose assignment triggered the propagation. In CNF-SAT, this subset is easy to identify as it consists of *all* literals of the unit clause, except the one which has been propagated. In ZOLCS-SAT, however, we have to take into account that a threshold clause is not necessarily satisfied after propagation and may even become propagating more than once. Hence, the state of its literals at the time of conflict analysis may not coincide its literals' state at the time of propagation. Blindly selecting assigned literals from a clause to reconstruct a cause for a certain propagation may thus introduce acausal relationships or even cycles in the propagation graph.

To avoid this, our implementation associates a timestamp to each variable assignment. The timestamp records the point in time when the variable was assigned; it is reset to zero upon unassignment of the variable. Let $\sum_{i \in M} a_i x_i \geq k$, $M \subseteq \mathbb{N}$ be a threshold clause and x_p a literal propagated by this clause. For each $i \in M$ let t_i denote the timestamp associated with literal x_i. To determine a cause for the propagation of x_p, our implementation chooses a minimal subset of literals with indices $R \subseteq M$ such that $(\sum_{i \in M \setminus R} a_i) - a_p < k$ and $(\sum_{i \in M \setminus R} a_i) + a_p \geq k$ hold and, furthermore, for each $r \in R$ the literal x_r has been assigned false with timestamp $t_r \leq t_p$.

The propagation graph is built by recursively relating propagated literals to their causes, where the latter are determined according to the above rules. Once the propagation graph has been constructed, the algorithm for conflict analysis and learning is equal to the one used in CNF-SAT. In particular, the clauses learned are CNF clauses. We do not support learning of more general clauses right now. Recently, a more general learning scheme learning restricted forms of threshold clauses has been proposed in [6].

5   Benchmark Results

In order to evaluate the proposed methods, we have developed Goblin, a new SAT solver for zero-one linear constraint systems, which employs lazy clause evaluation and conflict-driven learning as explained in section 4. For some experiments we used ZChaff, version 2001.2.17, as reference. Goblin, which is written in C++, shares several algorithmic features of the ZChaff solver, however, as opposed to Zchaff, it uses neither random restarts, nor deletion of learned conflict clauses to avoid memory explosion up to now, and it uses a less sophisticated decision strategy. All experiments were performed on a 1 GHz Pentium III machine with 640 MByte physical memory, running Linux.

The first group of experiments dealt with scheduling problems, originally formulated in discrete-time Duration Calculus. The propositional formulae used as input for the SAT engines are bounded model construction problems for Duration Calculus formulae, generated by the method proposed in [8]. Each SAT instance entails the search for a feasible schedule for three periodic tasks, where a feasible schedule corresponds to a satisfying valuation of the respective instance.

Table 1. Results of scheduling benchmarks.

	CNF			ZOLCS		
n	Clauses	Literals	ZChaff [s]	Clauses	Literals	Goblin [s]
1	56758	140637	0.19	21638	109054	0.23
2	107350	273069	0.40	22501	108703	0.25
3	157942	405501	1.97	21467	108193	0.25
4	208534	537933	20.24	21386	107536	0.26
5	259126	670365	153.56	21308	106744	0.25
6	309718	802797	163.45	21233	105829	0.25
7	360310	935229	219.42	21161	104803	0.24
8	410902	1067661	250.35	21092	103678	0.24
9	461494	1200093	277.04	21026	102466	0.24
10	512086	1332525	307.26	20963	101179	0.24

The individual instances only differ in the runtime n of the tasks involved in the corresponding task system.

The generation of the input formulae for Goblin exploits that a duration formula of shape $\int y \geq k$, which holds on an observation interval $O = [m, n]$ iff the accumulated duration of y being true over this interval exceeds k, can be directly translated into the threshold clause $\sum_m^n y_i \geq k$, where the y_i represent the values of y in the different time instants.

The results, presented in Table 1, show that this encoding yields ZOLCS which have size almost constant in n, whereas the size of the corresponding CNF-formulae grows rapidly with n. The same holds for the solving time. In total, Goblin finished all instances in less than three seconds, whereas ZChaff required more than 23 minutes to complete them.

The second group of experiments was carried out to assess the effectiveness of the proposed lazy clause evaluation scheme in terms of the average number of clause evaluations that have to be executed after each assignment performed. To this end, we translated integer arithmetic problems into ZOLCS, using a bit-wise encoding that replaces each occurence of an integer variable a with $\sum_{i=0}^{n-1} 2^i a_i$, where the a_i are propositional variables and n is the number of bits needed to represent a.

Consider for example the integer constraint $a^2 \geq 4$, where a is a 2-bit integer variable. The encoding sketched above yields $(2a_1 + a_0)(2a_1 + a_0) \geq 4$, i.e. $4a_1^2 + 4a_1 a_0 + a_0^2 \geq 4$, which can easily be transformed into a ZOLCS by replacing each nonlinear term $a_i a_j$ with an auxiliary variable h and imposing the additional constraint $h \rightarrow a_i \wedge a_j$, where the latter is expressed by $2\overline{h} + a_i + a_j \geq 2$.

Table 2 shows the integer formulae that were used in the experiments, as well as the size of the corresponding ZOLCS.

As a reference for these benchmarks we used a modified version of Goblin that watches *all* literals appearing in a threshold clause, thus mimicking the behaviour of a naive implementation of the DPLL algorithm, that, after each assignment, re-evaluates all clauses containing the literal falsified by that assignment.

Table 2. Integer arithmetic problems.

	Formula	Range	Clauses	Literals
a)	$a^3 + b^3 + c^3 = d^3$	$a, b, c, d \in [100; 200]$	1103	5352
b)	$a^3 + b^3 = c^3$	$a, b, c \in [100; 200]$	827	3952
c)	$a^3 + b^3 = 352 * a * b$	$a, b \in [100; 500]$	1018	4872
d)	$a^3 + b^3 = 517 * a * b$	$a, b \in [100; 500]$	1018	4872
e)	$(416 - a) * b^2 = a^3 \wedge a \neq b$	$a, b \in [100; 500]$	855	3915
f)	$(224 - a) * b^2 = a^3 \wedge a \neq b$	$a, b \in [100; 500]$	855	3915

Table 3. Results of integer problems.

	Solver Result	Naive Algorithm			Lazy Clause Evaluation		
		Time [s]	Assignments Evaluations	EpA	Time [s]	Assignments Evaluations	EpA
a)	$a = 108, b = 114,$ $c = 126, d = 168$	94.32	2716535 651362897	239.78	25.88	2853381 23950767	8.39
b)	UNSAT	105.25	2334859 732186876	313.59	21.97	2412304 24734089	10.25
c)	$a = 176, b = 176$	38.35	1273108 212213069	166.69	14.12	1291765 12169638	9.42
d)	UNSAT	268.96	2624583 1268553553	483.36	37.10	2628195 40664770	15.47
e)	$a = 288, b = 432$	8.27	425303 37606297	88.42	3.68	437408 2420138	5.53
f)	UNSAT	19.84	622024 98046695	157.63	6.47	647989 5633296	8.69

The results of the experiments are summarized in Table 3. "EpA" denotes the average number of clause evaluations per assignment required in the respective solver run. For all benchmarks performed, lazy clause evaluation is able to significantly reduce this value, as well as the runtime of the solver. The largest gain is obtained for benchmark d), where EpA is improved by a factor of 31.2, yielding a speed-up factor of 7.2. The reduction of EpA demonstrates that keeping the observation sets on backtracking does not lead to inefficiently large observation sets. It seems that the lower cost of backtracking gained from this strategy in fact outweighs the clause evaluation overhead caused by non-minimal observation sets, as our scheme provides considerable speedups even on general ZOLCS, like the arithmetic benchmarks. In contrast, Chai and Kuehlmann decided, based on benchmarking their implementation, to constrain lazy clause evaluation to CNF and cardinality clauses (i.e. clauses having only weights of 1) only [6].

6   Discussion

Our first experiments indicate that incorporating state-of-the-art SAT solver algorithmics, in particular lazy clause evaluation, into a ZOLCS satisfiability checker is efficient, with the overhead incurred from solving the more expressive source language being outweighed by the more concise input language. The empiric results are better than expected, given that they are based on a first prototype implementation that is lacking the perpetual refinement of many of its competitors, as well as on a limited set of benchmarks that have not been tuned to fully exploit the conciseness of zero-one linear constraint systems. Especially promising are the results obtained on integer arithmetic problems, a domain traditionally considered to be extremely challenging for propositional solvers, be it BDD-based or SAT-based solvers. It is worth noting that most of the arithmetic operations involved were non-linear such that they are out-of-scope of integer linear programming (ILP) procedures, unless bit-wise encoding is used, which yields poorly performing ILPs in general [16].

Planned optimizations and extensions to our implementation include, besides fine tuning of the various heuristics involved, a more cache-aware implementation which sorts clauses with similar high-weight literals into adjacent memory areas. Furthermore, we plan to exploit the straightforward relaxation of zero-one linear constraint systems into linear programs (LPs) for giving the variable selection strategy used in decision steps a reasonable seed: by occasionally — e.g., upon restarts — solving the relaxation of the ZOLCS with an LP solver, likely truth value assignments for some of the variables can be obtained, which provides guidance for selecting the variable and the initial truth value to be used within decision steps.

Acknowledgment

The authors would like to thank the Safety-Critical Embedded Systems Group of Oldenburg University and the ES/VT division of Kuratorium OFFIS e.V., Oldenburg, for many fruitful discussions.

References

1. Fadi A. Aloul, Arathi Ramani, Igor L. Markov, and Karem A. Sakallah. Generic ILP versus specialized 0-1 ILP: An update. In *Proc. ACM/IEEE Intl. Conf. Comp.-Aided Design (ICCAD)*, pages 450–457, November 2002.
2. L. Baptista, I. Lynce, and J. Marques-Silva. Complete search restart strategies for satisfiability. In *Proc. of the IJCAI'01 Workshop on Stochastic Search Algorithms (IJCAI-SSA)*, August 2001.
3. L. Baptista and J. P. Marques-Silva. Using randomization and learning to solve hard real-world instances of satisfiability. In *Proc. of the 6th International Conference on Principles and Practice of Constraint Programming*, 2000.
4. Peter Barth. A Davis-Putnam based enumeration algorithm for linear pseudo-boolean optimization. Technical Report MPI-I-95-2-003, Max-Planck-Institut für Informatik, Saarbrücken, Germany, 1995.
5. A. Biere, A. Cimatti, and Y. Zhu. Symbolic model checking without BDDs. In *TACAS'99*, volume 1579 of *Lecture Notes in Computer Science*. Springer-Verlag, 1999.

6. Donald Chai and Andreas Kuehlmann. A fast pseudo-boolean constraint solver. In *Proc. of the 40th Design Automation Conference (DAC 2003)*, pages 830–835, Anaheim (California, USA), June 2003. ACM.

7. M. Davis, G. Logemann, and D. Loveland. A machine program for theorem proving. *Communications of the ACM*, 5:394–397, 1962.

8. Martin Fränzle. Take it NP-easy: Bounded model construction for duration calculus. In Ernst-Rüdiger Olderog and Werner Damm, editors, *International Symposium on Formal Techniques in Real-Time and Fault-Tolerant systems (FTRTFT 2002)*, volume 2469 of *Lecture Notes in Computer Science*, pages 245–264. Springer-Verlag, 2002.

9. J. F. Groote and J. P. Warners. The propositional formula checker HeerHugo. Technical report SEN-R9905, CWI, 1999.

10. David Harel and Michal Politi. *Modeling Reactive Systems with Statecharts*. McGraw-Hill Inc., 1998.

11. Rainer Lochmann. Boosting the verification power of the statemate verification engine: on the perfomance benefits of integrating ProverCL. In preparation, 2003.

12. J. P. Marques-Silva. The impact of branching heuristics in propositional satisfiability algorithms. In *Proc. of the 9th Portuguese Conference on Artificial Intelligence (EPIA)*, September 1999.

13. J. P. Marques-Silva and K. A. Sakallah. GRASP: A search algorithm for propositional satisfiability. *IEEE Transactions on Computers*, 48(5):506–521, May 1999.

14. Matthew W. Moskewicz, Conor F. Madigan, Ying Zhao, Lintao Zhang, and Sharad Malik. Chaff: Engineering an Efficient SAT Solver. In *Proceedings of the 38th Design Automation Conference (DAC'01)*, June 2001.

15. Andreas Nonnengart and Christoph Weidenbach. Computing small clause normal forms. In Alen Robinson and Andrei Voronkov, editors, *Handbook of Automated Reasoning*. Elsevier Science B.V., 1999.

16. J. H. Owen and S. Mehrotra. On the value of binary expansions for general mixed-integer linear programs. *Operations Research*, 50(5):810–819, 2002.

17. G. Tseitin. On the complexity of derivations in propositional calculus. In A. Slisenko, editor, *Studies in Constructive Mathematics and Mathematical Logics*, 1968.

18. Joost P. Warners. A linear-time transformation of linear inequalities into conjunctive normal form. *Information Processing Letters*, 68(2):63–69, 1998.

19. Jesse Whittemore, Joonyoung Kim, and Karem Sakallah. SATIRE: A new incremental satisfiability engine. In *Proc. of the 38th Design Automation Conference (DAC 2001)*, pages 542–545, Las Vegas (Nevada, USA), June 2001.

20. H. Zhang. SATO: An efficient propositional prover. In *Proc. of the International Conference on Automated Deduction (CADE)*, volume 1249 of *LNAI*, pages 272–275. Springer, 1997.

21. H. Zhang and M. Stickel. An efficient algorithm for unit-propagation. In *Proc. of the International Symposium on Artificial Intelligence and Mathematics (AI-MATH'96)*, pages 166–169, Fort Lauderdale (Florida USA), 1996.

22. L. Zhang, C. F. Madigan, M. W. Moskewicz, and S. Malik. Efficient conflict driven learning in a Boolean satisfiability solver. In *Proc. of the International Conference on Computer-Aided Design (ICCAD'01)*, pages 279–285, November 2001.

NP-Completeness Results for Deductive Problems on Stratified Terms

Thierry Boy de la Tour and Mnacho Echenim

LEIBNIZ laboratory, IMAG – CNRS, INPG,
46 avenue Félix Viallet, F-38031 Grenoble Cedex,
Thierry.Boy-de-la-Tour@imag.fr, Mnacho.Echenim@imag.fr

Abstract. In [1] Avenhaus and Plaisted proposed the notion of *stratified* terms, in order to represent concisely the sets of consequences of clauses under *leaf permutative theories*. These theories contain variable-permuting equations, so that the consequences appear as simple "permuted" variants of each other. Deducing directly with stratified terms can reduce exponentially the search space, but we show that the problems involved (e.g. unifiability) are **NP**-complete. We use computational group theory to show membership in **NP**, while **NP**-hardness is obtained through an interesting problem in group theory.

1 Introduction

When dealing with an equational theory, it is often the case that *leaf permutative* equations are produced, i.e. equations that are invariant under some permutation of variables. For example, suppose an equational theory E contains the two following equations: $f(x, y, g(z, t)) = f(y, x, g(z, t))$ and $f(x, y, g(z, t)) = f(y, z, g(t, x))$. Then from a clause $C[f(t_1, t_2, g(t_3, t_4))]$ we can deduce any clause $C[f(t_{1\sigma}, t_{2\sigma}, g(t_{3\sigma}, t_{4\sigma}))]$, where σ is a permutation in the symmetric group $\text{Sym}(4)$, of cardinality 4!. Consequently, the number of resolvents modulo E can grow exponentially (depending on E). Different methods have been devised to handle this sort of problem, either by designing specialised unification algorithms, or by adding constraints to the theory (see e.g. [9]).

In [1], Avenhaus and Plaisted devise a new way to handle such theories, which intuitively consists in reasoning with a member of an equivalence class of terms instead of the terms themselves, thus avoiding the exponential space overhead. More precisely, any formula is considered modulo its consequences modulo leaf permutative equational theories, which are finite, and are defined in [1] through "stratified" rewriting. Of course, reasoning modulo such equivalence classes requires the modification of basic deduction algorithms such as unification, subsumption or factorisation. Unfortunately, the algorithms in [1] all have exponential time complexity. We show in the present paper that they all solve **NP**-hard problems.

We develop in the next section a formalism for terms that is based on occurrences. In section 3 we add a representation of leaf permutative theories as

M.Y. Vardi and A. Voronkov (Eds.): LPAR 2003, LNAI 2850, pp. 317–331, 2003.

labels in terms, yielding (our version of) the *stratified terms* of [1]. In this context we give a simple definition of stratified rewriting (section 4) and reach our aim of expressing equivalence classes as orbits[1]. The deductive problems defined in section 5 are then easily proved to be in **NP** (except one), by a well known result from computational group theory. In section 6, the easiest of these deductive problems is shown to be powerful enough to solve a problem on group constraints. Finally, we prove in section 7 that solving these group constraints is **NP**-hard.

A Word on Notations. The operation in permutation groups is the inverse of function composition, i.e. $\sigma\sigma' = \sigma' \circ \sigma$. The exponential notation (e.g. T^π) is usual for group actions, including function application, i.e. if σ is an integer permutation and i an integer, then $i^\sigma = \sigma(i)$. id is the identity function and $I = \{\text{id}\}$ is the trivial group. Permutations are written in cycle notations and implicitly extended with fix-points, e.g. $3^{(1\ 2)} = 3$. We write ε for the empty string.

2   Occurrence Terms

It is an essential idea of [1] that leaf permutative equations provide generators for permutation groups. Our aim is to exploit further this idea by using group-theoretic tools (see e.g. [7] or [4]) to manipulate these permutative equations and the equivalence classes they generate. We first focus on defining a suitable group and action (an *action* of a group G on a set A is a function from $A \times G$ to A such that $\forall a \in A, a^{\text{id}} = a$ and $\forall \sigma, \sigma' \in G, (a^\sigma)^{\sigma'} = a^{\sigma\sigma'}$, see [7], or the simple introduction in [2], section 3), so that these equivalence classes appear as orbits (a *G-orbit* in A is some $a^G = \{a^\sigma/\sigma \in G\}$).

But defining an action on terms gives rise to a first difficulty: how do we determine precisely the image of a term by a given permutation? For example, given a commutative function symbol g, how can we identify the basic operation of swapping a and b in the two equivalent terms $g(g(a,b),c)$ and $g(c,g(a,b))$, since $g(a,b)$ occurs at different positions? In [1] a distinctive mark labels each occurrence of g, which allows to keep track of "travelling" positions. This makes the swapping of a and b *relative* to a mark, which is not very convenient to obtain a simple group-theoretic framework.

This is why our formalism departs from [1], starting with a simple observation: considering the usual computer representation of the two terms above (e.g. in LISP), they may both contain the *same* pointer to $g(a,b)$. Hence the action we are looking for boils down to a simple kind of pointer manipulations. This justifies the notion of terms developed here, where "occurrences" are the fundamental objects (like vertices in graphs).

Definition 1. *A Σ-term t is a finite algebra (O, s, a), with $s : O \to \Sigma$ and $a : O \to O^\star$ such that $\forall v \in O$, the length of the word $a(v)$ is the arity of $s(v)$, and the directed graph $(O, \{\langle v, v' \rangle \in O^2 | v'$ occurs in $a(v)\})$ is a tree. The*

---
[1] These first sections are improved from [3].

elements of O *are the* occurrences *of* t. *We call the* root *of* t *the root of this tree,*
and note it root(t).

We also define desc : $O \to O^\star$, the descent of an occurrence in a (implicit)
term t, *by* $\forall v \in O, a(v) = v_1 \ldots v_n \Rightarrow$ desc(v) $= v.$desc(v_1)$\ldots$desc(v_n). *We*
note desc(t) *for* desc(root(t)). *We may also use* desc(v) *to denote the* set *of*
occurrences appearing in desc(v); *the same holds for other strings, such as* a(v).

If $t = (O, s, a)$ *is a* Σ*-term and* $v \in O$, *we note* $t.v = ($desc(v)$, s', a')$ *the*
subterm *of* t *at* v, *where* s' *and* a' *are the restrictions of* s *and* a *to* desc(v). *The*
reader may check that $t.v$ *is a* Σ*-term, and that* root($t.v$) $= v$, $t.$root(t) $= t$, *and*
$\forall u \in$ desc(v)$, (t.v).u = t.u$.

For any Σ*-term* t, *with* $r =$ root(t)*, if* $a(r) = v_1 \ldots v_n \neq \varepsilon$, *let* string($t$) $=$
$s(r)($string(v_1)$, \ldots,$ string(v_n))*, otherwise* string(t) $= s(r)$.

So, an occurrence v can be considered as the address of a structure that
contains a label, $s(v)$, and a list of pointers to other occurrences: $a(v)$. string(t)
on the other hand returns a term in the usual sense (say, a term-as-string).

Example 1. Let $f(b, g(b, c))$ be a Σ-term in the usual sense. This term is composed of two binary functions f and g, and two constant symbols, b and c. Take
$O = \{0, \ldots, 4\}$ and define the functions s and a by:

	0	1	2	3	4
s	f	b	g	b	c
a	1.2	ε	3.4	ε	ε

Then $t = (O, s, a)$ is one representation with occurrences of the term, desc(t)
$= 0.1.2.3.4$, and string(t) $= f(b, g(b, c))$. One should notice that we impose two
distinct occurrences labelled by the constant b, although in a computer there
could be two pointers to the same occurrence. This is done to keep a tree-like
structure. Figure 1 is a graphical representation of t.

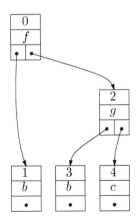

Fig. 1. A representation of $f(b, g(b, c))$

It should be noted that terms-as-strings have a unique mathematical representation, like integers. This is not the case here, and two different terms may represent the same term-as-string. Strictly speaking, terms-as-strings may be identified with *isomorphism classes* of terms.

Definition 2. *For a term $t = (O, s, a)$ and a bijection $\eta : O \to O'$, we define $\eta(t) = (O', s', a')$ by $\forall v \in O, s'(\eta(v)) = s(v)$ and $a'(\eta(v)) = \eta(a(v))$ (i.e. the function η is applied to each letter in $a(v)$). Two terms t and t' are isomorphic, noted $t \simeq t'$ iff there is an isomorphism η from t to t', noted $\eta : t \simeq t'$, that is a bijection such that $t' = \eta(t)$.*

Isomorphism testing can be performed in linear time; it is easy to see that $t \simeq t'$ iff $\text{string}(t) = \text{string}(t')$. Two isomorphic terms are joined by a unique isomorphism, so that $\eta(t) = \eta'(t)$ iff $\eta = \eta'$.

Definition 3. *A Σ-context c is a $(\Sigma \uplus \{[]\})$-term, where $[]$ is a constant known as "the hole".*
   From a term $t = (O, s, a)$ and $H \subseteq O$ such that $\forall h, h' \in H, h \neq h' \Rightarrow \text{desc}(h) \cap \text{desc}(h') = \emptyset$ (i.e. H is an antichain in t w.r.t. the subterm order), we define the context $t \setminus H$ by replacing the occurrences in H by holes: $t \setminus H = (O' \cup H, s', a')$, where $O' = O \setminus \bigcup_{h \in H} \text{desc}(h)$, and $\forall v \in O', s'(v) = s(v), a'(v) = a(v)$, and $\forall h \in H, s'(h) = [], a'(h) = \varepsilon$.
   A term t is an instance of c *iff there is a H such that $t \setminus H \simeq c$; this set H is of course unique.*

Example 2. It is easy to build a Σ-context c corresponding to the string $f([], g([], []))$. The term t of Example 1 is an instance of c, since with $H = \{1, 3, 4\}$, we have $t \setminus H \simeq c$.

3   Stratified Terms

The manner of controlling rewriting adopted in [1] is to rewrite so-called stratified terms, where function symbols are labelled with permutative equational theories and unique integers to avoid possible ambiguities. Our focus on occurrences makes this integer superfluous, and the theory is essentially a context and a group permuting the holes of this context.

Definition 4. *Let Σ' be the set of tuples $\langle f, c, G \rangle$ where $f \in \Sigma$, c is a Σ-context such that $s(\text{root}(c)) = f$, and G is a subgroup of $\text{Sym}(m)$, where m is the number of holes in c. A stratified term T is a $(\Sigma \uplus \Sigma')$-term (O, s, a) such that $\forall v \in O$, if $s(v) \in \Sigma'$, let $\langle f, c, G \rangle = s(v)$, then $T.v$ is an instance of c', which is c with $s(\text{root}(c))$ replaced by $\langle f, c, G \rangle$.*
   We get the meaning of a stratified term by removing the labels c, G, or "unmarking" it. Let um be the projection from $\Sigma \uplus \Sigma'$ onto Σ defined by $\forall \langle f, c, G \rangle \in \Sigma', \text{um}(\langle f, c, G \rangle) = f$. It can trivially be extended to a projection from $(\Sigma \uplus \Sigma')$-terms to Σ-terms, also noted um.

Example 3. We consider the leaf permutative theory E axiomatised by the equation $\forall x, y, z, f(x, g(y, z)) = f(y, g(z, x))$. Using the context from Example 2, we can write it $c[x, y, z] = c[y, z, x]$. This means that the first hole moves to the third position, the second to the first, the third to the second. So we represent the equation by c and the permutation $\sigma = (1\ 3\ 2)$. The theory E is represented by the symbol $F = \langle f, c, G \rangle$, where G is the group generated[2] by σ. By replacing f by F in Figure 1, we obtain a stratified term T. Indeed, $T \setminus H$ is isomorphic to the context c', with $\text{string}(c') = F([], g([], []))$. We have $\text{um}(T) = t$.

The next section will show that rewriting with permutative equations will only be allowed in stratified terms at occurrences v such that $s(v) \in \Sigma'$. In Example 3, supposing g is commutative, we will not be allowed to swap the arguments of g in T. Hence a choice between overlapping equations may be necessary when building a stratified term, but never when rewriting it.

Definition 5. *Given a stratified term $T = (O, s, a)$, we first define a function $\text{H}_T : O \to O^*$. $\forall v \in O$, if $s(v) \in \Sigma$, then $\text{H}_T(v) = \varepsilon$. Otherwise, let $\langle f, c, G \rangle = s(v)$ and c' be the context obtained from c as in Definition 4. Let $H \subseteq O$ such that $T.v \setminus H \simeq c'$; if $v_1, \ldots, v_m$ are the elements of H, given in the order in which they appear in $\text{desc}(T)$, then $\text{H}_T(v) = v_1 \ldots v_m$.*

Next, we define a function $\Phi_T^v : \text{Sym}(m) \to \text{Sym}(O)$, where $m = |\text{H}_T(v)|$. Let $v_1 \ldots v_m = \text{H}_T(v)$ and $\sigma \in \text{Sym}(m)$, let $\pi \in \text{Sym}(O)$ be defined by $\forall i, (v_i)^\pi = v_{i^\sigma}$, and π is the identity on $O \setminus \text{H}_T(v)$; we let $\Phi_T^v(\sigma) = \pi$. The reader may check that Φ_T^v is a group isomorphism.

Finally, for any $v \in O$ we define a group $\text{G}_T(v)$, equal to I if $s(v) \in \Sigma$, and to $\Phi_T^v(G)$ if $s(v) = \langle f, c, G \rangle$.

Example 4. Following our example, we have $\text{H}_T(0) = 1.3.4$, so $v_1 = 1, v_2 = 3$ and $v_3 = 4$. Let $\pi = \Phi_T^0(\sigma)$, we have $1^\pi = v_{1^\sigma} = v_3 = 4, 3^\pi = v_{2^\sigma} = 1$ and $4^\pi = v_{3^\sigma} = 3$, so $\pi = (1\ 4\ 3)$.

Intuitively, $\text{H}_T(v)$ represents the pointers that the leaf permutative theory at v can modify, and each permutation in $\text{G}_T(v)$ corresponds to a way these pointers can be modified.

Definition 6. *For $T = (O, s, a)$, $v \in O$ and $\pi \in \text{G}_T(v)$, let $T^\pi = (O, s, a^\pi)$, where $\forall v \in O, a^\pi(v) = a(v)^\pi$, i.e. π is applied to each letter in $a(v)$.*

Example 5. We may apply $\pi = (1\ 4\ 3)$ to T, simply by replacing a by a^π. We have $a^\pi(0) = (1.2)^\pi = 4.2$ and $a^\pi(2) = (3.4)^\pi = 1.3$. See the result on Figure 2.

The reader may check that T^π is a term, since a^π still defines a tree-like structure; this is due to the fact that $\text{G}_T(v)$ only permutes occurrences from $\text{H}_T(v)$, which is an antichain in T (cf. Definition 3). It is obvious that $\forall \pi, \rho \in \text{G}_T(v)$, we have $T^{\pi\rho} = (T^\pi)^\rho$, and that $T^{\text{id}} = T$. Hence we have defined an action of $\text{G}_T(v)$ on stratified terms built on O and s, if however we are certain that

---
[2] An implementation would contain a concise representation of G, i.e. basically some set of generators.

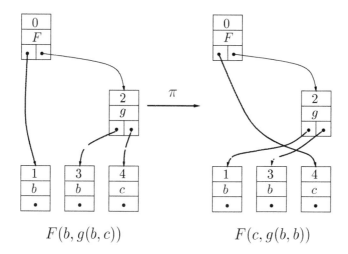

Fig. 2. The action of $\pi = (1\ 4\ 3)$ on T

T^π is indeed a stratified term. This is not obvious since a random permutation on occurrences may disrupt the contexts (try e.g. $\pi = (1\ 2)$ in Example 5; then $\text{string}(T^\pi) = F(g(b, c), b)$ which is not stratified). We first establish some results valid for any stratified term $T = (O, s, a)$.

Lemma 1. *If $u, v \in O, u \neq v, s(u) \in \Sigma'$ then $\mathrm{H}_T(v) \cap \mathrm{desc}(T.u \setminus \mathrm{H}_T(u)) \subseteq \{u\}$ and consequently $\mathrm{H}_T(u) \cap \mathrm{H}_T(v) = \emptyset$.*

Proof. The latter is a trivial consequence of the former, since $u \notin \mathrm{H}_T(u) \subseteq \mathrm{desc}(T.u \setminus \mathrm{H}_T(u))$. If $s(v) \in \Sigma$ then $\mathrm{H}_T(v)$ is empty, and the result is trivial, so suppose that $s(v) \in \Sigma'$, and let $\langle f, c, G \rangle = s(v)$. Either one of $T.u, T.v$ may be a subterm of the other, or $\{u, v\}$ is an antichain in T, i.e. $\mathrm{desc}(u) \cap \mathrm{desc}(v) = \emptyset$, but then the result is obvious (since $\mathrm{H}_T(v) \subseteq \mathrm{desc}(v)$, etc.)

If $T.u$ is a subterm of $T.v$, then it is a subterm of some $T.w$ with $w \in \mathrm{H}_T(v)$, since c is a Σ-context, i.e. v is the only occurrence in $\mathrm{desc}(T.v \setminus \mathrm{H}_T(v))$ such that $s(v) \in \Sigma'$. We therefore have $\mathrm{H}_T(v) \cap \mathrm{desc}(u) \subseteq \{u\}$, and the result follows.

If $T.v$ is a subterm of $T.u$, then it is a subterm of some $T.w$ with $w \in \mathrm{H}_T(u)$, as above. We therefore have $\mathrm{desc}(T.u \setminus \mathrm{H}_T(u)) \cap \mathrm{desc}(v) \subseteq \{v\}$, but $v \notin \mathrm{H}_T(v) \subseteq \mathrm{desc}(v)$, thus $\mathrm{H}_T(v) \cap \mathrm{desc}(T.u \setminus \mathrm{H}_T(u)) = \emptyset$. ∎

Lemma 2. *For all $u, v \in O$ and $\pi \in \mathrm{G}_T(v)$ we have*

(1) if $u \neq v$ and $s(u) \in \Sigma'$, then $T^\pi.u \setminus \mathrm{H}_T(u) = T.u \setminus \mathrm{H}_T(u)$,
(2) $\pi : T.v \setminus \mathrm{H}_T(v) \simeq T^\pi.v \setminus \mathrm{H}_T(v)$,
(3) $\mathrm{H}_{T^\pi}(u) = \mathrm{H}_T(u)^\pi$.

Proof. (1) π is a permutation of $\mathrm{H}_T(v)$, hence by Lemma 1, π is the identity on $\mathrm{desc}(T.u \setminus \mathrm{H}_T(u)) \setminus \{u\}$, and therefore (1) holds. Moreover, we have $\mathrm{H}_{T^\pi}(u) = \mathrm{H}_T(u) = \mathrm{H}_T(u)^\pi$.

(2) $\forall u \in \mathrm{desc}(T.v \setminus \mathrm{H}_T(v))$, either $u \in \mathrm{H}_T(v)$, and then $\pi(u) \in \mathrm{H}_T(v)$ and $s(u) = s(\pi(u)) = []$; or $u \notin \mathrm{H}_T(v)$, and then $\pi(u) = u$, hence $s(\pi(u)) = s(u)$ and $a^\pi(\pi(u)) = a^\pi(u) = \pi(a(u))$. This proves $\pi(T.v \setminus \mathrm{H}_T(v)) = T^\pi.v \setminus \mathrm{H}_T(v)$.

(3) Trivial when $s(u) \in \Sigma$, and proved in (1) when $s(u) \in \Sigma'$, $u \neq v$. For $u = v$, we have $\mathrm{desc}(\pi(T.v)) = \mathrm{desc}(T.v)^\pi$, so by (2) we get $\mathrm{desc}(T^\pi.v \setminus \mathrm{H}_T(v)) = \mathrm{desc}(T.v \setminus \mathrm{H}_T(v))^\pi$, hence $\mathrm{H}_{T^\pi}(v) = \mathrm{H}_T(v)^\pi$.

Theorem 1. $\forall v \in O, \forall \pi \in \mathrm{G}_T(v)$, T^π is stratified.

Proof. For $u \in O$ such that $s(u) \in \Sigma'$, by Lemma 2 we have

$$T^\pi.u \setminus \mathrm{H}_{T^\pi}(u) = T^\pi.u \setminus \mathrm{H}_T(u) \simeq T.u \setminus \mathrm{H}_T(u).$$

Another important consequence of Lemmata 1 and 2 is the invariance of the groups $\mathrm{G}_T(u)$ under the action of $\mathrm{G}_T(v)$.

Lemma 3. $\forall u, v \in O, \forall \pi \in \mathrm{G}_T(v), \mathrm{G}_{T^\pi}(u) = \mathrm{G}_T(u)$.

Proof. If $s(u) \in \Sigma$, then $\mathrm{G}_{T^\pi}(u) = \mathrm{I} = \mathrm{G}_T(u)$. If $s(u) \in \Sigma'$, let G be the group in $s(u)$, we have $\mathrm{G}_T(u) = \Phi_T^u(G)$, $\mathrm{G}_{T^\pi}(u) = \Phi_{T^\pi}^u(G)$ and $\mathrm{H}_{T^\pi}(u) = \mathrm{H}_T(u)^\pi$.

If $u \neq v$, then π is the identity on $\mathrm{H}_T(u)$, so that $\Phi_{T^\pi}^u = \Phi_T^u$, hence $\mathrm{G}_{T^\pi}(u) = \mathrm{G}_T(u)$. If $u = v$, let $v_1 \ldots v_m = \mathrm{H}_T(v)$, and for all $\sigma \in G$, let $\rho = \Phi_{T^\pi}^v(\sigma)$, by definition we have $\pi(v_i)^\rho = \pi(v_{i^\sigma})$, thus $v_i^{\pi \rho \pi^{-1}} = v_{i^\sigma}$, which proves that $\pi \rho \pi^{-1} = \Phi_T^v(\sigma)$, i.e. $\Phi_{T^\pi}^v(\sigma) = \pi^{-1} \Phi_T^v(\sigma) \pi$. Hence $\mathrm{G}_{T^\pi}(v) = \pi^{-1} \mathrm{G}_T(v) \pi = \mathrm{G}_T(v)$ since $\pi \in \mathrm{G}_T(v)$.

4   Stratified Rewriting

So, we have an action of $\mathrm{G}_T(v)$ on stratified terms built on O and s, which now we use to define the rewriting of T at an occurrence v, through the theory specified in $s(v)$.

Definition 7. *We say that T rewrites at v into T', noted $T \to^{v,*} T'$, iff $\exists \pi \in \mathrm{G}_T(v), T' = T^\pi$. We write $\to$ for $\bigcup_{v \in O} \to^{v,*}$, and $\to^*$ its reflexive and transitive closure[3]. Since the relation $\to^{v,*}$ is symmetric, so are $\to$ and $\to^*$.*

The stratified set of T, noted $[T]_s$, is the equivalence class of T modulo $\to^*$. We also define $\mathrm{S}[T] = \mathrm{string}(\mathrm{um}([T]_s))$.

Our aim is now to build a group that will yield stratified sets as orbits. We will be able to construct such a group from the $\mathrm{G}_T(v)$'s, thanks to this

Lemma 4. $\forall u, v \in O, \mathrm{G}_T(u)\mathrm{G}_T(v) = \mathrm{G}_T(v)\mathrm{G}_T(u)$.

Proof. If $u = v$ this is obvious, so suppose that $u \neq v$, then $\mathrm{H}_T(u) \cap \mathrm{H}_T(v) = \emptyset$, so that $\forall \pi \in \mathrm{G}_T(u), \forall \pi' \in \mathrm{G}_T(v)$, π and π' have disjoint cycles, hence $\pi \pi' = \pi' \pi$.

---

[3] The relation $\to^{v,*}$ corresponds to the relation $\to_i^{s,*}$ of [1], but is defined on occurrence terms rather than terms-as-strings.

This allows the definition of the following product.

Definition 8. *Let* $G(T) = \prod_{v \in O} G_T(v)$. *By supposing that occurrences are linearly ordered, say* $O = \{v_1, \ldots, v_n\}$, *then for* $\pi = \prod_{i=1}^{n} \pi_i \in G(T)$, *where* $\pi_i \in G_T(v_i)$, *we define* $T^\pi = (\cdots (T^{\pi_1})^{\pi_2} \cdots)^{\pi_n}$.

The definition of T^π is correct: Lemma 3 yields $\pi_2 \in G_T(v_2) = G_{T^{\pi_1}}(v_2)$, etc. In fact, Lemma 3 shows that $\forall v \in O, \forall \pi \in G_T(v)$, we have $G(T^\pi) = G(T)$. But then, a trivial induction proves that $\forall \pi \in G(T), G(T^\pi) = G(T)$.

Example 6. In our example, $G(T)$ is the group generated by π, thus containing the three elements $\pi, \pi^2 = (1\ 3\ 4)$ and $\pi^3 = $ id. Hence $S[T] = \{f(b, g(b, c)), f(c, g(b, b)), f(b, g(c, b))\}$.

It is obvious from Theorem 1 that $\forall \pi \in G(T), T^\pi$ is a stratified term. We now prove that this defines an action of $G(T)$ on the set of stratified terms built on O and s.

Theorem 2. *We have* $T^{\mathrm{id}} = T$ *and* $\forall \pi, \pi' \in G(T), (T^\pi)^{\pi'} = T^{(\pi\pi')}$.

Proof. $T^{\mathrm{id}} = T$ is obvious. Let $\{v_1, \ldots, v_n\} = O$, and $\pi, \pi' \in G(T)$, with $\pi = \prod_{i=1}^{n} \pi_i, \pi' = \prod_{i=1}^{n} \pi_i'$ where $\forall i, \pi_i, \pi_i' \in G_T(v_i)$. As in the proof of Lemma 4, if $i \neq j$ then $\pi_i \pi_j' = \pi_j' \pi_i$. Hence $\pi\pi' = \prod_{i=1}^{n} \pi_i \pi_i'$, and by definition $T^{(\pi\pi')} = (\cdots T^{(\pi_1\pi_1')} \cdots)^{(\pi_n\pi_n')}$. But it is easy to see that, if $i \neq j$, $(T^{\pi_i})^{\pi_j'} = (T^{\pi_j'})^{\pi_i}$ (since $\forall u \in O, (a^{\pi_i})^{\pi_j'}(u) = a^{(\pi_i\pi_j')}(u)$), i.e. the actions of $G_T(v_i)$ and $G_T(v_j)$ commute. Successive applications of this commutation yields $(T^\pi)^{\pi'} = ((\cdots (T^{\pi_1})^{\pi_1'} \cdots)^{\pi_n})^{\pi_n'} = (\cdots T^{(\pi_1\pi_1')} \cdots)^{(\pi_n\pi_n')} = T^{(\pi\pi')}$.

This proves that rewritings at different occurrences are essentially independent, even if one occurrence appears in a subterm of the other one. We are now going to use the $G(T)$-orbit of T, but we must first note that it is not quite standard to consider the orbit of an element w.r.t. a group that *depends* on this element. This does not allow us, for instance, to speak of the *orbit partition* of the set of stratified terms, since many different groups are involved. But wherever the group $G(T)$ is invariant, we do have an action. More precisely, we have defined a one-orbit action on any stratified set.

Theorem 3. $[T]_s = T^{G(T)}$.

Proof. We first show by induction that $\forall i \in \mathbb{N}$, if $T \to^i T'$ then $\exists \pi \in G(T)$ such that $T' = T^\pi$. This is trivial for $i = 0$, with $\pi = $ id. If true for i, and $T \to^{i+1} T'$, then by induction hypothesis $\exists \pi \in G(T), \exists v \in O$ such that $T \to^i T^\pi \to^{v,\star} T'$, and by definition $\exists \rho \in G_{T^\pi}(v) = G_T(v)$ (by Lemma 3) such that $T' = (T^\pi)^\rho = T^{\pi\rho}$ (by Theorem 2). We have $\pi\rho \in G(T)$, which completes the induction, and proves $[T]_s \subseteq T^{G(T)}$.

Conversely, $\forall \pi \in G(T)$, let $\{v_1, \ldots, v_n\} = O$, then $\forall i, \exists \pi_i \in G_T(v_i)$ such that $\pi = \pi_1 \cdots \pi_n$. Let $T_1 = T$ and $T_{i+1} = T_i^{\pi_i}$ for $i = 1 \ldots n$, suppose $T \to^\star T_i$ (which is true for $i = 1$), since $\pi_i \in G_T(v_i) = G_{T_i}(v_i)$ by Lemma 3, then $T_i \to^{v_i,\star} T_i^{\pi_i}$, thus $T_i \to T_{i+1}$, and therefore $T \to^\star T_{i+1}$. This proves by induction that $T \to^\star T_{n+1} = T^\pi$, yielding $T^\pi \in [T]_s$.

5 Deductive Problems

Lifting resolution and paramodulation to stratified clauses is not a trivial task, and requires complex algorithms as provided in [1]. One obvious requirement is unification of stratified terms, but less noble tasks are also required for paramodulation or subsumption, and appear quite complex on their own. Even membership in $S[T]$ is performed in [1] by an exponential time algorithm.

The following decision problems are expressed directly on stratified terms, which may be specified by strings. Since the transformation from strings to occurrences (and back) is linear in time and space, we may omit the distinction between t and $string(t)$. Unification is defined by considering some constant symbols (those in $\mathcal{V}$) as variables.

n°	problem	instance	question
1	STRATIFIED_MEMBERSHIP	t, T	$t \in S[T]$
2	STRATIFIED_SUBTERM	t, T	$\exists t' \in S[T]/t$ is a subterm of t'
3	STRATIFIED_INTERSECTION	T_1, T_2	$S[T_1] \cap S[T_2] \neq \emptyset$
4	STRATIFIED_UNIFIABLE	$T_1, T_2, \mathcal{V}$	$\exists t_1 \in S[T_1], \exists t_2 \in S[T_2]/$ t_1 and t_2 are unifiable
5	STRATIFIED_INCLUSION	T_1, T_2	$S[T_1] \subseteq S[T_2]$

There are a number of trivial relationships among these problems. The relation of reduction by polynomial transformation is noted $\propto$, see [6].

Lemma 5.

(ı) STRATIFIED_MEMBERSHIP $\propto$ STRATIFIED_INCLUSION *and* STRATIFIED_MEMBERSHIP $\propto$ STRATIFIED_INTERSECTION,

(ıı) STRATIFIED_MEMBERSHIP $\propto$ STRATIFIED_SUBTERM,

(ııı) STRATIFIED_INTERSECTION $\propto$ STRATIFIED_UNIFIABLE.

Proof. (ı) By considering t as a stratified term, we have $S[t] = \{t\}$, so that $t \in S[T] \Leftrightarrow S[t] \subseteq S[T] \Leftrightarrow S[t] \cap S[T] \neq \emptyset$.

(ıı) If t and T have the same number of occurrences, let $t' = t$, else let t' be some new constant symbol. The transformation from t, T to t', T is polynomial, and we have $t \in S[T]$ iff t' is a subterm of a member of $S[T]$.

(ııı) We consistently replace all variables in T_1, T_2 by new constant symbols, yielding T_1', T_2' which are unifiable iff $S[T_1]$ and $S[T_2]$ have a common element.

We will now prove that the first four problems are in **NP**. We therefore need to find polynomial witnesses for these problems. For this we consider the GROUP_MEMBERSHIP problem, defined on sequences $\sigma, \sigma_1, \ldots, \sigma_m$ of permutations of $\{1, \ldots, n\}$, that asks whether σ is a member of the group generated by $\sigma_1, \ldots, \sigma_m$. Now is the time to reap the benefits of the first half of the paper (on oracle Turing machines and non-deterministic polynomial Turing reduction, see [6]).

Lemma 6. *The problems 1 to 4 are all in* **NP**$^{\text{GROUP\_MEMBERSHIP}}$.

Proof. We prove it for STRATIFIED_MEMBERSHIP, and the reader can see that the same result follows for the three other problems (since testing unifiability of standard terms is polynomial, etc.). By Theorem 3 we know that $S[T] = \text{string}(\text{um}(T^{G(T)}))$, so that $t \in S[T]$ iff $\exists \pi \in G(T)$ such that $t = \text{string}(\text{um}(T^\pi))$. So given t and T, we first represent T on the set of occurrences $O = \{1, \ldots, n\}$, and we only have to guess a $\pi \in \text{Sym}(O)$ and first check that $t = \text{string}(\text{um}(T^\pi))$, which is trivially polynomial.

If this first test succeeds we proceed as follows. The symbols of Σ' appearing in T contain generators of permutations groups, so by computing their image by the morphism Φ^v_T we get generators for $G_v(T)$ for all $v \in O$. Therefore the set $\{\pi_1, \ldots, \pi_m\}$ of all these permutations is a generator set for $G(T) = \prod_{v \in O} G_T(v)$, and can be computed in time polynomial in the size of T. We can call the oracle GROUP_MEMBERSHIP on $\pi, \pi_1, \ldots, \pi_m$, and accept if the test succeeds. This yields the required non-deterministic polynomial Turing reduction from STRATIFIED_MEMBERSHIP to GROUP_MEMBERSHIP.

Of course, the whole point is that GROUP_MEMBERSHIP is polynomial, which is a well-known result from computational group theory (see [5]). We have therefore proved that problems 1 to 4 are in $\mathbf{NP^P} = \mathbf{NP}$.

6   Group Constraints and Stratified Terms

We now consider the GROUP_CONSTRAINT problem, defined on a list of generators of a group $G < \text{Sym}(n)$ and a list of non-empty subsets $J_1, \ldots, J_n$ of $\{1, \ldots, n\}$, that asks whether there exists a permutation $\sigma \in G$ such that $\forall i \in \{1, \ldots, n\}, i^\sigma \in J_i$. This is clearly a generalisation of GROUP_MEMBERSHIP, which can be seen as the particular case where the J_i's are singletons, and mutually disjoint (i.e. they specify a unique permutation).

We now prove that such group constraints can be solved as a membership problem on quite simple stratified terms.

Theorem 4. GROUP_CONSTRAINT $\propto$ STRATIFIED_MEMBERSHIP.

Proof. We are given a group G by its generators, and subsets $J_1, \ldots, J_n$ of $\{1, \ldots, n\}$. We build a membership problem on stratified terms on the signature $\Sigma = \{f, g, 0, 1\}$ where $0, 1$ are constants and f, g have arity n. We will also use the Σ-contexts $c_f = f([], \ldots, [])$ and $c_g = g([], \ldots, [])$, and the groups $G_j = \text{Sym}(I_j)$, where $I_j = \{i / j \in J_i\}$.

Let $t_i = g(0, \ldots, 0, 1, 0, \ldots, 0)$, where the 1 occurs as the ith argument of g. Similarly, let $T_j = \langle g, c_g, G_j \rangle(0, \ldots, 0, 1, 0, \ldots, 0)$, where the 1 occurs as the $(\min I_j)^{th}$ argument of $\langle g, c_g, G_j \rangle$. We have:

$$t_i \in S[T_j] \Leftrightarrow \exists \pi \in G(T_j), \text{um}(T_j^\pi) = t_i$$
$$\Leftrightarrow \exists \sigma \in G_j, (\min I_j)^\sigma = i$$
$$\Leftrightarrow i \in I_j$$
$$\Leftrightarrow j \in J_i .$$

We therefore build the terms $t = f(t_1, \ldots, t_n)$ and $T = \langle f, c_f, G \rangle (T_1, \ldots, T_n)$. Let O be the set of occurrences of T, with $r = \mathrm{root}(T)$ and o_j the occurrence corresponding to T_j; we have $\mathrm{G}(T) = \mathrm{G}_T(r) \mathrm{G}_T(o_1) \cdots \mathrm{G}_T(o_n)$. Moreover, we have $\mathrm{G}_T(r) = \Phi_T^r(G)$ and $\mathrm{G}_T(o_j) = \mathrm{G}(T_j)$, and therefore

$$
\begin{aligned}
t \in \mathrm{S}[T] &\Leftrightarrow \exists \pi \in \mathrm{G}(T), \mathrm{um}(T^\pi) = t \\
&\Leftrightarrow \exists \sigma \in G, \forall i, \exists \pi_i \in \mathrm{G}(T_{i^\sigma}), \mathrm{um}(\langle f, c_f, G \rangle ((T_{1^\sigma})^{\pi_1}, \ldots, (T_{n^\sigma})^{\pi_n})) = t \\
&\Leftrightarrow \exists \sigma \in G, \forall i, \exists \pi_i \in \mathrm{G}(T_{i^\sigma}), \mathrm{um}((T_{i^\sigma})^{\pi_i}) = t_i \\
&\Leftrightarrow \exists \sigma \in G, \forall i, t_i \in \mathrm{S}[T_{i^\sigma}] \\
&\Leftrightarrow \exists \sigma \in G, \forall i, i^\sigma \in J_i \; .
\end{aligned}
$$

This transformation from GROUP_CONSTRAINT to STRATIFIED_MEMBERSHIP is clearly polynomial: T contains the given generators of G, and no more than two generators[4] for each G_j.

7 Solving Group Constraints Is NP-Hard

Not all problems on groups can be solved in polynomial time like GROUP_MEMBERSHIP. Computational group theory also provides efficient though non-polynomial algorithms for many difficult problems on groups, which are known to be *isomorphism-complete* (i.e. polynomially equivalent to the problem of detecting an isomorphism between two graphs, see [7]), and therefore not **NP**-complete (unless the polynomial hierarchy collapses to $\Sigma_2^{\mathbf{P}}$, see chapters 16 to 18 in [10]). Hence the announced result may seem surprising. However, **NP**-completeness results have already been obtained by slight generalisations of isomorphism-complete problems, see [8]. Our proof similarly proceeds by a reduction from 3-SAT.

We are given a finite set S of 3-clauses. We denote by $\mathcal{A}$ the set of atoms appearing in S, and $\mathcal{L}$ the set of literals built on $\mathcal{A}$. We will use the usual notion of complementation: $\forall x \in \mathcal{A}, \bar{x} = \neg x$ and $\overline{\neg x} = x$. We suppose there is a linear order $<$ on $\mathcal{L}$. An interpretation is represented as a subset I of $\mathcal{A}$, meaning that the members of I are true and the members of $\mathcal{A} \setminus I$ are false. Hence $I \models C$ iff $\exists x \in C$ such that $x \in I$ or $\bar{x} \in \mathcal{A} \setminus I$.

The intuitive idea behind this proof is that there are 8 ways to evaluate all three variables of a clause, 7 of which render the clause satisfiable. We will construct a group G such that every permutation in it corresponds to an instanciation, and, for a clause C, put the 7 instanciations that satisfy C in the set J_C. Then the set S of clauses will be satisfiable if and only if there is a solution to GROUP_CONSTRAINT over G and the J_C's.

Definition 9. *To a 3-clause C we associate its* cube $C^\Pi = \{\langle C, i, j, k \rangle | i, j, k \in \{0, 1\}\}$. *To a finite set S of 3-clauses we associate the set $S^\Pi = \bigcup_{C \in S} C^\Pi$. Each member of C^Π can be interpreted as a 3-clause in the following way:*

---

[4] $\mathrm{Sym}(n)$ is generated by $(1\ 2)$ and $(2 \cdots n)$.

$J\langle\{x_1, x_2, x_3\}, a_1, a_2, a_3\rangle K = \{x_i/a_i = 0\} \cup \{\overline{x_i}/a_i = 1\}$, where $x_1 < x_2 < x_3$. The negative corner of C^Π (or: of C) is the $c \in C^\Pi$ such that JcK contains only negated atoms, and we let $P_C = C^\Pi \setminus \{c\}$.

Example 7. If we consider the clause $C = \{\neg x, y, z\}$ where $\neg x < y < z$, then its negative corner is $\langle C, 0, 1, 1\rangle$, since $J\langle C, 0, 1, 1\rangle K = \{\neg x, \neg y, \neg z\}$.

We now show how an interpretation selects a corner in each cube.

Definition 10. *Let $I \subseteq A$ and $C = \{x_1, x_2, x_3\} \in S$, where $x_1 < x_2 < x_3$, then $\iota(C, I) = \langle C, a_1, a_2, a_3\rangle$, where $a_i = 0$ if $x_i \in I$ or $\overline{x_i} \in I$, and $a_i = 1$ otherwise.*

Example 8. In the clause of Example 7, if we take $I = \{x\}$, then $\iota(C, I) = \langle C, 0, 1, 1\rangle$, which is the negative corner of C. Note that C is false in I, and this is why we have obtained the negative corner with $\iota(C, I)$.

P_C will contain the 7 assignments that render C satisfiable, as proven in the following lemma:

Lemma 7. $\forall I \subseteq A, I \models C$ *iff* $\iota(C, I) \in P_C$.

Proof. Let $C = \{x_1, x_2, x_3\}$ with $x_1 < x_2 < x_3$, and let a_1, a_2, a_3 such that $\iota(C, I) = \langle C, a_1, a_2, a_3\rangle$. We have

$$\langle C, a_1, a_2, a_3\rangle \in P_C \Leftrightarrow \exists i, (x_i \in A \wedge a_i = 0) \vee (\overline{x_i} \in A \wedge a_i = 1)$$
$$\Leftrightarrow \exists i, (x_i \in A \wedge x_i \in I) \vee (\overline{x_i} \in A \wedge \overline{x_i} \notin I)$$
$$\Leftrightarrow I \models C.$$

We are now going to establish a correspondence between interpretations and the elements of a group of permutations on S^Π. In order to define this group we first describe its generators.

Definition 11. *For any $x \in A, C \in S$ and $a, b \in \{0, 1\}$, we define the transposition $\tau_x^C(a, b) \in \mathrm{Sym}(S^\Pi)$ as follows: suppose $C = \{x_1, x_2, x_3\}$ with $x_1 < x_2 < x_3$. If there is an i such that $x_i = x$ or $x_i = \neg x$; then let $j < k$ such that $\{i, j, k\} = \{1, 2, 3\}$, and let*

$$\tau_x^C(a, b) = (\langle C, a_1, a_2, a_3\rangle \; \langle C, b_1, b_2, b_3\rangle) \; where \begin{cases} a_i = 0, b_i = 1, \\ a_j = b_j = a, \\ a_k = b_k = b. \end{cases}$$

Otherwise we let $\tau_x^C(a, b) = \mathrm{id}$. Moreover, we let

$$\sigma_x^C = \tau_x^C(0, 0)\tau_x^C(0, 1)\tau_x^C(1, 0)\tau_x^C(1, 1) \; and \; \sigma_x = \prod_{C \in S} \sigma_x^C.$$

Note that for $C \neq C'$, we have $\sigma_x^C \sigma_x^{C'} = \sigma_x^{C'} \sigma_x^C$, since their cycles are disjoint, hence σ_x is well defined. Finally, let $\mathcal{G}_S$ be the group generated by $\{\sigma_x/x \in A\}$.

Example 9. Following Example 7, where y occurs as the second literal in C, then

$$
\begin{aligned}
\sigma_y^C &= \tau_y^C(0,0)\tau_y^C(0,1)\tau_y^C(1,0)\tau_y^C(1,1) \\
&= (\langle C,0,0,0\rangle\ \langle C,0,1,0\rangle)(\langle C,0,0,1\rangle\ \langle C,0,1,1\rangle) \\
&\quad (\langle C,1,0,0\rangle\ \langle C,1,1,0\rangle)(\langle C,1,0,1\rangle\ \langle C,1,1,1\rangle)\ .
\end{aligned}
$$

So obviously, if x occurs in C, then σ_x^C is a permutation of C^Π without fix-point. Geometrically speaking, σ_x^C swaps the corners of C^Π along the dimension specified by x, i.e. it moves corners along the x axis.

Lemma 8. $\forall x, y \in \mathcal{A}, \sigma_x^2 = \mathrm{id}$ *and* $\sigma_x \sigma_y = \sigma_y \sigma_x$.

Proof. It is obvious that $\forall C \in S, (\sigma_x^C)^2 = \mathrm{id}$ and since the σ_x^C's have disjoint cycles, we also have $\sigma_x^2 = \mathrm{id}$. We now prove that $\forall c \in S^\Pi, c^{\sigma_x \sigma_y} = c^{\sigma_y \sigma_x}$, for $x \neq y$. Let $\langle C, a_1, a_2, a_3\rangle = c$, we clearly have $c^{\sigma_x \sigma_y} = c^{\sigma_x^C \sigma_y^C}$, so we need only prove $c^{\sigma_x^C \sigma_y^C} = c^{\sigma_y^C \sigma_x^C}$. If either x or y does not occur in C, then either $\sigma_x^C = \mathrm{id}$ or $\sigma_y^C = \mathrm{id}$, and the equality is obvious. Suppose now that x and y both occur in C, then $c^{\sigma_x^C \sigma_y^C}$ is the corner obtained from c by moving first along the x axis, then along the y axis. We obviously reach the same corner if we start along the y axis, and then along the x axis.

A consequence of this lemma is that the order in which the generators are composed is irrelevant. Another important property is that, if a dimension is used only once, the move is consequently one-way.

Lemma 9. *If* $X \subseteq \mathcal{A}, X \neq \emptyset$, *then* $\sigma = \prod_{x \in X} \sigma_x \neq \mathrm{id}$.

Proof. There is a $x \in X$, and a clause $C \in S$ in which x occurs. Let y, z be the other two atoms occurring in C, and $c \in C^\Pi$. We have $c^\sigma = c^{\sigma_x^C} \sigma'$ where $\sigma' = \prod_{u \in \{y,z\} \cap X} \sigma_u^C$. The permutation σ_x^C moves c along the x axis (i.e. swaps the plane $x = 0$ with the plane $x = 1$), while σ' does not (i.e. it stabilizes both planes $x = 0$ and $x = 1$), and therefore of c and c^σ one is in the plane $x = 0$, the other in the plane $x = 1$, hence $c^\sigma \neq c$.

We can now establish the correspondence between $\mathcal{G}_S$ and $2^{\mathcal{A}}$.

Theorem 5. $\forall \sigma \in \mathcal{G}_S, \exists! X \subseteq \mathcal{A}, \sigma = \prod_{x \in X} \sigma_x$.

Proof. Every element of $\mathcal{G}_S$ is a product of generators, so $\forall \sigma \in \mathcal{G}_S$, there is a finite sequence $x_1, \ldots, x_n$ of elements of $\mathcal{A}$ such that $\sigma = \sigma_{x_1} \cdots \sigma_{x_n}$. For any $x \in \mathcal{A}$, let $I_x = \{i \in \{1, \ldots, n\}/x_i = x\}$, $J_x = \{1, \ldots, n\} \setminus I_x$ and $n_x = |I_x|$. By Lemma 8 we have $\sigma = \prod_{i \in I_x} \sigma_{x_i} \prod_{j \in J_x} \sigma_{x_j}$. But clearly we have $\prod_{i \in I_x} \sigma_{x_i} = (\sigma_x)^{n_x}$, and by iterating the process we get $\sigma = \prod_{x \in \mathcal{A}} (\sigma_x)^{n_x}$. But $\sigma_x^2 = \mathrm{id}$, so that $(\sigma_x)^{n_x} = \sigma_x$ if n_x is odd, and $(\sigma_x)^{n_x} = \mathrm{id}$ if n_x is even. Let $X = \{x \in \mathcal{A}/n_x$ is odd$\}$, we have $\sigma = \prod_{x \in X} \sigma_x$.

Suppose now that $\prod_{x \in Y} \sigma_x = \prod_{x \in X} \sigma_x$, then we have

$$
\left(\prod_{x \in X} \sigma_x\right)^2 = \mathrm{id} = \prod_{x \in X} \sigma_x \prod_{x \in Y} \sigma_x = \prod_{x \in (X \setminus Y) \cup (Y \setminus X)} \sigma_x\ .
$$

By Lemma 9 this implies that $(X \setminus Y) \cup (Y \setminus X) = \emptyset$, i.e. that $X = Y$.

Definition 12. *To any $I \subseteq A$ we associate $\Psi(I) = \prod_{x \in A \setminus I} \sigma_x \in \mathcal{G}_S$.*

Theorem 5 clearly shows that Ψ is bijective. The choice of the complementation in the definition of Ψ comes from the following correspondence between the action of $\Psi(I)$ and the selection operated by I.

Lemma 10. $\forall C \in S, \forall I \subseteq A, \langle C, 0, 0, 0 \rangle^{\Psi(I)} = \iota(C, I)$.

Proof. Let $C = \{x_1, x_2, x_3\}$ with $x_1 < x_2 < x_3$, and $c = \langle C, 0, 0, 0 \rangle$. Let y_i be the atom in x_i, as in the proof of Lemma 9 we have $c^{\Psi(I)} = c^\sigma$ where $\sigma = \prod_{u \in \{y_1, y_2, y_3\} \cap (A \setminus I)} \sigma_u^C$. Since $\{y_1, y_2, y_3\} \cap (A \setminus I) = \{y_1, y_2, y_3\} \setminus I$, if we let $\langle C, a_1, a_2, a_3 \rangle = c^\sigma$, we have $a_i = 1$ iff $y_i \notin I$ iff $x_i \notin I \wedge \overline{x_i} \notin I$, hence by Definition 10 we get $c^\sigma = \iota(C, I)$.

Hence we can characterize the elements of the group $\mathcal{G}_S$ that correspond to models of S.

Theorem 6. $S \in 3\text{-SAT}$ *iff* $\exists \sigma \in \mathcal{G}_S$ *such that* $\forall C \in S, \langle C, 0, 0, 0 \rangle^\sigma \in P_C$.

Proof.

$$
\begin{aligned}
S \in 3\text{-SAT} \quad &\text{iff} \quad \exists I \subseteq A, \forall C \in S, I \models C \\
&\text{iff} \quad \exists I \subseteq A, \forall C \in S, \iota(C, I) \in P_C &&\text{(Lemma 7)} \\
&\text{iff} \quad \exists I \subseteq A, \forall C \in S, \langle C, 0, 0, 0 \rangle^{\Psi(I)} \in P_C &&\text{(Lemma 10)} \\
&\text{iff} \quad \exists \sigma \in \mathcal{G}_S, \forall C \in S, \langle C, 0, 0, 0 \rangle^\sigma \in P_C &&\text{(Theorem 5)}
\end{aligned}
$$

Corollary 1. $3\text{-SAT} \propto \text{GROUP\_CONSTRAINT}$

Proof. Let $n = |A|$ and $m = |S|$. $\mathcal{G}_S$ is a permutation group on S^Π, which has cardinality $8m$, and each element of S^Π has a fixed size; hence S^Π can be represented by the integers form 1 to $8m$, say by a function g. The group is represented by the n generators σ_x for $x \in A$, and each generator can be represented by the sequence $g(g^{-1}(1)^{\sigma_x}), \ldots, g(g^{-1}(8m)^{\sigma_x})$. For each $C \in S$, the set linked to $g(\langle C, 0, 0, 0 \rangle)$ is $g(P_C)$ (of fixed cardinality 7), while the set linked to $g(\langle C, a_1, a_2, a_3 \rangle)$, where some $a_i = 1$, is $g(C^\Pi)$ (i.e. it is unconstrained).

This transformation is clearly polynomial, and reduces 3-SAT to GROUP_CONSTRAINT by Theorem 6.

8   Conclusion

We have therefore established the **NP**-completeness of problems 1 to 4^5, and of GROUP_CONSTRAINT, and the **NP**-hardness of STRATIFIED_INCLUSION (by Lemma 5). It is actually easy to bound the complexity of this last problem in the polynomial hierarchy (see [6], or [10]).

Theorem 7. STRATIFIED_INCLUSION $\in \Pi_2^P$.

---

[5] An anonymous referee mentions that **NP**-hardness of problem 4 also results from the **NP**-hardness of commutative unifiability, see [6, problem AN16].

Proof. We have $S[T_1] \not\subseteq S[T_2]$ iff there is a t such that $t \in S[T_1]$ and $t \notin S[T_2]$, so we can solve this problem by guessing t and call an oracle for STRATIFIED_MEMBERSHIP first on t, T_1, then on t, T_2; we accept if the first test succeeds and the second fails. This provides a non-deterministic polynomial Turing reduction to a problem in **NP**, hence **co**−STRATIFIED_INCLUSION $\in$ $\mathbf{NP^{NP}} = \Sigma_2^P$, and therefore STRATIFIED_INCLUSION $\in$ **co**−$\Sigma_2^P = \Pi_2^P$.

These results explain why the algorithms given in [1] have exponential time complexity. They do not mean that deduction on stratified terms is less efficient than deduction on terms: the exponential behaviour is due to the complexity of solving group constraints, but remember that each element of $G(T)$ corresponds to a term that would be deduced if leaf permutative equations were to be used bluntly. Trading space complexity for time complexity is certainly advantageous, especially in a theorem prover.

We should also note that in the proof of Theorem 4, we have used a function symbol g with many different groups (the $\mathrm{Sym}(I_j)$'s), but with the same context. From a logical point of view, this does not make sense: it would mean that the equations generating a $\mathrm{Sym}(I_j)$ are valid in a subterm but not in another. Hence problems 1,2,3 and 5 could be restricted to a more meaningful notion of stratified terms, and thence see their complexity reduced.

References

1. Avenhaus and Plaisted. General algorithms for permutations in equational inference. *JAR: Journal of Automated Reasoning*, 26, 2001.
2. Thierry Boy de la Tour. A note on symmetry heuristics in SEM. In Andrei Voronkov, editor, *Proceedings of CADE-18*, LNAI 2392. Springer Verlag, 2002.
3. Thierry Boy de la Tour and Mnacho Echenim. On leaf permutative theories and occurrence permutation groups. In Ingo Dahn and Laurent Vigneron, editors, *4th International Workshop on First-Order Theorem Proving FTP'2003*, Electronic Notes in Theoretical Computer Science, 2003.
4. G. Butler. *Fundamental algorithms for permutation groups*. Lecture Notes in Computer Science 559. Springer Verlag, 1991.
5. M. Furst, J. Hopcroft, and E. Luks. Polynomial time algorithms for permutation groups. In *Proceedings 21st Annual Symposium on the Foundations of Computer Science*, pages 36–41, October 1980.
6. M. Garey and D. S. Johnson. *Computers and intractability: a guide to the theory of* **NP***-completeness*. Freeman, San Francisco, California, 1979.
7. C. Hoffmann. *Group-theoretic algorithms and graph isomorphism*. Lecture Notes in Computer Science 136. Springer Verlag, 1981.
8. Anna Lubiw. Some **NP**-complete problems similar to graph isomorphism. *SIAM Journal on Computing*, 10(1):11–21, 1981.
9. D. Plaisted. Equational reasoning and term rewriting systems. *Handbook of Logic in Artificial Intelligence and Logic Programming*, 1:273–364, 1993.
10. Uwe Schöning and Randall Pruim. *Gems of Theoretical Computer Science*. Springer-Verlag, 1998.

Is Cantor's Theorem Automatic?

Dietrich Kuske

Institut für Algebra, Technische Universität Dresden, D-01062 Dresden, Germany,
kuske@math.tu-dresden.de

Abstract. A regular language L together with a binary relation $\leq_L$ on L is an automatic presentation of the rationals iff $(L, \leq_L)$ is isomorphic to $(\mathbb{Q}, \leq)$ and $\leq_L$ can be accepted by a synchronous two-tape automaton. An automorphism of $(L, \leq_L)$ is automatic iff it can be computed by a synchronous two-tape automaton. We show (1) that the canonical presentation from [5] is automatic-homogeneous (any tuple can be mapped to any other tuple by an automatic automorphism), (2) that there are presentations which are not automatic-homogeneous, and (3) that there are automatic linear orders that are not isomorphic to any regular subset of the canonical presentation. This last result disproves a conjecture from [5].

Classically, model theory as a branch of mathematical logic investigates structural properties of algebraic structures. A typical[1] result is Cantor's theorem: Any countable linear order $(L, \leq)$ is isomorphic to a set X of rational numbers ("the rational numbers are universal"). In effective model theory [7], interest shifts to the computational content of classical model theory. In the example of Cantor's theorem, one is only interested in linear orders $(L, \leq)$ that are recursive (i.e., the set L is a recursive set of natural numbers and the relation $\leq \subseteq \mathbb{N} \times \mathbb{N}$ is decidable). Then, one asks whether X can be chosen to be decidable under a suitable encoding of the rationals.[2] If, in the example above, we restrict L, $\leq$ and X further to, say, sets decidable in a certain complexity class C, we arrive at complexity theoretic model theory. Here, Cantor's theorem holds only under severe restrictions on the encoding of $(L, \leq)$ in the natural numbers and for certain complexity classes C (see [4] for a survey on this and many other results). Khoussainov and Nerode [11] initiated the investigation of automatic structures; in the light of the explanation above, this means that the complexity class C is the set of regular languages. Since these automatic structures are intimately linked with finite automata, the rich theory of finite automata is at the core of understanding this field. For instance, complementation and projection of finite automata allows to show that the first-order theory of any automatic structure is decidable [8]. This implies, e.g., the decidability of Pressburger's arithmetic [2] (using the same ideas, this decidability was also

---

[1] Untypical, as far as difficulty of proof is concerned.
[2] A thorough analysis of Cantor's proof reveals that all the steps can be performed effectively; hence the effective version of Cantor's Theorem holds.

M.Y. Vardi and A. Voronkov (Eds.): LPAR 2003, LNAI 2850, pp. 332–345, 2003.
© Springer-Verlag Berlin Heidelberg 2003

shown by Elgot [6]) or of the first-order theory of the configuration graph with transitive closure of a pushdown automaton. One line of research attempts to identify all automatic structures [1, 5, 10, 12, 14] and investigates definability questions [13]. Khoussainov, Rubin and Stephan and, independently, Delhommé (personal communication) showed that many universal homogeneous structures are not automatic. Coming back to Cantor's theorem, Delhommé, Goranko and Knapik prove that a large class of automatic linear orders are order isomorphic to a regular subset of their canonical presentation of the rationals. Then they conjecture that this holds for all automatic linear orders [5]. Theorem 5.4 of the paper at hand disproves this conjecture. Since results on automatic structures depend on how the structure is encoded by automata, the complete result is:

– For any automatic presentation $(L, \leq)$ of a linear order, there exists an automatic presentation of the rational numbers $(Q, \sqsubseteq)$ and a synchronous rational transduction from L into Q that is a continuous order embedding (Theorem 5.1).
– There is an automatic linear order that is not order-isomorphic to any regular subset of the canonical representation from [5] (Theorem 5.4).

Cantor did not only show the universality of the rational numbers, but also their homogeneity: for any two tuples $x_1 < x_2 \cdots < x_n$ and $y_1 < y_2 \cdots < y_n$ of rational numbers, there is an automorphism $f : (\mathbb{Q}, \leq) \to (\mathbb{Q}, \leq)$ with $f(x_i) = y_i$ for $i \leq n$. Again, an effective version holds and complexity-theoretic investigations can be found in [17]. The first part of this paper investigates whether the canonical representation of the rational numbers is "automatic-homogeneous": can we choose the mapping f above such that it can be computed by a finite automaton? Again, the answer is two-fold:

– The canonical representation of the rational numbers is automatic-homogeneous (Corollary 3.5).
– There is an automatic presentation of the rational numbers which is not automatic-homogeneous (Corollary 4.3).

1   Definitions

For an alphabet Σ, let $\Sigma_\perp = \Sigma \cup \{\perp\}$ where we will make sure that $\perp \notin \Sigma$. The *convolution* $u \otimes v$ of two words $u = a_1 a_2 \ldots a_n$ and $v = b_1 b_2 \ldots b_m$ over Σ is defined by $u \otimes v = (a_1', b_1')(a_2', b_2') \ldots (a_k', b_k') \in (\Sigma_\perp^2)^*$ where $k = \max(m, n)$ and

$$a_i' = \begin{cases} a_i & \text{if } i \leq n \\ \perp & \text{otherwise} \end{cases} \text{ and } b_i' = \begin{cases} b_i & \text{if } i \leq m \\ \perp & \text{otherwise} \end{cases}$$

For a binary relation $R \subseteq (\Sigma^*)^2$ let $R^\otimes = \{u \otimes v \mid (u, v) \in R\}$ denote the convolution of R. For a (partial) mapping $f : \Sigma^* \to \Sigma^*$, let $f^\otimes$ denote the convolution of the graph of f.

Lemma 1.1. *Let R, S be binary relations on Σ^* such that $R^\otimes$ and $S^\otimes$ are regular. Assume furthermore that there is $k \in \mathbb{N}$ such that $-k \leq |u| - |v| \leq k$ for any $(u, v) \in R$. Then $(R \cdot S)^\otimes = \{u_1 u_2 \otimes v_1 v_2 \mid (u_1, v_1) \in R, (u_2, v_2) \in S\}$ is regular.*

Proof. Let $u, v \in \Sigma^*$. To determine whether $(u, v) \in R \cdot S$, the automaton guesses positions in u and v which determine factorizations $u = u_1 u_2$ and $v = v_1 v_2$ such that $(u_1, v_1) \in R$ and $(u_2, v_2) \in S$. By our assumption on k and R, these two positions can only be k positions apart. Thus, remembering at most k letters from one of the tapes, an automaton can check whether $u \otimes v \in (R \cdot S)^\otimes$. $\qquad\square$

An *automatic presentation* is a tuple $(L, R_0, \ldots, R_n)$ with $L \subseteq \Gamma^*$ and $R_i \subseteq (\Gamma^*)^2$ such that L and $(R_i)^\otimes$ are regular languages. A structure is *automatic* if there exists an isomorphic automatic presentation.

We next prepare the definition of an automatic presentation of $(\mathbb{Q}, \leq)$ that has been considered in [5] (in another context, it can also be found in [17]). For two words u and v, let $u \wedge v$ denote the *largest common prefix* of u and v. The *length* of a word u is denoted $|u|$. Then the *distance* $d(u, v)$ between u and v is $|u| + |v| - 2|u \wedge v|$. Alternatively, $d(u, v) = |x| + |y|$ where x and y are words uniquely given by $u = (u \wedge v)x$ and $v = (u \wedge v)y$.

From now on, let $\Sigma = \{0, 1\}$. For $u, v \in \Sigma^*$, let $u \sqsubset v$ iff $(u \wedge v)0$ is a prefix of u or $(u \wedge v)1$ is a prefix of v. Note that $u \sqsubset v$ iff

1. $u = x0y$ and $v = x1z$ for some $x, y, z \in \Sigma^*$ (i.e., u is lexicographically smaller than v), or
2. $u = v0x$ for some $x \in \Sigma^*$, or
3. $v = u1x$ for some $x \in \Sigma^*$.

The relation $\sqsubset$ is transitive and antisymmetric, i.e., $\sqsubseteq = (\sqsubset \cup =)$ is a linear order on the set Σ^*. Since $v0 \sqsubset v \sqsubset v1$ for any $v \in \Sigma^*$, it does not have endpoints. Furthermore, whenever $u \sqsubset v$, then $u \sqsubset u1 \sqsubset v$ (in the first two cases) or $u \sqsubset v0 \sqsubset v$ (in the first and in the last case). Hence the countable linear order $(\Sigma^*, \sqsubseteq)$ is dense without endpoints and therefore isomorphic to $(\mathbb{Q}, \leq)$ [3]. Furthermore, it is easily checked that $\sqsubseteq^\otimes$ is regular:

$$\sqsubseteq^\otimes = \left[\{(0, 0), (1, 1)\}^* \cdot \{(0, 1), (0, \bot), (\bot, 1)\} \cdot (\Sigma_\bot^2)^*\right] \cap \left[\Sigma^*\{\bot\}^* \times \Sigma^*\{\bot\}^*\right]^\otimes.$$

Thus, $(\Sigma^*, \sqsubseteq)$ is an automatic presentation of $(\mathbb{Q}, \leq)$.

2   An Automatic Automorphism of $(\Sigma^*, \sqsubseteq)$

Let $(L, \preceq)$ be an automatic presentation of $(\mathbb{Q}, \leq)$. An automorphism f of $(L, \preceq)$ is *automatic* provided $f^\otimes$ is regular. Before we actually construct the automatic automorphism, we need two auxiliary properties of the interplay between $(\Sigma^*, \sqsubseteq)$ and the tree structure on Σ^*.

Lemma 2.1. *Let $h \in \Sigma^*$. Then the set $h\Sigma^*$ is convex in $(\Sigma^*, \sqsubseteq)$.*

Proof. Let $x, y, z \in \Sigma^*$ with $x \sqsubseteq y \sqsubseteq z$ and $x, z \in h\Sigma^*$. If $x \wedge z$ is a prefix of y, then $y \in h\Sigma^*$ since h is a prefix of $x \wedge z$. If $x \wedge z$ is no prefix of y, then $u := x \wedge y = y \wedge z$ since the prefixes of $x \wedge z$ form a chain. Furthermore, u has to be a proper prefix of $x \wedge z$ for otherwise $x \wedge z$ was a prefix of y. Hence u is a proper prefix of x and of z. From $x \sqsubseteq y$, it then follows that $u0$ is a prefix of x. Similarly, $y \sqsubseteq z$ implies that $u1$ is a prefix of z. But then $u = x \wedge z$ which contradicts the assumption that $x \wedge z$ is no prefix of y. □

Lemma 2.2. *Let $a \in \Sigma^*$ and $n \in \mathbb{N}$. Then the set $X = a0\Sigma^* \cup \{a\} \cup a10^n\Sigma^*$ is convex in $(\Sigma^*, \sqsubseteq)$.*

Proof. Let $x, z \in X$ and let $y \in \Sigma^*$ with $x \sqsubseteq y \sqsubseteq z$. Note that, for $x \in a0\Sigma^* \cup \{a\}$ and $z \in \{a\} \cup a10^n\Sigma^*$, we always have $x \sqsubseteq z$. Making x smaller and z larger if necessary, we can assume $x \in a0\Sigma^*$ and $z \in a10^n\Sigma^*$. Since, by Lemma 2.1, the set $a\Sigma^*$ is convex, we obtain $y \in a\Sigma^*$. If $y \in a0\Sigma^* \cup \{a\}$, we are done. So let $y \in a1\Sigma^*$. Let $m \in \mathbb{N}$ be maximal with $y \in a10^m\Sigma^*$. If $m < n$, then $z \sqsubseteq a10^m \sqsubseteq y$ since $a10^{m+1}$ is a prefix of z. Hence $m \geq n$ implying $y \in a10^n\Sigma^*$. □

Next, we construct the announced automatic automorphism: let $a \in \Sigma^*$ and $n \in \mathbb{N}$. We define a function $g_{a,n} : \Sigma^* \to \Sigma^*$ as follows:

$$g_{a,n}(x) = \begin{cases} a & \text{if } x = a10^n \\ a0 & \text{if } x = a \\ a10^n z & \text{if } x = a10^n 1z \\ a01z & \text{if } x = a10^n 0z \\ a00z & \text{if } x = a0z \\ x & \text{otherwise} \end{cases}$$

To visualize the effect of $g_{a,n}$, consider Figure 1. On the left, one sees a small portion of the tree Σ^*. The same portion is depicted on the right, but now the labels indicate what is mapped to this node: a simple label x (like $a10^n$ on the root) denotes that this node equals $g_{a,n}(x)$. A label $x\!\Uparrow$ (like $a0\!\Uparrow$) denotes not only that this node is $g_{a,n}(x)$, but that any node above is the image of the corresponding node above x. In the right tree, I added two dashed arrows. They indicate two particular movements of points wrt. the mapping $g_{a,n}$; these two movements will be used frequently in later proofs and indicated in the corresponding pictures.

Lemma 2.3. *For $a \in \Sigma^*$ and $n \in \mathbb{N}$, the mapping $g_{a,n}$ is an automatic automorphism of $(\Sigma^*, \sqsubseteq)$.*

Proof. The support (i.e., the set of words $w \in \Sigma^*$ with $g_{a,n}(w) \neq w$) of $g_{a,n}$ is

$$\{a\} \cup \underbrace{\{a10^n\} \cup a10^n 1\Sigma^* \cup a10^n 0\Sigma^*}_{=a10^n\Sigma^*} \cup a0\Sigma^*$$

and the image of this set equals

$$\{a\} \cup a10^n\Sigma^* \cup \underbrace{\{a0\} \cup a01\Sigma^* \cup a00\Sigma^*}_{=a0\Sigma^*}$$

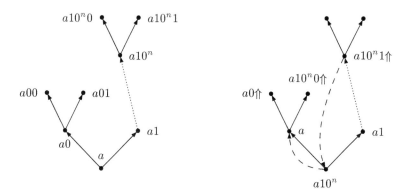

Fig. 1. The automorphism $g_{a,n}$

Thus, $g_{a,n}$ maps its support onto its support and is therefore surjective. In order to show that $g_{a,n}$ is injective, it suffices to check that it acts injectively on its support: $\{a10^n, a\}$ is mapped injectively onto $\{a, a0\}$, $a10^n1\Sigma^*$ onto $a10^n\Sigma^*$, $a10^n0\Sigma^*$ onto $a01\Sigma^*$ and $a0\Sigma^*$ onto $a00\Sigma^*$. Thus, $g_{a,n}$ is bijective.

By Lemma 2.2, the support $a0\Sigma^* \cup \{a\} \cup a10^n\Sigma^*$ of $g_{a,n}$ is convex. To show that $g_{a,n}$ is an automorphism, it therefore suffices to show that its restriction to its support $\mathrm{supp}(g_{a,n})$ is order preserving. So let $b, c \in \mathrm{supp}(g_{a,n})$ with $b \sqsubset c$. We proceed by case distinction:

$b = a10^n$. Then $c \in a10^n1\Sigma^*$ because of $b \sqsubset c$ and therefore $g_{a,n}(c) \in a1\Sigma^*$. Since $g_{a,n}(b) = a$, we obtain $g_{a,n}(b) \sqsubset g_{a,n}(c)$.

$b = a$. Then $c \in a10^n\Sigma^*$ and therefore $g_{a,n}(c) \in \{a\} \cup a1\Sigma^* \cup a01\Sigma^*$. Now $g_{a,n}(b) = a0$ implies $g_{a,n}(b) \sqsubset g_{a,n}(c)$.

$b \in a10^n1\Sigma^*$. Then $c \in a10^n1\Sigma^*$ implies $g_{a,n}(b) \sqsubset g_{a,n}(c)$ since the restriction of $g_{a,n}$ to the filter $a10^n1\Sigma^*$ is a tree isomorphism.

$b \in a10^n0\Sigma^*$. Then $c \in a10^n\Sigma^*$. If $c \in a10^n0\Sigma^*$, the same argument as before implies $g_{a,n}(b) \sqsubset g_{a,n}(c)$. If $c \in a10^n1\Sigma^*$, then $g_{a,n}(c) \in a1\Sigma^*$ and $g_{a,n}(b) \in a0\Sigma^*$, hence $g_{a,n}(b) \sqsubset g_{a,n}(c)$. If, finally, $c = a10^n$, then $g_{a,n}(b) \sqsubset a = g_{a,n}(c)$.

$b \in a0\Sigma^*$. The case $c \in a0\Sigma^*$ is dealt with as before. Otherwise, $g_{a,n}(c) \in \{a, a0\} \cup a10^n\Sigma^* \cup a01\Sigma^*$ and $g_{a,n}(b) \in a00\Sigma^*$ implying $g_{a,n}(b) \sqsubset g_{a,n}(c)$.

This finishes the proof that $g_{a,n}$ is an automorphism of $(\Sigma^*, \sqsubseteq)$.

It remains to be shown that $g_{a,n}^{\otimes}$ is regular: this set is the union of the sets $\{a10^n \otimes a, a \otimes a0\}$, $(a10^n \otimes a10^n) \cdot \{1z \otimes z \mid z \in \Sigma^*\}$, $(a1 \otimes a0) \cdot \{0^{n+1}z \otimes 1z \mid z \in \Sigma^*\}$, $(a0 \otimes a0) \cdot \{z \otimes 0z \mid z \in \Sigma^*\}$, and $\{x \otimes x \mid x \notin \mathrm{supp}(g_{a,n})\}$. Each of these sets is regular, hence g is an automatic automorphism.   □

Two groups are *elementarily equivalent* if they satisfy the same closed first-order formulas. Morozov and Truss [16, Cor. 2.21] showed that for any principal ideal of Turing degrees $\mathbf{I}$ containing an arithmetical set, the group of $\mathbf{I}$-recursive automorphisms of $(\mathbb{Q}, \leq)$ is not elementarily equivalent with the full automorphism group of $(\mathbb{Q}, \leq)$. One particular first-order formula is $\forall g \exists f (f^{-1} g f = g^2)$. From a more general result by Holland [9], it follows that this formula holds in the group of all automorphisms of the rational numbers. Using the automorphism $g_{\varepsilon,0}$, we now show that this formula is violated in the group of automatic automorphisms of $(\Sigma^*, \sqsubseteq)$.

Lemma 2.4. *For any automatic automorphism f of $(\Sigma^*, \sqsubseteq)$, there is $n \in \mathbb{N}$ such that $f^{-1} g_{\varepsilon,0}^n f(1^{2n}) \neq g_{\varepsilon,0}^{2n}(1^{2n})$.*

Proof. Since f is an automatic injection, there is $n_f \in \mathbb{N}$ such that, for any $x \in \Sigma^*$, the lengths of the words $f(x)$ and x differ by at most n_f. Let $n = 2n_f + 1$ and $w = 1^{2n}$. Note that the lengths of w and $f(w)$ and those of $f^{-1} g_{\varepsilon,0}^n f(w)$ and $g_{\varepsilon,0}^n f(w)$ differ by at most n_f. Furthermore, for any $x \in \Sigma^*$, the lengths of $g_{\varepsilon,0}(x)$ and x differ by at most 1. Hence the lengths of w and $f^{-1} g_{\varepsilon,0}^n f(w)$ differ by at most $2n_f + n < 2n$ implying $f^{-1} g_{\varepsilon,0}^n f(w) \neq \varepsilon = g_{\varepsilon,0}^{2n}(w)$. □

Theorem 2.5. *The group of automatic automorphisms of $(\Sigma^*, \sqsubseteq)$ is not elementarily equivalent with the full automorphism group of $(\mathbb{Q}, \leq)$.*

Proof. The formula $\forall g \exists f : f^{-1} g f = g^2$ holds in the full automorphism group of $(\mathbb{Q}, \leq)$. Suppose it holds in the group of automatic automorphisms and let $g = g_{\varepsilon,0}$. Then there is an automatic automorphism f with $f^{-1} g f = g^2$. Hence, for any $n \in \mathbb{N}$, we have $f^{-1} g^n f = (f^{-1} g f)^n = g^{2n}$. With the natural number n from the previous lemma, this contradicts $f^{-1} g^n f(1^{2n}) \neq g^{2n}(1^{2n})$. □

3 $(\Sigma^*, \sqsubseteq)$ Is an Automatic-Homogeneous Presentations of $(\mathbb{Q}, \leq)$

Let $(L, \preceq)$ be an automatic presentation of $(\mathbb{Q}, \leq)$. The automatic presentation $(L, \preceq)$ is *automatic-homogeneous* if, for any $x_1 \prec x_2 \cdots \prec x_n$ and $y_1 \prec y_2 \cdots \prec y_n$ words in L, there exists an automatic automorphism of $(L, \preceq)$ with $f(x_i) = y_i$ for $1 \leq i \leq n$. In this section, we show that the automatic presentation $(\Sigma^*, \sqsubseteq)$ is automatic-homogeneous.

Lemma 3.1. *Let $x, y, z \in \Sigma^*$ with $x \sqsubset y \sqsubset z$. Then there exists an automorphism f of $(\Sigma^*, \sqsubseteq)$ such that*

(1) $d(x,y) > d(x, f(y))$,
(2) $f(z') = z'$ for $z \sqsubseteq z' \in \Sigma^*$, and
(3) f is a finite product of automorphisms of the form $g_{u,n}$ and their inverses.

Proof. To prove the lemma, we distinguish three cases according to the prefix relation between the words x, y, and z. In all these cases, we will construct a finite product $f = g_n \circ g_{n-1} \cdots \circ g_1$ of automorphisms g_i of the form $g_{u,m}$ and their inverses such that f moves y closer to x. Even more, any of these factors g_i

will move $g_{i-1} \cdots \circ g_1(y)$ and fix z. Recall that the support $\text{supp}(g_{u,m})$ is convex by Lemma 2.2. Hence, we get automatically that f fixes anything to the right of z.

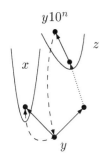

First let y be a prefix of x. Then, from $x \sqsubset y \sqsubset z$, we get $x \in y0\Sigma^*$. Let $n \in \mathbb{N}$ with $z \notin y10^n\Sigma^*$ and set $f = g_{y,n}$. Then $f(y) = y0$ is closer to x than y, i.e., (1) holds. By $y \sqsubset z$ and our choice of n, we have $z \notin y0\Sigma^* \cup \{y\} \cup y10^n\Sigma^*$ which is the support of $g_{y,n}$. Hence $f(z) = z$.

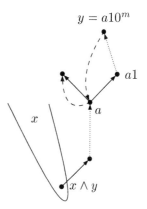

Let y be neither a prefix of x nor of z. Since $x \sqsubset y$, we have $y \in (x \wedge y)1\Sigma^* \cup \{x \wedge y\}$. Since y is no prefix of x, we obtain $y \in (x \wedge y)1\Sigma^*$. Hence there is $m \in \mathbb{N}$ and $a \in (x \wedge y)1\Sigma^* \cup \{x \wedge y\}$ with $y = a10^m$ (the picture indicates $a \neq x \wedge y$, but equality is possible as well). From $x \sqsubset y$, we obtain $x \in (x \wedge y)0\Sigma^* \cup \{x \wedge y\}$. Hence a lies on the path from x to y in the tree Σ^* which implies $d(x,a) < d(x,y)$. Setting $f = g_{a,m}$ therefore moves y closer to x. Then the support of f is $y\Sigma^* \cup \{a\} \cup a0\Sigma^*$. But z cannot belong to $y\Sigma^*$ since y is no prefix of z. Nor can z belong to $\{a\} \cup a0\Sigma^*$ since any element of this set lies to the left of y. Thus, the automorphism f fixes z.

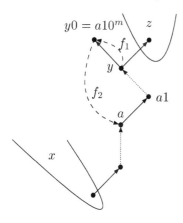

Now suppose y is a prefix of z but not of x. Since $y \sqsubset z$ is a prefix of z, we get $z \in y1\Sigma^*$. Choose $n \in \mathbb{N}$ such that $y10^n$ is no prefix of z and set $f_1 = g_{y,n}$. Then $f_1(y) = y0$ and $f_1(z) = z$ (see the first case, first picture). Since y is no prefix of x, the word $x \wedge y$ is a proper prefix of y. Then $x \sqsubset y$ implies that $(x \wedge y)1$ is a prefix of y. Hence there are $a \in \Sigma^*$ and $m \in \mathbb{N}$ such that $a10^{m-1} = y$ (the picture indicates $a \neq x \wedge y$ which is not necessarily the case). Let $f_2 = g_{a,m}$. Then $f_2(y0) = f_2(a10^m) = a$. Since a lies on the path from $x \wedge y$ to y and is a proper prefix of y, we get $d(x,y) > d(x,a) = d(x, f_2 \circ f_1(y))$. Since neither $a0$ nor $a10^m$ is a prefix of z, we get $f_2(z) = z$. Hence $f = f_2 \circ f_1$ has the desired properties. $\square$

The lemma above allows to move the inner point y towards the left margin while fixing the right margin. Next, we will move the left margin towards the inner point while still fixing the right margin.

Lemma 3.2. *Let $x, y, z \in \Sigma^*$ with $x \sqsubset y \sqsubset z$. Then there exists an automorphism f of $(\Sigma^*, \sqsubseteq)$ such that*

(1) $d(x,y) > d(f(x), y)$,

(2) $f(z') = z'$ for $z \sqsubseteq z' \in \Sigma^*$, and
(3) f is a finite product of automorphisms of the form $g_{u,n}$ and their inverses.

Proof. We proceed similarly to the previous proof.

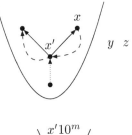

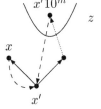

First suppose x is neither a prefix of y nor of z. Then $x \neq \varepsilon$, i.e., there is $x' \in \Sigma^*$ with $x \in x'\Sigma$. First consider the case $x = x'1$ (cf. first picture). Setting $f = g_{x',0}^{-1}$ moves x to x' and therefore closer to y. Since $x \sqsubset z$, the word x' cannot be a prefix of z. Hence z is fixed since the support of f is $x'\Sigma^*$. Now we deal with the case $x = x'0$ (cf. second picture). Let $m \in \mathbb{N}$ such that $x'10^m$ is no prefix of z and set $f = g_{x',m}^{-1}$. Then $x = x'0$ gets moved to x' and therefore closer to y. Note that $z \neq x'$ for otherwise $x'0 = x \sqsubset y \sqsubset z = x'$ would imply $y \in x\Sigma^*$. Since neither $x = x'0$ nor $x'10^m$ is a prefix of z, we obtain $z \notin \{x'\} \cup x'0\Sigma^* \cup x'10^m\Sigma^*$. Hence f fixes z.

If x Is a Prefix of y but Not of z, then $x1$ is a prefix of y that is closer to y than x is. Hence $f = g_{x,0}^{-1}$ moves x towards y. The support of this mapping is $x\Sigma^*$ which does not contain z, hence z is fixed.

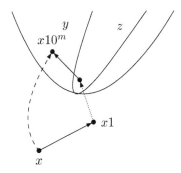

If x Is a Prefix of z, then $x1$ is a prefix of z since $x \sqsubset z$. Now $x \sqsubset y \sqsubset z$ implies that $x1$ has to be a prefix of y as well. Let $m \in \mathbb{N}$ be maximal such that $x10^{m-1}$ is a prefix of z. Then $x10^{m-1}$ is a prefix of y since $y \sqsubset z$ is an extension of $x1$. Now consider $f_1 = g_{x,m}^{-1}$. Since neither $x0$ nor $x10^m$ is a prefix of z, the mapping f_1 fixes z. Since $x10^{m-1}$ is a prefix of y, we obtain $d(f_1(x), y) = d(x10^m, y) \leq 1 + d(x10^{m-1}, y) \leq 1 + d(x1, y) = d(x, y)$. Note that $f_1(x) \sqsubset y \sqsubset z$ and $f_1(x)$ is no prefix of y or of z. Hence, by the first case, there is an automatic automorphism f_2 that moves $f_1(x)$ closer to y and fixes z. Now $f = f_2 \circ f_1$ has the desired properties. $\square$

Lemma 3.3. *Let $a, b, z \in \Sigma^*$ with $a, b \sqsubset z$. Then there exists an automorphism f of $(\Sigma^*, \sqsubseteq)$ such that*

(1) $f(a) = b$,
(2) $f(z') = z'$ for $z \sqsubseteq z' \in \Sigma^*$, and
(3) f is a finite product of automorphisms of the form $g_{u,n}$ and their inverses.

Proof. The lemma is shown by induction on $d(a, b)$. The case $d(a, b) = 0$ is trivial, so let $d(a, b) = n + 1$. Then depending on whether $a \sqsupset b$ or $a \sqsubset b$, we use Lemma 3.1 or 3.2 to obtain an automorphism f_1 that moves a closer to b and satisfies (2) and (3). Since $d(f_1(a), b) < d(a, b) = n + 1$ the induction hypothesis yields an automorphism f_2 that moves $f_1(a)$ to b and satisfies (2) and (3). Hence $f = f_2 \circ f_1$ has the desired properties. □

Theorem 3.4. *Let* $x_1 \sqsubset x_2 \cdots \sqsubset x_n \sqsubset z$ *and* $y_1 \sqsubset y_2 \cdots \sqsubset y_n \sqsubset z$ *be words from* Σ^*. *Then there exists an automorphism* f *of* $(\Sigma^*, \sqsubseteq)$ *such that*

(a) $f(x_i) = y_i$ *for* $1 \le i \le n$ *and*
(b) $f(z') = z'$ *for* $z \sqsubseteq z' \in \Sigma^*$, *and*
(c) f *is a finite product of automorphisms of the form* $g_{u,m}$ *and their inverses.*

Proof. The theorem is shown by induction on n, the base case $n = 0$ being trivial. By Lemma 3.3, there exists an automorphism f_1 that moves x_n to y_n and satisfies (b) and (c). Then $f_1(x_1) \sqsubset f_1(x_2) \cdots \sqsubset f_1(x_{n-1}) \sqsubset f_1(x_n) = y_n$. Hence, by the induction hypothesis, there exists an automorphism f_2 with $f_2(f_1(x_i)) = y_i$ for $1 \le i \le n - 1$ that fixes anything to the right of y_n (which includes y_n, hence $f_2(f_1(x_n)) = f_2(y_n) = y_n$) and satisfies (c). Now $f = f_2 \circ f_1$ has the desired properties. □

Corollary 3.5. *The group generated by the automorphisms* $g_{u,m}$ *acts homogeneously on* $(\Sigma^*, \sqsubseteq)$. *Hence the automatic presentation* $(\Sigma^*, \sqsubseteq)$ *is automatic-homogeneous.*

Proof. Recall that automorphisms of the form $g_{u,m}$ are automatic by Lemma 2.3. Furthermore, automatic automorphisms are closed under catenation. Hence the result follows immediately from the previous theorem. □

Let $(L, \preceq)$ be an automatic presentation of $(\mathbb{Q}, \le)$ such that there exists an order isomorphism $f : (L, \preceq) \to (\Sigma^*, \sqsubseteq)$ with $f^\otimes$ regular. Then it is an easy exercise to show that $(L, \preceq)$ is automatic-homogeneous as well.

4   A Non-automatic-homogeneous Presentation of $(\mathbb{Q}, \le)$

Let $\Gamma = \{a, b\}$ and let R denote the regular set $\Gamma^* bab \backslash \Gamma^* bab\Gamma^+$. Furthermore, let $\le_{\text{lex}}$ denote the lexicographic order on the set R. By [11, Prop. 2.2], the structure $(R, \le_{\text{lex}})$ is an automatic presentation of $(\mathbb{Q}, \le)$. The following theorem shows that there is no automatic isomorphism from $(R, \le_{\text{lex}})$ to $(\Sigma^*, \sqsubseteq)$.

Theorem 4.1. *There is no order-embedding* $f : (\Sigma^*, \sqsubseteq) \to (R, \le_{\text{lex}})$ *with* $f^\otimes$ *regular.*

Remark 4.2. Conversely, the mapping $a \mapsto 0$ and $b \mapsto 1$ defines an order-embedding $g : (R, \le_{\text{lex}}) \to (\Sigma^*, \sqsubseteq)$ with $g^\otimes$ regular.

Proof. Suppose, to the contrary, that f is such an embedding. Since it is an automatic injection, there is $k \in \mathbb{N}$ with $-k \le |u| - |f(u)| \le k$ for any word $u \in \Sigma^*$. Thus, the words of length at most n in Σ^* are mapped to words of length at most $n + k$ in R. Since f is injective, there are at least $2^{n+1} - 1$ words of length at most $n + k$ in R.

Let r_n be the number of words of length $n+3$ in R. Hence $r_0 = 1$ and $r_1 = 2$. Then r_n is the number of words of length n in $R' = \Gamma^* \setminus (\Gamma^* bab \Gamma^* \cup \Gamma^* ba)$. Now let $u \in \Gamma^*$ and $\alpha, \beta \in \Gamma$. Then $u\alpha\beta \in R'$ iff one of the following statements holds

1. $u\alpha \in R'$ and $\beta = b$, or
2. $u \in R'$ and $\alpha\beta = aa$, or
3. $u \in R'ba$ and $\alpha\beta = aa$.

Note that these three cases are pairwise disjoint. Hence $r_{n+4} = r_{n+3} + r_{n+2} + r_n \leq r_{n+3} + r_{n+2} + r_{n+1}$. This proves that r_n is bounded from above by the Tribonacci number T_{n+2}. Asymptotically, the sequence $(T_n)_{n \in \mathbb{N}}$ is bounded by 1.9^n [15]. Hence the number of words of length at most $n + k - 3$ in R' is asymptotically bounded from above by

$$\sum_{i=0}^{n+k-3} 1.9^i = \frac{1.9^{n+b-2} - 1}{0.9}.$$

Thus, for large n, the number of words in R of length at most $n + k$ is properly smaller than $2^{n+1} - 1$, i.e., we derived a contradiction. □

We do not know whether $(R, \leq_{\mathrm{lex}})$ is automatic-homogeneous, but from the above theorem we can infer that the combination of $(R, \leq_{\mathrm{lex}})$ and $(\Sigma^*, \sqsubseteq)$ is not. So let $L = R \cup \Sigma^*$ and, for $u, v \in L$, set $u \preceq v$ iff $u, v \in R$ with $u \leq_{\mathrm{lex}} v$, or $u, v \in \Sigma^*$ and $u \sqsubseteq v$, or $u \in R$ and $v \in \Sigma^*$ (i.e., $\preceq = (\leq_{\mathrm{lex}} \cup \sqsubseteq \cup R \times \Sigma^*)$). Then $(L, \preceq)$ is another automatic presentation of $(\mathbb{Q}, \leq)$.

Corollary 4.3. *The automatic presentation $(L, \preceq)$ is not automatic-homogeneous.*

Proof. Suppose f is an automatic automorphism of $(L, \preceq)$ with $f(\varepsilon) = bab$. Then, for any word $w \in 0\Sigma^*$, we get $f(w) \preceq f(\varepsilon) = bab$ and therefore $f(w) \in R$. Let $g : \Sigma^* \to R$ be given by $g(u) = f(0u)$. Since the mapping $h : \Sigma^* \to \Sigma^* : u \mapsto 0u$ is automatic, $g = f \circ h$ is automatic as well. Since $u \sqsubseteq v$ iff $0u \sqsubseteq 0v$ for any $u, v \in \Sigma^*$, the mapping g is an embedding of $(\Sigma^*, \sqsubseteq)$ into $(R, \leq_{\mathrm{lex}})$, contradicting the previous theorem. □

5   Automatic-Universality

Cantor [3] showed that any countable linear order can be embedded into $(\mathbb{Q}, \leq)$, i.e., the rationals are *universal* for the class of countable linear orders. In this section, we show that similarly any automatic linear order L can be embedded into $(\mathbb{Q}, \leq)$ by an automatic embedding. For this, we construct an automatic presentation of $(\mathbb{Q}, \leq)$ from the automatic presentation for L. The second result is that there are automatic linear orders that cannot be embedded into either $(\Sigma^*, \sqsubseteq)$ or $(R, \leq_{\mathrm{lex}})$ by an automatic embedding (this disproves the conjecture by Delhommé, Goranko and Knapik from [5]).

An order embedding $f : (L, \leq_L) \to (K, \leq_K)$ is *continuous* if, for any set $X \subseteq L$ that has a least upper bound x in $(L, \leq_L)$, the element $f(x)$ is the least upper bound of $f(X)$ in $(K, \leq_K)$.

Theorem 5.1. *Let* $(L, \leq_L)$ *be an automatic presentation of a linear order (with* $L \subseteq \Delta^*$ *and* $\Sigma \cap \Delta = \emptyset$*). Then there exists an automatic presentation* $(K, \leq_K)$ *of* $(\mathbb{Q}, \leq)$ *and a mapping* $f : L \to K$ *such that*

1. f *is a continuous embedding of* $(L, \leq_L)$ *into* $(K, \leq_K)$, *and*
2. $f^\otimes$ *is regular in* $((\Delta \cup \Sigma \cup \{\bot\})^2)^*$.

Remark 5.2. Without the requirement on f to be continuous, one could easily choose $K = L \cdot \Sigma^*$ with $u_1 v_1 <_K u_2 v_2$ iff $u_1 <_L u_2$ or $u_1 = u_2$ and $v_1 \sqsubset v_2$. The continuity of f requires some more effort.

Proof. Let $L_1 \subseteq L$ be the set of elements of L that cannot be approximated from the left, i.e., $w \in L_1$ iff

$$\exists u \in L(u <_L w \wedge \neg \exists v \in L(u <_L v <_L w)) \vee \neg \exists u \in L(u <_L w)$$

This set is first-order definable in $(L, \leq_L)$ and the same holds for the set L_2 of elements of L that cannot be approximated from the right. Now let K be the set

$$L \cup L_1 \cdot 0\Sigma^* \cup L_2 \cdot 1\Sigma^*$$

Since Δ and Σ are disjoint, any word w from K splits uniquely into words $w_\Delta \in L$ and $w_\Sigma \in \Sigma^*$. This splitting allows to view K as a subset of the lexicographic product of the chains $(L, \leq_L)$ and $(\Sigma^*, \sqsubseteq)$: $u \leq_K v$ iff $u_\Delta \leq_L v_\Delta$ or $u_\Delta = v_\Delta$ and $u_\Sigma \sqsubseteq v_\Sigma$.

Since L_1 is first-order definable in the automatic presentation $(L, \leq_L)$, it is regular and the same holds for L_2. Hence K is regular. Since $(\leq_L)^\otimes$ and $\sqsubseteq^\otimes$ are regular sets, the set

$$(\leq_K)^\otimes = [(<_L \cdot (\Sigma^* \times \Sigma^*))^\otimes \cup \{u \otimes u \mid u \in L\} \cdot \sqsubseteq^\otimes] \cap K \otimes K$$

is regular as well, i.e., $(K, \leq_K)$ is an infinite automatic presentation. Furthermore, the identity mapping $f : L \hookrightarrow K$ is an order embedding with $f^\otimes$ regular.

Now let w_i be an increasing chain of elements of L that tend to $w \in L$ (i.e., $w = \sup_{\leq_L} w_i$). Suppose $w = w_i$ for some $i \in \mathbb{N}$. Then $f(w)$ is an element and an upper bound of the chain $(f(w_i))_{i \in \mathbb{N}}$ in $(K, \leq_K)$, hence it is the supremum of this chain. Now suppose $w_i <_L w$ for any $i \in \mathbb{N}$. Since w is the supremum of the chain $(w_i)_{i \in \mathbb{N}}$, we get $w \notin L_1$. Now let $u \in K$ be some upper bound of the chain $(w_i)_{i \in \mathbb{N}}$ in $(K, \leq_K)$. Then, for any $i \in \mathbb{N}$, we get $(w_i)_\Delta \leq_L u_\Delta$. Since $w = \sup_{\leq_L} w_i$ and $w_i = (w_i)_\Delta$, this implies $w \leq_L u_\Delta$. If $w <_L u_\Delta$, we obtain $w \leq_K u$. If $w = u_\Delta$, then $u \in \{w\} \cup w1\Sigma^*$ since $w \notin L_1$ implies $K \cap w0\Sigma^* = \emptyset$. Hence $w \leq_K u$ implying $f(w) = w = \sup_{\leq_K} f(w_i)$. Thus, indeed, f is continuous.

To see that $(K, \leq_K)$ is an automatic presentation of $(\mathbb{Q}, \leq)$, let $u, w \in K$ with $u <_K w$. First, let $u_\Delta <_L w_\Delta$. If there is $v \in L$ with $u_\Delta <_L v <_L w_\Delta$, then

$u <_K v <_K w$. If there is no element of L between u_Δ and w_Δ, then $u_\Delta \in L_2$. Hence there exists $u' \in 1\Sigma^*$ with $u_\Sigma \sqsubseteq u'$ and therefore $u = u_\Delta u_\Sigma <_K u_\Delta u'$. Thus, we found $v = u_\Delta u' \in K$ with $u <_K v <_K w$, i.e., the linearly ordered set $(K, \leq_K)$ is dense. Similarly, one can show that it does not have endpoints, i.e., it is isomorphic to $(\mathbb{Q}, \leq)$. $\qquad\square$

Let $(K, \leq)$ be a linearly ordered set. Two elements $x, y \in K$ are *equivalent* $(x \equiv y)$ if the interval $[\min(x,y), \max(x,y)]$ is finite. A *block* is an equivalence class with respect to $\equiv$.[3] A block size $n \in \mathbb{N} \cup \{\omega\}$ is *realized* in the linear order $(K, \leq)$ if there exists a block of size n.

Lemma 5.3. *Let $L \subseteq \Sigma^*$ be regular. Then the linear order $(L, \sqsubseteq \restriction_L)$ realizes only finitely many block sizes.*

Proof. Let B_1 and B_2 be two distinct blocks in $(L, \sqsubseteq)$. Furthermore, let b_i be the longest common prefix of the elements of B_i. Then $b_i \in B_i$ or there are words $b_i 0x, b_i 1y \in B_i$. Hence b_i belongs to the convex closure of B_i in $(\Sigma^*, \sqsubseteq)$. Since B_1 and B_2 are disjoint and convex in $(L, \sqsubseteq)$, we obtain $b_1 \neq b_2$.

Now suppose, by contradiction, that $(L, \sqsubseteq)$ realizes infinitely many block sizes. Then there are blocks B_i for $i \in \mathbb{N}$ of mutually different size. For $i \in \mathbb{N}$, let b_i be the longest common prefix of the elements of B_i. Then, as shown above, the words b_i are mutually distinct.

Let $\mathcal{A} = (Q, T, \iota, F)$ be a deterministic automaton accepting L. Then we can further assume that $\iota.b_i = \iota.b_j$ for any $i, j \in \mathbb{N}$. For $i \in \mathbb{N}$ let $L_i = b_i \Sigma^* \cap L$. Then $f_{i,j} : L_i \to L_j$ with $f_{i,j}(b_i u) = b_j u$ is a bijection since $b_i u \in L$ iff $\iota.b_i u \in F$ iff $\iota.b_j u \in F$ iff $b_j u \in L$. Due to the special form of the linear order $\sqsubseteq$, it is even an order isomorphism between $(L_i, \sqsubseteq \restriction_{L_i})$ and $(L_j, \sqsubseteq \restriction_{L_j})$. Recall that b_i is contained in the convex closure of B_i in $(\Sigma^*, \sqsubseteq)$. Hence, by the definition of $f_{i,j}$, the convex closure of the image $f_{i,j}(B_i)$ contains b_j. Thus, the convex closures (in $(\Sigma^*, \sqsubseteq)$) of B_j and $f_{i,j}(B_i)$ overlap. In $(L, \sqsubseteq)$, these two sets are convex implying that B_j and $f_{i,j}(B_i)$ overlap. Since $f_{i,j}(B_i)$ is convex in L, its elements are mutually equivalent with respect to $\equiv$. Thus, $f_{i,j}(B_i) \subseteq B_j$, i.e., $|B_i| \leq |B_j|$. Since, symmetrically, $|B_j| \leq |B_i|$, we obtain $|B_i| = |B_j|$, a contradiction. $\qquad\square$

Now we disprove [5, Conjecture 4.6]:

Theorem 5.4. *There exists an automatic linear order $(K, \leq)$ such that no restriction of $(\Sigma^*, \sqsubseteq)$ or $(R, \leq_{\mathrm{lex}})$ to a regular set is order-isomorphic to $(K, \leq)$.*

Proof. By [10], there exists a permutation σ of $\mathbb{N}$ such that $\mathbb{Q} + \sum_{i \in \mathbb{N}}([\sigma(i)] + \mathbb{Q})$ has an automatic presentation $(K, \leq)$ (where $[n]$ denotes the n-elements linear order). Suppose $f : K \to \Sigma^*$ was a rational embedding into $(\Sigma^*, \sqsubseteq)$. Then the image $L = f(K)$ is regular and $(L, \sqsubseteq) \cong \mathbb{Q} + \sum_{i \in \mathbb{N}}([\sigma(i)] + \mathbb{Q})$. But this linear order realizes infinitely many block sizes.

The statement for $(R, \leq_{\mathrm{lex}})$ follows since R is a regular subset of Σ^* and $\leq_{\mathrm{lex}}$ is the restriction of $\sqsubseteq$ to R. $\qquad\square$

---

[3] The set of blocks is, in a natural way, linearly ordered. Calling this linear order $c_{CF}(K, \leq)$, Khoussainov, Rubin, and Stephan [14] show that for any automatic linear order $c_{CF}^n(K, \leq) = c_{CF}^{n+1}(K, \leq)$ for some natural number n.

6   Open Questions

So far, only one automatic-homogeneous presentation of the rationals is known, in particular, we do not know whether $(R, \leq_{\text{lex}})$ is automatic-homogeneous.

We showed that any automatic presentation of a linear order can be embedded into some automatic presentation of $(\mathbb{Q}, \leq)$ by an automatic embedding. It is not clear to me whether there is one automatic presentation of $(\mathbb{Q}, \leq)$ that embeds *all* automatic presentations of linear orders by an automatic embedding.

The conjecture from [5] that $(\Sigma^*, \sqsubseteq)$ serves this purpose was refuted by Theorem 5.4. On the other hand Delhommé, Goranko and Knapik [5] showed that any linear order from $\mathcal{M}$ (see [18]) embeds via an automatic embedding into $(\Sigma^*, \sqsubseteq)$. So the new conjecture by Delhommé (personal communication) is that this is a characterization of the class $\mathcal{M}$.

References

1. A. Blumensath. Automatic structures. Technical report, RWTH Aachen, 1999.

2. A. Blumensath and E. Grädel. Automatic Structures. In *LICS'00*, pages 51–62, 2000.

3. G. Cantor. Beiträge zur Begründung der transfiniten Mengenlehre, II. *Math. Annalen*, 49:207–246, 1897.

4. D. Cenzer and J.B. Remmel. Complexity theoretic model theory and algebra. In *[7], Chapter 10*. 1998.

5. C. Delhommé, V. Goranko, and T. Knapik. Automatic linear orderings, 2003. Manuscript.

6. C.C. Elgot. Decision problems of finite automata design and related arithmetics. *Trans. Am. Math. Soc.*, 98:21–51, 1961.

7. Yu.L. Ershov, S.S. Goncharov, A. Nerode, and J.B. Remmel. *Handbook of Recursive Mathematics I and II*. Elsevier, 1998.

8. B.R. Hodgson. On direct products of automaton decidable theories. *Theoretical Comp. Science*, 19:331–335, 1982.

9. C. Holland. The lattice-ordered groups of automorphisms of an ordered set. *Michigan Math. J.*, 10:399–408, 1963.

10. I. Ishihara, B. Khoussainov, and S. Rubin. Some results on automatic structures. In *LICS'02*, pages 235–244, 2002.

11. B. Khoussainov and A. Nerode. Automatic presentations of structures. In *Logic and Computational Complexity*, Lecture Notes in Comp. Science vol. 960, pages 367–392. Springer, 1995.

12. B. Khoussainov and S. Rubin. Graphs with automatic presentations over a unary alphabet. *J. Autom. Lang. Comb.*, 6:467–480, 2001.

13. B. Khoussainov, S. Rubin, and F. Stephan. Definability and regularity in automatic presentations of subsystems of arithmetic, 2003. Manuscript.

14. B. Khoussainov, S. Rubin, and F. Stephan. On automatic partial orders, 2003. accepted for LICS'03.

15. C.P. McCarty. A formula for Tribonacci numbers. *Fibonacci Quarterly*, 19:391–393, 1981.

16. A.S. Morozov and J.K. Truss. On computable automorphisms of the rational numbers. *J. Symb. Logic*, 66(3):1458–1470, 2001.

17. J.B. Remmel. Polynomial time categoricity and linear orderings. *Progress in Computer Science and Applied Logic (Papers from Conference in honor of Anil Nerod's 60th birthday)*, 12:713–746, 1993.

18. J.G. Rosenstein. *Linear Orderings*. Academic Press, 1982.

Automatic Structures of Bounded Degree

Markus Lohrey

Institut für Formale Methoden der Informatik, Universität Stuttgart,
Universitätsstr. 38, 70569 Stuttgart, Germany,
lohrey@informatik.uni-stuttgart.de

Abstract. The first-order theory of an automatic structure is known to
be decidable but there are examples of automatic structures with nonelementary first-order theories. We prove that the first-order theory of an
automatic structure of bounded degree (meaning that the corresponding
Gaifman-graph has bounded degree) is elementary decidable. More precisely, we prove an upper bound of triply exponential alternating time
with a linear number of alternations. We also present an automatic structure of bounded degree such that the corresponding first-order theory
has a lower bound of doubly exponential time with a linear number of
alternations. We prove similar results also for tree automatic structures.

1 Introduction

Automatic structures were introduced in [13, 15]. The idea goes back to the concept of automatic groups [8]. Roughly speaking, a structure is called automatic if
the elements of the universe can be represented as words from a regular language
and every relation of the structure can be recognized by a finite state automaton
with several heads that proceed synchronously. Automatic structures received
increasing interest during the last years [1, 3, 14, 16–18]. One of the main motivations for investigating automatic structures is the fact that every automatic
structure has a decidable first-order theory. On the other hand it is known that
there exist automatic structures with a nonelementary first-order theory [3]. This
motivates the search for subclasses of automatic structures for which the first-
order theory becomes elementary decidable. In this paper we will present such
a subclass, namely automatic structures of bounded degree, where the bounded
degree property refers to the Gaifman-graph of the structure. Using a method
of Ferrante and Rackoff [9] (see Section 3), we show in Section 4 that for every
automatic structure of bounded degree the first-order theory can be decided in
triply exponential alternating time with a linear number of alternations (Theorem 3). We are currently not able to match this upper bound by a sharp lower
bound. But in Section 6 we will construct an example of an automatic structure
of bounded degree such that the corresponding first-order theory has a lower
bound of doubly exponential time with a linear number of alternations (Theorem 5). Finally, in Section 7 we will briefly discuss the extension of our results
from Section 4 to tree automatic structures [2].

M.Y. Vardi and A. Voronkov (Eds.): LPAR 2003, LNAI 2850, pp. 346–360, 2003.

2   Preliminaries

General Notations. Let Γ be a finite alphabet and $w \in \Gamma^*$ be a finite word over Γ. The length of w is denoted by $|w|$. We also write $\Gamma^n = \{w \in \Gamma^* \mid n = |w|\}$ and $\Gamma^{\leq n} = \{w \in \Gamma^* \mid n \geq |w|\}$. Let us define $\exp(0, x) = x$ and $\exp(n + 1, x) = 2^{\exp(n,x)}$ for $x \in \mathbb{N}$. A computational problem is called *elementary* if it can be solved in time $\exp(c, n)$ for some constant $c \in \mathbb{N}$.

In this paper we will deal with alternating complexity classes, see [5, 19] for more details. Roughly speaking, an *alternating Turing-machine* is a nondeterministic Turing-machine, where the set of states is partitioned into existential and universal states. A configuration with a universal (resp. existential) state is accepting if every (resp. some) successor state is accepting. An alternation in a computation of an alternating Turing-machine is a transition from a universal state to an existential state or vice versa. For functions $t(n)$ and $a(n)$ with $a(n) \leq t(n)$ for all $n \geq 0$ let $\mathrm{ATIME}(a(n), t(n))$ denote the class of all problems that can be solved on an alternating Turing-machine in time $t(n)$ with at most $a(n)$ alternations. It is known that $\mathrm{ATIME}(t(n), t(n))$ is contained in $\mathrm{DSPACE}(t(n))$ if $t(n) \geq n$ [5].

Structures. The notion of a structure (or model) is defined as usual in logic. Here we only consider *relational structures*. Sometimes, we will also use constants, but a constant c can be always replaced by the unary relation $\{c\}$. Let us fix a relational structure $\mathcal{A} = (A, (R_i)_{i \in J})$, where $R_i \subseteq A^{n_i}$, $i \in J$. For $B \subseteq A$ we define the restriction $\mathcal{A}{\restriction}B = (B, (R_i \cap B^{n_i})_{i \in J})$. Given further constants $c_1, \dots, c_n \in A$, we write $(\mathcal{A}, c_1, \dots, c_n)$ for the structure $(A, (R_i)_{i \in J}, c_1, \dots, c_n)$.

The *Gaifman-graph* $G_{\mathcal{A}}$ of the structure $\mathcal{A}$ is the following undirected graph:

$$G_{\mathcal{A}} = (A, \{(a, b) \in A \times A \mid \bigvee_{i \in J} \exists (c_1, \dots, c_{n_i}) \in R_i \, \exists j, k : c_j = a \neq b = c_k\}).$$

Thus, the set of nodes is the universe of $\mathcal{A}$ and there is an edge between two elements, if and only if they are contained in some tuple belonging to one of the relations of $\mathcal{A}$. With $d_{\mathcal{A}}(a, b)$, where $a, b \in A$, we denote the distance between a and b in $G_{\mathcal{A}}$, i.e., it is the length of a shortest path connecting a and b in $G_{\mathcal{A}}$. For $a \in A$ and $r \geq 0$ we denote with $S_{\mathcal{A}}(r, a) = \{b \in A \mid d_{\mathcal{A}}(a, b) \leq r\}$ the r-sphere around a. If $\widetilde{a} = (a_1, \dots, a_n) \in A^n$ is a tuple, then $S_{\mathcal{A}}(r, \widetilde{a}) = \bigcup_{i=1}^{n} S_{\mathcal{A}}(r, a_i)$. The substructure of $\mathcal{A}$ that is induced by $S_{\mathcal{A}}(r, \widetilde{a})$ is denoted by $N_{\mathcal{A}}(r, \widetilde{a})$, i.e., $N_{\mathcal{A}}(r, \widetilde{a}) = \mathcal{A}{\restriction}S_{\mathcal{A}}(r, \widetilde{a})$. A *connected component* of the structure $\mathcal{A}$ is any induced substructure $\mathcal{A}{\restriction}C$, where C is a connected component of the Gaifman-graph $G_{\mathcal{A}}$. We say that the structure $\mathcal{A}$ has *bounded degree*, if its Gaifman-graph $G_{\mathcal{A}}$ has bounded degree, i.e., there exists a constant d such that every $a \in A$ is adjacent to at most d other nodes in $G_{\mathcal{A}}$.

First-Order Logic. For more details concerning first-order logic see e.g. [12]. Let us fix a structure $\mathcal{A} = (A, (R_i)_{i \in J})$, where $R_i \subseteq A^{n_i}$. The *signature of* $\mathcal{A}$ contains for each $i \in J$ a relation symbol of arity n_i that we denote without risk of confusion by R_i as well. Let $\mathbb{V}$ be a countable infinite set of variables, which evaluate to elements from the universe A. *First-order formulas* over the signature of $\mathcal{A}$ are constructed from the atomic formulas $x = y$ and $R_i(x_1, \ldots, x_{n_i})$, where $i \in J$ and $x, y, x_1, \ldots, x_{n_i} \in \mathbb{V}$, using Boolean connectives and quantifications over variables from $\mathbb{V}$. The notion of a free variable is defined as usual. The *quantifier-depth* of a formula ϕ is the maximal number of nested quantifiers in ϕ. A first-order formula without free variables is called a *first-order sentence*. If $\varphi(x_1, \ldots, x_n)$ is a first-order formula with free variables among $x_1, \ldots, x_n$ and $a_1, \ldots, a_n \in A$, then $\mathcal{A} \models \varphi(a_1, \ldots, a_n)$ means that φ evaluates to true in $\mathcal{A}$ when the free variable x_i evaluates to a_i. The *first-order theory* of $\mathcal{A}$, denoted by $\mathrm{FOTh}(\mathcal{A})$, is the set of all first-order sentences φ such that $\mathcal{A} \models \varphi$. Given a formula $\varphi(x_1, \ldots, x_n, y_1, \ldots, y_m)$ and $b_1, \ldots, b_m \in A$, $\varphi(x_1, \ldots, x_n, b_1, \ldots, b_m)^{\mathcal{A}}$ denotes the n-ary relation $\{(a_1, \ldots, a_n) \in A^n \mid \mathcal{A} \models \varphi(a_1, \ldots, a_n, b_1, \ldots, b_m)\}$. Let Σ be an arbitrary set of first-order sentences over some fixed signature $\mathcal{S}$. A *model* of Σ is a structure $\mathcal{A}$ with signature $\mathcal{S}$ such that $\mathcal{A} \models \psi$ for every $\psi \in \Sigma$. With $\mathrm{sat}(\Sigma)$ we denote the set of all first-order sentences ϕ over the signature $\mathcal{S}$ such that $\mathcal{A} \models \phi$ for some model $\mathcal{A}$ of Σ. The set of all sentences ϕ such that $\mathcal{A} \models \phi$ for every model $\mathcal{A}$ of Σ is denoted by $\mathrm{val}(\Sigma)$. Note that if Σ is *complete*, i.e., for every first-order sentence ϕ either $\phi \in \Sigma$ or $\neg\phi \in \Sigma$ (this holds in particular if $\Sigma = \mathrm{FOTh}(\mathcal{A})$ for some structure $\mathcal{A}$), then $\mathrm{sat}(\Sigma) = \mathrm{val}(\Sigma)$.

Let C be some complexity class. We say that C is a *hereditary lower bound* for a theory $\mathrm{FOTh}(\mathcal{A})$ if for every $\Sigma \subseteq \mathrm{FOTh}(\mathcal{A})$ neither $\mathrm{sat}(\Sigma)$ nor $\mathrm{val}(\Sigma)$ is in C [6]. Thus, in particular $\mathrm{FOTh}(\mathcal{A})$ does not belong to the class C.

Automatic Structures. See [3, 15] for more details concerning automatic structures. Let us fix $n \in \mathbb{N}$ and a finite alphabet Γ. Let $\# \notin \Gamma$ be an additional padding symbol. For words $w_1, \ldots, w_n \in \Gamma^*$ we define the *convolution* $w_1 \otimes w_2 \otimes \cdots \otimes w_n$, which is a word over the alphabet $\prod_{i=1}^{n}(\Gamma \cup \{\#\})$, as follows: Let $w_i = a_{i,1} a_{i,2} \cdots a_{i,k_i}$ with $a_{i,j} \in \Gamma$ and $k = \max\{k_1, \ldots, k_n\}$. For $k_i < j \le k$ define $a_{i,j} = \#$. Then

$$w_1 \otimes \cdots \otimes w_n = (a_{1,1}, \ldots, a_{n,1}) \cdots (a_{1,k}, \ldots, a_{n,k}).$$

Thus, for instance $aba \otimes bbabb = (a, b)(b, b)(a, a)(\#, b)(\#, b)$. An n-ary relation $R \subseteq (\Gamma^*)^n$ is called automatic if the language $\{w_1 \otimes \cdots \otimes w_n \mid (w_1, \ldots, w_n) \in R\}$ is a regular language.

Now let $\mathcal{A} = (A, (R_i)_{i \in J})$ be an arbitrary relational structure with finitely many relations, where $R_i \subseteq A^{n_i}$. A tuple (Γ, L, h) is called an *automatic presentation* for $\mathcal{A}$ if

- Γ is a finite alphabet,
- $L \subseteq \Gamma^*$ is a regular language,
- $h : L \to A$ is a surjective function,
- the relation $\{(u, v) \in L \times L \mid h(u) = h(v)\}$ is automatic, and
- the relation $\{(u_1, \ldots, u_{n_i}) \in L^{n_i} \mid (h(u_1), \ldots, h(u_{n_i})) \in R_i\}$ is automatic for every $i \in J$.

We say that $\mathcal{A}$ is *automatic* if there exists an automatic presentation for $\mathcal{A}$. The following result from [15] can be shown by induction on the structure of the formula φ.

Proposition 1 (cf [15]). *Let (Γ, L, h) be an automatic presentation for the structure $\mathcal{A}$ and let $\varphi(x_1, \ldots, x_n)$ be a first-order formula over the signature of $\mathcal{A}$. Then the relation $\{(u_1, \ldots, u_n) \in L^n \mid \mathcal{A} \models \varphi(h(u_1), \ldots, h(u_n))\}$ is automatic.*

This proposition implies the following result, which is one of the main motivations for investigating automatic structures.

Theorem 1 (cf [15]). *If $\mathcal{A}$ is automatic, then $\mathrm{FOTh}(\mathcal{A})$ is decidable.*

In [3] it was shown that even the extension of first-order logic, which allows to say that there are infinitely many x with $\phi(x)$, is decidable. On the other hand there are automatic structures with a nonelementary first-order theory [3]. For instance the structure $(\{0,1\}^*, s_0, s_1, \preceq)$, where $s_i(w) = wi$ for $w \in \{0,1\}^*$ and $i \in \{0,1\}$ and $\preceq$ is the prefix order on finite words, has a nonelementary first-order theory, see e.g. [6, Example 8.3]. In Section 4 we will show that for automatic structures of bounded degree this cannot happen: in this case the first-order theory is in $\mathrm{ATIME}(O(n), \exp(3, O(n)))$.

Let us end this section with two typical examples for automatic structures of bounded degree:

Transition Graphs of Machines like Turing-Machines or Counter Machines: Let $\mathcal{M}$ be such a machine, $\mathcal{C}(\mathcal{M})$ the set of all possible configurations of $\mathcal{M}$, and $\Rightarrow_\mathcal{M}$ the one-step transition relation between configurations. Then $(\mathcal{C}(\mathcal{M}), \Rightarrow_\mathcal{M})$ is the transition graph of $\mathcal{M}$ and easily seen to be automatic.

Cayley-Graphs of Automatic Groups [8] or more general *Cayley-graphs of automatic monoids of finite geometric type* [20]: Let $\mathcal{M} = (M, \circ)$ be a finitely generated monoid and Γ a finite generating set for $\mathcal{M}$. Then the Cayley-graph of $\mathcal{M}$ with respect to Γ is the structure $(M, (\{(x, x \circ a) \mid x \in M, a \in \Gamma\})_{a \in \Gamma})$. It can be viewed as a Γ-labeled directed graph: there is an a-labeled edge from x to y if and only if $y = x \circ a$. Automatic monoids [4] have the property that their Cayley-graphs are automatic, but in general these graphs may have unbounded degree (more precisely, a node may have unbounded indegree). On the other hand, if the Cayley-graph of $\mathcal{M}$ has bounded degree with respect to some finite generating set, then it is easy to see that this holds for every finite generating set of $\mathcal{M}$. In this case, the monoid $\mathcal{M}$ is of finite geometric type [20]. This is in particular the case for right-cancellative monoids and hence for groups.

Moreover, the class of automatic structures of bounded degree is closed under operations like for instance disjoint union or direct product [3].

3   The Method of Ferrante and Rackoff

In order to prove that the first-order theory of an automatic structure of bounded degree is elementary, we have to introduce a general method from [9].

Let us fix a structure $\mathcal{A}$ with universe A. Roughly speaking, Gaifman's Theorem [11] states that first-order logic only allows to express local properties of structures, see [7] for a recent account of this result. For our use, the following weaker statement is sufficient, which is an immediate consequence of the main theorem in [11].

Theorem 2 (cf. [11]). *Let* $\tilde{a} = (a_1, a_2, \ldots, a_k)$ *and* $\tilde{b} = (b_1, b_2, \ldots, b_k)$, *where* $a_i, b_i \in A$, *such that* $(N_{\mathcal{A}}(7^n, \tilde{a}), \tilde{a}) \cong (N_{\mathcal{A}}(7^n, \tilde{b}), \tilde{b})$.[1] *Then, for any first-order formula* $\varphi(x_1, \ldots, x_k)$ *of quantifier-depth at most* n, *we have* $\mathcal{A} \models \varphi(\tilde{a})$ *if and only if* $\mathcal{A} \models \varphi(\tilde{b})$.

A *norm function* on $\mathcal{A}$ is just a function $\lambda : A \rightarrow \mathbb{N}$. Let us fix a norm function λ on $\mathcal{A}$. We write $\mathcal{A} \models \exists x \leq n : \varphi$ in order to express that there exists $a \in A$ such that $\lambda(a) \leq n$ and $\mathcal{A} \models \varphi(a)$, and similarly for $\forall x \leq n : \varphi$. Let $H : \{(j, d) \in \mathbb{N} \times \mathbb{N} \mid j \leq d\} \rightarrow \mathbb{N}$ be a function such that the following holds: For all $j \leq d \in \mathbb{N}$, all $\tilde{a} = (a_1, a_2, \ldots, a_{j-1}) \in A^{j-1}$ with $\lambda(a_i) \leq H(i, d)$, and all $a \in A$, there exists $a_j \in A$ with $\lambda(a_j) \leq H(j, d)$ and

$$(N_{\mathcal{A}}(7^{d-j}, \tilde{a}, a), \tilde{a}, a) \cong (N_{\mathcal{A}}(7^{d-j}, \tilde{a}, a_j), \tilde{a}, a_j).$$

Then $\mathcal{A}$ is called *H-bounded* (with respect to the norm function λ). This definition is a slight variant of the definition in [9] that suits our needs much better than the original formulation. The following corollary to Theorem 2 was shown by Ferrante and Rackoff for their version of H-bounded structures.

Corollary 1 (cf. [9]). *Let* $\mathcal{A}$ *be a relational structure with universe* A *and norm* λ *and let* $H : \{(j, d) \in \mathbb{N} \times \mathbb{N} \mid j \leq d\} \rightarrow \mathbb{N}$ *be a function such that* $\mathcal{A}$ *is* H-*bounded. Then for any first-order formula* $\varphi \equiv Q_1 x_1 \, Q_2 x_2 \cdots Q_d x_d : \psi$ *where* ψ *is quantifier free and* $Q_i \in \{\exists, \forall\}$, *we have* $\mathcal{A} \models \varphi$ *if and only if*

$$\mathcal{A} \models Q_1 x_1 \leq H(1, d) \, Q_2 x_2 \leq H(2, d) \cdots Q_d x_d \leq H(d, d) : \psi.$$

Proof. For $j \leq d$, let ψ_j denote the formula $Q_j x_j \, Q_{j+1} x_{j+1} \cdots Q_d x_d : \psi$ and let φ_j stand for the sentence

$$Q_1 x_1 \leq H(1, d) \cdots Q_{j-1} x_{j-1} \leq H(j-1, d) \, \psi_j.$$

Thus, $\varphi_1 \equiv \varphi$. We show that $\mathcal{A} \models \varphi_j$ if and only if $\mathcal{A} \models \varphi_{j+1}$, which then proves the corollary.

Let $\tilde{a} = (a_1, \ldots, a_{j-1}) \in A^{j-1}$ with $\lambda(a_i) \leq H(i, d)$. First assume $Q_j = \exists$, i.e., $\psi_j \equiv \exists x_j : \psi_{j+1}$. If $\mathcal{A} \models \psi_j(\tilde{a})$, then there is $a \in A$ with $\mathcal{A} \models \psi_{j+1}(\tilde{a}, a)$. By our assumption on the norm function λ, we find $a_j \in A$ with $\lambda(a_j) \leq H(j, d)$ and

$$(N_{\mathcal{A}}(7^{d-j}, \tilde{a}, a), \tilde{a}, a) \cong (N_{\mathcal{A}}(7^{d-j}, \tilde{a}, a_j), \tilde{a}, a_j). \tag{1}$$

Since the quantifier depth of ψ_{j+1} is $d - j$, Theorem 2 implies $\mathcal{A} \models \psi_{j+1}(\tilde{a}, a_j)$. Thus, $\mathcal{A} \models (\exists x_j \leq H(j, d) : \psi_{j+1})(\tilde{a})$. If, conversely, $\mathcal{A} \models (\exists x_j \leq H(j, d) : \psi_{j+1})(\tilde{a})$, we have trivially $\mathcal{A} \models \psi_j(\tilde{a})$.

---

[1] Thus, there exists a bijection $f : S_{\mathcal{A}}(7^n, \tilde{a}) \rightarrow S_{\mathcal{A}}(7^n, \tilde{b})$, which preserves all relations from $\mathcal{A}$ and such that $f(a_i) = b_i$ for $1 \leq i \leq k$.

Assume now that $Q_j = \forall$, i.e., $\psi_j \equiv \forall x_j : \psi_{j+1}$. If $\mathcal{A} \models \psi_j(\tilde{a})$, then of course also $\mathcal{A} \models (\forall x_j \leq H(j,d) : \psi_{j+1})(\tilde{a})$. Now assume that

$$\mathcal{A} \models (\forall x_j \leq H(j,d) : \psi_{j+1})(\tilde{a}) \tag{2}$$

and let $a \in A$ be arbitrary. We have to show that $\mathcal{A} \models \psi_{j+1}(\tilde{a}, a)$. The case $\lambda(a) \leq H(j,d)$ is clear. Thus, assume that $\lambda(a) > H(j,d)$. Then there exists $a_j \in A$ with $\lambda(a_j) \leq H(j,d)$ and (1). Since $\lambda(a_j) \leq H(j,d)$, (2) implies $\mathcal{A} \models \psi_{j+1}(\tilde{a}, a_j)$. Finally, Theorem 2 implies $\mathcal{A} \models \psi_{j+1}(\tilde{a}, a)$. $\qquad\square$

4 An Upper Bound

In this section we apply the method of Ferrante and Rackoff in order to prove the following result:

Theorem 3. *If $\mathcal{A}$ is an automatic structure of bounded degree, then* $\mathrm{FOTh}(\mathcal{A})$ *can be decided in* $\mathrm{ATIME}(O(n), \exp(3, O(n)))$.

Proof. Fix an automatic presentation (Γ, L, h) for $\mathcal{A}$ and let the degree of the Gaifman-graph $G_{\mathcal{A}}$ be bounded by δ. By [15] we can assume that $h : L \to \mathcal{A}$ is injective and thus bijective. Hence, we may assume that L is the universe of $\mathcal{A}$ (and h is the identity function). Let E be the edge relation of $G_{\mathcal{A}}$. Since this relation is first-order definable in $\mathcal{A}$, Proposition 1 implies that the relation E is automatic. Let γ be the number of states of a finite automaton A_E for the language $\{u \otimes v \mid (u, v) \in E\}$.

Claim 1. If $(u, v) \in E$, then $|(|u| - |v|)| \leq \gamma$.

In order to deduce a contradiction, assume w.l.o.g. that $(u, v) \in E$ and $|v| - |u| > \gamma$. Then a simple pumping argument shows that the automaton A_E accepts an infinite number of words of the form $u \otimes w$ with $w \in L$ and $|w| \geq |v|$. It follows that the Gaifman-graph $G_{\mathcal{A}}$ has infinite degree, which is a contradiction.

Claim 2. Let $r \in \mathbb{N}$ and $u \in L$. Then there exists a finite automaton $A_{r,u}$ with $\exp(2, O(r))$ many states such that

$$L(A_{r,u}) = \{v \in L \mid (N_{\mathcal{A}}(r, u), u) \cong (N_{\mathcal{A}}(r, v), v)\}.$$

Thus, the automaton $A_{r,u}$ accepts a word $v \in L$ if and only if the r-sphere around v is isomorphic to the r-sphere around u (with u mapped to v). For the proof of Claim 2 first notice that since $G_{\mathcal{A}}$ has bounded degree, $|S_{\mathcal{A}}(r, u)| \in 2^{O(r)}$. We will use this in order to describe the finite substructure $N_{\mathcal{A}}(r, u)$ by a formula of size $2^{O(r)}$ over the signature of $\mathcal{A}$:

First, for $0 \leq n \leq \delta$ (δ bounds the degree of the Gaifman-graph) let the formula $\deg_n(x)$ express that the degree of x in the Gaifman-graph $G_{\mathcal{A}}$ is exactly n. Thus, $\deg_n(x)$ is a fixed first-order formula over the signature of $\mathcal{A}$. Next take $m = |S_{\mathcal{A}}(r, u)| \in 2^{O(r)}$ many variables $x_1, \ldots, x_m$, where x_i represents the element $u_i \in S_{\mathcal{A}}(r, u)$ ($u_i \neq u_j$ for $i \neq j$) and w.l.o.g. $u = u_1$. Then write down the conjunction of the following formulas, where R is an arbitrary relation of $\mathcal{A}$ and $0 \leq n \leq \delta$:

- $x_i \neq x_j$ for $i \neq j$,
- $R(x_{i_1}, \ldots, x_{i_n})$ if $(u_{i_1}, \ldots, u_{i_n}) \in R$,
- $\neg R(x_{i_1}, \ldots, x_{i_n})$ if $(u_{i_1}, \ldots, u_{i_n}) \notin R$, and
- $\deg_n(x_i)$ if the degree of u_i in $G_{\mathcal{A}}$ is precisely n.

Finally we quantify the variables $x_2, \ldots, x_m$ existentially. Let $\phi(x_1)$ be the resulting formula. It is easy to see that $\mathcal{A} \models \phi(v)$ if and only if $(N_{\mathcal{A}}(r, u), u) \cong (N_{\mathcal{A}}(r, v), v)$. Only the use of the formulas $\deg_n(x_i)$ needs some explanation. If we would omit these formulas, then $\mathcal{A} \models \phi(v)$ would only express that $(N_{\mathcal{A}}(r, u), u)$ is isomorphic to some induced substructure of $(N_{\mathcal{A}}(r, v), v)$ (with u mapped to v). But by fixing the degree of every x_i we exclude the possibility that there exists $y \in S_{\mathcal{A}}(r, x_1)$ with $y \neq x_i$ for all $1 \leq i \leq m$.[2]

Now the automaton $A_{r,u}$ is obtained by translating the formula $\phi(x_1)$ into an automaton using the standard construction for automatic structures, see e.g. [15]: each of the predicates listed above can be translated into an automaton of fixed size (recall that $\deg_n$ is a formula of fixed size). Since we have $2^{O(r)}$ such predicates, their conjunction can be described by a product automaton of size $\exp(2, O(r))$ working on $2^{O(r)}$ tracks (one for each variable x_i). Finally, the existential quantification over the variables $x_2, \ldots, x_m$ means that we have to project this automaton onto the track corresponding to the variable x_1. The resulting automaton is $A_{r,u}$, it still has $\exp(2, O(r))$ states and only one track. This proves Claim 2.

For the next claim we define the norm of an element $u \in L$ as its length $|u|$.

Claim 3. $\mathcal{A}$ is H-bounded by a function H satisfying $H(j, d) \in \exp(3, O(d))$ for all $j \leq d \in \mathbb{N}$.

Proof of Claim 3. By Claim 2, the size of the automaton $A_{r,u}$ is bounded by $\exp(2, c \cdot r)$, where c is some fixed constant. Define the function H by

$$H(j, d) = H(j - 1, d) + 2 \cdot \gamma \cdot \exp(2, c \cdot 7^{d-j}),$$

where γ is the constant from Claim 1 and $H(0, d)$ is set to 0. Note that $H(d, d) \in \exp(3, O(d))$. Now let $1 \leq j \leq d$ and $\tilde{u} = (u_1, \ldots, u_{j-1}) \in L^{j-1}$ with $|u_i| \leq H(i, d)$. Let furthermore $u \in L$ with $|u| > H(j, d)$. Thus, $|u| - |u_i| > 2 \cdot \gamma \cdot \exp(2, c \cdot 7^{d-j})$ for every $1 \leq i \leq j-1$, which by Claim 1 implies that the distance between u and every u_i in the Gaifman-graph is larger than $2 \cdot \exp(2, c \cdot 7^{d-j})$. Thus, the spheres $S_{\mathcal{A}}(7^{d-j}, \tilde{u})$ and $S_{\mathcal{A}}(7^{d-j}, u)$ are certainly disjoint and there is no edge in $G_{\mathcal{A}}$ between these two spheres.

---

[2] The standard solution of this problem is to say that there does not exist $y \notin \{x_1, \ldots, x_m\}$ which is in $G_{\mathcal{A}}$ adjacent to some x_i with $d_{\mathcal{A}}(x_1, x_i) \leq r - 1$, see e.g. the proof of [22, Corollary 4.9]. But this would introduce a quantifier alternation that we want to avoid.

Now consider the automaton $A_{7^{d-j},u}$ from Claim 2. It has at most $\exp(2, c \cdot 7^{d-j})$ states. Since u is accepted by $A_{7^{d-j},u}$, it accepts a word of length larger than $H(j,d) = H(j-1,d) + 2 \cdot \gamma \cdot \exp(2, c \cdot 7^{d-j})$. Thus, a simple pumping argument shows that $A_{7^{d-j},u}$ also accepts a word $u_j \in L$ with

$$H(j-1,d) + \gamma \cdot \exp(2, c \cdot 7^{d-j}) \leq |u_j| \leq H(j-1,d) + 2 \cdot \gamma \cdot \exp(2, c \cdot 7^{d-j}) = H(j,d)$$

(note that $\gamma \geq 1$). Since $|u_j| \geq H(j-1,d) + \gamma \cdot \exp(2, c \cdot 7^{d-j})$, Claim 1 implies that the distance between u_j and u_i $(1 \leq i < j)$ in the Gaifman-graph is at least $\exp(2, c \cdot 7^{d-j})$. Thus, also the spheres $S_A(7^{d-j}, \widetilde{u})$ and $S_A(7^{d-j}, u_j)$ are disjoint and there is no edge in G_A between these two spheres. Finally, since by definition of the automaton $A_{7^{d-j},u}$ we have $(N_A(7^{d-j}, u), u) \cong (N_A(7^{d-j}, u_j), u_j)$, we obtain $(N_A(7^{d-j}, \widetilde{u}, u), \widetilde{u}, u) \cong (N_A(7^{d-j}, \widetilde{u}, u_j), \widetilde{u}, u_j)$. Thus, A is H-bounded.

Now we can finish the proof of the theorem. Let

$$\varphi \equiv Q_1 x_1 Q_2 x_2 \cdots Q_d x_d : \psi(x_1, \ldots, x_d)$$

be a first-order sentence over the signature of A with d quantifiers $Q_i \in \{\exists, \forall\}$. Then, by Corollary 1, $A \models \varphi$ if and only if

$$A \models Q_1 x_1 \leq H(1,d) \, Q_2 x_2 \leq H(2,d) \cdots Q_d x_d \leq H(d,d) : \psi(x_1, \ldots, x_d). \quad (3)$$

Since $H(i,d) \in \exp(3, O(|\varphi|))$, this implies the statement of the theorem: In order to verify (3), we guess (either in an existential or a universal state) words $u_i \in L$ with $|u_i| \leq H(i,d)$. Every quantifier alternation leads to one alternation in our alternating Turing-machine. After having guessed every word u_i, we verify whether $A \models \psi(u_1, \ldots, u_d)$ by running the automata given by the automatic presentation of A. This needs deterministic triply exponential time. This concludes the proof.   □

Remark 1. The proof of Theorem 3 shows also another result. Assume that the premises of Theorem 3 are satisfied. If moreover the Gaifman-graph G_A has polynomial growth, i.e., for every $u \in L$, the size of the r-sphere $S_A(r, u)$ is bounded by $r^{O(1)}$, then the size of the automaton $A_{r,u}$ from Claim 2 is bounded by $2^{(n^{O(1)})}$. It follows that FOTh(A) can be decided in ATIME($O(n), \exp(2, n^{O(1)})$).

Remark 2. Theorem 3 can be easily generalized to a larger class of automatic structures: By Proposition 1, the class of automatic structures is closed under first-order interpretations (see [3] for the definition). Moreover, it is easy to see that a first-order interpretation between two structures leads to a polynomial time reduction between the corresponding first-order theories. Thus, every automatic structure that is first-order interpretable in an automatic structure of bounded degree has a first-order theory in ATIME($O(n), \exp(3, O(n))$). Moreover, the resulting class of automatic structures strictly contains the class of automatic structures of bounded degree.

5   The Method of Compton and Henson

In order to prove lower bounds for theories of automatic structures of bounded degree, we will use a method of Compton and Henson, which will be introduced in this section.

For every $i \geq 0$ let C_i be a class of structures over some signature $(R_j)_{j \in J}$, which is the same for all structures in $\bigcup_{i \geq 0} C_i$. Assume that R_j has arity n_j. Let furthermore $\mathcal{A}$ be an additional structure with universe A. We say that $(C_i)_{i \geq 0}$ has a *monadic interpretation* in the structure $\mathcal{A}$ [6] if for every $i \geq 0$ there exist formulas

$$\phi_i(x, r), \ (\psi_{i,j}(x_1, \ldots, x_{n_j}, r))_{j \in J}, \ \mu_i(x, r, s) \tag{4}$$

over the signature of $\mathcal{A}$ such that for every structure $\mathcal{B} \in C_i$ there exists $a \in A$ with:

- $\mathcal{B}$ is isomorphic to the structure $(\phi_i(x, a)^{\mathcal{A}}, (\psi_{i,j}(x_1, \ldots, x_{n_j}, a)^{\mathcal{A}})_{j \in J})$,
- $\mu_i(x, a, b)^{\mathcal{A}}$ is a subset of $\phi_i(x, a)^{\mathcal{A}}$ for every $b \in A$, and moreover every subset of $\phi_i(x, a)^{\mathcal{A}}$ is of the form $\mu_i(x, a, b)^{\mathcal{A}}$ for some $b \in A$.

Thus, by varying the parameter r in (4), we obtain all structures from C_i. In [6] it is also allowed to use a sequence $r_1, \ldots, r_k$ of parameters instead of a single parameter r. We will not need this more general notion of monadic interpretations.

In order to derive complexity lower bounds using monadic interpretations, one has to require that given $i \geq 0$ in unary notation (i.e., $\$^i$), the formulas in (4) can be computed efficiently. Following [6], we require that these formulas are *reset log-lin computable* from $\$^i$. This means that there exists a deterministic Turing-machine operating in linear time and logarithmic working space that computes (4) from $\$^i$. Moreover the input-head always moves one cell to the right except for k transitions (where k is some fixed constant), where the input-head is reset to the left end of the input. This technical extra condition was introduced in [6] in order to obtain a transitive notion of reducibility.[3] In the following we will always restrict implicitly to reset log-lin computable functions in the context of monadic interpretations. The following theorem was shown in [6, Thm. 7.2].

Theorem 4 (cf. [6]). *Let $T(n)$ be a time resource bound such that for some d between 0 and 1, $T(dn) \in o(T(n))$. Let C_n be the class of all structures of the form $(\{0, \ldots, m\}, \mathrm{plus})$ with $m < T(n)$ and $\mathrm{plus}(x, y, z)$ if and only if $x + y = z$. If there is a monadic interpretation of $(C_n)_{n \geq 0}$ in a structure $\mathcal{A}$, then for some constant c, $\mathrm{ATIME}(cn, T(cn))$ is a hereditary lower bound for $\mathrm{FOTh}(\mathcal{A})$.[4]*

---

[3] Reset log-lin reductions should not be confused with the log-lin reductions from [21], where it is only assumed that the output length is linearly bounded in the input length.

[4] From the proofs in [6] it is easy to see that this statement is also true if C_n is the singleton class $\{(\{0, \ldots, T(n) - 1\}, \mathrm{plus})\}$.

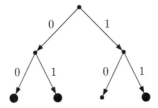

Fig. 1. A tree of height 2 with marked leafs

6   A Lower Bound

A binary tree of height n with marked leafs is a structure of the form

$$(\{0,1\}^{\leq n}, s_0, s_1, P),$$

where $s_i = \{(w, wi) \mid w \in \{0,1\}^*, |w| < n\}$ and $P \subseteq \{0,1\}^n$ is an additional unary predicate on the leafs. Let $\mathcal{T}_n$ be the set of all these structures and let $\mathcal{T} = \bigcup_{n \geq 0} \mathcal{T}_n$. Figure 1 shows a member of $\mathcal{T}_2$, where the leafs 00, 01, and 11 are marked.

Binary trees with additional unary predicates were used in [10] in order to derive lower bounds on the parametrized complexity of first-order model checking. Here we will use these trees in connection with the method of Compton and Henson from the preceding section. First we have to prove the following lemma:

Lemma 1. *There exists an automatic structure* $\mathcal{A} = (A, s_0, s_1, P)$ *with* $s_i \subseteq A \times A$ *and* $P \subseteq A$ *such that*

- *every connected component of* $\mathcal{A}$ *is isomorphic to a structure from* $\mathcal{T}$, *and*
- *every structure from* $\mathcal{T}$ *is isomorphic to a connected component of* $\mathcal{A}$.

Proof. Let $\Sigma = \{0, 1, \#, a, a', b, b'\}$ and let $A = (\{a, a', b, b'\}^*\{0, 1\}^*\#)^*$, which is regular. Let $s_0 \subseteq A \times A$ contain all pairs of the form

$$(u_1\alpha_1v_1\#u_2\alpha_2v_2\cdots\#u_n\alpha_nv_n\#,\ u_1\beta_1v_1\#u_2\beta_2v_2\cdots\#u_n\beta_nv_n\#)$$

such that

- $u_i \in \{a, a', b, b'\}^*$, $\alpha_i \in \{0, 1\}$, $\beta_i \in \{a, a', b, b'\}$, $v_i \in \{0, 1\}^*$, and
- if $\alpha_i = 0$ then $\beta_i = a$, and if $\alpha_i = 1$ then $\beta_i = b'$.

This relation is clearly automatic. The relation $s_1 \subseteq A \times A$ is defined analogously, we only replace the second condition above by $\beta_i = b$ if $\alpha_i = 1$ and $\beta_i = a'$ if $\alpha_i = 0$. Finally define the regular language $P \subseteq A$ by

$$P = \{w_1\#w_2\#\cdots w_n\# \in A \mid w_i \in \{a, b\}^* \text{ for some } i\}.$$

This finishes the definition of the automatic structure $\mathcal{A} = (A, s_0, s_1, P)$. It is easy to see that $\mathcal{A}$ has indeed the properties stated in the lemma. In Figure 2, it is shown, how the tree from Figure 1 is generated. Marked leafs are underlined. Note that the same tree is for instance also rooted at words from $\{a, b\}^*00\#\{a, b\}^*01\#\{a, b\}^*11\#(\{a, a', b, b'\}^*\{0, 1\}^{\geq 3}\#)^*$.

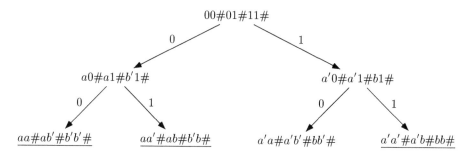

Fig. 2. A connected component from the structure $\mathcal{A}$ in Lemma 1

Lemma 2. *Let $\mathcal{A}$ be the structure from Lemma 1. Let $\mathcal{C}_n$ be the class of all structures of the form $(\{0,\ldots,m\},\text{plus})$ with $m < 2^{2^n}$. Then there exists a monadic interpretation of $(\mathcal{C}_n)_{n\geq 0}$ in the structure $\mathcal{A}$.*

Proof. Let $\mathcal{A} = (A, s_0, s_1, P)$ be the structure from Lemma 1. Given $a, b \in A$ we say that b is a successor of a or a is a predecessor of b if there exists a directed path in the relation $s_0 \cup s_1$ from a to b. This directed path defines a word over $\{0,1\}$ in the canonical way. If, e.g., $s_0(a,c)$ and $s_1(c,b)$, then the path from a to b defines the word 01.   □

Our aim is to construct formulas

$$\phi_n(x,r), \ \text{plus}_n(x,y,z,r), \ \mu_n(x,r,s)$$

that are reset log-lin computable from $\$^n$ and that witness a monadic interpretation of $(\mathcal{C}_n)_{n\geq 0}$ in the structure $\mathcal{A}$. First, we define a few auxiliary formulas that define relations in the structure $\mathcal{A}$. Let us fix $n \geq 0$. For every $0 \leq i \leq n$, the formula $\pi_i(x_0, x_1, y_0, y_1)$ expresses that x_0 is a predecessor of x_1, y_0 is a predecessor of y_1, and the unique path leading in $\mathcal{A}$ from x_0 to x_1 has length at most 2^i and is labeled with the same word over $\{0,1\}$ as the unique path leading in $\mathcal{A}$ from y_0 to y_1:

$$\pi_0(x_0, x_1, y_0, y_1) \equiv$$
$$(x_0 = x_1 \wedge y_0 = y_1) \vee (s_0(x_0,x_1) \wedge s_0(y_0,y_1)) \vee (s_1(x_0,x_1) \wedge s_1(y_0,y_1))$$
$$\pi_{i+1}(x_0, x_1, y_0, y_1) \equiv$$
$$\exists x_2 \exists y_2 \, \forall x \, \forall x' \, \forall y \, \forall y'$$
$$\left\{ \left(\begin{array}{l} (x = x_0 \wedge x' = x_2 \wedge y = y_0 \wedge y' = y_2) \vee \\ (x = x_2 \wedge x' = x_1 \wedge y = y_2 \wedge y' = y_1) \end{array} \right) \rightarrow \pi_i(x, x', y, y') \right\}$$

Here we use the usual trick for replacing two occurrences of π_i in the definition of π_{i+1} by a single occurrence of π_i [9], which is necessary in order to obtain formulas of linear size. It is easy to see that π_i is reset log-lin computable from $\$^i$ (see [6] for a class of reset log-lin computable formula sequences that contains the sequence $(\pi_i)_{i \geq 0}$. In the same way we can construct reset log-lin computable formulas, which express the following:

- $\preceq_i(x, y)$ if and only if x is a predecessor of y and the unique path from x to y has length at most 2^i. Instead of $\preceq_i(x, y)$ we will write $x \preceq_i y$. We write $x \prec_i y$ if $x \preceq_i y$ and $x \neq y$.
- $\mathrm{dist}_i(x_0, x_1, y_0, y_1)$ if and only if $x_0 \prec_i x_1$, $y_0 \prec_i y_1$, and the unique path from x_0 to x_1 has the same length as the unique path from y_0 to y_1. We write $\lambda_i(x, y, z)$ for $\mathrm{dist}_i(x, y, x, z)$.

We will represent an interval $\{0, \ldots, m\}$ with $m < 2^{2^n}$ by the leafs of a binary tree of height $k \leq 2^n$ rooted at the node $r \in A$.[5] The set of these nodes can be defined by the formula

$$\phi_n(x, r) \equiv r \preceq_n x \wedge \neg \exists y \{s_0(x, y) \vee s_1(x, y)\}$$

(thus, for most $a \in A$ we have $\phi_n(x, a)^A = \emptyset$). The word from $\{0, 1\}^k$ ($k \leq 2^n$) labeling the path from the root r to a leaf x can be interpreted as the binary coding of x. In order to define addition on these leafs let y be another leaf of the tree rooted at r. Let $u \neq r$ (resp. $v \neq r$) be a node on the unique path from r to x (resp. r to y). Assume that $\lambda_n(r, u, v)$ holds. We first define a formula $\psi_n(u, v, r)$, expressing that adding x and y leads to a carry over from a previous position at the position corresponding to u (and v). For $i \in \{0, 1\}$ let $\beta_i(x) \equiv \exists y : s_i(y, x)$. Then we can define $\psi_n(u, v, r)$ as follows:

$$\psi_n(u, v, r) \equiv \exists p \exists q \left\{ \begin{array}{l} \lambda_n(r, p, q) \wedge p \prec_n u \wedge q \prec_n v \wedge \beta_1(p) \wedge \beta_1(q) \wedge \\ \forall s \forall t \left\{ \left(\begin{array}{l} \lambda_n(r, s, t) \wedge \\ p \preceq_n s \prec_n u \wedge \\ q \preceq_n t \prec_n v \end{array} \right) \rightarrow (\beta_1(s) \vee \beta_1(t)) \right\} \end{array} \right\}$$

Using the formula

$$\varphi_n(u, v, w, r) \equiv \bigvee_{\substack{i,j,k \in \{0,1\} \\ i+j+1 \equiv k \bmod 2}} (\beta_i(u) \wedge \beta_j(v) \wedge \psi_n(u, v, r) \wedge \beta_k(w)) \vee$$

$$\bigvee_{\substack{i,j,k \in \{0,1\} \\ i+j \equiv k \bmod 2}} (\beta_i(u) \wedge \beta_j(v) \wedge \neg\psi_n(u, v, r) \wedge \beta_k(w))$$

we can define $\mathrm{plus}_n(x, y, z, r)$ as follows:

$$\mathrm{plus}_n(x, y, z, r) \equiv \phi_n(x, r) \wedge \phi_n(y, r) \wedge \phi_n(z, r) \wedge$$

$$\forall u \forall v \forall w \left\{ \left(\begin{array}{l} \lambda_n(r, u, v) \wedge \lambda_n(r, v, w) \wedge \\ u \preceq_n x \wedge v \preceq_n y \wedge w \preceq_n z \end{array} \right) \rightarrow \varphi_n(u, v, w, r) \right\}$$

---

[5] In this way we represent only those intervals whose size is a power of two, which is not crucial, see the footnote in Theorem 4.

Finally, arbitrary subsets of the set of leafs in the tree rooted at r can be defined by varying s in the following formula:

$$\mu_n(x, r, s) \equiv \phi_n(x, r) \wedge \exists y \{s \preceq_n y \wedge \pi_n(r, x, s, y) \wedge P(y)\}$$

This formula selects those leafs from the tree rooted at r such that the corresponding leaf in the tree rooted at s satisfies the unary predicate P.   □

Lemma 1 and 2 combined with Theorem 4 give us the main result of this section:

Theorem 5. *There exists an automatic structure $\mathcal{A}$ of bounded degree such that for some constant c,* $\mathrm{ATIME}(cn, \exp(2, cn))$ *is a hereditary lower bound for* $\mathrm{FOTh}(\mathcal{A})$.

7   Tree Automatic Structures

Tree automatic structures were introduced in [2], they generalize automatic structures. Let Γ be a finite alphabet. A *finite binary tree* over Γ is a mapping $t : \mathrm{dom}(t) \to \Gamma$, where $\mathrm{dom}(t) \subseteq \{0,1\}^*$ is finite and satisfies the following closure condition for all $w \in \{0,1\}^*$ and $i \in \{0,1\}$: if $wi \in \mathrm{dom}(t)$, then also $w \in \mathrm{dom}(t)$ and $wj \in \mathrm{dom}(t)$ for all $j \in \{0,1\}$. Those $w \in \mathrm{dom}(t)$ such that $w0 \notin \mathrm{dom}(t)$ (and hence also $w1 \notin \mathrm{dom}(t)$) are called the *leafs* of t. With T_Γ we denote the set of all finite binary trees over Γ. We define the *height* of the tree t by $\mathrm{height}(t) = \max\{|w| \mid w \in \mathrm{dom}(t)\}$. A *tree automaton* over Γ is a tuple $A = (Q, \delta, I, F)$, where Q is the finite set of states, $I \subseteq Q$ (resp. $F \subseteq Q$) is the set of initial (resp. final) states, and $\delta \subseteq Q \times Q \times \Gamma \times Q$. A *successful run* of A on a tree t is a mapping $\rho : \mathrm{dom}(t) \to Q$ such that: (i) $\rho(w) \in I$ if w is a leaf of t, (ii) $\rho(\epsilon) \in F$, and (iii) $(\rho(w0), \rho(w1), t(w), \rho(w)) \in \delta$ if $w \in \mathrm{dom}(t)$ is not a leaf. With $T(A)$ we denote the set of all finite binary trees t such that there exists a successful run of A on t. A set $L \subseteq T_\Gamma$ is called *recognizable* if there exists a finite tree automaton A with $L = T(A)$. Recognizable tree languages allow similar pumping arguments as regular word languages. More precisely, if A is a finite tree automaton with n states and $T(A) \neq \emptyset$, then $T(A)$ contains a tree of height at most n.

Let $t_1, \ldots, t_n \in T_\Gamma$. We define the convolution $t = t_1 \otimes \cdots \otimes t_n$, which is a finite binary tree over $\prod_{i=1}^n (\Gamma \cup \{\#\})$, as follows: $\mathrm{dom}(t) = \bigcup_{i=1}^n \mathrm{dom}(t_i)$ and for all $w \in \bigcup_{i=1}^n \mathrm{dom}(t_i)$ we define $t(w) = (a_1, \ldots, a_n)$, where $a_i = t_i(w)$ if $w \in \mathrm{dom}(t_i)$ and $a_i = \#$ otherwise. An n-ary relation R over T_Γ is called *tree-automatic* if the language $\{t_1 \otimes \cdots \otimes t_n \mid (t_1, \ldots, t_n) \in R\}$ is recognizable. Using this definition we can define the notion of a *tree automatic presentation* analogously to the word case in Section 2: A tree automatic presentation of the structure $\mathcal{A} = (A, (R_i)_{i \in J})$, where $R_i \subseteq A^{n_i}$, is a tuple (Γ, L, h) such that

- Γ is a finite alphabet,
- $L \subseteq T_\Gamma$ is recognizable,
- $h : L \to A$ is a surjective function,
- the relation $\{(u, v) \in L \times L \mid h(u) = h(v)\}$ is tree automatic, and

– the relation $\{(u_1, \ldots, u_{n_i}) \in L^{n_i} \mid (h(u_1), \ldots, h(u_{n_i})) \in R_i\}$ is tree automatic for every $i \in J$.

We say that $\mathcal{A}$ is *tree automatic* if there exists a tree automatic presentation for $\mathcal{A}$. An example of a tree automatic structure, which is not automatic is $(\mathbb{N}, \cdot)$, i.e., the natural numbers with multiplication [2].

Many results for automatic structures carry over to tree automatic structures. For instance the first-order theory of a tree automatic structure is still decidable [2]. Analogously to Theorem 3 we can prove the following result:

Theorem 6. *If $\mathcal{A}$ is a tree automatic structure of bounded degree, then* $\mathrm{FOTh}(\mathcal{A})$ *can be decided in* $\mathrm{ATIME}(O(n), \exp(4, O(n)))$.

Proof. We copy the proof of Theorem 3. Thus, let (Γ, L, h) be a tree automatic presentation for $\mathcal{A}$, where h can be assumed to be bijective (see [2, Theorem 3.4]). For an element $t \in L$, we define its norm as $\mathrm{height}(t)$. Then, analogously to Claim 1 in the proof of Theorem 3 it follows that if (t, t') is an edge in the Gaifman-graph $G_{\mathcal{A}}$, then $|\mathrm{height}(t) - \mathrm{height}(t')| \leq \gamma$. Then also Claim 2 and 3 from the proof of Theorem 3 carry over easily to the tree automatic case. Thus $\mathcal{A}$ is H bounded by a function H satisfying $H(j, d) \in \exp(3, O(d))$ for all $j \leq d \in \mathbb{N}$. We can conclude as in the word case. The only difference is that a binary tree, whose height is bounded by $\exp(3, O(n))$ needs $\exp(4, O(n))$ many bits for its specification in the worst case. This is the reason for the $\mathrm{ATIME}(O(n), \exp(4, O(n)))$ upper bound in the theorem. $\qquad\square$

8 Open Problems

Several open problems remain for (tree) automatic structures of bounded degree:

– Does there exist an automatic structure $\mathcal{A}$ of bounded degree such that $\mathrm{ATIME}(O(n), \exp(3, O(n)))$ is a (hereditary) lower bound for $\mathrm{FOTh}(\mathcal{A})$, or is $\mathrm{ATIME}(O(n), \exp(2, O(n)))$ always an upper bound? The same open problem remains for tree automatic structures, there the gap is even larger (between $\mathrm{ATIME}(O(n), \exp(2, O(n)))$ and $\mathrm{ATIME}(O(n), \exp(4, O(n)))$).
– Is there a tree automatic structure of bounded degree, which is not automatic? Without the restriction to structures of bounded degree this is true, see Section 7.

Acknowledgments

I am grateful to Dietrich Kuske for many fruitful discussions on the topic of this paper.

References

1. M. Benedikt, L. Libkin, T. Schwentick, and L. Segoufin. A model-theoretic approach to regular string relations. In *Proceedings of the 16th Annual IEEE Symposium on Logic in Computer Science (LICS'2001)*, pages 431–440. IEEE Computer Society Press, 2001.

2. A. Blumensath. Automatic structures. Diploma thesis, RWTH Aachen, 1999.
3. A. Blumensath and E. Grädel. Automatic structures. In *Proceedings of the 15th Annual IEEE Symposium on Logic in Computer Science (LICS'2000)*, pages 51–62. IEEE Computer Society Press, 2000.
4. C. M. Campbell, E. F. Robertson, N. Ruškuc, and R. M. Thomas. Automatic semigroups. *Theoretical Computer Science*, 250(1-2):365–391, 2001.
5. A. K. Chandra, D. C. Kozen, and L. J. Stockmeyer. Alternation. *Journal of the Association for Computing Machinery*, 28(1):114–133, 1981.
6. K. J. Compton and C. W. Henson. A uniform method for proving lower bounds on the computational complexity of logical theories. *Annals of Pure and Applied Logic*, 48:1–79, 1990.
7. H.-D. Ebbinghaus and J. Flum. *Finite Model Theory*. Springer, 1991.
8. D. B. A. Epstein, J. W. Cannon, D. F. Holt, S. V. F. Levy, M. S. Paterson, and W. P. Thurston. *Word processing in groups*. Jones and Bartlett, Boston, 1992.
9. J. Ferrante and C. Rackoff. *The Computational Complexity of Logical Theories*. Number 718 in Lecture Notes in Mathematics. Springer, 1979.
10. M. Frick and M. Grohe. The complexity of first-order and monadic second-order logic revisited. In *Proceedings of the 17th Annual IEEE Symposium on Logic in Computer Science (LICS'2002)*, pages 215–224. IEEE Computer Society Press, 2002.
11. H. Gaifman. On local and nonlocal properties. In J. Stern, editor, *Logic Colloquium '81*, pages 105–135. North Holland, 1982.
12. W. Hodges. *Model Theory*. Cambridge University Press, 1993.
13. B. R. Hodgson. On direct products of automaton decidable theories. *Theoretical Computer Science*, 19:331–335, 1982.
14. H. Ishihara, B. Khoussainov, and S. Rubin. Some results on automatic structures. In *Proceedings of the 17th Annual IEEE Symposium on Logic in Computer Science (LICS'2002)*, pages 235–244. IEEE Computer Society Press, 2002.
15. B. Khoussainov and A. Nerode. Automatic presentations of structures. In *LCC: International Workshop on Logic and Computational Complexity*, number 960 in Lecture Notes in Computer Science, pages 367–392, 1994.
16. B. Khoussainov and S. Rubin. Graphs with automatic presentations over a unary alphabet. *Journal of Automata, Languages and Combinatorics*, 6(4):467–480, 2001.
17. B. Khoussainov, S. Rubin, and F. Stephan. Automatic partial orders. To appear in *Proceedings of the 18th Annual IEEE Symposium on Logic in Computer Science (LICS'2003)*, 2003.
18. D. Kuske. Is Cantor's Theorem automatic. In *Proceedings of the 10th International Conference on Logic for Programming, Artificial Intelligence, and Reasoning (LPAR 2003), Almaty (Kazakhstan)*, 2003. this volume.
19. C. H. Papadimitriou. *Computational Complexity*. Addison Wesley, 1994.
20. P. V. Silva and B. Steinberg. A geometric characterization of automatic monoids. Technical Report CMUP 2000-03, University of Porto, 2001.
21. L. J. Stockmeyer and A. R. Meyer. Word problems requiring exponential time (preliminary report). In *Proceedings of the 5th Annual ACM Symposium on Theory of Computing (STOCS 73)*, pages 1–9. ACM Press, 1973.
22. W. Thomas. Languages, automata, and logic. In G. Rozenberg and A. Salomaa, editors, *Handbook of Formal Languages, volume III*, pages 389–455. Springer, 1997.

An Optimal Automata Approach
to LTL Model Checking of Probabilistic Systems

Jean-Michel Couvreur[1], Nasser Saheb[2], and Grégoire Sutre[2]

[1] LSV, ENS Cachan, Cachan, France,
couvreur@lsv.ens-cachan.fr|
[2] LaBRI, Université de Bordeaux I, Talence, France,
{saheb,sutre}@labri.fr

Abstract. Most verification problems on finite systems may be formulated and solved optimally using automata based techniques. Nonetheless LTL verification of (finite) probabilistic systems, i.e. deciding whether a probabilistic system almost surely satisfies an LTL formula, remains one of the few exceptions to this rule. As a matter of fact, existing automata-based solutions to this problem lead to double EXPTIME algorithms, while Courcoubetis and Yannakakis provide an optimal one in single EX-PTIME. In this study, we remedy this exception. Our optimal automata based method proceeds in two steps: we present a minimal translation from LTL to ω-automata and point out appropriate properties on these automata; we then show that checking whether a probabilistic system satisfies an ω-automaton with positive probability can be solved in linear time for this kind of automata. Moreover we extend our study to the evaluation of this probability. Finally, we discuss some experimentations with our implementation of these techniques: the ProbaTaf tool.

1 Introduction

Many techniques have been introduced to check algorithmically that a system satisfies a given set of required properties. These properties are usually specified by formulas in some temporal logic. The automata approach to model checking basically consists in (1) translating temporal formulas into some sort of automata and (2) checking that the behavior of the system (usually given as an infinite branching tree or as a set of linear infinite traces) is "accepted" by this automaton [5, 8]. This approach has been successfully applied by many authors in the area of verification, and it turns out that most verification problems on (non probabilistic) finite-state systems can be solved optimally using automata-based techniques.

Randomized algorithms are designed in numerous field of computer science in particular in the synchronization of concurrent processes and that of distributed computation. In fact, in these areas there are problems that admit no satisfactory deterministic algorithms and, therefore the randomization tool becomes a necessity. It would be desirable to develop efficient techniques for the verification of concurrent probabilistic systems.

M.Y. Vardi and A. Voronkov (Eds.): LPAR 2003, LNAI 2850, pp. 361–375, 2003.
© Springer-Verlag Berlin Heidelberg 2003

Verification of probabilistic systems usually consists in checking that a given property is satisfied with probability 1. The standard automata approach to model checking LTL formulas on probabilistic systems require a determinization of the Büchi ω-automata obtained from LTL formulas [7]. This leads to a doubly exponential time complexity. Courcoubetis and Yannakakis [1] developed another (non automata based) algorithm that runs in single exponential time and polynomial space, which is proven to be optimal.

We present in this paper an automata based method to model-checking LTL formulas on probabilistic systems, that meets the optimal complexity bounds of [1]. As in the non probabilistic case, we synchronize the system with the automaton corresponding to the (negation of) the LTL formula. However, we use a translation from LTL to ω-automata [3] that yields ω-automata with specific properties. We then exploit these properties to avoid determinization of these ω-automata, which is the crucial step leading to a doubly exponential time complexity in [7].

Basic concepts on measures over the set of infinite words and on probabilistic systems are introduced in Section 2. In Section 3, we introduce LTL formulas and the related ω-automata. The probabilistic verification and probabilistic satisfaction problems are discussed in Section 4. Probabilistic evaluation is the subject of Section 5. We finally show some experimentation on ProbaTaf in Section 6. In this short paper, proofs are omitted and left for a complete version of the paper.

2   Probabilistic Systems

2.1   Words and Measurability

Let Σ be an *alphabet* (a finite non empty set of *letters*). We write Σ^* (resp. Σ^ω) for the set of all *finite words* $a_0 a_1 \cdots a_n$ (resp. *infinite words* $a_0 a_1 \cdots a_n \cdots$) over Σ, and ε denotes the empty (finite) word. A *word* is any finite or infinite word, and we write Σ^∞ for the set of all words. A subset of Σ^∞ is called a *language*.

Given a finite word x and a word y, $x \cdot y$ (shortly written xy) is their *concatenation*. A finite word y is a *left factor* of a (finite or infinite) word x, written $y \leq x$, if $x = y \cdot z$ for some word z and moreover we write $z = y^{-1}x$. These operations are classically extended over languages: for any $X \subseteq \Sigma^*$ and $Y \subseteq \Sigma^\infty$, $X \cdot Y = \{xy \mid x \in X, y \in Y\}$ and $X^{-1}Y = \{x^{-1}y \mid x \in X, y \in Y\}$.

Recall that a σ-*algebra* on a set X is a subset $\mathcal{A}$ of $\mathbb{P}(X)$ such that $\emptyset \in \mathcal{A}$, $\mathcal{A}$ is closed under complementation, and $\mathcal{A}$ is closed under countable union. The pair $(X, \mathcal{A})$ is then called a *measurable space*, and elements of $\mathcal{A}$ are called *measurable sets*. Given two measurable spaces $(X_1, \mathcal{A}_1)$ and $(X_2, \mathcal{A}_2)$, a mapping $f : X_1 \to X_2$ is called a *measurable mapping* if the inverse image $f^{-1}(Y_2)$ of any measurable subset Y_2 of X_2 is a measurable subset of X_1.

A *measure* μ over a measurable space $(X, \mathcal{A})$ is any mapping from $\mathcal{A}$ to $\mathbb{R}^+$ such that (1) $\mu(\emptyset) = 0$, and (2) for any countable sequence $(A_n)_{n \in \mathbb{N}}$ of pairwise disjoint sets in $\mathcal{A}$, $\mu(\bigcup_{n \in \mathbb{N}} A_n) = \sum_{n \in \mathbb{N}} \mu(A_n)$. A *probability measure* over $(X, \mathcal{A})$ is a measure μ over $(X, \mathcal{A})$ such that $\mu(X) = 1$.

Given an alphabet Σ, we denote by $\mathcal{C}_\Sigma$ the set of all *basic cylindric sets* $w \cdot \Sigma^\omega$ with $w \in \Sigma^*$, and by $\mathcal{B}_\Sigma$ the σ-algebra (on Σ^ω) generated by $\mathcal{C}_\Sigma$. For the rest of the paper, $(\Sigma^\omega, \mathcal{B}_\Sigma)$ will be the considered *measurable space* (where Σ will depend on the context).

Proposition 2.1. *Let Σ be an alphabet. For any language $L \subseteq \Sigma^\omega$, the following assertions are equivalent:*

  i) L is measurable
  ii) $K \cdot L$ is measurable for every language $K \subseteq \Sigma^*$
  iii) $w \cdot L$ is measurable for some finite word $w \in \Sigma^*$
  iv) $K^{-1}L$ is measurable for every language $K \subseteq \Sigma^*$
  v) $a^{-1}L$ is measurable for every letter $a \in \Sigma$.

For the rest of this section, we consider two alphabets Σ_1 and Σ_2.

Definition 2.2. *For any mapping $f : \Sigma_1 \to \Sigma_2$, the ω-extension $\bar{f}$ of f is the mapping $\bar{f} : \Sigma_1^\omega \to \Sigma_2^\omega$ defined by $\bar{f}(a_0 a_1 \cdots a_n \cdots) = f(a_0)f(a_1) \cdots f(a_n) \cdots$.*

Proposition 2.3. *The ω-extension of any mapping $f : \Sigma_1 \to \Sigma_2$ is measurable.*

Notation. In the remaining of the paper, we will shortly write f instead of $\bar{f}$.

Theorem 2.4 (Measure Extension). *For any mapping $f : \mathcal{C}_\Sigma \to \mathbb{R}^+$, the following assertions are equivalent:*

  i) we have $f(w \cdot \Sigma^\omega) = \sum_{a \in \Sigma} f(wa \cdot \Sigma^\omega)$ for every $w \in \Sigma^*$
  ii) there exists a unique measure μ over $(\Sigma^\omega, \mathcal{B}_\Sigma)$ such that μ and f are equal on $\mathcal{C}_\Sigma$.

2.2   Finite Graphs

Probabilistic systems and ω-automata will later be defined as "enriched" finite labeled graphs. Transitions in these graphs will play a major role in the rest of the paper (for instance, the measurable space associated with a probabilistic system and acceptance conditions in ω-automata will be defined in terms of transitions). Hence we choose to represent transitions in graphs explicitly (instead of the usual representation of transitions as tuples). Moreover, thanks to this representation, probabilistic systems can contain two times the same transition with different probabilities attached to them.

A *finite labeled graph* (over Σ) is a 5-tuple $G = \langle V, T, \alpha, \beta, \lambda \rangle$ where V is a finite set of *vertices*, T is a finite set of *transitions*, $\alpha : T \to V$ and $\beta : T \to V$ are the *source* and the *target* mappings, and $\lambda : T \to \Sigma$ is a *transition labeling*.

Notation. We will use throughout the paper the following notations:

 – for any transition $t \in T$, the source $\alpha(t)$ of t is shortly written $^\bullet t$ and the target $\beta(t)$ of t is shortly written $t^\bullet$.
 – for any vertex $v \in V$, the set $\beta^{-1}(v)$ of transitions entering v is denoted by $^\bullet v$ and the set $\alpha^{-1}(v)$ of transitions leaving v is denoted by $v^\bullet$.

- we will also write $^\bullet X$ and $X^\bullet$ when $X \subseteq V$ or $X \subseteq T$: $^\bullet X$ and $X^\bullet$ are then defined as expected (e.g. $^\bullet X = \{^\bullet x \mid x \in X\}$ if $X \subseteq T$).

The *transition relation* $\to$ of G is the relation on V defined by: $v \to v'$ if $v^\bullet \cap {}^\bullet v' \neq \emptyset$. We denote by $\xrightarrow{+}$ (resp. $\xrightarrow{*}$) the transitive closure of $\to$ (resp. the reflexive and transitive closure of $\to$). Observe that $\xrightarrow{*}$ is a preorder on V. A *finite path* (resp. *infinite path*) in G is any non empty finite word $\rho = t_0 t_1 \cdots t_n$ (resp. any infinite word $\rho = t_0 t_1 \cdots t_n \cdots$) over T such that $t_i^\bullet = {}^\bullet t_{i+1}$ for all $i \leq n - 1$ (resp. for all $i \in \mathbb{N}$). Moreover, we say that ρ is a finite (resp. infinite) path *originating from* v_0, where $v_0 = {}^\bullet t_0$. We write $Path^*(G)$ (resp. $Path^*(G,v)$, $Path^\omega(G)$, $Path^\omega(G,v)$) for the set of all finite paths (resp. finite paths from v, infinite paths, infinite paths from v) in G. The sets $Trace^*(G)$ of all *finite traces*, $Trace^*(G,v)$ of all *finite traces from* v, $Trace^\omega(G)$ of all *infinite traces* and $Trace^\omega(G,v)$ of all *infinite traces from* v are the image under λ of the corresponding sets of infinite paths (e.g. $Trace^*(G) = \lambda(Path^*(G))$).

Proposition 2.5. *Given a finite labeled graph G and a vertex v of G, the sets $Path^\omega(G)$, $Path^\omega(G,v)$, $Trace^\omega(G)$ and $Trace^\omega(G,v)$ are measurable.*

A *strongly connected component* (shortly *SCC*) in G is any equivalence class for the equivalence relation $\overset{*}{\leftrightarrow}$ on V defined by: $v \overset{*}{\leftrightarrow} v'$ if $v \xrightarrow{*} v'$ and $v' \xrightarrow{*} v$. Given a vertex v, we write $SCC(v)$ for the SCC containing v (in other words $SCC(v)$ is the equivalence class of v). We denote by $SCC(G)$ the set of all SCCs in G (in other words $SCC(G)$ is the quotient set $V/\overset{*}{\leftrightarrow}$). Observe that $\xrightarrow{*}$ is a partial order on $SCC(G)$. An SCC C is called *maximal* when it is maximal with respect to $\xrightarrow{*}$.

Given a function $f : X \to Y$ and a subset $X' \subseteq X$, we denote by $f_{|X'}$ the *restriction of* f *to* X'. Given a subset $V' \subseteq V$, the *restriction of* G *to* V' is the graph $G_{|V'} = \langle V', T', \alpha', \beta', \lambda' \rangle$ where $T' = {}^\bullet V' \cap V'^\bullet$, $\alpha' = \alpha_{|V'}$, $\beta' = \beta_{|V'}$ and $\lambda' = \lambda_{|V'}$.

We will use finite labeled graphs to define ω-automata and probabilistic systems. Vertices of an ω-automaton (resp. probabilistic system) will be called *locations* (resp. *states*) and they will be denoted by $q, q_0, q_1, \ldots$ (resp. $s, s_0, s_1, \ldots$).

2.3   Probabilistic Systems

A *probabilistic system* (over Σ) is a 7-tuple $M = \langle S, T, \alpha, \beta, \lambda, P_0, P \rangle$ where:

1. $\langle S, T, \alpha, \beta, \lambda \rangle$ is a finite labeled graph over Σ, and
2. $P_0 : S \to [0,1]$ is an *initial probability distribution* satisfying $\sum_{s \in S} P_0(s) = 1$,
3. $P : T \to]0,1]$ is a *transition probability function* satisfying $\sum_{t \in s^\bullet} P(t) = 1$, for all $s \in S$.

Observe that the third condition above enforces every state to be the source of at least one transition (there is no "deadlock state").

Following Theorem 2.4, we define μ_M as the unique *probability measure* over $(T^\omega, \mathcal{B}_T)$ defined on basic cylindric sets by:

1. $\mu_M(T^\omega) = 1$, and
2. for any non empty word $t_0 t_1 \cdots t_n \in T^*$,

$$\mu_M(t_0 t_1 \cdots t_n \cdot T^\omega) = \begin{cases} P_0(\bullet t_0) P(t_0) P(t_1) \cdots P(t_n) \text{ if } t_0 t_1 \cdots t_n \in Path^*(M) \\ 0 \text{ otherwise.} \end{cases}$$

For the rest of the paper, $(T^\omega, \mathcal{B}_T, \mu_M)$ will be the considered *probability space*.

Proposition 2.6. *We have* $\mu_M(Path^\omega(M)) = 1$.

The states $s \in S$ such that $P_0(s) > 0$ are called *initial states*. Given a state s, we denote by $M[s]$ the probabilistic system M with s as unique initial state (i.e. the initial probability distribution P_0' of $M[s]$ is such that $P_0'(s) = 1$). The following observation easily follows from the uniqueness of μ_M:

Proposition 2.7. *For every measurable language* $L \subseteq T^\omega$, *we have:*

$$\mu_M(L) = \sum_{s \in S_0} P_0(s) \cdot \mu_{M[s]}(L).$$

Proposition 2.8. *For any state s, we have* $\mu_{M[s]}(Path^\omega(M, s)) = 1$.

Proposition 2.9. *For every state s and for every measurable language* $L \subseteq T^\omega$, *we have:*

$$\mu_{M[s]}(L) = \sum_{t \in s^\bullet} P(t) \cdot \mu_{M[t^\bullet]}(t^{-1}L).$$

Lemma 2.10. *Let* $K \subseteq T^*$. *If there is* $k \in \mathbb{N}$ *such that for all* $\sigma \in Path^*(M)$ *we have* $\sigma \cdot \sigma' \in K \cdot T^*$ *for some* $\sigma' \in T^k$, *then we have* $\mu_M(K \cdot T^\omega) = 1$.

The two following propositions follow from Lemma 2.10, and state strong equity properties of (finite) probabilistic systems: (1) a path ends almost surely in a maximal SCC, and (2) an infinite path in a maximal SCC visits almost surely infinitely often all finite paths of the SCC.

Proposition 2.11. *Let* $Path_{max}^*$ *denote the set of all finite paths ending in a maximal SCC. We have* $\mu_M(Path_{max}^* \cdot T^\omega) = 1$.

Proposition 2.12. *Let ρ be a finite path contained in some maximal SCC C, and let $s \in C$. We have* $\mu_{M[s]}((T^* \cdot \rho)^\omega) = 1$.

3   Temporal Properties

3.1   LTL

We review the basic definitions of *linear temporal logic* (LTL). Formulas in LTL are build from letters of a given alphabet Σ, the boolean operators, the unary temporal operator X (Next) and the binary temporal operator U (Until). The formulas in LTL are interpreted over infinite words in Σ^ω. For an infinite word $w = w_0 \cdot w_1 \cdots$ and a position i, we define the satisfaction of a formula f by w at position i (denoted $w, i \models f$) inductively on the structure of f as follows:

- $w, i \models a$ iff $w_i = a$,
- $w, i \models f \vee g$ iff $w, i \models f$ or $w, i \models g$,
- $w, i \models \neg f$ iff not $w, i \models f$,
- $w, i \models Xf$ iff $w, i+1 \models f$,
- $w, i \models fUg$ iff for some $j \geq i$, $w, i \models g$ and for all k, $j > k \geq i$, $w, k \models f$.

We say that a word w *satisfies* a formula f, denoted $w \models f$, iff $w, 0 \models f$. The set of all infinite words satisfying f, called the *language of f*, is denoted $L(f)$.

Usual boolean constants and connectives are defined classically (e.g. *true* is defined as $a \vee \neg a$ for some given letter $a \in \Sigma$).

3.2   Automata on Infinite Words

An ω-*automaton* (over Σ) is a 7-tuple $A = \langle Q, T, \alpha, \beta, \lambda, Q_0, Acc \rangle$ where:

1. $\langle Q, T, \alpha, \beta, \lambda \rangle$ is a finite labeled graph over Σ, and
2. $Q_0 \subseteq Q$ is a set of *initial locations*, and
3. $Acc \subseteq 2^T$ is an *acceptance condition*.

A *run* of A over an infinite word $w \in \Sigma^\omega$ is an infinite path ρ from some initial location $q_0 \in Q_0$ such that $\lambda(\rho) = w$. Acceptance of runs is defined in terms of limits of transition sets. Given a run $\rho = t_0 t_1 \cdots t_n \cdots$ (over some infinite word), the set $lim(\rho)$ of all transitions that appear infinitely often in ρ is defined by $lim(\rho) = \bigcap_{n \in \mathbb{N}} \{t_i \mid i \geq n\}$. A run ρ is *accepting* if $lim(r) \in Acc$.

An infinite word $w \in \Sigma^\omega$ is *accepted* by A if there exists an accepting run ρ over w. The set of all infinite words accepted by A, called the *language of A*, is denoted $L(A)$. Given an ω-automaton A and a state q, we denote $A[q]$ the ω-automaton A with q as unique initial location. Observe that $L(A) = \bigcup_{q \in Q_0} L(A[q])$. If $Acc = 2^T$ then we have $L(A[q]) = Trace^\omega(A, q)$ for all $q \in Q_0$.

Recall that languages of ω-automata are measurable:

Theorem 3.1 ([7]). *For any ω-automaton A, the language $L(A)$ is a measurable subset of Σ^ω.*

We then deduce that the set of infinite paths (of a probabilistic system) satisfying an LTL formula is measurable, and hence its probability is well defined.

Corollary 3.2. *Given an ω-automaton A and a probabilistic system M, the set of infinite paths of M "accepted" by A (i.e. $Path^\omega(M) \cap \lambda^{-1}(L(A))$) is a measurable subset of T^ω.*

Probabilistic verification can be applied efficiently only when the considered ω-automata fulfill some structural properties. We will in particular consider upward closed acceptance conditions: an acceptance condition $Acc \subseteq 2^T$ is said to be *upward closed* if for every $U \in Acc$ we have $U' \in Acc$ for every $U' \supseteq U$. Observe that the usual Büchi and multi-Büchi acceptance conditions are upward closed. Local properties on the automaton's graph will also be helpful.

- A is *deterministic* if for every $t_1, t_2 \in T$ such that $^\bullet t_1 = {}^\bullet t_2$ and $\lambda(t_1) = \lambda(t_2)$ we have $t_1 = t_2$.

- A is *unambiguous* if for every $t_1, t_2 \in T$ such that ${}^\bullet t_1 = {}^\bullet t_2$ and $\lambda(t_1) = \lambda(t_2)$ we have $t_1 = t_2$ or $L(A[t_1{}^\bullet]) \cap L(A[t_2{}^\bullet]) = \emptyset$.
- A is *separated* if for every $q_1, q_2 \in Q$ such that $q_1 \neq q_2$ we have $L(A[q_1]) \cap L(A[q_2]) = \emptyset$.
- A is *transition duplicate free* if for every $t_1, t_2 \in T$ such that ${}^\bullet t_1 = {}^\bullet t_2$, $t_1{}^\bullet = t_2{}^\bullet$ and $\lambda(t_1) = \lambda(t_2)$ we have $t_1 = t_2$.

Given a subset $Q' \subseteq Q$, the *restriction of A to Q'* is the ω-automaton $A_{|Q'} = \langle Q', T', \alpha', \beta', \lambda', Q'_0, Acc' \rangle$ where $T' = {}^\bullet V' \cap V'{}^\bullet$, $\alpha' = \alpha_{|V'}$, $\beta' = \beta_{|V'}$, $\lambda' = \lambda_{|V'}$, $Q'_0 = Q_0 \cap Q'$ and $Acc' = \{X \subseteq T' \mid X \in Acc\}$. We say that A is *deterministic on Q'* (resp. *unambiguous on Q', separated on Q'*) if $A_{|Q'}$ is deterministic (resp. unambiguous, separated).

Proposition 3.3. *Let A be an ω-automaton. The three following assertions hold:*

  i) if A is deterministic then A is unambiguous,
  ii) if A is separated and transition duplicate free then A is unambiguous.

3.3   From LTL to Automata

We briefly present an adaptation of a translation from LTL to ω-automata given in [3]. This method produces ω-automata which are unambiguous, separated, and with upward closed acceptance conditions. The construction described here is slightly different than the classical ones (as [8]) by the notion of closure of a formula (interesting sub formulas): it contains only formulas associated to temporal operators. As a result, our technique produces automata with only $O(2^{|cl(f)|})$ states and $O(|\,\Sigma\,| \cdot 2^{|cl(f)|})$ transitions; this point is crucial to state the time complexity of the probabilistic verification.

Let f be an LTL formula. We define the *closure* of f as follows:

$$cl(a) = \emptyset \text{ when } a \in \Sigma$$
$$cl(\neg f) = cl(f)$$
$$cl(f \vee g) = cl(f) \cup cl(g)$$
$$cl(Xf) = \{f\} \cup cl(f)$$
$$cl(fUg) = \{fUg\} \cup cl(f) \cup cl(g).$$

Any LTL formula g can be expended as a boolean combination of letters and next formulas (Xh with $h \in cl(g)$). Letters represent what has to be true immediatly, and next formulas represent what has to be true in the next state. The fundamental assertion, which is used for this expansion, is: $gUh \equiv h \vee (g \wedge X(gUh))$. Based on this principle, we define, for any subformula g of f, the next predicate $\Phi_g(b, v)$, with $b \in \Sigma$ and $v \in 2^{cl(f)}$ as follows:

$$\Phi_a(b, v) = \mathrm{P}_a(b, v) \text{ when } a \in \Sigma$$
$$\Phi_{\neg g}(b, v) = \neg \Phi_g(b, v)$$
$$\Phi_{g \vee h}(b, v) = \Phi_g(b, v) \vee \Phi_h(b, v)$$
$$\Phi_{Xg}(b, v) = \mathrm{Next}_g(b, v)$$
$$\Phi_{gUh}(b, v) = \Phi_h(b, v) \vee (\Phi_g(b, v) \wedge \mathrm{Next}_{gUh}(b, v))$$

where $P_a(b, v)$ and $\text{Next}_g(b, v)$ are two predicates defined by: $P_a(b, v) = (a = b)$ and $\text{Next}_g(b, v) = g \in v$.

The interpretation of next predicate is made clear with the following proposition.

Lemma 3.4. *Let* $w = a_0 a_1 \cdots a_i \cdots$ *be an infinite word over* Σ. *Then, for any subformula* g *of* f, *and for any position* i:

$$w, i \models g \quad \text{iff} \quad \Phi_g(a_i, \{h \in cl(f) \mid w, i+1 \models h\}) \text{ is satisfied.}$$

For the automaton construction, each location is labelled by a set of formulas, and each transition is designed using the next predicate in accordance with lemma 3.4. Moreover, the acceptance takes into account the fair constraint of the "until" formulas. Given an LTL formula f, we define the ω-automaton $A_f = \langle Q, T, \alpha, \beta, \lambda, Q_0, Acc \rangle$ as follows:

- $Q = \{f\} \cup 2^{cl(f)}$,
- $T = \{(f, a, v) \in \{f\} \times \Sigma \times 2^{cl(f)} \mid \Phi_f(a, v)\} \cup$
  $\{(u, a, v) \in 2^{cl(f)} \times \Sigma \times 2^{cl(f)} \mid \forall g \in cl(f), g \in u \text{ iff } \Phi_g(a, v)\}$,
- for all $(u, a, v) \in T$, $\alpha(u, a, v) = u$, $\beta(u, a, v) = v$, and $\lambda(u, a, v) = a$,
- $Q_0 = \{f\}$,
- for all $R \subseteq T$, $R \in Acc$ if $R \cap Acc_{gUh} \neq \emptyset$ for every $gUh \in cl(f)$, where
  $Acc_{gUh} = \{(u, a, v) \in T \mid u \in 2^{cl(f)} \wedge (gUh) \in u \Rightarrow \Phi_h(a, v)\}$.

Proposition 3.5. *For every LTL formula* f, *we have* $L(f) = L(A_f)$. *Moreover,* A_f *is unambiguous, separated on each SCC, and has an upward closed acceptance condition.*

The acceptance condition Acc of A_f is entirely defined by the sets Acc_{gUh} with $gUh \in cl(f)$. Hence, in the following proposition, the size of Acc is defined as the size of these sets.

Proposition 3.6. *For every LTL formula* f, *the size of* $A(f)$ *and its computation time are in* $O(|\Sigma| \cdot |cl(f)| \cdot 2^{|cl(f)|})$.

4   Probabilistic Verification

This section presents our optimal automata based approach to verification of probabilistic systems.

Linear time probabilistic verification consists in checking that the set of all paths in a given probabilistic system almost surely satisfies a given (linear time) specification. Formally, the *LTL probabilistic verification problem* (resp. *ω-regular probabilistic verification problem*) is the set of all pairs (M, f) (resp. (M, A)) where M is a probabilistic system and f is an LTL formula (resp. A is an ω-automaton) such that $\mu_M(Path^\omega(M) \cap \lambda_M^{-1}(L(f))) = 1$ (resp. such that $\mu_M(Path^\omega(M) \cap \lambda_M^{-1}(L(A))) = 1$).

Automata based approaches to verification usually consider the dual problem, where the negation of the specification is considered. We follow the same principles, and we reduce the probabilistic verification problem to the so-called probabilistic satisfaction problem, which consists in checking that the set of all paths in a given probabilistic system satisfies a given (linear time) specification with positive probability. Formally, the *LTL probabilistic satisfaction problem* (resp. *ω-regular probabilistic satisfaction problem*) is the set of all pairs (M, f) (resp. (M, A)) where M is a probabilistic system and f is an LTL formula (resp. A is an ω-automaton) such that $\mu_M(Path^\omega(M) \cap \lambda_M^{-1}(L(f))) > 0$ (resp. such that $\mu_M(Path^\omega(M) \cap \lambda_M^{-1}(L(A))) > 0$).

4.1 Synchronized Product

Classical automata based verification methods first construct the synchronized product of the system and of the (negated) specification ω-automaton. This synchronized product is basically a cartesian product of the two graphs, keeping only the transition pairs having the same label; viewed as an ω-automaton over transitions of the system, it recognizes precisely the set of all infinite paths in the system which fulfill the specification ω-automaton. We give the definition of the synchronized product, recall some basic properties and fix some notations.

From now on, we will consider a probabilistic system $M = \langle S, T_M, \alpha_M, \beta_M, \lambda_M, P_0, P \rangle$ and an ω-automaton $A = \langle Q, T_A, \alpha_A, \beta_A, \lambda_A, Q_0, Acc \rangle$.

The *projection onto M* (resp. *projection onto A*) is the mapping π_M (resp. π_A) defined on $(S \times Q) \cup (T_M \times T_A)$ by $\pi_M(z_M, z_A) = z_M$ (resp. $\pi_A(z_M, z_A) = z_A$).

Definition 4.1. *The* synchronized product *of M and A is the ω-automaton $M \otimes A = \langle S \times Q, T_\otimes, \alpha_\otimes, \beta_\otimes, \lambda_\otimes, S_0 \times Q_0, Acc_\otimes \rangle$ where:*

- $T_\otimes$ *is defined by* $T_\otimes = \{(t_M, t_A) \in T_M \times T_A \mid \lambda_M(t_M) = \lambda_A(t_A)\}$, *and*
- $\alpha_\otimes$ *and* $\beta_\otimes$ *are defined by* ${}^\bullet(t_M, t_A) = ({}^\bullet t_M, {}^\bullet t_A)$ *and* $(t_M, t_A)^\bullet = (t_M{}^\bullet, t_A{}^\bullet)$, *and*
- $\lambda_\otimes$ *is the restriction of π_M to $T_\otimes$, and*
- $Acc_\otimes$ *is equal to* $\{U \subseteq T_\otimes \mid \pi_A(U) \in Acc\}$.

Remark 4.2. As expected, we have the following equality:

$$L(M \otimes A) = Path^\omega(M) \cap \lambda_M^{-1}(L(A)).$$

We want to determine whether M satisfies A with positive probability, i.e. whether $\mu_M(L(M \otimes A)) > 0$. The language $L(M \otimes A)$ can be written as a union of $L(M \otimes A[s, q])$ where (s, q) are initial locations. Hence, the probabilistic satisfaction problem reduces to checking whether $\mu_M(L(M \otimes A[s, q])) > 0$ for some $(s, q) \in S_0 \times Q_0$.

For convenience, we will shortly write $L(s, q)$ instead of $L(M \otimes A[s, q])$, and we define the mapping $V : S \times Q \to [0, +\infty[$ as $V(s, q) = \mu_{M[s]}(L(s, q))$. Note that we also have: $L(s, q) = Path^\omega(M[s]) \cap \lambda^{-1}(L(A[q]))$. Moreover, as $M \otimes A$ is an ω-automaton, it is readily seen that for all $(s, q) \in S \times Q$, we have:

$$L(s, q) = \bigcup_{(t_M, t_A) \in (s,q)^\bullet} t_M \cdot L(t_M{}^\bullet, t_A{}^\bullet).$$

We deduce from the previous equality that $V(s, q) > 0$ iff $V(s', q') > 0$ for some (s', q') reachable from (s, q) (i.e. $(s, q) \xrightarrow{*} (s', q')$). Hence, we obtain that $V^{-1}(]0, +\infty[)$ is downward closed w.r.t. $\xrightarrow{*}$, and each SCC is either contained in $V^{-1}(]0, +\infty[)$ or contained in $V^{-1}(\{0\})$. We come to the following fundamental definitions:

Definition 4.3. *An SCC C of $M \otimes A$ is called:*

- null *if $C \subseteq V^{-1}(\{0\})$,*
- persistent *if C is an SCC which is maximal among the non null SCCs,*
- transient *otherwise.*

It turns out that probabilistic verification reduces to checking the existence of a reachable non null SCC, or, equivalently, a reachable persistent SCC. Unfortunately, these notions are not *local*: for instance, persistence of a given SCC depends on the other SCCs of $M \otimes A$. In order to perform probabilistic verification efficiently, we investigate local notions on SCCs.

Given a SCC C of $M \otimes A$ and a location $(s, q) \in C$, we define $L_C(s, q)$ and $V_C(s, q)$ by: $L_C(s, q) = L((M \otimes A)_{|C}[s, q])$ and $V_C(s, q) = \mu_{M[s]}(L_C(s, q))$.

Definition 4.4. *An SCC C of $M \otimes A$ is called* locally positive *if $V_C(s, q) > 0$ for all $(s, q) \in C$.*

Remark 4.5. Any SCC C is locally positive iff $V_C(s, q) > 0$ for some $(s, q) \in C$.

It is readily seen that every persistent SCC is locally positive. The converse does not hold, however every locally positive SCC is non null. Hence, we come to the following proposition:

Proposition 4.6. *We have $\mu_M(L(M \otimes A)) > 0$ iff there exists a locally positive SCC C that is reachable from an initial location of $M \otimes A$.*

4.2   Probabilistic Satisfaction

As locally positive SCCs play a major role in probabilistic verification, we look for an easily checkable characterization of locally positive SCCs. This characterization is based on two properties on SCCs: *completeness* and *acceptance*. We show that when A is unambiguous on each SCC or has an upward closed acceptance condition, then for any SCC C of $M \otimes A$, C is locally positive iff C is complete and accepted. We then prove that completeness and acceptance can be checked efficiently when A is unambiguous and separated (which is the case for ω-automata obtained through our translation of LTL formulas).

Definition 4.7. *Let C be an SCC in $M \otimes A$. C is said to be* complete *if for all $s \in \pi_M(C)$, we have:*

$$Path^*(M, s) = \bigcup_{q \in Q \mid (s,q) \in C} Trace^*((M \otimes A)_{|C}, (s, q)). \tag{1}$$

Remark 4.8. Any SCC C is complete iff (1) is satisfied for some $s \in \pi_M(C)$.

We say that an SCC C is accepted when the set of transitions of A that are "contained" in C fulfills the acceptance condition of A, formally:

Definition 4.9. *An SCC C in $M \otimes A$ is accepted if $({}^\bullet C \cap C^\bullet) \in Acc_\otimes$.*

The following result shows that every complete and accepted SCC is locally positive. The proposition actually states a stronger result that will prove useful for evaluation.

Proposition 4.10. *Let C be an SCC in $M \otimes A$. If C is both complete and accepted, then for all $s \in \pi_M(C)$ we have:*

$$\mu_{M[s]} \left(\bigcup_{q \in Q \ | \ (s,q) \in C} L_C(s,q) \right) = 1.$$

The two following propositions show that the converse holds when A is unambiguous on each SCC or has an upward closed acceptance condition.

Proposition 4.11. *If C is a locally positive SCC in $M \otimes A$, then C is complete.*

Proposition 4.12. *If A is unambiguous on C or A has an upward closed acceptance condition and if C is locally positive then C is accepted.*

We have proved so far that when A is unambiguous on each SCC or has an upward closed acceptance condition, then the two following assertions are equivalent:

i) M satisfies A with positive probability,
ii) there exists a complete and accepted SCC reachable from some initial location.

Observe that checking whether an SCC C is accepted amounts to checking whether $({}^\bullet C \cap C^\bullet) \in Acc_\otimes$. We now show that completeness of an SCC can also be checked efficiently when for every SCC C of $M \otimes A$, $M \otimes A$ is both unambiguous and separated on C, or deterministic on C. Basically, under these assumptions, completeness checking reduces to counting transitions, as expressed by the following lemmas.

Lemma 4.13. *Let C be an SCC in $M \otimes A$. If $M \otimes A$ is deterministic on C then the two following properties are equivalent:*

– C is complete,
– for all $(s,q) \in C$ and $t_M \in s^\bullet$, we have $| \pi_M^{-1}(t_M) \cap (s,q)^\bullet \cap {}^\bullet C | = 1$.

Lemma 4.14. *Let C be an SCC in $M \otimes A$. If $M \otimes A$ is unambiguous on C and separated on C then the two following properties are equivalent:*

– C is complete

– *for all* $(s, q) \in C$, $SCC(s)$ *is maximal and*

$$\sum_{s \in \pi_M(C)} | {}^\bullet s \cap SCC(s)^\bullet | \cdot | \pi_M^{-1}(s) \cap C | = | {}^\bullet C \cap C^\bullet | .$$

The following theorems follow from the previous propositions, and from the translation from LTL to ω-automata presented in section 3.3.

Theorem 4.15. *Assume that for every SCC C of $M \otimes A$, $M \otimes A$ is both unambiguous and separated on C, or deterministic on C. Then checking whether M satisfies A with positive probability can be done in $K_{Acc} \cdot O(| M \otimes A |)$.*

Theorem 4.16. *Let f be an LTL formula. Checking whether M satisfies f with positive probability can be done in $O(| cl(f) |) \cdot O(| M |) \cdot O(2^{|cl(f)|})$.*

Remark 4.17. Checking whether M satisfies f with positive probability can be done in polynomial space.

5   Probabilistic Evaluation

The evaluation problem may be studied reasonably when automata are non ambiguous: this property induces that $V(s, q)$ probabilities fulfill a linear equation system. The system may be solved on each non null SCC with respect to a topology order. We state the nature of this linear equation system: for transient SCC, the system has a unique solution, while for persistent SCC, only one equation is necessary to complete the resolution. We give some missing linear properties when the persistent SCC is separated or deterministic. One can notice that these results lead to a technique for the evaluation problem for non ambiguous and SCC separated automaton, in particularly a method to evaluate LTL formulas.

Proposition 5.1. *Let A be unambiguous. Let C be strongly connected component in $M \otimes A$. Let E_C be the equation system*

$$V(s, q) = \sum_{(t_M, t_A) \in (s,q)^\bullet} P(t_M) \cdot V(t_M^\bullet, t_A^\bullet)$$

with $(s, q) \in C$. If C is persistent then $rank(E_C) = |C| - 1$. If C is transient then $rank(E_C) = |C|$.

Proposition 5.2. *Let C be a persistent component in $M \otimes A$. Then*

– *if C is deterministic: $\forall (s, q) \in C : V(s, q) = 1$,*
– *if C is separated: $\sum_{q:(s,q) \in C} V(s, q) = 1$.*

6   Experimentation, the Tool ProbaTaf

We have implemented our techniques in the ProbaTaf tool. The probabilistic systems are described by (bounded) Petri nets. The LTL formulas are defined from transitions, propositions on marking (e. g. "P" for Place P marked) and proposition *dead* for each dead transition attach to any dead markings. The tool allows checking the satisfaction of a formula and its evaluation. Several advanced techniques have been applied:

- Binary decision diagram (bdd) technology to compute, to store and to simplify the ω-automaton for a formula. The enumeration of the successor locations for a given location and values of the propositions may be obtained directly from the bdd structure after some bdd operations.
- An on-the-fly algorithm based on [2].
- A simple Gauss elimination algorithm to solve linear systems associated to each persistent and transient SCC: we may select all pivots on the diagonal.

We conclude the study with two illustrative examples of applications. They are not exhaustive and do not present elaborated use of the techniques. Our goal is rather to display shortly the scope of the presented models.

Example 6.1. The first example is borrowed from a paper by Knuth and Yao [4]. They introduce a number of essential questions related to the generation of random variables with nonuniform distributions. The first tackled technique is on the generation of a uniform random variable taking values in a finite set. We consider a variant of their introductory example. Suppose that one wants to simulate a (uniform) dice game by a number of flips of a possibly biased coin. We toss four times the coin and discard the result if the numbers of heads and that of tails differ. Otherwise (two heads and two tails) we let: $0011 \rightarrow o$, $0101 \rightarrow oo$, $0110 \rightarrow ooo$, $1001 \rightarrow oooo$, $1010 \rightarrow ooooo$, $1100 \rightarrow oooooo$ (head is encoded as 1 and tail as 0). When the three first tosses are identical, we preventively discard the result.

Using the ProbaTaf tool, we easily verify the uniform property of the game for possibly biased coin. However, we have observed that the expected number of flips grows with the biasness of the coin. To confirm this assertion, we have considered the property "get a value with at most n flips", expressed in LTL by the formula $X^n dead$, and computed its probability for different biased coins. However, the satisfaction and the evaluation of this formula lead to an exponential time computation (see Table 1 where times are expressed in milliseconds). Indeed, the automata, produced by our techniques, have an exponential number of states. Adding the tautology $G(dead \Rightarrow X dead)$ to our formula lead to linear time computation (see Table 1): the automata have linear sizes. This

Table 1. Time performance of sat. and eval. problem applied to dice game

n		3	4	5	6	7	8	9	10	11	12	13
$X^n dead$	sat	2	2	11	46	99	268	836	1815	4205	9713	19686
	eval	10	24	36	73	161	378	977	2114	5053	9665	21057
$X^n dead \wedge G(dead \Rightarrow X dead)$	sat	1	1	2	4	3	6	10	6	10	13	9
	eval	2	6	6	8	11	23	26	32	40	50	56

experimentation brings to the fore the well-known state explosion problem of model-checking. This problem may be partially solved by adapting the classical LTL automata construction (as [2]) to produce non-ambiguous automata.

Example 6.2. In [6], the authors design a probabilistic one-passage distributed algorithm in trees which eliminates leaves one-by-one until the tree is reduced to a single vertex, considered as the elected vertex. The main particularity of the election algorithm is that it assigns to *all* vertices of the tree graph the same probability of being elected, by giving to each leaf or vertex which has become a leaf a life duration exponentially distributed with a parameter computed as follows. Initially all vertices have the same weight 1. Any leaf of the tree generates its lifetime, which is a positive-real-valued random variable with an exponential distribution of parameter equal to its weight. Once the lifetime has expired the leaf is eliminated and its father recuperates the weight of the removed son. The process continues until the tree is reduced to one vertex.

Using the ProbaTaf tool, we observe the uniform property of the election algorithm for some trees. This experimental verification consists in evaluating the probability of formula $F(dead \land E_i)$ where E_i states that the vertex i is still a candidate. By accident, during our experimentation, we obtained a surprising result: for a given tree, the probability of being a finalist vertex (i.e. one of the two last candidate) depends only on the degree of the vertex. A formal proof of this result is out the scope of our study and is left as a conjecture. We observe this property on Table 2 for the balanced binary tree of depth 5, where the index i represents the depth of a vertex.

Some performance experimentation has been over made the election algorithm applied to balanced binary trees. The size of the probabilistic system grows in double exponential with the depth of the tree and leads to 459829 states and 3599198 transitions for the depth 5. Table 3 displays the time computation for the satisfaction and evaluation algorithm. The time performance difference between these two problems is mainly explained by the on-the-fly technology used to solve the satisfaction problem, amplified by the cost of linear systems to be solved for the evaluation problem.

Table 2. Probability to be second on balanced binary tree of depth 5

i	0	1	2	3	4
$F(E_i \land X(dead \land \neg E_i))$	0.034	0.068	0.068	0.068	0.0010

Table 3. Time performance for sat. and eval. problems applied to election algorithm

deaph		2	3	4	5
$F(dead \land E_0)$	sat	3	7	8	4841
	eval	21	19	94	99797
$F(E_0 \land X(dead \land \neg E_0))$	sat	3	3	19	4894
	eval	17	28	242	336821

References

[1] Costas Courcoubetis and Mihalis Yannakakis. The complexity of probabilistic verification. *Journal of the ACM*, 42(4):857–907, July 1995.

[2] Jean-Michel Couvreur. On-the-fly verification of linear temporal logic. In *FM'99— Formal Methods, Volume I*, volume 1708 of *Lecture Notes in Computer Science*, pages 253–271. Springer, 1999.

[3] Jean-Michel Couvreur. Un point de vue symbolique sur la logique temporelle linéaire. In *Actes du Colloque LaCIM 2000*, volume 27 of *Publications du LaCIM*, pages 131–140. Université du Québec à Montréal, August 2000.

[4] Knuth and Yao. The complexity of nonuniform random number generation. In *Algorithms and Complexity: New Directions and Recent Results, Ed. J. F. Traub*. Academic Press, 1976.

[5] Orna Kupferman, Moshe Y. Vardi, and Pierre Wolper. An automata-theoretic approach to branching-time model checking. *Journal of the ACM*, 47(2):312–360, March 2000.

[6] Yves Métivier, Nasser Saheb, and Akka Zemmari. A uniform randomized election in trees. In *SIROCCO 10*, volume 17 of *Proceedings in Informatics*, pages 259–274. Carleton Scientific, 2003.

[7] Moshe Y. Vardi. Automatic verification of probabilistic concurrent finite-state programs. In *focs85*, pages 327–338, 1985.

[8] Moshe Y. Vardi and Pierre Wolper. Reasoning about infinite computations. *Information and Computation*, 115(1):1–37, November 1994.

A Logical Study on Qualitative Default Reasoning with Probabilities*

Christoph Beierle and Gabriele Kern-Isberner

Praktische Informatik VIII – Wissensbasierte Systeme, Fachbereich Informatik,
FernUniversität Hagen, 58084 Hagen, Germany,
{christoph.beierle|gabriele.kern-isberner}@fernuni-hagen.de

Abstract. Only very special subclasses of probability distributions can be used for qualitative reasoning that meets basic logical demands. Snow's *atomic bound systems* (*big-stepped probabilities*) provide one positive example for such a subclass. This paper presents a thorough investigation of the formal logical relationships between qualitative and probabilistic default reasoning. We start with formalizing qualitative conditional logic, as well as both standard and big-stepped probabilistic logic as abstract logical systems, using the notion of *institutions*. The institution of big-stepped probabilities turns out to be a proper combination of the other two. Moreover, the framework of institutions offers the possibility to elaborate exactly the properties that make probability distributions suitable for qualitative reasoning.

1 Introduction

Default reasoning means walking on unstable logical grounds: Conclusions are drawn only defeasibly and may be revised when new information becomes evident. So the resulting logics are nonmonotonic [Mak94] and are closely related to belief revision theory [MG91]. On the other hand, they also make use of results and techniques from conditional logics [BDP97]. Indeed, a conditional relationship "If A then B", formally often denoted as $(B|A)$, is a most concise and complex piece of information. It may represent a default rule, a plausible relationship, a nonmonotonic inference, or a revision policy, depending on the context in which it is used [KI01]. So conditional logics [NC02], devised as logical systems to deal with if-then-statements in a non-classical way, have interesting connections to central concerns of Artificial Intelligence.

Roughly, two ways of conditional reasoning may be distinguished: qualitative approaches, aiming at following the traditions of symbolic logics, and quantitative approaches, making use of numerical information to handle conditionals. The oldest and most founded quantitative conditional theory is based on conditional probabilities. Whereas classical logics proved to be unable to represent conditionals properly, probability theory offered a convincing concept to deal with uncertain rules. In fact, one principal motivation for qualitative conditional reasoning was to handle conditionals in a non-classical way as easily and properly as probability theory does, but without probabilities. On the other hand, the rich expressiveness of probabilistics is sometimes perceived

---

* The research reported here was partially supported by the DFG – Deutsche Forschungsgemeinschaft within the CONDOW-project under grant BE 1700/5-1.

M.Y. Vardi and A. Voronkov (Eds.): LPAR 2003, LNAI 2850, pp. 376–388, 2003.

as a burden, so probabilists have attempted to use probabilities for a more qualitative kind of reasoning; the *comparative probabilities* of de Finetti [dF37, DP96] provide an early example for this. A more recent approach are the *atomic bound systems* of Snow [Sno94], more intuitively called *big-stepped probabilities*. A big-stepped probability distribution accepts a conditional $(B|A)$ iff its confirmation, $A \wedge B$, is more probable than its refutation, $A \wedge \neg B$; its specific probabilistic structure makes this compatible with basic standards of symbolic nonmonotonic reasoning.

This paper presents a rigorous logical investigation of qualitative reasoning with probabilities. Although qualitative and probabilistic conditional logics are substantially different, there is a framework broad enough to provide logical grounds for both of them. This is the framework of *institutions* which were introduced in [GB92] as a general framework for logical systems. Institutions are based on category theory and abstract from logical details, thus opening a unifying view on fundamental logical features. An institution formalizes the informal notion of a logical system, including syntax, semantics, and the relation of satisfaction between them. The latter poses the major requirement for an institution: that the satisfaction relation is consistent under the change of notation.

We will show in this paper, that not only qualitative and probabilistic conditional logics, but also the conditional logic of big-stepped probabilities can be formalized as institutions. Hereby, we build on work previously done [BKI02]. Then, by using the notion of institution morphisms [GR02], we study formal logical relationships between the institution of big-stepped probabilities, and the institution of qualitative conditional logic, being based on a semantics of total preorders. It will turn out, that there is exactly one such institution morphism that takes obvious similarities between both approaches properly into account. Furthermore, we raise a more general question that can be handled most adequately in the framework of institutions: Which probability distributions can be used to realize qualitative conditional reasoning? In this paper, we give an exact answer to this question, yielding a slight generalization of big-stepped probabilities.

The organization of this paper is as follows: In Section 2, we recall some basic definitions and facts from the theory of institutions. Section 3 gives a very brief overview on semantics for conditionals and shows how ordinal conditional logic and probabilistic conditional logic can be formalized as institutions. Section 4 then deals with qualitative probabilistic approaches; the institution of big-stepped probabilistic logic is set up as a combination of ordinal and probabilistic conditional logics. We investigate formal relationships between the institutions of big-stepped probabilistic logic and ordinal conditional logic, respectively, in Section 5. Section 6 summarizes the main results and points out further work.

2   The Framework of Institutions

Institutions will provide the general framework for this paper. After recalling some basic concepts of category theory and institutions, we present propositional logic as an institution. This will serve as a simple example, and provides us with useful notations.

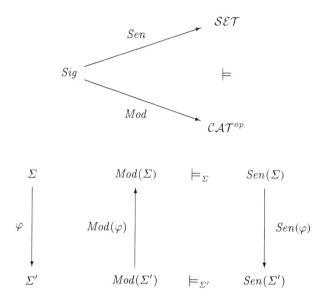

Fig. 1. Relationships within an institution $Inst = \langle\, Sig,\ Mod,\ Sen,\ \models\,\rangle$ [GB92]

2.1 Preliminaries: Basic Definitions and Notations

If C is a category, $|C|$ denotes the objects of C and $/C/$ its morphisms; for both objects $c \in |C|$ and morphisms $\varphi \in /C/$, we also write just $c \in C$ and $\varphi \in C$, respectively. C^{op} is the opposite category of C, with the direction of all morphisms reversed. The composition of two functors $F : C \to C'$ and $G : C' \to C''$ is denoted by $G \circ F$ (first apply F, then G). For functors $F, G : C \to C'$, a *natural transformation* η from F to G, denoted by $\eta : F \Longrightarrow G$, assigns to each object $c \in |C|$ a morphism $\eta_c : F(C) \to G(C) \in /C'/$ such that for every morphism $\varphi : c \to d \in /C/$ we have $\eta_d \circ F(\varphi) = G(\varphi) \circ \eta_c$. $\mathcal{SET}$ and $\mathcal{CAT}$ denote the categories of sets and of categories, respectively. (For more information about categories, see e.g. [HS73].) The central institution definition is the following (cf. Figure 1 that visualizes the relationships within an institution):

Definition 1. [GB92] *An institution is a quadruple* $Inst = \langle\, Sig,\ Mod,\ Sen,\ \models\,\rangle$ *with a category Sig of signatures as objects, a functor* $Mod : Sig \to \mathcal{CAT}^{op}$ *yielding the category of* Σ*-models for each signature* Σ*, a functor* $Sen : Sig \to \mathcal{SET}$ *yielding the sentences over a signature, and a* $|Sig|$*-indexed relation* $\models_\Sigma\ \subseteq\ |Mod(\Sigma)| \times Sen(\Sigma)$ *such that for each signature morphism* $\varphi : \Sigma \to \Sigma' \in /Sig/$*, for each* $m' \in |Mod(\Sigma')|$*, and for each* $f \in Sen(\Sigma)$ *the following* satisfaction condition *holds:*
$$m' \models_{\Sigma'} Sen(\varphi)(f) \quad \text{iff} \quad Mod(\varphi)(m') \models_\Sigma f.$$

For sets F, G of Σ-sentences and a Σ-model m we write $m \models_\Sigma F$ iff $m \models_\Sigma f$ for all $f \in F$. The satisfaction relation is lifted to semantical entailment $\models_\Sigma$ between sentences by defining $F \models_\Sigma G$ iff for all Σ-models m with $m \models_\Sigma F$ we have $m \models_\Sigma G$. $F^\bullet = \{f \in Sen(\Sigma) \mid F \models_\Sigma f\}$ is called the *closure* of F, and F is *closed* if $F = F^\bullet$.

The closure operator fulfils the *closure lemma* $\varphi(F^\bullet) \subseteq \varphi(F)^\bullet$ and various other nice properties like $\varphi(F^\bullet)^\bullet = \varphi(F)^\bullet$ or $(F^\bullet \cup G)^\bullet = (F \cup G)^\bullet$. A consequence of the closure lemma is that entailment is preserved under change of notation carried out by a signature morphism, i.e. $F \models_\Sigma G$ implies $\varphi(F) \models_{\varphi(\Sigma)} \varphi(G)$ (but not vice versa).

2.2   The Institution of Propositional Logic

In all circumstances, propositional logic seems to be the most basic logic. The components of its institution $Inst_\mathcal{B} = \langle\, Sig_\mathcal{B},\, Mod_\mathcal{B},\, Sen_\mathcal{B},\, \models_\mathcal{B} \,\rangle$ will be defined in the following.

Signatures: $Sig_\mathcal{B}$ is the category of propositional signatures. A propositional signature $\Sigma \in |Sig_\mathcal{B}|$ is a (finite) set of propositional variables, $\Sigma = \{a_1, a_2, \ldots\}$. A propositional signature morphism $\varphi : \Sigma \to \Sigma' \in /Sig_\mathcal{B}/$ is an injective function mapping propositional variables to propositional variables, allowing for the renaming of variables in a larger context.

Models: For each signature $\Sigma \in Sig_\mathcal{B}$, $Mod_\mathcal{B}(\Sigma)$ contains the set of all propositional interpretations for Σ, i.e. $|Mod_\mathcal{B}(\Sigma)| = \{I \mid I : \Sigma \to Bool\}$ where $Bool = \{true, false\}$. Due to its simple structure, the only morphisms in $Mod_\mathcal{B}(\Sigma)$ are the identity morphisms. For each signature morphism $\varphi : \Sigma \to \Sigma' \in Sig_\mathcal{B}$, we define the morphism (i.e. the functor in $\mathcal{CAT}^{op}$) $Mod_\mathcal{B}(\varphi) : Mod_\mathcal{B}(\Sigma') \to Mod_\mathcal{B}(\Sigma)$ by $(Mod_\mathcal{B}(\varphi)(I'))(a_i) := I'(\varphi(a_i))$ where $I' \in Mod_\mathcal{B}(\Sigma')$ and $a_i \in \Sigma$.

Sentences: For each signature $\Sigma \in Sig_\mathcal{B}$, the set $Sen_\mathcal{B}(\Sigma)$ contains the usual propositional formulas constructed from the propositional variables in Σ and the logical connectives $\wedge$ (and), $\vee$ (or), and $\neg$ (not). The symbols $\top$ and $\bot$ denote a tautology (like $a \vee \neg a$) and a contradiction (like $a \wedge \neg a$), respectively.

For each signature morphism $\varphi : \Sigma \to \Sigma' \in Sig_\mathcal{B}$, the function $Sen_\mathcal{B}(\varphi) : Sen_\mathcal{B}(\Sigma) \to Sen_\mathcal{B}(\Sigma')$ is defined by straightforward inductive extension on the structure of the formulas; e.g., $Sen_\mathcal{B}(\varphi)(a_i) = \varphi(a_i)$ and $Sen_\mathcal{B}(\varphi)(A \wedge B) = Sen_\mathcal{B}(\varphi)(A) \wedge Sen_\mathcal{B}(\varphi)(B)$. In the following, we will abbreviate $Sen_\mathcal{B}(\varphi)(A)$ by just writing $\varphi(A)$. In order to simplify notations, we will often replace conjunction by juxtaposition and indicate negation of a formula by barring it, i.e. $AB = A \wedge B$ and $\overline{A} = \neg A$. An *atomic formula* is a formula consisting of just a propositional variable, a *literal* is a positive or a negated atomic formula, and a *complete conjunction* is a conjunction of literals where all atomic formulas appear once, either in positive or in negated form. Ω_Σ denotes the set of all complete conjunctions over a signature Σ. Note that there is an obvious bijection between $|Mod_\mathcal{B}(\Sigma)|$ and Ω_Σ, so we will not distinguish between both sets.

Throughout the paper, two evident facts on formulas of the form $\varphi(\omega)$, where φ is a signature morphism, and ω is a complete conjunction, will often be used implicitly. First, $\varphi(\omega) \not\equiv \bot$, since φ is injective. Second, for two distinct complete conjunctions $\omega_1, \omega_2 \in \Omega_\Sigma$, the formulas $\varphi(\omega_1)$ and $\varphi(\omega_2)$ are exclusive, i.e. $\varphi(\omega_1)\varphi(\omega_2) \equiv \bot$.

Satisfaction Relation: For any $\Sigma \in |Sig_\mathcal{B}|$, the satisfaction relation $\models_{\mathcal{B},\Sigma} \subseteq |Mod_\mathcal{B}(\Sigma)| \times Sen_\mathcal{B}(\Sigma)$ is defined as expected for propositional logic, e.g. $I \models_{\mathcal{B},\Sigma} a_i$ iff $I(a_i) = true$

and $I \models_{\mathcal{B}, \Sigma} A \wedge B$ iff $I \models_{\mathcal{B}, \Sigma} A$ and $I \models_{\mathcal{B}, \Sigma} B$ for $a_i \in \Sigma$ and $A, B \in Sen_{\mathcal{B}}(\Sigma)$. For ease of notation, we will write $\models$ instead of $\models_{\mathcal{B}, \Sigma}$, if no confusion arises.

It is easy to check that $Inst_{\mathcal{B}} = \langle Sig_{\mathcal{B}}, Mod_{\mathcal{B}}, Sen_{\mathcal{B}}, \models_{\mathcal{B}} \rangle$ is indeed an institution.

Example 1. Let $\Sigma = \{s, u\}$ and $\Sigma' = \{a, b, c\}$ be two propositional signatures with the atomic propositions s – *being a scholar*, u – *being single* and a – *being a student*, b – *being young*, c – *being unmarried*. Let I' be the Σ'-model with $I'(a) = true$, $I'(b) = true$, $I'(c) = false$. Let $\varphi : \Sigma \to \Sigma' \in Sig_{\mathcal{B}}$ be the signature morphism with $\varphi(s) = a$, $\varphi(u) = c$. The functor $Mod_{\mathcal{B}}(\varphi)$ takes I' to the Σ-model $I := Mod_{\mathcal{B}}(\varphi)(I')$, yielding $I(s) = I'(a) = true$ and $I(u) = I'(c) = false$.

2.3   Institution Morphisms

An institution morphism Φ expresses a relation between two institutions *Inst* und *Inst'* such that the satisfaction condition of *Inst* may be computed by the satisfaction condition of *Inst'* if we translate it according to Φ. The translation is done by relating every *Inst*-signature Σ to an *Inst'*-signature Σ', each Σ'-sentence to a Σ-sentence, and each Σ-model to a Σ'-model.

Definition 2. [GB92] *Let*

$$Inst = \langle Sig, Mod, Sen, \models \rangle$$

and

$$Inst' = \langle Sig', Mod', Sen', \models' \rangle$$

be two institutions. An institution morphism Φ *from Inst to Inst' is a triple* $\langle \phi, \alpha, \beta \rangle$ *with a functor* $\phi : Sig \to Sig'$, *a natural transformation* $\alpha : Sen' \circ \phi \implies Sen$, *and a natural transformation* $\beta : Mod \implies Mod' \circ \phi$ *such that for each* $\Sigma \in |Sig|$, *for each* $m \in |Mod(\Sigma)|$, *and for each* $f' \in Sen'(\phi(\Sigma))$ *the following* satisfaction condition (for institution morphisms) *holds:*

$$m \models_{\Sigma} \alpha_{\Sigma}(f') \quad \textit{iff} \quad \beta_{\Sigma}(m) \models'_{\phi(\Sigma)} f'$$

Figure 2 illustrates the relationships within an institution morphism.

3   Semantics for Conditionals

Conditionals $(B|A)$ (with propositional antecedent and consequent) can not be properly evaluated in classical logical environments. Instead, they substantially need the possibility to having their confirmation, AB, compared to their refutation, $A\overline{B}$, with respect to normality, plausibility, probability, and the like. This comparison can be done directly by using (pre)orders on formulas, or indirectly via appropriate numerical degrees of belief. In this section, we will present two well-known semantics for conditionals in the institution framework, namely, a qualitative semantics based on total preorders, and the usual probabilistic semantics making use of conditional probabilities. These results are based on work previously done [BKI02], but are briefly summarized here, since their notations and techniques will be used in the sequel.

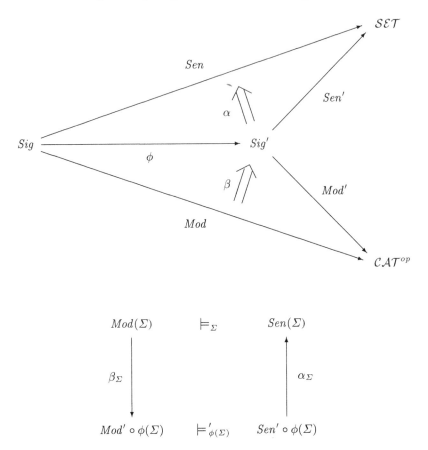

Fig. 2. Relationships within an institution morphism $\langle \phi, \alpha, \beta \rangle : \langle Sig, Mod, Sen, \models \rangle \longrightarrow$ $\langle Sig', Mod', Sen', \models' \rangle$

3.1   The Institution of Qualitative Conditional Logic

Various types of models have been proposed to interpret conditionals adequately within a formal system (cf. e.g. [NC02]). Many of them are based on considering possible worlds which can be thought of as being represented by classical logical interpretations $|Mod_{\mathcal{B}}(\Sigma)|$, or complete conjunctions $\omega \in \Omega_\Sigma$ (as defined in Sec. 2.2), respectively. One of the most prominent approaches is the *system-of-spheres* model of Lewis [Lew73] which makes use of a notion of similarity between possible worlds. This idea of comparing worlds and evaluating conditionals with respect to the "nearest" or "best" worlds (which are somehow selected) is common to very many approaches in conditional logics.

The institution $Inst_\mathcal{K} = \langle Sig_\mathcal{K}, Mod_\mathcal{K}, Sen_\mathcal{K}, \models_\mathcal{K} \rangle$, as specified in the following, provides a formal logical framework to carry out qualitative conditional reasoning.

Signatures: $Sig_\mathcal{K}$ is identical to the category of propositional signatures, i.e. $Sig_\mathcal{K} = Sig_\mathcal{B}$.

Models: In order to base our conditional logic on quite a general semantics, we take the models to be total preorders[1] over possible worlds, ordering them according to their *plausibility*, i.e.

$$|Mod_\mathcal{K}(\Sigma)| = \{R \mid R \text{ is a total preorder on } \Omega_\Sigma\}$$

By convention, the least worlds are the most plausible worlds. We will also use the infix notation $\omega_1 \preceq_R \omega_2$ instead of $(\omega_1, \omega_2) \in R$. As usual, we introduce the $\prec_R$-relation by saying that $\omega_1 \prec_R \omega_2$ iff $\omega_1 \preceq_R \omega_2$ and not $\omega_2 \preceq_R \omega_1$. Furthermore, $\omega_1 \approx_R \omega_2$ means that both $\omega_1 \preceq_R \omega_2$ and $\omega_2 \preceq_R \omega_1$ hold.

Each $R \in Mod_\mathcal{K}(\Sigma)$ induces a partitioning $\Omega_0, \Omega_1, \ldots$ of Ω, such that all worlds in the same partitioning subset are considered equally plausible ($\omega_1 \approx_R \omega_2$ for $\omega_1, \omega_2 \in \Omega_j$), and whenever $\omega_1 \in \Omega_i$ and $\omega_2 \in \Omega_k$ with $i < k$, then $\omega_1 \prec_R \omega_2$. Moreover, each $R \in Mod_\mathcal{K}(\Sigma)$ gives rise to a total preorder on $Sen_\mathcal{B}(\Sigma)$ by setting

$$A \preceq_R B \text{ iff } \exists \omega_0 \models A, \forall \omega \models B : \omega_0 \preceq_R \omega \tag{1}$$

So, A is considered to be at least as plausible as B (with respect to R) iff the most plausible worlds satisfying A are at least as plausible as any world satisfying B. Again, $A \prec_R B$ means both $A \preceq_R B$ and not $B \preceq_R A$. Note that $A \prec_R \bot$ for all $A \not\equiv \bot$. As before, we only consider the identity morphisms in $Mod_\mathcal{K}(\Sigma)$ for this paper.

For each signature morphism $\varphi : \Sigma \to \Sigma'$, we define a functor $Mod_\mathcal{K}(\varphi) : Mod_\mathcal{K}(\Sigma') \to Mod_\mathcal{K}(\Sigma)$ by mapping a (total) preorder R' over $Mod_\mathcal{B}(\Sigma')$ to a (total) preorder $Mod_\mathcal{K}(\varphi)(R')$ over $Mod_\mathcal{B}(\Sigma)$ in the following way:

$$\omega_1 \preceq_{Mod_\mathcal{K}(\varphi)(R')} \omega_2 \quad \text{iff} \quad \varphi(\omega_1) \preceq_{R'} \varphi(\omega_2) \tag{2}$$

Sentences: For each signature Σ, the set $Sen_\mathcal{K}(\Sigma)$ contains (*propositional*) *conditionals* of the form $(B|A)$ where $A, B \in Sen_\mathcal{B}(\Sigma)$ are propositional formulas from $Inst_\mathcal{B}$. For $\varphi : \Sigma \to \Sigma'$, the extension $Sen_\mathcal{K}(\varphi)$ is defined as usual by $Sen_\mathcal{K}(\varphi)((B|A)) = (\varphi(B)|\varphi(A))$.

Satisfaction Relation: The satisfaction relation $\models_{\mathcal{K},\Sigma} \subseteq |Mod_\mathcal{K}(\Sigma)| \times Sen_\mathcal{K}(\Sigma)$ is defined, for any $\Sigma \in |Sig_\mathcal{K}|$, by

$$R \models_{\mathcal{K},\Sigma} (B|A) \quad \text{iff} \quad AB \prec_R A\overline{B}$$

Therefore, a conditional $(B|A)$ is satisfied (or accepted) by the plausibility preorder R iff its confirmation AB is more plausible than its refutation $A\overline{B}$.

---

[1] A total preorder R is a reflexive and transitive relation such that for any two elements ω_1, ω_2, we have $(\omega_1, \omega_2) \in R$ or $(\omega_2, \omega_1) \in R$ (possibly both).

Example 2. We continue our student-example in this qualitative conditional environment, so let Σ, Σ', φ be as defined in Example 1. Let R' be the following total preorder on Ω':

$$R' : \quad \overline{a}\overline{b}\overline{c} \prec_{R'} abc \approx_{R'} \overline{a}bc$$
$$\prec_{R'} ab\overline{c} \approx_{R'} a\overline{b}c \approx_{R'} a\overline{b}\overline{c} \approx_{R'} \overline{a}b\overline{c} \approx_{R'} \overline{a}\overline{b}c$$

For instance $R' \models_{\mathcal{K},\Sigma'} (c|a)$ – *students* are supposed to be *unmarried* since under R', ac is more plausible than $a\overline{c}$. Under $Mod_{\mathcal{K}}(\varphi)$, R' is mapped onto $R = Mod_{\mathcal{K}}(\varphi)(R')$ where R is the following total preorder on Ω:

$$R : \quad \overline{s}\,\overline{u} \prec_R \overline{s}u \approx_R su \prec_R s\overline{u}$$

As expected, the conditional $(u|s)$ that corresponds to $(c|a)$ in $Sen_{\mathcal{K}}(\Sigma')$ under φ, is satisfied by R – here, *scholars* are supposed to be *single*.

3.2   The Institution of Probabilistic Conditional Logic

A full probabilistic semantics for conditionals with precise probability values is provided by standard probability distributions P and conditional probabilities. In the language of institutions, the corresponding institution is given by $Inst_C = \langle Sig_C, Mod_C, Sen_C, \models_C \rangle$ with the following components: $Sig_C = Sig_B$ is the category of propositional signatures. The model functor Mod_C assigns to each signature Σ the category of probability distributions over Σ (with trivial morphisms). For each signature morphism $\varphi : \Sigma \to \Sigma'$, we define a functor $Mod_C(\varphi) : Mod_C(\Sigma') \to Mod_C(\Sigma)$ by mapping each distribution P' over Σ' to a distribution $Mod_C(\varphi)(P')$ over Σ. $Mod_C(\varphi)(P')$ is defined by giving its value for all complete conjunctions ω over Σ:

$$(Mod_C(\varphi)(P'))(\omega) := P'(\varphi(\omega)) \tag{3}$$

The set $Sen_C(\Sigma)$ of sentences consists of *probabilistic conditionals* of the form $(B|A)[x]$ with propositional formulas A, B and probabilities $x \in [0,1]$. For each signature morphism $\varphi : \Sigma \to \Sigma'$, the extension $Sen_C(\varphi) : Sen_C(\Sigma) \to Sen_C(\Sigma')$ is defined by straightforward inductive extension on the structure of the formulas: $Sen_C(\varphi)((B|A)[x]) = (\varphi(B)|\varphi(A))[x]$. Finally, the satisfaction relation $\models_{C,\Sigma} \subseteq |Mod_C(\Sigma)| \times Sen_C(\Sigma)$ is defined, for any $\Sigma \in |Sig_C|$, by

$$P \models_{C,\Sigma} (B|A)[x] \quad \text{iff} \quad P(A) > 0 \text{ and } P(B|A) = \frac{P(AB)}{P(A)} = x$$

For more details and examples for $Inst_C$, we refer to [BKI02].

4   Qualitative Probabilities

Adams was the first to present a probabilistic framework for qualitative default reasoning. In his work [Ada75], he used an infinitesimal approach to define "reasonable (probabilistic) consequences". On these ideas, Pearl later based his ϵ-*semantics* [Pea89] which turned out to be the same as *preferential semantics* and can be characterized by the properties of *system P* [KLM90]. Therefore, the infinitesimal ϵ-semantics provides a probabilistic semantics for system P.

This seemed hardly possible to realize within a standard probabilistic framework. An obvious way to interpret a default rule "usually, if A then B", or "from A, defeasibly infer B" (written as $A \hspace{1pt}\vrule\hspace{-3pt}\sim B$) by a probability distribution P would be to postulate $P(AB) > P(A\overline{B})$ (which is equivalent to $P(B|A) > 0.5$). I.e. given A, the presence of B should be more probable than its absence. This interpretation, however, is not generally compatible with system P, it may conflict, for instance, with the *OR*-postulate of system P:

$$OR \qquad \text{if } A \hspace{1pt}\vrule\hspace{-3pt}\sim C \text{ and } B \hspace{1pt}\vrule\hspace{-3pt}\sim C \text{ then } A \vee B \hspace{1pt}\vrule\hspace{-3pt}\sim C$$

Indeed, it is easy to find counterexamples where $P(AC) > P(A\overline{C})$ and $P(BC) > P(B\overline{C})$, but $P((A \vee B)C) < P((A \vee B)\overline{C})$. So, in order to give reasonable probabilistic meanings to defaults, one has to focus on special subclasses of probability distributions.

Atomic bound systems, introduced by Snow in [Sno94], turned out to be such proper subclasses. Their distributions are also known as *big-stepped probabilities* (this more intuitive name was coined by Benferhat, Dubois & Prade, see [BDP99]).

Definition 3. *A* big-stepped probability distribution P over a signature Σ *is a probability distribution on* Ω_Σ *such that the following conditions are satisfied for all* $\omega, \omega_0, \omega_1, \omega_2 \in \Omega_\Sigma$:

$$P(\omega) > 0 \tag{4}$$

$$P(\omega_1) = P(\omega_2) \quad iff \quad \omega_1 = \omega_2 \tag{5}$$

$$P(\omega_0) > \sum_{\omega : P(\omega_0) > P(\omega)} P(\omega) \tag{6}$$

The set of all big-stepped probability distributions over Σ *is denoted by* $\mathcal{P}_{BS}(\Sigma)$.

The last condition (6) explains the attribute "big-stepped": In a big-stepped probability distribution, the probability of each possible world is bigger than the sum of all probabilities of less probable worlds. Big-stepped probabilities actually provide a standard probabilistic semantics for system P, as was shown in [BDP99], by interpreting conditionals in the intended way:

$$P \models_{BS} (B|A) \quad iff \quad P(AB) > P(A\overline{B}) \tag{7}$$

for $P \in \mathcal{P}_{BS}$. The following two lemmata give a more detailed impression of properties of big-stepped probabilities, and of their resemblance to ordinal presentations of belief; their proofs are straightforward.

Lemma 1. *Let* $P \in \mathcal{P}_{BS}(\Sigma)$ *be a big-stepped probability distribution over a signature* Σ, *and let* A, B *be two propositional formulas. Then* $P(A) = P(B)$ *iff* $A \equiv B$.

Lemma 2. *Let* $P \in \mathcal{P}_{BS}(\Sigma)$ *be a big-stepped probability distribution over a signature* Σ, *and let* A, B *be two non-contradictory, exclusive propositional formulas. Then*

$$P(A) > P(B) \text{ iff } \exists \omega_0 \models A, \forall \omega \models B : P(\omega_0) > P(\omega) \tag{8}$$

These lemmata will prove useful in the sequel. We are now ready to set up the institution $Inst_S$ of big-stepped probabilities by deriving its components both from $Inst_C$ and $Inst_K$:

- $Sig_S = Sig_B$, i.e. the signatures are propositional signatures.
- $Mod_S(\Sigma)$ is the full subcategory obtained from $Mod_C(\Sigma)$ by restriction to the big-stepped probability distributions $\mathcal{P}_{BS}(\Sigma)$; for each signature morphism $\varphi :$ $\Sigma \to \Sigma'$, the functor $Mod_S(\varphi)$ is the restriction and corestriction of $Mod_C(\varphi)$ to $Mod_S(\Sigma')$ and $Mod_S(\Sigma)$.
- $Sen_S = Sen_K$, i.e. the sentences are conditionals as in $Inst_K$ with corresponding sentence translation.
- In correspondence to (7), the satisfaction relation is defined by: $P \models_{S,\Sigma} (B|A)$ iff $P(AB) > P(A\overline{B})$.

Proposition 1. $Inst_S = \langle Sig_S, Mod_S, Sen_S, \models_S \rangle$ *is an institution.*

Proof. With the help of Lemmata 1 and 2, and the injectivity of φ, it is straightforward to check that $Mod_S(\varphi)$ is well-defined, i.e. mapping big-stepped probability distributions over Σ' to big-stepped probability distributions over Σ. (Note that the presupposition that signature morphisms are injective is crucial for this; otherwise, $\varphi(\omega)$ may be contradictory for possible worlds ω, in which case zero probabilities would arise.) What remains to be shown is that the satisfaction condition from Definition 1 is satisfied, which in this case requires

$$P' \models_{S,\Sigma'} Sen_S(\varphi)(B|A) \text{ iff } Mod_S(\varphi)(P') \models_{S,\Sigma} (B|A)$$

to hold. But this is trivial, since $Sen_S(\varphi)(B|A) = (\varphi(B)|\varphi(A))$ and $Mod_S(\varphi)(P')(B|A)$ $= P'(\varphi(B)|\varphi(A))$.

5   Relating Ordinal and Probabilistic Qualitative Logics

Now that we have formalized both ordinal and qualitative probabilistic logics for conditionals as institutions, we can use institution morphisms (cf. Section 2.3) to study formal logical relationships between them. In fact, the resemblance between $Inst_K$ and $Inst_S$ is quite close: Both have identical syntax, provided by propositional signatures $Sig_K = Sig_S = Sig_B$ and conditional sentences $Sen_K = Sen_S$, but differ with respect to the semantics defined by the model functors Mod_K and Mod_S, and the satisfaction relations $\models_K$ and $\models_S$, respectively. Therefore, we will focus on institution morphisms $\langle \phi, \alpha, \beta \rangle$ that take this resemblance into account by having $\phi = id_{Sig_B}$ and $\alpha = id_{Sen_K}$. So, only appropriate natural transformations β relating the different semantics have to be studied. In view of the similarity of the crucial relations (1) and (8), this might be expected to be trivial. However, a first negative result is stated in the following proposition:

Proposition 2. *There is no institution morphism* $\langle id_{Sig_B}, id_{Sen_K}, \beta \rangle : Inst_K \to Inst_S$.

Proof. Assume there is such an institution morphism $\langle id_{Sig_B}, id_{Sen_K}, \beta \rangle : Inst_K \to Inst_S$. Then for each $R \in Mod_K(\Sigma)$, $P_R := \beta_\Sigma(R) \in Mod_S(\Sigma)$ is a big-stepped probability distribution. The satisfaction condition (for morphisms) requires $R \models_{K,\Sigma} (B|A)$ iff $P_R \models_{S,\Sigma} (B|A)$, i.e. $AB \prec_R A\overline{B}$ iff $P_R(AB) > P_R(A\overline{B})$, which implies $\omega_1 \prec_R \omega_2$ iff $P_R(\omega_1) > P_R(\omega_2)$ for $\omega_1, \omega_2 \in \Omega_\Sigma$. Now, it is obvious that we can choose an R such that $\omega_1 \approx_R \omega_2$ and $\omega_1 \neq \omega_2$, yielding $P(\omega_1) = P(\omega_2)$, which is impossible in $Inst_S$.

Thus, there is no way of mapping ordinal models from $Inst_K$ to big-stepped probabilistic models in $Inst_S$ within such an institution morphism.

Fortunately, institution morphisms in the other direction turn out to be feasible. An obvious way to define a natural transformation $\beta : Mod_S \implies Mod_K$ is to associate to each big-stepped probability $P \in Mod_S(\Sigma)$ a total preorder $R_P \in Mod_K(\Sigma)$ via

$$\omega_1 \preceq_{R_P} \omega_2 \text{ iff } P(\omega_1) \geqslant P(\omega_2) \tag{9}$$

The next proposition shows this to be (uniquely) successful.

Proposition 3. $\langle id_{Sig_B}, id_{Sen_K}, \beta_{S/K} \rangle : Inst_S \to Inst_K$ *with* $\beta_{S/K,\Sigma}(P) := R_P$ *as defined in (9) for each* $\Sigma \in Sig_B$ *and* $P \in Mod_S(\Sigma)$ *is the only institution morphism from* $Inst_S$ *to* $Inst_K$.

It is straightforward to check that $\langle id_{Sig_B}, id_{Sen_K}, \beta_{S/K} \rangle$ is indeed an institution morphism, and that the satisfaction condition leaves no other possibility.

So, also on formal logical grounds, the big-stepped probability distributions prove to be adequate to implement qualitative conditional reasoning. The institution morphism from $Inst_S$ to $Inst_K$ makes probabilistic reasoning with big-stepped probabilities fully compatible to qualitative reasoning based on total preorders.

With the instruments of institutions and institution morphisms at hand, we may also consider a more general question concerning qualitative probabilities: Which are the properties that make probability distributions adequate for qualitative reasoning? More exactly, which subclasses $Mod_Q(\Sigma)$ of $Mod_C(\Sigma)$ are apt to base an institution $Inst_Q$ on them, similarly to $Inst_S$ (in particular, with a qualitative satisfaction relation corresponding to (7)) and also allowing a morphism from $Inst_Q$ to $Inst_K$? The following proposition gives a comprehensive answer to this question.

Proposition 4. *Let* $Inst_Q = \langle Sig_Q, Mod_Q, Sen_Q, \models_Q \rangle$ *be an institution with* $Sig_Q = Sig_B$, $|Mod_Q(\Sigma)| \subseteq |Mod_C(\Sigma)|$, $Mod_Q(\varphi)$ *the restriction and corestriction of* $Mod_C(\varphi)$, $Sen_Q = Sen_K$, *and* $\models_Q$ *in accordance with (7).*
If there is an institution morphism

$$\langle id_{Sig_B}, id_{Sen_K}, \beta \rangle : Inst_Q \to Inst_K$$

then the probability distributions P from $|Mod_Q(\Sigma)|$ have to satisfy the properties (4) and (6), and for all $\omega_1, \omega_2 \in \Omega$, it holds that

$$
P(\omega_1) = P(\omega_2) \text{ iff } \omega_1 = \omega_2, \text{ or for all}
$$
$$
\omega \in \Omega_\Sigma \backslash \{\omega_1, \omega_2\}, P(\omega) > P(\omega_1) = P(\omega_2) \tag{10}
$$

Conversely, the subclass of $|Mod_C(\Sigma)|$ consisting of all probability distributions with properties (4), (6), and (10) gives rise to an institution in the specified way.

Proof. The presupposed existence of the institution morphism from $Inst_\mathcal{Q}$ to $Inst_\mathcal{K}$ ensures that with each probability distribution $P \in Mod_\mathcal{Q}(\Sigma)$, a total preorder $\preceq_P :=$ $\beta_\Sigma(P)$ on Ω_Σ is associated such that $P \models_{\mathcal{Q},\Sigma} (B|A)$ iff $\beta_\Sigma(P) \models_{\mathcal{K},\Sigma} (B|A)$, i.e.

$$P(AB) > P(A\overline{B}) \quad \text{iff} \quad AB \prec_P A\overline{B} \tag{11}$$

The condition (11) has important consequences. First, considering the conditional $(\omega|\omega)$ yields $P(\omega) > 0$, since $\omega \prec_P \bot$ for all $\omega \in \Omega$. Furthermore, for $\omega_1, \omega_2 \in \Omega$, we obtain $P(\omega_1) > P(\omega_2)$ iff $\omega_1 \prec_P \omega_2$ by setting $A = \omega_1 \vee \omega_2, B = \omega_1$. In order to recover the crucial property (6), we consider $\omega_0 \in \Omega$ and set

$$A := \omega_0 \vee \bigvee \{\omega \mid P(\omega) < P(\omega_0)\}, \quad B := \omega_0.$$

Then $AB = \omega_0$, $A\overline{B} = \{\omega \mid P(\omega) < P(\omega_0)\}$. Since for all $\omega \in A\overline{B}$, we have $P(\omega) < P(\omega_0)$, which implies $\omega_0 \prec_P \omega$, it holds that $AB \prec_P A\overline{B}$. Due to (11), we obtain

$$P(\omega_0) > \sum_{P(\omega_0) > P(\omega)} P(\omega)$$

which is (6). The property (10) is shown similarly, by considering suitable conditionals. Finally, it is straightforward to prove that the class of probability distributions so defined is apt to provide the basis for an institution $Inst_\mathcal{Q}$, and that the natural transformation β with $\beta_\Sigma(P) := R_P$ as in (9) again defines an institution morphism in the required way.

The postulated institutional compatibility of probabilities with qualitative default reasoning produces a slightly generalized version of big-stepped probability distributions: Instead of assuming that all probabilities are different (and hence linearly ordered), the probabilities of two possible worlds may now be identical, but this probability has to be the least one. This is the utmost concession that can be made; otherwise, the compatibility of the additive probabilistic structure with qualitative reasoning gets lost.

6   Summary and Further Work

This paper presented a thorough logical formalizations of different logics for conditionals. The concept of institutions, introduced by Goguen and Burstall [GB92], made it possible not only to study qualitative and probabilistic conditional logic within one framework, but also to combine them in order to specify the components of a qualitative probabilistic logic based on big-stepped probabilities. Moreover, the formal relationship to qualitative conditional logic via institution morphisms allows a precise characterization of those probability distributions which can be used for qualitative probabilistic reasoning.

As representative for qualitative conditional logics, we used a logic whose semantics is based on total preorders on possible worlds. In fact, there are many other well-known semantics for conditionals, for instance, the ordinal conditional functions of Spohn [Spo88], or possibilistic semantics (cf. e.g. [BDP99]). It is also possible to consider these logics as institutions, and the study of relationships between these different qualitative conditional logics via institution morphisms shows them to be quite similar. A thorough investigation of these aspects is subject of our current work.

Acknowledgements

We thank the anonymous referees of this paper for their helpful comments. The research reported here was partially supported by the DFG – Deutsche Forschungsgemeinschaft within the CONDOR-project under grant BE 1700/5-1.

References

[Ada75]   E.W. Adams. *The Logic of Conditionals*. D. Reidel, Dordrecht, 1975.

[BDP97]   S. Benferhat, D. Dubois, and H. Prade. Nonmonotonic reasoning, conditional objects and possibility theory. *Artificial Intelligence*, 92:259–276, 1997.

[BDP99]   S. Benferhat, D. Dubois, and H. Prade. Possibilistic and standard probabilistic semantics of conditional knowledge bases. *Journal of Logic and Computation*, 9(6):873–895, 1999.

[BKI02]   C. Beierle and G. Kern-Isberner. Using institutions for the study of qualitative and quantitative conditional logics. In *Proceedings of the 8th European Conference on Logics in Artificial Intelligence, JELIA'02*. Springer, LNCS Vol. 2424, 2002.

[dF37]   B. de Finetti. La prévision, ses lois logiques et ses sources subjectives. In *Ann. Inst. H. Poincaré*, volume 7. 1937. English translation in *Studies in Subjective Probability*, ed. H. Kyburg and H.E. Smokler, 1964, 93-158. New York: Wiley.

[DP96]   D. Dubois and H. Prade. Non-standard theories of uncertainty in plausible reasoning. In G. Brewka, editor, *Principles of Knowledge Representation*. CSLI Publications, 1996.

[GB92]   J. Goguen and R. Burstall. Institutions: Abstract model theory for specification and programming. *Journal of the ACM*, 39(1):95–146, January 1992.

[GR02]   J. A. Goguen and G. Rosu. Institution morphisms. *Formal Aspects of Computing*, 13(3–5):274–307, 2002.

[HS73]   H. Herrlich and G. E. Strecker. *Category theory*. Allyn and Bacon, Boston, 1973.

[KI01]   G. Kern-Isberner. *Conditionals in nonmonotonic reasoning and belief revision*. Springer, Lecture Notes in Artificial Intelligence LNAI 2087, 2001.

[KLM90]   S. Kraus, D. Lehmann, and M. Magidor. Nonmonotonic reasoning, preferential models and cumulative logics. *Artificial Intelligence*, 44:167–207, 1990.

[Lew73]   D. Lewis. *Counterfactuals*. Harvard University Press, Cambridge, Mass., 1973.

[Mak94]   D. Makinson. General patterns in nonmonotonic reasoning. In D.M. Gabbay, C.H. Hogger, and J.A. Robinson, editors, *Handbook of Logic in Artificial Intelligence and Logic Programming*, volume 3, pages 35–110. Oxford University Press, 1994.

[MG91]   D. Makinson and P. Gärdenfors. Relations between the logic of theory change and nonmonotonic logic. In *Proceedings Workshop The Logic of Theory Change, Konstanz, Germany, 1989*, pages 185–205, Berlin Heidelberg New York, 1991. Springer.

[NC02]   D. Nute and C.B. Cross. Conditional logic. In D.M. Gabbay and F. Guenther, editors, *Handbook of Philosophical Logic*, volume 4, pages 1–98. Kluwer Academic Publishers, second edition, 2002.

[Pea89]   J. Pearl. Probabilistic semantics for nonmonotonic reasoning: A survey. In G. Shafer and J. Pearl, editors, *Readings in uncertain reasoning*, pages 699–710. Morgan Kaufmann, San Mateo, CA., 1989.

[Sno94]   P. Snow. The emergence of ordered belief from initial ignorance. In *Proceedings AAAI-94*, pages 281–286, Seattle, WA, 1994.

[Spo88]   W. Spohn. Ordinal conditional functions: a dynamic theory of epistemic states. In W.L. Harper and B. Skyrms, editors, *Causation in Decision, Belief Change, and Statistics, II*, pages 105–134. Kluwer Academic Publishers, 1988.

On Structuring Proof Search
for First Order Linear Logic

Paola Bruscoli and Alessio Guglielmi

Technische Universität Dresden, Hans-Grundig-Str. 25, 01062 Dresden, Germany,
Paola.Bruscoli@Inf.TU-Dresden.DE, Alessio.Guglielmi@Inf.TU-Dresden.DE

Abstract. We start from the Forum presentation of first order linear logic to design an equivalent system for which proof search is highly structured. We restrict formulae to a language of clauses and goals, without losing expressivity, in such a way that formulae have the same structure of Forum sequents. This means having a very big generalised connective that suffices for all of linear logic. We can then design a system with only two big rules, a left one and a right one. The behaviour of such system in proof search is operationally interesting and makes it suitable for further semantic investigations. We test the mutual harmony of the new rules by showing a cut elimination theorem.

1 Introduction

Forum [9] is a presentation of linear logic which only produces uniform proofs. This guarantees that a sensible operational interpretation of proof search is possible. Surprisingly, Forum is complete for linear logic; this contrasts with the situation in classical logic, where a complete presentation that only produces uniform proofs is not possible. Given the linguistic flexibility of linear logic, i.e., its ability of interpreting a broad range of computational situations, Forum represents a major step forward towards practical applications.

This research is motivated by the search for adequate operational models of Forum, especially behavioural models like labelled event structures, which describe causal relations. These are particularly important for the domains of applications of Forum, namely the modelling of computations in concurrency and planning.

A proof in Forum mainly consists of small, deterministic steps, corresponding to applying each of several inference rules. This determinism is, of course, not a surprise, since Forum has been designed precisely for the purpose of reducing and isolating non-determinism. One soon realises that, in order to obtain sensible models, one must abstract away from situations in which several steps occur one after another and no choice at all is actually possible: when no choice is available, causality becomes trivial and uninteresting. It is of course possible to make this abstraction after a proof is produced, but it is desirable to design a system that makes the abstraction since the beginning. In other words, one wonders whether it is possible to carry Forum one step ahead: making further restrictions that,

M.Y. Vardi and A. Voronkov (Eds.): LPAR 2003, LNAI 2850, pp. 389–406, 2003.

without losing expressivity, provide the right level of abstraction directly in the
proof theory.

To get Forum, Miller imposed certain restrictions on the sequents, inference
rules, and possible connectives of linear logic, but he left formula building free.
In this paper we restrict the class of allowed formulae, along lines already imag-
ined by Miller in [9], and we design correspondingly a system called G-Forum.
By doing this, we have that formulae drive the construction of proofs in a very
structured way, which allows us to individuate big chunks of derivations that essentially behave in a deterministic way: these will be the building blocks of our
desired behavioural semantics. The restriction of formulae makes them isomorphic to the sequents in Forum. Of course, in order to claim that this is "good"
proof theory, one has to test the internal harmony of G-Forum. We do it the
classical way: we prove a cut elimination theorem for the new system, and we
show that it is not necessary to resort to Forum in the intermediate steps of the
cut elimination procedure: G-Forum is enough, meaning that the new granularity
of rules genuinely corresponds to what we can consider a generalised connective.

We leave the development of the behavioural semantics to a future paper
(the reader can consult [6] for some preliminary results); in this paper we limit
ourselves to defining G-Forum and show cut elimination for it. In Sect. 2 we give
a quick account of Forum, then we develop G-Forum in Sect. 3.

The cut elimination proof is in the appendix.

2   First Order Forum

We deal with first order formal systems, and the following conventions apply.

2.1 Definition. *First order variables* are denoted by x, y and z; *terms* are
denoted by t, *atoms* by $a, b, c, \ldots, a(t_1, \ldots, t_h), b(\ldots), c(\ldots), \ldots$ *Sequences* are
denoted in vector notation, as in $\forall \vec{x}.a(\vec{t})$. *Formulae* are denoted by F and other
letters which will be introduced later on. Formulae are considered equal under
α-conversion.

This work is founded on linear logic; we are mainly interested in its first order
sequent calculus presentation. We refer to the literature for details, especially to
[5].

2.2 Definition. The formal system of full *first order linear logic*, in its Gentzen's
sequents presentation, and its language, are both denoted by FOLL. Formulae
in FOLL are freely built from first order atoms and *constants* 1, $\bot$, $\top$, 0 by
using *binary connectives* $\otimes$, $\parr$, $\&$, $\oplus$, $\multimap$, *modalities* !, ?, *negation* $^{\bot}$ and the
quantifiers $\forall$ and $\exists$. Constants 1, $\bot$ and connectives $\otimes$, $\parr$ and $\multimap$ are called the
multiplicatives; $\top$, 0, $\&$ and $\oplus$ are called the *additives*. *Equivalence* is written $\equiv$.
In linear logic $F \equiv F'$ iff $(F \multimap F') \& (F' \multimap F)$ is provable.

Intuitionistic implication $\Rightarrow$ admits the well-known decomposition $F \Rightarrow F' \equiv$
$!F \multimap F'$; we can consider $\Rightarrow$ part of the calculus.

2.3 Definition. The *binary connective* $\Rightarrow$ is introduced such that $F \Rightarrow F'$ is equivalent to $!F \multimap F'$.

2.4 Definition. Multiplicative connectives, except $\multimap$, take precedence over additive ones; implications are the weakest connectives; modalities and quantifiers are stronger than binary connectives; negation takes precedence over everything. Implications associate to the right. Whenever possible, we omit parentheses.

For example, $!\forall x.a^\perp \multimap b \,\&\, c \,⅋\, d \Rightarrow e$ stands for $(!(\forall x.(a^\perp))) \multimap ((b \,\&\, (c \,⅋\, d)) \Rightarrow e)$.

We briefly introduce the Forum formal system. The presentation corresponds to the one in [8], restricted to the first order case and with some minor modifications. An alternative and more detailed exposition can be found in [9].

2.5 Definition. The language of *first order* Forum is the subset of FOLL freely built over atoms and the constants $\bot$ and $\top$ by use of the binary connectives $⅋$, $\&$, $\multimap$ and $\Rightarrow$ and of the quantifier $\forall$. We will say "Forum" instead of "first order Forum." Generic Forum formulae are denoted by A and B.

So, Forum presents fewer connectives than FOLL, by getting rid of some of the redundant ones. It is not difficult to prove the following equivalences in FOLL:

$$1 \equiv \bot^\perp, \qquad\qquad 0 \equiv \top^\perp,$$
$$F \otimes F' \equiv (F^\perp ⅋ F'^\perp)^\perp, \qquad F \oplus F' \equiv (F^\perp \& F'^\perp)^\perp,$$
$$!F \equiv (F \Rightarrow \bot)^\perp, \qquad\qquad ?F \equiv F^\perp \Rightarrow \bot,$$

$$\exists x.F \equiv (\forall x.F^\perp)^\perp,$$
$$F^\perp \equiv F \multimap \bot.$$

Then, one can equivalently write any FOLL formula into the Forum language.

2.6 Definition. *Sequents* are expressions of the form

$$\begin{bmatrix} \Psi \\ \Gamma \end{bmatrix} A \vdash \begin{bmatrix} \\ \Lambda \end{bmatrix} \quad \text{or} \quad \begin{bmatrix} \Psi \\ \Gamma \end{bmatrix} \vdash \begin{bmatrix} \Xi \\ \Lambda \end{bmatrix},$$

where all formulae are Forum formulae and Ψ is a finite multiset of formulae (the *left classical context* or *classical program*); Γ is a finite multiset of formulae (the *left linear context* or *linear program*); A is a formula (the *left focused formula*); Ξ is a finite sequence of formulae (the *right linear context*); Λ is a finite multiset of atoms (the *atomic context*). Γ, Ξ and Λ are collectively referred to as the *linear context*. Ψ and Γ together are called the *program*. In the following Ψ, Γ, Ξ and Λ respectively stand for multisets, multisets and sequences of formulae and multisets of atoms. We write "Γ, A", or "A, Γ", instead of "$\Gamma \uplus \{A\}_+$" and "Γ, Γ'" instead of "$\Gamma \uplus \Gamma'$", where $\uplus$ is multiset union. Sequents are denoted by Σ. Sequents where no focused formula is present and Ξ is empty are called *state sequents*, are written

$$\begin{bmatrix} \Psi \\ \Gamma \end{bmatrix} \vdash \begin{bmatrix} \\ \Lambda \end{bmatrix}$$

and are denoted by S and R.

2.7 Definition. An *inference rule* is an expression of the form $r\dfrac{\Sigma_1 \ \cdots \ \Sigma_h}{\Sigma}$, where $h \geq 0$, sequents $\Sigma_1, \ldots, \Sigma_h$ are the *premises* of the rule, Σ is its *conclusion* and r is the *name* of the rule. An inference rule with no premises is called an *axiom*.

2.8 Definition. Let Forum be the first order proof system defined by inference rule schemes in Fig. 1. Structural rules are: i (*initial*), d_L (*decide linear*), d_C (*decide classical*), a (*atom*). Logical rules, divided into left and right ones, are: $\perp_L$, $\perp_R$ (*bottom*); $\top_R$ (*top*, there is no left rule); $\otimes_L$, $\otimes_R$ (*par*); $\&_{LL}$, $\&_{LR}$, $\&_R$ (*with*); $\multimap_L$, $\multimap_R$ (*linear implication*); $\Rightarrow_L$, $\Rightarrow_R$ (*intuitionistic implication*); $\forall_L$, $\forall_R$ (*universal quantification*).

Consider proofs in Forum in a bottom-up reading. In absence of a left focused formula, the right linear context is acted upon by right rules until it is empty; at that point a formula becomes focused, in a d_L or d_C rule. Then left rules only are applicable, until new formulae reach the right linear context, through $\multimap_L$ and $\Rightarrow_L$ rules. Proofs in Forum are said to be *uniform* [8–10].

Our system's major differences with Forum as presented in [8] are: 1) our classical context is a multiset while in [8] it is a set; 2) our atomic context is a multiset while in [8] it is a sequence. These differences do not affect provability (and uniformity of proofs), as it can be proved trivially.

Representing derivations as directed trees whose nodes are sequents is typographically advantageous, especially in the cut elimination proof. The direction of the arrows corresponds to the tree growth during the search for a proof. It should be clear that there is no difference between this notation and the usual one.

2.9 Definition. To every instance of an inference rule $r\dfrac{\Sigma_1 \ \cdots \ \Sigma_h}{\Sigma}$, when $h > 0$ an *elementary derivation*

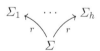

corresponds, *i.e.* a labeled directed tree whose root is labeled Σ, whose leaves are labeled $\Sigma_1, \ldots, \Sigma_h$ and whose arcs are labeled r; when $h = 0$ the corresponding elementary derivation is

$$r\uparrow^{\circ}_{\Sigma} \ ,$$

where $\circ$ is a mark distinct from every sequent. *Derivations* are non-empty, finite directed trees whose root is labeled by a sequent and whose other nodes are labeled by sequents or $\circ$ marks and such that every maximal subtree of depth 1 is an elementary derivation. Derivations are denoted by Δ. Given a derivation Δ, we say that Δ' is a *subderivation* of Δ if Δ' is a derivation and a subtree of Δ. Δ' is a *principal subderivation* of Δ if it is a subderivation of Δ and the roots of Δ and Δ' coincide. Given Δ, its *premises* are the labels of the leaves of Δ

Structural Rules

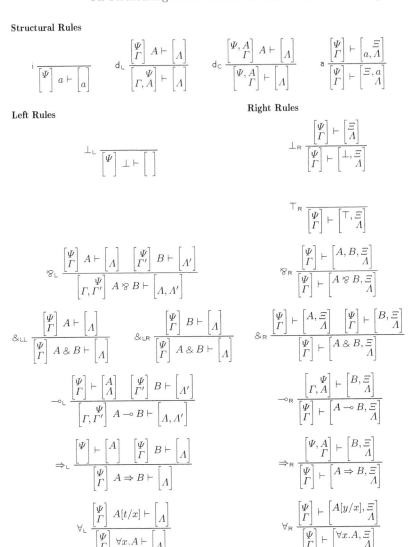

Left Rules

Right Rules

Fig. 1. The first order Forum proof system

other than ∘; its *conclusion* is the sequent labeling the root of Δ. The multiset of premises of Δ is indicated by $\tilde{\Delta}$. A sequent Σ is a derivation (of depth 0) whose premise and conclusion is Σ. A derivation Δ such that its premises are $\Sigma_1, \ldots, \Sigma_h$ and its conclusion is Σ can be represented as

$$\overset{\Sigma_1 \;\cdots\; \Sigma_h}{\underset{\Sigma}{\overbrace{\Delta}}}.$$

Sometimes the name of the derivation is not shown. If Δ is the derivation

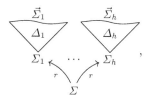

where $h \geq 0$, we define its *depth* $\mathsf{d}(\Delta)$ as max $\{\mathsf{d}(\Delta_1), \ldots, \mathsf{d}(\Delta_h)\} + 1$, where, for every sequent Σ, it holds $\mathsf{d}(\Sigma) = \mathsf{d}(\circ) = 0$. If Δ has no premises we say that Δ is a *proof*. Proofs are denoted by Π. We say that Π *proves* (or *is a proof of*) its conclusion. We say that a formula A is *provable* in Forum, or that Forum *proves* A, if a proof of $\left[\,\right] \vdash \left[A\right]$ exists.

The premises of the derivation in Fig. 2 are $\left\{\left[\,\right] a \vdash \left[a\right], \left[\,\right] a \vdash \left[a\right]\right\}_+$, and its conclusion is $\left[\,\right] a \,\bindnasrepma\, (b \,\bindnasrepma\, a) \vdash \left[a, a, b\right]$. This derivation can be completed into a proof by applying two initial rules to its premises.

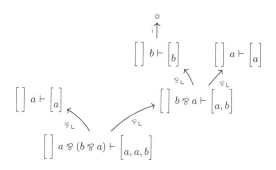

Fig. 2. Example of derivation

Arcs are not independent in the growth process of a derivation: all arcs propagating from a node correspond to the application of the same inference rule.

By looking at Fig. 1 it is clear that if we make the classical context a set (as Miller does), derivability is not affected. In fact, the only impact is on the $\Rightarrow_R$ rule, but things do not change, because the classical context is implicitly subject to weakening in all axioms.

2.10 Theorem. *Every* Forum *formula is provable in* Forum *if and only if it is provable in* FOLL. (Miller [8, 9])

3   Derivations at a Higher Level of Abstraction

Consider a formula $\delta = G_1 \Rightarrow \cdots \Rightarrow G_{k''} \Rightarrow H_1 \multimap \cdots \multimap H_{k'} \multimap a_1 \otimes \cdots \otimes a_k$.
In Forum, in a bottom-up construction of a derivation, from $\begin{bmatrix} \\ \end{bmatrix} \vdash \begin{bmatrix} \delta \\ \end{bmatrix}$ we

are always led to the state sequents $\begin{bmatrix} G_1, \ldots, G_{k''} \\ H_1, \ldots, H_{k'} \end{bmatrix} \vdash \begin{bmatrix} \\ a_1, \ldots, a_k \end{bmatrix}$. Let us

call *clauses* formulae like δ, where formulae G_i and H_j (*goals*) are of the form $\forall \vec{x}.(\delta_1 \& \cdots \& \delta_h)$, and where in the $\&$ conjunction only clauses are allowed.

In this section we derive a proof system equivalent to FOLL. The new proof system is in fact the old Forum proof system seen at a coarser abstraction level: rules are essentially macro derivations composed of many Forum rules, and the only formulae allowed are goals (and clauses).

3.1   Goals and Clauses

We define goals and clauses, which are Forum formulae of a constrained shape; then we show that their language is equivalent to Forum and then to FOLL.

3.1.1 Definition. Goals and clauses are recursively defined this way:

1) A *goal* is a formula of the form

$$\forall \vec{x}.(\delta_1 \& \cdots \& \delta_h),$$

where $\vec{x}$ can be empty, $h \geq 0$ and every δ_i is a clause. When $h = 0$ a goal is $\forall \vec{x}.\top$.

2) A *clause* δ is a formula of the form

$$G_1 \Rightarrow \cdots \Rightarrow G_{k''} \Rightarrow H_1 \multimap \cdots \multimap H_{k'} \multimap a_1 \otimes \cdots \otimes a_k,$$

where $k, k', k'' \geq 0$, formulae G_i and H_i are goals and formulae a_i are atoms. Goals G_i are called the *classical premises* of δ, goals H_i are its *linear premises* and $a_1 \otimes \cdots \otimes a_k$ is the *head* of the clause. We define $\mathsf{hd}(\delta) = \{a_1, \ldots, a_k\}_+$, $\mathsf{lp}(\delta) = \{H_1, \ldots, H_{k'}\}_+$ and $\mathsf{cp}(\delta) = \{G_1, \ldots, G_{k''}\}_+$. When $k = 0$ the head is $\bot$. When $k' = 0$ and $k'' = 0$ clauses assume the following special forms, respectively:

$$G_1 \Rightarrow \cdots \Rightarrow G_{k''} \Rightarrow a_1 \otimes \cdots \otimes a_k \quad \text{and}$$
$$H_1 \multimap \cdots \multimap H_{k'} \multimap a_1 \otimes \cdots \otimes a_k.$$

Goals are denoted by G and H, clauses by δ and γ.

Clearly, a clause is also a goal.

3.1.2 Theorem. *Every formula in* FOLL *is equivalent to a goal in* Forum.

Proof. We show that, taken any formula in Forum, we can exhibit an equivalent goal.

We use the following absorption equivalences:

1) $F \otimes \bot \equiv F$;
2) $F \otimes \top \equiv \top$;
3) $F \& \top \equiv F$.

We also use the following equivalences:

4) $F \otimes (F' \& F'') \equiv (F \otimes F') \& (F \otimes F'')$;
5) $\forall x.F \otimes F' \equiv \forall x.(F \otimes F')$, whenever x is not free in F' and
6) $\forall x.F \& F' \equiv \forall x.(F \& F')$, whenever x is not free in F'.

Let A be a formula in Forum: the proof is by induction on its structure. The base cases being trivial, consider given B and B'; by the induction hypothesis we suppose we are also given two goals G and G' such that

$$B \equiv G = \forall \vec{x}.(\delta_1 \& \cdots \& \delta_h),$$
$$B' \equiv G' = \forall \vec{y}.(\delta'_1 \& \cdots \& \delta'_{h'}),$$

where $\vec{x}$ and $\vec{y}$ may be empty and h and h' may be 0. The following cases may occur.

- $A = B \otimes B'$. By applications of equivalence 5 and renaming of bounded variables, if necessary, we get

$$A \equiv \forall \vec{z}.\big((\delta_1 \& \cdots \& \delta_h) \otimes (\delta'_1 \& \cdots \& \delta'_{h'})\big).$$

If $h = 0$ or $h' = 0$ we can conclude that $A \equiv \forall \vec{z}.\top$, by making use of equivalence 2. Otherwise, we may repeatedly apply equivalence 4 above, and we get:

$$A \equiv \forall \vec{z}.\Big(\big((\delta_1 \otimes \delta'_1) \& \cdots \& (\delta_h \otimes \delta'_1)\big) \& \cdots \& \big((\delta_1 \otimes \delta'_{h'}) \& \cdots \& (\delta_h \otimes \delta'_{h'})\big)\Big).$$

For $1 \leq i \leq h$ and $1 \leq j \leq h'$, let

$$\delta_i = G_1^i \Rightarrow \cdots \Rightarrow G_{h''_i}^i \Rightarrow H_1^i \multimap \cdots \multimap H_{h'_i}^i \multimap a_1^i \otimes \cdots \otimes a_{h_i}^i,$$
$$\delta'_j = G_1'^j \Rightarrow \cdots \Rightarrow G_{k''_j}'^j \Rightarrow H_1'^j \multimap \cdots \multimap H_{k'_j}'^j \multimap a_1'^j \otimes \cdots \otimes a_{k_j}'^j.$$

Since $F \Rightarrow F' \equiv {!}F \multimap F'$ and $F \multimap F' \equiv F^\perp \otimes F'$, commutativity of $\otimes$ suffices to show that

$$\delta_i \otimes \delta'_j \equiv G_1^i \Rightarrow \cdots \Rightarrow G_{h''_i}^i \Rightarrow G_1'^j \Rightarrow \cdots \Rightarrow G_{k''_j}'^j \Rightarrow$$
$$H_1^i \multimap \cdots \multimap H_{h'_i}^i \multimap H_1'^j \multimap \cdots \multimap H_{k'_j}'^j \multimap$$
$$a_1^i \otimes \cdots \otimes a_{h_i}^i \otimes a_1'^j \otimes \cdots \otimes a_{k_j}'^j.$$

Special cases where $h_i = 0$ or $k_j = 0$ are handled by equivalence 1 above.

- $A = B \,\&\, B'$. By applications of equivalence 6 and renaming of bounded variables, if necessary, we get

$$A \equiv \forall \vec{z}.(\delta_1 \,\&\, \cdots \,\&\, \delta_h \,\&\, \delta'_1 \,\&\, \cdots \,\&\, \delta'_h).$$

If $h = 0$ or $h' = 0$ use equivalence 3.

- $A = B \multimap B'$. By using equivalences 5 and 4, and by renaming bounded variables if necessary, we have:

$$\begin{aligned}
A &\equiv G^{\perp} \,\&\, \forall \vec{y}.(\delta'_1 \,\&\, \cdots \,\&\, \delta'_h) \\
&\equiv \forall \vec{z}.(G^{\perp} \,\&\, (\delta'_1 \,\&\, \cdots \,\&\, \delta'_h)) \\
&\equiv \forall \vec{z}.((G^{\perp} \,\&\, \delta'_1) \,\&\, \cdots \,\&\, (G^{\perp} \,\&\, \delta'_h)).
\end{aligned}$$

By commutativity of $\,\&\,$ it is easily seen that every $(G^{\perp} \,\&\, \delta'_i)$ is a clause. If $B' \equiv \top$ then $A \equiv \top$.

- $A = B \Rightarrow B'$. The argument goes as in the previous case.
- $A = \forall x.B$. Trivial. □

3.1.3 Corollary. *Every formula in* FOLL *is equivalent to a clause.*

Proof. Let F be a formula and $G \equiv F$, where G is obtained as in th. 3.1.2. Then, $(G \multimap \perp) \multimap \perp$ is a clause equivalent to G.

From the proof of th. 3.1.2 an obvious algorithm can be derived to transform a Forum formula into a goal. Please note that if A is a Forum formula and G the equivalent goal found by the given procedure, then the set of logical constants appearing in G is not greater than that of A. In fact, in none of the cases considered new connectives are introduced. If G is not a clause, and a clause is required, then $(G \multimap \perp) \multimap \perp$ introduces $\perp$, not necessarily present in A. It could be possible to prove the result in a shorter way, but we would have to give up this separation property.

Not introducing new connectives in the translation to a goal has obvious benefits concerning modularity. In particular, this property takes care of some concerns of Miller in [8] about clauses (similar to ours) with degenerate head $\perp$. Clauses of that kind, when at the left of $\vdash$, are always available to rewritings, what is of course cause of explosion of the search space of proofs.

3.2 Deriving in the Right Context

3.2.1 Definition. Let δ_R be the following *clause reduction right* inference rule, shown in Fig. 3 in terms of Forum rules:

$$\delta_R \frac{\left[\begin{array}{c} \Psi, \mathsf{cp}(\delta) \\ \Gamma, \mathsf{lp}(\delta) \end{array}\right] \vdash \left[\begin{array}{c} \Xi \\ \mathsf{hd}(\delta), \Lambda \end{array}\right]}{\left[\begin{array}{c} \Psi \\ \Gamma \end{array}\right] \vdash \left[\begin{array}{c} \delta, \Xi \\ \Lambda \end{array}\right]}.$$

In the figure $k > 0$ and $k', k'' \geq 0$. Starred inference rule names mean repeated application of the rule, or no application at all; ($\,\&_R$ or a) stands for "application of one of either $\,\&_R$ or a." In the special case where $k = 0$ the upper sequence of ($\,\&_R$ or a) rules is replaced by a single application of $\perp_R$.

$$
\cfrac{
\cfrac{
\cfrac{
\cfrac{
\left[\begin{matrix}\Psi \\ \Gamma\end{matrix}\right] \vdash \left[G_1 \Rightarrow \cdots \Rightarrow G_{k''} \Rightarrow H_1 \multimap \cdots \multimap H_{k'} \multimap a_1 \,\invamp\, \cdots \,\invamp\, a_k, \begin{matrix}\Xi \\ \Lambda\end{matrix}\right]
}{
\left[\begin{matrix}\Psi \\ \Gamma\end{matrix}\right] \vdash \left[H_1 \multimap \cdots \multimap H_{k'} \multimap a_1 \,\invamp\, \cdots \,\invamp\, a_k, \begin{matrix}\Xi \\ \Lambda\end{matrix}\right]
}{\;\Rightarrow_R^{\,\star}\uparrow}
}{
\left[\begin{matrix}\Psi, G_1, \ldots, G_{k''} \\ \Gamma, H_1, \ldots, H_{k'}\end{matrix}\right] \vdash \left[a_1 \,\invamp\, \cdots \,\invamp\, a_k, \begin{matrix}\Xi \\ \Lambda\end{matrix}\right]
}{\;\multimap_R^{\,\star}\uparrow}
}{
\left[\begin{matrix}\Psi, G_1, \ldots, G_{k''} \\ \Gamma, H_1, \ldots, H_{k'}\end{matrix}\right] \vdash \left[\begin{matrix}\Xi \\ a_1, \ldots, a_k, \Lambda\end{matrix}\right]
}{(\invamp_R \text{ or } \mathbf{a})^{\star}\uparrow}
$$

Fig. 3. Clause reduction right inference rule δ_R

3.2.2 Proposition. *Every proof of* $\left[\begin{matrix}\Psi \\ \Gamma\end{matrix}\right] \vdash \left[\begin{matrix}\delta, \Xi \\ \Lambda\end{matrix}\right]$ *has shape*
$$
\cfrac{
\nabla \atop \left[\begin{matrix}\Psi' \\ \Gamma'\end{matrix}\right] \vdash \left[\begin{matrix}\Xi \\ \Lambda'\end{matrix}\right]
}{
\left[\begin{matrix}\Psi \\ \Gamma\end{matrix}\right] \vdash \left[\begin{matrix}\delta, \Xi \\ \Lambda\end{matrix}\right]
}{\delta_R\uparrow}\;.
$$

Proof. By reasoning bottom-up, each application of an inference rule is compulsory. □

All Forum inference rules applied in δ_R are right ones. This is of course an aspect of the fact that Forum produces only uniform proofs (see [8–10]). Rules $\top_R$, $\&_R$ and $\forall_R$ are still missing: they will appear in the reduction of goals.

We can build on δ_R an inference rule which reduces goals in the right linear context.

3.2.3 Definition. Let G_R be the following *goal reduction right* inference rule, shown in Fig. 4 in terms of δ_R and Forum rules:

$$
G_R \cfrac{
\left[\begin{matrix}\Psi, \mathsf{cp}(\delta_1\rho) \\ \Gamma, \mathsf{lp}(\delta_1\rho)\end{matrix}\right] \vdash \left[\begin{matrix}\Xi \\ \mathsf{hd}(\delta_1\rho), \Lambda\end{matrix}\right] \quad \cdots \quad \left[\begin{matrix}\Psi, \mathsf{cp}(\delta_h\rho) \\ \Gamma, \mathsf{lp}(\delta_h\rho)\end{matrix}\right] \vdash \left[\begin{matrix}\Xi \\ \mathsf{hd}(\delta_h\rho), \Lambda\end{matrix}\right]
}{
\left[\begin{matrix}\Psi \\ \Gamma\end{matrix}\right] \vdash \left[\begin{matrix}\forall \vec{x}.(\delta_1 \& \cdots \& \delta_h), \Xi \\ \Lambda\end{matrix}\right]
}\;,
$$

where $\vec{x}$ can be empty, ρ is an appropriate renaming substitution and $h \geq 0$. In the figure only one choice among the possible associations of $\&$ connectives has been considered, but every choice leads to the same multiset of premises.

This whole reduction phase is deterministic: in the end a goal is reduced to pieces with no choice about the possible outcome, except for the rather immaterial choice of eigenvariables in G_R rules. The Forum system has been designed to reduce choices to a minimum, in a bottom-up construction of a proof. Still, some "unnecessary" sequentialization exists: in the case above it resides in the binary treatment of associative connectives. We can consider the G_R rule at the

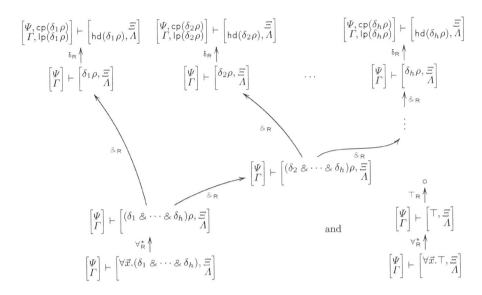

Fig. 4. Goal reduction right inference rule G_R when $h > 0$ and $h = 0$

abstraction level in which all premises are reached at the same time in a parallel way, thus hiding the sequentialization at the Forum's level of abstraction. In other words we can consider every instance of the G_R rule a representative of an equivalence class of derivations, differing only on the associations of & connectives.

We can perform on the G_R rule the same kind of simple reasoning we did for δ_R in prop. 3.2.2.

3.2.4 Proposition. *Every proof of* $\begin{bmatrix} \Psi \\ \Gamma \end{bmatrix} \vdash \begin{bmatrix} G, \Xi \\ \Lambda \end{bmatrix}$ *has shape*

G_R defines the behaviour of goals when they appear at the right of $\vdash$. They generate as many threads in the computation as there are clauses in the conjunction. These threads are independent, and can be considered *parallel* computations. When G_R is applied to a $\forall \vec{x}.\top$, it just *terminates* a (thread of a) computation.

3.2.5 Definition. A G-*state sequent* is a state sequent of the kind $\begin{bmatrix} \Psi \\ \Gamma \end{bmatrix} \vdash \begin{bmatrix} \\ \Lambda \end{bmatrix}$, where all formulae in Ψ and Γ are goals.

By 3.1.2 and 3.2.4 we can always reduce provability of a Forum formula (therefore of a FOLL's one, by 2.10) to provability of some G-state sequents. Moreover, we can always reduce provability of a given formula to the provability of exactly one G-state sequent by employing the double negation equivalence $G \equiv (G \multimap \bot) \multimap \bot$: this last formula is a clause.

3.3   Deriving in the Left Context

G-State sequents embody the natural notion of state of our computations. A G-state sequent represents state at a certain level of abstraction; to proceed, clauses from its program must be applied to its atomic context. Left rules come into play: application of clauses is mainly accomplished by $\multimap_L$ and $\Rightarrow_L$ rules.

3.3.1 Definition. Let h be the following *head matching* inference rule, where $k \geq 0$:

$$h \frac{}{\begin{bmatrix} \Psi \\ \end{bmatrix} a_1 \,\text{⅋}\cdots\text{⅋}\, a_k \vdash \begin{bmatrix} \\ a_1,\ldots,a_k \end{bmatrix}} \ .$$

Fig. 5 shows how h corresponds to Forum inference rules. The same considerations made above about the associativity of & hold here for ⅋.

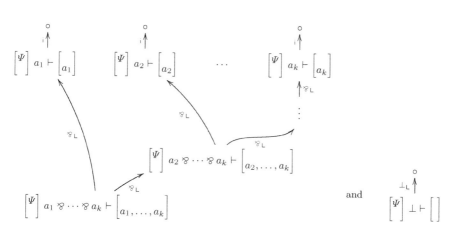

Fig. 5. Head matching inference rule h when $k > 0$ and $k = 0$

3.3.2 Proposition. *If the sequent* $\begin{bmatrix} \Psi \\ \Gamma \end{bmatrix} a_1 \,\mathbf{\gamma}\cdots\mathbf{\gamma}\, a_k \vdash \begin{bmatrix} \\ \Lambda \end{bmatrix}$ *is provable, then* Γ

is empty, $\Lambda = \{a_1, \ldots, a_k\}_+$ *and the only proof is* $\mathsf{h}\, \overline{\begin{bmatrix} \Psi \\ \end{bmatrix} a_1 \,\mathbf{\gamma}\cdots\mathbf{\gamma}\, a_k \vdash \begin{bmatrix} \\ a_1, \ldots, a_k \end{bmatrix}}$.

3.3.3 Definition. Let δ_L be the following *clause reduction left* inference rule, shown in Fig. 6 in terms of h and Forum rules:

$$\delta_\mathsf{L} \frac{\begin{bmatrix} \Psi \\ \end{bmatrix} \vdash \begin{bmatrix} G_1 \\ \end{bmatrix} \;\cdots\; \begin{bmatrix} \Psi \\ \end{bmatrix} \vdash \begin{bmatrix} G_{k''} \\ \end{bmatrix} \quad \begin{bmatrix} \Psi \\ \Gamma_1 \end{bmatrix} \vdash \begin{bmatrix} H_1 \\ \Lambda_1 \end{bmatrix} \;\cdots\; \begin{bmatrix} \Psi \\ \Gamma_{k'} \end{bmatrix} \vdash \begin{bmatrix} H_{k'} \\ \Lambda_{k'} \end{bmatrix}}{\begin{bmatrix} \Psi \\ \Gamma \end{bmatrix} \delta \vdash \begin{bmatrix} \\ \Lambda \end{bmatrix}},$$

where $\delta = G_1 \Rightarrow \cdots \Rightarrow G_{k''} \Rightarrow H_1 \multimap \cdots \multimap H_{k'} \multimap a_1 \,\mathbf{\gamma}\cdots\mathbf{\gamma}\, a_k$, and $k, k', k'' \geq 0$, and where $\Gamma_1 \uplus \cdots \uplus \Gamma_{k'} = \Gamma$ and $\Lambda_1 \uplus \cdots \uplus \Lambda_{k'} \uplus \{a_1, \ldots, a_k\}_+ = \Lambda$.

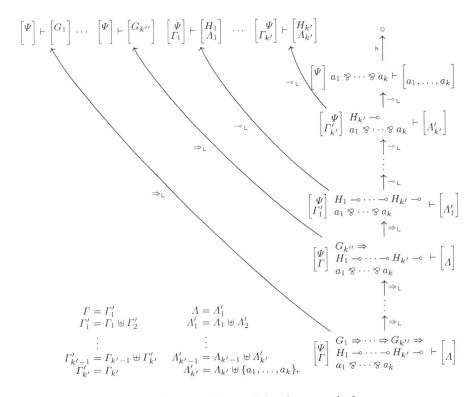

Fig. 6. Clause reduction left inference rule δ_L

$$\left[\begin{matrix}\Psi\\\Gamma\end{matrix}\right]\delta_l\sigma\vdash\left[\Lambda\right] \qquad\qquad \left[\begin{matrix}\Psi,G\\\Gamma\end{matrix}\right]\delta_l\sigma\vdash\left[\Lambda\right]$$

$$\text{(\&}_{LL}\text{ or \&}_{LR}\text{)}^\ast\uparrow \qquad\qquad \text{(\&}_{LL}\text{ or \&}_{LR}\text{)}^\ast\uparrow$$

$$\left[\begin{matrix}\Psi\\\Gamma\end{matrix}\right]\delta_1\sigma\,\&\ldots\&\,\delta_h\sigma\vdash\left[\Lambda\right] \qquad \left[\begin{matrix}\Psi,G\\\Gamma\end{matrix}\right]\delta_1\sigma\,\&\ldots\&\,\delta_h\sigma\vdash\left[\Lambda\right]$$

$$\forall_L^\ast\uparrow \qquad\qquad\qquad\qquad \forall_L^\ast\uparrow$$

$$\quad\text{or}$$

$$\left[\begin{matrix}\Psi\\\Gamma\end{matrix}\right]G\vdash\left[\Lambda\right] \qquad\qquad \left[\begin{matrix}\Psi,G\\\Gamma\end{matrix}\right]G\vdash\left[\Lambda\right]$$

$$d_L\uparrow \qquad\qquad\qquad\qquad d_C\uparrow$$

$$\left[\begin{matrix}\Psi\\\Gamma,G\end{matrix}\right]\vdash\left[\Lambda\right] \qquad\qquad \left[\begin{matrix}\Psi,G\\\Gamma\end{matrix}\right]\vdash\left[\Lambda\right]$$

Fig. 7. Decision inference rule d in its two possibilities

As an outcome of the reduction of the left focused clause, we have a multiset of premises which will be further reduced by as many G_R rules. They, in turn, will produce G-state sequents. The most degenerate instances of δ_L have no premises. Special cases where there are no classical or linear premises are easily inferable from the general scheme provided. Thanks to uniform provability, all non-determinism in searching for Forum proofs resides in left rules. Much of it can be concentrated into a decision rule, but one should notice that δ_L is also nondeterministic in the splitting of the linear contexts.

3.3.4 Definition. Let d be the *decision* inference rule, defined in the following two (non-mutually exclusive) cases, and shown in Fig. 7 in terms of Forum rules:

$$d\frac{\left[\begin{matrix}\Psi\\\Gamma\end{matrix}\right]\delta_l\sigma\vdash\left[\Lambda\right]}{\left[\begin{matrix}\Psi\\\Gamma,G\end{matrix}\right]\vdash\left[\Lambda\right]} \quad\text{or}\quad d\frac{\left[\begin{matrix}\Psi,G\\\Gamma\end{matrix}\right]\delta_l\sigma\vdash\left[\Lambda\right]}{\left[\begin{matrix}\Psi,G\\\Gamma\end{matrix}\right]\vdash\left[\Lambda\right]},$$

where the conclusions are G-state sequents. In the first case Γ, G is the *selected context*, in the second it is Ψ, G. $G = \forall\vec{x}.(\delta_1\,\&\ldots\&\,\delta_h)$, where $h > 0$ and $\vec{x}$ can be empty, is the *selected goal*; $\delta_l\sigma$ is the *selected clause*, $1 \le l \le h$, and σ is a substitution whose domain is $\vec{x}$.

3.3.5 Proposition. *All proofs of* $\left[\begin{matrix}\Psi\\\Gamma\end{matrix}\right]\vdash\left[\Lambda\right]$ *have shape* $\begin{matrix}\bigtriangledown\\\left[\begin{matrix}\Psi\\\Gamma'\end{matrix}\right]\delta\vdash\left[\Lambda\right]\\d\uparrow\\\left[\begin{matrix}\Psi\\\Gamma\end{matrix}\right]\vdash\left[\Lambda\right]\end{matrix}$ *, for*

some Γ', and the inference rule above d is δ_L.

We can build on d and δ_L an inference rule which reduces goals in the program.

3.3.6 Definition. Let G_L be the *goal reduction left* inference rule, defined in the following two (non-mutually exclusive) cases and shown in Fig. 8 in terms of d and δ_L rules:

$$
G_L \frac{\left[\begin{matrix}\Psi\\ \end{matrix}\right] \vdash \left[\begin{matrix}G_1\\ \end{matrix}\right] \cdots \left[\begin{matrix}\Psi\\ \end{matrix}\right] \vdash \left[\begin{matrix}G_{k''}\\ \end{matrix}\right] \quad \left[\begin{matrix}\Psi\\ \Gamma_1\end{matrix}\right] \vdash \left[\begin{matrix}H_1\\ \Lambda_1\end{matrix}\right] \cdots \left[\begin{matrix}\Psi\\ \Gamma_{k'}\end{matrix}\right] \vdash \left[\begin{matrix}H_{k'}\\ \Lambda_{k'}\end{matrix}\right]}{\left[\begin{matrix}\Psi\\ \Gamma,G\end{matrix}\right] \vdash \left[\begin{matrix}\Lambda\\ \end{matrix}\right]} \quad \text{or}
$$

$$
G_L \frac{\left[\begin{matrix}\Psi,G\\ \end{matrix}\right] \vdash \left[\begin{matrix}G_1\\ \end{matrix}\right] \cdots \left[\begin{matrix}\Psi,G\\ \end{matrix}\right] \vdash \left[\begin{matrix}G_{k''}\\ \end{matrix}\right] \quad \left[\begin{matrix}\Psi,G\\ \Gamma_1\end{matrix}\right] \vdash \left[\begin{matrix}H_1\\ \Lambda_1\end{matrix}\right] \cdots \left[\begin{matrix}\Psi,G\\ \Gamma_{k'}\end{matrix}\right] \vdash \left[\begin{matrix}H_{k'}\\ \Lambda_{k'}\end{matrix}\right]}{\left[\begin{matrix}\Psi,G\\ \Gamma\end{matrix}\right] \vdash \left[\begin{matrix}\Lambda\\ \end{matrix}\right]},
$$

where $G = \forall \vec{x}.(\delta_1 \& \ldots \& \delta_h)$, $\vec{x}$ can be empty, $\delta_l \sigma = G_1 \Rightarrow \cdots \Rightarrow G_{k''} \Rightarrow H_1 \multimap \cdots \multimap H_{k'} \multimap a_1 \,\otimes\, \cdots \otimes a_k$, for $1 \leq l \leq h$ and $k, k', k'' \geq 0$, and where $\Gamma_1 \uplus \cdots \uplus \Gamma_{k'} = \Gamma$ and $\Lambda_1 \uplus \cdots \uplus \Lambda_{k'} \uplus \{a_1, \ldots, a_k\}_+ = \Lambda$.

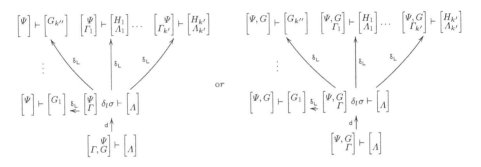

Fig. 8. Goal reduction left inference rule G_L in its two possibilities

3.4 A System for Goals

In the previous section we built two big inference rules, a left one and a right one. Their definition might look complex, but it is in fact rather straightforward once one knows the (operational) meaning of linear logic connectives. One should notice that if the language of formulae were not restricted to goals, such an enterprise would really be cumbersome and complex, and probably pointless. Our point is, instead, that goals in Forum actually define sort of a 'generalised' connective. In the sequent calculus, connectives are defined by inference rules, and of course inference rules should behave correctly. An important technical meaning of this last requirement is that the rules allow for a cut elimination theorem.

We know already cut elimination from linear logic, but that theorem is proved inside the sequent system where all the usual connectives are defined. Even if we know that cut is admissible in our system, in order to test its internal harmony we have to provide a cut elimination proof that does not appeal to the underlying 'small' connectives. In this section we expose the main ideas, the details are available in the journal version of the paper [3].

3.4.1 Definition. Let G-Forum be the formal system whose sequents are G-state sequents or sequents of the form $\begin{bmatrix} \Psi \\ \Gamma \end{bmatrix} \vdash \begin{bmatrix} G \\ \Lambda \end{bmatrix}$, where Ψ and Γ contain goals, and whose inference rules are $\mathsf{G_L}$ and $\mathsf{G_R}$.

Let us first define two natural cut rules for G-Forum.

3.4.2 Definition. The following inference rules $\bowtie_L$ and $\bowtie_C$ are respectively called *cut linear* and *cut classical*:

$$\bowtie_L \dfrac{\begin{bmatrix} \Psi \\ \Gamma \end{bmatrix} \vdash \begin{bmatrix} G \\ \Lambda \end{bmatrix} \quad \begin{bmatrix} \Psi' \\ G, \Gamma' \end{bmatrix} \vdash \begin{bmatrix} \Xi' \\ \Lambda' \end{bmatrix}}{\begin{bmatrix} \Psi, \Psi' \\ \Gamma, \Gamma' \end{bmatrix} \vdash \begin{bmatrix} \Xi' \\ \Lambda, \Lambda' \end{bmatrix}} \quad \text{and} \quad \bowtie_C \dfrac{\begin{bmatrix} \Psi \\ \ \end{bmatrix} \vdash \begin{bmatrix} G \\ \ \end{bmatrix} \quad \begin{bmatrix} G, \Psi' \\ \Gamma' \end{bmatrix} \vdash \begin{bmatrix} \Xi' \\ \Lambda' \end{bmatrix}}{\begin{bmatrix} \Psi, \Psi' \\ \Gamma' \end{bmatrix} \vdash \begin{bmatrix} \Xi' \\ \Lambda' \end{bmatrix}}.$$

Ξ' is either empty or a singleton. In both rules G is called the eigenformula. System G-Forum$^{\bowtie_L, \bowtie_C}$ is G-Forum where $\bowtie_L$, $\bowtie_C$ are allowed in proofs.

The following is the cut elimination theorem. Its proof follows a traditional argument in which one deals with contraction by a generalised cut rule that cuts on several copies of the same eigenformula (see for example [4]). We use the cut classical rule, in a certain generalisation $\bowtie'_C$, together with a contraction rule, to make G-Forum$^{\bowtie_L, \bowtie_C}$ more general, and then we prove cut elimination on this more general system. The core of the proof is the elimination of the $\bowtie_L$ rule. Actually, the design of the rules $\mathsf{G_L}$ and $\mathsf{G_R}$, and the crucial decisions about the exact definition of goals, all come from a careful analysis of what is needed in this part of the cut elimination argument. The induction measure is based on cut-rank.

3.4.3 Theorem. *For every proof in* G-Forum$^{\bowtie_L, \bowtie_C}$ *there exists a proof in* G-Forum *with the same conclusion.*

Proof (Sketch). We consider a contraction rule, $>$, and a cut classical rule in a more general form, $\bowtie'_C$, and we show that they hold:

$$\text{G-Forum}^{>, \bowtie_L, \bowtie'_C} \to \text{G-Forum}^{>, \bowtie_L} \to \text{G-Forum}^{>} \to \text{G-Forum},$$

i.e., a proof in a left system can be transformed into a proof in a system at its right, having the same conclusion. The leftmost system is more general than G-Forum$^{\bowtie_L, \bowtie_C}$, what yields the result.   □

4   Conclusions

In this paper we showed G-Forum, an asymmetrical sequent system for linear logic, and we proved cut elimination for it. Like in the case of Forum, the left-right asymmetry of sequents is motivated by the necessity of limiting proof search to uniform proofs. We also imposed an asymmetry to formulae, in such a way that their structure matches that of sequents. This new asymmetry is motivated by the desire of structuring proofs by easily definable, big building blocks, suitable to semantic understanding. We consider the situation where two asymmetries match rather pleasant, and more symmetric than the same in Forum, where the structure of formulae is symmetric, so at odds with that of sequents.

The result is a system for which it is natural to define cut rules and for which it is possible to prove cut elimination by a procedure that rewrites proofs inside the system, without resorting to Forum or plain linear logic. This guarantees that the new system has a good proof theoretical standing, which usually means that it is a good basis for further, fruitful research.

In a forthcoming paper we will show how to associate to G-Forum a labelled event structure semantics, i.e., a behavioural model of computation, along the lines initiated in [6]. In another paper we will apply G-Forum and its semantics to problems of partial order planning.

The methods in this paper are about studying the structure of proofs at a coarser abstraction level than the one provided by the sequent calculus. In another research project we are pursuing about the calculus of structures [1, 2, 7, 11] (see also our web site at http://www.ki.inf.tu-dresden.de/~guglielm/Research), we study proofs at a *finer* level than provided by the sequent calculus. We do so for exploring properties of locality and modularity, which are important for computer science, that are otherwise not available. In the future, we plan to adapt the techniques in this paper to the calculus of structures (for example, of linear logic), in order to cover the full range of abstractions: from the finer, suitable for distributed implementation, to the coarser, suitable for semantics.

References

1. Kai Brünnler and Alwen Fernanto Tiu. A local system for classical logic. In R. Nieuwenhuis and A. Voronkov, editors, *LPAR 2001*, volume 2250 of *Lecture Notes in Artificial Intelligence*, pages 347–361. Springer-Verlag, 2001. URL: http://www.ki.inf.uni-dresden.de/~kai/LocalClassicalLogic-lpar.pdf.

2. Paola Bruscoli. A purely logical account of sequentiality in proof search. In Peter J. Stuckey, editor, *Logic Programming, 18th International Conference*, volume 2401 of *Lecture Notes in Artificial Intelligence*, pages 302–316. Springer-Verlag, 2002. URL: http://www.ki.inf.uni-dresden.de/~paola/bvl/bvl.pdf.

3. Paola Bruscoli and Alessio Guglielmi. On structuring proof search for first order linear logic. Technical Report WV-03-10, Technische Universität Dresden, 2003. URL: http://www.ki.inf.uni-dresden.de/~paola/sps/sps.pdf.

4. Jean Gallier. Constructive logics. Part I: A tutorial on proof systems and typed λ-calculi. *Theoretical Computer Science*, 110:249–339, 1993.

5. Jean-Yves Girard. Linear logic. *Theoretical Computer Science*, 50:1–102, 1987.

6. Alessio Guglielmi. *Abstract Logic Programming in Linear Logic—Independence and Causality in a First Order Calculus*. PhD thesis, Università di Pisa, 1996.

7. Alessio Guglielmi. A system of interaction and structure. Technical Report WV-02-10, Technische Universität Dresden, 2002. Submitted to ACM Transactions on Computational Logic. URL: http://www.ki.inf.uni-dresden.de/~guglielm/Research/Gug/Gug.pdf.

8. Dale Miller. A multiple-conclusion meta-logic. In S. Abramsky, editor, *Ninth Annual IEEE Symp. on Logic in Computer Science*, pages 272–281, Paris, July 1994.

9. Dale Miller. Forum: A multiple-conclusion specification logic. *Theoretical Computer Science*, 165:201–232, 1996.

10. Dale Miller, Gopalan Nadathur, Frank Pfenning, and Andre Scedrov. Uniform proofs as a foundation for logic programming. *Annals of Pure and Applied Logic*, 51:125–157, 1991.

11. Lutz Straßburger. MELL in the calculus of structures. Technical Report WV-01-03, Technische Universität Dresden, 2001. URL: http://www.ki.inf.uni-dresden.de/~lutz/els.pdf, to appear in Theoretical Computer Science.

Strict Geometry of Interaction Graph Models[*]

Furio Honsell[1], Marina Lenisa[1], and Rekha Redamalla[1,2]

[1] Dipartimento di Matematica e Informatica, Università di Udine,
Via delle Scienze 206, 33100 Udine, Italy,
tel. +39 0432 558417, fax: +39 0432 558499,
{honsell,lenisa}@dimi.uniud.it
[2] B.M. Birla Science Center,
Adarsh Nagar, Hyderabad, 500 063 A.P., India,
tel. +91(40)3235081, fax: +91(40)3237266,
rrekhareddy@yahoo.com

Abstract. We study a class of *"wave-style" Geometry of Interaction* (GoI) λ-models based on the category *Rel* of sets and relations. Wave GoI models arise when Abramsky's GoI axiomatization, which generalizes Girard's original GoI, is applied to a traced monoidal category with the *categorical product* as tensor, using "countable power" as the traced strong monoidal functor !. Abramsky hinted that the category *Rel* is the basic setting for traditional denotational "static semantics". However, *Rel*, together with the cartesian product, apparently escapes Abramsky's original GoI construction. Here we show that *Rel* can be axiomatized as a *strict GoI situation*, i.e. a strict variant of Abramsky's GoI situation, which gives rise to a rich class of *strict graph models*. These are models of *restricted* λ-calculi in the sense of [HL99], such as Church's λ-I-calculus and the $\lambda\beta_{KN}$-calculus.

Keywords: (linear) graph model, traced monoidal category, weak linear category, categorical geometry of interaction.

Introduction

In [Abr96], Abramsky provides a categorical axiomatization/generalization of Girard's *Geometry of Interaction* (GoI) [Gir89], embracing previous axiomatic approaches, such as that based on *dynamic algebras* [DR93, DR95] and the one in [AJ94]. This generalization is based on traced monoidal categories, [JSV96], and it consists in building a compact closed category $\mathcal{G}(\mathcal{C})$ (*GoI category*) starting from a traced symmetric monoidal category $\mathcal{C}$. In [AHS02], the construction is extended to exponentials, which, in a general categorical setting, are captured by a strong monoidal functor ! on the traced category $\mathcal{C}$, together with some additional structure. Under these conditions on $\mathcal{C}$, the GoI category $\mathcal{G}(\mathcal{C})$ is a *weak linear category* (WLC), i.e. a weakening of a linear category (see [BBPH92]).

[*] Research supported by the MIUR Projects COFIN 2001013518 COMETA and 20022018192_002 PROTOCOLLO, and by the UE Project IST-2000-29001 TYPES.

M.Y. Vardi and A. Voronkov (Eds.): LPAR 2003, LNAI 2850, pp. 407–421, 2003.
© Springer-Verlag Berlin Heidelberg 2003

Moreover, every reflexive object in a WLC gives rise to a *linear combinatory algebra* (LCA).

Following [Abr96], there are two main instantiations of the GoI axiomatization. In the "particle-style" GoI, the tensor on the underlying category is a coproduct and the strong monoidal functor is a *countable* copower. Girard's GoI is an instance of this. Composition in the GoI category can be intuitively understood by simulating the flow of a particle around a network. Dually, in the "wave-style" GoI, the tensor is a product and the strong monoidal functor is a *countable* power. Composition in the GoI category is defined now statically and globally. In [Abr96], the category $(Rel, +)$ was suggested as the "basic setting" for particle/*dynamic semantics*, while $(Rel, \times)$ as the "basic setting" for wave/*static semantics*. This is clearly the case for the former which underlies many game categories in the [AJM00]-style, [Abr96], and contains as subalgebras those fruitfully used in [AL00, AL00a, AL01]. On the other hand, the thesis that $(Rel, \times)$ is the basic setting for static semantics is less immediate, also because $(Rel, \times)$ itself escapes the original GoI axiomatization.

The connection between traditional (static) semantics and wave GoI has not received much attention in the literature, apart from the investigations of some special wave-style models in [BDER97, AM99]. In the present paper and in [HL03], a companion paper to the present one, this connection has been taken seriously, and categories of relations in the wave-style have been explored, *vis-à-vis* graph models. In particular, in [HL03], a weaker axiomatization of the *GoI situation* of [AHS02] has been introduced, which still ensures that a GoI category is a WLC. This axiomatization allows to capture the case of Rel^*, i.e. the category of pointed sets and relations preserving the distinguished point, which otherwise escapes the original axiomatization. GoI algebras arising from Rel^* have then been shown to amount to (a variant of) graph models à la Scott-Plotkin-Engeler, [Sco80, Plo93].

In this paper, we focus directly on the basic setting for wave GoI, i.e. $(Rel, \times)$. This apparently escapes both the original axiomatization of the GoI situation of [AHS02] and the weaker axiomatization of [HL03]. In order to recover the case of Rel, we introduce a *strict* variant of the GoI situation. LCAs arising from a strict GoI situation are strict, i.e. application is *strict* w.r.t. a distinguished element $\bot$, and only a *restricted* form of K combinator is available, which allows to erase only non-$\bot$ elements. In particular, we show that GoI algebras on $(Rel, \times)$ are *strict graph models*. These are models of *restricted* λ-calculi, such as the λI-calculus and the $\lambda\beta_{KN}$-calculus of [HL99].

The paper consists of three parts.

In the first part (Section 1), we introduce strict versions of (linear) combinatory algebras, (linear) combinatory λ-models, and (linear) graph models, and we study the relations between them. In particular, we show that the somewhat unexpected fact that every graph model (GM) can be recovered from a linear graph model (LGM) via standardisation, proved in [HL03], extends also to the strict case. An important consequence is that all strict λ-theories induced by strict GM's can be captured by strict LGMs.

In the second part of the paper (Section 2), we study strict LGMs from a categorical point of view. In particular, we introduce the notion of *order-enriched strict* WLC, and we show that many strict LGMs can be captured as strict WLCs in the wave-style.

In the third part of the paper (Sections 3 and 4), we study *strict* wave GoI algebras. In particular, we introduce a strict variant for the axiomatization of the GoI situation of [AHS02]. Our axiomatization ensures that a GoI category is a *strict* WLC, and hence it allows to build a *strict* GoI algebra. This axiomatization allows us to capture the case of $(Rel, \times)$. In particular, we show that the class of GoI algebras induced by $(Rel, \times)$ are strict LGMs. Finally, we show that there are wave GoI models realizing non-sensible λ-theories, as was the case for Rel^*. This should be contrasted with the fact that, in [DFH99], it has been shown that game models capture only a very limited number of λ-theories, related to Böhm trees and Levy-Longo trees.

Basic categorical definitions used in the paper appear in Appendix A.

Notation. Let $\mathcal{P}_{<\kappa}^-$, for a cardinal κ, denote the powerset of all non-empty sets with cardinality less than κ. In particular, $\mathcal{P}_{<\omega}^-$ denotes the finite non-empty powerset. Let $\subseteq_{fne}$ denote finite non-empty subset inclusion. Let U, V be objects in a category $\mathcal{C}$. We denote by $\tau : U \lhd V : \tau'$ a retraction of U in V, i.e. $\tau' \circ \tau = id_U$. Let Rel be the category of sets and relations. Relations $f \subseteq A \times B$ will be also denoted by $f : A \dashrightarrow B$. Let $PO_\perp$ denote the category of partial orders with bottom element and monotone maps as morphisms. The sets of finite streams and the set of infinite streams on a set A will be denoted by $A_{<\omega}$ and A_ω, respectively. Streams in A_ω will be denoted by $\boldsymbol{a}, \boldsymbol{b}, \ldots$ The i-th component of a (finite) stream $\boldsymbol{a}$ is denoted by a_i; a^ω denotes the infinite stream whose components are all equal to a.

1   Strict Linear Combinatory Algebras and Graph Models

In this section, we introduce *strict* versions of *(linear) combinatory algebras*, *(linear) combinatory λ-models*, and *(linear) graph models*, and we study the relations between them. In particular, we show that every strict graph model is induced by a strict linear one.

We start by defining the notion of *strict combinatory algebra* (in the Curry style), which arises from a *strict applicative structure*, and where only a restricted form of the K combinator is available, which allows to erase only non-$\perp$ elements:

Definition 1 (Strict Combinatory Algebra). *i) A strict applicative structure is an applicative structure $(A, \cdot)$ with a distinguished element $\perp \in A$ and a strict notion of application, i.e. $x \cdot \perp = \perp$ and $\perp \cdot x = \perp$, for all $x \in A$.*

ii) A strict combinatory algebra (strict CA) $\mathcal{A} = (A, \cdot)$ is a strict applicative structure together with distinguished elements (combinators) B, C, I, K, W satisfying the following equations (we associate $\cdot$ to the left): for all $x, y, z \in A$,

$Bxyz = x(yz)$ *(Composition, Cut)* $Cxyz = (xz)y$ *(Exchange)*

$Ix = x$ *(Identity)* $Wxy = xyy$ *(Contraction)*

$Kxy = x$, *if $y \neq \perp$ (Restricted Weakening)*

The notion of linear combinatory algebra of Abramsky refines the notion of combinatory algebra, in that it has an extra unary operation ! and a set of combinators, refining Curry's original set of combinators. Strict linear combinatory algebras are the linear counterpart of strict CA's:

Definition 2 (Strict Linear Combinatory Algebra). *A strict linear combinatory algebra (strict LCA)* $\mathcal{A} = (A, \cdot, !)$ *is a strict applicative structure* $(A, \cdot)$ *with a unary (injective) operation ! which is strict, i.e.* $! \perp = \perp$, *and combinators* $B, C, I, K, W, D, \delta, F$ *satisfying the following equations (we associate · to the left and we assume ! to have order of precedence greater than ·): for all* $x, y, z \in A$,

$Bxyz = x(yz)$ *(Composition, Cut)* $Cxyz = (xz)y$ *(Exchange)*

$Ix = x$ *(Identity)* $Kx!y = x$, *if* $y \neq \perp$ *(Restricted Weakening)*

$Wx!y = x!y!y$ *(Contraction)* $D!x = x$ *(Dereliction)*

$\delta!x = !!x$ *(Comultiplication)* $F!x!y = !(xy)$ *(Monoidal Functoriality)*

The *standardisation* procedure for building a standard combinatory algebra (CA) from a LCA extends to the strict case:

Proposition 1 (Standardisation). *Let* $(A, \cdot, !)$ *be a strict LCA. Then* $(A, \cdot_s)$, *where* $x \cdot_s y \triangleq x \cdot !y$, *is a strict CA with combinators* B_s, C_s, I_s, K_s, W_s *defined by:*

$C_s \triangleq D' \cdot C$ $B_s \triangleq C \cdot (B \cdot (B \cdot B \cdot B) \cdot (D' \cdot I)) \cdot (C \cdot ((B \cdot B) \cdot F) \cdot \delta)$

$I_s \triangleq D' \cdot I$ $K_s \triangleq D' \cdot K$ $W_s \triangleq D' \cdot W$,

where $D' \triangleq C(BBI)(BDI)$ *is such that, for all* x, y, $D'x!y = xy$.

It is well known that λ-models à la Hindley-Longo can be characterized as *combinatory* λ-*models*, i.e. CAs with an extra *selector* combinator (see e.g. [Bar84]). One can give a notion of strict combinatory λ-model arising from a strict CA:

Definition 3 (Strict Combinatory λ-Model). *A strict CA* $\mathcal{A} = (A, \cdot)$ *is a strict combinatory λ-model if there exists an extra selector combinator* ϵ *such that, for all* $x, y \in A$,

$$\epsilon xy = xy \quad and \quad (\forall z. \ xz = yz) \Rightarrow \epsilon x = \epsilon y .$$

Here is the strict version of the notion of linear combinatory λ-model introduced in [HL03]:

Definition 4 (Strict Combinatory Linear λ-Model). *A strict LCA* $\mathcal{A} = (A, \cdot, !)$ *is a strict combinatory linear λ-model if there exist linear selector* ϵ *and selector combinator* ϵ_s *such that, for all* $x, y \in A$,

$$\epsilon xy = xy \quad and \quad (\forall z. \ xz = yz) \Rightarrow \epsilon x = \epsilon y$$
$$\epsilon_s !x!y = x!y \quad and \quad (\forall z. \ x!z = y!z) \Rightarrow \epsilon_s !x = \epsilon_s !y \ .$$

Then we have:

Proposition 2. *Every strict combinatory linear λ-model gives rise by standardisation to a strict combinatory λ-model.*

Strict combinatory λ-models yield models of restricted λ-calculi, such as the $\lambda\beta_{KN}$-calculus of [HL99]. The $\lambda\beta_{KN}$-calculus is the λ-calculus, where the notion of β-reduction is substituted by the β_{KN}-reduction, which allows to erase an argument only when it is a closed β-normal form or a variable. I.e.: $(\lambda x.M)N \to_{\beta_{KN}} M[N/x]$, if $(\lambda x.M)N$ is either a $I\beta$-redex[1] or a $K\beta$-redex[2], whose argument is a closed normal form or a variable. Hence, in particular strict λ-models give models of the λI-calculus, the original calculus introduced by Church, where only strict λ-abstractions are available (i.e. the abstracted variable appears in the body). The notion of β_{KN}-reduction is correct w.r.t. observational equivalences induced by perpetual strategies (see [HL99] for more details).

Graph Models à la Scott-Plotkin-Engeler and Abramsky's *linear graph models* are examples of combinatory (linear) λ-models. Here we present strict versions of them, which give rise to strict combinatory (linear) λ-models. Notice that, in the definition of graph models below, we allow retractions to be relations instead of simply partial functions, thus generalizing original definitions, and capturing also some constructions in [Sco80] and some weak variants of filter models of [BCD83].

Definition 5 (Strict (Linear) Graph Model). *A strict graph model (S-GM) $\mathcal{U}$ is an applicative structure $(\mathcal{P}(U), \cdot_\tau)$, where U is a (infinite) set with a retraction in* Rel *$\tau : \mathcal{P}^-_{<\omega}(U) \times U \lhd U$, and the application $\cdot_\tau$ is defined by:*

$$\text{for all } x, y \in \mathcal{P}(U), \quad x \cdot_\tau y \triangleq \{a \mid \exists u \subseteq_{fne} y.\exists b \in x.\ ((u,a),b) \in \tau\} \ .$$

A strict linear graph model (S-LGM) is a structure $\mathcal{U} = (\mathcal{P}(U), \cdot_{\tau_1}, !_{\tau_2})$, where U is a (infinite) set with retractions in Rel *$\tau_1 : U \times U \lhd U$ and $\tau_2 : \mathcal{P}^-_{<\omega}(U) \lhd U$, and linear application $\cdot_{\tau_1}$ and $!_{\tau_2}$ are defined by: for all $x, y \in \mathcal{P}(U)$,*

$$x \cdot_{\tau_1} y \triangleq \{a \mid \exists b \in y.\exists c \in x.\ ((b,a),c) \in \tau_1\} \ , \quad !_{\tau_2} x \triangleq \{a \mid \exists u \subseteq_{fne} x.\ (u,a) \in \tau_2\} \ .$$

One can define combinators on strict (linear) graph models in such a way that:

Proposition 3. *Every strict (L)GM is a strict combinatory (linear) λ-model.*

As one expects, given a strict LGM, by standardisation, we get a strict GM:

Proposition 4. *Let $\mathcal{U} \triangleq (\mathcal{P}(U), \cdot_{\tau_1}, !_{\tau_2})$ be a S-LGM with retractions $\tau_1 : U \times U \lhd U$ and $\tau_2 : \mathcal{P}^-_{<\omega}(U) \lhd U$. Then by standardisation we get a S-GM $\mathcal{S}(\mathcal{U}) \triangleq (\mathcal{P}(U), \cdot_\tau)$, where the retraction $\tau : \mathcal{P}^-_{<\omega}(U) \times U \lhd U$ is defined by $\tau_1 \circ (\tau_2 \times id_U)$.*

The construction for building a LGM from a GM for which standardisation is an inverse, introduced in [HL03], extends to the strict case:

Proposition 5. *For any S-GM $\mathcal{U}$, there is a S-LGM $\mathcal{L}(\mathcal{U})$ such that $\mathcal{S}(\mathcal{L}(\mathcal{U})) = \mathcal{U}$.*

---

[1] I.e. the variable x occurs in the body M of the λ-abstraction.

[2] I.e. the variable x does not occur in the body M.

Proof. Let $\mathcal{U} \triangleq (\mathcal{P}(U), \cdot_\tau)$ be a S-GM. For any bijection $\xi : U \to \mathcal{P}^-_{<\omega}(U)$ (which exists by cardinality reasons), the retractions $\tau_1 : U \times U \lhd U$, $\tau_1 \triangleq \tau \circ (\xi \times id_U)$, and $\tau_2 : \mathcal{P}^-_{<\omega}(U) \lhd U$, $\tau_2 \triangleq \xi^{-1}$ induce a S-LGM $(\mathcal{P}(U), \cdot_{\tau_1}, !_{\tau_2})$. We take such LGM as $\mathcal{L}(\mathcal{U})$. □

From the point of view of strict λ-theories, we have the following important consequence:

Corollary 1. *The class of strict λ-theories induced by S-GMs coincides with the class of strict λ-theories induced by S-GMs obtained from S-LGMs via standardisation.*

Remark 1. Notice that, in the spirit of [Sco75], the above constructions of strict (L)GMs go through even if we consider $\mathcal{P}^-_{<\kappa}$, for any cardinal κ, in place of $\mathcal{P}^-_{<\omega}$.

2 Strict Weak Linear Categories and Linear Graph Models

In this section, we introduce a *strict* version of Abramsky's axiomatization of an LCA from a *weak linear category* (WLC). WLCs are the counterpart for linear combinatory algebras of the notion of linear category for linear λ-models (see [BBPH92]). In this section, we show that the category *Rel* with the cartesian product as tensor, together with suitable stream-based functors turns out to be a *strict* WLC. Moreover, the LCAs arising from the strict WLC *Rel* are S-LGMs.

We start by introducing a strict variant of Abramsky's notion of WLC. A strict WLC is a WLC which is also a $PO_\perp$-*enriched category*, [SP82], where strictness conditions of tensor, composition and ! are required, and only a restricted form of weakening is required. We recall that a $PO_\perp$-enriched category is a category where all spaces of morphisms form a partial order with $\perp$, and composition is monotone.

Definition 6 (Strict Weak Linear Category). *Let $(\mathcal{C}, \otimes)$ be a $PO_\perp$-enriched symmetric monoidal closed category together with a symmetric monoidal closed functor $! : \mathcal{C} \to \mathcal{C}$. Then $(\mathcal{C}, \otimes, !)$ is a strict weak linear category (strict WLC) if*

- *for all $f \in \mathcal{C}(A,B)$, for all C, D,*
  - $f \otimes \perp_{C,D} = \perp_{A \otimes C, B \otimes D}$ *and* $\perp_{C,D} \otimes f = \perp_{C \otimes A, D \otimes B}$
  - $\perp_{B,C} \circ f = \perp_{A,C}$ *and* $f \circ \perp_{C,A} = \perp_{C,B}$
  - $! \perp_{A,B} = \perp_{!A, !B};$
- *there exist monoidal pointwise natural transformations:*
  der : $! \Rightarrow Id$ (dereliction) $\delta : ! \Rightarrow !!$ (comultiplication)
  con : $! \Rightarrow ! \otimes !$ (contraction);
- *there exists a monoidal pointwise natural transformation up-to-$\perp$ (i.e. the naturality condition is not required on $\perp$):*
  weak : $! \Rightarrow \mathcal{K}_I$ (weakening) ,   where $\mathcal{K}_I$ is the constant I functor.

Definition 7. *A reflexive object in a (strict) WLC $\mathcal{C}$ is an object V in $\mathcal{C}$ with the following retracts: $V \multimap V \lhd V$ $!V \lhd V$ $I \lhd V$.*

The construction of [AHS02] of a LCA from a WLC can be tailored to the strict case:

Theorem 1. *Let $(\mathcal{C}, \otimes, !)$ be a strict WLC and V be a reflexive object in $\mathcal{C}$ with retracts $\theta_1 : V \multimap V \lhd V : \theta_1'$ and $\theta_2 : !V \lhd V : \theta_2'$. Then $(\mathcal{C}(I, V), \cdot, !)$ is a strict LCA, where $\cdot$ and $!$ are defined by: for $f, g \in \mathcal{C}(I, V)$,*

$$ f \cdot g \triangleq ev \circ ((\theta_1' \circ f) \otimes g) \circ \rho_I^{-1} \qquad !f \triangleq \theta_2 \circ (!f) \circ \phi_I' \ , $$

where $\rho_I : I \otimes I \simeq I$ and $\phi_I' : I \to !I$ is the morphism associated to the monoidal functor $!$ (see Appendix A).

We are now in the position of proving that the category *Rel* together with any of the following symmetric monoidal functors based on streams is a strict WLC:

Definition 8. *i) Let $(\ )_{<\omega} : Rel \to Rel$ be the functor defined by: for any set A, $(A)_{<\omega} \triangleq A_{<\omega}$, where $A_{<\omega}$ is the set of finite streams; for any $f : A \multimap B$, let $(f)_{<\omega} \triangleq f_{<\omega} : A_{<\omega} \multimap B_{<\omega}$, $(\boldsymbol{a}, \boldsymbol{b}) \in f_{<\omega}$ iff $|\boldsymbol{a}| = |\boldsymbol{b}|$ and $\forall i. (a_i, b_i) \in f$.*
ii) Let $(\ )_\omega : Rel \to Rel$ be defined by: for any set A, $(A)_\omega \triangleq A_\omega$, where A_ω is the set of (infinite) streams; the definition on arrows is similar to (i).
iii) Let $(\ )_\omega^f : Rel \to Rel$ be defined by: for any set A, $(A)_\omega^f \triangleq A_\omega^f$, where A_ω^f is the restriction of A_ω to the streams with finite codomain; the definition on arrows is similar to (i).

Proposition 6. *$(Rel, \times, !)$, where $!$ is either $(\ )_{<\omega}$ or $(\ )_\omega^f$ or $(\ )_\omega$, is a strict WLC.*

Proof. The proof of the fact that $(Rel, \times)$ is symmetric monoidal closed, with right adjoint of $\times$ the product $\times$ itself, and that the functors of Definition 8 are monoidal closed is routine. Moreover, one can easily check that *Rel* is $PO_\perp$-enriched w.r.t. set-theoretic inclusion, with the empty relation being $\perp$, satisfying the appropriate strictness conditions. Let $con : (\ )_\omega \Rightarrow (\ )_\omega \times (\ )_\omega$, $con_A : (A)_\omega \multimap (A)_\omega \times (A)_\omega$ be defined by $con_A \triangleq \{(a, (a', a'')) \mid a, a', a'' \in A_\omega \land \forall i \geq 0. a_{2i+1}'' = a_i \land \forall i \geq 1. a_{2i}'' = a_i'\}$. Weakening is a natural transformation only up-to the empty relation: $weak_A : A_\omega \to A$, $weak_A \triangleq \{(a^\omega, *) \mid a \in A\}$. We omit the definitions of the other natural transformations and the discussion of the other !-functors. □

Theorem 2. *The LCAs generated by reflexive objects in the strict WLC $(Rel, \times, !)$, where $!$ is either $(\ )_{<\omega}$ or $(\ )_\omega^f$ or $(\ )_\omega$, are (isomorphic to) strict LGMs.*

Proof. We consider the case $! = (\ )_{<\omega}$. The other cases can be dealt with similarly. Using Theorem 1, one can easily check that any set U with retracts $\theta_1 : U \times U \lhd U$ and $\theta_2 : U_{<\omega} \lhd U$ gives rise to a LCA isomorphic, via the canonical isomorphism $\lambda_U : I \times U \to U$ (see Appendix A), to the LCA $(\mathcal{P}(U), \cdot, !)$, where application $\cdot$ is the application on a LGM w.r.t. coding θ_1, and $!f \triangleq \{\theta_2(\boldsymbol{a}) \mid \forall i \in \{1, \dots, |\boldsymbol{a}|\}. a_i \in f\}$. Let $\xi : \mathcal{P}_{<\omega}^- U \multimap U_{<\omega}$ be the injective

Table 1.

WLC	CODINGS	LCA
$(Rel, \times, (\ )_{<\omega})$	$\theta_1 : U \times U \lhd U, \ \theta_2 : U_{<\omega} \lhd U \ \Rightarrow$	$\exists \xi : \mathcal{P}^-_{<\omega} U \lhd U_{<\omega}$ s.t. $(\mathcal{P}U, \cdot_{\theta_1}, !_{\theta_2 \circ \xi})$ strict LGM
$(Rel, \times, (\ )^f_\omega)$	$\theta_1 : U \times U \lhd U, \ \theta_2 : U^f_\omega \lhd U \ \Rightarrow$	$\exists \xi : \mathcal{P}^-_{<\omega} U \lhd U^f_\omega$ s.t. $(\mathcal{P}U, \cdot_{\theta_1}, !_{\theta_2 \circ \xi})$ strict LGM
$(Rel, \times, (\ )_\omega)$	$\theta_1 : U \times U \lhd U, \ \theta_2 : U_\omega \lhd U \ \Rightarrow$	$\exists \xi : \mathcal{P}^-_{<\omega_1} U \lhd U_\omega$ s.t. $(\mathcal{P}U, \cdot_{\theta_1}, !_{\theta_2 \circ \xi})$ ω_1-strict LGM

relation defined by $(u, \boldsymbol{a}) \in \xi$ iff, for all i, $a_i \in u$ and for all $b \in u$ there exists i s.t. $a_i = b$. Then $\tau_2 : \mathcal{P}^-_{<\omega} U \multimap U$, $\tau_2 \triangleq \theta_2 \circ \xi$ is s.t. $!_{\tau_2} f = \{\tau_2(u) \mid u \subseteq_{fne} f\} = !f$, i.e. the LCA $(\mathcal{P}(U), \cdot, !)$ is a strict LGM with codings θ_1, τ_2. Notice that the coding τ_2 in the proof above is forced to be non functional. □

The situation is summarized in Table 1. Notice that, in the cases of infinite streams (possibly with finite codomain), the cardinality of U is at least $2^{\aleph_0}$. Moreover, for $! = (\ )_\omega$, we get an ω_1-strict LGM.

Remark 2. Notice that the category *Rel* fails to be a WLC in the original sense of [AHS02], since the "natural" definition of weakening (see the proof of Proposition 6 above) is *not* natural on the *empty* relation.

Somewhat unexpectedly, the powerset functor $\mathcal{P}^-_{<\omega}$ fails to induce a structure of (strict) WLC on *Rel*. Namely, the "natural" definition of dereliction, i.e. $der_A : \mathcal{P}^-_{<\omega}(A) \multimap A$, $der_A \triangleq \{(\{a\}, a) \mid a \in A\}$, is not natural.

3   The Geometry of Interaction Construction

The categorical axiomatization of the *Geometry of Interaction* (GoI) due to [Abr96, AHS02] is based on traced categories of [JSV96]. Any traced monoidal category gives rise, by the construction of [Abr96], to a *GoI category*. If moreover the traced category we start from has a strong traced monoidal functor together with suitable retractions, then the GoI category is a WLC, and hence every suitable reflexive object generates a (GoI) LCA. This situation, called *GoI situation*, is axiomatized and studied in [AHS02]. In this section, we introduce the notion of *strict GoI situation*, which gives rise to a GoI category which is a strict WLC. Our axiomatization of strict GoI situation is based on the weaker axiomatization of GoI situation given in [HL03]. In the next section, we will see that this notion of strict GoI situation captures the basic examples of wave models arising from *Rel*.

GoI categories arise from traced symmetric monoidal categories by the following construction:

Proposition 7 (Geometry of Interaction Construction, [Abr96]). *Given a traced symmetric monoidal category $\mathcal{C}$, we define a GoI category $\mathcal{G}(\mathcal{C})$ by:*

– **Objects:** *pairs of objects of $\mathcal{C}$, denoted by (A^+, A^-), where A^+ and A^- are objects of $\mathcal{C}$.*

- **Arrows**: *an arrow* $f : (A^+, A^-) \to (B^+, B^-)$ *in* $\mathcal{G}(\mathcal{C})$ *is* $f : A^+ \otimes B^- \to A^- \otimes B^+$ *in* $\mathcal{C}$.
- **Identity**: $id_{(A^+, A^-)} = \sigma_{A^+, A^-}$.
- **Composition**: *it is given by* symmetric feedback. *Given* $f : (A^+, A^-) \to (B^+, B^-)$ *and* $g : (B^+, B^-) \to (C^+, C^-)$, $g \circ f : (A^+, A^-) \to (C^+, C^-)$ *is given by:* $g \circ f \triangleq Tr_{A^+ \otimes C^-, A^- \otimes C^+}^{B^- \otimes B^+}(\gamma' \circ (f \otimes g) \circ \gamma)$, *where* $\gamma \triangleq (id_{A^+} \otimes id_{B^-} \otimes \sigma_{C^-, B^+}) \circ (id_{A^+} \otimes \sigma_{C^-, B^-} \otimes id_{B^+})$ *and* $\gamma' \triangleq (id_{A^-} \otimes id_{C^+} \otimes \sigma_{B^+, B^-}) \circ (id_{A^-} \otimes \sigma_{B^+, C^+} \otimes id_{B^-}) \circ (id_{A^-} \otimes id_{B^+} \otimes \sigma_{B^-, C^+})$.
- **Tensor**: $(A^+, A^-) \otimes (B^+, B^-) \triangleq (A^+ \otimes B^+, A^- \otimes B^-)$, *and, for any* $f : (A^+, A^-) \to (B^+, B^-)$ *and* $g : (C^+, C^-) \to (D^+, D^-)$, $f \otimes g \triangleq (id_{A^-} \otimes \sigma_{B^+, C^-} \otimes id_{D^+}) \circ (f \otimes g) \circ (id_{A^+} \otimes \sigma_{C^+, B^-} \otimes id_{D^-})$.
- **Unit**: (I, I).

Then $\mathcal{G}(\mathcal{C})$ *is compact closed. Moreover,* $F : \mathcal{C} \to \mathcal{G}(\mathcal{C})$ *with* $F(A) = (A, I)$ *and* $F(f) = f$ *is a full and faithful embedding.*

In [AHS02], sufficient conditions are given on the traced monoidal category $\mathcal{C}$ for $\mathcal{G}(\mathcal{C})$ to be a WLC, and hence to give rise to a GoI LCA. Here we give a strict version of this construction. First of all notice that:

Lemma 1. *If* $(\mathcal{C}, \otimes)$ *is a* $PO_\perp$*-enriched traced symmetric monoidal category with monotone tensor and monotone trace operator, then* $\mathcal{G}(\mathcal{C})$ *is a compact closed* $PO_\perp$*-enriched category.*

Now we are in the position of introducing the notion of *strict GoI situation*. This is based on the weak axiomatization of GoI situation given in [HL03], which generalizes the original GoI situation of [AHS02], by requiring the existence of suitable retractions which are natural only in a weak sense. This generalization of a GoI situation still ensures that the GoI category is a WLC. It is necessary in order to capture categories based on relations, where some retractions in the definition of GoI situation fail to be natural in the full sense.

Definition 9 (Strict GoI Situation). *A* strict GoI situation *is a triple* $(\mathcal{C}, T, U)$, *where:*

- $\mathcal{C}$ *is a* $PO_\perp$*-enriched traced symmetric monoidal category with monotone tensor and monotone trace operator such that, for all* $f \in \mathcal{C}(A, B)$, *for all* C, D,
  - $f \otimes \perp_{C,D} = \perp_{A \otimes C, B \otimes D}$ *and* $\perp_{C,D} \otimes f = \perp_{C \otimes A, D \otimes B}$
  - $\perp_{B,C} \circ f = \perp_{A,C}$ *and* $f \circ \perp_{C,A} = \perp_{C,B}$
  - $Tr_{A,B}^C(\perp_{A \otimes C, B \otimes C}) = \perp_{A,B}$;
- $T : \mathcal{C} \to \mathcal{C}$ *is a traced strong symmetric monoidal functor such that, for all* A, B, $T(\perp_{A,B}) = \perp_{!_A, !_B}$; *moreover, there exist retractions comultiplication, dereliction, contraction, which satisfy a weak form of naturality, which we call* naturality up-to retraction, *and furthermore a retraction* weakening, *which is natural up-to-retraction and up-to-*$\perp$, *i.e.:*
  1. $\{e_A : TTA \lhd TA : e_A'\}_A$ *(Comultiplication) is a family of monoidal retractions s.t., for all* $f : A \to B$, $e_B' \circ Tf \circ e_A = f$;

2. $\{d_A : A \lhd TA : d'_A\}_A$ (Dereliction) *is a family of monoidal retractions s.t., for all* $f : A \to B$, $d'_B \circ Tf \circ d_A = f$;
3. $\{c_A : TA \otimes TA \lhd TA : c'_A\}_A$ (Contraction) *is a family of monoidal retractions s.t., for all* $f : A \to B$, $c'_B \circ Tf \circ c_A = f$;
4. $\{w_A : I \lhd TA : w'_A\}_A$ (Weakening) *is a family of monoidal retractions s.t., for all* $f : A \to B$, $f \neq \bot_{A,B}$, $w'_B \circ Tf \circ w_A = f$.

- U *is an object of* $\mathcal{C}$, *called a* GoI reflexive object, *with retractions*
  1. $\theta_1 : U \otimes U \lhd U : \theta'_1$
  2. $I \lhd U$
  3. $\theta_2 : TU \lhd U : \theta'_2$.

Theorem 3. *Let* $(\mathcal{C}, T, U)$ *be a strict GoI situation. Then*
i) $(\mathcal{G}(\mathcal{C}), !)$ *is a strict WLC with* $! : \mathcal{G}(\mathcal{C}) \to \mathcal{G}(\mathcal{C})$ *defined as follows:* $!(A^+, A^-) \triangleq (TA^+, TA^-)$, *and, for* $f : (A^+, A^-) \to (B^+, B^-)$, $!f \triangleq TA^+ \otimes TB^- \overset{\sim}{\to} T(A^+ \otimes B^-) \overset{Tf}{\to} T(A^- \otimes B^+) \overset{\sim}{\to} TA^- \otimes TB^+$.
ii) $(\mathcal{C}(U, U), \cdot, !)$ *is a strict LCA, where for any* $f, g \in \mathcal{C}(U, U)$, $f \cdot g \triangleq Tr_{U,U}^U((id_U \otimes g) \circ (\theta'_1 \circ f \circ \theta_1))$, *and* $!f \triangleq \theta_2 \circ Tf \circ \theta'_2$.

4   Strict Wave GoI Algebras and Linear Graph Models

We show that the traced category $(Rel, \times)$, together with stream functors, gives rise to a strict GoI situation. Moreover, the GoI algebras induced by $(Rel, \times)$ are strict linear graph models. Finally, we show that such wave models can induce restricted λ-theories in the sense of [HL99], where not all unsolvables of order 0 are equated.

4.1   GoI Algebras on $(Rel, \times)$

The category $(Rel, \times)$ is traced with the trace operator $Tr_{A,B}^U(\ )$ defined by: for $f : A \times U \nrightarrow B \times U$,

$$Tr_{A,B}^U(f) \triangleq \{(a, b) \mid \exists u. \ (a, u, b, u) \in f\} \ .$$

Both the functor of streams $(\ )_\omega$ and that of streams with finite codomain $(\ )_\omega^f$ induce on $(Rel, \times)$ a strict GoI situation. We focus on $(\ )_\omega^f$.

Proposition 8. *For any GoI reflexive object* U *in* Rel, $(Rel, \times, (\ )_\omega^f, U)$ *is a strict GoI situation.*

Proof. We only sketch the definitions of the retractions:
- $e_A : (A_\omega^f)_\omega^f \to A_\omega^f$, $e_A \triangleq \xi \circ \chi_A$, where $\chi_A : [\mathbf{N} \to_{fcod} [\mathbf{N} \to_{fcod} A]] \lhd [\mathbf{N} \times \mathbf{N} \to_{fcod} A]$ is a component of the retraction natural in A induced by curryfication, and $\xi \triangleq \lambda f \in [\mathbf{N} \times \mathbf{N} \to_{fcod} A].\lambda n \in \mathbf{N}.f(\epsilon^{-1}(n))$, where $\epsilon : \mathbf{N} \times \mathbf{N} \simeq \mathbf{N}$ is any bijective coding of pairs;
- $c_A : A_\omega^f \times A_\omega^f \to A_\omega^f$, $c_A(\boldsymbol{a}, \boldsymbol{a}') = \boldsymbol{a}''$, where, for all $i \geq 0$, $a''_{2i+1} = a_i$ and, for all $i \geq 1$, $a''_{2i} = a'_i$;
- $d_A : A \to A_\omega^f$, $d_A(a) = a^\omega$, $d'_A : A_\omega^f \to A$, $d'_A(a^\omega) = a$;
- $w_A : I \nrightarrow A_\omega^f$, $w_A \triangleq \{(*, a^\omega) \mid a \in A\}$, $w'_A : A_\omega^f \to I$, $w'_A \triangleq \{(a^\omega, *) \mid a \in A\}$.
□

Notice that d in the proof above is natural up-to retraction, but not in the full sense; while w_A is natural only up-to the empty relation. Then we have:

Proposition 9. *i) The GoI category $\mathcal{G}(Rel, \times, (\ )^f_\omega)$ is a strict WLC.*
ii) Let U be a GoI reflexive object in Rel, with retractions $\theta_1 : U \times U \lhd U$, $\theta_2 : U^f_\omega \lhd U$. Then $(\mathcal{P}(U \times U), \cdot_{\theta_1}, !_{\theta_2})$ is a LCA, where, for all $x, y \in \mathcal{P}(U \times U)$
- $x \cdot_{\theta_1} y = \{(a, b) \mid \exists (c, d) \in y.\ (\theta_1(a, d), \theta_1(b, c)) \in x\}$;
- $!_{\theta_2} x = \{(\theta_2(\boldsymbol{a}), \theta_2(\boldsymbol{b})) \mid \boldsymbol{a}, \boldsymbol{b} \in U^f_\omega \wedge \forall i.(a_i, b_i) \in x\}$.

A crucial fact for our purposes is that all the GoI algebras of Proposition 9 give rise, for a suitable choice of the coding relations, to strict LGMs:

Theorem 4. *Let $\mathcal{U} = (\mathcal{P}(U \times U), \cdot_{\theta_1}, !_{\theta_2})$ be a GoI algebra induced by $(Rel, \times,$ $(\ )^f_\omega)$, with $\theta_1 : U \times U \lhd U$, $\theta_2 : U^f_\omega \lhd U$. Then $\mathcal{U}$ coincides with the strict LGM $\mathcal{U}' = (\mathcal{P}(U'), \cdot_{\tau_1}, !_{\tau_2})$, where $U' \triangleq U \times U$, $\tau_1 : U' \times U' \lhd U'$ and $\tau_2 : \mathcal{P}^-_{<\omega}(U') \lhd U'$ are defined by:*

$$\tau_1 \triangleq \langle \theta_1 \circ (\pi_1 \circ \pi_2 \times \pi_2 \circ \pi_1), \theta_1 \circ (\pi_2 \circ \pi_2 \times \pi_1 \circ \pi_1) \rangle, \quad \tau_2 \triangleq (\theta_2 \times \theta_2) \circ \zeta,$$

where $\zeta : \mathcal{P}^-_{<\omega}(U \times U) \multimap U^f_\omega \times U^f_\omega$ is the injective relation defined by $(u, (\boldsymbol{a}, \boldsymbol{b})) \in \zeta$ iff for all i, $(a_i, b_i) \in u$ and for all $(c, d) \in u$ there exists i such that $a_i = c$ and $b_i = d$.

Proof. Let $x, y \in \mathcal{P}(U \times U)$. By Proposition 9, $x \cdot_{\theta_1} y = \{(a, b) \mid \exists (c, d) \in y.\ (\theta_1(a, d), \theta_1(b, c)) \in x\} = \{(a, b) \mid \exists (c, d) \in y.\ \tau_1((c, d), (a, b)) \in x\}$, by definition of τ_1; i.e. $\cdot_{\theta_1}$ is the application on the LGM $\mathcal{U}'$. Moreover, by Proposition 9, $!_{\theta_2} x = \{(\theta_2(\boldsymbol{a}), \theta_2(\boldsymbol{b})) \mid \boldsymbol{a}, \boldsymbol{b} \in U^f_\omega \wedge \forall i.(a_i, b_i) \in x\} = \{(\theta_2(\boldsymbol{a}), \theta_2(\boldsymbol{b})) \mid \boldsymbol{a}, \boldsymbol{b} \in U^f_\omega \wedge \exists u \subseteq_{fne} x.\ \forall i.(a_i, b_i) \in u \wedge \forall (c, d) \in u\ \exists i.(a_i = c \wedge b_i = d)\} = \{(\theta_2 \times \theta_2)(\zeta(u)) \mid u \subseteq_{fne} x\} = \{\tau_2(u) \mid u \subseteq_{fne} x\}$, by definition of τ_2; i.e. $!_{\theta_2}$ is the ! operator on the LGM $\mathcal{U}'$. $\square$

Remark 3. Finally, notice that both the finite powerset functor $\mathcal{P}^-_{<\omega}$ and the finite stream functor $(\ )_{<\omega}$ fail to be strong monoidal, and hence they do not give a GoI situation on *Rel*.

4.2   Strict Wave GoI λ-Theories

The class of strict λ-theories induced by wave models is quite rich, or at least it goes beyond theories where all unsolvable of order 0 are equated in the bottom element. Namely:

Lemma 2. *For any $k \geq 0$, there exists a GoI algebra on $(Rel, \times, (\ )^f_\omega)$ with k self-singletons, i.e. elements $a \in U$ such that $\theta_1(a, a) = a$ and $\theta_2(\{a\}) = a$.*

One can easily check that any self-singleton a belongs to the interpretation of a term iff it reduces to a closed λ-term (see [HR92]). Therefore:

Theorem 5. *There is a strict wave model in which*

$$[\![\lambda xy.\Delta \Delta xy]\!] \neq [\![\lambda xy.\Delta \Delta(xy)]\!].$$

5   Conclusions and Future Work

Building on [Abr96, AHS02, HL03], we have investigated the connections between graph models and wave GoI models arising in the basic setting of $(Rel, \times)$. The category $(Rel, \times)$ apparently fails to give a WLC and a GoI situation, because weakening is not well-behaved on the empty relation. However, we have shown that it induces a *strict* WLC and a *strict* GoI situation, where only a restricted form of weakening is available. Correspondingly, GoI algebras arising from $(Rel, \times)$ amount to a strict version of LGMs, where only a restricted K-combinator is present, allowing to erase non-$\perp$ elements. These are models for restricted λ-calculi, such as Church's λI-calculus and the $\lambda\beta_{KN}$-calculus of [HL99].

The notion of strict linear combinatory algebra in Definition 2 captures also models of *call-by-value* λ-calculus. However, strict combinatory λ-models in Definitions 3 and 4 rule this out. It would be interesting to explore GoI models for call-by-value λ-calculus or Moggi's computational λ-calculus.

Finally, here is a list of intriguing open questions. Definitive answers or even well-motivated conjectures to these appear to be rather difficult.
- Many classes of graph-like models have been considered in the literature, see [DH93]. Do they all induce the same λ-theories as the class of standard GMs?
- Can original LGMs and the generalizations of graph models in [DH93] be captured as possibly modified wave WLCs?
- Are all the theories of GMs induced by wave GoI algebras? Which theories escape GoI characterizations?
- Can standard graph models be "naturally" extracted from strict graph models?
- Finally, an interesting issue to be investigated is that of giving a logical characterization via *intersection types* to the graph models arising from wave GoI constructions. We feel that this will shed more light both on intersection types and on wave models.

References

[Abr96]   S.Abramsky. Retracing some paths in Process Algebra, *Concur'96*, U. Montanari and V. Sassone eds., 1996, 1–17.

[AHS02]   S.Abramsky, E.Haghverdi, P.Scott. Geometry of Interaction and Linear Combinatory Algebras, *Math.Struct. in Comp.Science* **12**(5), 2002, 625–665.

[AJ94]   S.Abramsky, R.Jagadeesan. New foundations for the Geometry of Interaction, *Inf. and Comp.* **111**(1), 1994, 53–119.

[AJM00]   S.Abramsky, R.Jagadeesan, P.Malacaria. Full Abstraction for PCF, *Inf. and Comp.* **163**, 2000, 409–470.

[AL00]   S.Abramsky, M.Lenisa. A Fully-complete PER Model for ML Polymorphic Types, *CSL'00*, LNCS **1862**, 2000, 140–155.

[AL01]   S.Abramsky, M.Lenisa. Fully Complete Minimal PER Models for the Simply Typed λ-calculus, *CSL'01*, LNCS **2142**, 2001, 443–457.

[AL00a]   S.Abramsky, J.Longley. Realizability models based on history-free strategies, draft, 2000.

[AM99]   S.Abramsky, P.Mellies. Concurrent Games and Full Completeness, *LICS'99*.

[BDER97]   P.Baillot, V.Danos, T.Ehrard, L.Regnier. *Timeless games, CSL'97*, LNCS **1414**, 1997,

[Bar84]   H.Barendregt. *The Lambda Calculus, its Syntax and Semantics*, North Holland, Amsterdam, 1984.

[BCD83]   H.Barendregt, M.Coppo, M.Dezani. A filter lambda model and the completeness of type assignment system, *J. Symbolic Logic* **48**, 1983, 931–940.

[BBPH92]   P.Benton, G.Bierman, V. de Paiva, M.Hyland. Term assignment for intuitionistic linear logic, TR **262**, Computer Laboratory, Cambridge, 1992.

[DFH99]   P.Di Gianantonio, G.Franco, F.Honsell. Game Semantics for Untyped λ-calculus, *TLCA'99*, LNCS **1581**, 1999, 114–128.

[DH93]   P.Di Gianantonio, F.Honsell. An abstract notion of application, *TLCA'93*, LNCS **664**, 124–138.

[DR93]   V.Danos, L.Regnier. Local and Asynchronous beta-reduction (An analysis of Girard's Execution Formula), *LICS'93*, 296–306.

[DR95]   V.Danos, L.Regnier. Proof-nets and the Hilbert space, in J.-Y.Girard et al. eds., *Advances in linear Logic*, London Math. Soc. Series **222**, Cambridge University Press, 307–328.

[Gir89]   J.-Y.Girard. Geometry of Interaction I: Interpretation of System F, *Logic Colloquium'88*, R.Ferro et al. eds., North Holland, 221–260.

[HL99]   F.Honsell, M.Lenisa. Semantical Analysis of Perpetual Strategies in lambda-calculus, *TCS*, **212**, 1999, 183–209.

[HL03]   F.Honsell, M.Lenisa. "Wave-style" Geometry of Interaction Models are Graph-like λ-models, available at: http://www.dimi.uniud.it/~lenisa/Papers/Soft-copy-pdf/pointed.pdf

[HR92]   F.Honsell, S.Ronchi Della Rocca. An approximation theorem for topological lambda models and the topological incompleteness of lambda models, *J. Comp. System Sci.* **45**, 1992, 49–75.

[HO00]   M.Hyland, L.Ong. On full abstraction for PCF, *Inf. and Comp.* **163**, 2000.

[JSV96]   A.Joyal, R.Street, D.Verity. Traced monoidal categories, *Math. Proc. Comb. Phil. Soc.* **119**, 1996, 447–468.

[Plo93]   G.Plotkin. Set-theoretical and other elementary models of the λ-calculus, *Volume in Honour of Corrado Böhm*, M.Dezani et al. eds., Elsevier, 351–410.

[Sco75]   D.Scott. Combinators and classes, *λ-calculus and Computer Science Theory*, LNCS **37**, 1–26.

[Sco80]   D.Scott. Lambda calculus: some models, some philosophy, *Proc. The Kleene Symp.*, J.Barwise ed., North Holland, Amsterdam, 1980.

[SP82]   M.Smith, G.Plotkin. The category-theoretic solution of recursive domain equations, *SIAM J. of Computing* **11**(5), 1982, 761–783.

A   Categorical Definitions

We collect some categorical definitions. For more details, see e.g. [AHS02, JSV96].

Definition 10 (Monoidal Category). *A monoidal category is a tuple* $(\mathcal{C}, \otimes, I, \alpha, \lambda, \rho)$ *consisting of a category* $\mathcal{C}$, *an object* I *of* $\mathcal{C}$ *called the* unit, *a bifunctor* $\otimes : \mathcal{C} \times \mathcal{C} \to \mathcal{C}$, *and natural isomorphisms* α, λ, ρ *with components*

$$\alpha_{A,B,C} : A \otimes (B \otimes C) \simeq (A \otimes B) \otimes C \qquad \lambda_A : I \otimes A \simeq A \qquad \rho_A : A \otimes I \simeq A$$
such that the two diagrams below commute.

$$
\begin{array}{ccc}
A \otimes (B \otimes (C \otimes D)) & \xrightarrow{\alpha} (A \otimes B) \otimes (C \otimes D) \xrightarrow{\alpha} ((A \otimes B) \otimes C) \otimes D \\
id_A \otimes \alpha \downarrow & \uparrow \alpha \otimes id_D \\
A \otimes ((B \otimes C) \otimes D) & \xrightarrow{\hspace{4cm}\alpha\hspace{4cm}} (A \otimes (B \otimes C)) \otimes D
\end{array}
$$

$$
\begin{array}{ccc}
A \otimes (I \otimes B) & \xrightarrow{\alpha} & (A \otimes I) \otimes B \\
& {}_{id_A \otimes \lambda} \searrow \quad \swarrow {}_{\rho \otimes id_B} & \\
& A \otimes B &
\end{array}
$$

A symmetric *monoidal category* is a monoidal category equipped with a natu-
ral *isomorphism* σ with components $\sigma_{A,B} : A \otimes B \to B \otimes A$ such that $\sigma_{B,A} \circ \sigma_{A,B} = id_{A \otimes B}$, $\rho_A = \lambda_A \circ \sigma_{A,I}$ and the diagram below commutes

$$
\begin{array}{ccc}
A \otimes (B \otimes C) & \xrightarrow{\alpha} (A \otimes B) \otimes C \xrightarrow{\sigma} C \otimes (A \otimes B) \\
id_A \otimes \sigma \downarrow & \downarrow \alpha \\
A \otimes (C \otimes B) \xrightarrow{\alpha} (A \otimes C) \otimes B & \xrightarrow{\sigma \otimes id_B} (\otimes A) \times B
\end{array}
$$

A *symmetric monoidal category* $\mathcal{C}$ is closed *if, for each object B in $\mathcal{C}$, the
functor $\_ \otimes B : \mathcal{C} \to \mathcal{C}$ has a right adjoint, $B \multimap \_ : \mathcal{C} \to \mathcal{C}$.*

Definition 11 (Traced Symmetric Monoidal Category). *A* traced sym-
mentric monoidal category *is a symmetric monoidal category* $(\mathcal{C}, \otimes, I, \sigma)$ *with a
family of functions* $Tr_{A,B}^U : \mathcal{C}(A \otimes U, B \otimes U) \to \mathcal{C}(A, B)$, *called a* trace, *satisfying
the following conditions:*

- **Natural** *in A:* $Tr_{A,B}^U(f) \circ g = Tr_{C,B}^U(f \circ (g \otimes id_U))$, *where* $f : A \otimes U \to B \otimes U$,
  $g : C \to A$;
- **Natural** *in B:* $g \circ Tr_{A,B}^U(f) = Tr_{A,C}^U((g \otimes id_U) \circ f)$, *where* $f : A \otimes U \to B \otimes U$,
  $g : B \to C$;
- **Dinatural** *in U:* $Tr_{A,B}^U((id_B \otimes g) \circ f) = Tr_{A,B}^{U'}(f \circ (id_a \otimes g))$, *where* $f :$
  $A \otimes U \to B \otimes U'$, $g : U' \to U$;
- **Vanishing:** $Tr_{A,B}^I(f) = f$ *and* $Tr_{A,B}^{U \otimes V}(g) = Tr_{A,B}^U(Tr_{A \otimes U, B \otimes U}^V)$, *for* $f :$
  $A \otimes I \to B \otimes I$ *and* $g : A \otimes U \otimes V \to B \otimes U \otimes V$;
- **Superposing:** $g \otimes Tr_{A,B}^U(f) = Tr_{C \otimes A, D \otimes B}^U(g \otimes f)$, *for* $f : A \otimes U \to B \otimes U$
  and $g : C \to D$;
- **Yanking:** $Tr_{U,U}^U(\sigma_{U,U}) = id_U$.

A *geometrical* representation of traced symmetric monoidal categories can
be given using the language of "boxes and wires" (see [JSV96, AHS02] for more
details).

Definition 12 (Monoidal Functor, Monoidal Natural Transformation).
A monoidal functor between monoidal categories $\mathcal{C}$ and $\mathcal{D}$ is a triple (F, ϕ, ϕ'_I), where $F : \mathcal{C} \to \mathcal{D}$ is a functor, ϕ is a natural transformation with componenents $\phi_{A,B} : FA \otimes FB \to F(A \otimes B)$ and $\phi'_I : I \to FI$ is a morphism in $\mathcal{D}$ such that the following diagrams commute

$$
\begin{array}{ccccc}
FA \otimes (FB \otimes FC) & \xrightarrow{id_{FA} \otimes \phi} & FA \otimes F(B \otimes C) & \xrightarrow{\phi} & F(A \otimes (B \otimes C)) \\
\downarrow{\scriptstyle \alpha} & & & & \downarrow{\scriptstyle F\alpha} \\
(FA \otimes FB) \otimes FC & \xrightarrow{\phi \otimes id_{FC}} & F(A \otimes B) \otimes FC & \xrightarrow{\phi} & F((A \otimes B) \otimes C)
\end{array}
$$

$$
\begin{array}{ccc}
I \otimes FA & \xrightarrow{\lambda} & FA \\
\downarrow{\scriptstyle \phi'_I \otimes id_{FA}} & & \uparrow{\scriptstyle F\lambda} \\
FI \otimes FA & \xrightarrow{\phi} & F(I \otimes A)
\end{array}
\qquad
\begin{array}{ccc}
FA \otimes I & \xrightarrow{\rho} & FA \\
\downarrow{\scriptstyle id_{FA} \otimes \phi'_I} & & \uparrow{\scriptstyle F\rho} \\
FA \otimes FI & \xrightarrow{\phi} & F(A \otimes I)
\end{array}
$$

A monoidal functor is strong *when ϕ is a natural isomorphism and ϕ' is an isomorphism.*

A monoidal functor $F : \mathcal{C} \to \mathcal{D}$, with $\mathcal{C}$ and $\mathcal{D}$ symmetric monoidal categories, is symmetric *if the following diagram commutes:*

$$
\begin{array}{ccc}
FA \otimes FB & \xrightarrow{\phi_{A,B}} & F(A \otimes B) \\
\downarrow{\scriptstyle \sigma_{FA,FB}} & & \downarrow{\scriptstyle F\sigma_{A,B}} \\
FB \otimes FA & \xrightarrow{\phi_{B,A}} & F(B \otimes A)
\end{array}
$$

A symmetric monoidal functor $F : \mathcal{C} \to \mathcal{D}$ is traced *if, for all $f : A \otimes U \to B \otimes U$, $Tr^{FU}_{FA,FB}(\phi^{-1}_{B,U} \circ Ff \circ \phi_{A,U}) = F(Tr^{U}_{A,B}(f))$.*

A monoidal natural transformation *m between monoidal functors (F, ϕ, ϕ'_I) and (G, ψ, ψ'_I) is a natural transformation $m : F \Rightarrow G$ s.t. the following diagrams commute:*

$$
\begin{array}{ccc}
FA \otimes FB & \xrightarrow{\phi_{A,B}} & F(A \otimes B) \\
\downarrow{\scriptstyle m_A \otimes m_B} & & \downarrow{\scriptstyle m_{A \otimes B}} \\
GA \otimes GB & \xrightarrow{\psi_{A,B}} & G(A \otimes B)
\end{array}
\qquad
\begin{array}{ccc}
I & \xrightarrow{\phi'_I} & FI \\
& {\scriptstyle \psi'_I} \searrow & \downarrow{\scriptstyle m_I} \\
& & GI
\end{array}
$$

A monoidal pointwise *natural transformation is a family of maps $m_A : FA \to GA$ s.t. the naturality diagram commutes for morphisms of the form $f : I \to A$, for all object A.*

Connection-Based Proof Construction in Non-commutative Logic

D. Galmiche and J.-M. Notin

LORIA – Université Henri Poincaré, 54506 Vandœuvre-lès-Nancy Cedex, France,
{galmiche,notin}@loria.fr

Abstract. We propose a connection-based characterization of the multiplicative fragment of non-commutative logic (MNL), that is a conservative extension of both commutative (MLL) and non-commutative or cyclic (MCyLL) linear logic. It is based on a characterization for MLL together with the introduction of labels and constraints from a formula polarization process. We also study a similar characterization for the intuitionistic fragment of MNL. Finally, we consider the relationships between these results and proof nets construction in MNL based on labels and constraints.

1 Introduction

Since last years there is an increasing amount of interest for logical systems that are resource sensitive (linear logic [10] with its resource consumption interpretation and bunched implications logic [16] with its resource sharing interpretation) but also order-aware (non-commutative logic [1]). As specification logics, they can represent features as interaction, resource distribution and mobility, nondeterminism, sequentiality or coordination of entities. Here, we focus on this order-awareness in the Non-Commutative Logic (NL) [1, 17] that incorporates, in a conservative way, the notion of order into Linear Logic. This logic is motivated by a fine logical characterization of operational aspects of concurrent constraint programming (CC) [18]. It allows to analyze how to manage coordination in the access to resources and information [3]. Its intuitionistic fragment also allows to specify and verify the TCP/IP protocol [12] for which one needs a linear implication that consumes its premise in a particular order, together with a commutative conjunction.

In this paper we focus on proof construction in the multiplicative fragment of Non-Commutative Logic (MNL), that is a conservative extension of both commutative (MLL) and non-commutative or cyclic (MCyLL) linear logic. Non-Commutative Logic is mainly characterized by two equivalent sequent calculi that are enriched with a structure of order, the first with an order variety [1] and the second with bunches of formulae including a commutative and a non-commutative separators [17]. Proof search is difficult in such settings in particular because of the management of context splitting. Recent works on MNL proof search are based on particular treatments of order varieties and the introduction of the focusing principle. We can mention a cluster calculus with a simple

M.Y. Vardi and A. Voronkov (Eds.): LPAR 2003, LNAI 2850, pp. 422–436, 2003.

way to propagate the order structure [4] and a bipolar sequent calculus that allows to deal with partial information, through specific constraints, during proof construction [2]. The later approach has been also adapted to the proof net construction [3]. Independently, we have studied proof construction in MNL through the construction of labelled proof nets [7], the labels allowing to fix constraints and/or to propagate information necessary to guide and control the construction process. But the labels were not clearly related to the MNL semantics and cannot help for instance for countermodel generation. We recently proposed new sequent and proof net calculi with dependency relations (on formulae) and in this setting the provability of a MNL formula A is studied through the provability of the corresponding MLL formula (A without distinction between commutative and non-commutative connectives) and the verification of some conditions on a set of dependency relations generated during the proof search process [8]. All these works come from, or are influenced by, the definition of NL with order varieties. An alternative way consists in studying proof search from the MNL sequent calculus with bunches [17] and its phase semantics. Because of the presence of two context separators and two structural rules, this calculus is not well adapted to the design of an automatic theorem prover of MNL.

Therefore, we propose a connection-based characterization of provability in MNL, starting from our previous works on connection methods for MLL and proof nets construction [5]. It is based on the introduction of polarities on formulae, of labels and label constraints in order to deal with bunched contexts and thus to capture the specific interactions between commutative and non-commutative connectives. The use of labels and constraints for designing a connection method has been already studied in the setting of a bunched logic, namely BI logic [16], in which labels and constraints are counterparts of the resource semantics [6]. Here an essential preliminary step is the computation of a polarization, which implicitly allows us to consider an intuitionistic encoding of the formula to prove. Moreover, we can naturally define a similar connection-based characterization of provability for the intuitionistic fragment of MNL (IMNL). A consequence of both characterizations is a new characterization of proof nets for both MNL logics and a new procedure for MNL proof nets construction that can be considered as an alternative connection method [5] and a verification method for MNL proof nets [14].

2   The Non-commutative Logic

The MNL formulae are built from literals $p, q, \ldots, p^\perp, q^\perp, \ldots$ with commutative connectives (conjunction $\otimes$ and disjunction $\mathfrak{P}$) and non-commutative connectives (conjunction $\odot$ and disjunction $\lhd$). The negation is defined as follows with the De Morgan laws: $(p)^\perp = p^\perp$, $(p^\perp)^\perp = p$, $(A \odot B)^\perp = B^\perp \lhd A^\perp$, $(A \lhd B)^\perp = B^\perp \odot A^\perp$, $(A \otimes B)^\perp = B^\perp \mathfrak{P} A^\perp$, $(A \mathfrak{P} B)^\perp = B^\perp \otimes A^\perp$. The MLL (resp. MCyLL) formulae are built from literals and the connectives $\otimes$ and $\mathfrak{P}$ (resp. $\odot$ and $\lhd$). The MNL sequent calculus, given in Figure 1, is based on bunches with two formula separators (a commutative ',' and a non-commutative ';'). Moreover, it includes

$$\frac{}{\vdash A, A^{\perp}} \ (Ax.) \qquad \frac{\vdash \Gamma, A \quad \vdash A^{\perp}, \Delta}{\vdash \Gamma, \Delta} \ (Cut) \qquad \frac{\vdash \Gamma, A \quad \vdash \Delta, B}{\vdash \Delta, \Gamma, A \otimes B} \ (\otimes)$$

$$\frac{\vdash \Gamma, A \quad \vdash \Delta, B}{\vdash (\Delta; \Gamma), A \odot B} \ (\odot) \qquad \frac{\vdash \Gamma, A, B}{\vdash \Gamma, A \,\mathbin{⅋}\, B} \ (⅋) \qquad \frac{\vdash \Gamma, (A; B)}{\vdash \Gamma, A \vartriangleleft B} \ (\vartriangleleft)$$

$$\frac{\vdash \Gamma[\Delta; \Sigma]}{\vdash \Gamma[\Delta, \Sigma]} \ (Entropy) \qquad \frac{\vdash \Gamma, \Delta}{\vdash \Gamma; \Delta} \ (Seesaw) \qquad \frac{\vdash \Gamma; \Delta}{\vdash \Gamma, \Delta} \ (CoSeesaw)$$

Fig. 1. A sequent calculus for MNL

some explicit structural rules (Entropy and Seesaw) that establish relationships between both separators. We have added a restricted case of entropy, namely the rule *CoSeesaw*, that is the opposite of the *Seesaw* rule. More details are given in [17]. The phase semantics of MNL is defined as follows:

Definition 1 (Non-commutative Phase Space). *A* non-commutative phase space *is a sextuplet* $\mathcal{P} = (P, \cdot, \star, 1, \leq, \perp)$ *such that:*
- *$(P, \cdot, 1)$ is a monoid,*
- *$(P, \star, 1)$ is a commutative monoid,*
- *$\leq$ is a partial order on P, compatible with both monoidal structures and such that: $\forall x, y \in P \ x \star y \leq x \cdot y$,*
- *$\perp \subseteq P$ is an order ideal such that: $\forall x, y \in P \ x \cdot y \in \perp \Leftrightarrow x \star y \in \perp$.*

Given a phase space $\mathcal{P}$, $F \subseteq P$ and $G \subseteq P$, we define the following operations:
$F \otimes G = (F \star G)^{\perp\perp}$; $F \odot G = (F \cdot G)^{\perp\perp}$; $F \,⅋\, G = (G^{\perp} \star F^{\perp})^{\perp}$ and $F \vartriangleleft G = (G^{\perp} \cdot F^{\perp})^{\perp}$

Definition 2 (Validity). *Given a phase space $\mathcal{P}$ and a valuation S that assigns a fact of P to any propositional symbol, we define the interpretation* $J \cdot K_S^P$ *as usual. A formula F is* valid *if and only if $1 \in \mathrm{JFK}_S^P$ for every phase space $\mathcal{P}$ and every interpretation S.*

Theorem 1. *The sequent calculus with explicit structural rules is sound and complete w.r.t. the phase semantics.*

Proof. The complete proof is given in [17].

We aim to start from the sequent calculus with bunches and its proof-theoretical results in order to study proof search in MNL. Because of the presence of two context separators and two structural rules, this calculus is not well adapted for the design of proof search methods. For instance, the context splitting problem is hardened by the structure of sequents (see $\otimes$ and $\odot$ rules).

    The structural rules impose an order between the sequent formulae modulo cyclicity. There is no explicit rule for cyclicity, but it can be recovered through applications of *Seesaw* and *Entropy* rules. In fact, in that case, we consider a restricted case of entropy through the rule *CoSeesaw* (see Figure 1).

As an example, we consider the sequent $\vdash A, (B; (C, D))$. It can be derived from $\vdash (A; B), C, D$ by a reversible sequence of *Seesaw* and *Entropy* rules. Both sequents can be considered to be equivalent modulo cyclicity.

In order to represent sequents that are equivalent modulo reversible applications of *Seesaw* and *CoSeesaw* rules (ie modulo cyclicity), we consider sequents through a "viewpoint". Considering a family $\mathcal{F}$ of sequents that are equivalent modulo cyclicity, we represent $\mathcal{F}$ by $\vdash \Gamma, A$ that is an element of $\mathcal{F}$ with A an arbitrary formula. Thanks to the following theorem any formula of any sequent of $\mathcal{F}$ can be considered as a "viewpoint".

Theorem 2. *Let $\vdash \Gamma$ be a MNL sequent and A be a formula in Γ, we can built from Γ a reversible derivation of $\vdash \Delta, A$ by using only Entropy and Seesaw rules.*

Proof. Given in detail in [17].

Sequent calculi without structural rules have been proposed for MNL [17]. The structure of formulae in such sequents is expressed through *order varieties*, that are a refinement of cyclic orders. Proof search in these calculi has been studied through the focalization and bipolar calculus [2, 4].

Our aim is to propose proof search methods based on simple (algorithmic) structures, that can be easily handled in an automated proof search procedure. In this perspective, order varieties (and their operations) as mathematical structures seem not to be appropriate for the design of useful proof search methods for MNL. Our previous works based on sequents and proof nets with formulae dependencies [7, 8] were a first step to find alternative and useful semantical structures. A key point of our approach is to separate in a simple way the linearity and non-commutativity aspects.

3   A Matrix Characterization for MNL

We define a matrix characterization for MNL by extending one characterization for MLL [5, 13] with specific labels and constraints that capture the interactions between commutative and non-commutative connectives. In fact, the label calculus allow to express in a simple way constraints on formulae ordering inside a context.

3.1   Dealing with Linearity

First, we consider the matrix characterization for MLL of [5], by ignoring the structure of the context, and by seeing $\odot$ as $\otimes$, and $\lhd$ as $\mathfrak{P}$. As usual in matrix characterizations, we first define the formula tree and thus consider the decomposition tree of the formula F to prove, where nodes are called positions (denoted $a_0, a_1, \ldots$). A position u exactly identifies a subformula of F. We identify two types of nodes, α and β: a node is of type α (resp. β) if the principal connective is $\mathfrak{P}$ or $\lhd$ (resp. $\otimes$ or $\odot$). Now, we define the notion of a path through a formula F, knowing that u denotes a position and $l(u)$ (resp. $r(u)$) denotes the left (resp. right) premise of u.

a_0	F_0
a_1	$(B^\perp \,\invamp\, C^\perp) \odot D^\perp$
a_2	$B^\perp \,\invamp\, C^\perp$
a_3	$B^\perp$
a_4	$C^\perp$
a_5	$D^\perp$
a_6	$(D \lhd [(C \otimes B) \odot A]) \,\invamp\, A^\perp$
a_7	$D \lhd [(C \otimes B) \odot A]$
a_8	D
a_9	$(C \otimes B) \odot A$
a_{10}	$C \otimes B$
a_{11}	C
a_{12}	B
a_{13}	A
a_{14}	$A^\perp$

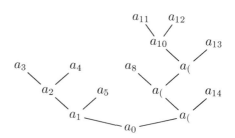

Fig. 2. An example of formula tree

Definition 3. *Let F be a MNL formula, the set of paths through F is the smallest set of positions such that:*
- *$\{a_0\}$ is a path;*
- *if $\{s, u\}$ is a path then:*
    if $type(u) = \alpha$ then $\{s, l(u), r(u)\}$ is a path;
    if $type(u) = \beta$ then $\{s, l(u)\}$ and $\{s, r(u)\}$ are paths.
An atomic path is a path that contains only atomic positions.

Definition 4. *Given a MNL formula F, a set of connections $\mathcal{SC}$ linearly spans F if and only if*
- *all literals in the formula tree appear exactly once in $\mathcal{SC}$;*
- *if (a, b) and (c, d) are distinct elements of $\mathcal{SC}$ then $a \neq c$ and $b \neq d$;*
- *every atomic path contains a connection from $\mathcal{SC}$;*
- *no proper subset of $\mathcal{SC}$ spans F.*

This definition is the one for MLL [5] without distinction between commutative and non-commutative connectives in the construction process of atomic paths. Thus, if a MNL formula F is such that there exists a set of connections $\mathcal{SC}$ that linearly spans F then the commutative version of F is provable in MLL.

In order to illustrate the different steps of the characterization, we consider the following MNL formula: $F_0 = (B^\perp \,\invamp\, C^\perp) \odot D^\perp \,\invamp\, (D \lhd [(C \otimes B) \odot A]) \,\invamp\, A^\perp$.

From this first step we obtain the indexed formula tree of F_0 (see Figure 2) and build the set of paths following Definition 3. The set of atomic paths of F_0 is:

$$\left\{ \begin{array}{l} \{a_3, a_4, a_8, a_{11}, a_{14}\}, \{a_3, a_4, a_8, a_{12}, a_{14}\}, \{a_3, a_4, a_8, a_{13}, a_{14}\}, \\ \{a_5, a_8, a_{11}, a_{14}\}, \{a_5, a_8, a_{12}, a_{14}\}, \{a_5, a_8, a_{13}, a_{14}\} \end{array} \right\}$$

The set of connections $\{(a_{14}, a_{13}), (a_3, a_{12}), (a_4, a_{11}), (a_8, a_5)\}$ linearly spans F_0.

3.2   Dealing with the Non-commutativity

In order to deal with ordering constraints within subformulae, we define label and constraints for MNL that in fact capture the semantics and allow us to encode the structure of MNL sequents, and to express constraints on it. Labels are computed w.r.t. a polarization of the formula that informally defines a "viewpoint" of a sequent.

Definition 5. *A polarization pol for a MNL formula F is a function that associates a polarity (+ or −) to F and all its subformulae.*

Definition 6. *Given a formula F and a polarization pol for F, pol is* node-correct *if and only if, for every subformula of F it respects the following inductive rules:*

$$pol(A \otimes B) = + \Rightarrow pol(A) = pol(B) = +; pol(A \otimes B) = - \Rightarrow pol(A) \neq pol(B);$$
$$pol(A \odot B) = + \Rightarrow pol(A) = pol(B) = +; pol(A \odot B) = - \Rightarrow pol(A) \neq pol(B);$$
$$pol(A \,⅋\, B) = - \Rightarrow pol(A) = pol(B) = -; \quad pol(A \,⅋\, B) = + \Rightarrow pol(A) \neq pol(B);$$
$$pol(A \lhd B) = - \Rightarrow pol(A) = pol(B) = -; pol(A \lhd B) = + \Rightarrow pol(A) \neq pol(B);$$

Definition 7. *Given a formula F, a set of connections $\mathcal{SC}$ and a polarization pol, pol is* admissible *if and only if it is node-correct and for every connection $(a, b) \in \mathcal{SC}$, $pol(a) \neq pol(b)$.*

Theorem 3. *Given a formula F, if there exists a set of connections $\mathcal{SC}$ that linearly spans F then there exists an admissible polarization for F.*

Proof. Following [15], we can give a linear algorithm that, given a MNL formula, a set of connections and a DR-switching, builds a polarization for F.

Given a polarization of a formula to prove F, we define the notion of label. A label structure is a tuple $\mathcal{L} = (\Sigma, \star, \cdot, 1)$ such that: Σ is a set of so called simple labels, denoted a, b, c, ...; $\star$ is a commutative monoidal operator; $\cdot$ is a monoidal operator; 1 is a unit for both $\star$ and $\cdot$.

Labels are considered modulo associativity of $\star$ and $\cdot$, and commutativity of $\star$. A label is said *linear* when it contains no repetition of the same simple label.

We express constraints on the structure of contexts through label constraints of the form $x \leq y$ and the resolution of such constraints is performed using the inference rules given in Figure 3. Given a set of constraints $\mathcal{H}$ and a constraint E, we write $\mathcal{H} \approx E$ to express that there exists a derivation tree starting from E, by using inferences given in Figure 3 and such that each branch ends with a Ax-rule, a Ent-rule or with a constraint of $\mathcal{H}$. If $\mathcal{E}$ is a set of constraints, we write $\mathcal{H} \approx \mathcal{E}$ to express that, for all $E \in \mathcal{E}$ we have $\mathcal{H} \approx E$.

$$\frac{x \leq y \quad x' \leq y'}{x \star x' \leq y \star y'} (Comp_\star) \qquad \frac{x \leq y \quad x' \leq y'}{x \cdot x' \leq y \cdot y'} (Comp.)$$

$$\frac{}{x \star y \leq x \cdot y} (Ent) \qquad \frac{}{x \leq x} (Ax) \qquad \frac{x \leq y \quad y \leq z}{x \leq z} (Tr)$$

Fig. 3. Inference rules for constraint resolution

u	$type(u)$	$lbl(u)$	$lbl(l(u))$	$lbl(r(u))$	$Cont(u)$
$A^+ \otimes^+ B^+$	β	x	y	z	$x \leq y \star z$
$A^+ \otimes^- B^-$	β	l	x	$x \star l$	
$A^- \otimes^- B^+$	β	l	$x \star l$	x	
$A^+ \odot^+ B^+$	β	x	y	z	$x \leq y \cdot z$
$A^+ \odot^- B^-$	β	l	x	$l \cdot x$	
$A^- \odot^- B^+$	β	l	$x \cdot l$	x	
$A^+ \mathbin{⅋}^+ B^-$	α	x	$b \star x$	b	
$A^- \mathbin{⅋}^+ B^+$	α	x	a	$a \star x$	
$A^- \mathbin{⅋}^- B^-$	α	l	a	b	$l \leq b \star a$
$A^+ \lhd^+ B^-$	α	x	$x \cdot b$	b	
$A^- \lhd^+ B^+$	α	x	a	$a \cdot x$	
$A^- \lhd^- B^-$	α	l	a	b	$l \leq b \cdot a$

Fig. 4. Inductive rules for label computation

Given a MNL formula F and a node-correct polarization for F, we can compute the polarities of F subformulae by starting from F with the polarity $+$ and the label 1 and by applying the rules given in Figure 4.

The labels associated with premises of $\otimes^+$ or $\odot^+$ nodes and to the positive premise of $\otimes^-$ or $\odot^-$ nodes are considered as *variables*. The labels associated with premises of $⅋^-$ or $\lhd^-$ nodes, and to the negative premise of $⅋^+$ or $\lhd^+$ nodes are considered as *constants* (simple labels). A substitution σ is an application that associates a label l to a variable x such that l is a element of the label structure $(\mathcal{C}, \star, \cdot, 1)$, where $\mathcal{C}$ denotes the set of constants.

In some cases, we generate label constraints that are splitted into two sets: the set of *assertions* (Ass) that are introduced by $⅋^-$ or $\lhd^-$ nodes, and the set of *requirements* (Req) that are introduced by $\otimes^+$ and $\odot^+$ nodes. The assertions are axioms in the calculus on constraints.

We can notice that label constraints express some constraints on the formulae structure inside a sequent. Therefore, one could expect to have also such constraints associated to $⅋^+$, $\lhd^+$, $\otimes^-$ and $\odot^-$. For these nodes, constraints are expressed through the way the premise labels are computed and the constraints derived from connections.

Definition 8. *A formula F of MNL is connection-provable if and only if*
i) there exists a set of connections $\mathcal{SC}$ such that linearly spans F;
ii) there exists an admissible polarization pol and a substitution σ such that:
  - For every connection (a^+, a^-) of $\mathcal{SC}$, $\sigma(Ass) \approx \sigma(a^+ \leq a^-)$,
  - $\sigma(Ass) \approx \sigma(Req)$.

Coming back to our example, we can now enrich its formula tree with labels. The polarity and the label associated to each subformula of F_0 are given in the labelled formula tree of F_0 are given in Figure 5. Moreover we have some label constraints. Among them, we can distinguish an assertion: $s \cdot e \leq b \star c$, two requirements: $d \cdot (a \star e) \leq t \cdot x$ and $t \leq z \star y$ and constraints coming from

u	Pol(u)	lbl(u)	Cont(u)	u	Pol(u)	lbl(u)	Cont(u)
				a_7	$+$	$a \star e$	
a_0	$+$	1		a_8	$-$	d	
a_1	$-$	e		a_9	$+$	$d \cdot (a \star e)$	$d \cdot (a \star e) \leq t \cdot x$
a_2	$-$	$s \cdot e$	$s \cdot e \leq b \star c$	a_{10}	$+$	t	$t \leq z \star y$
a_3	$-$	b		a_{11}	$+$	z	
a_4	$-$	c		a_{12}	$+$	y	
a_5	$+$	s		a_{13}	$+$	x	
a_6	$+$	e		a_{14}	$-$	a	

Fig. 5. An example of labelled formula tree

connections: $x \leq a$, $y \leq b$, $z \leq c$ and $s \leq d$. In these constraints, $\{a, b, c, d, e\}$ are constants (simple labels), and $\{x, y, z, s, t\}$ are variables.

In order to solve these constraints, we can easily deduce, from the constraints obtained from connections, a partial substitution: $\{x \mapsto a, y \mapsto b, z \mapsto c, s \mapsto d\}$. Moreover, the requirement $t \leq z \star y$ becomes $t \leq c \star b$ and thus can be satisfied if we consider $t \mapsto b \star c$. Then, this substitution trivially satisfies constraints from connections and the requirement $t \leq z \star y$. We have now to verify that it also satisfies the last requirement $d \cdot (a \star e) \leq t \cdot x$. Using inference rules of Figure 3 we can obtain the following proof:

$$\cfrac{\cfrac{d \leq d \quad a \star e \leq e \cdot a}{d \cdot (a \star e) \leq d \cdot e \cdot a}\ (Comp) \qquad \cfrac{d \cdot e \leq b \star c \quad a \leq a}{d \cdot e \cdot a \leq (b \star c) \cdot a}\ (Comp)}{d \cdot (a \star e) \leq (b \star c) \cdot a}\ (Tr)$$

Let us remark that the label constraints capture the constraints on the bunched context for rule applications in the MNL sequent calculus. For instance, the constraint $a \star e \leq e \cdot a$ corresponds to the use of the *Entropy* rule in the sequent calculus. Finally, we check that the MNL formula of our example is connection-provable and in fact valid (see next subsection).

Let us consider now the formula $G_0 = (B^{\perp} \mathfrak{N} C^{\perp}) \odot D^{\perp} \mathfrak{N} (D \lhd [(C \otimes B) \otimes A]) \mathfrak{N} A^{\perp}$ that is obtained from the previous one by changing $(C \otimes B) \odot A$ to $(C \otimes B) \otimes A$. If we take the same polarization as for F_0, we obtain the same computed labels. But the requirement generated by the subformula $(C \otimes B) \otimes A$ is now $d \cdot (a \star e) \leq t \star x$. Using the substitution, we obtain the constraint $d \cdot (a \star e) \leq b \star c \star a$, that cannot be satisfied.

Taking another admissible polarization changes the labels and the constraints associated to subformulae, but the set of constraints does not admit a solution. Then, as we have no other choice for the set of connections, we can state that G_0 is not connection-provable, and consequently is not valid in MNL.

3.3   Properties of the Characterization

Let us show that our characterization is correct and complete w.r.t. the MNL sequent calculus with bunches. It is mainly based on: a) a polarization of the

$$\dfrac{\dfrac{\quad}{\vdash [\mathbf{e} : (B^{\perp}\,\mathfrak{N}\,C^{\perp}) \odot D^{\perp}; \mathbf{d} : D], \mathbf{t} : C \otimes B \quad \overline{\vdash \mathbf{x} : A, \mathbf{a} : A^{\perp}}}{\begin{array}{l} S_1 : \vdash [\mathbf{a} : A^{\perp}; \mathbf{e} : (B^{\perp}\,\mathfrak{N}\,C^{\perp}) \odot D^{\perp}; \mathbf{d} : D], \mathbf{d} \cdot (\mathbf{a} \star \mathbf{e}) : (C \otimes B) \odot A \\ \hline S_2' : \vdash [(\mathbf{a} : A^{\perp}, \mathbf{e} : (B^{\perp}\,\mathfrak{N}\,C^{\perp}) \odot D^{\perp}); \mathbf{d} : D], \mathbf{d} \cdot (\mathbf{a} \star \mathbf{e}) : (C \otimes B) \odot A \\ \hline \vdash [\mathbf{a} : A^{\perp}, \mathbf{e} : (B^{\perp}\,\mathfrak{N}\,C^{\perp}) \odot D^{\perp}]; \mathbf{d} : D; \mathbf{d} \cdot (\mathbf{a} \star \mathbf{e}) : (C \otimes B) \odot A \\ \hline S_2 : \vdash \mathbf{e} : (B^{\perp}\,\mathfrak{N}\,C^{\perp}) \odot D^{\perp}, (\mathbf{d} : D; \mathbf{d} \cdot (\mathbf{a} \star \mathbf{e}) : (C \otimes B) \odot A), \mathbf{a} : A^{\perp} \end{array}}$$

(Ax.) (⊙) (Entropy) (Seesaw) (Ent.)

Fig. 6. A part of proof with labels

sequent in order to deal with irrelevant (reversible) applications of (co-)seesaw rules; b) labels to represent the structure of formulae inside a sequent; c) constraints on labels to deal with applications of the *Entropy* rule in the sequent calculus.

A key point is that provability is independent from the choice of an admissible polarization. If, for such a choice, the set of constraints has no solution then we can claim the non-provability for the given set of connections and thus try another one if possible. An admissible polarization for F is defined in such a way that if $\vdash \Gamma$ is a sequent that can be derived from F, then there exists exactly one positive formula in $\vdash \Gamma$. In some way, our polarization gives a "viewpoint" of a MNL sequent, as defined in the previous section. The structure of formulae within a sequent $\vdash \Delta$ is considered w.r.t. the structure of $\vdash \Gamma^{-}, A^{+}$, where $\vdash \Gamma, A$ is equivalent to $\vdash \Delta$ modulo cyclicity. Moreover, labels are computed w.r.t. the polarization in such a way that, given a set of connections $\mathcal{SC}$, the sets of constraints generated from a choice of an admissible polarization are all equivalent. This is related to the fact that, in the MNL sequent calculus, sequents are equivalent modulo cyclicity (as said in previous section). As an example, we consider the part of the proof of F_0 (see Figure 6). Each formula inside a sequent is together with its label. We can easily see that the label $d \cdot (a \star e)$ (associated with $(C \otimes B) \odot A$, that is the positive formula of S_2 and S_2') represents the structure of both S_2 and S_2'.

Now, we illustrate how label constraints are related to ordering constraints within a sequent. Let us consider the sequent $\vdash \Sigma, A \odot B$. In order to apply a ⊙-rule we need to turn the context Σ into the form $\Delta; \Gamma$. This transformation is not reversible in general and induces some constraints on (the structure of) Γ and Δ. Let us consider the way labels and constraints are computed for $\odot^{+}$. The requirement $l \leq x \cdot y$ expresses that Σ has to be turned into the particular form $\Delta; \Gamma$, and thus some constraints on variables x and y. In the case of $\odot^{-}$, we have to compute labels in a different way taking into account the polarization. Constraints on contexts are expressed by the way labels are computed and by equations coming from connections.

In our example, we have to apply an *Entropy* rule to obtain the sequent S_1 from S_2. The structure of S_1 would be represented by the label $d \cdot e \cdot a$. In our characterization, we associate a constraint $d \cdot (a \star e) \leq t \cdot x$ to $(C \otimes B) \odot A$. We have to use an entropy relation namely $a \star e \leq e \cdot a$, to solve this constraint.

Let us remind that a MNL sequent $\vdash \Gamma$ is provable in MNL if and only if $Dis(\Gamma)$ is connection-provable, where $Dis : Context \mapsto Formula$ is defined by: $Dis(A) = A$ if A is a formula; $Dis(\Gamma, \Delta) = Dis(\Gamma) \otimes Dis(\Delta)$; $Dis(\Gamma; \Delta) = Dis(\Gamma) \lhd Dis(\Delta)$.

Theorem 4 (Correctness). *If a MNL formula F is connection-provable then it is provable in the MNL sequent calculus.*

Proof. At first, the existence of a set of connections that linearly spans F gives a proof in MLL of the commutative version of F. It provides a skeleton for the proof of F in MNL. Then, we need to attach a structure to each sequent of this skeleton. For that, we use the label associated to each formulae. In fact, the label of the positive formula induces an order between other (negative) formulae. The existence of a solution such that label constraints are satisfied ensures that we can insert structural rules, between each inference of the skeleton, such that the proof construction leads to a MNL proof.

Theorem 5 (Completeness). *If a MNL formula F is provable in the MNL sequent calculus then F is connection-provable.*

Proof. If the formula F is provable, then there exists a proof of F in the MNL sequent calculus. From this proof, we can deduce a set of connections that linearly spans F (see [5] for more details).

We can then compute an admissible polarization for F and by linearity, in any sequent appearing in the proof there is exactly one positive formula (other formulae of the sequent being negative). Thus, the polarization gives a so-called viewpoint in any sequent, and the label associated to the positive formula represents the structure of the negative formulae. Then, given this viewpoint, we can relate the rule of structural entropy with the corresponding *Entropy* rule in the calculus of constraints.

3.4   The Related Connection Method

From this characterization we can define a connection-based proof search method with the following main steps: 1) to compute the atomic paths and choose a spanning set of connections like in MLL [5, 13]; 2) to compute, from the set of connections, an admissible polarity and then labels and constraints; 3) to compute a substitution that is a solution for the set of constraints (connection constraints and requirements satisfied from assertions).

Steps 1) and 2) being standard and without difficulty we aim to analyze the step 3) and its main problem, that is to find a substitution such that requirements can be proved from assertions using some particular inference rules. Given these rules, constraints of the form $x \leq a$ (where x is a variable and a is a constant) are satisfied if and only if $\sigma(x) = a$. The way in which constraints are generated makes constraint resolution relatively easy. Moreover, we can use the linearity of labels to reduce the search space.

Assertions are of the form $l \leq a \square b$, where a and b are constants (simple labels) and l is a label composed of variables and constants (l does not contain a or b). Requirements are of the form $l \leq x \square y$, where x and y are (fresh) variables. Thus, variables have a very restricted set of possible instantiations. Moreover, labels attached to positive formulae always appear on the left-hand side of a constraint (generated by a connection or by a $\otimes^+$ or $\odot^+$ rule). However, when created, variables are attached to positive premise (for instance, see the construction of labels for $\otimes^+$ in Figure 4). As a result, variables always appear in the right-hand side of a constraint and on the left-hand side of another one. This means that the set of admissible values of each variable is strongly restricted by the constraints.

Coming back to our example, the variable t appears on the left-hand side of $t \leq z \star y$ (y and z appear in the constraint $y \leq b$ and $z \leq c$). It also appears on the right-hand side of $d \cdot (a \star e) \leq t \cdot x$. Thus, from this requirement (and taking into account that $\sigma(x) = a$, we can deduce the following constraint $d \cdot e \leq t$, using compatibility and entropy rules. Then, the choices of values for t are strongly reduced because of the constraint $d \cdot e \leq t \leq b \star c$ that admits a solution because we have an assertion $d \cdot e \leq b \star c$. In our example, we have seen that $\sigma(t) = b \star c$ satisfies requirements and that $\sigma(t) = d \cdot e$ is also a solution for t. These two solutions for t can be considered equivalent, as they are deducible from each other using the assertion. The choice between $b \star c$ and $d \cdot e$ depends on strategies applied to compute a substitution. A smart choice of substitution can strongly reduce the complexity of constraints resolution.

4   A Characterization for Intuitionistic MNL

From the previous results on MNL, we aim to analyze what happens in the case of Intuitionistic MNL (IMNL). This work is inspired from the relationships between MLL and MILL described in [15]. IMNL formulae are built from propositional variables p, q, ... and commutative connectives $\otimes$ and $\multimap$, and non-commutative ones $\odot$, $\multimapdot$ and $\bullet\!\!-$. The corresponding sequent calculus is given in Figure 7.

$$\frac{}{A \vdash A} \, (Ax.) \qquad \frac{\Gamma[\Delta; \Sigma] \vdash C}{\Gamma[\Delta, \Sigma] \vdash C} \, (Ent.) \qquad \frac{\Gamma \vdash A \quad \Delta \vdash B}{\Gamma, \Delta \vdash A \otimes B} \, (\otimes R)$$

$$\frac{\Gamma[A, B] \vdash C}{\Gamma[A \otimes B] \vdash C} \, (\otimes L) \qquad \frac{\Gamma \vdash A \quad \Delta \vdash B}{\Gamma; \Delta \vdash A \odot B} \, (\odot R) \qquad \frac{\Gamma[A; B] \vdash C}{\Gamma[A \odot B] \vdash C} \, (\odot L)$$

$$\frac{\Gamma \vdash A \quad \Delta[B] \vdash C}{\Delta[\Gamma, A \multimap B] \vdash C} \, (\multimap L) \qquad \frac{A, \Gamma \vdash B}{\Gamma \vdash A \multimap B} \, (\multimap R) \qquad \frac{\Gamma \vdash A \quad \Delta[B] \vdash C}{\Delta[\Gamma; A \multimapdot B] \vdash C} \, (\multimapdot L)$$

$$\frac{A; \Gamma \vdash B}{\Gamma \vdash A \multimapdot B} \, (\multimapdot R) \qquad \frac{\Gamma \vdash A \quad \Delta[B] \vdash C}{\Delta[B \bullet\!\!- A; \Gamma] \vdash C} \, (\bullet\!\!- L) \qquad \frac{\Gamma; A \vdash B}{\Gamma \vdash B \bullet\!\!- A} \, (\bullet\!\!- R)$$

Fig. 7. A sequent calculus for IMNL

There exists a strong relationship between MLL and intuitionistic MLL [15] that can be extended to MNL. In fact, any IMNL formula can be translated to a MNL formula using De Morgan laws and the equalities: $A \multimap B = A^{\perp} \gamma B$, $A \mathbin{\text{---}\bullet} B = A^{\perp} \vartriangleleft B$ and $B \bullet\!\!\text{---} A = B \vartriangleleft A^{\perp}$. For that, given a IMNL formula A, we define its classical counterpart $\overline{A}$ (and $\underline{A}$).

Let A be an IMNL formula, we define its classical counterpart $\overline{A}$ (and $\underline{A}$) as follows:

$$\overline{a} = a \qquad\qquad \underline{a} = a^{\perp} \qquad \overline{A \otimes B} = \overline{A} \otimes \overline{B} \quad \underline{A \otimes B} = \underline{B} \gamma \underline{A}$$

$$\overline{A \odot B} = \overline{A} \odot \overline{B} \quad \underline{A \odot B} = \underline{B} \vartriangleleft \underline{A} \quad \overline{A \multimap B} = \underline{A} \gamma \overline{B} \quad \underline{A \multimap B} = \underline{B} \otimes \overline{A}$$

$$\overline{A \mathbin{\text{---}\bullet} B} = \underline{A} \vartriangleleft \overline{B} \quad \underline{A \mathbin{\text{---}\bullet} B} = \underline{B} \odot \overline{A} \quad \overline{B \bullet\!\!\text{---} A} = \overline{B} \vartriangleleft \underline{A} \quad \underline{B \bullet\!\!\text{---} A} = \overline{A} \odot \underline{B}$$

From this definition we have the following result

Theorem 6. *A IMNL sequent $H_1, \ldots, H_n \vdash C$ is provable if and only if the sequent MNL $\vdash \underline{H_1}, \ldots, \underline{H_n}, \overline{C}$ is provable.*

Proof. We build a proof of $H_1, \ldots, H_n \vdash C$ from a proof of $\vdash \underline{H_1}, \ldots, \underline{H_n}, \overline{C}$ and conversely. An intuitionistic sequent $\Gamma \vdash A$, where Γ is a context with bunches, can be easily turned into a one-sided sequent, using negation and De Morgan laws. Moreover, as stated in theorem 2, any sequent $\vdash \Delta[A]$ can be reversibly turned into the form $\vdash \Gamma, A$.

Consequently, any linearly balanced IMNL formula A can be transformed to a variant MNL formula which is built from polarized atoms and polarized connectives in the following way

$$\ulcorner a \urcorner = a^{+} \qquad\qquad \llcorner a \lrcorner = a^{-} \qquad\qquad \ulcorner A \otimes B \urcorner = \ulcorner A \urcorner \otimes^{+} \ulcorner B \urcorner$$

$$\llcorner A \otimes B \lrcorner = \llcorner B \lrcorner \gamma^{-} \llcorner A \lrcorner \quad \ulcorner A \odot B \urcorner = \ulcorner A \urcorner \odot^{+} \ulcorner B \urcorner \quad \llcorner A \odot B \lrcorner = \llcorner B \lrcorner \vartriangleleft^{-} \llcorner A \lrcorner$$

$$\ulcorner A \multimap B \urcorner = \llcorner A \lrcorner \gamma^{+} \ulcorner B \urcorner \quad \llcorner A \multimap B \lrcorner = \llcorner B \lrcorner \otimes^{-} \ulcorner A \urcorner \quad \ulcorner A \mathbin{\text{---}\bullet} B \urcorner = \llcorner A \lrcorner \vartriangleleft^{+} \ulcorner B \urcorner$$

$$\llcorner A \mathbin{\text{---}\bullet} B \lrcorner = \llcorner B \lrcorner \odot^{-} \ulcorner A \urcorner \quad \ulcorner B \bullet\!\!\text{---} A \urcorner = \ulcorner B \urcorner \vartriangleleft^{+} \llcorner A \lrcorner \quad \llcorner B \bullet\!\!\text{---} A \lrcorner = \ulcorner A \urcorner \odot^{-} \llcorner B \lrcorner$$

The transformation of a one-sided sequent into a two-sided (intuitionistic) sequent corresponds to a polarization of the sequent, as previously defined. In fact, a node-correct polarization follows De Morgan laws, and the definition of linear implication(s). Given a IMNL formula A we built a MNL formula $\ulcorner A \urcorner$ formula with a unique polarization, denoted $ipol(A)$, derived from the above construction. It is easy to verify that it is node-correct. From now, we can apply the connection-based method of MNL and derive the following definition:

Definition 9. *A formula F of IMNL is connection-provable if and only if*
i) there exists a set of connections $\mathcal{SC}$ such that linearly spans $\ulcorner A \urcorner$.
ii) given the polarization $ipol(A)$, there exists a substitution σ such that:
   - for every connection (a^{+}, a^{-}) of $\mathcal{SC}$, $\sigma(Ass) \approx \sigma(a^{+} \leq a^{-})$,
   - $\sigma(Ass) \approx \sigma(Req)$.

It means that a formula A of IMNL is connection-provable if and only if $\ulcorner A \urcorner$ is connection-provable in MNL but with a fixed polarization $ipol(A)$.

Theorem 7. *A IMNL formula A is valid if and only if A is connection-provable.*

Proof. Similar to the proof for MNL with $ipol(A)$ as an admissible polarization.

As an example, we can consider $A, D\multimap(C \otimes B) \vdash D\multimap[(C \otimes B) \odot A]$. Its translation into an equivalent polarized MNL formula leads to the formula F_0 with the polarization given in Figure 5.

5   MNL Proof Nets

The notion of *proof net* has been introduced by Girard [11] in order to cope with the problems due to the intrinsic concurrency of the linear sequent calculus. It corresponds to a concise graph-theoretic representation of linear logic deductions. This concept, initially defined for MLL, has been defined for various LL fragments and then for MNL [1]. We can define a proof structure from a pair (*Dectree, Axlinks*) where, for a given sequent, *Dectree* is the set of its subformulae arranged as a decomposition tree and *Axlinks* is a set of axiom-links (or connections) between positive and negative occurrences of the same atomic formula. Such a pair is a proof structure if each atom of *Dectree* is the conclusion of exactly one axiom-link.

There exist various correctness criteria that decides if a proof structure of a LL fragment corresponds to a (graphical) proof of a given sequent or not, i.e., if a proof structure is a proof net. It is known that a based-on connection characterization of MLL directly provides a new correctness criterion for MLL proof nets [5]. Moreover, an algorithm that builds a MLL proof net provides a connection method that builds in parallel a sequent proof and a proof net, in case of provability [5, 9].

Correctness and Verification of Proof Nets

As a first consequence of our based-on connection characterization of MNL we can straightforwardly deduce a new correctness criterion for MNL proof nets based on a criterion for MLL with the computation of a polarization, the generation of labels and constraints and the satisfaction of requirements from assertions. Thus, we can design an algorithm for the verification of a MNL proof structure, starting by the verification of the MLL proof structure associated to the MNL one (without difference between commutative and non-commutative connectives), for instance with a linear algorithm [15]. The proof structure including a given set of connections, we can compute in parallel an admissible polarization for it (following [15]), and then compute labels attached to nodes (subformulae) of the proof structure and the set of constraints to satisfy.

Proof Nets Construction

Given a MLL formula F, there exists an algorithm [5] that automatically builds a set of axiom-links (or connections) such that the decomposition tree of F, together with this set of axiom-links is a proof net. It directly provides a particular connection method for MLL. We can easily adapt this algorithm to compute a set of connections that linearly spans a given MNL formula F. Then, as for the verification, we compute, in parallel with the construction of axiom-links, an admissible polarization for F and then generate the labels attached to subformulae (or nodes) in the proof structure. Finally, we solve the requirements from the assertions and check if there is a solution for the set of constraints. This algorithm can be adapted to intuitionistic MNL proof nets by only checking polarities during the axiom-links construction.

6   Conclusion and Perspectives

We present a connection-based characterization of the multiplicative fragment of Non-Commutative logic (MNL). It is related to a MNL sequent calculus with bunches and its phase semantics [17]. Its main steps are: to consider a MNL formula, first without distinction between commutative and non-commutative connectives; to introduce a polarization, that means to consider MNL through its intuitionistic fragment; to build labels and constraints that are syntactic counterparts of the semantics; to characterize provability through the resolution of constraint. Because of the central role of polarization, we can naturally derive a similar connection-based characterization for the intuitionistic fragment of MNL. Compared to other works on MNL proof construction, that are based on order varieties and the focusing principle [2, 4] and that deal with partial information in a specific way, our approach tends to separate the linearity from the non-commutativity during the proof construction process with the help of labels, constraints and constraint resolution. A similar approach has been already studied for the BI logic [16], in which additive and multiplicative connectives cohabit, but with different labels and constraints that capture a different semantics [6]. Moreover, we can derive a new correctness criterion for MNL proof nets and propose algorithms for the verification and the construction of MNL proof nets from our previous works on MLL [5].

In further work, we will focus on the constraint resolution process that deals with simple labels and particular constraints. Moreover, we will study the complexity of MNL proof net verification from our new criterion, in comparison with the quadratic one of [14]. The labels and constraints being syntactic counterparts of the semantics, we will also consider the problem of countermodel generation in MNL in case of non-provability.

References

1. M. Abrusci and P. Ruet. Non-commutative logic I : the multiplicative fragment. *Annals of Pure and Applied Logic*, 101:29–64, 2000.
2. J.M. Andreoli. Focussing and Proof construction. *Annals of Pure and Applied Logic*, 107:131–163, 2001.

3. J.M. Andreoli. Focusing proof-net construction as a middleware paradigm. In *18th Int. Conference on Automated Deduction, CADE-18, LNAI 2392*, pages 501–516, 2002. Copenhagen, Danemark.

4. C. Faggian. Proof construction and non-commutativity: a cluster calculus. In *International Conference on Principles and Practice of Declarative Programming, PPDP 2000*, 2000. ACM Press.

5. D. Galmiche. Connection Methods in Linear Logic and Proof nets Construction. *Theoretical Computer Science*, 232(1-2):231–272, 2000.

6. D. Galmiche and D. Méry. Connection-based proof search in propositional BI logic. In *18th Int. Conference on Automated Deduction, CADE-18, LNAI 2392*, pages 111–128, 2002. Copenhagen, Danemark.

7. D. Galmiche and J.M. Notin. Proof-search and Proof nets in Mixed Linear Logic. *Electronic Notes in Theoretical Computer Science*, 37, 2000.

8. D. Galmiche and J.M. Notin. Calculi with Dependency Relations for Mixed Linear Logic. In *International Workshop on Logic and Complexity in Computer Science, LCCS'2001*, pages 81–102, Créteil, France, 2001.

9. D. Galmiche and G. Perrier. A procedure for automatic proof nets construction. In *LPAR'92, International Conference on Logic Programming and Automated Reasoning, LNAI 624*, pages 42–53, St. Petersburg, Russia, July 1992.

10. J.Y. Girard. Linear Logic: its Syntax and Semantics. In J.Y. Girard, Y. Lafont, and L. Regnier, editors, *Advances in Linear Logic*, pages 1–42. Cambridge University Press, 1995.

11. J.Y. Girard. Proof nets: the parallel syntax for proof theory. In A. Ursini and P. Agliano, editors, *Logic and Algebra*, New York, 1995. M. Dekker.

12. D. Gray, G. Hamilton, J. Power, and D. Sinclair. Specifying and verifying TCP/IP using Mixed Intuitionistic Linear Logic. Technical report, Dublin City Univ., 2001.

13. C. Kreitz, H. Mantel, J. Otten, and S. Schmitt. Connection-based proof construction in Linear Logic. In *14th Int. Conference on Automated Deduction, CADE-14, LNCS 1249*, pages 207–221, Townsville, North Queensland, Australia, 1997.

14. V. Mogbil. Quadratic correctness criterion for non commutative logic. In *15th Int. Workshop on Computer Science Logic, CSL 2001, LNCS 2142*, pages 69–83, Paris, France, 2001.

15. A. S. Murawski and C.-H. L. Ong. Dominator trees and fast verification of proof net. In *15th IEEE Symposium on Logic in Computer Science*, Santa Barbara, California, June 2000.

16. P.W. O'Hearn and D. Pym. The Logic of Bunched Implications. *Bulletin of Symbolic Logic*, 5(2):215–244, 1999.

17. P. Ruet. Non-commutative logic II : sequent calculus and phase semantics. *Math. Struct. in Comp. Science*, 10:277–312, 2000.

18. P. Ruet and F. Fages. Concurrent constraint programming and non-commutative logic. In *11th Int. Workshop on Computer Science Logic, CSL'97, LNCS 1414*, pages 406–423, Aarhus, Denmark, August 1997.

Author Index

Alonso, J.A.   49
Autexier, S.   33

Baader, F.   1
Baaz, M.   107
Badaev, S.   213
Bao Vo, Q.   274
Beierle, C.   376
Berwanger, D.   229
Boy de la Tour, T.   317
Brandt, S.   122
Bruscoli, P.   389

Ciaffaglione, A.   59
Couvreur, J.-M.   361

Degtyarev, A.   214

Echenim, M.   317

Falke, S.   167
Fermüller, C.G.   107
Fisher, M.   214
Foo, N.   274
Fränzle, M.   302

Galmiche, D.   422
Ghilardi, S.   152
Giesl, J.   167
Grädel, E.   229
Guglielmi, A.   389

Heinemann, B.   137
Herde, C.   302
Hidalgo, M.J.   49
Hladik, J.   1
Honsell, F.   407

Inoue, K.   259

Kern-Isberner, G.   376
Konev, B.   214
Korovina, M.   290

Kreutzer, S.   229
Küsters, R.   122
Kuske, D.   332

Lenisa, M.   407
Liquori, L.   59
Lohrey, M.   346
Lutz, C.   1

Martín–Mateos, F.J.   49
Miculan, M.   59
Morawska, B.   198

Nayak, A.   274
Nieuwenborgh, D. Van   244
Nieuwenhuis, R.   78
Nitta, K.   259
Notin, J.-M.   422

Oliveras, A.   78

Redamalla, R.   407
Ruiz–Reina, J.L.   49

Saheb, N.   361
Sakama, C.   259
Santocanale, L.   152
Schneider-Kamp, P.   167
Schürmann, C.   33
Schweitzer, S.   91
Sutre, G.   361

Thiemann, R.   167
Turhan, A.-Y.   122

Verma, K.N.   183
Vermeir, D.   244

Wakaki, T.   259
Walther, C.   91
Wilke, T.   289
Wolter, F.   1